Ancient Ryukyu

Ancient Ryukyu

Frontispiece. Chinese ceramics from the Kyōnouchi area, Shuri Gusuku, dating from the fourteenth and fifteenth centuries AD (see page 251). Courtesy of Okinawa Kenritsu Maizō Bunkazai Sentā. Color printing courtesy of the Sainsbury Institute for the Study of Japanese Arts and Cultures, Norwich and London, UK.

Ancient Ryukyu

An Archaeological Study of Island Communities

Richard Pearson

HAWAI

University of Hawai'i Press
Honolulu

Publication of this book has been supported by a grant from the Center for Okinawan Studies, University of Hawaiʻi at Mānoa.

Printed in the United States of America

18 17 16 15 14 13 6 5 4 3 2 1

Library of Congress Cataloging-in-Publication Data
Pearson, Richard J., author.
Ancient Ryukyu : an archaeological study of island communities / Richard Pearson.
pages cm
Includes bibliographical references and index.
ISBN 978-0-8248-3712-9 (cloth : alk. paper)
1. Ryukyu Islands—Antiquities. 2. Ryukyu Islands—History—To 1879. I. Title.
DS895.R935P43 2014
952'.29—dc23 2013012417

University of Hawaiʻi Press books are printed on acid-free paper and meet the guidelines for permanence and durability of the Council on Library Resources.

Designed by Integrated Composition Systems, Spokane, Washington

Contents

Figures

Tables

Acknowledgments

I am deeply indebted to countless individuals and institutions for assistance, support, and encouragement during fifty years of research in the Ryukyu Islands. It is impossible to express my gratitude to each and every one of them. A fortunate chance meeting in 1961 with George Kerr, historian of Okinawa, began my long association with the Ryukyus. Since that time many specialists and government agencies have made it possible for me to gain firsthand experience and to secure precious excavation reports.

The writing of this book was assisted by research support in 2007 and 2008 from the Sainsbury Institute for the Study of Japanese Arts and Cultures, Norwich and London, United Kingdom. I am grateful to Nicole Rousmaniere, Director, and Simon Kaner, Assistant Director, for making this support possible. The first draft of the book was based on three lectures given in the Toshiba Lectures on Japanese Art in 2007. I offer sincerest thanks to the Toshiba International Foundation for providing this valuable opportunity to consider the broader aspects of Ryukyu archaeology.

I wish to thank the University of British Columbia and the Social Sciences and Humanities Research Council of Canada for providing various opportunities from 1971 to 2000 to conduct research on the archaeology of the Ryukyus.

Sincere thanks are offered for assistance and friendship to the following individuals (in alphabetical order): Ankei Yūji, Anzai Eiji, Ari Naoji, Asato Shijun, Asato Susumu, China Teijun, Chinen Isamu, Gotō Masahiko, Goya Yoshikatsu, Hung Hsaio-chun, Ikeda Yoshifumi, Itō Shinji, Kamei Meitoku, Kan Hironobu, Kanaseki Hiroshi, Kin Seiki, Kinjō Kamenobu, Kinoshita Naoko, Kishimoto Yoshihiko, Kōmoto Masayuki, Kuo Su-chiu, Kurozumi Taiji, Maesako Ryōichi, Miyagi Hiroki, Miyara Yoshikazu, Miyashita Takahiro, Morimura

Ken'ichi, Nakasone Motomu, Nakayama Kiyomi, Judith McNeill, Ōhama Eisen, Ono Masatoshi, Seki Toshihiko, Seto Tetsuya, Shimabukuro Ayano, Shimoji Kazuhiro, Shintō Kōichi, Shinzato Akito, Shinzato Takayuki, Shiroma Yoshiaki, Sumida Naotoshi, Sunabe Kazumasa, Takamiya Hiroe, Takamiya Hiroto, Tōma Shi'ichi, Uehara Shizuka, Uezato Takashi, and David Welch.

I offer special thanks to the editors at the University of Hawai'i Press, Pamela Kelley, Cheri Dunn, and Susan Stone.

Finally, words cannot express my thanks to my wife, Kazue Miyazaki Pearson, without whose compassionate support none of my work would have been possible.

Chapter 1

Introduction

The Archaeology of Ryukyu Islanders

This book is an archaeological study of the prehistory and early history of the Ryukyu Islands, which are the southwest extension of the Japanese island chain (Figure 1.1). Dealing with earliest times up to about AD 1600, I describe the life of the islanders from the point of view of their island communities, livelihood, and political organization. I emphasize the environment of the Ryukyus, its development, and its interrelationship with local history.

In brief, the first archaeological record of human habitation occurred at the end of the Pleistocene, some 20,000 to 30,000 years ago, when sea level was about 140 meters lower than at present (Figure 1.2). In the Holocene Period, colonizing populations from divergent directions inhabited the northern and central Ryukyus from about 9,000 years ago, and the southern Ryukyus from about 4,500 years ago. Whereas the southern islands remained in comparative isolation until the eleventh century AD, the northern and central islanders were in almost continuous contact with the Japanese main islands. With the sweeping changes of the East Asian Mediaeval Period beginning in the tenth and eleventh centuries AD, the islanders were affected by changes in Japan and China, particularly the development of navigation and commerce in the Chinese Song dynasty (AD 960 to 1279). Social, technological, and economic changes were also brought about by migrants from the Japanese main islands. The cultivation of rice, wheat, barley, and other crops and the raising of livestock were introduced, and contact with the coast of China became more frequent. Small polities emerged on Okinawa to form the Ryukyu Kingdom in the fourteenth and fifteenth centuries. Culturally distinctive and independent, it became a trading entrepôt for all of East Asia and extended its power to the surrounding islands. With changes in the nature of East Asian maritime trade at

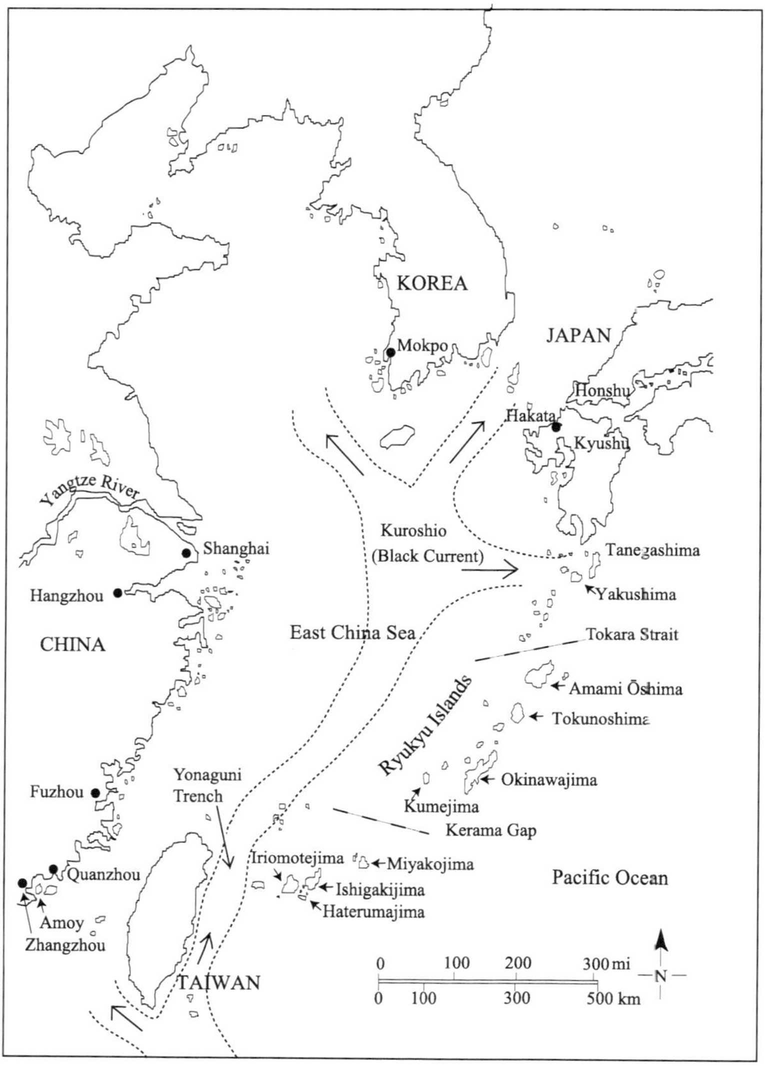

Figure 1.1. The Ryukyu Islands and surrounding areas. The Kuroshio (Black Current) is indicated by dotted lines.

the end of the sixteenth century AD and domination by the Satsuma Fiefdom of southern Kyushu in AD 1609, the islands entered a new stage of their history, which marks the end of discussion in this book.

Although this book is partially based on translation of Japanese-language sources and I have attempted to showcase the extensive work of local archaeologists, the discourse that I use is different from that used in Japan, with the excep-

Approximate Dates	Central Ryukyus (Okinawa) Period	Southern Ryukyus (Sakishima) Period
ca. 18,000 BC	Palaeolithic 32,000 to 16,000 BC?	Palaeolithic 25,000 to 16,000 BC?
7000 BC 5000 BC	Early Shellmound Period 7000 BC to 300 BC	
3000 BC		Shimotabaru Period 2900 to 2000 BC Gap 2000 BC to 900 BC
1000 BC	(hunter-gatherer subsistence to ca. AD 800)	
AD 1	(shell exchange ca. 600 BC to AD 1200)	Non-Ceramic Period 900 BC to AD 1100
AD 500	Late Shellmound Period 300 BC to AD 1050 (beginning of cultivation ca. AD 800)	
AD 1000		
	Gusuku Period AD 1050 to 1422 (major castle building, small states)	Shinzato Period AD 1100 to 1300
		Nakamori Period AD 1300 to 1600 (invasion of Yaeyama by Ryukyu Kingdom AD 1500)
AD 1500	Early Ryukyu Kingdom Period AD 1429 to 1609. (independent Ryukyu Kingdom)(AD 1609, Satsuma control begins)	
	Late Ryukyu Kingdom Period AD 1609 to 1879	Panari Period AD 1600 to 1800 part of Ryukyu Kingdom AD 1500 to 1879
AD 2000	Meiji Period AD 1868 to 1912	

Figure 1.2. Archaeological chronology of the Okinawa and Sakishima Islands

tion of the work of Takamiya Hiroto, who is US-trained. I modify the temporal framework and use my own interpretive terms, and disagree with prevailing interpretations on several occasions.

I use the Japanese suffix *-jima or -shima* (island) instead of repeating the English term "island." I use the terms Northern, Central, and Southern Ryukyus for the islands of Ōsumi-Tokara, Amami-Okinawa, and Sakishima respectively. I retain the term Amami Ōshima for Amami Island and use the term Amami Islands and Okinawa Islands to refer to these big islands together with their surrounding smaller islands.

Research Framework

There are many forms in which to describe and debate the archaeology of the Ryukyu Islands. Although the islanders were not politically part of the Japanese state until AD 1879, their story is often told from the point of view of centralized

Japan, using the traditional periods of Japanese prehistory and history such as the Jōmon, Yayoi, and Kofun. These time periods fit poorly the actual events and processes that took place in the Ryukyus, but they provide a framework that facilitates communication among Okinawan, Japanese, and foreign scholars. The Ryukyus can be described in terms of their unique tropical and Indo-Pacific environment and location, as tropical island laboratories. Their history can also be told from the point of view of the people and things that came to them from outside—a history of trade and foreign contacts. My intention is to describe maritime communities, linked to each other and to adjacent land masses in variable and constantly changing configurations. Processes of colonization, migration, interaction, assimilation, trade and tribute, commodification, and subjugation have all had effects on the shaping of Ryukyu communities. Researchers are just beginning to search for the natural and human agents that drew islanders together and connected them to the larger land masses of Asia. A further step will be to link the formation of these communities to changes in seafaring. For instance, in the Japanese main islands there is direct evidence of Jōmon Period (14,000 to 1,000 BC) canoes, used on rivers and lakes, from waterlogged deposits but evidence of sea going craft is only indirect, in the form of the remains of deep sea resources and evidence of interaction with the Korean Peninsula. Since the Jōmon Period voyagers must have used seagoing craft to reach Hokkaido and the southern Kuriles (Fitzhugh et al. 2002), the Izu Islands south of Tokyo (Imamura 1996, 62), and Sado Island (Tatsuo Kobayashi 2004, 60).

In the Yayoi Period (1000 BC to AD 250) there are finds of boat planks and drawings on pottery of boats with many oars and sails. It is possible that the increase in population at the end of the Jōmon Period and in Early Yayoi noted by Hiroto Takamiya (2006a) is related to improved navigation. These boats must have facilitated travel in the Ryukyu region. In the subsequent Kofun Period (AD 250 to 600) there are clay *haniwa* replicas of boats with raised fore and aft decks (Habu 2010). The rise of trade with China in the tenth to twelfth centuries AD appears to be related to the formidable navigation skills of the merchant traders of the Song dynasty. While each new island appears before sight of the previous island is lost as one proceeds from Kyushu as far south as Okinawajima (in daylight and good weather!), such "intervisibility" does not occur in sailing on to the Sakishima Islands, which are separated from Okinawajima by the Kerama Gap, a stretch of 270 km of open sea. Similar gaps in interisland visibility have been noted in the Mediterranean (Manning and Hulin 2005) and the Caribbean (Torres and Ramos 2008). The water compass, recorded in China from the eleventh century AD, must have been a crucial invention for the rise of Ryukyu trade. Common sense would predict that islands in a long chain were progressively colonized in a stepping stone progression; however, the Ryukyu evidence seems to indicate that, as in other parts of the world (Anderson 2005) this did not always happen. Puzzling cases in the Early Shellmound Period of the Central Ryukyus and the prehistory of the Southern Ryukyus are discussed in Chapter 4.

In writing this book I use a broad theoretical perspective, incorporating points from recent discussions of island archaeology, island political economy, and historical ecology. The approach of island archaeology was first applied to the Ryukyus by Hiroto Takamiya (1997; 2004; 2006a,b) to examine subsistence and carrying capacity and to compare the Ryukyus with the islands of the Caribbean and the Mediterranean. My approach supplements considerations of island ecology, marine ecosystems, and biogeography with a concern for human agency, interaction, and cultural choice. I attempt to show the social dynamics of the interactions that underlie the distributions of artifacts and the effect of changes in the social and physical environment, including volcanic eruptions and rising sea level. It is also important to consider the social and political choices that the islanders made in response to dynamic social, economic, political, and religious conditions within the islands and on the adjacent mainland. In earlier work my approach was to consider the Ryukyus as examples of isolated islands similar to the islands of Remote Oceania (Pearson 1969). I stressed the isolation of the Ryukyu Islands and the bounded nature of resources within particular islands (Pearson 1981a). However, more recent approaches reject the idea that islands are analytical isolates or that many of them have ever been truly isolated (Terrell 1997; Cherry 2004, 243–244; Spriggs 2008). Recently there has been a move to create a discourse of island archaeology as a worldwide analytical domain. As Broodbank notes, there is a "need to go beyond interpretive paradigms characterized by adaptive models and simple static concepts of insularity, to develop more complex and culturally driven perspectives that recognize the extent to which the islanders have consciously fashioned and refashioned their own identities and worlds" (2000, 1). Broodbank (2000) and Rainbird (2007) advocate the importance of seeing islands and archipelagoes as communities with shifting boundaries in which communication, navigation, and identity play an important role. Artifacts should be considered not just as markers of periods or cultural groups but as signifiers of island social practice. Rainbird (2007) and Torres and Ramos (2008) advocate a study of the history of maritime communities connected rather than isolated by the sea. Similarly, Barker (2005, 49) speaks of the "connectivity of the Mediterranean landscape" in which Mediterranean islands were connected to each other and to the mainland at an early date. Knapp and Blake (2005, 10) state that insularity must be seen in relative and dynamic terms, being "historically contingent and culturally constructed, like island identities themselves." The Ryukyus share many features with the islands of the Caribbean and the Mediterranean, being linked to continental land masses whose people were in continuous interaction with the islanders.

My treatment of the Ryukyus begins with island hunter-gatherers and ends with the maturation of the Ryukyu Kingdom. Can a single approach be applied to communities of radically different organization and complexity? The approach of historical ecology allows me to stress the subsistence practices and adaptations of island communities and the political economy of island kingdoms within one conceptual framework. By studying a long time span I can discuss long-term trends in the region, such as the effect of the Kuroshio (Black Current), the dynamic relations between the Japanese Islands and the continent, and the effects of contacts from the south and the continent, as they are played out in the Ryukyus. The islands lie to the east of the Asian continent in the East China Sea, part of an inner sea running from the far north to the tropics. Trade was a key factor for the island political economy of the Ryukyus, as with all island political economies.

In the approach of historical ecology, rather than cultural ecology, the adaptation of humans to the environment is seen as a dialogue, not a dichotomy (Balee 1998, 13). Historical, not evolutionary, events are responsible for the principal changes in relationships between human societies and their immediate environments (ibid., 13). Whitehead advocates a style of reasoning about ecology that puts persons, not organic systems, at the center of explanation of changing ecological relationships through time. He states that "the point of a methodology of historical ecology must be to make human decision making, and the consciousness that drives it, the independent variable in our analysis of environmental dynamics" (1998, 36). According to Balee, "political economies play a key role in affecting ecosystems both present and future and both political economies and ecosystems affect future systems" (1998, 14). I take this to mean that within wide environmental parameters humans have choice and may actually affect environmental outcomes.

We should also consider the archaeology of island kingdoms. Many island kingdoms are small-scale secondary states using sea-lanes to support elites whose land resources may be limited. Port and palace have a particular relationship. Ideologies may include original islanders and later migrants as well as a paradise across the sea.

Keegan and Diamond (1987) raised a number of issues relevant to the study of island archaeology. Were islands reached accidentally or on purpose? Did the discovery of some islands lead to the expectation of more islands to be discovered (autocalysis)? Did land-bridge islands on continental shelves connected to nearby mainland areas at times of lower sea level present different living conditions from oceanic islands? What is the relationship among older and more recently arriving populations? What are the phases of the colonization process and the ecological adjustments necessary to exploit past environments? What kinds of risks were faced by small, early colonizing groups? Keegan (2004) has added several additional considerations. How do lifelines connecting the colony to a parent community increase the chance of survival of a colonizing community? What is the effect of a nursery area, in which colonizing communities develop?

Further questions can be added to those of Keegan. What was the nature of the voyages of discovery that likely occurred before the settlement of any island? Is there a general pattern of push or pull? Were people forced to leave the mainland, or were they attracted to the islands? How did people adjust their own settlement strategy to those employed by the people who preceded them?

How did islanders express their cultural distinctiveness? In his study of Malta, Robb (2001) found that a low degree of interaction with neighbors was a means of expressing identity. At the same time the choice of expressing identity by emphasizing differences from neighbors implies a strong measure of interaction and a knowledge of them.

Was the practice of horticulture essential for tropical or subtropical island colonization? In the Caribbean nonhorticultural peoples apparently found sufficient resources to support independent populations for thousands of years (Fitzpatrick and Keegan 2007). Anderson concludes that the practice of cultivation was a sufficient but not necessary cause of island colonization in Oceania, since Early Lapita people of Fiji and West Polynesia subsisted on an essentially foraging economy. Some of the islands of the Mediterranean were settled before food production occurred, as were islands of the Caribbean (Anderson 2004, 262–263). Were hunter-gatherer populations able to survive in the Ryukyus for long periods of time? While humans seem to have survived at low population density on islands for thousands of years, exponential growth could only occur with cultivation (Hiroto Takamiya 2006b). Some islands in the high latitudes were home to large sea mammals that provided abundant protein for island hunter-gatherers, enabling population increase and the rise of social complexity. Other islands were close enough to large land masses that islanders could commute to obtain food. Hiroto Takamiya (2006b) has proposed that isolated islands must be around 10,000 sq km or more in area to support hunter-gatherers for long time periods. In rare cases such as the Aleutian Islands, high densities of sea mammals may have created high population densities of hunter-gatherers (M. Hudson, personal communication).

Although historical linguistics and archaeology are often linked in island studies, I make only brief reference to historical linguistics in Chapter 10, since I am not competent in this field.

Geographic Setting

The subtropical Ryukyu Islands (Ryūkyū Rettō or Nansei Shotō in Japanese) are part of the island flank of Asia. There are fifty-five major islands with a total area of 3,090 sq km, or 1,193 square miles (Table 1.1). Formed at the boundary between the Eurasian and Philippine Plates, they extend from Japan's southernmost main island of Kyushu to Taiwan. The northern island of Tanegashima is about 60 km from the main island of Kyushu and was connected to Kyushu during the Late Pleistocene, while Yonagunijima is about 60 km from the east coast of Taiwan but has been separated from Taiwan for a long time. To the east of them lies the Pacific Ocean and to the west, the East China Sea. More than a century ago Yoshiwara (1901, 66) noted that the islands share many features with the Andamans, Nicobars, and Lesser Antilles. The Ryukyu Islands are composed of a line of old sea mounts, separate from the continental shelf. To the east of this line is the extremely deep Ryukyu Trench, and to the west of the islands is a line of volcanoes, flanked on their west by the Okinawa Trough (see Chapter 2). Lying from north latitude 24 degrees to 31 degrees and strongly affected by the warm Pacific Black Current (Kuroshio) flowing from the Philippines, the islands have a subtropical climate under the regime of the East Asian monsoon. Annual rainfall on Okinawa is 2,223 mm (87.5 in) with heaviest precipitation in the summer monsoon months and autumn typhoons. Many of the islands are surrounded by extensive coral reefs, which increase in width from north to south (Kinoshita 2009a). At present the northern part of the chain, from Yakushima and Tanegashima to Yoronjima, is part of Kagoshima Prefecture. There is one exception. The island of Iō Torishima, sometimes called Tokara Iōjima, to the northeast of the Amami Islands, a source of sulfur traded to China by the Ryukyu Kingdom, belongs to Kumejima City in Okinawa Prefecture. The area extending from the islands of Okinawa, including Iheyajima and Izenajima, which lie north of Okinawa, to southernmost Yonagunijima constitutes Okinawa Prefecture, which has a population of 1.384 million people. Population density on Okinawajima is 1,015 persons per sq km, or 2,630 persons per square mile, whereas the density on the smaller offlying islands is much lower.

Some of the islands are configured in symbiotic clusters of low and high islands. The low islands, of limestone coral, are well drained; with no standing water, they are relatively free of malaria. The high islands have dense forests with stands of tall, straight timber, fresh water, and moist alluvial soils for paddy cultivation, as well as suitable raw material for stone artifacts, but their wet environment was often malarial. Interdependent groupings of high and low islands can be seen in the case of Amami Ōshima and Kikaigashima; Ishigakijima and

TABLE 1.1 Island Groups in the Ryukyus

Ōsumi	Yakushima (504 sq km, 1935 m), Tanegashima (445 sq km, 263 m), Kuchinoerabujima (36 sq km), Suwanosejima (28 sq km)
Amami Tokara	Amami Ōshima (712 sq km, 699 m), Tokunoshima (247 sq km, 642 m), Okinoerabujima (94 sq km), Kakeromajima (77 sq km), Kikaigashima (57 sq km), Yoronjima
Okinawa	Okinawajima (1,204 sq km, 503 m), Kumejima (59 sq km, 310 m), Izenajima, Iheyajima, Iejima, Agunijima, Kerama Rettō, Kudakajima, Tsukenjima, Hamahigajima, Henzajima, etc.
Sakishima Miyako Group	Miyakojima (159 sq km, 115 m), Irabujima (29 sq km), Ikemajima, Ōgamijima, Kurimajima, Minnajima, Taramajima
Sakishima Yaeyama Group	Iriomotejima (289 sq km, 442 m), Ishigakijima (222 sq km, 512 m), Yonagunijima (29 sq km), Taketomijma, Kobamajima, Hatomajima, Aragusukujima, Kayamajima, Haterumajima, Kuroshimajima

Notes: Island area and maximum elevations are given for largest islands. Island areas are from the Japanese language website http://www.ja.wikipedia.org/wiki/島の一覧 (*shima no ichiran*), accessed May 1, 2012. Island elevations (approximate) are from Pearson 1969, 16.

Miyakojima; Okinawa, Kudakajima and Tsukenjima; and Iriomotejima, Hatomajima, Haterumashima, and Kobamajima. In some cases coral limestone and volcanic materials are found in the same island, as in Amami Ōshima, Tokunoshima, Okinawajima, Kumejima, Ishigakijima, and others.

In summary the islands of the Ryukyus are interwoven strands of sea mounts and coral caps separated from the continental shelf by the Okinawa Trough, washed by the Black Current, battered by typhoons in late summer, and affected by the East Asian monsoon.

Archaeologists usually group the Ryukyus into Northern, Central, and Southern Ryukyus. The Northern group includes the islands between Amami Ōshima and Kyushu, while the Central Ryukyus include the islands from Amami Ōshima and Kikaigashima to Okinawajima and all of its offliers. The Southern Ryukyus consist of the Sakishima Islands. Sakishima can be divided into the Miyako Islands and the Yaeyama Islands, the latter comprising Ishigakijima, Iriomotejima, and their respective offliers, as well as Yonagunijima. Two deep ocean trenches, the Tokara Strait to the north of Amami Ōshima and the Kerama Gap to the south of Okinawajima, form natural boundaries within the islands. Because of their depth they prevented the crossing of certain animals in the past.

Historical Overview of the Ryukyus

For the reader who is unfamiliar with the Ryukyus, a general historical overview may be useful. The earliest evidence of human occupation in the Ryukyus consists of Late Pleistocene modern *Homo sapiens* skeletons dated to as early as 32,000 years ago. The latest date for this group is around 16,000 years ago, after which there is a hiatus of about 8,000 years without archaeological remains. Following this hiatus, around 7,000 BC, the northern islands were colonized by groups from Kyushu, while the Sakishima Islands were inhabited by around 2900 BC by groups from some as yet undetermined location to the south. Agriculture began surprisingly late, around AD 800. Around AD 1429 a unified maritime state, the Ryukyu Kingdom, emerged on Okinawajima. (I use the term Chūzan Kingdom to refer to the central Okinawan polity of Chūzan up to AD 1429 and Ryukyu Kingdom to refer to the unified kingdom that emerged with Chūzan's victory over its northern and southern rivals.) After roughly two centuries of independence the Ryukyu Kingdom was dominated by the Satsuma Fiefdom of southern Kyushu in AD 1609 (Kerr 1958, 183–190). Sweet potatoes and sugarcane were introduced to the islands shortly after AD 1600; the former became an important crop for subsistence, and the latter became a profitable export commodity tightly controlled by Satsuma. In AD 1879 the islands were taken over by Meiji Japan, and in AD 1945, with the defeat of Japan in World War II, the Central and Southern Ryukyus, from Amami Ōshima to Sakishima, became an American military dependency, with residual Japanese sovereignty. Amami Ōshima and surrounding islands as far south as Yoronjima were returned to Japan in 1953, and the rest of the Ryukyus were returned in 1972. Although it may seem that the Ryukyus are marginal to the Asian continent, they occupy a central position, being equidistant from China, Korea, and Japan. The strategic position of Okinawa in East Asia has been realized since the Ming dynasty (AD 1368 to 1644) and was an important factor in the movement by Japan to protect its own hegemony in the nineteenth century AD. The location and maintenance of Okinawan military bases remain critical international issues in 2014 (Johnson 2004, 2010).

Chronological Framework

An archaeological chronology can be built using various kinds of relative and absolute dating (Figure 1.3). Geological events such as the Kikai eruption and deposition of Akahoya Ash (7280 BP) and the Meiwa Tsunami of AD 1771, which produced pumice deposits and moved large porite boulders inland (Atsushi Suzuki et al. 2008), have also been used. Chinese coins from various

Date	Period JMI	Sub-division	Takamiya Chronology	Pottery Type		Decoration (Itō Shinji 2000)	Important Trade Items	Important Sites
pre 10,000 BC	Palaeo-lithic	Palaeo-lithic						Minatogawa Fissure
	JŌMON	Incipient	Okinawan Neolithic	Noguni Shellmound Group IV				
		Earliest	ESM I	Yabuchi Agaribaru		Tsumegata thumbnail		Noguni Shellmounds Toguchi Agaribaru
ca. 4000 BC ca.3000 BC		Early	ESM II	Jōkonmon Murokawa Lower Layer Sobata Kamino A Kamino B		Jōkonmon	Sobata Pottery (Toguchi Agaribaru Site)	
		Middle	ESM III	Omonawa I (Gushikawa I) Omonawa II (Gushikawa II) Omonawa III (Gushikawa III) Omonawa IV (Gushikawa IV) Omonawa V (Gushikawa V)		applied strip		Kogachibaru Kamino
ca. 2000 BC ca. 1000 BC		Late	ESM IV	Kamino D Kamino E Iha, Nakadomari Ogidō Ōyama Murokawa		punctate	Izumi Pottery Ichiki Pottery (Urasoe Shellmound)	Attabaru Mēbaru Murokawa
		Latest	ESM V	Murokawa Upper Layer, Kayauchibanta Uzahama Nakahara		thickened rim	pottery types parallel to Kurokawa Yan knife coin	Shinugudō
300 BC BC ------ AD	YAYOI	Early	LSM I	Maezato	Nakahara Aharen Ura Layer IV	plain pointed bottom	Itazuke II Type (Maezato SM) Kamenoko Type (Kusatobaru Site)	Toguchi Momenbaru
		Middle	LSM II	Gushibaru	Hamayabaru		Yuriki Pottery Yamanokuchi Pottery Itazuke Pottery	Gushiken Kamon Uken
200		Late	LSM III	Akajangā	Ufutōbaru		Menda Type Pottery (Gushibaru Shellmound)	Heshikiya Tōbaru
500	KOFUN to beginning of HEIAN		LSM IV	Fensa Lower Layer	Akajangā Fensa Lower Layer	constriction above flat foot	Kaigen Tsūhō coins mainland type *sueki* Kamuiyaki gray stoneware	Nazakibaru Fensa Gusuku
	HEIAN to MUROMACHI		Ko Ryukyu	Gusuku Period	Gusuku Pottery	wide-bottom type	Nagasaki steatite cauldrons Chinese thick-lip whiteware lotus petal celadon bowl	Isamaebaru No. 1 Layers 8,9

Figure 1.3. Chronology of the Shellmound Period of the Central Ryukyus (Okinawa Islands). The abbreviations ESM and LSM stand for Early Shellmound Period and Late Shellmound Period respectively, and JMI stands for the four major Japanese main islands. After Okinawa Kenritsu Maizō 2001a, 137.

periods are found in the Ryukyus. The earliest are Meitōsen knife coins of the state of Yan, Warring States Period (475–221 BC). Goshusen coins were minted in the Han dynasty (202 BC to AD 220) and again in the Sui dynasty (AD 581–618). Kaigen Tsūhō coins (of the Tang dynasty, minted in the seventh and ninth centuries) have also been found (Zaidan 2003, 227–231). These coins can be used to give a minimum date for their time of manufacture, but the length of time these coins were held before entering archaeological deposits is not clear. They could have been used for a longer or shorter period after they were made.

With the publication of a careful review of carbon dates from the Ryukyus (Najima et al. 2008), a new stage of chronology building in the Ryukyus was achieved. Before this no systematic tabulation of dates was available. Dates were often published without their complete laboratory identification number, range of variation, or recalibration. Najima et al. (2008) have tabulated a total of 409 dates from Amami (68), Okinawa (266), and Sakishima (75) with recalibration. I have used some of these dates in chronological discussions in several chapters. Radiocarbon dates (14C) are often expressed in years BP (before AD 1950) as well as in years BC or AD. I have tried to use calibrated dates, indicated as "cal BP," as often as possible; however, often the precise recalibration curve is not given. Readers who are not familiar with the proper use of radiocarbon dates should check one of the many standard references that are available.

The archaeological chronology has been built up through relative dating of pottery types and stratigraphy. Cross-dating of Jōmon and Yayoi pottery sherds from Kyushu found in sites of the Northern and Central Ryukyus has been has been carried out extensively (Itō Shinji 2000; Shinzato Takayuki 2000). Chronologies based on East Asian mediaeval trade ceramics are also employed. Many Okinawan scholars cross-date Ryukyu finds with the Dazaifu and Hakata sites of northern Kyushu, from which meticulous stylistic typologies of Chinese, Korean, and Southeast Asian ceramics have been correlated with historically dated stratigraphic layers (Arakaki and Seto 2005; Seto et al. 2007). Since sites where particular ceramics were used will always be later than sites where the same ceramics were produced, it is more reliable to build a chronology for use sites by selecting other use sites that can be independently dated than by selecting dated production sites. Thus Ryukyu sites are usually dated by a chronology built up in Japan, rather than from Chinese or Southeast Asian production sites.

The history of the earliest Okinawan kingdoms up to and including the Ryukyu Kingdom, the *Chūzan seikan* (Haneji 1983) was first written by the Okinawans themselves in the seventeenth century AD. It contains records of events such as the great fires in Shuri Gusuku in AD 1453 and 1459. No earlier historical documents written by the Okinawans have survived. The dynastic histories of China and Korea provide some information for the tribute missions and associated events in the fourteenth and fifteenth centuries AD (Wada 2006). Japanese historical documents have also been used to shed light on the sites of the fifteenth and sixteenth centuries AD.

The basic divisions of the chronology of the Central Ryukyus used in the book are Palaeolithic, Shellmound Period, Gusuku Period, Early Ryukyu Kingdom, and Late Ryukyu Kingdom. The extreme northern Ryukyus, including Yakushima and Tanegashima, follow the chronology of Kyushu and the main islands of Japan (Kyushu, Honshu, Shikoku, and Hokkaido)—Palaeolithic, Jōmon, Yayoi, Kofun, and so on—while the Southern Ryukyus have a separate chronology reflecting their isolation from the Japanese main islands.

Based on carbon dates from fissure and cave deposits in association with human fossils but without associated artifacts, people termed "Palaeolithic" are thought to have inhabited Late Pleistocene islands from around 30,000 BC to around 16,000 BC. A gap of some eight to nine thousand years separates this period from the Shellmound Period, which dates from 7000 BC to AD 1050. The Shellmound Period is often referred to as Neolithic by Japanese archaeologists, in keeping with the Japanese and Northeast Asian tradition of referring to cultures with pottery and polished stone tools as Neolithic. However, there is no conclusive evidence of cultivated plants, the usual hallmark of the Neolithic in Western archaeology, until the end of the Shellmound Period. This long period is divided into Early and Late Shellmound Periods, the dividing line set at about 300 BC. This date was the old dividing line between Jōmon and Yayoi, and in the Ryukyus it is the approximate time of a gradual shift from Jōmon-like wares to Yayoi-like wares. However, this dating does not take into account the revision of the Jōmon-Yayoi chronology based on AMS dates (Harunari and Imamura 2004, 11; Ōnuki 2005). The transition from Jōmon to Yayoi is placed at around 1000 BC, Earliest Yayoi at 1000 to 800 BC, Early Yayoi at 800 to 450 BC, Middle Yayoi at 450 BC to AD 50, and Late Yayoi at AD 50 to 250. Since it is thought that the Jōmon and Yayoi may have coexisted in Kyushu for as long as five hundred years, a date of 300 BC may be appropriate as the dividing line between Jōmon and Yayoi in the Northern and Central Ryukyus.

Although the Okinawan relative chronology is amply supported by cross-dating of artifacts from Japan, it is a relative, general chronology that has only recently been matched with an absolute radiocarbon chronology of modern standards. Many Okinawan archaeologists use the standard chronology of the Japanese main islands to discuss the archaeological record of the Northern and Central Ryukyus, rather than the system of Early and Late Shellmound Periods, since many readers are more familiar with it. The authoritative review of Okinawan archaeology published in the *History of Okinawa Prefecture* (Zaidan 2003) also uses the Jōmon subperiods rather than subperiods of the Shellmound Period.

In general, the Early Shellmound Period coincides with the Jōmon culture of the Japanese main islands. It is divided into five arbitrary time periods, the first of about three thousand years and the remaining periods of about one thousand years each. Takamiya Hiroe divided his Early Shellmound Period into five subperiods (1994, 24, table 1–2), which are roughly equivalent to five of the six subperiods of the Jōmon chronology of the Japanese main islands. In my treatment I have tried to indicate a specific period in both the Shellmound Period and Jōmon chronologies.

An alternative chronology for the Shellmound Period created four large divisions, Earliest, Early, Middle, and Late (Okinawa Kenritsu Maizō 2005a, 3). As seen in Figure 1.4, these periods are aligned with the larger temporal divisions of Takamiya Hiroe. The Late Shellmound Period is divided into four time

Asato Chronology		Society and Culture	Site Location	Pottery Types	Present Chronology	Takamiya Chronology	Japan	Date
Palaeolithic		Unknown			Palaeolithic	Palaeolithic	Palaeolithic	
Neolithic							Incipient Initial	8000 BC
Neolithic	Migration 1	Jōmon people arrive from north, some settlement, culture like Kyushu	shoreline	Nail-Impressed (Tsumegata)	Shellmound Period: Earliest, Early	Early Shellmound: I	Jōmon: Early	4000 BC
Neolithic	Migration 2	Jōmon people arrive from north, Kyushu style culture plus distinctive features	shoreline, below cliffs	Jōkonmon Murokawa Lower Sobata	Shellmound Period: Earliest, Mid	Early Shellmound: II	Jōmon: Middle	3000 BC
Neolithic	Adaptation	adaptation and local features	shoreline, below cliffs	Omonawa Zentei	Shellmound Period: Earliest, Late	Early Shellmound: III	Jōmon: Late	2000 BC
Neolithic	Diffusion	basic adaptation, spread to all islands, continuation of distinctive features	below terraces, beach	Nakadomari Iha Ōgido Ōyama Murokawa	Shellmound Period: Early	Early Shellmound: IV	Jōmon: Late	1000 BC
Neolithic	Development 1	population increase, development of villages	terrace periphery	Kayauchibanta Uzahama Nakahara	Shellmound Period: Middle	Early Shellmound: V	Jōmon: Final	
Neolithic	Development 2	development of villages, marine adaptation, exchange	beach	Ufutōbaru Maezato Gushibaru Akajangā	Shellmound Period: Late	Late Shellmound: I to IV	Yayoi: Early, Middle, Late; Kofun; Heian	AD 1; AD 800
Neolithic	Class Society	spread of agriculture, iron artifacts, emergence of chief class, construction of *gusuku*	low hills	Kamuiyaki Gusuku Pottery trade ceramics	Gusuku Period	Gusuku Period	Kamakura Muromachi	AD 1100

Figure 1.4. Interpretive chronology of the Shellmound Period for the Okinawa Islands. After Asato Shijun, Okinawa Kenritsu Maizō 2005a, 3.

periods, three of which match the traditional Early, Middle, and Late of the Yayoi Period of the main islands of Japan, while the Late Shellmound Period IV extends from roughly AD 300 to 850 (Kofun Period to the early part of the Heian Period).

A major transition follows the Shellmound Period with the Gusuku Period (AD 1050 to 1429). This is a period of rapid social change brought about by the adoption of cultivation, substantial immigration, and widespread mediaeval trade in the East China Sea region, and the emergence of contending chiefdoms and small states. Although Kin (1998) has proposed three transitional periods instead of a single period, in the interests of simplicity I have opted for a single period. The period begins at about the time of the beginning of the appearance of Chinese whitewares (Appendix 1) and the establishment of the Kamuiyaki kilns on Tokunoshima in the eleventh century and ends with the unification of the Okinawa Islands by the Chūzan Kingdom in AD 1429. From around the beginning of the thirteenth century AD to the beginning of the fifteenth century AD, the Shunten Dynasty, (AD 1187 to 1259), Eiso Dynasty (AD 1260 to 1349), and Satto Dynasties (AD 1350 to 1405) are recorded in the *Chūzan seikan*. While little is known about the Shunten Dynasty, research on Urasoe Gusuku has provided historical information on King Eiso (AD 1260 to 1299) (Asato Susumu 2006) (Appendix 2). Although a case can be made that unification took place in AD 1422 (Wada 2006, 50–51), I have decided to use the date preferred by most scholars, AD 1429 (Takara 1987). The subsequent period (AD 1429 to 1609) covers the time of the fluorescence of the Chūzan Kingdom, from the unification and consolidation of its power until the invasion of Satsuma. The First Shō Dynasty (also referred to as the Shō Shishō Dynasty after its founder) extended from AD 1406 to 1469. It was followed by the Second Shō or Shō En Dynasty, from AD 1470 to 1879. The major turning point, the loss of independence in AD 1609 when the Satsuma Fiefdom of Kagoshima invaded and subjugated the Ryukyu Kingdom, marks a change to Early Modern (Kinsei) Ryukyu, which I have termed the Late Ryukyu Kingdom. This period lies beyond the scope of this book.

The chronology of the Southern Ryukyus (Sakishima Islands) has some gaps that may be filled in with subsequent research. It is in its formative stages. Following finds of fossil humans in the Late Pleistocene, there is a hiatus until around 2900 BC, when the Shimotabaru Culture (about 2900 BC to 2000 BC) appears. A chronological gap of about 1,100 years exists between the Shimotabaru Period and the Non-Ceramic Period (about 900 BC to AD 1100 AD), a period marked by the complete absence of pottery. At the end of the period, interaction with the Central Ryukyus and the Japanese main islands expanded rapidly, and the islanders were brought under the formal control of the Ryukyu Kingdom around the end of the fifteenth century AD.

Chapter Outline

In the chapter that follows, Chapter 2, I discuss the features of the islands that have had the most profound impacts on human settlement: geomorphology, climate, and vegetation. In Chapter 3, the earliest human inhabitants of the islands are introduced. In the Northern Ryukyus, there is artifactual evidence of Palaeolithic occupation. In Okinawa and Sakishima, however, bones have been recovered, but we have few clues about their origins and life patterns. Chapter 4 is concerned with the arrival of Jōmon hunter-gatherers in the period from 7000 to 300 BC, the conditions under which they migrated, and their life in the islands. What lured them to the Ryukyus, and what were the choices necessary for their survival? The shifting boundaries of their island communities in interaction with their Kyushu homeland are explored in that chapter. In Chapter 5,

I discuss their life on the islands and their food-getting strategies. From the last few centuries BC to the end of the first millennium AD, one of the most important activities linking these communities in the East China Sea was the exchange of tropical marine shells. The choice of species, the objects fashioned from them, and the groups who traded them changed at various times. This important theme in the life of the islanders is discussed in Chapter 6. Around the end of the first millennium AD, quantum changes, linked to changes in the Japanese main islands, took place throughout the Ryukyus. The arrival of new groups brought cereal cultivation, which was rapidly adopted. Trade with mediaeval China, Japan, and Korea opened the Ryukyus to increased interaction, and societies within the Ryukyus showed increased social hierarchy. These changes are covered in Chapter 7. Since trade is a crucial topic in understanding the development of the Chūzan and later Ryukyu Kingdoms), I devote a separate chapter, Chapter 8, to exploring its dynamics and context. In Chapter 9, the "classic" Ryukyu Kingdom, from the fifteenth to sixteenth centuries AD, is covered. An entirely new kind of community, a maritime city-state, arose in central Okinawa and subsequently expanded to control all of the Central and Southern Ryukyus. The archaeology of castle complexes such as Shuri and Nakijin is discussed as well as the complex web of maritime trade that sustained the life of the kingdom. The political economy of the Ryukyu Kingdom was intricately adapted to island life.

In the concluding chapter, Chapter 10, I focus on several aspects of Ryukyu archaeology that are significant for world archaeology and the archaeology of islands. These aspects include (1) human choices in adapting to the islands, (2) the shifting nature of human communities and islandscapes in the Ryukyus, (3) the development of systems of trade, (4) the political economy and production of culture in the maritime Ryukyu Kingdom, (5) the strategic position of the Ryukyu Kingdom in East Asia and its implications for contemporary geopolitics, and (6) comparisons with similar island arcs in other parts of the world.

Since the discussion of the Gusuku and Early Ryukyu Kingdom Periods relies heavily on a chronology based on East Asian trade ceramics, I include a discussion of the ceramic chronology in Appendix 1. A chronology of the rulers of the Ryukyu Kingdom and its predecessors is provided in Appendix 2.

Chapter 2

The Active Environment of the Ryukyus

The active role of the environment in shaping human communities in the Ryukyus may seem obvious to Western readers. However, the historical typological approach of Japanese archaeology relegates the environment to a passive background role if it is mentioned at all. While there are exceptions, Holocene environmental change is often ignored in site reports and surveys. There is much to be done to fully integrate environmental data into the archaeological discourse of the Ryukyus; this chapter is a preliminary effort.

The Ryukyu Islands form a chain 1,100 km long. In east-west cross-section, from the Pacific Ocean, they are composed of the following components: the Ryukyu Trench, the main island arc of sea mounts, an inner line of volcanoes, the Okinawa Trough, and the continental shelf. The line of volcanoes extends between the western side of the Ryukyu Islands and the Okinawa Trough, and can be seen in the Tokara Islands and Iō Torishima. From these islands it continues under the sea as far south as Yonagunijima. As mentioned in Chapter 1, the islands are divided into three groups, northern, central, and southern, divided by the Tokara and Kerama Gaps. Some special features of the islands have played important roles in the development of living patterns in the region. These features are the unique combination of inland broadleaf evergreen forest with Indo-Pacific strand flora and coral reefs, the East Asian monsoon, the Kuroshio (Black Current), and seasonal typhoons.

Geological Formation

Although the earliest humans who lived in the Ryukyus date to about 32,000 years ago, it is useful to know something about the history of earlier geological periods in order to comprehend the environment of the islands and their animal and plant resources.

In brief, the geological basement of the Ryukyus consists of metamorphic rocks of the Ishigaki Group, the Tomuru or Fuzaki Layers, which have been dated to between 159 and 175 million years ago (Early to Middle Jurassic) by potassium argon dating. The Tomuru Layer, the oldest in the Ryukyus, is distributed only in Yaeyama and the sea bottom near Miyakojima. Stone from the Tomuru Formation was ideal for stone tools of the later Sakishima islanders. Other very old formations of roughly similar age are the chert formations (also prized as raw materials for stone artifacts) in the Motobu Region of Okinawa and on Amami Ōshima. On top of these formations there are metamorphosed rocks of the earlier Cenozoic, dating from 66 million years ago to 1.8 million years ago, and silts, sandstones, tuffs, and mudstone, which were deposited during the Miocene and Pliocene (23.7 to 1.6 million years ago). These deposits, termed the Shimajiri Group, are up to 2,000 m thick. They were laid down in what is termed the Shimajiri Sea. These underlie the thick layer of Ryukyu Limestone, dating from 1.6 million years ago (Kizaki 1985).

The limestone formations and reefs defining Ryukyu topography were formed in the Pleistocene Period, dated from 1.8 million years ago to about 12,000 years ago. At that time marine transgressions and regressions on the continental shelf, which extended to within roughly 200 km of the Ryukyu Island Arc, the deepening and extension of the Okinawa Trough, and the building up of limestone over the islands, in both deep and shallow seas, took place. (A revision in 2009 of Pleistocene dating by the International Union of Geological Sciences set the beginning of the Pleistocene at 2.588 million years ago, but this revision has not yet found its way into the literature on the Ryukyus. The following discussion is mostly concerned with the end of the Pleistocene.) The Okinawa Trough is a submarine rift valley that formed to the west of the Ryukyus, separating the island arc from the continental shelf. It serves as a trap for the sediment deposited by Chinese rivers into the East China Sea, protecting the coral reefs of the Ryukyus from land-derived deposits that would kill the coral. Volcanic activity was particularly important in the Northern Ryukyus. The successive warm and cold periods and changes in the topography of ocean floors created dramatic changes in sea level, high sea levels coinciding with warm climatic periods and glacial melting, and low sea levels coinciding with cold periods and glacial expansion. High sea level diminished the size of the islands, whereas low levels created large island masses and even land bridges between the islands and the continent. In the Early Pleistocene (1.3 million years ago to 700,000 years ago), the Ryukyus consisted of five large islands, separated from each other and from Kyushu and Taiwan. Around 400,000 years ago, the Uruma Crustal Movement created sharp subsidence, deepening the Kerama Gap between Okinawajima and Miyakojima, and around 200,000 years ago, the Yonaguni Trench deepened the separation between Taiwan and Yonagunijima.

In the case of the Ryukyus, the Tokara Strait to the north of the Amami Islands persisted as a water barrier throughout the Pleistocene, but there was a land bridge joining the southern Ryukyus to Taiwan on at least one occasion. A recent volume of the *History of Okinawa Prefecture* (*Okinawa Ken shi*) (Okinawa Ken Bunka Shinkōkai 2006, 19) shows only one such land bridge during the Pleistocene but offers no supporting evidence for there being only one. Zoologists Otsuka and Takahashi (2000) propose three Pleistocene land bridges. Although they cite specific fossil assemblages, the dating of the assemblages is imprecise. It appears that the imprecise dating of the assemblages may be the basis for different interpretations. The *History of Okinawa Prefecture* states that there have been no land bridges linking the southern Ryukyus to the continent for the past 200,000 years (Okinawa Ken Bunka Shinkōkai 2006, 19).

For archaeologists the main point is that, whatever the Pleistocene date, the southern land bridge(s) from what is now Taiwan to the Ryukyus allowed continental animals to migrate into the Ryukyus as far as the Tokara Strait so that by the time of the earliest human communities there was a surprising range of animals to hunt. The main species was the Ryukyu deer (*Cervus astyolodon*), which flourished during the Pleistocene and finally became extinct "some time in the Late Pleistocene" (Otsuka and Takahashi 2000, 29) or "just after the last Glacial Period" (Minagawa et al. 2005, 93). In addition there were muntjac deer, which also became extinct. Endemic wild boar (*Sus riukiuanus*) and two genera of poisonous snakes for which the Ryukyus are famous were also present and survive to present times. According to Otsuka and Takahashi there is also a characteristic fossil assemblage of Miyakojima vertebrates, including another deer species (*Capreolus miyakoensis*).

At the height of the last cold episode of the Pleistocene, around 20,000 years ago, sea level was about 140 m below its current level. Many islands sharing the same underwater mountain ridge coalesced into larger islands.

The islands took their present shape the beginning of the Holocene Period, roughly 12,000 years ago to the present. According to the above scenario, *Homo sapiens,* dated to the Late Pleistocene (see Chapter 3), would have had to cross from the Asian mainland to the Southern and Central Ryukyus by water. A second gap, the Tokara Strait, existed north of the Amami Islands (see Figure 2.1). Apparently humans did not cross the Tokara Strait at this time. Deposits that span the transition between the Terminal Pleistocene and the Holocene have recently been excavated in caves in southern Okinawa (Okinawa Ken-

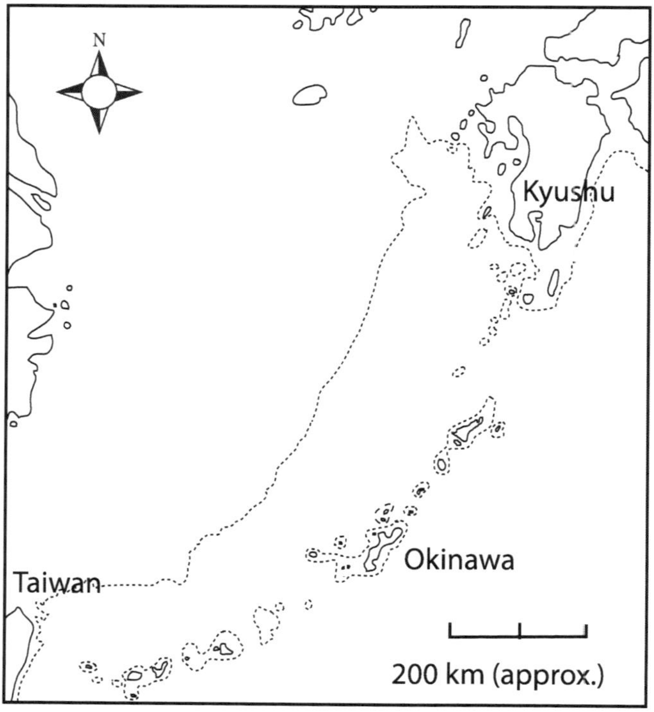

Figure 2.1. The Ryukyu Islands in the Late Pleistocene at about 20,000 BP. The dotted lines indicate Pleistocene shorelines. Redrawn from Okinawa Ken Bunka Shinkōkai 2006, 19.

ritsu Hakubutsukan 2010). They may shed light on early human populations and faunal extinctions.

A Late Land Bridge?

In the Mid-Pleistocene, according to Kamiya (2007, 180), the Amami Islands were separated from Yakushima and Tanegashima by the wide Tokara Strait, and the Okinawa Islands were separated from the Southern Ryukyus by the narrow Kerama Gap. However, Kimura (1996) has postulated the existence of Pleistocene land bridges, based on drill cores and submarine exploration. In the period from 200,000 to 20,000 years ago, Kimura postulates that the two gaps were land or possibly channels as narrow as 1 km over which animals could migrate at low tide (1996, 277). Kimura has concluded that the land bridges were broken at a late date by very sharp subsidence. Although this hypothesis is accepted by Otsuka and Takahashi (2000, 33), other authors do not appear to accept it. Kamiya (2007, 176) does not show the late Pleistocene land bridges postulated by Kimura (1996). Kamiya indicates that the Yonaguni Trench, a deep sea channel between Yonaguni and Taiwan, was present by 20,000 BP (see Figure 1.1). But, as mentioned above, a recent volume on land forms in the *History of Okinawa* (Okinawa Ken Bunka Shinkōkai 2006, 19) does not indicate the presence of such late land bridges.

Changes in Sea Level

During the Pleistocene, substantial changes in sea level occurred along with shifts in the relative elevation of the islands created by changes in the earth's crust. According to Qin et al. (1996, 152–156) three cycles of transgression occurred in the East China Sea shelf and its adjacent areas within the last 100,000 years. Based on several lines of evidence, Qin et al. proposed a period of high sea level from 100,000 to 70,000 BP followed by a period of low sea level from 70,000 to 39,000 BP, high sea level from 39,000 to 23,000 BP, and regression from 23,000 to 18,000 BP, at the height of the Wurm Glaciation. They propose that during this regression sea level was lower than present mean sea level by more than 130 m. During the last glacial maximum the Okinawa Trough changed from an open sea environment to a semi-enclosed marginal basin because of this sea level change. The Kuroshio flowed on the western side of the Ryukyus through the Ryukyu Trench until 7500 BP. This is based on the absence of the *Pulleniatina* group of prehistoric Foraminifera, most characteristic of the warm water temperature of the Kuroshio Current (Ujiie et al. 1991). Sea level began to rise around 18,000 BP.

Recent research on Late Pleistocene sea level records from reef sites in the Bahamas Islands and Tahiti show a rapid rise of about 14 to 18 m in less than five hundred years, between 14,650 and 14,310 years ago (Deschamps et al. 2012), at the time of the Bolling Warming. Such a dramatic rise, created by rapidly melting ice sheets, must have had a great impact on Pleistocene Period Ryukyu islanders. No finds have been recorded from this time period. If they moved to higher ground, why have their remains not been found?

Sea level of the East China and Yellow Seas rose from 36 m to 16 m below modern sea level from 9500 to 9200 cal kyr BP (Xiang et al. 2008) and continued to rise to the present level at 7500 cal kyr BP, reaching a high sea level of +2 to 3 m at about 7000 cal yr BP (Xiang et al. 2007). Hongo and Kayanne (2010, 143) identified Mid-Holocene high sea level at 3 plus or minus 2.5 m above present mean sea level at 5000 cal years BP.

At the same time that Holocene sea levels changed, uplift occurred. Notches created by wave action on coral outcrops show changes in sea level as islands were pushed up by Holocene hydro-isostatic uplift. A many as six separate notches can be seen. Hydro-isostasis occurs in interglacials and the Holocene when the sea bottom is pushed down by the weight of an increased volume of water. Accompanying this downward push is an upward push on adjacent land masses. This upward push is greater for the large islands of the Ryukyus such as Okinawajima and Ishigakijima than for smaller islands with less mass. Therefore relative sea level on large and small islands may differ because of hydro-isostasis (Kamiya 2007, 31). A few islands in the Northern Ryukyus show degrees of emergence from 6 to 14 m from local additional tectonic uplift (Koba et al. 1982). Holocene sea levels not only affect settlement choices of ancient islanders, but also obliterate or remove archaeological sites from their primary context.

The Kuroshio Current

The Kuroshio is the largest boundary surface current in the western Pacific (Hsueh 2000) (see Figure 1.1). Its impact on the Ryukyus is profound, affecting climate, marine resources, and geological constituents. It is also responsible for the constant flow of organisms that create and support the Okinawan reefs. It is 1.0 km thick, 150 to 200 km wide, with a high temperature of 28 to 29 degrees Centigrade in summer and 22 to 25 degrees Centigrade in winter. Relatively little is known about it compared to the Gulf Stream of the Atlantic, since research on the current requires sea bottom cores from very great depths. Where it passes between the eastern side of Taiwan and the southern part of the Ryukyu Island Arc, it is deflected upward as it approaches the Ilan Ridge. Then it flows northeast into the Okinawa Trough. Information on the Holocene history of the Kuroshio from deep sea cores from the bottom of the Okinawa Trough provides insights into Holocene climatic change.

Data from two sediment cores, A7 and EO17, in the middle Okinawa Trough show a sudden drop in sedimentation at 11,200 cal BP owing to a rapid rise of sea level after the Younger Dryas, which submerged the large continental shelf of the East China Sea and decreased the effect of the estuaries that provided sediment to the basin (Xiang et al. 2007). In addition, data from two cores, numbers 255 and B-3GC, from the southern and northern Okinawa Trough respectively, have confirmed cyclical changes in the strength of the Kuroshio in the Holocene (Jian et al. 2000). These resulted in lower temperatures in at least the Ryukyus and Japan. Jian et al. found that winter sea surface temperatures increased at 7500 to 7300 cal BP in parallel with an increase in warm water planktonic Foraminifera, *Pulleniatina obliquiloculata*. They concluded that this indicates the reentry of the Kuroshio into the Okinawa Trough, as did Ujiie and Ujiie (1999). Other scientists have concluded that the current was already flowing through the Okinawa Trough but increased in strength at this time (Liu et al. 2007; Xiang et al. 2007). Several episodes of weakening of the Kuroshio have been noted around 600, 1700, 3300, 4600, 5900, 8100, and 9400 cal BP (Yu et al. 2008; Jian et al. 2000, 315; Xiang et al. 2008). The four recent cooling events at 4600, 3300, 1700, and 700 cal BP have been correlated with the Middle/Late Jōmon Cold Stage, Latest Jōmon Cold Stage, Kofun Cold Stage, and Little Ice Age. According to Jian et al. (2000, 317) the mean pacing of these events is around 1,500 years, and they are correlated with events in the North Atlantic, Arabian Sea, and South China Sea marine sediment cores and Greenland ice cores. These cooling episodes were caused by increases in the strength of the winter monsoon, which cooled surface sea water temperatures.

Ujiie has recorded that the *Pulleniatina* group also disappeared from the Okinawa Trough area between 4,400 and 3,300 years ago, "indicating the appearance of a barrier that prevented the prominent flowing of the Kuroshio Current through the Okinawa Trough" (1998, 249). The eastward turning of the Kuroshio Current at the south of the southern Ryukyu Arc seems to have enhanced a cooling period in the Middle Jōmon Period (Ujiie and Ujiie 1999, 38). Further research is needed to correlate these trends. An absence of *Pulleniatina* was also recognized in a core from the South China Sea (Li et al. 1997, 66), although it was not as distinct as the East China Sea case. Li et al. (1997) regard both cases as evidence of climatic cooling rather than obstruction of the Kuroshio, and Ujiie and Ujiie (1999, 38) acknowledge that there is room for such an alternative explanation, subject to more precise core investigations. The same sharp cooling event is noted in pollen studies (see Table 2.2 below). Another perspective is provided by Kawahata and Ohshima (2004), who found in their sea core from the northern edge of the East China Sea the pollen of *Phyllocladus,* a podocarp found in modern times in the mountains of New Guinea, Indonesia, and the Philippines. Since this pollen is never found in Quaternary-Tertiary sediments in Japan, they state that it must have been carried by the Kuroshio flowing through the East China Sea in "last glacial times." They do not think that there was an eastward deflection of the Kuroshio (Kawahata and Ohshima 2004, 269), but instead there was a Late Pleistocene cooling event (see also Li et al. 1997). They admit that it is difficult to quantify the *Phyllocladus* data at present (Kawahata and Ohshima 2004, 269). (The dates in Ujiie's studies have been calibrated using CALIB 3.03; however, other dates in this discussion have not been calibrated, to my knowledge.) Kurozumi noted that at the time of the Jōmon Transgression, three species of shell that are found in China appeared in the Ryukyus and Kyushu (2008). Their distribution is independent of the Kuroshio. They may be indicative of environmental changes that are not understood at present.

Zhang et al. (2008) noted a weakening of the summer monsoon from AD 850 to 940 and a strengthening of the summer monsoon from AD 1020 to 1340, followed by a subsequent weakening from AD 1360 to 1850. Fluctuations in the summer monsoon must have affected rainfall during the growing season, increasing yields during the Chinese Song dynasty (AD 960 to 1279) and the Ryukyu Gusuku Period. The precise change in mean temperature is very difficult to calculate because of ranges of variation in the counting of warm and cool temperature Foraminifera, dating, and temperature determination. From Chinese historical records, the climate of the cold period of about 1,700 years ago was 2 to 4 degrees C lower than today (Liu et al. 2007).

The significance of these fluctuations for the inhabitants of the Ryukyu Islands lies not only in changes in mean annual temperature, but also in the strength of the winter and summer monsoon, which must have affected rainfall patterns, shoreline settlement, and navigation as well as crop yields. Although it is difficult at present to provide a synthetic interpretation of the effects of these changes on human settlement, I believe that in the near future the full value of these palaeoenvironmental data sets for archaeology will be realized.

Soils

Although contemporary studies of Okinawan soils are directed at modern agriculture, particularly sugarcane and rice (Kokudo Chōsa 1983), they provide clues concerning the development of Okinawan prehistoric cultivation and subsistence practices. Major soil types, shown in Table 2.1, can be divided into four groups based on their parent materials. Most of the soils can only be used for upland, dry-crop cultivation; they have been in use since the Gusuku Period.

1. Reddish soils (Okin. *māji*) are found overlying karst uplands formed of Ryukyu Limestone.
2. Soils derived from Tertiary congealed lava (Okin. *kucha*) are found on low hills and terraces. The Tertiary Period (65 million years ago to 1.8 million years ago) precedes the Quaternary Period, which comprises the Pleistocene and Holocene.
3. Lowland soils derived from weathered Tertiary shale and sandstone (Okin. *jyagaru*) are found in shoreline and valley bottom localities. These are used for irrigated rice and taro fields. They make up a very small portion of the agricultural land of the Ryukyus.
4. Brown soils derived from marine coral, which formed in a few shoreline localities, are used for dryland crops.

TABLE 2.1 Relations between Surface Geology, Topography, and Soil

Period		*Surface Geology*		*Geological Phase*	*Topography*	*Soil*
Tertiary	Pliocene	Shimajiri Group	Shinzato Layer	sandstone, mudstone interbedded with congealed lava		gray upland soil, gray lowland soil, brown lowland soil (*jagaru* regosol)
			Yonabaru Layer	thick mudstone (shale) and sandstone, congealed lavas (*kucha*)	gradual and steep slopes	
			Tomigusuku Layer	upper sandstone, lower shale		
		Chinen sandstone		limestone sand layer	no exposed surfaces	
		Kunigami gravel		uncompacted layer	middle elevations, faults and blocks	Shimajiri *māji* (lithosol)
		Ryukyu Limestone		surface layer up to 10 m thick, recrystallized, consolidated, lower part sandy, interspersed compacted and uncompacted layers	limestone terraces	
		reddish brown soil		Shimajiri *māji*, limestone in elevated areas		reddish yellow clay soil (lithosol)
Quaternary	Pleistocene	limestone terraces		brown-colored clay sandy limestone compacted in layers found at high elevations in southeast, low in northwest	lower and middle terraces 5–60 m	yellow-brown soil

TABLE 2.1 *(continued)*

Period	*Surface Geology*	*Geological Phase*	*Topography*	*Soil*
	alluvial layer	brown mud, sand, mixed with pieces of coral and marine fossils unconsolidated	low alluvial deposits	gray low lying soil (alluvium)
	recent sand dune layer	sand derived from limestone, unconsolidated with humus layers	sand dunes	sand, immature soils
Holocene	modern coral deposit	mixed coral, compacted clay in lagoon bottom; unconsolidated clay, silt, sand, gravel	coral reef	no soil development

Source: Data from Kokudo Chōsa Okinawa Ken 1983, 17.

Only a small proportion of Okinawan soils (about 3 percent) is suitable for irrigated crops. Most soils, derived from Quaternary Ryukyu Limestone, are suitable for dryland cultivation, which was devoted to millet, wheat, and barley in early historic times.

Holocene Climate

While data on palaeo-climate are not available from locations within the Ryukyus, abundant data are available from recent analyses in coastal China and the Japanese main islands. Data in Table 2.2 show climatic trends in the region from the time of the Younger Dryas Event, dated from 12,800 to 11,500 cal BP. There is a slight discrepancy between the usual date for the end of the Pleistocene, 12,000 BP, and the date of 11,500 BP quoted by Nakazawa et al. (2011).

Following the Younger Dryas Event, climate moderated, but there was a substantial cooling event around 8200 cal BP, which has been been noted in other parts of the world. Warmer conditions prevailed until a cooling period around 4000 BP, which had a sharp impact on Chinese Neolithic cultures and the cultures of the Late Jōmon Period of the Japanese main islands. Cool and warm periods alternated in the Common Era. Climate in the Ryukyus must have been moderated by the East China Sea and would not be the same as that of surrounding areas; however, relative trends are similar. This can be seen in the case of the analysis of quartz particles in core samples spanning 2,100 years, taken from the distal mud area of the continental shelf in the East China Sea. The winter monsoon transports wind-blown dust from coastal and interior China across the sea, more sediment being carried when the winter monsoon is stronger and the climate cooler. Quartz particles increased in the cores from 2100 to 1520 cal BP and 720 to 220 cal BP, coinciding with the Kofun Cold Period and the Little Ice Age (Qiao et al. 2011). Chinese historical records describe the drastic effects of the Little Ice Age in detail (Brook 2010, 53–73). Within two phases of cold climate, from AD 1270 to 1370 and AD 1450 to 1715, there were nine subperiods of cold each lasting several years, during which hard freezes were common in the Yangtze Basin, causing hardship and economic losses.

During the strong winter monsoon, which indicates cool climate, cold, dry air pushes from the Asian continent southward across the East China Sea. The surface temperature of the ocean is lowered, affecting the distribution of marine life. The north wind also makes it possible to sail southward. Ships sailing from Japan and the Ryukyus to the China coast embarked on the winter monsoon and returned on the summer monsoon, which blows from south to north. The strong winter monsoon pushed migrants and drifting mariners to the south.

TABLE 2.2 Holocene Climate in the Ryukyus

Period/Event, Location	*Date*	*Type of Evidence*	*Description*	*Reference*
Younger Dryas Cooling Event, Japan, Yangtze Delta (end of Pleistocene)	12,800–11,500 cal BP	varves, pollen	several parts of Japan; Yangtze Delta, mild climate, more precipitation (SWM)	Nakazawa et al. 2011
8,200 cal BP cooling event, Middle Okinawa Trough	8200 cal BP	O isotopes, alkenone-surface seawater temperature, planktonic Foraminifera, piston cores	cooling of upper 30–40 m of local sea surface water (SWM)	Yu et al. 2008; Xiang et al. 2007
Early Holocene Optimum (Yangtze Delta)	8000–7800 BP	pollen of evergreen tree species	warmest climate of the Holocene	Z. Chen et al. 2005
Mid-Holocene Optimum (Yangtze Delta)	7500–5000 BP	pollen of *Castanopsis*, *Cyclobalanopsis*	warm climate	Z. Chen et al. 2005
sharp cooling event, Yangtze Delta, Hebei, Kanto area	4200–4000 BP (1) 4600–4300 BP (2)	*Fagus* pollen in delta samples; trends in Hebei, Kanto pollen samples	cool climate (decline of Chinese Neolithic cultures) (SWM)	(1) Z. Chen et al. 2005 (2) Jin and Liu 2002; Kudō 2007
cooler conditions with five warm spells	4000–3050 BP	Kanto region	pollen changes	Adhikari et al. 2002
Jōmon-Yayoi Warm Period	3000–1750 BP	lake sediments in Nagano	Jōmon-Yayoi transition, warmer climate, also in Greenland	Adhikari et al. 2002

Kofun Cold Stage	1700–1250 BP (AD 250–700)	Japanese pollen samples	temperature change comparable to Little Ice Age (SWM)	Adhikari et al. 2002
Mediaeval Warm Period	700–1200 BP (AD 750–1250)	Japan, Europe, pollen; lake sediments stalagmite analysis, Gansu Province	warm period, strong summer monsoon AD 1020–1340, weaker AD 850–940	Adhikari et al. 2002; Zhang et al. 2008
"Little Ice Age"	650–480 BP, 250–190 BP (AD 1300–1470, AD 1700–1760)	lake sediments	cooling climate (SWM)	Adhikari et al. 2002; Zhang et al. 2008

SWM = Strong Winter Monsoon

Periods of strong summer monsoon brought warmer climate and increased precipitation. These periods, such as the Jōmon-Yayoi Warm Period and the Mediaeval Warm Period may have been important for human communities experimenting with cultivation.

Vegetation

The high islands of the Ryukyus are covered with broadleaf evergreen forest, an extension of the East Asian broadleaf evergreen forest zone of southwestern Japan and Taiwan (Hotta 1981; Pearson 1981a, b). While it includes edible chestnuts and yams, rice, millet, wheat, barley, and edible taro are not indigenous to this zone. Raised limestone coral areas also support a distinctive broadleaf evergreen forest of limestone-adapted species. The shoreline vegetation shares many species with other areas of the Indo-Pacific.

Because of the length of the Ryukyu island chain, it is difficult to present a general picture of vegetation change in the Holocene from samples taken at a single location. However, one sea core bottom 33.6 m long, from the northern end of the East China Sea, about 150 km from Kyushu and 650 km from the modern coastline of China (Kawahata and Ohshima 2004) has provided information on terrestrial and ocean environments during the past 40,000 years. Based on changes in planktonic Foraminifera assemblages, it is estimated that during the Last Glacial Maximum, sea surface temperature was 2 to 3 degrees C lower in winter than at present. Zone 1, from 42,000 to 40,500 years, showed cooler conditions than at present, with fairly high rainfall. Zone 2, from 40,500 to 17,000 years, shows a predominance of nonarboreal pollen from vegetation on the exposed continental shelf, a lowland with lakes and marshes. However, a core from Izenajima, north of Okinawa, at 22,900 years, showed a warm temperate pollen assemblage with pine and subtropical evergreen broadleaf trees such as *Cyclobalanopsis, Castanopsis-Pasania,* and *Podocarpus.* Zone 3, 17,000 to 14,000 years, showed nonarboreal species living on exposed land, but also warm temperate subtropical evergreen broad-leaved trees such as *Cyclobalanopsis* and *Castanopsis-Pasania,* indicating a warming trend. Zone 4, 14,000 to 8000 years, showed the rapid increase of pollen of warm temperate subtropical evergreen broad-leaved trees, indicating a warm temperate climate. Zone 5, from 8,000 to 1,200 years, shows further sea-level rise and a decreased abundance of nonarboreal pollen as well as the pollen of warm temperate evergreen species (*Castanopsis, Pasania-Cyclobalanopsis*) and pollen of the warm temperate evergreen conifer *Podocarpus.* This corresponds to the Holocene Optimum. A pollen core from the Kanna Dam Site, Ginoza, Okinawajima, showed that the climate in the period around 20,000 BP was not so much cooler than present but was definitely drier. A section of another other pollen core from Izenajima, with an uncalibrated radiocarbon date of 6970±100 (Gak 15946) shows predominance of evergreen oak (*Cyclobalanopsis* and *Shiia* species) and a minimum of pine or nonarboreal pollen, indicating broadleaf evergreen forest (Kuroda and Ōzawa 1996).

Vulcanism—the Kikai Akahoya Eruption, 7280 BP

The calibrated date of the Kikai Akahoya eruption is 7300 cal BP, and by detailed counting of sedimentary layers with ash from Lake Suigetsu, north of Kyoto, the eruption has been dated at 7280 BP (Machida and Sugiyama 2002, 316). The Kikai eruption was one of the three largest eruptions in the world of the last ten thousand years, along with Changbaishan in North Korea (ninth or early tenth century AD) and Crater Lake, Oregon (4895 BC). The caldera is the

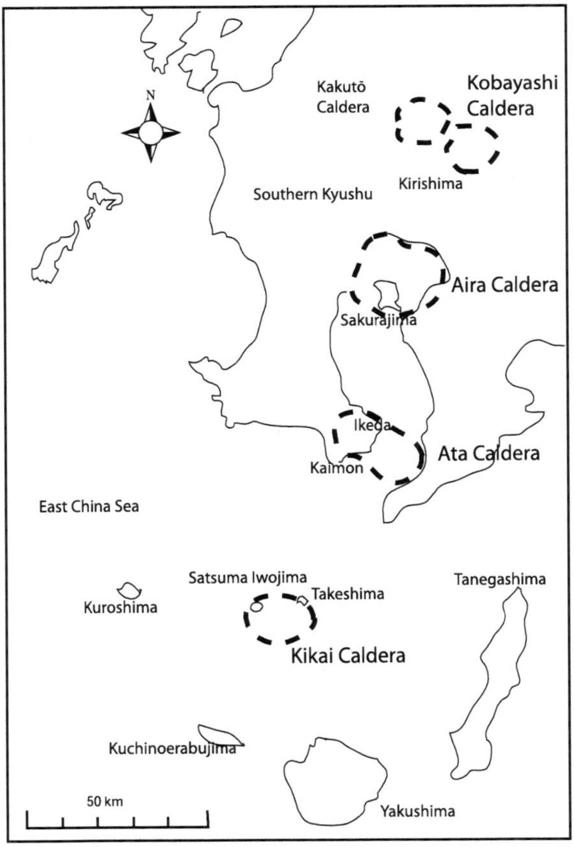

Figure 2.2. The location of the Kikai Caldera and neighboring calderas. Redrawn from Maeno and Taniguchi 2010.

most southerly in a line of four, lying in the Kagoshima volcanic depression, which extends 150 km from north to south (Figure 2.2).

It had a maximum diameter of 20 km and ejected a volume of ash of 150 cu km. In the Osaka area the deposited ash layer, termed the Akahoya Ash Layer, was up to 30 cm deep (Machida and Sugiyama 2002, 314). This ash deposit can be seen in soil profiles from the Ryukyus, Japanese main islands, and Korea. It created a decline in the broadleaf evergreen forests of western Japan for eight hundred to nine hundred years. Deforestation occurred as far away as the Kii Peninsula and Shikoku, and a decline in shellfish populations as far away as Chiba has been noted (ibid., 320). While there has been some disagreement on its local impact, Machida concluded that people in southern Kyushu either perished or were pushed to the north. The distinctive cylindrical pottery vessels with shell impression (Senokan type) and roller-impressed (*oshigata mon*) pottery types of the Incipient Jōmon disappeared and were replaced by Sobata and Todoroki types, which moved into southern Kyushu from the north (Shimoyama 2002). The Kikai eruption occurred at the height of the Jōmon Transgression (Machida and Sugiyama 2002, 316). The eruption was of a totally different magnitude from other volcanic activity in the region (Shimoyama 2002). Southern Kyushu was covered not by ash but by pyroclastic flow, and phytolith samples from the southernmost part of Kyushu show a total absence of Gramineae, Bambusoideae, and arboreal species for several hundred years (Machida and Sugiyama 2002, 323, 319).

Tokara Iōshima (Sulfur Island) has been active in historic times, producing sulfur that was sent to China as tribute from Japan in the eleventh to twelfth centuries AD (Yamauchi 2009) and from Chūzan and Ryukyu from the late fourteenth century AD (Wada 1975, 20).

Coral Reefs

The development of Holocene coral reefs is of the utmost importance for the life of Ryukyu islanders, past and present. While uplifted Pleistocene coral reefs provided caves for shelter and burial and limestone building material used by mediaeval islanders for construction, the Holocene reefs provided protection from storms and tidal waves for humans and animals, and their lagoons and barrier reefs housed diverse varieties of marine food. The coral reefs of the Ryukyus are unique in East Asia. While shallow, warm water required for the growth of coral is found in south China, for instance, alluvium from large rivers and run off prevent the extensive growth of coral reefs.

Surrounding reefs and protected lagoons were only achieved after the Mid-Holocene. Coral had either to keep up with rising sea levels or to catch up in a delayed fashion, depending on factors affecting coral growth. In conditions of adequate warmth, salinity, and sunlight, coral growth is largely controlled by ocean swells and local winds.

Through the study of a cut 8 m × 630 m through the fringing reef of Tonakijima, an outlier in the Okinawa Group, made in 1989 to widen access for boats, Kan and his team (Kan et al. 1997) were able to study and date the development of the reef, in which the combination of coral accretion and sea level fall was a key factor. Around 5800 cal BP the reef is said to have been affected by a high-energy window. This may have been caused by a strengthening of the winter monsoon. The fringing reef that created a protected lagoon was complete around 3900 cal BP. Evidence from several points in the Western Pacific, including Tonakijima indicates that there was a fall in sea level of about 1 m around 3650 BP. The achievement of the fringing reef of Tonakijima coincides in general with the completion of other reef building in the Western Pacific such as the Great Barrier Reef (Kan et al. 1997, 14) (Figure 2.3). Koba et al. (1982, 231) noted that

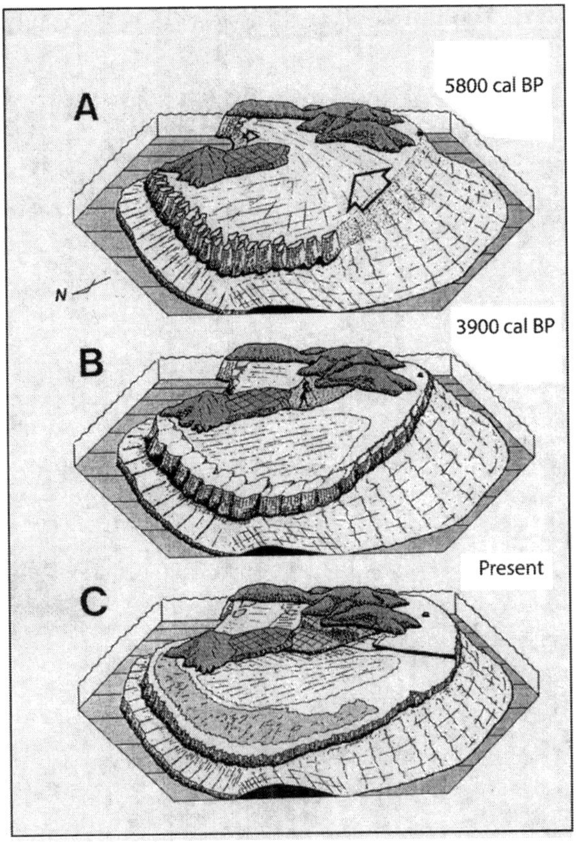

Figure 2.3. The formation of the ringing reef of Tonakijima, Central Ryukyus. The arrows in A indicate the Holocene high-energy window occurring at around 5800 cal BP. Adapted, with new information from Professor Kan Hironobu (personal communication), from Kan et al. 1997, 15. Courtesy of Kan Hironobu.

sea level in the Ryukyus from 3500 to 1700 BP was stable but was up to 1 m higher than at present.

In their study of dated cores from the Sekisei Reef, a reef that is 30 km in circumference and only 20 m deep at maximum, which surrounds Ishigakijima and Iriomotejima, Kan and Kawana (2006) found that the fringing reef began some time after 9500 cal years BP, when sea level first reached the -20 m level and the island shelf was inundated. At first a thick palaeosol would have made the water too turbid for coral growth. By 7500 sea level had nearly reached its present position, and by 6500 cal BP the reefs had grown up to reach sea level. The fact that the pace of reef formation varied throughout the Ryukyus necessitates a local approach to subsistence ecology. Hongo and Kayanne (2009, 70) state that sea level in the Ryukyus stabilized in a range between 7000 and 4000 cal years BP. For Ishigakijima the date is 5280 cal years BP; for Okinoerabujima, 4700 years BP; and for Yoronjima 4300 cal years BP. The variation is explained by the hydro-isostatic response of islands according to their size. Ishigakijima is one of the larger of the Ryukyu Islands; therefore, sea level would have stabilized relatively early. The sea-level curve for Ishigakijima matches those from Tahiti and Palau, indicating that the history of sea-level change for islands of this size was similar over the entire tropical and subtropical western Pacific Ocean. Coral reefs develop more rapidly along windward coasts where wave action creates high energy. Therefore, windward reefs reached maturity earlier than leeward reefs. For instance, the upper portions of the windward reef of Ishigakijima at Ibaruma are dated to 4750 cal BP, while those of the leeward reef are dated to 1870 cal BP (Hongo and Kayanne 2009).

Tsunami

Tidal waves have had a huge impact on the Ryukyus. The most famous, the Meiwa Tsunami of AD 1771, killed about 12,000 people in the southern Ryukyus, with an aftermath that continued for decades (Makino 1968; Kawana 2008). Through radiocarbon dating of aragonite in large coral boulders broken from the reef and carried inland by major tsunami, Kawana and Nakata (1994) and Suzuki et al. (2008) were able to create a chronology of tidal waves. Major tsunami occurred in the Sakishima Islands in the following time periods: 200 years ago (Meiwa Tsunami), 500 to 650 years ago, 1,000 to 1,200 years ago, 1,950 to 2,100 years ago, 2,300 to 2,500 years ago, 3,750 years ago, and 4,350 to 4,450 years ago (uncalibrated). In particular a powerful tsunami occurring about two thousand years ago affected a wide area from Miyakojima to Ishigakijima (Okinawa Kenritsu Maizō 2009a, 43). These tsunami originated through earthquake activity in the Ryukyu Trench and Okinawa Trough, affecting different sections of coastline. While all of the studies above deal only with Sakishima, other tidal waves affected the rest of the Ryukyus, obliterating coastal settlements and wiping out records of ancient coastal sites, the damaged areas differing according to their direction and magnitude.

Subsequent chapters will introduce the ways in which islanders harvested the products of forests and reef, and coped with volcanic events, the monsoon, typhoons, and tidal waves.

Chapter 3

Pleistocene Inhabitants

In this chapter I describe the earliest archaeological finds from the Ryukyus and discuss their significance for the study of early migrations, the relations of island populations to continental populations, and their place in the history of the Ryukyu islanders. I briefly introduce comparative studies with ancient and modern populations that have brought up many questions. The locations of major sites discussed in this chapter and in Chapters 4 to 6 are shown in Figure 3.1.

The earliest evidence of human groups in the Ryukyu region consists of late Pleistocene fossils, the most extensive assemblage found in all of Japan and Taiwan. Although they are very important for understanding the osteology of early populations of the China Sea area, their archaeological value is limited. They are finds of fossil bones in contexts that are not living sites and do not produce artifacts or other cultural debris. They range in date from 32,000 to 16,000 years ago. From 23,000 to 18,000 BP, at the height of the Wurm Glaciation, sea level was lower by about 140 m; consequently, a large land mass was available for habitation by people whose remains were found in Minatogawa and other sites. As mentioned in Chapter 2, Late Pleistocene *Homo sapiens* had to cross water to reach the few large islands of the Ryukyus in the Late Pleistocene. Between the Late Pleistocene discoveries and subsequent Holocene archaeological sites there is a gap of about eight thousand to nine thousand years.

Sites in the Northern Ryukyus and the Amami Islands

Several sites belonging to the Late Palaeolithic have been found on Tanegashima, to the south of the main island of Kyushu. During the Late Glacial Maximum it was joined to the main island of Kyushu. The Yokomine C Site (see Figure 3.1d),

Figure 3.1a–d. Location of major sites of the Palaeolithic and Shellmound Periods mentioned in the text.

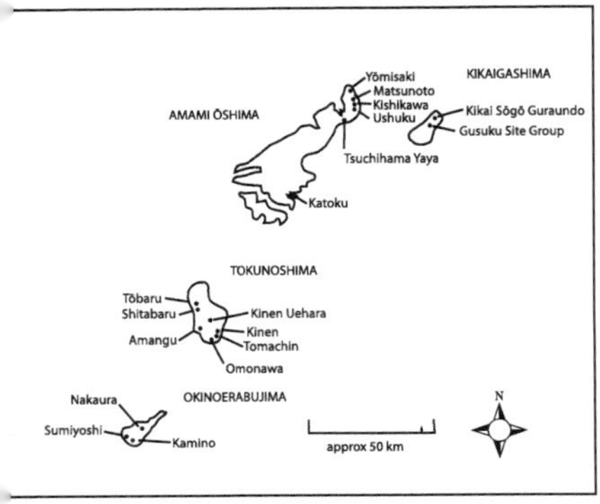

(a) *Amami Islands.*

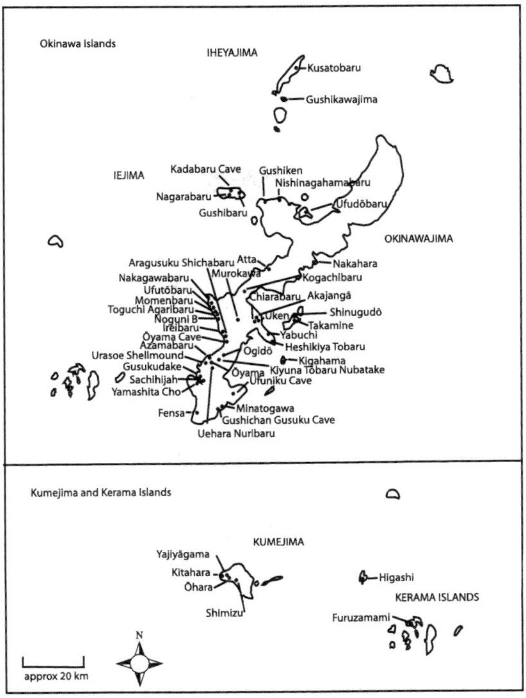

(b) *Okinawa Islands, Kumejima and Kerama Islands.*

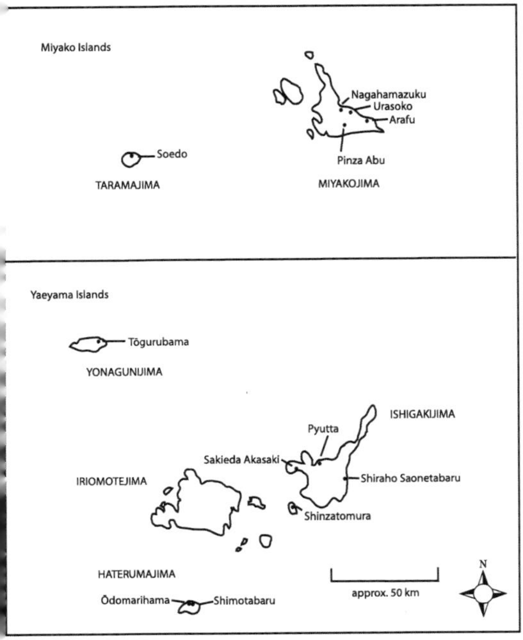

(c) *Location of major sites of the Palaeolithic and Early Periods, Sakishima Islands.*

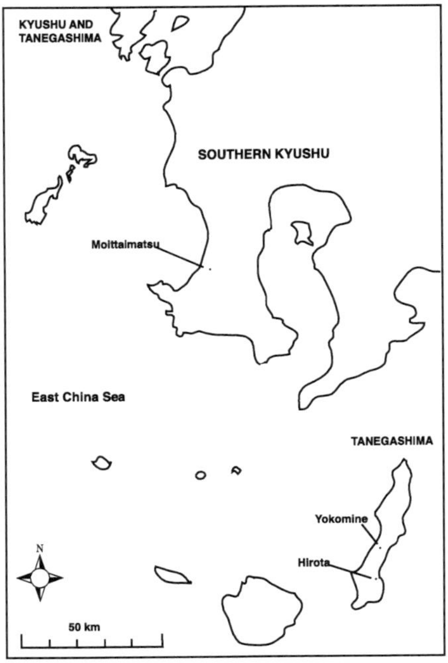

(d) *Location of sites of various periods in Kyushu and on Tanegashima.*

dated between 25,000 and 30,000 BP (Kuwahata and Okubo 2000), contains evidence of processing of plant foods and cooking in earth ovens (Nakamura 2006) in the form of mortars and round grinding stones, hammer stones, gravel clusters, and pits. Rhyolite from Miyazaki Prefecture in nearby Kyushu was found in this site in pebble form, showing that exchange existed at this time (Oda 1999; Kuwahata and Okubo 2000).

Three sites in the Amami islands have yielded chert flakes that are somewhat similar to the flakes found in Japanese Late Palaeolithic sites; however, the evidence from each site is insufficient for conclusive confirmation of Palaeolithic occupation (Nakayama 2009, 19–20). The Kishikawa Site, on the Kasari Peninsula, Amami Ōshima, yielded chert flakes in a pitlike feature lying below a layer of Akahoya Ash dated to 7280 BP; however, no other artifacts or cultural remains were found. The Tsuchihama Yanya Site, Amami Ōshima, has yielded a shale pointed tool associated with a 14C date of 18,000 BP as well as flakes, raw material fragments, and three artifacts with traces of grinding, from a layer dated to 21,400 BP (Takamiya Hiroe 1990, 112). Small, regular, chert flakes, which resemble flakes produced in the Palaeolithic of the Japanese main islands, were recovered from the Amangusuku Site, located on a terrace in southern Tokunoshima. However, a clearly defined cultural layer could not be determined.

Fossil Finds

Vertebrate fossils have been found in at least 104 locations in the Ryukyus, both from Tertiary and Quaternary contexts, and *Homo sapiens* fossils have been found in at least seven localities. The most typical context is a deposit of brownish clay, mixed with angular limestone fragments, either in cave floor deposits or in limestone fissures. Fossil assemblages generally consist of a wide range of species including elephant, deer, wild boar, wild cat, fruit bat, rat, frog, and reptile and bird species.

The most prominent find occurred in a limestone fissure at Minatogawa in southern Okinawa, which is about 15 m deep and 40 cm to 1.5 m in width. Part of the fissure area has been quarried, leading to the discovery of human fossils. From 1968 to 1974 three excavations yielded *Homo sapiens* bones belonging to between five and nine individuals. Radiocarbon dates of 18,250±650 years BP (TK-99) and 16,600±300 years BP (TK-142) were determined (H. Kobayashi et al. 1974; Kizaki 1985, 228). The Minatogawa specimens were considered to be similar to the Liujiang skeleton of Guangxi, China (Baba and Narasaki 1991), which is dated between 10,000 and 30,000 years ago. The degree of tooth wear was much greater than that usually seen in Holocene hunter-gatherers (Kaifu 2007). Baba (2000) pointed out a number of traits that he regarded as archaic:

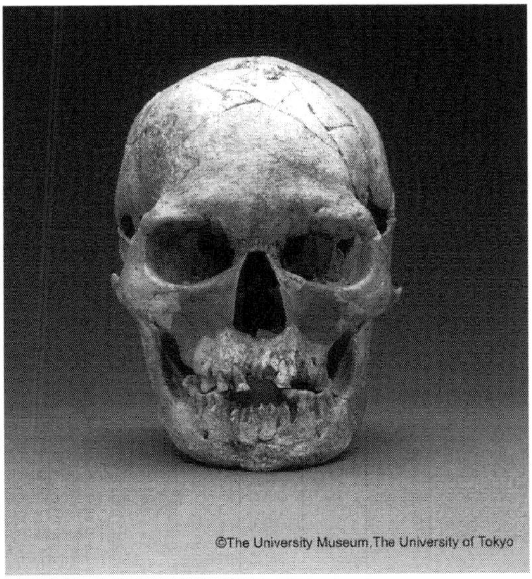

Figure 3.2. Human Skull No. 1, Minatogawa Fissure Site, southern Okinawajima. Photo provided by the University Museum, University of Tokyo.

thick cranial vault, a rugged profile, prominent glabella, inclined frontal bones, and medially oriented mastoid processes (Figure 3.2). Small and slender upper bodies, with limited muscle development of the upper limbs, and signs of interrupted bone growth in childhood indicated adaptation to stressful island conditions (2000, 236). I would suggest that slender build may foster mobility in dense forests.

Some writers state that one of the Minatogawa specimens shows ritual tooth ablation (removal) of the lower central incisors, a custom that is most common in Japan in Middle Jōmon (about 3500–2500 BC) (Kokuritsu Kagaku Hakubutsukan 1988, 45). However, the evidence of tooth extraction is considered inconclusive by Baba (2003, 549). Cranial bones from two individuals show perforations thought by Hisashi Suzuki to indicate some violent force to the head (1982, 39). While some doubt has been expressed that the mandible and cranium of Minatogawa I belong to the same individual, Kaifu (2007) confirms that they are from one individual.

From a cave site at Yamashita Chō, in a low limestone ridge near Naha Harbor, Okinawajima, fragments of a tibia and a femur belonging to a juvenile female *Homo sapiens* were recovered from the upper part of Layer IV. From a pooled sample of charcoal from Layers III and V, a radiocarbon date of 32,100±1000 years BP (TK-78) was determined (Takamiya Hiroe 1990, 61; Takemoto and Asato 1993, 56). Other sites yielding *Homo sapiens* fossils have been reported. Takamiya (1990, 5) includes Kadabaru Cave, Iejima, and Ōyama Cave, Ginowan City, Okinawa. Fossilized bone fragments belonging to a one-year-old infant have also been found in the Yajiyāgama Cave Site, Kumejima (Kizaki 1985, 230). Some discussions of Late Pleistocene *Homo sapiens* from the Ryukyus consider only the Minatogawa finds and set the dating at about 17,000 BP (Hanihara and Ishida 2009). Although these constitute the most complete collection, they are not from a sealed deposit.

Fragments of human cranium and vertebrae as well as a deciduous tooth were found in the Pinza Abu cave deposit on Miyakojima (Sakura 1981), after water screening some 10 metric tons of fossil-bearing clay. Associated faunal materials include deer, boar, wild cat, and rats, all of which are extinct. Although radiocarbon dates of 25,800±900 BP (TK-535) and 26,800±1300 BP (TK-605) were determined from charcoal in the upper clay layer of the site, the relationship of these dates to the fossils is not entirely clear; the authors of the site report suggest a date of around 20,000 years ago and conclude that the Pinza Abu specimens were "morphologically slightly older" than those of Minatogawa (Okinawa Ken Kyōiku Iinkai 1985a, 178, 182). Sakura (1981, 5) concludes that the specimens from Pinza Abu and Minatogawa represent a single population that inhabited the Ryukyus in the Late Pleistocene Period. A new discovery from the Shiraho Saonetabaru Cave, at the edge of the construction site of the new airport on Ishigakijima, is the first to provide actual dating of human bones, rather than dating of material found near the bones, often in a context that shows secondary deposition. Collagen AMS dating of six bone fragments found in a secondary deposit provided the first dates of actual individuals instead of associated materials (Nakagawa et al. 2010; Ishigaki Shiritsu 2010; Yamazaki et al. 2010). Two specimens, Nos. 2 and 4, gave dates of 20,416±113 (MTC 12820) and 18752±100 (MTC 13228) respectively, while other specimens were dated to later time periods in the Holocene. The direct dating of the bones of *Homo sapiens* to a Late Pleistocene context is a positive step, but there are still some problems regarding the geomorphological interpretation of the deposits.

A major problem with Pleistocene finds in the Ryukyus is the absence of artifact assemblages. The Minatogawa fissure did not yield any artifactual material. The Iejima and the Yamashita Chō sites yielded modified fragments of deer antler, mandible, and leg bones (femur, tibia, and tarsal). Antler fragments consist of the basal portion of the antler with a small portion of surrounding cranium, or antler tips. The long bone fragments are usually notched at one or both ends and are referred to as double-notched bone artifacts. From the Yamashita Chō site Takamiya Hiroe identified three stone specimens thought to be tools (Takamiya 1990, 47). One piece is said to resemble a chopper, while the other two are stone spherical-shaped objects 7 to 8 cm in diameter. The lithic material of these three objects is local Tertiary sandstone (1990, 66). However, most scholars do not consider these to be artifacts.

Katō (1979) has concluded that the so-called bone artifacts have been created by the gnawing of deer, based on the arguments of Sutcliffe (1973). In other localities such as Zhoukoudian, China, bone modification was created by the chewing of carnivores; however, carnivores were not present on Okinawan sites, judging from the bone assemblages. Takamiya Hiroe has surveyed bone assemblages of the late Pleistocene and Early Holocene from surrounding regions in East and Southeast Asia (1990, 83–112). Some of these may also have been created by the chewing of carnivores or deer, and others, with convincing evidence of human modification into well-recognized artifact types, are later in age. Takemoto and Asato (1993, 203) state that since not one stone tool of the Palaeolithic has been found on Okinawa Island, this makes the assertion that there is any Palaeolithic culture (*Kyūsekki bunka*) south of the Amami Islands very weak. However, there is some indication that stone tools may be found in the future. With the possible exception of the sites from Amami Ōshima, sites discussed above are not living sites showing daily activities. When such sites are discovered, archaeological comparisons with surrounding regions will become possible.

Hisashi Suzuki (1982, 39) mentioned the mixed nature of the Minatogawa deposit, in which human and animal bones were found together. He thought that the humans may have died from a natural disaster or been thrown into the fissure by other humans, and proposed that the fragmentation was the result of cannibalization. The single complete skeleton, Minatogawa I, was found in an almost articulated state but was "standing on its head" (1982, 5). Fluorine assays of 8 samples of human fossils and 33 fragments of deer and wild boar bone showed dispersion within all three categories, the deer having higher fluorine content than the wild boar and being close to the values for the human bone (Matsu'ura 1982, 206). Matsu'ura was careful not to give absolute dates and concluded that the chronological relation between the radiocarbon-dated charcoal specimens and the human bones could not be established from the available evidence. Hasegawa (1980) has classified the palaeontological deposits of the Ryukyus into two stratigraphic layers, based on mammalian fauna, especially deer and wild boar, fluorine content of the bones, and radiocarbon dates. The older layer yields deer and is dated to about 30,000 BP. It includes Yamashita Chō and Gohezu Cave. The upper, more recent layers yield only wild boar (Nagarabaru, Iejima, and the Upper Minatogawa Deposit). The intermediate of these two layers, in which deer and boar remains occur together, corresponds to the horizon of the Minatogawa human fossils (Lower Minatogawa Deposit). Two deer species, *Cervus astylodon* and a muntjac deer (Muntjacinae) of undetermined species, were found in the Minatogawa deposits (Matsu'ura 1982, 205). As noted in Chapter 2, deer are reported to have become extinct in the early

Holocene (Minagawa et al. 2005). The cause of their extinction has received little attention. Did they die out as the land mass of the Ryukyus contracted through rising sea levels? Deer populations generally seem to be very adaptable, in the absence of human predators. Did human populations hunt them to extinction in the Early Holocene before the earliest recorded Holocene sites, from which deer are absent. In future, the finding of undisturbed cultural layers dating to the Late Pleistocene may make it possible to answer these and other questions.

Relations to Early Continental Asians and Japanese Populations

Hisashi Suzuki (1982, 37) found several characteristics of the Minatogawa specimens to be shared with specimens from the Upper Cave Locality at Zhoukoudian, north China, such as a narrow, pinched nasal bone, a "saber-hilt-shaped" zygomatic arc, and a transverse occipital torus. These traits are not found in Jōmon specimens. Suzuki concluded that Minatogawa people were "descended from a generalized Pleistocene proto Mongoloid of the Asian continent." He proposed that Minatogawa specimens resembled the Liujiang skull of Guangxi Province, China, and that Liujiang must be an ancestor of Minatogawa. He further proposed that around 18,000 years ago descendants of a proto-Mongoloid stock migrated to Okinawa and western Japan, and that populations represented by Minatogawa and Japanese finds at Ushikawa, Mikkabi, and Hamakita were all related. He concluded that "present day Okinawans are without doubt the direct descendants of Minatogawa humans" (1982, 37).

In a subsequent review, Baba et al. (1998) introduced new data and presented some different interpretations. They identified the presence of archaic features such as thick bones of the cranial vault, rugged facial profile, prominent glabella, inclined frontal bones, and medially oriented mastoid process. They noted that the Zhoukoudian Upper Cave and Liujiang specimens have recently been dated later than Minatogawa and thus cannot be ancestral (1998, 31). A comparison of nineteen cranial morphological characters indicated to them wide differences from Zhoukoudian Upper Cave Specimens 101 and 102, and a relative closeness between Minatogawa and specimens from Wadjak (Java). Their analysis did not show a close similarity between Minatogawa and Liujiang. They concluded that Late Pleistocene people in China, Japan, and insular Southeast Asia evolved more or less independently without major migrations within the region (1998, 41). The discussion above is related to the Minatogawa finds. But what about the substantially earlier tibia and femur fragments from Yamashita Chō? In their analysis of the Yamashita Chō specimens, Trinkaus and Ruff (1996) found a mosaic pattern of robust characters of archaic *Homo* with features of early modern humans, which they found to be consistent with the radiocarbon dating. Baba (2000) noted features that might indicate stress from poor nutrient conditions as well as small body size, slenderness of postcranial bones, and narrowness of vertebrae that could be the result of adaptation to an island environment.

In his dual structure population hypothesis for explaining the peopling of the Japanese islands, Hanihara (1991) proposed that Japan was first populated by Palaeolithic people from Southeast Asia who became the Jōmon people. Jōmon people developed into three groups: Ainu, Ryukyu, and modern Japanese. However, the group developing into modern Japanese were greatly affected by mixing with Yayoi immigrants from Northeast Asia. In this scenario, the first inhabitants of the Ryukyu Islands would be people who migrated on a Late Pleistocene land bridge connecting Taiwan and south China to the Japanese main islands (with some gaps), with the inhabitants of the land bridge forming a community ancestral to modern Ryukyu islanders. Ryukyu islanders should have strong connections to Jōmon and Ainu people. Suzuki and Hanihara (1982, 37) concluded that the present-day Okinawans are the direct descendants of the Minatogawa population and that the Minatogawa people are the "remote ancestors of Jōmon age man" (1982, 37), affected by a "long period of isolation and gene flow" that took place in the Late Pleistocene and the Early Post-Pleistocene (1982, 37). Baba and Narasaki (1991, 221) reach a more tentative conclusion, stating that Minatogawa man "might be an ancestor of the Jōmon people." Baba (2003, 569) concluded his review of the evidence by saying that he believes that modern Okinawan populations carry some genes from the Minatogawa population (i.e., there is not a complete break between Minatogawa and modern Okinawans). However, examination of the Minatogawa mandible No. 1 by Fujita and Kaifu (2010, 6) and digital imaging by Kōno (2010) led these researchers to propose that the facial structure is closer to that of populations from Australia and New Guinea than to that of East and Southeast Asian populations. They also proposed that the Minatogawa population is distinct from Jōmon populations. These studies of the jaw and facial structure diverge from Turner's (1990; 2006) analysis of the cusps, facets, root form, and other characters of teeth. Turner proposed that Minatogawa and Jōmon populations were all part of an ancient population of "Sundadonts," who evolved into "Sinodonts" represented by post-Jōmon and northern Chinese populations. Thus it seems that Minatogawa and Jōmon populations may share some general features, but Minatogawa is not ancestral to Jōmon.

The absence of human sites from about 16,000 to about 7000 BC may indicate that prehistoric occupation of the Ryukyus was discontinuous (Hiroto Takamiya 1997), and substantial mixing with later occupations from the Japanese main islands makes it very difficult to affirm that the Ryukyu islanders,

Ainu, and Jōmon were all part of one ancient population. It is likely that rising sea levels have obliterated and submerged sites occupied during the chronological gap. It is also possible that Ryukyu islanders and the people of the Japanese main islands have separate origins in East Asia. As we shall see in Chapter 4, it is also clear that a new population entered the Ryukyus from Kyushu in the Jōmon Period.

Based on the nature of Late Palaeolithic knife cultures of Kyushu, which can be said to extend as far south as Amami Ōshima (from briefly reported finds at the Tsuchihama Yanya and Kishikawa sites), and the absence of any Palaeolithc tools from the Central and Southern Ryukyus, Hiroto Takamiya and Obata (2002, 498) concluded that Kyushu was probably populated from Northeast Asia (north China and Korea), whereas the Central and Southern Ryukyus were populated from south China. While Pleistocene skeletons have been found in Kyushu and possibly the Northern Ryukyus, the general similarity of Late Palaeolithic-type artifacts in Kyushu and Northeast Asia and the lack of Palaelolithic artifacts in Okinawa indicate that these areas were probably populated by separate groups (Oda 2007). Recent studies of mitochondrial DNA (mtDNA) of Jōmon skeletons suggest that the Jōmon of Hokkaido may be derived from Northeast Asia and that the total Japanese Jōmon population may be more diverse than previously anticipated (Shinoda and Adachi 2010; T. Hanihara and Ishida 2009). Hanihara Kazurō's postulate of a Southeast Asian origin of Palaeolithic and Jōmon populations is called into question (Kazuro Hanihara 1991). In scenarios of the peopling of the Japanese islands up to 2005, a population input from the south China area through Taiwan and the Ryukyus was proposed. A revision in 2010 shows an input from the south as far as Okinawa but with the new interpretation that Minatogawa is not ancestral to Jōmon and that Jōmon groups may have come from Northeast Asia (Mizoguchi 2010).

After reviewing various cases around the world, Hiroto Takamiya (2011, 28–29) concluded that Palaeolithic *Homo sapiens* could not have survived on the limited resources of small islands, despite their larger area with lower Late Pleistocene sea levels. The lack of finds dating to the Final Pleistocene and Early Holocene appears to support his conclusion. Since shoreline settlements from this period would be submerged by rising sea levels, the only way to disprove this conclusion is to find materials in inland caves or rock shelters, which are being explored at present.

The Late Pleistocene finds from the Ryukyus show that the first episode of the formation of Ryukyu communities comprised people who arrived in the Ryukyus by watercraft. Since voyaging and deep-sea fishing were carried out in the Sunda-Sahul region as early as 40,000 to 46,000 BP (O'Connell et al. 2010), crossing the Kerama Gap should not be seen as unusual. Osteological comparisons with adjacent populations show something of their origins but raise questions about their relations to other groups. A lack of human fossils of similar general age to the Minatogawa finds makes it difficult to reconstruct the pedigree of the first inhabitants of the Ryukyu region, and subsequent mixing complicates attempts to compare ancient populations.

Humans lived on the east coast of Taiwan at roughly the same time period as that of the Ryukyu finds (Tsang 2000, 53–56). A group of cave sites in a massive coastal outcrop at Baxiandong, north of Taidong City, has yielded cultural layers containing flake tools with radiocarbon dates in in three ranges, 20,000 to 25,000 BP, 15,000 to 18,000 BP, and around 5000 BP (Tsang 2011; Tsang et al. 2011). The Pleistocene sites yield a variety of simple flake tools. Connections between these two groups of Palaeolithic finds are not clear at present.

Comparison of Modern Ryukyu Islanders to Other Modern Populations

In the dual structure population scenario of Hanihara (1991), Jōmon formed the basis for Ainu, Ryukyu, and modern Japanese populations with the latter receiving substantial input from Yayoi immigrants. One would expect that the three early populations would show substantial physical similarities. However, early studies showed that Okinawa populations are closer to Honshu and Kyushu Japanese than to Ainu (Tagaya and Ikeda 1976). Doi's analysis (Doi 2003; Asato Susumu and Doi 1999) showed that, as a result of substantial migration from the Japanese main islands at the beginning of the Mediaeval Period (generally dated around the beginning of the eleventh century AD), modern Okinawan populations resemble modern Japanese populations from western Japan. Genetic studies show some distance between Ainu and Okinawan groups, indicating that they were separate groups even in the Jōmon Period (Doi 2003, 577). In mtDNA studies of Ainu, Japanese main islands Japanese, Koreans, and Chinese, Ainu and Japanese do not share any common types (ibid). Also, Pietrusewsky's multivariate comparisons of male and female series from the Ryukyus and Japan showed that the modern Ryukyu series are closest to a cluster consisting of Yayoi, Kofun, and mediaeval Kamakura cranial series (Pietrusewsky 2004). Studies of facial flatness of Ryukyu and Ainu skeletons by Dodo et al. (1998) showed no indication of a close affinity between Ryukyu and Ainu. However, the authors acknowledge that there are close affinities in somatological traits such as fingerprints, palm patterns, earwax, earlobes, and eyelids.

Analysis of absolute and relative dental size by Takashi Tōma et al. (2007) did not show any direct genetic continuity between Jōmon or Ainu and Ryukyu islanders. Ryukyu islanders were distinct among eastern Asian groups but also show substantial internal diversity. They found that different patterns of gene flow from outside the Ryukyus, geographical isolation, and genetic drift on each island of the Ryukyus produced contemporary patterns of morphological variation.

Although the picture is not yet clear, the following tentative conclusions can be proposed. (1) There is a physical discontinuity between the Late Pleistocene populations and later populations. (2) The relationships between Ainu and Ryukyu islanders seem to be complex.

As we shall see in the next chapter, ceramic data show that the Northern and Central Ryukyus were colonized repeatedly from Kyushu. It appears that substantial interaction in the post-Jōmon period had a pronounced effect on the physical and cultural characteristics of the Ryukyu islanders. Doi's general conclusion (2010) is that the Ryukyu islanders are a Jōmon population with an intrusion in the Japanese Mediaeval Period and possible mixing from the south, from the Kuroshio. In addition, internal evolution may account for some distinctive Ryukyu attributes, but this aspect is still debated.

Chapter 4

Arriving and Settling

Island Hunter-Gatherer Colonization and Interaction

In the previous chapter, the scant archaeological record of Late Pleistocene *Homo sapiens* confirmed their presence in the Ryukyus but provided little basis for the reconstruction of island communities. Fossil bones were found without artifacts or cultural context in sites dispersed through thousands of years. However, sites left by groups living in the Shellmound Period of the Central and Northern Ryukyus and the Shimotabaru and Non-Ceramic Periods of the Southern Ryukyus (see Figures 1.2, 1.3) are relatively rich and permit some social interpretations. In this chapter, I summarize the cultural chronology for the two regions and describe some key characteristics of early prehistoric island communities along the lines suggested by Broodbank (2000) and Rainbird (2007). At least five types of interaction among communities can be identified: exploration, migration, exchange, innovation, and emulation. A lack of interaction, that is isolation, should also be considered and explored. The discussion is based on analyses of ceramics, ornaments, stone tools, and exotic materials. Following the long tradition of prehistoric pottery typology in Japan, Okinawan archaeologists have created stylistic types based primarily on decoration and surface treatment. In most instances, the vessels, used for cooking and storage, are wide-mouthed jars (*hachi*), small and crude compared to the classic Jōmon jars of the Japanese main islands. I have reduced the pottery descriptions to a bare minimum, giving a few details to show similarities and differences.

The habitation of the islands by nonagricultural hunter-gatherers in the Holocene Period is the second major episode in the archaeology of the Ryukyus, following the settlement by Pleistocene populations. It is now thought that the Ryukyus were colonized from the north by groups from Kyushu as early as 7000 BC. Subsequently, small groups from Kyushu arrived at intervals, indicated by several intrusive pottery types. From roughly 7000 BC to around AD 800, people of the Northern and Central Ryukyu were hunter-gatherers, subsisting on terrestrial and marine plants and animals. Although the people of Kyushu, with whom they interacted almost continuously, began to adopt cultivation some time after 500 BC, the islanders did not adopt cultivation until around AD 800 to 900. Similarly, in the Southern Ryukyus, a nonagricultural subsistence pattern was practiced by the first Holocene inhabitants, who lived in the islands from around 2900 BC to 2000 BC. The colonization of the Southern Ryukyus is not easy to trace through clear similarities in appropriately dated artifacts from surrounding regions. There were interesting differences between the North-Central and Southern Ryukyus, which are discussed below. By about AD 1050, trade throughout the Ryukyus and the adoption of cultivation transformed earlier patterns of settlement and subsistence, and the Gusuku Period began.

Northern and Central Ryukyus

For the Central Ryukyus, Asato has proposed four major periods: Migration, Adaptation, Diffusion, and Development, which can be correlated with the chronological divisions of the Shellmound Period used by Okinawan archaeologists (see Figure 1.4; Okinawa Kenritsu Maizō 2005a). In the Earliest Shellmound Period, from around 7000 BC to 2000 BC, groups arrived in the Amami and Okinawa Islands, and over the course of 5,000 years their culture developed local features but population remained low. In the light of recent finds from the Ufuniku Cave Site, southern Okinawa (see below), we should push the date for the earliest Holocene occupation back to 7000 BC. In Asato's Early Shellmound Period, roughly 2000 to 1000 BC, a distinctive Central Ryukyu culture with local styles of pottery and ornament emerged, and sites increased dramatically. In the Middle (1000 BC to 300 BC) and Late Shellmound (300 BC to AD 1050) Periods, pottery shows influence from the Yayoi styles of Kyushu, but differences in subsistence, settlement, and artifacts continue to deepen, despite interaction with many groups of Kyushu shell traders, This divergence, particularly in the Central Ryukyus, was not produced by isolation but through adaptation to island conditions and the growth of island communities that were culturally separate from Kyushu. Itō Shinji (2000, 159) notes that the Ryukyus and the Japanese main islands were separate psychological worlds, judging from differences in ornaments and ritual objects. He speaks of a Ryukyuan subtropical variant of Jōmon culture. Asato's interpretive chronology, shown in Figure 1.4, divides the Shellmound Period into four subperiods. However, Hiroe Takamiya's chronology, shown in Figure 1.3, divides the Shellmound Period into nine subperiods. The relationship between the two systems is shown in Figure 1.4. With its finer resolution, Takamiya's chronology is appropriate for the discussion of pottery chronology in this chapter, whereas Asato's broader sequence of adaptation fits the discussion in Chapter 5.

The Pottery Chronology of the North and Central Ryukyus

Pottery types provide evidence of cultural groups arriving and settling in the Ryukyus, assuming that different decorative styles reflect social subgroups. At the same time, the sequence of pottery types provides an important means of building a chronology, which has recently been supported by well-documented radiocarbon dates. The chronology of the Shellmound Period of the Northern and Central Ryukyus presented in Figure 1.3 has been built up through the relative dating of pottery types (Takamiya Hiroe 1993; 1994, 23–43) or wares (*yōshiki*) (Itō Shinji 2000; 2003) and cross-dating with types in southern Kyushu. The major pottery types established by Okinawan archaeologists are shown in Figure 4.1. These pottery types have been grouped into wares (*yōshiki*) by Itō Shinji (2000; 2003), as shown in Figure 4.2. To simplify the discussion in this chapter, I refer mainly to the wares rather than individual pottery types.

I have pushed back the dates for the Earliest Shellmound Period to 7000 BC to accommodate the new discoveries from Ufuniku Cave discussed below. From 291 dates compiled by Najima et al. (2008), the Plain Pottery Type is dated 5000 to 6000 BC; Nail-Impressed or Tsumegata Type, 5000 to 4000 BC; Sobata Type, 3500 to 3000 BC; Iha/Ogidō Types, 1500 to 1000 BC; Kayauchibanta/Nakahara Types, ca. 1000 BC; Fensa Lower Layer Type, AD 600 to 1000; and Ufutōbaru Type, AD 700 to 1000. Kawana (2011) groups some of the dates from the Okinawa Islands by pottery type (Table 4.1a, b). Kawana selected a subset of dates from Najima's tabulation, choosing samples from well-known recent excavations. The range presented in Table 4.1b is simply my summary of the few dates that he presented and should be used with caution. There are slight differences in the proposed range of each pottery type. It is useful to have one tabulation prepared by archaeologists (Najima et al. 2008) and one prepared by a geologist (Kawana 2011) and to find general agreement. In the discussion of pottery types in this chapter, I refer to the local Okinawan chronology and the chronology of the Japanese main islands. Okinawan archaeologists distinguish between sites with extensive shell deposits (shellmounds, Japanese *kaizuka*) and sites without shell deposits (sites, Japanese *iseki*). I have maintained this distinction in my discussion.

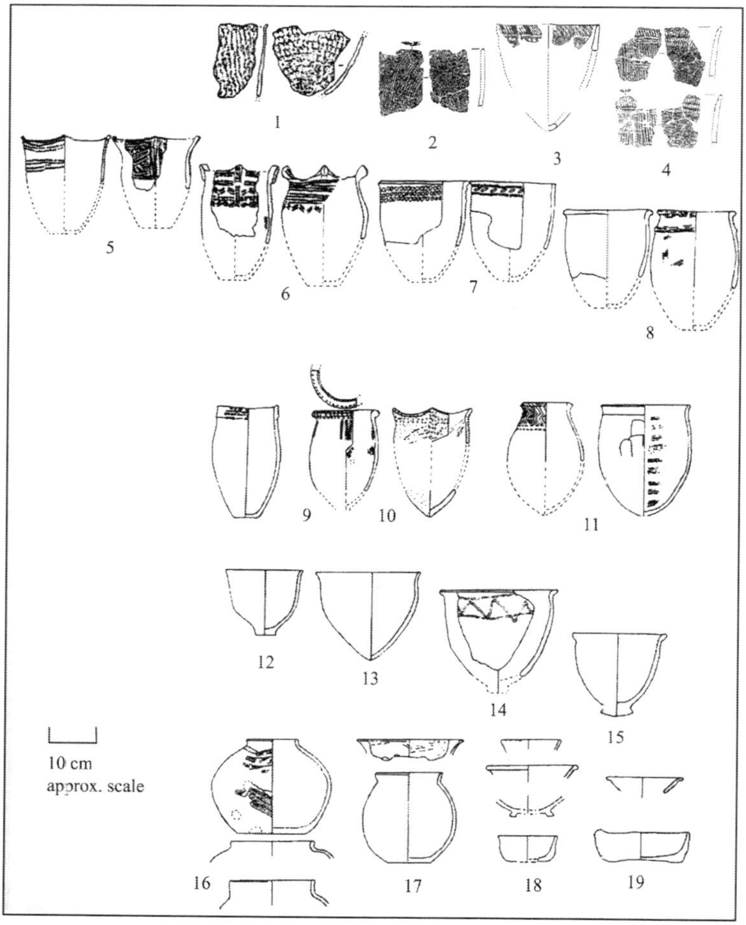

Figure 4.1. Diagnostic pottery types from Okinawajima. Redrawn from Kinjō Kamenobu 1990, Miyagi Eishō and Takamiya Hiroe 1983, and Takamiya Hiroe 1994.

1. Nail-Impressed (*tsumegata mon*) Type pottery from Yabuchi Cave.
2. Nail-Impressed Type pottery from the Toguchi Agaribaru Site.
3. Murokawa Upper Layer Type.
4. Sobata Type.
5. Iha Type.
6. Ogidō Type.
7. Ōyama Type.
8. Murokawa Lower Layer Type.
9. Kayauchibanta Type.
10. Murokawa Upper Layer Type.
11. Uzahama Type.
12. Maezato Type (height of vessel 18.5 cm).
13. Gushibaru Type (with pointed bottom) (height of vessel 23.5 cm).
14. Akajangā Type (height of vessel 23.5 cm).
15. Fensa Lower Layer Type.
16. Gusuku Type, constricted-neck (*tsubo*) form.
17. Gusuku Type, (upper) open-mouth cauldron (*nabe*) form, (lower) jar (*kame*) form.
18. Gusuku Type, shallow bowl (*wan*) form.
19. Gusuku Type, plate (*sara*) form. For Gusuku Types, no scale is available, and no chronological distinctions within the period are indicated.

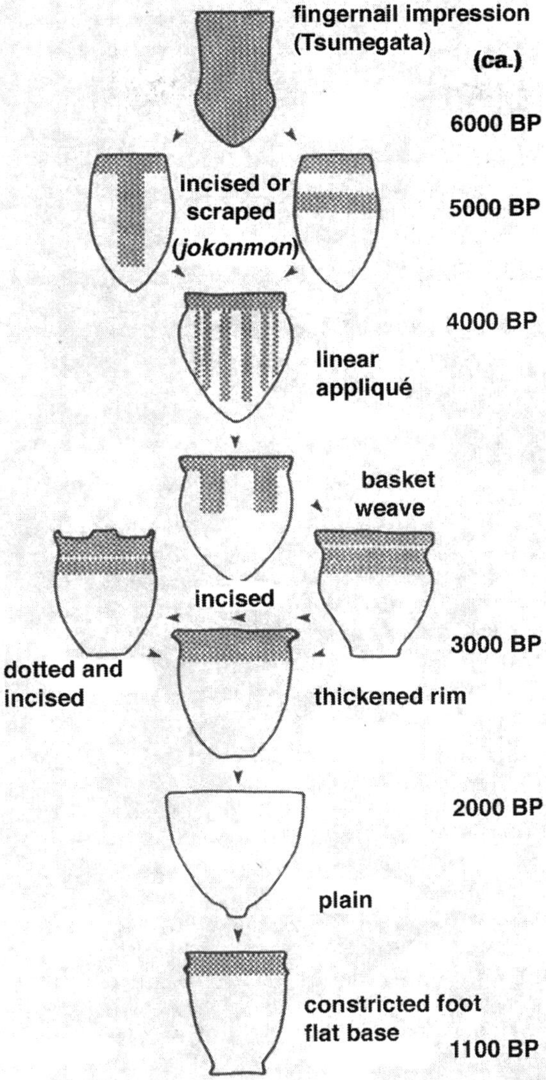

Figure 4.2. Pottery wares (*yōshiki*) of the Central Ryukyus. From Itō 2000, 32; 2003, 64. Itō's dating is shown. Courtesy of Itō Shinji.

TABLE 4.1A Calibrated Dates for Pottery Types of the Shellmound Period of the Okinawa Islands

Kyushu	*Period*	*Subperiod*	*Pottery Type*	*Cal Date* BP 1σ *(no. of dates)*	*Site Name*	*Site Location*
			Plain Pottery	ca. 7900–7700 *** (1)	Noguni Shellmound Loc B	base of terrace near sea
	ESMP I		Plain, Tsumegata Types	ca. 7300–6800* (3)	Aragusuku Shichabaru II	shoreline low area
			Tsumegata Type	ca. 7600–7200 ** (2)	Toguchi Agaribaru	base of terrace near sea
		Earliest		ca. 7000–6500 ** (2)	Noguni Shellmound Loc B	
	ESMP II		Sobata Type	ca. 6200– 5700* (7)	Ireibaru Wet Area	base of terrace near sea,
				ca. 5800–5500**** (1)	Toguchi Agaribaru	shoreline low area
	ESMP III		Omonawa Zentei?	ca. 5300–4900* (3)	Ireibaru Wet Area	shoreline low area
				ca. 4200–3900* (2)	Ginoza Mēbaru	sloping terrain,
				ca. 3600–3200** (3)	Kigahama Shellmound	base of cliff, inland from sea
Jōmon	ESMP IV		Iha, Ogidō	ca. 3500–2900* (2)	Nishinagahamabaru	shoreline low area
				ca. 3300–2900* (2)	Ginoza Mēbaru	
		Early		ca. 3400–2900* (1)	Busena Minami Shelllmound	
	ESMP IV, V		Iha, Ōyama, Murokawa Uzahama	Iha, Ōyama, Murokawa Uzahama Types ca. 3300–2900* (5)	Kayauchibanta	high terraces
				Murokawa, Uzahama Types ca. 3400–2900* (4)	Ōyama Fukumoribaru II	

	ESMP V		Kayauchibanta,	Kayauchibanta Type	Ōyamadake no Saku I	high terraces
			Nakahara	ca. 3400–3200* (2)		slopes
			Nakahara	ca. 3300–2900** (2)	Shinugudō, Kiyūna	shoreline low area
					Higashi	
		Middle			Nubataki	
			Nakahara?	ca. 2800–2700* (1)	Ireibaru Wet Area	
			Type unknown	ca. 1900–1400** (2)	Mēbaru II	
	LSMP I		Hamayabaru,	ca. 2300–1900* (2)	Ginoza Mēbaru	
	LSMP II		Ufutōbaru			coastal low areas and dunes
Yayoi	LSMP III	Late	Ufutōbaru	ca. 1600–1500* (1)	Tsuken Shellmound	
			Ufutōbaru	ca. 2200–1900*(1)	Heshikiya Tōbaru	
				ca. 1300–900** (2)	Heshikiya Tōbaru	
Kofun			Ufutōbaru, Akajangā	ca. 1900–1300* (3)	Ginoza Mēbaru	
	LSMP IV		Akajangā	ca. 1400 * (1)	Tsuken Shellmound	
Heian			Fensa Lower Layer	ca. 1100–900* (2)	Ireibaru Wet Area	

Source: Kawana 2011, 67.

ESMP = Early Shellmound Period; LSMP = Late Shellmound Period

* based on Najima et al. 2008 with two standard deviations, calibrated with calib 501.

** from Najima et al. 2008 (charcoal and carbonized material), not adjusted for 13C, calibrated with calib 501.

*** from Furukawa 1984, shell date.

**** from Furukawa and Oshiro 1977, not adjusted for 13C, but calibrated with calib 501.

TABLE 4.1B Range of Dates for Major Early Shellmound Period Pottery Types Found in the Okinawa Islands

Type	*Range (cal years BP)*	*Range (cal years BC)*
Plain Pottery	7900–7700	5950–5750
Plain and Tsumegata	7300–6500	5350–4550
Sobata	6200–5500	4259–3550
Omonawa Zentei	5300–4900	3350–2950
Iha, Ogidō	4200–2900	2250–950
Murokawa	3300–2900	1350–950
Kayauchibanta	3300–2900	1350–950
Nakahara	2800–2700	850–750

The Oldest Pottery in the Okinawa Islands

The Ufuniku Cave Site, in Nanjō City, southern Okinawajima, has yielded pottery sherds that resemble pottery of the Incipient Jōmon Period (13,680 to 9250 cal BC) of Kyushu (Yamazaki et al. 2010). The style of pottery and the site location are different from other early finds of Okinawajima, which are found on low-lying shorelines. This site is located at an elevation of 130 m, 2 km inland from the present shoreline. Associated shells have given AMS dates of (uncal) 9000 to 10,000 BP, leading the authors to assign a date of at least 9000 BP for the pottery. In 1998 a four-month excavation of the Minatogawa Fissure was undertaken in hopes of recovering more Pleistocene materials. Although no Pleistocene materials were forthcoming, a single pointed bottom vessel with incised wavy lines near the rim and a *Conus* shell were found in red clay soil in the upper part of the fissure deposit. The shell was dated at 8640±90 BP (Tka 12090), while humus soil from the same layer was dated at 8550±290 BP (Tka 12364) (Oda 2009, 10). Similar pottery was found in the Nakaura Cave Site, Okinoerabujima (Yamazaki et al. 2010, 122). Generally, writers refer to the Plain and Nail-Impressed Types discussed below as the earliest in Okinawa, but these finds supersede them.

Plain Pottery

Until the recent findings from Ufuniku Cave mentioned above, the oldest pottery found in Okinawa was the plain pottery termed Group IV, in Layer VII, the lowest layer of the Noguni B Site. (Although some dates assessed by the Gakushuin Laboratory have been considered unreliable, Spriggs and Anderson

[1993, 207] found no problems with samples numbered above 4500, which includes the above date.) Plain pottery also occurs in two contexts in the Aragusuku Shichabaru No. 2 Site. It was found together with Sobata Type pottery from Kyushu, in Layer IX, and one fragment was found with wild boar bones in Layer XIIIa. At present, it appears that a small group of plain pottery makers may have lived in Okinawa for a short period. These finds can be grouped into a Plain Pottery Type. The origin of the Okinawan early Plain Pottery Type is unknown. Itō Kei (2006; 2007a) states that this type of pottery may be an independent invention since no immediate antecedents have been found in the surrounding East China Sea area. Associated stone tools are variable. The adzes from Toguchi Agaribaru are chipped on all surfaces, whereas those from Noguni B show edge grinding. The raw material for the adzes is thought to have come from the Kerama Islands, which lie 32 km to the west of southern Okinawa. Shell arrowheads are recorded, but stone arrowheads are absent. (Because the sherds are small and lack distinguishing features of vessel shape or decoration, they have not been illustrated in Figure 4.1.)

Nail-Impressed: Early Shellmound Period I (Takamiya Chronology)

Itō Kei (2007a) lists a total of sixteen sites in the Central Ryukyus that have yielded Nail-Impressed Type pottery. Two subtypes have been identified. In the Yabuchi Type, "fingernail impressions" (*tsumegata mon*) are rare, but "fingertip" impressions are common. (These so-called impressions were probably made with a spatula, but the descriptive names are used as a convention.) For convenience I have used the term "Nail-Impressed." The outer surface and sometimes the inner surface as well show shallow, irregular impressions. The walls of the vessels are thin (5 mm), and the vessel shape is postulated to be a wide-mouthed jar, with pointed bottom and sharply sloping sides. The Agaribaru Type has the same shape, but the walls are thicker and the decoration is more frequently made by instruments than by finger impressions. While early writers postulated that the Ryukyu Nail-Impressed *tsumegata mon* was similar to the Incipient Jōmon *tsumegata mon* of southern Kyushu, it is now clear that it is unrelated and of a later date. Its origins are not known.

Incised: Early Shellmound Period II/ Early Jōmon (Takamiya Chronology)

Incised (*jōkonmon*) pottery is found in the Todoroki, Sobata, Jōkonmon, Kamino A, and Murokawa Lower Layer Types. While *jōkonmon* is usually translated as "incised," the surface treatment is actually closer to scraping. The outer edge of a shell that has transverse ridges on its exterior is scraped over the surface of the vessel, the teeth leaving shallow incisions or scraping marks. In many cases the scraping was subsequently smoothed over and linear appliqué or incision was applied to the surface.

The origin of this type is in the Early Jōmon Todoroki Type of Kyushu, which occurs at the beginning of Early Jōmon (7250 to 5400 cal BP). In western Kyushu, particularly Kumamoto and Kagoshima Prefectures, two subtypes of Todoroki occur. Todoroki A is the older type. On the vessel rim there are traces of scraping in either a weave or a zigzag pattern. This type of decoration is followed by Todoroki B, on which the scraping marks have been partially erased, and horizontal or vertical thin strips of clay have been applied. Todoroki B is often found with Sobata pottery, which has decoration composed of parallel incised lines in geometric patterns. Sobata is thought to have been influenced by the Comb Pattern Pottery of the Korean Peninsula. In site excavations in southern Kyushu, the layers that contain Todoroki A and those that contain Todoroki B and Sobata Types are often separated by the Akahoya Ash Layer (Kuwahata Mitsuhiro 2002).

Todoroki sherds were found in the Toguchi Agaribaru and Noguni Sites, and Sobata Type has been recovered from Ireibaru C and Toguchi Agaribaru. In each case these two types form the total ceramic assemblage of a single layer, suggesting a small colonizing group. As indicated in Table 4.1, Sobata pottery at the Ireibaru C Site has been dated to around 4000 BC. Some vessels have tempering of steatite, which occurs in Kyushu but not in Okinawa.

Three local types appear to develop from Sobata and Todoroki in Amami and Okinawa: Jōkonmon, Murokawa Lower Layer, and Kamino A. They retain the scraping and incising of the former imported types and indicate that the colonizing population of Sobata/Todoroki began to develop local pottery types in the Central Ryukyus.

Jōkonmon pottery shows signs of shell scraping on both the interior and exterior surfaces. The vessel shape is a straight-sided deep jar with a straight or slightly everted mouth and probably a pointed bottom (few recognizable base sherds have been recovered). Vessel height is not clear, but mouth diameter is around 24 cm. Surface treatment consisted of several steps. Following shell scraping, rows of punctates or incisions were applied. Short incised lines were sometimes arranged in a "feather" pattern (Tamaki Chōken et al. 1981, 105–115). This type of pottery has been found in small quantities in the Gushikawajima and Toguchi Agaribaru Sites and the lowest layer of the Kusatobaru Site, Izenajima. At the Sōgō Guraundo Site, Kikaigashima, in a deposit of alluvium almost 7 m from the present surface, two intact vessels and some sherds with horizontal linear incision and rows of push-pull impressions on the rim and neck and unidentified animal bones were found. The associated bones produced an AMS calibrated date of 5967 BC (Sumida et al. 2003, 31). The uncalibrated date is reported to be 6998±32, with no lab data.

The Murokawa Lower Layer Type was first found in the Murokawa Site, Okinawa, where it was the only type in the lowest cultural layer. The main form is a deep jar with pointed or nipple-shaped base. The shell scraping was generally erased before the application of decoration, from the rim to the upper body of the vessel, with the edge of a shell or a spatula, sometimes in combination. Rows of punctates (pierced small holes) or long incisions were also applied. Through experiment, Yoko'o (2008) found that the regular rows of punctates were made by impressing the toothed edge of the bivalve shell *Fragrum unedo* into the leather-hard clay. The rare Kamino A Type, found primarily in the Kamino Shellmound, Okinoerabujima, has similar rows of continuous incisions or impressions on the exterior of the lip (Itō Shinji 2000, 16).

Linear Decoration (Nakadomari Type)

Vessels of the Nakadomari Type with linear decoration (*chinsenmon*) are globular, with a pointed bottom and rows of incision on the exterior lip.

Linear Appliqué or Applied Band (Kamino B, Omonawa Zentei Types): Early Shellmound Period III/Middle Jōmon (Takamiya Chronology)

Several types with linear appliqué or applied strips or ridges (*ryūtaimon*) were first recognized in excavations on Okinoerabujima and Tokunoshima. They are a series of related types termed Omonawa after the Omonawa Shellmound, a large and very important type site in southern Tokunoshima, which is actually a group of sites, including East and West Caves, Foreground (Zentei) Area, and other localities. Excavations at the Kamino Shellmound, southern Okinoerabujima, and comparison of materials from early excavations at Omonawa Shellmound No. 4, southern Tokunoshima, provide materials from the Middle Jōmon. The center of distribution of these types is in the Amami Islands, and sites of this period are rare in the Okinawa Islands, which has been interpreted as an indicator of very low population. The rarity of the linear appliqué type and sites of the Middle Jōmon in general has been noted by Takamiya Hiroe (1994, 30) and Hiroto Takamiya (1996, 146).

The Omonawa Zentei Type is of great interest because of its links to the Amami Islands and its comparative rarity in Okinawa. Takamiya Hiroe found it to fill the Middle Jōmon gap in his chronology. Its presence in Okinawa was recognized in the 1976 excavations on Gushikawajima, an island between Iheyajima and Izenajima. Most of the sherds that were later included in the Omonawa

Zentei Type were originally placed in a separate type, the Gushikawa Type. It appears that the surface was first scraped with a shell and subsequently partially smoothed, before being decorated with linear appliqué. The applied thin strips of clay were usually incised or impressed with the edge of a shell, after which groups of linear incisions were sometimes applied. In the small excavation of the East Area of Gushikawajima, Omonawa Zentei was the sole type in Layers 8 and 9, while above it in Layers 6 and 7 were the Iha and Ogidō Types, succeeded by Late Shellmound Period plain pottery in Layers 1 and 5. (Layers 2, 3, and 4 were sterile.)

Dotted and Incised Lines: Early Shellmound Period IV/ Late Jōmon (Takamiya Chronology)

Following the Linear Appliqué or Applied Band Ware are the Iha and Ogidō Types with dotted or incised lines (*tenkokumon*), originating in Okinawa rather than Kyushu. Tatsuo Kobayashi (2004, 30) refers to them as the Okinawa Incised Style. They are roughly contemporary with the Basket Pattern of Amami (Omonawa East Cave Type). Distinctive wares and types existed in Okinawa and Amami at this time, showing the rise of distinctive groups. Local variations are the Kamino D and E and Murokawa Types. These types were based on a deep jar (*fukabachi*) with flat bottom and four knoblike projections on the rim, but there were also narrow-necked jars (*tsubo*). The shift to a flat bottom reflects trends in Kyushu. Differences between Iha and Ogidō are mainly in the rim profile and style of the projection. The rims of the Iha Type show a slight flare, and the widest diameter is at the mouth of the vessel. The decoration is usually repeated in three rows around the rim. Sometimes there are two rows separated by a blank row. It is usually executed with a forked instrument. The diameter of the mouth of the deep jars is variable. From Kusatobaru there are instances of vessels with diameters of 10, 15, and 20 cm.

The Ogidō Type is distinguished by its enlarged overhanging castellations on the rim. The decoration below the lip, often in four rows or registers, is composed of elements such as a sawtooth pattern or rows of dots created by a dentate instrument. The most common tool for applying the decoration is a single pointed bamboo spatula, which is used to create a push-pull or stab and drag motif. There are also some undecorated rims.

The rim of Ogidō vessels is slightly constricted, leaving the widest diameter in the upper part of the body. Incised lines on the upper neck were made with a pointed or forked tool, the latter being used more frequently. The Ōyama Type follows the Ogidō Type. Rim projections disappear, and the rims become flat. Vessels of this type often contain calcareous tempering material. There is a narrow band of decoration composed of push and drag incisions or a broad raised band (*tottaimon*), which is found on contemporary Kyushu types.

Basket Weave: Early Shellmound Period IV/ Late Jōmon (Takamiya Chronology)

In general the Amami Basket Weave (*kagomemon*) types resemble the pottery of southern Kagoshima in sharpness and complexity of decoration, and repetition of motifs.

The Omonawa East Cave Type is primarily a flat-bottomed deep jar with a thickened rim decorated with push-pull thumbnail impressions. There is also a narrow-neck *tsubo* form. The decorating tool has two or three teeth, and some vessels have a criss-cross basket weave decoration. Other vessels are decorated with rows of push-pull punctates separated by thin incised lines. The type appears to be related to types from the Late Jōmon of Kyushu and the pottery of the Ushuku and Katoku Sites of Amami (Ōnishi 1998).

The Katoku Type shows little change from Omonawa East Cave. Vessels are deep jars with flat bottoms. The chief motif is a basket weave criss-cross pattern. The body is well fired, and often the top of the rim is decorated with curved punctates like thick thumbnail impressions. The surface has been smoothed.

Two other types were first found in the extensive excavations of the multicomponent site of Omonawa. The Omonawa West Cave Type has a constriction below the thickened rim. The Omonawa Zentei Type has a raised band on the rim and incisions on the neck and shoulder. Other types from Tokunoshima and Amami Ōshima are the Kinen and Ushuku Upper Layer Types. The Kinen I Type has a thickened rim decorated with raised linear appliqué, zones of slanting parallel fine incisions, and punctates. Many of the vessels are narrow-necked *tsubo*. The Ushuku Upper Layer Type has a smoothed surface and thickened lip, which is triangular in cross-section. It resembles the Okinawa Kayauchibanta Type.

Thickened Rim: Early Shellmound Period V/ Final Jōmon (Takamiya Chronology)

Included in the group of vessels with thickened rims are the Murokawa, Murokawa Upper Layer, Kayauchibanta, Uzahama, and Nakahara Types in the Okinawa Islands and the Omonawa West Cave, Inutabu, Kinen I, and Ushuku Upper Layer Types in the Amami Islands. Within the thickened rim (*hikō kōsen*) types there are common elements shared by the Okinawa and Amami Islands as well as distinctive variants. The surface of the Murokawa Upper Type is porous, and the lip is thickened. The most common form is a deep jar with flat rim and small flat base about 3 to 5 cm in diameter. The paste contains very little temper, which appears to be coral sand as well as quartz that does not seem to have been added intentionally. This type is predominantly plain, but there is some incision made with a single pointed tool. Some lugs have been found, but they have become separated from the vessels and their precise point of attachment is not known. The subsequent Uzahama Type has a thickened rim, triangular or rounded in section, and a slightly constricted mouth. The surface paste is coarse, with heavy quartz temper, and the surface is plain. The Uzahama Type of the Okinawa Islands seems to be connected to the Ushuku Upper Type, which is found in the Amami and Tokara Islands.

Plain with Pointed Base: Late Shellmound Period I, II/Late Yayoi, Kofun Period (Takamiya Chronology)

Following the Thickened Rim Ware, Plain Pointed Base Ware (*mumon sentei*) appears in Okinawa, represented by the Nakahara Type. There are probably other types that date to the beginning of the Late Shellmound Period, but they are not well described. The Nakahara Type consists of both deep jars and *tsubo.* Distinguishing features are the plain rim treatment with a flangelike horizontal ridge and the lack of decoration. The Hamayabaru Type is also generally plain, with a pointed or constricted foot. Occasionally vessels have a lug near the neck. The outer surface shows traces of wiping, while the inner surface shows traces of smoothing with fingertips, features that are derived from Yayoi pottery (Kishimoto et al. 2000).

Constricted Foot Flat Base: Late Shellmound Period III, IV (Takamiya Chronology)

The Constricted Foot Flat Base (*kubirehirasoko*) variety can be seen in two types, the Fensa Lower Layer Type in Okinawa and the Kaneku Type of Amami. Two types not included by Itō are the Ufutōbaru and Akajangā Types (Takamiya Hiroe et al. 1993). The Ufutōbaru Type has continuous ridges formed by smoothing, all over the surface, which resemble smoothing after coil building. Vessel forms include deep jars, narrow-neck jars, plates, and miniature vessels. The Akajangā Type, first found in the Akajangā Site, Okinawajima, has a flat base or constricted foot. The main forms are wide- and narrow-mouth jars (*kame* and *tsubo*). The paste is sandy and reddish brown. Decoration consists of incision, punctates, or ridges (*tottaimon*), which are decorated by cutting or punctates. Incised net pattern decoration also appears. Rows of short incisions in sawtooth or wave patterns also occur. Fensa Lower Layer Pottery was first recognized in Layer III of the Fensa Site, Okinawajima. It is an immediate precursor of the pottery of the Gusuku Period, typified by the Fensa Upper Layer Type. There are decorated and plain variants of wide- and narrow-mouth jars of the Lower Layer Type. The foot is constricted. This vessel shape is based on prototypes from the Yayoi Period of Kyushu. It appears to have changed little until the advent of flat-bottom pottery of the Gusuku Period. While the Central Ryukyus, as far north as the Tokara Islands, maintained the constricted-foot form until the end of the Shellmound Period, the people of Kyushu adopted new forms of pottery in the Kofun Period, with flat bottoms and a variety of pastes, including earthenware (*hajiki*) and stoneware (*sue*).

Island Relations and Communities

Throughout the Shellmound Period the islands of the Northern and Central Ryukyus were in virtually constant contact with Kyushu and each other. Takamiya Hiroe (1994, 32–35) has shown how pottery groupings emerged in the Northern and Central Ryukyus (Figure 4.3).

The nature and intensity of the interaction and the boundaries of the communities shifted over time, and communication took various forms. While pottery is often considered the basis for studying communities and interaction, it is not the only means. Studies of nonceramic artifact styles and raw materials, faunal materials, and palaeoenvironment all shed light on these communities, as described below.

Stylistic analysis of pottery has provided clues to island interrelationships. Pottery types that have been brought from outside the region may be present as the majority type or in large quantities, indicating a migration; small quantities of exotic pottery, in contrast, may indicate more limited migration at the subcommunity level, or exchange. The relative quantity of each type of pottery in the total assemblage is important. A different level of communication or interaction may be indicated by the development of distinctive locally made pottery. The general vessel form and technique and location of decoration on the vessel may show close resemblance between sites and regions as well as reflecting group identity. Groupings of pottery based on these general similarities are termed *yōshiki* (lit. style or ware) in Jōmon studies. Typological groupings, based on specific decorative motifs, represent a more localized community.

Stylistic analysis of pottery has been the most common method of studying the movement of people in the Ryukyus. Studies of the geochemical components of pottery sherds to determine their origin have also produced promising results (Takamiya Hiroto et al. 1991; Fitzpatrick et al. 2006). A recent study by

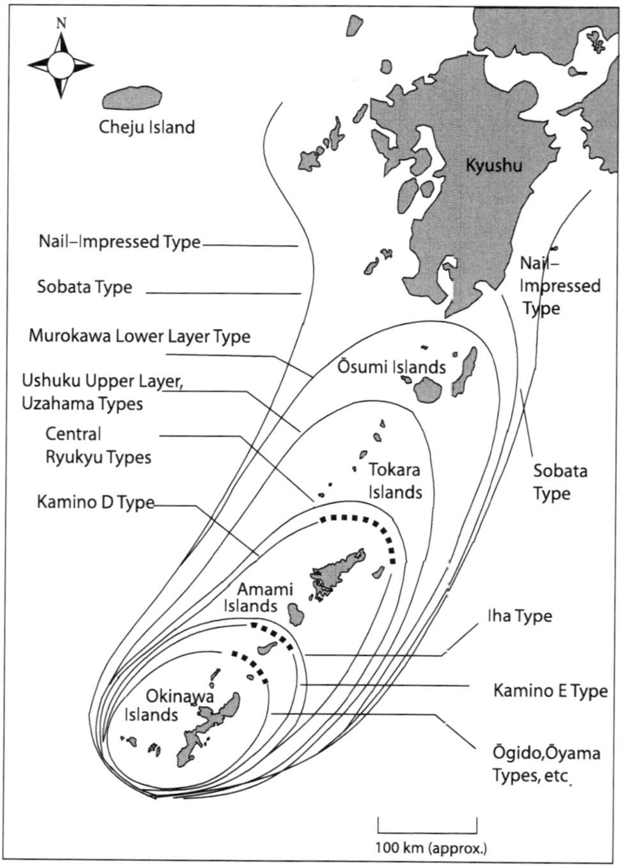

Figure 4.3. Pottery groupings, first proposed by Takamiya Hiroe (1994). After Zaidan 2003, 104. Courtesy of Okinawa Ken Kyōiku Cho, Bunkazai Ka.

Ueda Kei'ichi et al. (2009) sheds light on Sobata Type pottery and the Kinen Type of pottery from Tokunoshima (see below).

The following sections identify some of the major archaeologically recognizable communities and the most important interactive processes that promoted their formation.

Early Explorers

It would seem natural that Kyushu islanders would explore the Northern and Central Ryukyus before settling on them. They may have come in search of food or raw materials. During the Incipient Jōmon of southern Kyushu, (13,680 to 9250 cal BC), substantial communities existed in southern Kagoshima Prefecture and on Tanegashima (Pearson 2006). Permanent houses, central villages, very early pottery making, and an elaborate ritual life are well documented

(Mithen 2004, 370–380). While the first dated Holocene settlements of the Northern and Central Ryukyus are dated to between 6000 and 7000 BC, it is quite possible that earlier settlement occurred. Since sea levels rose during the first half of the Holocene and later, coastal sites from this time period may now be submerged. However, depending on the degree of hydro-isostatic rebound, the islands or parts of them may have been pushed up by the added weight of seawater created by rising sea levels (Kamiya 2007, 31), and shoreline sites may have been preserved

Early groups must have explored the Northern and Central Ryukyus for some time before establishing permanent settlements. The recent finds from Ufuniku Cave of pottery similar to Incipient Jōmon pottery from Kyushu seem to confirm this possibility. At present the evidence for early exploration is inconclusive but tantalizing. In the Incipient Jōmon of southern Kyushu, coastal sites are absent, covered by rising sea levels; therefore, little evidence of maritime technology remains. While Incipient Jōmon pottery has not been found in the islands south of Tanegashima, surface finds of Kakoinohara-type adzes have been made in a number of locations as far south as Okinawa Island. Oda (1997) has proposed that they are part of a southern stone tool tradition extending from Southeast Asia as far north as Kagoshima Prefecture. He proposes that their gouge form indicates that they were used in boat building. However, this type of adze has not been found in Sakishima, and no close parallels are known from Taiwan or Southeast Asia, particularly at this early date. Thus the evidence for a southern origin is lacking at this time. The fact that Late Palaeolithic people voyaged offshore from Honshu to Kōzu Island to obtain obsidian as well as the wide distribution of Kakoinohara adzes would indicate that people navigated around coastal Japan and in the Ryukyus. Probably the Northern and Central Ryukyus were being explored and colonized in the period equivalent to the Incipient Jōmon.

Dating of the Plain Pottery is tentative, but it may have been deposited within a few centuries of the eruption of the Kikai caldera, which had an enormous impact on the Northern Ryukyus (Chapter 2).

The Kikai eruption was of a totally different magnitude from other volcanic activity in the region (Shimoyama 2002). Southern Kyushu was covered not by ash but by pyroclastic flow, and phytolith samples from the southernmost part of Kyushu show a total absence of Gramineae, Bambusoideae, and arboreal species for several hundred years (Machida and Sugiyama 2002, 323, 319).

Following the Kikai eruption (7280 BP or 5320 BC), the distinctive cylindrical vessels with shell impression (Senokan Type) and roller-impressed (*oshigata mon*) pottery types of the Incipient Jōmon disappeared and were replaced by Sobata and Todoroki Types, which moved into southern Kyushu from the north

(Shimoyama 2002). The Kikai eruption occurred at the height of the Jōmon Transgression (Machida and Sugiyama 2002, 316).

Given the magnitude of the Kikai eruption and its refined dating, the dating of sites around 7000 BP (calib.) and the finding of Nail-Impressed Type pottery (Yabuchi Type) above the Akahoya Ash layer at the Kishikawa Site, Kasari Chō, Amami Ōshima (Kishimoto 1991, 8; Zaidan 2003, 163), it seems that many of the oldest pottery types found in Amami and Okinawa must be from people who inhabited the islands shortly after the eruption. Torrence and Grattan (2002) caution against assigning causality in cultural change to extreme natural events simply on the basis of synchronicity. Emphasizing problems in the interpretation of the effects of volcanic eruptions, they stress the need for independent analyses of the natural and cultural data as well as dating. Whereas the Akahoya Ash Layer has been used to confirm the chronology of Jōmon pottery, dating of the Okinawan sites is independent, based on radiocarbon and local geomorphology, and the general effects of the eruption are known from nonarchaeological, geomorphological, and palaeoenvironmental studies. Therefore, the effects of the Kikai eruption on island populations can be assessed from independent bodies of data. I believe that survivors of the Kikai eruption were pushed southward into the Ryukyus.

Sojourners

Sojourning is indicated by deposits exclusively of an exotic type of pottery on a few small sites of relatively short duration. The predominance of one type of pottery in a deposit distinguishes this situation from exchange, in which we would expect to find limited quantities of one or more types of pottery in a larger assemblage. In the period from roughly 6000 to 4000 BC, three types of pottery are found in small settlements. These are Plain Pottery, Nail-Impressed, and Sobata pottery. Small quantities of a fourth type, Kyushu Todoroki, are also found, as well as the pottery vessels from the Sōgō Guraundo Site of Kikaigashima.

Deposits at sixteen Ryukyu sites have yielded Nail-Impressed pottery (Itō Kei 2007b) in stratigraphic contexts above the Akahoya pumice, indicating the arrival of a small group to the Okinawa and Amami Islands, but the precise source of the pottery is unknown.

Todoroki and Sobata pottery types of the southern Kyushu Early Jōmon occur in a number of sites in the Ryukyus as the predominant type within a layer, suggesting migration from Kyushu and the establishment of communities of short duration. Both types are hallmarks of the movement of people into southern Kagoshima from the Kumamoto region following the devastation of the Kikai eruption (Machida and Sugiyama 2002). In Amami and Okinawa they are followed by Murokawa Lower Type (Takamiya Hiroe 1994, 28; Kamimura 1999), which is thought to have developed from Sobata Type pottery.

In sites of southern Kyushu, the Akahoya pumice layer marks the boundary between Initial and Earliest Jōmon. The Todoroki Type, named for the type site in Kumamoto Prefecture, is the first type to occur above the ash layer, and it is followed by the Sobata Type (Yokoyama 1986, 82). In Kyushu, the diagnostic type of Todoroki is Todoroki B, which has a thin horizontal appliqué band, decorated with nicks and notches, below the lip. The body shows lines of scraping, sometimes with a shell. A comparative petrographic study of Sobata sherds from sites in Kagoshima and Kumamoto and from Ufudōbaru, Toguchi Agaribaru, and Ireibaru C sites in Okinawa showed that the Okinawa Sobata sherds were made in Kyushu (with inclusions of Kyushu steatite), the Northern Ryukyus (with volcanic glass and limestone coral inclusions), and Okinawa Island (with inclusions of chert from the Nago Layer) (Ueda et al. 2009).

At present, the concentration of sites on Okinawajima on the central west coast, suggests that this may have been the initial point of colonization. The density of sherds and large number of individuals of *Sus* indicates that members of a small settlement hunted wild boar/pigs.

Faunal data also raise interesting issues about the life of early sojourners in the Ryukyus. From the Noguni B site, remains of some four hundred individuals of wild boars or pigs were found in a concentrated area in Layers IV and V. Metric analysis showed that the suid bones were 10 percent smaller than those of modern Ryukyu wild boars (Kawashima and Muraoka 1984). The authors did not make a final decision on whether they were domesticated. A study of the diet of the suids, using analysis of stable carbon and nitrogen isotopes from collagen (Minagawa et al. 2005), showed a vertical range of values for the isotope 15N, suggesting that some of the animals had been fed on C4 plants. These are plants that have a particular path of photosynthesis; included in this group are grasses and grains (such as rice, millet, barley, and wheat). They generally retain less 15N than woody C3 plants. The wide vertical range of 15N values suggests that plants from both groups were consumed. A separate small group of *Sus* found in the Ryukyu sites had similar 13C/15N values to wild animals in the Japanese main islands. To explain all of this variability, Minagawa et al. concluded that some of the pigs must have been domesticated and traded to the Ryukyus, and those with lower values of 15N must have been allowed to become feral. At the time of one of these sites, Noguni B (see above), the only human groups with domesticated C4 plants and pigs in the vicinity lived in coastal China. However, the source of the Noguni B suids remains unclear. Although suids properly belong in the discussion of subsistence in Chapter 5, the genealogical puzzle of the Noguni pigs is also relevant to consideration of the origins and migrations of human populations (unless the pigs swam on their own or crossed on Kimura's land bridge discussed in Chapter 2).

Colonizers

Colonization is identified by substantial deposits of exotic pottery in relatively deep deposits. I refer to colonization generally, leaving the discussion of unsuccessful and successful colonization to the next chapter, in which subsistence is the central topic. In the first stage of colonization, the artifact assemblage is basically that of the colonizing population. As the colonies become established, divergences such as new pottery types emerge.

In the Ryukyus the Jōkonmon Type is found in a number of sites from Okinawa north to the Satsunan Islands. It appears to be a local subtype of Todoroki. Whereas there is no doubt that substantial amounts of Sobata Type were carried as far south as Okinawa, Jōkonmon Type pottery appears to be a local development. It is not clear if Jōkonmon is the product of colonization or of emulation. Subsequent pottery types, Omonawa Zentei and Kamino D and E, show the development of local types leading to Ogidō and Iha. Two elements from Todoroki seem to become separated: scraping and decorated appliqué. Omonawa Zentei adopts the decorated rim, while Kamino types have linear scraping.

Relations between Amami and Okinawa

In the analysis of the pottery from the Kusatobaru Shellmound, Iheyajima, Tamaki Chōken et al. (1981) explored relationships between pottery types from the Amami and Okinawa Islands. The majority of sherds from Kusatobaru date to 3,000 to 2,000 years ago, the Early Shellmound Period IV and V. In general, pottery types from the Amami Islands show greater similarity to the Jōmon pottery of Kyushu than do Okinawan types. The paste is more refined, and decoration is often composed of more than one motif or technique, such as scraping, linear appliqué, and incision of the Omonawa Zentei Type. Incision is sharper, crisper, and finer than the incision found on Okinawan types. About 20 percent of a sample of 688 sherds from four cultural layers were of Amami types. In a petrographic study of pottery from Izena, which, with Iheyajima, lies to the north of Okinawajima, Ueda Kei'ichi et al. (2009) found evidence that the so-called Amami types such as Kinen contained inclusions of granite, found to the north in Amami

Ōshima, Okinoerabujima, and Tokunoshima, but not in Iheyajima, Izenajima, or Okinawajima. Another group of sherds contained volcanic glass, which could have only come from one of the large volcanoes to the north of Amami.

Communities with Strong Local Identity

Communities with a strong local identity were stable, growing communities with distinctive material culture and abundant sites with thick cultural layers. By this time (around 1500 BC) pottery types with strong local identity such as the Ōgido and Iha Types of the Late Jōmon Period or Early Shellmound Period IV appeared in the Okinawa Islands. The zone of stylistic distinctiveness contracted gradually, from the Northern and Central Ryukyus at the time of Nail-Impressed Type pottery, to the Central Ryukyus with types such as Murokawa, to the Okinawan Islands (Takamiya Hiroe et al. 1985).

Trading or exchange is indicated by the presence of minority exotic wares in ceramic assemblages and may be corroborated by evidence of exchange of other items such as lithics (Kamimura 2004). The Late Jōmon Ichiki Type of southern Kyushu is found as a minority ware in the Ushuku Shellmound of Amami Ōshima (Nakayama 1995) and the Urasoe Shellmound of Okinawa. It can be distinguished from pottery produced in Okinawa by its darker color, finer paste, and deeper and more precise incising. Sherds of the Ichiki Type have been found in more than forty sites in the Ryukyus, indicating considerable interaction. The interaction is of a lesser scale than that indicated by the distribution of Sobata and Todoroki Types (Kamimura 1999, 321). Simple models of dugout boats fashioned from pumice found in sites yielding Ichiki Type pottery in Kagoshima indicate to Kamimura that the makers of Ichiki pottery were maritime oriented (1999, 324). The Urasoe Shellmound, excavated in 1969 and 1970, contained several kinds of pottery from Amami: the Omonawa Zentei Type, with raised bands decorated with bivalve shell impressions; the Nakadomari Type; and the Ushuku Lower Layer Type, with push-pull decoration. In addition, some hammerstones were made from Kyushu lithic material (Nitta et al. 2005).

At the time of the appearance of Ichiki Type pottery in the Ryukyus, there was exchange of nephrite and obsidian. Nephrite from Itoigawa, Niigata Prefecture, in central Honshu, Japanese main islands, has been found, usually in the form of small beads, in at least eight sites on Okinawa, dating to the Late and Latest Jōmon. It is thought to have reached Okinawa via southern Kyushu (Tōma Kenji 2009).

Obata et al. (2010) reported that, during the middle Late Jōmon, a small-scale exchange of obsidian took place. An estimated gross weight of 360 grams of obsidian from Koshidake, Nagasaki Prefecture, Kyushu, has been found on thirty-six sites in the Okinawa Islands as far south as Kerama. Obata et al. concluded that it was probably occasional exchange carried out by a few people. Obsidian, imported as unprocessed nodules or as flaked material, was worked into small flake tools from a wedge-shaped core, using a bipolar technique. Since the raw material was rare and probably not continuously available, a technique that conserved the resource was used (Yamazaki 2008).

At the end of the Earliest Shellmound Period, the Omonawa Zentei Type was shared in the Amami and Okinawa Islands, forming a large area of interaction. In the subsequent Early Shellmound Period (Late Jōmon), at the time of the Iha/Ogidō Types, the area of interaction contracted to the Okinawa Islands. This distinctive group has been termed Okinawan Incised by Tatsuo Kobayashi (2004, 30). Despite the distinctive qualities of these pottery types, their connection to the Ichiki Type of Kyushu can be seen in their overhanging collar and castellations. The subsequent Ōyama Type also shows connections to Kyushu. Its thickened lip seems to show emulation of the thickened lip of the Latest Jōmon Kurokawa Type of southern Kyushu. Distinctive animal- and butterfly-shape ornaments, mostly made from dugong bone, were made in Okinawa Island in the time period of the Iha, Ogidō, and Ōyama Types. Kin (1986) believed that their form was similar to the bilaterally symmetrical motifs of the China mainland. No similar ornaments have been found in Kyushu. Animal pendants fashioned in shell are known from eleven sites in the central and southern parts of Okinawa (Shimabukuro 2009). They are usually made from the curved outer portion of the *Conus* shell, although stone examples are known. These stone ornaments seem to be particularly associated with Iha Type pottery and confirm the emergence of a distinctive culture area in Okinawa at this time. At the same time, the Late Jōmon Issō Type was shared among communities in the Northern Ryukyus from the Ōsumi Peninsula to the Kasari Peninsula of Amami Ōshima. It appears to indicate the emergence of a particular style in the Northern Ryukyus at the same time as the Iha and Ogidō Types of Okinawa Island.

Takamiya Hiroe (1994, 293) proposed that the sphere of interaction expanded after the Early Shellmound Period, since Uzahama Type pottery of Early Shellmound Period V (dated to around 1000 BC) is found in a wide area from Okinawa to northern Kyushu.

Local Development on Okinawa Island in the Late Shellmound Period

In the Late Shellmound Period, communities in the Northern and Central Ryukyus remained in contact with Kyushu through the exchange of shells, which is discussed in Chapter 6. While there were slight changes in pottery styles, their pottery generally retains the shapes of Yayoi Period jars. The islanders did not follow the profound social and economic changes of the Yayoi and Kofun Periods of the Japanese main islands.

The Nagarabaru Nishi Shellmound is situated in sand dunes on the south shore of Iejima adjacent to a well-developed reef lagoon on the leeward side of the island. Part of the site was destroyed by the removal of beach sand for construction; in the remaining section an excavation of 30 m × 12 m was carried out in 1977 and 1978. The site is thought to date to the middle of the Late Shellmound Period. Radiocarbon dates from the bottom of the cultural deposit, Layer VII, of *Tridacna* shell and wood charcoal (details are not given), are 2080±80 BP and 2060±80 BP (Ie Son 1979, 2); in addition, there is an aspartic acid racemization date on human bone of 1750 BP (Ie Son 1979, 274). Groups of postholes in the sand dune show a shift to dwellings erected on the ground surface rather than the pit house type of the Early and Middle Shellmound Periods.

The ceramics show a shift from the pointed bottoms of the Early and Middle Shellmound Periods to the flat-bottomed vessels of the Gusuku Period, and the surfaces of most of the vessels are plain. Decorated sherds account for less than 10 percent of the total sample, the decoration consisting of curvilinear appliqué on the neck or a row of punctates below the lip. One example with a horizontal luglike handle on the exterior is thought to be an imitation of a Kyushu soapstone cooking vessel. One sherd has a lip rim to accommodate a lid. This is the only example known from the Ryukyu Islands and may be a copy of a Kofun Period *sue* vessel. Shell artifacts include plaques made of pieces of *Conus* (*imogai*) shells and perforated limpet (*Penepatella* or *otsutanoha*) shells. Stone adzes, hammerstones, querns, and bone awls and a bone polished bladelike tool, perhaps used for cleaning fish, were also recovered.

The Uken Shellmound, on the east coast of Okinawa Island, immediately behind coastal sand dunes, was first excavated in 1979 (Okinawa Ken Gushikawa Shi 1980). The cultural layer was 10 to 30 cm thick. From 25 to 66 percent of the pottery sherds from different excavation units were Yayoi pottery from northern Kyushu of the Yamanokuchi and Menda types, as determined by analysis of style and tempering materials. Most of the local pottery bases were pointed, like those of earlier periods, but there were also a small number of flat bottoms. The authors of the site report noted that the variety of forms (narrow-necked storage vessels, footed serving stands, shallow individual eating bowls, and small narrow-necked jars for the storage of precious substances) correspond to Yayoi functional types and indicate substantial Yayoi influence.

The Akajangā Shellmound is situated on a sand dune about 4 m above sea level, some 200 m inland from the shore. From excavations in 1959 and 1979 (Okinawa Ken Gushikawa Shi 1980), it is dated to the first half of the Late Shellmound Period. An unusual small shallow-pit house, with clay spread on the floor, was discovered there, for the first time in Japan. In addition, two round surface dwellings were recovered, each surrounded by about twelve postholes. Less than 1 percent of the pottery was decorated. A few vessels with elevated bases resembling pottery stands were thought to show Yayoi influence. Some vessels had thickened bases with a constriction above the foot (*kubirehira-soko*), a style common toward the end of the Late Shellmound Period. The site yielded beads and pendants of *Conus* and other types of shells.

The Kitahara Shellmound is located on the extreme western tip of Kume-jima, an island about 90 km to the west of Okinawa, in close proximity to a shallow lagoon formed by coral reefs (Pearson et al. 1980; Ryūkyū Archaeological Research Team 1981; Pearson et al. 1990). The site yielded an undisturbed cultural layer from 80 to 100 cm in depth, containing artifacts, shells, and abundant organic materials. Three radiocarbon dates are available for this site. One of the dates is out of sequence and is too early; the other two dates are 1980±100 BP (KAERI-82) and 1190±50 (KAERI-84) (unrecalibrated). With doubled standard deviations and calibrated, they are 140 BC–AD 260 (KAERI-82) and AD 720–920 (KAERI-84). Layer III can be dated from the second century to the eighth century AD using a variety of dating methods, including the presence of a Kaigen Tsūhō coin and changes in local pottery styles. Excavations in 1973 and 1992 confirmed that in some parts of the site below Layer III there was an intervening white sand sterile layer and another cultural layer, Layer IV, which yielded Iha Type pottery, dating to Early Shellmound Period IV (Okinawa Ken 1995a).

Post molds were found in the sterile beach sand immediately below the cultural layer. They are thought to be associated with it. They may be the remains of two structures, of unclear shape, about 3 m in diameter. No distinctly excavated floors similar to those of Yayoi houses could be detected. Artifacts recovered from the site included hammerstones, mortars and pestles, and adzes. Shell knives or scrapers were fashioned from the opercula of large *Turbo* shells by direct percussion along their edges. Shell weights were manufactured by perforating bivalve shells. Pottery was present in small quantities, but no intact vessels were recovered; it is probable that basketry was used extensively. Three vessel forms, *kame, hachi,* and *tsubo*—the wide-mouthed jar, straight-sided jar, and constricted-neck jar—were distinguished. The bases of the vessels took several forms, which seem generally to reflect Yayoi pottery: a flat bottom with curving sides, a flat foot set off from the body of the vessel by a constriction, and a gradually pointed base. The surfaces of the vessels were smooth, with traces of scraping or wiping. A total of thirty-four sherds, identified as coming from the Yayoi of Kyushu, were found in Layer III.

In this summary of the ceramic chronology, primarily of the Central Ryukyus, I have attempted to describe the major pottery types and explore the social implications of their distributions. The situation for the Sakishima Islands is presented below.

The Southern Ryukyus

Sakishima Chronology

The Sakishima Islands, the southernmost of the Ryukyu Archipelago, lie at the southern edge of the East China Sea. Isolated from the rest of the Ryukyus in prehistory, they are separated from the Okinawa Islands by a stretch of about 270 km of open sea. They were probably colonized twice in prehistory and became linked to the entire Ryukyu Archipelago through trade and further colonization in the eleventh century AD.

In Chapter 3 I reviewed evidence for human Pleistocene habitation in Sakishima at Pinza Abu, Miyakojima, and Shiraho Saonetabaru, Ishigakijima. Holocene populations first lived in Sakishima around 4,850 years ago, judging from recently calibrated radiocarbon dates (Najima et al. 2008; Summerhayes and Anderson 2009) (Table 4.2). Five archaeological periods are recognized (Kin 1994; Ōhama 1999) (Table 4.3). The first two periods are prehistoric and are discussed here. The unusual sequence of Ceramic to Non-Ceramic in Periods 1 (Shimotabaru Period) and 2 (Non-Ceramic Period) (Kin 1994) is peculiar to the Sakishima Islands within the Ryukyus. At present there is a hiatus of 1,100 years between carbon-dated sites of Periods 1 and 2 (Ōhama 1999), and the relationship between the people of Period 1 and the people of Period 2 is unclear. The chronological gap raises many questions. Did the people of the Shimotabaru Period become extinct, leaving the islands to be recolonized, or have some sites been obliterated by typhoons or tsunami? Did population levels decrease drastically, reducing the chance of finding sites dating to the apparent hiatus? The possibility of continuous occupation from the Shimotabaru to Non-Ceramic Periods on Miyakojima has recently been proposed by Mark Hudson (personal communication) on the basis of recent excavations of the Nagabaka Site, Miyakojima.

Period 1: The Shimotabaru Period

The earliest evidence of colonization of Sakishima occurred in the Shimotabaru Period (Ishigaki Shi Sōmubu 2007; 2008a). Unlike the rest of the Ryukyus, the

TABLE 4.2 Selected Calibrated Sakishima Radiocarbon Dates

Lab No.	*Site*	*14C Date Date BP*	*Cal Date BC*	*Details*
		SHIMOTABARU PERIOD		
Geo Beta 3426–97153	Pyutta Layer III	4250±50	2890–2833 cal BC	AMS, carbonized material
Geo Beta 3427–97154	Pyutta Layer IV	3870±50	2499–2281 cal BC	AMS, carbonized material
N++++ (number not available)	Shimotabaru G-58 Layer III	3630±80		Beta, wood charcoal
		NON-CERAMIC PERIOD		
Beta 171944	Arafu 1-11, Layer 2 House 3	2270±40	387–197 cal BC	AMS, carbonized material
Beta 171946	Arafu 1-10, Layer 1 stone feature	1930±40	83–236 cal AD	AMS, carbonized material
Beta 171945	Arafu 1-9/10, Layer 2 bottom of layer	2320±40	418–349 cal BC	AMS, carbonized material
Beta 158578	Arafu J-9, Layer 3	2790±40	1002–825 cal BC	AMS, carbonized material

Source: Najima et al. 2008, 45.

TABLE 4.3 Summary of the Archaeological Periods of the Sakishima Islands

Period	*Date*	*Major Characteristics*
Shimotabaru Period	2900 to 2000 BC	Coarse ceramics, low straight-sided bowls, with some incision. Chipped, also semipolished stone adzes, remains of wild boar, shellfish, no cultivation. Sites behind low coastal dunes near fresh water.
Non-Ceramic Period	900 BC to AD 1100	Diagnostic *Tridacna* and chipped, also semipolished stone adzes. Remains of wild boar, shellfish. Tang coins, no cultivation, no pottery. Sites behind low coastal dunes near fresh water. Cooking using heated sandstone rocks.
Shinzato Period	AD 1100 to 1300	Reddish earthenware, rectangular mouth, 4 external lugs, flat bottom, imitates imported soapstone cauldron. Southern Song (few Northern) ceramics, stone tools, cultivation of rice, millet.
Nakamori Period	AD 1300 to 1600	Reddish earthenware, flaring mouth, lugs slightly lower on body than Shinzato Period. Some steatite tempered vessels. Yuan, Ming trade ceramics, walled settlements. Iron slag, tuyeres, bone tools, no stone tools. Cultivated rice, millet. Song to Ming coins.
Panari Period	AD 1600 to 1800	Panari shell tempered pottery, shapes imitate Okinawan hard-fired ceramics. Okinawan, Yaeyama, Japanese hard-fired ceramics. Iron slag, tuyeres, bone tools. Cultivated rice, millet, no stone tools.

Source: Based on Pearson 2003, 98; Ishigaki Shi Sōmubu 2008a, 2.

Holocene colonizers were not part of the Jōmon cultures that extended through most of the Japanese Islands. Fourteen sites belonging to the Shimotabaru Period have been recorded, including the Tōgurubama Site of Yonagunijima, found during airport expansion. This site does not have any pottery, but the stone tools are of the same type as those found in other Shimotabaru Period sites, and the radiocarbon dates are compatible with the Shimotabaru Period (Asato Shijun 2003). A date of 4000 cal BP from the lower layers of the Nagabaka Site, Miyakojima (Mark Hudson, personal communication), confirms Shimotabaru Period settlement, and one site, Soedō, has been found on the island of Taramajima between the Miyako and Yaeyama Groups. Otherwise all of the sites are found in Yaeyama. Is there some reason for the lack of sites on Miyakojima (Shimoji Kazuhiro 2010)? Since the marine resources of the two island groups are similar, the differences may relate to greater abundance of edible chestnuts, roots, and wild boar on the high, densely forested islands of Ishigaki and Iriomote than on the limestone islands of Miyako.

Shimotabaru Type pottery is distinctive from the pottery of the Central and Northern Ryukyus since the basic vessel form is a low globular jar 10 to 25 cm in diameter, with wide mouth and horizontal lugs, completely different from the straight-sided deep jar that is the basic prehistoric form throughout Northeast Asia (Asato Shijun 2010, 163). Decoration is rare: in a few cases, in the area between the mouth and the shoulder there is a vertical row of "thumbnail" (crescent) or small horizontal incisions, or there may be vertical rows of punctates and slab and drag marks. Occasionally there is a groove below the lip. The vessel wall is thick, over 1.1 cm, and the unrefined clay contains inclusions such as quartz. Since relatively few, small sherds of this pottery have been found, it is thought that its use was limited. Associated adzes are variable, with triangular and oval cross-sections. Many have a chipped body and polished assymetrical bit (Asato Shijun 2010). The actual span of the Shimotabaru Period based on published AMS dates is approximately 2900 to 2500 BC. The date from the Nagabaka site mentioned above would extend the span to 2900 to about 2000 BC. This dating should be taken as an approximation.

Period 2: Non-Ceramic Period

The Non-Ceramic Period is thought to begin around 900 BC, judging from recently excavated sites on Miyakojima, and to end around AD 1100. Miyakojima sites yielding shell adzes, such as Nagamazuku and Urasoko, have tended to give rather early dates (Ishigaki Shi Sōmubu 2009a, b).

The absence of pottery sets this period apart from most of contemporary East Asia, and the chronological gap between the Shimotabaru and Non-Ceramic Periods makes it difficult to determine whether the absence of ceramics is the result of change within one cultural group or replacement by another. A cache of Tang coins, Kaigen Tsūhō, at the Sakieda Akasaki Site, Ishigakijima (Takemoto and Asato 1993, 248), raises the strong possibility of direct contact with Chinese traders. Since most of the Sakishima coins come from one site, it is possible that they came from a shipwreck rather than from continuous trading. Asato Shijun (2010, 175) notes that shell adzes are not found in sites yielding

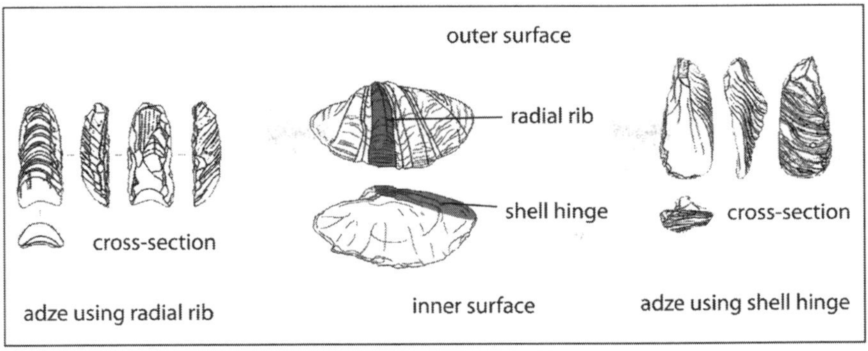

Figure 4.4. Shell adzes of the Non-Ceramic Period, Sakishima. Original by Anzai Eisuke. Adapted from Ishigaki Shi Sōmubu 2009b, 17. Courtesy of Anzai Eisuke and Miyara Yoshikazu of Ishigaki Shi Sōmubu Shishi Henshūka.

Kaigen Tsūhō Tang dynasty coins, suggesting that the shell adzes had died out by the seventh century AD.

The production of unique *Tridacna* shell adzes also raises many questions about the nature of Sakishima Island communities. They were fashioned either from the thick rib or edge near the hinge of the *Tridacna* shell (Figure 4.4). Some three hundred adzes have been reported from forty-three sites, the largest numbers coming from Miyakojima, which, being a coral limestone island, lacks suitable stone material for adzes. Nevertheless, some stone adzes of material from lithic material from Yaeyama have been found. Along the north-facing coast of triangular Miyakojima, there are several Non-Ceramic Period sites on the narrow coastal plain below limestone cliffs from which springs provide ample water. These coastal strips have been altered for sugarcane cultivation. Originally they consisted of a back marsh or low-lying area facing a substantial sloping dune and reef lagoon about 500 m wide.

One particularly large site is Urasoko, Miyakojima. It is an ancient village site covering an area of 300 m × 50 m, dating to 2,500 to 1,800 years ago. Two very similar layers with over a hundred cooking areas of burned soil and rocks were found. The site yielded two hundred shell adzes. In a similar protected location, inland from the shoreline sand dune, the Nagamazuku Site of Miyakojima also produced many shell adzes, while the Nagura Bay area of Ishigakijima yielded about thirty specimens. The Arafu Site, on the northeast shore of Miyakojima, is located in a sand dune on Aragusuku Beach, near an inlet with a small stream. The reef in front of the site is 500 m wide. The site did not yield any pottery, but excavators recovered stone tools made of Yaeyama lithics, wild boar bones, and burned rock. Dates from the site cover a one-thousand-year span, from about

900 BC to 80 AD (Egami 2009). In the bottom layer, Layer IV, dated at 2200 years BP, four shell adzes were found in a cache along with a piece of branch coral. The adzes appear to have been buried in a shallow wooden container. One is gouge-shaped (*marunomi kaifu*), two are hand adzes with beveled bits, and the fourth is a planing tool. From comparison with ethnographic examples from the Marshall Islands, Egami concluded that they were probably types used for making canoes (Egami 2009). Egami found in fieldwork in Indonesia that at the completion of canoe construction artisans ritually disposed of the tools. He proposed that the cache of shell adzes at the Arafu Site also indicates ritual disposal. A cooking area of burned soil and rocks was also found.

The Nagabaka Site is a habitation site in the Shimajiri area of Miyakojima, on sloping ground immediately in front of a later rock overhang "wind burial" site, Nagabaka Fūsōbo. Investigated in 2005 and 2006, the main site belongs to the Non-Ceramic Period. Radiocarbon dates indicate occupation from the third to eighth centuries AD. The site yielded four *Tridacna* adzes, six pierced shark tooth ornaments, and seventeen shell beads. Pottery was absent. While all of the other Non -Ceramic Period sites are coastal sand dune sites, this site is 1 km inland at the base of a limestone slope. In 2007 human bone fragments were found in a lower layer (Ishigaki Shi Sōmubu 2009b, 28–30; Hudson and Taneishi 2007).

Formation of Island Communities in Sakishima

Since the origins of the people of the Shimotabaru and Non-Ceramic Periods are not clear, it is difficult to discuss the processes by which island communities formed. The most logical place to look for the ancestors of the early inhabitants of Sakishima is the east coast of Taiwan; however, a comparison between the two areas turns up few striking similarities in artifacts or subsistence patterns. In Taiwan, prehistoric farming cultures are thought to have appeared as early as 5000 to 4500 BP with the latter part of the Early Neolithic Dabenkeng Culture (Tsang 2000; Chi and Hung 2010; 2011), characterized by thick cord-marked pottery. The typical shape of pottery vessels has a globular body, flaring rim, and ring foot. As of 2001, Dabenkeng pottery was found in eleven sites, including the lower layers of stratified sites (Li and Yeh 2001, 40). While Dabengkeng-type sites are rare on the east coast of Taiwan, sites of the subsequent Middle Neolithic East Coast Fushan Culture are relatively abundant and date from 4500 to 3500 BP. The pottery has a fine paste and is decorated with fine cord marking. Notable cultural traits are the use of large pieces of slate to make coffins and the production of ornaments from local jade. From 3500 to 2000 BP, the Beinan (Late Neolithic) Culture flourished on the east coast. It is characterized by fine cord-marked and coarse sandy pottery with external lugs and a wide variety of elaborate ornaments and some adzes of local nephrite. These adzes and ornaments are found on the offlying islands of Lü Dao and Lan Yu but are not found in Sakishima. Roughly contemporary with the Beinan Culture is the Qilin Culture. These two cultures share the use of large pieces of local slate for house supports and coffins. The Sanhe Culture (2500 to 1200 BP) has pottery decorated by elaborate stamping and punctuating, particular stone ornaments in the form of a split ring with three triangular protrusions, termed *lingling-o,* and glass beads (Kuo 2010). An extensive exchange system extending from southern Taiwan to mainland Southeast Asia, the Philippines, and Borneo included the Sanhe Culture (Hung and Bellwood 2010).

Significant differences in the artifact assemblages of the two areas would indicate that a very few people accidentally drifted away from the east coast to Sakishima and were unable to replicate the diagnostic features of their culture in their new homeland. They survived for several centuries before becoming extinct. Also the occurrence of a small number of completely polished rectangular adzes in the Nagamazuku Site, Miyako Island, suggests that Sakishima was contacted sporadically by accidental voyagers who were unable to return to Taiwan.

While common sense might dictate that groups from the Philippines drifted north to Sakishima on the Kuroshio, creating a continuum of culturally similar populations and cultures, genetic and linguistic evidence do not show such widespread similarities, but instead trading occurred between Luzon and the Batanes, and Taiwan and Lan Yu (Loo et al. 2011).

Anderson (2005) has proposed that the Kuroshio may have been an obstacle to movement from Taiwan to the Philippines and that early voyagers to the Philippines may have departed from the southern tip of Taiwan, to the west of the Kuroshio, rather than from the east coast of Taiwan, to avoid being pushed back to Taiwan by the current. The source regions of populations moving to the south from Taiwan and drifting to Sakishima may have been separate.

Origins of the Inhabitants of Sakishima: Austronesian Migrations?

While the thick brown low-fired paste of Shimotabaru pottery does not resemble closely the more varied and sophisticated prehistoric pottery from the east coast of Taiwan, external lugs are present in the pottery of both areas, and the chipped adzes without polishing, which must have been digging tools, are identical in both areas. Therefore, some archaeologists think that the first populations from Sakishima came from the east coast of Taiwan (Summerhayes and Anderson 2009). Since Taiwan is the nearest landfall to Sakishima, with only a distance of 108 km from Taiwan to Yonagunijima, it may seem irrational not to accept it as the source of Sakishima populations. However, strong differences in the assemblages of the two areas must be accounted for. Many items from Taiwan cultures are absent in the Shimotabaru Culture: these include bark-cloth beaters, pottery spindle whorls, jade ornaments, and glass beads. Hallmarks of the Taiwan pottery tradition, ring feet and footed strands, as well as virtually every type of surface treatment, are absent. We need to explain these absences. Chen Yupei (2009) concludes that Neolithic populations from Taiwan did not colonize the Ryukyus because conditions on the islands were difficult for agriculture.

In addition, eastern Taiwan is considered by some scholars to be the homeland of the Austronesian people, who migrated through Southeast Asia to faraway islands such as Polynesia and Madagascar. The postulated Austronesian migration is thought to have begun in the third millennium BC. Did Austronesian peoples also populate Sakishima? A recent critique does not support the idea of a continuous Austronesian migration but favors the concept of exchange links between Taiwan and the Philippines (Donohue and Denham 2010). There is still much debate concerning the place of Taiwan in the expansion of Austronesian speakers. Debates continue regarding the link between artifacts and language speakers, the patterns of migration, and the role of farming in the expansion (Bellwood and Dizon 2005; Anderson 2005). Eastern Taiwan was the center of a trading network in jade that extended far into the Philippines. It is now known that green jade, used to make adzes and ornaments found in the Philippine islands of Luzon and Palawan, comes from Fengtian in eastern Taiwan (Hung 2005; Hung et al. 2007); however, objects of Fengtian jade have not been found in Sakishima.

The occurrence of *Tridacna* shell adzes in Sakishima has stimulated discussion about possible migration into the area from Micronesia or the Philippines. However, the available archaeological evidence from the Philippines is from far to the south, and chronological correspondences cannot be confirmed. Shell adzes found in the Balobok Rock Shelter, Sangasanga Island, Tawi Tawi Islands, in the extreme south of the Philippines, occur in Layer III, which is a mixed deposit containing shell adzes and a gouge but also a socketed bronze axe and an opaque glass bead. Despite a single early date of 5140 ±710 (3190 BC) (Ronquilllo 2003, 36), the dating is unreliable because of the mixing of artifacts in the deposit. The second dated occurrence of shell adzes is from a burial in Duyong Cave, Palawan, dated to 4630±250 (2680 BC). This flexed male burial contained a stone adze, four polished shell *Tridacna* adzes, two ear discs and a pendant made from the perforated base of a *Conus* shell, and six lime containers made from *Arca* shells (Ronquillo 2003, 35). They are earlier than the Sakishima adzes. At present most archaeologists have concluded that the most logical source of the Sakishima adzes is somewhere in the Philippines, but conclusive evidence has yet to be found. However, it would seem that people bringing shell adzes into Sakishima would have left other artifactual evidence of their origins. In the absence of such evidence, Takayama's conclusion (2001) that they were invented independently may be the most economical for the present.

A recent study of Sakishima Islanders and Taiwan indigenous people, using mtDNA, Y Chromosome, and autosomal short tandem repeat loci found that the proposed Neolithic expansion from Taiwan did not contribute to the gene pool of modern Sakishima Islanders and that the male lineage of Ryukyu Islanders shares a common linkage with Hokkaido Ainu who are presumably direct descendants of the Jōmon people (Matsukusa et al. 2010, 211). As in the study of the Lan Yu and Ivatan Islanders by Loo et al. (2011), frequent reciprocal gene flow within the islands has masked traces of common ancestry in the Ryukyu chain. Because of the break between the Shimotabaru and Non-Ceramic Periods and substantial migrations from the north around the eleventh century AD, there is no reason to expect genetic continuity between the Taiwan aborigines and modern Sakishima Islanders. Although studies of Taiwan prehistoric adzes have failed to turn up any specimens with a Ryukyu geological signature (Hung 2004; Summerhayes and Anderson 2009, 88), similar studies of lithics in Sakishima should also be undertaken to look for exotic materials. Similarly, comparative genetic studies of palaeobotanical and palaeofaunal (suid) materials are overdue.

The Shimotabaru Period is roughly dated to 4850 to 4000 BP (2900 to 2000 BC), while the Non-Ceramic Period is dated to 1,800 years ago up to the twelfth century AD. The hiatus of 1,100 years (900 BC to AD 1100) between the two periods and the unusual nonceramic assemblage left by the new colonizers makes the archaeological interpretation of ancient island communities challenging. In the Non-Ceramic Period, small communities lived in the Sakishima Islands in isolation from Taiwan and the Central and Northern Ryukyus.

Shimoji Kazuhiro (2008, 328) notes that the dates for the Non-Ceramic Period in the Miyako Islands cover a span from about 2,500 to 1,800 years ago, ending earlier than in the Yaeyama Islands. However, recently the Nagabaka Site has yielded dates from AD 435 to 735. This suggests that the gap between the Non-Ceramic and Gusuku Period will be filled in with further research and that the Miyako Islands were continuously inhabited from the Non-Ceramic Period to later historic periods.

The islandscapes of Sakishima were created by experiences of colonization and adaptation that were different from those of people living in the rest of the Ryukyus. Colonization was from the south, although the precise source of the first populations remains unknown. Until the eleventh century AD the islanders had no significant contact with the cultures of the Central Ryukyus or Kyushu. Nor were they involved in the shell trade linking the rest of the Ryukyus to Yayoi and later cultures of the Japanese main islands. At present these distinctive local cultures do not seem to have close connections with known cultures of Taiwan or the Philippines, nor did they participate in the long-distance exchange network linking southern Taiwan and Southeast Asia described by Hung and Bellwood (2010).

In the first millennium AD there is evidence of contact between Yaeyama and mainland China. Some forty Tang coins, mostly Kaigen Tsūhō, including thirty-three specimens from the Sakieda Akasaki Site on Ishigaki Island, by far the largest concentration found in the Ryukyus, are thought by Ōhama (2008) to have been brought by ships sailing from Japan to China on the Japanese tribute missions (*kentōshi*). Several routes were taken to sail from Hakata to China. Ōhama contends that the southern route, through the Ryukyus, was used between 702 and 752 (2008, 352). Iron ships' nails or chisels (perhaps nails reused as chisels) have also been found. Two small plates of Chinese Tang dynasty Changsha ware, unique in the Ryukyus, which were long disregarded by archaeologists because their exact provenience on Iriomote Island could not be confirmed, have recently been reported to have come from an *utaki* (local shrine) in the Sonai area of Iriomote. Kinoshita (2000) concluded that itinerant Chinese traders must have visited the islands of Sakishima, seeking to obtain mother of pearl (*Turbo*) shell. In the Japanese main islands Kaigen Tsūhō coins are usually found in shrines, temples, or burials; however, in the Ryukyus they are found in village sites.

According to Ōhama (2008), navigation skills and technology gradually became available to the islanders in the period from AD 700 to 1000, but it was not until the eleventh century AD that changes from hunting and gathering to cultivation took place. In the twelfth to thirteenth centuries AD, small groups from the Central and Northern Ryukyus migrated to the islands.

Conclusions

The Holocene colonization of the Northern and Central Ryukyus took place over several millennia with the arrival of small groups recognizable by their pottery. The relative duration and distribution of pottery types and other types of artifacts vary according to the nature of social groups. While maintaining contact with Jōmon and Yayoi groups in Kyushu, the islanders formed social groups with shifting boundaries. In the Middle Shellmound Period they developed distinctive styles of pottery and ornaments. Different communities of the Shellmound Period, along with those from other periods, are described in Chapter 10. The archaeological record of the Sakishima Islands is more difficult to interpret since the homeland of the colonizing populations has not been identified. The puzzling gap between the Shimotabaru and Non-Ceramic Periods appears to indicate that the original colonizing group died out and the islands were recolonized. This gap supports Takamiya Hiroto's conclusions (2005) that it is difficult for subtropical hunter-gatherers to survive on small islands. It is possible that small populations were devastated by tsunami and fell below the size required for continuous reproduction.

Chapter 5

Surviving in the Archipelago

Island Hunter-Gatherer Subsistence

In this chapter I examine hunter-gatherer subsistence patterns throughout the Ryukyus, based on brief descriptions of sites from each subperiod and summaries of analyses of faunal and floral remains, site locations, archaeological features, and diet.

As people colonized the Ryukyus in the Middle and Late Holocene, their subsistence patterns adapted to local conditions. These subsistence changes are the subject of research in a variety of fields. How did islanders adapt to the developing coral reefs that grew to surround the islands? Did they hunt wild boar, or transport boar or pigs from the Japanese main islands or the Asian mainland? (In my discussion I use the general term "suid" to refer to both wild boar and domesticated pigs.) Is there evidence of stress on resources? When did the islanders adopt cultivation, and how was it adapted to island subtropical conditions? In addition to these general issues, there are specific questions concerning the Southern Ryukyus. What is the meaning of the gap between the Shimotabaru Period and the Non-Ceramic Period, and the disappearance of pottery? Did small island populations become extinct?

Takamiya Hiroto emphasizes that it is difficult for hunter-gatherers to survive on small islands since they require substantial territories from which to secure enough food in the absence of cultivated plants; otherwise they cannot sustain a viable population (Takamiya 2004). The largest mammals in the Ryukyus at this time were wild boar/feral pigs, as deer became extinct in the Latest Pleistocene (Minagawa et al. 2005, 93). Takamiya (2006b) concluded that it was the combination of reef fishes and shellfish and edible chestnuts that provided protein and carbohydrates for the islanders and that this successful adaptation was actually sustainable. This survival of human communities on islands for relatively long periods of time without cultivation or rich, storable marine resources is unusual and raises questions about how the Ryukyu islanders were able to survive. It also raises questions about whether they had some sort of noncereal crop cultivation or domestication that is difficult to detect archaeologically (Ankei Yūji 2007; Itō Kei 2007a).

Subsistence in the Northern and Central Ryukyus

From roughly 7000 BC to about AD 800, Northern and Central Ryukyu islanders are thought to have lived as hunter-gatherers, despite interaction with farmers from the main islands of Japan and possibly other regions of East Asia. There is some evidence suggesting that, on Okinawa, cultivation may have been adopted substantially earlier than AD 800 to 1000, as discussed below. Subsistence patterns have been relatively well studied, with a substantial number of faunal and floral analyses based on flotation and water screening. An interpretive framework for the Shellmound Period of the Central Ryukyus, identifying some of the main trends in island settlement and community formation was proposed by Shijun Asato in 2002 (Okinawa Kenritsu Maizō 2005a) (see Figure 1.4). He proposed four periods for the Northern and Central Ryukyus—Migration, Adaptation, Diffusion, and Development—to describe how human groups gradually settled in the islands, adapted to local conditions, and established a distinctive culture. In the following section I expand Asato's description and summarize data relevant to the discussion of hunter-gatherer subsistence. His four periods coincide with the four temporal divisions within the Shellmound Period: Initial Shellmound Period (7000 to 2000 BC), Early Shellmound Period (2000 to 1000 BC), Middle Shellmound Period (1000 to 300 BC), and Late Shellmound Period (300 BC to AD 1050) (Okinawa Kenritsu Maizo 2005a, 2005). I have extended the date of the Initial Shellmound Period back to 9000 BP to include the new finds from Ufuniku Cave.

Earliest Subsistence Patterns: Initial Shellmound Period (Asato Chronology)

As described in Chapter 4, from as early as 9,000 years ago small groups reaching the Ryukyus were marked by distinctive pottery types, including Jōmon Plain, Nail-Impressed, and Sobata Types, in addition to others that are less common. None of these groups formed large stable populations producing later descendants (Asato Shijun 2009) showing progressive population growth. Itō Shinji (2011b) described settlement in this period as mobile and seasonal.

A group of sites near freshwater streams flowing from Ryukyu limestone into the East China Sea in Ginowan, Central Okinawa, provide a glimpse into the life of the people of the Initial Shellmound Period. With the exception of the Ufuniku Cave Site, which is inland, sites of this period appear to be restricted to riverine/coastal locations and are rare in the southern Okinawan coral limestone regions.

TOGUCHI AGARIBARU SITE

In the Toguchi Agaribaru Site the geologist Furukawa identified Layer VI as the bottom layer. It was laid down during the Jōmon Transgression (7400 to 5900 uncal BP), when sea level was thought to be 1 to 2 m higher than at present. Nail-Impressed pottery, of two types, I ("fingertip impressed") and II ("fingertip and fingernail impressed"), is found in sand and limestone coral gravel, washed out from a nearby terrace, and broken shells. This is considered to be a secondary deposit with no cultural features. The primary occupation in Layer VI must have occurred before the transgression, judging from this site and Aragusuku Shichabaru II (see below), and then become washed out as the Jōmon Transgression proceeded. Layer III, which contained Sobata Type pottery, is dated to the height of the Jōmon Transgression, based on data from Sobata finds in Kyushu. Stone tools from Toguchi Agaribaru consist of adzes, grindstones, scrapers, and flakes (Yomitan Son 1977).

NOGUNI B SITE

Located on the central-west coast of Okinawa near Kadena and the mouth of the Noguni Stream, Noguni B is important for its very early cultural layers (Okinawa Ken Kyōiku Iinkai 1984). Excavated in 1981, it is one of a cluster of three sites comprising the Noguni Shellmound Group. Locality A, largely destroyed by dredging, dates to the Late Shellmound Period and yielded Kaigen Tsūhō coins, while Locality C has yielded sherds of the Ōyama and Iha Types of the Late Shellmound Period (Takemoto and Asato 1993, 118). Noguni B is situated in a low-lying dune at an elevation above sea level of 0 to 2 m. The excavators did not find features such as houses. The cultural layer is about 2 m thick and was composed of seven layers. Below Layer I was the undisturbed primary cultural deposit. Four periods are represented by different groups of pottery. Layer Ib was a mixed deposit of artifacts from various periods and pottery of the end of the Early Shellmound Period (Group 1). In Layers II and III Incised pottery (*jōkonmon*) and Murokawa Lower Layer Types (Group 2) were chiefly found; these belong to the Early Shellmound Period II (Early Jōmon). The upper part of this layer had been damaged by construction. The layer is relatively thick, but artifacts are few. Some adzes and chert fragments were recovered. Most of the pottery was incised (*jōkonmon*) Murokawa Lower Layer; and even though the site is within a few kilometers of the Toguchi Agaribaru Site, which produced a substantial amount of Sobata Type pottery, this site produced none. Layers IV and V produced about 5,700 sherds of Nail-Impressed Type pottery. The mouth is straight or outward flaring, with a gently pointed bottom and slight waist. Four subvariants were noted. Other tools included edge-polished adzes, and hammerstones and whetstones for sharpening adzes. Many flakes showed the use of hand hammer technique. Some adzes had bilateral polish. Stone tools were generally similar to those from Toguchi Agaribaru. A polished shell arrowhead was also recovered from the Yabuchi Cave Site, and a polished stone arrowhead was recovered from Noguni B. *Kubomi ishi,* stones with circular depressions, appear to have been used for processing nuts.

Hiroto Takamiya stated that in this period shellfish utilization seems to have focused on large shellfish such as *Tectus maximus* and *Lunatica marmorata,* which he considered risky and costly to harvest because they inhabit submerged outcrops and the outer sea slope of the coral reef (2006b, 60–61). However, at this time reef formation was incomplete so that the shellfish of the lagoon would not have been abundant, and shellfish from rocky outcrops may have been the most available. The absence of reef species in Initial Shell-mound Period sites is probably related to the undeveloped nature of the coral reefs at this time. However Kurozumi (2008) noted that *magakigai* (*Conomurex liukiuanus*), a small gastropod that lives in lagoons, predominated in Noguni B. He believes that, although the areas were small, lagoons had formed by this period. The most common shellfish species found in Ryukyu sites are shown in Figure 5.1.

A very large quantity of wild boar bones (some 611 individuals, 19 percent of which were juveniles) were found (Kawashima and Muraoka 1984, 181–188). One would expect a high reliance on wild boar if humans arrived after a hiatus of thousands of years and found wild boar populations that had not been subject to predators. As indicated in Chapter 4 and discussed later in this chapter, there is a possibility that some of these suids were introduced into the Ryukyus and were not local wild boar.

IREIBARU SITE

The Ireibaru Site is located on the eastern (inland) edge of the coastal alluvial flat at Chatan, on the west coast of Okinawa, immediately adjacent to an extensive ridge of limestone coral. A stream flowing from the limestone has created a

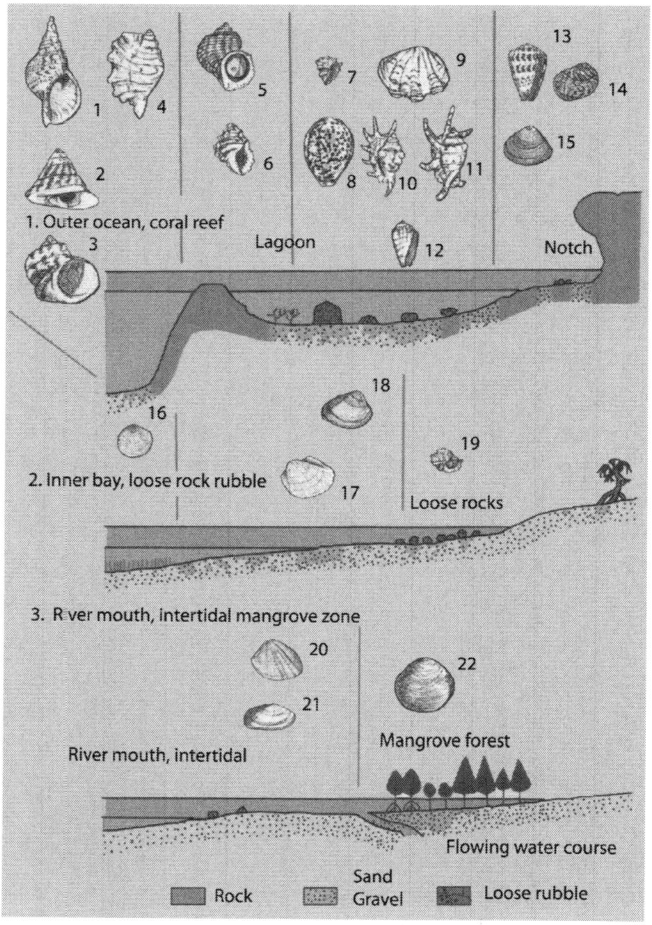

Figure 5.1. Major marine shells found in archaeological sites and their environments. Adapted from Ishigaki Shi Sōmubu 2009b, 10. Original prepared by Ayano Shimabukuro and Kurozumi Taiji. Courtesy of Ayano Shimabukuro, Kurozumi Taiji, and Miyara Yoshikazu of Ishigaki Shi Sōmubu Shishi Henshūka.

Key to Names

No.	Name (scientific, Japanese)	No.	Name (scientific, Japanese)
1	*Charonia tritonis* (*horagai*)	12	*Strombus luhuanus* (*magakigai*)
2	*Trochus niloticus* (*sarasabatei*)	13	*Conus ebreaus* (*madara imogai*)
3	*Turbo marmoratus* (*yakōgai*)	14	*Ritena striata* (*koshitaka amagai*)
4	*Lambis truncata* (*rakudagai*)	15	*Atactodea striata* (*iso hamaguri*)
5	*Turbo argyrostomus* (*chōsen sazae*)	16	*Codakia paytenorum* (*ura kishigai*)
6	*Bursa bufonis* (*okinishi*)	17	*Anadara antiquata* (*Ryūkyū sarabōgai*)
7	*Vasum turbinellum* (*konikobushigai*)	18	*Katelysia japonica* (*sudare hamaguri*)
8	*Cypraea tigris* (*oshidakaragai*)	19	*Lunella moniliformis* (*kangiku*)
9	*Hippopus hippopus* (*shakōgai*)	20	*Gafrarium tumidum* (*arasuji kemangai*)
10	*Lambis lambis* (*kumogai*)	21	*Psammotaea elongata* (*masuogai*)
11	*Harpago chiragra* (*suijigai*)	22	*Geloina erosa* (*shirenami shijimi*)

wet area originally termed Ireibaru C, next to which there is an old coastal dune, originally termed Ireibaru A. Since 2006 both localities have been combined as the Ireibaru Site. Excavation took place from 2004 to 2006 (Chatan Chō 2004; 2007; Tōma Kenji 2009).

Layers 14 and 15, about 4 m below the present surface, contain waterlogged deposits from 5000 to 6000 cal BP. The site contains occupation layers from later periods up to the Gusuku Period.

Layer 15 is an olive gray color sandy layer 22 to 28 cm thick. On the surface of this layer, small sherds of Nail-Impressed Type pottery were found in an area 2 m square, in the center of which were remains of a fire. In the lower part of this layer, there was a thick layer of pumice, at the edge of which, where it thinned out, there was a line of Nail-Impressed Type sherds of the type found in the Toguchi Agaribaru Site, which showed signs of rolling, as if they had been washed by water. It is thought that they were deposited before a rise in sea level (Chatan Chō 2007, 567). Was the pumice layer deposited at the time of the Kikai eruption?

In Layer 14, three sublayers were identified, each containing water-worn rocks of limestone coral of human head size. In the uppermost layer there were sherds of the Middle Jōmon Omonawa Zentei Type and some sherds of Latest Jōmon pottery. The middle sublayer yielded substantial amounts of Sobata Type pottery with steatite tempering, indicating its origin in Kyushu, and a woven bamboo basket pegged at the corners, filled with edible acorns. Several species were present, but the most common were *Castanopsis* sp. (Japanese *shii*) and *Quercus miyagii* (Okinawan *jirogashi*). The nuts must be leached before they can be processed into edible flour. The specimens of *Castanopsis* tended to be fragmentary, as if they had been partially processed while those of *Quercus* were intact. The latter contain more tannin and require a longer period of leaching (Chatan Chō 2007, 563); they appear to have been left for leaching prior to crushing. This layer also yielded querns, adzes, and bones of fish and wild boar. Part of this sublayer appears to have been a living area at the time of Sobata Type pottery. In the adjacent sand dune area were layers containing the Middle Jōmon Omonawa East Cave, Omonawa Zentei, and Katoku Types as well as pit house remains. Carbon dates for the Sobata occupation ranged from 5000 to 5400 BP, while those for the Omonawa Zentei Type pottery were about 4400 BP.

ARAGUSUKU SHICHABARU NO. 2 SITE

The recently excavated Aragusuku Shichabaru No. 2 Site on the Ginowan alluvial plain in the Zukeran Military Base also yielded some of the earliest Jōmon finds from Okinawa (Okinawa Kenritsu Maizō 2006). Below three thick layers

(Layers VI, VII, and VIII) of almost 2 m of marine sand, deposited during the Jōmon Transgression, Layer IX, located right at sea level, yielded 125 sherds of Nail-Impressed Type pottery along with 43 sherds of Plain Type pottery, stone tools, shell artifacts, suid bones, and animal and plant remains. Pending further discoveries of early plain pottery predating the Jōmon Transgression, the significance of this distinctive pottery type is not clear, but, as mentioned in Chapter 4, it represents another small population who reached the Ryukyus. It was dated at 6077± 52 BP or 6997–6861 to 6821–6806 cal BP. The pottery was not abraded, but there were no features, indicating to the excavators that this is a secondary deposit (Okinawa Kenritsu Maizō 2006, 331–332). Artifacts included a stemmed shell arrowhead with curving sides and a shell knife. Both are unique finds in Okinawa. Bone tools include a spear point and bone needle. Stone tools consist of edge-ground adzes, hand-held abraders, large abraders, and hammerstones. Food remains include wild boar bones, burned shells of two large gastropods, *Turbo marmoratus* (turban shell) and *Batillus cornutus* (horned turban), and bird bones, but fish bones were very rare, despite the analysis of 250 liters of midden sample. Layer XII, separated from Layer IX by two sterile layers, Layers X and XI, yielded one sherd of plain pottery and suid bones. From Layer XIIIa, suid bones and one fragment of deer antler were found. Layer XIV yielded a 14C date of 6020±50 BP and Layer XIIIc, a date of 6410±50 BP. This reversal of dates may have been caused by contamination from Layer XIV.

The new information from this site clarifies the nature of deposits of Plain Type and Nail-Impressed Type pottery and the temporal relationship with Sobata Type pottery as well as giving information on geomorphology and context. The pattern of early sites established with the excavation of Noguni and Toguchi Agaribaru has been confirmed.

The stone tool assemblage from Noguni B Layer VII (the Plain Type pottery layer) includes one large, flat chipped adze, and two grinding stones. The latter suggest that the earliest inhabitants were already processing plant foods. Layers IV and V, which yielded Nail-Impressed Type sherds, also produced flat, thin chipped adzes with polished bits as well as small, flat edge-ground adzes around 12 cm in length, used for cutting, grindstones, and hammerstones. While grindstones are abundant, there are no chert flaked artifacts. However, in Toguchi Agaribaru chert scrapers, drills, flakes, and a spear point were found, but hammerstones were absent. This pattern might indicate special-purpose sites, similar to some Jōmon patterns in the Japanese main islands. In the Bugeidō Site unusual shell artifacts and cutting tools were discovered, as well as completely polished stone adzes, in association with Nail-Impressed and Sobata Types (Okinawa Kenritsu Hakubutsukan 2010). Thus, in the Early Shellmound Period there was a broad assemblage of stone tools derived from Jōmon types.

Early Shellmound Period (Asato Chronology)

As mentioned in the previous chapter, the Early Shellmound Period, which is parallel to the Late Jōmon, is poorly known. While the pottery chronology has been filled in by types from the Murokawa Site of Okinawa, the Kamino Site of Okinoerabujima, and the Omonawa No. 4 Site from southern Tokunoshima, these excavations were all relatively small research excavations that have not yielded a detailed picture of living patterns at this time. The excavation of the Sumiyoshi Shellmound, on the west coast of Okinoerabujima, from 2001 to 2004 provides some details on subsistence (Morita 2009). Fish bones included species from the reef but also from the deep sea, such as tuna and flying fish; whale and dugong bones were also recovered. Sites from this period are thought to have been small with low numbers of houses (Asato Shijun 2009). The Omonawa No. 4 Site yielded a small sample of polished adzes, one large chipped adze, four hammerstones, and a stone sickle. The polished adze is triangular in section, a form found in the Middle Jōmon and later periods (Zaidan 2003, 174).

KOGACHIBARU SITE

The Kogachibaru Site was excavated in 1983–1984 (Okinawa Ken 1987). It lay in the path of the construction of the Okinawa Expressway and was destroyed after salvage excavation. It is located on a high limestone terrace, some 1.5 km from Kin Bay, overlooking the islands of Henzajima, Hamahigajima, and Ikeijima. An area of 35 × 40 m plus numerous test pits were excavated. Two distinct areas of occupation, about 50 m apart, were found. The first was higher and relatively flat. It contained house pits and stone-lined fire pits. The second is a group of features lying to the south. In a bowl-shaped depression about 14 m × 16 m, there is a layer of burned earth, plus house pits and other pits, indicating a large hearth and surrounding structures. Some 23,400 pottery sherds were recovered. Most of the pottery is of the so-called Amami types, consisting of deep jars with pointed bottoms and flat bottom vessels. They include the Omonawa, Katoku, Kamino, Iha, and Ogidō Types and can generally be placed in the Early Shellmound Period IV, first half of Late Jōmon in the Takamiya chronology or in the Early Shellmound Period in the Asato chronology. Two groups of types were recovered: one of deep jar form with slightly everted neck, and one with flat bottom and flaring sides. They belong to the Early Shellmound Period IV (first half of Late Jōmon Period). Stone tools consisted of adzes (40 out of a total of 173 stone tools), chisels, hammerstones/pounders (105 out of a total of 173 stone tools), whetstones, and querns. There are also stone arrow points. The adzes are thought to have been used for woodworking. Many tools were used for crushing and grinding, presumably of plant materials. Bone tools were fashioned from the bones of birds, suids, whale, dugong, and porpoise. Four fragments of worked deer long bone were recovered. Since deer were extinct by the Holocene, bone material for artifacts must have been traded from Kyushu. Worked fragments of deer bone also have been recovered from the Ōyama and Akajangā Sites, Okinawajima (Okinawa Ken 1987, 318). A surprisingly large number of dogs (a minimum of twenty-seven), the bones of which were highly fragmented, were recovered from Kogachibaru, their fragmented state suggesting that they may have been used for food (Zaidan 2003, 177). The shellfish remains indicated the use of a number of aquatic zones, including riverine, tidal, and mangrove environments. The majority were *Terebralia palustris* and *Telescopium telescopium,* mangrove species that are not found or are extremely rare in the Ryukyus at present. The Ryukyus are the northernmost habitat for these species. Their disappearance may reflect cooling ocean temperatures after the Holocene Optimum, but this has not been determined for certain (Ohgaki and Kurozumi 2000). Another possible cause for their disappearance could be the alteration of their mangrove habitats. Small terrestrial gastropods indicated a forest rather than a cleared environment around the site.

MĒBARU SITE

The Mēbaru Site is located on the east coast of Okinawajima, near the mouth of the Fukuchi River. A wet area created by freshwater springs flowing through limestone has yielded a waterlogged deposit preserved by alkaline conditions. The adjacent ocean shallows is a traditional location for gathering seaweed, which flourishes in the brackish water. Layers IX to XI of this stratified site have yielded remains of a *mizuba* (waterside processing area), dated to roughly 4000 to 3,000 BP. Ogidō and Iha pottery types are present. In Okinawa today, traditional sites termed *kagua,* a paved area in shallow fresh water, for washing, are well known (Ginoza Son Kyōiku Iinkai 1999, 282–283); Mēbaru has provided a prehistoric example. Two adjacent paved areas at Mēbaru were roughly 5 m × 8 m, and some stones showed grooving from sharpening stone tools (China Teijun 2000). Storage pits filled with the nuts of Okinawa edible oak, primarily *Quercus miyagii,* were found as well as twined bamboo basket remains. These nuts must have been leached in the alkaline wet mud deposit. The excavators were not sure if the storage pits belonged to individual families or a larger social collective. Bones of suids and domesticated dog were recovered. The finding of a waterlogged waterside site, for washing, processing, and storage of edible nuts, is important for understanding the range of prehistoric subsistence activities. These finds along with the waterlogged site of Ireibaru demonstrate that nut processing and storage were important activities, and such sites were probably relatively common in suitable locations (Zaidan 2003, 120). The nuts found in the Mēbaru site require crushing and washing to leach away their tannin and render them edible. It is likely that the seeds of *Machilus (Persea) thunbergii* were also eaten (Zaidan 2003, 181).

Middle Shellmound Period (Asato Chronology)

A distinctive living pattern has been found in the Middle Shellmound Period. Sites are located inland, at relatively high elevations, even on small offshore islands (Okinawa Kenritsu Maizō 2005a). They are often on limestone hills and terraces open to the elements. Many are located at around 100 m elevation, while one site, the Kinen Uehara Site of Tokunoshima, is located at 235 m elevation. Interestingly enough, the earlier Omonawa Site Group lies below it, slightly above sea level. At least ten of these upland sites occur on the western coastal terraces of Tokunoshima, the most prominent being the Tōbaru (Amagi Chō 1988; Kagoshima Ken Amagi Chō 1999) and Shitabaru Sites (Kagoshima Ken Amagi Chō 2004). Located several hundred meters inland from the shoreline, these sites would presumably have been surrounded by dense broadleaf evergreen forests including *Castanopsis,* which would have flourished in the northern part of Tokunoshima, where the substrate is granite while the substrate of the southern portion is coral limestone. Since they contain rather substantial house pits, they seem to be base villages from which people may have moved to seasonal shoreline fishing camps. Itō Shinji (2011b) groups these sites and Shinugudō into what he calls the Sedentary Period from 4500 to 2500 BP.

SHINUGUDŌ SITE

Shinugudō serves as an illustration of sites of the Middle Shellmound Period. The site, larger and more complex than earlier trench excavations of Middle Shellmound Period sites indicated, is located on the raised limestone central plateau of Miyagi Island, at an elevation of 97 to 112 m (Okinawa Ken Kyōiku Iinkai 1985b). The central plateau of Miyagi Island, which has an area of about 130 ha and has been developed for modern dryland agriculture, consists of a series of five terraces that vary in elevation by about one meter. Shinugudō commands an imposing location, with strategic views along the east coast of Okinawa.

Shinugudō is roughly contemporary with the Late Jōmon of the Japanese main islands, dating to around 1000 BC. Four radiocarbon charcoal dates, run by Nihon Isotope, give calibrated dates of 2960±65 BP, 2770±90 BP, 2970±65 BP, and 3030±70 BP. They were taken from floor surfaces and fill of pit houses. No lab numbers or other data are provided in the report (Okinawa Ken Kyōiku Iinkai 1985b, 195). In addition to the pit houses, eighteen houses were built on the ground surface.

The site covers an estimated 14,000 sq m of which 1200 sq m was excavated. In addition to the Shinugudō Site, an associated shellmound has been found immediately to the east, below the limestone cliff. The Shinugudō Shellmound is 12,000 sq m in area, making a total of 26,000 sq m for both sites. The lower layer of the shellmound is said by the authors of the report to be "one period earlier" than the Shinugudō Site (Okinawa Ken Kyōiku Iinkai 1985b, 2). Nearby, flowing from the base of the cliff, is a substantial spring.

Forty-two house sites have been recovered. They are rectangular, with dimensions of 2 m to 5 m × 6 m and an average depth of 30 cm. Some of them are simply earth pits, while others have pits with stones lining some or all of the walls. Post molds 7 to 10 cm in diameter and 8 to 25 cm in depth are usually in rows of three along each side (making a total of eight posts). Some houses have coral gravel for paved floors. A hearth occurred at one end of the house. In addition to the semisubterranean pit houses, twelve houses were erected over stone pavements (Yonagusuku Son 1988, 17). They are rectangular, with dimensions of 2 to 3 m and 4 to 5 m. Cooking appears to have been conducted outside these houses.

Shinugudō is a major site of the entire Okinawan Shellmound Period, comparable to large Jōmon sites in other parts of Japan. Based on the fact that certain houses had postholes of similar depth, the excavators distinguished three separate, possibly internally contemporaneous, groupings of house remains of 15, 13, and 11 dwellings respectively. The total population living at the site is not clear. Abundant pottery recovered from the site was primarily of the Nakahara Type, which is undecorated, with an everted mouth, slightly constricted neck, long body, and pointed bottom. Shallow jars and vessels with tightly constricted necks were also recovered in small quantities. The pottery is thin and well fired, and the exterior has been scraped with a spatula. It shows a general resemblance to Late Jōmon pottery of Kyushu. The pointed-bottom vessels appear to have been used for boiling. Some incised pottery of earlier types was recovered from the house pit fill. Stone axes with bifacially polished bits as well as some assymetrical adzes were also recovered. They are made of basalt, which can be found in northern Okinawajima and the Kerama Islands. Grinding stones (complete and fragmentary) were recovered from many house floors. Two chert arrowheads were also recovered. Artifacts of wild boar and dugong bone included needles, spatulas, and awls. Ornaments were fashioned from dog and pig canine teeth as well as shark teeth. Shell artifacts included adzes, adzelike tools made of the disklike opercula of *Turbo,* and sharpened protrusions of the *Harpago* shell. Other containers and ornaments were fashioned from large gastropods. Terrestrial snails appeared to be more abundant that marine shellfish as food remains. Other food remains included marine fish, sea turtles, dugong, wild boar, shark, land tortoise, snake, shore bird, mouse, and dog.

Two Middle Shellmound Period sites on Ikeishima, the Nakahara and Takamine Sites, also yielded extensive dwelling remains. The Nakahara Site yielded five human skeletons, buried within houses (Yonagusuku Son 1988, 16). Burial in abandoned houses, while common in the Japanese main islands, is only known in Okinawa from this site. Thus, there are three imposing Middle Shellmound Period sites on two small offlying islands. The interrelationships of these three sites require further study.

Analyses of fish bones show that by this period exploitation of marine resources extended beyond the reef to the deep sea. Detailed comparison of pick-up samples and bagged midden samples that were water screened from the Middle Shellmound Period sites of Sumiyoshi on Okinoerabujima and Nishi Nagahama on the north shore of the Motobu Peninsula, Okinawa, revealed the presence of a number of species from the sea beyond the reef, including schooling fish such as flying fish (Tōizumi 2007c).

KIYŪNA TŌBARU NUBATAKE SITE

The remains of sixteen houses were excavated at the Kiyūna Tōbaru Nubatake Site. The houses are oval, about 2 to 3.5 m on a side. Three houses were particularly large. No. 101 was 8.9 m × 6.3 m, oval, with a central hearth. Buried in the floor of the house, on the north side near the wall, was a "stone rod" (*sekibō*), which had been burned (Zaidan 2003, 166–188). Such stone phalli are found in the Jōmon of the Japanese main islands but generally at much earlier dates. They are extremely rare in the Ryukyus. Convergences in burial patterns and ritual objects indicate continuing contacts between Okinawa and the Japanese main islands.

Late Shellmound Period (Asato Chronology)

The Late Shellmound Period extended from 2,500 years ago to about 1,000 years ago. Although fundamental social and cultural changes occurred in the Japanese main islands with the advent of wet rice cultivation, metallurgy, and state formation, Takamiya Hiroto concludes that in the Ryukyu Islands basic subsistence patterns of hunter-gatherers persisted until the end of the first millennium (Takamiya 2007).

AZAMABARU SITE GROUP

The Azamabaru No. 1 and No. 2 sites are extremely important in understanding the living patterns of the prehistoric peoples in Okinawa in the first half of the first millennium AD. Wide area excavations in the 1980s yielded extensive dwelling and burial remains (Ginowan Shi 1989, 64–79; Ikeda and Goya 1994, 99–104).

These two sites are situated on a strip of deep coastal alluvium on the west coast of Okinawa Island, near a series of springs flowing from the base of a central low ridge of coral limestone, to the south of early sites such as Aragusuku Shichabaru and Ireibaru. The sites are within 200 m of the present shoreline, which faces a wide sheltered reef that must have been very rich in marine resources. The surrounding area is now a heavily developed urban strip adjacent to large military bases.

The total area of the two sites is estimated to be about 10,000 sq m. In the 1980s 3,200 sq m were excavated. The village site dates roughly to 100 BC to AD 500. Yayoi sherds from Kyushu have been found in this deposit (see below), and 14C dates of 1700±75 and 1620±75 for the north side and 1550±75 for the south side have been received. No lab numbers or further details are provided (Ginowan Shi 1989, 100). Pit houses, stone cairns, a dog burial, and shell concentrations were recovered. The pit houses were rebuilt many times and varied in length from 2 to 4 m. The shell concentrations appear to be the remains of activities involving shellfish meat extraction and shell working, evidence of which included caches of unworked shells, shell debitage, and partially worked shell bracelets. Many pit features were found as well as some hearths that were outside the houses. The site also contained burials in two layers that are earlier than the period under discussion and a dwelling area with a group of features. The upper-layer burials, of which there are thirty-seven, can be dated by ceramic styles to roughly 1500 BC to 500 BC. The pottery from the lower-layer burials (of which there are ten), dates roughly to the first half of the Early Shellmound Period, around 3500 to 2500 BC. Most of the burials are extended and primary; some are in shallow pits in the sandy substratum, while others are in pits outlined or covered with chunks of coral. Secondary burials also occur.

Azamabaru Site No. 2 is about 180 m directly inland from the seashore and 50 m from Azamabaru Site No. 1. The date of this site falls within the time span of the Ufutōbaru Type of pottery (Takamiya Hiroe et al. 1993, 25), which is roughly AD 1 to 500. The excavated area is 1,410 sq m. Some 45 pit houses were discovered. Of these, 24 were square, 10 were square-oval, 1 was round, and the remainder are unclear. Two carbon dates from an unspecified pit house (no further details provided) are 1,430±75 and 1,280±75 years ago (Ginowan Shi 1989, 103).

Two burials of the same general date as the pit houses were found in a separate area from the pit houses. In one burial of a mature individual of undetermined sex, which was oriented to the south, the head and cervical vertebrae were missing. Outside the grave, opposite the place where the head should be, a perforated *Triton* shell was recovered. The burial was covered by pieces of coral and limestone. Only the backbone, right humerus, and left fibula were present in the second burial. Are these burials the remains of individuals who died away from the site? Were they shell traders? Does the preparation of their specific burial facilities indicate higher social status? This topic is discussed in Chapter 6.

The Azamabaru sites show that thriving, relatively large villages existed in favored locations in Okinawa in the first half of the first millennium AD and that some individuals were receiving distinctive burial treatment.

A preliminary analysis of carbon and nitrogen isotope rations (13C/15N) from the bones of eleven individuals from the upper-layer burials of Azamabaru No. 1 indicated that terrestrial resources were slightly more important than marine resources as sources of protein (Takamiya Hiroto 1997, 223).

YŌMISAKI SITE, AMAMI ŌSHIMA

The major cultural layers of the Yōmisaki Site are XVI and XIII, which are parallel to the Yayoi Period, and Layer VI, which has yielded Kaneku Type pottery. Tōizumi (2002) assigns it to the seventh century AD. Bones recovered were mainly fish, but there were also suids, sea turtle, frog, and snake. The latter two are not considered to have been collected for food, occurring naturally in the area. Suids were found in considerable numbers. The main feature of the fish assemblage is the diversity of species found in the reefs in front of the site and the open sea (Tōizumi 2002, 48). The most common were *Pronurus and Scarus* species, followed by Labridae (all bony reef fish). *Scarus* (parrot fish) is less frequent than from Okinawan sites, perhaps reflecting differences between Amami and Okinawan reefs or cultural preference (ibid., 51). Most of the fish, with the exception of those of Layer VIIIc, were small, in the range of 10 to 20 cm with a wide diversity of species. Layer VIIIc had relatively little associated shells or pottery, and seems to have been a fishing camp occupation. In Layer VIIIc the fish were predominantly large individuals. Because there are different size groups, Tōizumi infers that different fishing methods may have been used. Possible factors creating this size difference suggested by Tōizumi include the use of different fishing techniques, decline of fish size within the reef, or a rise in the numbers of people catching fish. Tōizumi (2002, 50) states that there was an adequate supply of fish for daily consumption and makes no allusion to food stress.

Tōizumi notes that there is greater diversity in the fish bone assemblages from the Amami sites of Kasari Chō, compared to sites from Okinawa, which may reflect special conditions in the Kasari region, where the reef is discontinuous. The Yōmisaki Site has a diversity of small fish, which were probably caught in nets since shell fishing weights have been recovered.

Analysis of shellfish remains from Yōmisaki and Nagarabaru Higashi showed the collection of small bivalves for soup as well as very large *Turbo* shellfish that are thought to have been consumed in feasting (Kurozumi 2006). *Turbo* prefer a substrate that is not coral limestone on the windward sides of islands. Kurozumi suggests that people of the Kasari Peninsula traveled to the volcanic Tokara Islands, which have limited reefs, to harvest *Turbo* shells. In both the Matsunoto and Nagarabaru Higashi Sites there were shells collected from mangrove environments that are located some distance from the sites; however, Tōizumi (2002, 59–62) found that fish from the deep ocean and mangrove were not of major importance.

KITAHARA SHELLMOUND, KUMEJIMA

Kitahara Shellmound is located on the extreme western tip of Kumejima, an island about 90 km to the west of Okinawa, in close proximity to a shallow lagoon formed by coral reefs (Pearson et al. 1980; Ryūkyū Archaeological Research Team 1981; Pearson et al. 1990). Subsequent excavations in 1973 and 1992 located a layer below Layer III, Layer IV (Okinawa Ken 1995a). However, this discussion deals only with the analysis of material from Layer III. The analysis of faunal remains, which can be dated from the second to eighth centuries AD (see Chapter 4), provides some insight into subsistence patterns.

While the bones of *Bos, Felis,* and *Canis* were found in the very top of Layer III, because of the disturbed nature of the surface of the layer, we concluded that these were intrusive. The bones of wild boar, now extinct on Kumejima, were found in Layer III, along with those of unidentified sea mammals. In the discussion of prehistoric subsistence later in this chapter, the possibility that the "wild boar" are domesticated pig will be reviewed. The surviving fish bones were mostly the mouth parts of coral-eating reef fish such as parrot fish. These are very thick and durable, and preserve well in sites. There does not seem to be any evidence of deep-sea fishing from the fish remains recovered.

Large numbers of terrestrial gastropods occurred in the cultural layer, being more abundant in the lowest levels within the layer. When we wrote the report, we postulated that there was a pronounced shift from the exploitation of terrestrial snails at the time of deposition of the lower portion of the cultural layer to marine molluscs from the intertidal and littoral zones at the time of deposition of the upper part of the layer. In hindsight I am not sure whether the high frequency of terrestrial snails indicates that they were a source of food brought to the site or whether they occurred naturally in the vegetation growing on the site when the site was not inhabited and were not eaten. We noted an overall decrease in the maximum diameters of all intact shells from the bottom levels to the top levels in Layer III. This may be the result of high rates of collecting, in which shellfish were collected before they could attain their maximum size, and could indicate some other environmental pressure on shellfish resources. The largest excavated portion of the site was a cluster of 1 m × 1 m excavation units termed Cluster 3. The cultural layer was excavated in eight 10 cm thick spits or arbitrary horizontal levels to detect changes in the percentages of different shellfish in different parts of the layer. All soil from the layers, with a small number of uncertain exceptions where data are missing, was screened through a screen of about 5 mm mesh. Twenty-eight identified mollusc types, plus a category of unidentified shells, were tabulated by percentage based on the number of identified individuals. Within this site a trend toward the collection of a wider variety of shellfish species from the lower layers to the upper layers was noted. The use of an index of diversity to display this pattern is described later in this chapter.

Suid bones were found to be less abundant in Layer V than in Layer III (Okinawa Ken 1995a). This trend may confirm Takamiya's hypothesis of food stress in the Late Shellmound Period, which led to more hunting of wild boar and collecting of large, heavy shellfish, both of which require comparatively greater effort to harvest. It could also be a trend limited to Kumejima. Further comparative research is required.

Subsistence in the Sakishima Islands

As discussed in Chapter 4, the colonizing populations of Sakishima were not derived from Kyushu. Also, pottery of the Shimotabaru Period and shell adzes in the Non-Ceramic Period are very different from artifacts found in the Northern and Central Ryukyus. However, the basic subsistence patterns throughout the Ryukyus and the functional stone and shell tool assemblages are actually quite similar, as noted by Shinzato Takayuki (2008b) (with the exception of the *Tridacna* shell adzes, which are found only in Sakishima).

Shimotabaru Period

At the beginning of the Shimotabaru Period, around 4850 BP, sea level was about 1.4 m above the present level, with variation created by local techtonics. About 3700 BP sea level was about the same as present, but reef formation was not yet complete, and shorelines were subject to strong wave action. The windward fringing reef was largely formed by about 4750 cal BP and the leeward reef by about 1870 cal BP (Hongo and Kayanne 2009; 2010). However, reef resources were already available, especially to the main cluster of Shimotabaru Period sites in the Nagura Bay area, since the adjoining Sekisei Reef had already begun to form. This reef, some 30 km in length, joins the large islands of Iriomote and Ishigaki, and encloses several offliers. On this large reef, by 6500 BP lagoonal reef patches reached the sea surface. In a manner typical of high latitude coral reefs, the barrier formed after the interior patches (Kan and Kawana 2006). The leeward Pyutta Site, Ishigakijima, is 5 m above sea level and 200 m from the present shoreline. It and the Soedō Site, Taramajima, are situated on old sand dunes; however, all of the remaining thirteen sites of the Shimotabaru Period are on the red clay found immediately inland from the shoreline, and their elevation ranges from 3 to 13 m above sea level (Ishigaki Shi Sōmubu 2008a, 39–41). Dating of Layer 7 of the Nagabaka Site, Miyakojima, to 4000 to 4200 cal BP indicates that Miyakojima was also inhabited in the Shimotabaru Period (Mark Hudson, personal communication). The most common marine shells found in these sites are mainly large gastropods from shallow water. However, mangrove species were also utilized, and bones of sea turtles and dugong are present. Suid bones are found in sites on Haterumajima, Yonagunijima, and Taramajima, where they were not native, as well as in sites on large high islands. The distances from these offlying islands to the nearest high islands is 25 km, 75 km, and 37 km respectively. It should be noted that the Tōgurubama Site of Yonagunijima and the Shimotabaru Site of Haterumajima are both on islands that lack substantial reefs, and Kobayashi Ryūta et al. (2010) have noted that Shimotabaru Period sites are generally clustered in the leeward areas of Ishigakijima, away from the most extensive windward reefs. There is no evidence of cultivation at this time period. Ethnographic research on Iriomotejima indicates that two species of yams (*Dioscorea*) are cultivated at present, and three more wild species are collected (Ishigaki Shi Sōmubu 2008a, 11). It seems quite possible that yams were cultivated in prehistory, but as yet there is no direct evidence. Many stone adzes were recovered from the type site, Shimotabaru, suggesting that digging tools were used extensively. Wild yams must have been an important part of the diet. The presence of querns and grinding stones indicates that nuts, probably edible acorns, and wild seeds were processed.

In general, sites show impermanent dwellings and cooking areas, with no recognizable storage or specialized production features. Houses were either built over shallow depressions or were post-supported houses built on the flat ground surface. The type site of Shimotabaru yielded part of a house, with post molds 15 to 50 cm in diameter and a depth of 10 to 30 cm. Six hearths were found, containing wood charcoal. Five of them were very small, about 50 cm in diameter, while the sixth was 1.7 m × 0.9 m. A shallow trench about 80 cm wide, 5 to 15 cm deep, and at least 36 m long was thought to provide drainage for the site. The Pyutta Site yielded a dark soil area, 1 m in diameter, containing chunks of coral limestone and cobbles of metamorphic rock from Iriomotejima, showing signs of strong heating. The cultural layer of the Soedō Site on Tarama Island, which is a coral island, also contained burned limestone chunks.

In a review of the presence and absence of major faunal species from 266 sites from Kagoshima to Sakishima from the Jōmon to Mediaeval Periods, Ishimaru and Arata (2011) noted that there were no dog remains from the Shimotabaru Period and only one occurrence from the Non-Ceramic Period. Dog remains have recently been found in the Nagabaka Site, Miyakojima (Mark Hudson, personal communication) and were reported from the Funaura Site, Iriomotejima (Pearson et al. 1980, 23).

Non-Ceramic Period

There is a gap of 1,100 years between the Shimotabaru Period and the Non-Ceramic Period discussed in Chapter 4. Although this may in part be an artifact of the destruction of coastal sites by fluctuating sea levels, typhoons, and tsunami, it seems unlikely that the entire temporal gap was caused by such forces. This suggests that the Shimotabaru people died out, perhaps being unable to sustain themselves as hunter-gatherers on small islands. However, recent dates from the Nagabaka Site, Miyakojima, hint that the gap between the Shimotabaru Period and the Non-Ceramic Period may have been shorter than anticipated. Analysis of faunal remains from the site indicate a constant predominance of parrot fish (*Calotomus* sp.), probabably taken in nets, whereas the Amitori Site, Iriomotejima, shows a broader range of fish (Mark Hudson, personal communication). Data that are independent of excavations, such as a pollen or geomorphological sequence, might provide a record of vegetation and sedimentation that would confirm the presence or absence of human populations during this apparent hiatus.

Scant evidence from sites of this period makes it difficult to reconstruct subsistence practices. Some forty-eight Non-Ceramic Period sites have been recorded in Sakishima. Sites in general show a higher proportion of shellfish species from lagoon environments than those of the Shimotabaru Period (Ishigaki Shi Sōmubu 2009b, 52). Perforated stone weights may be related to reef fishing. Scattered finds of shell adzes in the estuary of the Nagura River, Ishigakijima, indicate that the brackish waterways and sandbars must have been an important locale for hunting birds and fishing as well as making canoes. Although much of the Nagura environment has been irreparably damaged by land development for sugarcane cultivation, coring may yield geomorphological information regarding human activities.

The Ōdomaribama Site on Haterumajima provides an example of a site of the Non-Ceramic Period. The cultural deposit is 3.4 m thick, which is unusual for this period. It is located some 50 m to the east of the Shimotabaru Site. The top cultural layer dates to the twelfth century, at the very end of the Non-Ceramic Period, when trade goods such as steatite cauldrons and *kamuiyaki* were beginning to appear (Okinawa Ken 1986; Asato Susumu and Harunari 2001). Remains of rectangular dwellings, about 2.5. m × 2.0 m, were found. The floor was covered with coral rubble, and there were generally six posts to support the roof. The houses each had an internal central hearth. Non-Ceramic Period sites have concentrations of burned stone that appear to be cooking areas for food wrapped in leaves (in the absence of pottery). In the Ōdomaribama Site, the rock material used for large cooking stones was not local but came from Iriomotejima.

Uzawa et al. (2001) found that the faunal remains from the Ōdomaribama Site showed a strong dependency on wild boar and a relatively minor role for fishing. Could site formation processes account for this predominance of suid remains? Could fish bones be absent because of poor preservation or discarded in a separate location? From age determination of suid remains by tooth eruption, most individuals were slaughtered at an estimated age of 1.5 to 2 years. A similar trend was noted for the Shimotabaru Site. The authors propose that Haterumajima is too small to maintain a population of wild boar and that either domesticated pigs were tended on the island or wild boar/pigs were brought to the island from Iriomotejima.

Shinzatomura Period

Sites from the Shinzatomura Period yield charred grains and phytoliths of rice and millet, as well as cow and pig bones, from the Shinzatomura East Site (Ishigaki Shi Sōmubu 2009a, 14). Agriculture and stock breeding were introduced from the Central Ryukyus some time around AD 1100.

Discussion of Prehistoric Subsistence

The study of prehistoric subsistence patterns in the Ryukyus is of specific interest in understanding different patterns of livelihood within Japan and of general interest in island archaeology. One of the key questions in this field is how people managed to survive on small isolated islands with limited resources. Takamiya Hiroto (2007) contended that these islands were not a tropical paradise where living was easy. Although debates about earlier kinds of agriculture (described below) need to be considered carefully, the earliest evidence of cultivation to be accepted by many archaeologists is the occurrence of carbonized seeds in several sites in the Okinawa and Amami Islands. The seeds belong to rice (Japanese *ine*, *Oryza sativa*), wheat (*komugi*, *Triticum aestivum*), barley (*omugi*, *Hordeum vulgare*), millet (*awa*, *Setaria italica*), and broomcorn millet (*kibi*, *Panicum miliaceum*). Takamiya recovered seeds of these grains from the Nazakibaru Site, Okinawajima, along with evidence of forest clearing plus remains of ditches and hoe marks (2006b, 56) dated to AD 700 to 900. He stated that the quantities were small, which might be expected shortly after the introduction of cultivation. New finds of broomcorn millet seed impressions in pottery of Late Shellmound Period type, with constricted foot and flat bottom, and carbonized seeds in postholes, at the Yabumaedabaru Site, Okinawa, confirm the date for the adoption of cereal cultivation to be around AD 800 (Takamiya Hiroto et al. 2011; Chida 2010).

How could the Ryukyu Islanders have "failed" to adopt cultivation, when all around them East Asian populations, including some in close contact, made the shift long before the Common Era? Most islanders overcome the limitations created by small land masses by growing some of their food. Exceptions are islands that are close to large land masses or high-latitude islands where abundant large sea mammals provide ample large amounts of protein (Takamiya Hiroto 2006b). Is it possible that some kind of noncereal cultivation, archaeologically difficult to detect, was practiced? Did the islanders intensify hunting and gathering practices? Did they prosper and increase, or barely survive? Did they depend on continual migration from the outside to maintain their communities?

There are many aspects to the study of Ryukyu Island subsistence patterns. Rapid progress in so many specialties is a testament to the maturation of Okinawan archaeology. Below I introduce the following topics: changes in site location and their relation to subsistence; the role of wild boar and domesticated pigs; debates on the nature of prehistoric cultivation and the time of its adoption; the role of shellfish in subsistence; the role of fishing; the effect of environmental changes; and differing interpretations of adaptive patterns.

Although there are some differences between the Northern/Central Ryukyus and the Southern Ryukyus, many aspects of subsistence are the same. Therefore, I have chosen to treat them together in my discussion.

Changes in Site Location and Adapation

Important differences in settlement patterns distinguish the Early Shellmound Period from the Late Shellmound Period in the Northern and Central Ryukyus.

The shift to a different pattern takes place in the Middle Shellmound Period, dating from around 1000 BC to AD 100 in the chronology of Asato Shijun (Okinawa Kenritsu Maizō 2005a). Whereas sites in the Early Shellmound Period are usually at the foot of cliffs or inland, those of the Late Shellmound Period occur in sand dunes adjacent to the sea. Sites are larger and more numerous, suggesting an increase in population and a broadened subsistence base. The shell deposits are well defined, with greater numbers of large, thick shells, suggesting a more extensive use of lagoon resources. Pecked stone tools with depressions, used for processing nuts and shellfish, may indicate that local populations were devising new ways to process locally available foods. Stone tools generally show diversification, while adzes decline in frequency. The Late Shellmound Period has been termed the Epi-Jōmon by a number of authors since it is a continuation of Jōmon hunting and gathering subsistence patterns beyond the temporal limits of the Jōmon Period.

Several reasons have been proposed for the change in site location. It has been suggested that this was a period of rapid coastal dune formation, rendering coastal locations less desirable, or that there was a shift to inland horticulture. Geomorphological analysis of the sediments from layers V and VI of the Heshikiya Tōbaru Site indicate strong wave action and stable, high sea levels from 3,500 to 1,700 years ago (EAC 2008, 69; Kōmoto 2007). The occurrence of many flaked stone arrowheads may indicate warfare, in which case an elevated location would have been easier to defend (Okinawa Kenritsu Maizō 2005a). Not only are sites larger than earlier sites, but they also comprise larger pit houses and have distinctive artifact assemblages (Itō Shinji 2011b). The pit houses are mostly rectangular, with a fireplace dug into the floor and postholes. Each side of the houses is about 2 to 3 m in length, although there are some that are as large as 5 m to a side. Stone lines, apparently boundary markers, also occur. Grindstones, querns, and hammerstones/crushers were used to process nuts of edible chestnuts such as *Castanopsis*. Villages, much larger than those of earlier subperiods, generally have ten to thirty dwellings, not all occupied at one time. Each of the large Middle Shellmound Period sites has a small Early Shellmound Period component. The relationship of the populations of these earlier components to the people inhabiting the Middle Shellmound Period sites is not clear; however, the association of components from the two periods does not appear to be random. While sites of the Early Shellmound Period situated on low hills, such as Ogidō and Iha, usually have shell middens at their base, these associated middens are absent from Middle Shellmound Period sites. However, refuse remains, including shells, suid bones, and fish bones, have been recovered from pit houses. The reasons for this divergent disposal pattern are not clear.

A series of shallow depressions and ridges visible during excavation because of contrasting soil coloration and thought to be part of a dry field system associated with a shallow well-like feature and postulated water channel, have been found at Uehara Nūribaru, Uehara, Ginowan, Central Okinawa in a layer that has yielded pottery sherds from the Middle Shellmound Period (roughly 2,700 years ago) (Ginowan Shi 1993; Goya 2000; Itō Kei 2007a, 102). Stone tools that look like reaping knives, a whetstone, and a scraper have also been recovered. It has been suggested that these features are associated with horticulture; however, no remains of cultivated plants have been found from flotation of samples from many sites of this period (Takamiya Hiroto 2007), and many archaeologists question the horticulture hypothesis.

Stone adzes are substantially larger than those of previous periods and are thought to have been used for heavy woodworking. Chipped triangular arrowheads with concave bases, fashioned from obsidian or chert, are relatively abundant in this period, whereas they are rare in other subperiods. They may indicate an increase in hunting wild boar/feral pigs, rather than warfare, as proposed above. Abundant net weights made of perforated shells provide evidence of intensive fishing. In Sakishima a slight trend to locate sites closer to the seashore occurred in some areas.

The "Pig Puzzle": Suids, Wild Boar, Pigs

Early suid bones from archaeological sites in the Ryukyus hold many keys to understanding patterns of interaction as well as subsistence activities. The relationships between wild boar and domesticated pigs in East Asia, Japan, and the Ryukyus has been investigated through genetic and dietary studies. I use the term "suid" to refer to both wild boar and domesticated pigs. The term is convenient because it can include intermediate stages of domestication or cases in which wild or domesticated status is not determined. Virtually all studies up to 2009 are based on bones recovered from sites on the Okinawa Islands. In the future it will be important to include samples from archaeological and living populations in Sakishima and the Amami Islands.

First of all, the position of the Ryukyu wild boar is of interest since they are not closely related to Japanese wild boar. Studies of mtDNA show that the Ryukyu wild boar, *Sus scrofa riukiuanus,* forms a subclade separate from other Asian suids including the wild boar of Japan, *Sus scrofa leucomystax* and *Sus scrofa ussuricus* (Groves 2007; Watanobe et al. 2001). Related wild boar clades from Lan Yu Island, Taiwan, and the Ryukyus migrated from the Asian continent during the Pleistocene. It is important to note that this population is distinct from the wild boar found in the Japanese main islands.

Second, Larson et al. concluded that the domestic pigs of Japan were introduced from continental Asia and were not domesticated Japanese wild boar. They found that "no modern Japanese domestic pig samples to date possess the Japanese wild boar haplotype" (Larson et al. 2007, 36). Although the Japanese wild boar are not the ancestors of Japanese domesticated pigs, some level of management of wild boar was achieved in the Jōmon Period. From Earliest Jōmon there is evidence that wild boar were transported to the Izu Ōshima Islands, some 30 to 200 km from the Izu Peninsula, and released. Jōmon wild boar remains have been found in Hokkaido. These areas are outside of their natural distribution (Hongo et al. 2007; Matsui et al. 2005; Yamazaki et al. 2005). It was previously thought that they were similarly introduced to Sado Island, but the early Sado Island suids are now identified as an old indigenous population (Watanobe et al. 2004). Nevertheless, if the former examples are evidence of a general Jōmon pattern occurring on islands in various parts of Japan, then it would seem plausible that Ryukyu islanders may have transported suids and raised them in semidomestication from an early date.

Third, not only is there evidence that pigs in the Japanese main islands are not related to wild boar in the Japanese main islands, but there is evidence that at least some ancient domesticated pig in the Ryukyus are not descended from local wild boar but were introduced from the Asian continent, such as the Early Shellmound Period suids from Noguni mentioned above. These were domesticated pigs introduced to the Ryukyus from Japan or perhaps Korea. Analysis of mtDNA from a sample of 161 bone specimens from twelve archaeological sites in the Okinawa Islands ranging in date from Early Jōmon and Late Jōmon to Early Yayoi–Heian (AD 1 to 500) and recent (post–AD 1600) shows several groups of haplotypes, each with implications for relations between suids and humans (Watanobe et al. 2002). The haplotype sequences from the Early Jōmon from Kogachibaru, Noguni B, and Chiarabaru were too short to include in the total phylogenetic analysis, but some nucleotide sequences were more similar to nucleotide sequences of East Asian domestic pigs than Ryukyu and Japanese wild boar.

The third finding challenges notions of gradual human migration down the Ryukyu chain. It has been proposed that from the Early Shellmound Period "wild boar" bones found in archaeological sites are actually domesticated pigs that were carried from the Asian continent. (At this time period, domesticated pigs are only known from Chinese sites.) Minagawa et al. (2005) and Matsui et al. (2005) proposed that pigs were introduced in the Earliest Shellmound Period and that some of them lived near human sites before being killed. The suid remains from the Noguni B Shellmound now dated to around 6000 BC (see Table 4.1) are particularly interesting. Their relatively high 15N content indicated to Matsui et al. (2005) that they probably ate fish and other marine resources as well as human leftovers and excrement, supporting the conclusion that some animals were kept and fed. It should be emphasized, however, that while the Noguni suids provide evidence of unusual dietary patterning, their genetic affiliation could not be determined since the specimens did not yield adequate samples of mtDNA. Ryohei Takahashi et al. (2011) found that, based on the length and breadth of their lower third molars, the *Sus* specimens from the Noguni Shellmound were distinctly smaller than modern Ryukyu wild boar. (Reduction in tooth size is considered to be an indicator of domestication.) Although the nucleotide sequences were fragmentary, analysis of the D loop region of mtDNA of the Noguni specimens showed that the *Sus* from the Noguni Shellmound included populations that were different from populations of modern wild boar. Takahashi et al. proposed two hypotheses to explain these differences: first, that the Noguni *Sus* were introduced to Okinawajima from elsewhere; and, second, that prehistoric wild boar were morphologically and genetically more diverse than modern Ryukyu wild boar, some ancient mtDNA lineages having died out in the past. Their comparison of tooth size of Noguni specimens with those of later sites such as Gushibaru on Iejima confirmed that the specimens from Gushibaru and Ie Island were Ryukyu wild boar brought from Okinawajima (main island).

Domesticated pigs are usually fed on cultivated crops or human waste. However, cultivation may not have been adopted until the end of the Shellmound Period around AD 800. Therefore, they may have been managed in semiferal fashion similar to Jōmon practices proposed by Hongo et al. (2007). This requires further research. Pigs were transported within the Ryukyus, and it is likely that there were early attempts to tend them. Since it is difficult to store and preserve animal protein in subtropical and tropical environments, keeping of suids may have served the same function as storage. Itō Shinji (2000, 151) notes that substantial numbers of wild boar bones have been found in sites on very small offshore islands in the Early Shellmound Period, such as the Kigahama Shellmound on Tsukenjima (1.92 sq km in area) and the Higashi Site on Tonakishima (3.77 sq km in area), suggesting that wild boar were carried to these islands from Okinawa and released. In the first half of the Late Shellmound Period at the latest, it appears that pigs of continental origin reached the Ryukyus via Kyushu and were preferred over wild boar. In their analysis of suid bones from the Gushibaru Shellmound, dated roughly 2,500 years ago, Matsui et al. (2005, 150) found specimens that showed a high 13C diet and noted that some individuals showed significant enrichment of 13C; they concluded that these pigs must have been fed on C4 plants such as foxtail millet, barnyard millet, Chinese millet, or sorghum.

Determining the role of suids in the subsistence economy of the Late Shellmound Period is complicated because of the possibility that pigs were tended or managed in some fashion, rather than simply hunted. In this case the cost of harvesting them would be different from that of hunting wild boar, which is considered to be a dangerous occupation. This point is relevant to the "food stress hypothesis" of Takamiya (see below). The use of dogs and traps in wild boar hunting is also important and needs to be considered in assessing the relative cost of catching them. Ethnographic accounts provide important insights (Ebihara 2011).

Those of the Yayoi-Heian Period were generally similar to East Asian domesticated pigs, indicating introduction from either Kyushu or possibly China. Many archaeologists believe that cultivation of crops began in the latter half of the first millennium in the Okinawa Islands. If this is the case, then pigs introduced to the Ryukyus before that date were not fed on agricultural crops but may have been traded for food rather than locally raised. Or perhaps they were brought to Okinawa to be raised in semidomestication at the edge of human settlements. In this regard, tiny Iejima presents a puzzle. The island is very small (23 sq km in area), yet more than three hundred suid individuals have been excavated from several Early Yayoi–Heian Period sites, including the Gushibaru Shellmound mentioned above. Although theses sites span several centuries, the density of domesticated pigs is very high for the size of the island. This island was a center for manufacture and distribution of shell bracelets (see Chapter 6). Pigs may have been an important exchange item brought by Kyushu traders who came to secure shells.

A rare group of suids termed the Shimizu Boar Group from the Shimizu Shellmound (Late Shellmound Period), Kumejima, has unique mtDNA characteristics suggesting introduction from an unidentified area, possibly somewhere on the Asian continent some time in the first few centuries AD (Watanobe et al. 2002, 230).

The fact that no artifacts from Taiwan or Sakishima were associated with suid remains of the Yayoi–Heian Period indicates that the suids were not transported from those areas. As discussed in Chapters 6 and 8, the clustering of Kaigen Tsūhō coins and *Turbo* shell processing sites suggests that Kumejima islanders may have been in contact with the China coast in the seventh to eighth centuries AD.

The Debate on Cultivation in the Early Shellmound Period

There is no doubt that early cereal cultivation in Okinawa, as determined by identification of seeds from flotation, did not occur until the latter first millennium AD. From the twelfth century AD, carbonized remains of wheat, millet, and barnyard grass become abundant (Takamiya Hiroto 2005, 204; 2006a). No archaeological remains of early root crops have been found in the Ryukyus. However, several different lines of analysis have suggested that irrigated taro cultivation or swidden cultivation of root crops may have preceded cereal cultivation. Root crop cultivation plays a major role in both East and Southeast Asia, areas adjacent to the Ryukyus, and could have entered the Ryukyus from either of these regions (Ankei Yūji 2007, 2376; Matsuda 2002).

Historical accounts from Sakishima indicate that both wild and domestic forms of yams exist, and yam collecting is recorded from the fifteenth century (Ishigaki Shi Sōmubu 2008a, 11).

Kurozumi (2006, 128) has proposed that two particular species of terrestrial viviparous gastropods living in wet taro fields indicate the introduction of cultivation of irrigated taro in the Early to Middle Shellmound Period 3500 to 2500 BP. These are *Melanoides tuberculata* and Taiwan *Melanoides formosensis.* Since these species do not exist in Kyushu, Kurozumi has proposed that they must have been introduced from the south. However, at present there is no artifactual evidence to substantiate contact between Okinawa and Sakishima, Taiwan, or Southeast Asia in this time period. As mentioned above, soil features at the Uehara Nūribaru Site, Ginowan, Okinawa Island, have been interpreted by Goya as the remains of a swidden field of the Middle Shellmound Period (1000 BC to AD 100) (Ginowan Shi 1993; Goya 2000; Itō Kei 2007a, 102). Goya notes that the Middle Shellmound Period is a time of large upland sites such as Shinugudō, which have limited middens. As noted above, sites of similar type have been found in upland areas in Okinawajima and Tokunoshima. Sites of this time period also have large quantities of terrestrial snails, indicating forest clearance on limestone plateaus. The subsistence patterns of the Middle Shellmound Period may have been diverse, but this is still difficult to confirm since root crops are very perishable and usually cannot be confirmed through pollen analysis.

Takamiya Hiroto (2007) has stated that the only "hard data" for substantiating prehistoric cultivation in Okinawa were cereal seeds found in flotation. However, the malacological evidence presented by Kurozumi and data from the Uehara Nūribaru Site cannot be discounted simply because they do not yield macrofossils of cultivars. Further evidence or alternative explanations must be sought. At the same time, new ways of exploring the possibility of prehistoric yam cultivations in Sakishima should be explored. If changes in vegetation can be detected in future environmental studies and these show an increase in nonarboreal pollen and evidence of prehistoric alluviation, some kind of cultivation of root crops might be substantiated. Since root crops produce insufficient pollen to be detected directly in samples, it is only through these proxies that their cultivation can be detected. Admittedly, the evidence for cultivation in the Early Shellmound Period is tenuous at present (Shinzato Akito 2010).

The ethnographic research of Ankei Yūji and his colleagues on traditional agriculture shows that the archaeological record oversimplifies the picture. The early cultivation system of the Ryukyus had at least three components: wet rice cultivation, generally limited to high islands; dryland crops, particularly millet but also barnyard grass and wheat and barley; and root crops (*Colocasia* and *Dioscorea*). *Dioscorea* was both cultivated and collected in Yaeyama until recently (Ankei 2007, 218–237). The configuration of these three components varied temporally and spatially. For instance, in the early twentieth century in Yaeyama, irrigated rice cultivation was practiced on Iriomotejima, and rice served as a kind of currency and standard of wealth (ibid., 375). Some of the surrounding low islands exchanged seaweed, millet, and beans for rice. Islanders from Kuroshima exchanged wood charcoal, which was valued by the Iriomotejima paddy farmers as a source of potash for fertilizing paddies. Ankei reported that modern rice varieties developed on Okinawajima do not grow well on Iriomotejima and Ishigakijima, where farmers prefer varieties developed in Taiwan. He proposes that the ancient varieties of rice, now virtually extinct, may have come from Southeast Asia, whereas dryland crops such as millet, barley, and wheat were brought from the north.

Shellfish Analysis

Shellfish species are extremely abundant and diverse in the Ryukyu Islands. They occupy every available marine habitat and are also found in brackish and fresh water, rice paddies, and terrestrial habitats. Published analyses of shellfish remains commonly record one hundred to two hundred species, recorded as the number of identified specimens. Distribution patterns of shellfish remains have been used by Takamiya Hiroto (1997; 2006b) and Pearson (1994; 1997a) to reconstruct patterns of subsistence. The use of shellfish analysis to reconstruct human ecology rests on a number of assumptions and methodological choices. Shellfish may be a dietary staple, as in the Gilbert Islands of Micronesia (Thomas 2002), or of lesser caloric value as a condiment or constituent of soups as described by Keegan et al. (2003, 1615) for the Bahamas Islands of the Caribbean. They refer to stable isotope analysis that indicates that less than 10 percent of the diet of a sample of prehistoric inhabitants of the Bahamas Islands was obtained from mollusks (Keegan and de Niro 1988). Some shellfish, usually those with a large amount of meat, are used as high-status food, as in the case of *Turbo* meat served to visiting officials in the Sumiya Site, Miyakojima (referred to in Chapter 9), or they may be low-status food for times of famine. If the shellfish are an insignificant component of the total diet, then they are not appropriate subjects for reconstructing overall subsistence patterns, even if numerous and well preserved. In the Ryukyu case, many of the shellfish in midden samples come from species that are naturally small and provide low amounts of protein. However, when protein is scarce, even small amounts may be critical, despite the fact that they provide relatively few calories to the whole diet (Habu 2004, 73).

In Takamiya's analysis of twenty-two assemblages from the Okinawa Islands, the "top ten" abundant species for each site were selected, and using a technique adopted from palaeo-ethnobotany, species that were present in the highest number of sites of this group were considered core subsistence species. In Takamiya's analysis relative abundance in each site rather than absolute abundance was considered. However, it should be noted that most of the shell assemblages are dominated by one or two species that comprise most of the identified shells, so that, even within the "top ten" for each site, many shell species are present in very small numbers. Many sites contain species not found in the "top ten" of other sites, suggesting that collectors may have scooped up small gastropods in a random fashion. Takamiya proposed that, in sites of the Yayoi Period or its equivalent, the early part of the Late Shellmound Period, the occurrence of shells such as *Tridacna maxima* and *Lunatica (Turbo) marmorata* indicated food stress in the island population because these shells are large and heavy to carry and are difficult or dangerous to harvest, often occurring on the outer slope of the reef. *Tridacna* does occur in six of the ten sites, with a maximum of 18 percent of the Ara Shellmound, but otherwise it is always below 10 percent, and *Lunatica marmorata* occurs in two sites at frequencies of 6.7 percent and 1.6 percent. Thus the frequency of the large, heavy shellfish is very low. This would seem to indicate that their significance is also low.

I have examined frequencies, rather than presence/absence, in the shell data compiled by Takamiya Hiroto (1997, 252–262) and found several interesting trends (Table 5.1). Takamiya grouped the sites in a rough chronological sequence and divided them into two periods: Late Jōmon (Middle Shellmound Period) and Yayoi (first half of Late Shellmound Period). Eighteen sites (one with three separate areas) have samples in which the MNI (Minimum Number of Individuals) identified to the species level is over 1,000. I dropped two sites with samples below 1,000 individuals from the original sample of twenty sites. All of the species are generally small shellfish inhabiting mangroves and reef lagoons. Six of the eight Late Jōmon assemblages are dominated by a single species that comprised more than 70 percent of the MNI. In the Yayoi Period, two sites showed a similar pattern of very high predominance of one species. In the reexamination of Takamiya's data, I calculated percentages for the top twelve species from each site and ranked the species according to their percentages in Early or

TABLE 5.1 Percentages of the Most Common Shell Species in Okinawan Sites from the Latest Jōmon and Yayoi Periods

	Percent										
	SITES 1–10 (ROUGHLY 1000 BC TO 500 BC)										
Shell Species	1	2	3	4	5	6	7	8	9	10	*Average %*
Gafrarium tumidum	0.9			74.5	4.2	4.6	73.2				15.7
Conomurex luhuanus	0.9	81.2	1.9		4.5	29.4		10.1	5.6	18.1	15.2
Theliostyla albicilla			74.3	1.4				49.3			12.5
Terebralia palustris	87.3										8.7
Lunella coronata granulata			5.2	4.3	70.2		1.3	2.6			8.4
Marmarostoma argyrostoma	0.6	7.7	3.5		2.2	20.4		15.3	10.8	16.6	7.7
Semisulcospira libertina							4.4		50.9		5.5
Atactodea striata		2.6	2.8	4.5	10.4	14.3		3.3	9.3	3.6	5.1
atsushiro gai									23.7	2.4	
Asaphis dichotoma		0.7				5.8			9.3	5.9	2.2
Tectus maximus	1.3	2.7								17.0	2.1
Geloina papua	3.7					8.7			4.2	3.7	2.0
Total percent											87.5

	SITES 11–20 (ROUGHLY 500 BC TO 250 AD)										
	11	12	13	14	15	16	17	18	19	20	*Average %*
Conomurex luhuanus	38.1	38.8	21.1	19.8			15.9	44.7	3.1	44.3	22.6
Gafrarium tumidum					86.3	75.5					16.2
Tectus maximus	13.0	2.5	10.1	20.9			16.7	11.9	3.8	8.6	8.7
Marmarostoma argyrostoma	14.6		31.6	13.7				12.5	13.9	1.1	8.7
Tridacna crocea	5.4	22.0		9.2	1.2	0.9	20.0			4.9	6.4
Tridacna maxima	4.8		7.1	6.6			8.1	18.1		5.6	5
Atactodea striata	8.5	2.7				10.0	9.2		1.3	13.8	4.6
Theliostyla albicilla				5.3					27.4		3.3
Cellana testudinaria			8.0						24.5		3.3
Cellana nigrolineata									18.1		1.8
Geloina papua		15.8			0.6						1.6
Lunatica marmorata			6.7						1.6	6.8	1.5
Total percent											82.7

Source: Based on data from Takamiya Hiroto 1997, 252–262.

Late sites from most to least abundant. Six species were common to both groups, and *Conomurex luhuanus,* a small gastropod, and *Gafrarium tumidum,* a small bivalve, dominated the assemblages of both periods. *Theliostyla,* a very small snail; *Marmarostoma,* a medium size gastropod; and *Atactodea* and *Geloina,* small clams, were also common to both groups. One of the early sites was dominated by *Terebralia,* a small mangrove gastropod. As Takamiya's analysis indicated, sites of the Late Shellmound Period were distinguished by two species of *Tridacna, tectus and lunatica,* but their combined average percentage was about 20 percent of the total number of specimens.

To better understand this trend of reliance on a single or very few species an index of diversity is useful (Pearson 1994; 1997a). The diversity index was used by Kirch and Yen in their analysis of the shellfish remains from the Polynesian outlier of Tikopia (1982, 303). It is the same measure as Kirch's measure of Niche Width (Kirch 1980). It measures the degree of diversity of shellfish by the following formula: D.I. = $1/\text{sum}\ (pi)^2$, where *pi* is the percentage of weight contributed by species *i.* (A few species with high frequencies will make a high sum of square frequencies, resulting in a low index of diversity). Kirch and Yen noted that, for prehistoric sites in Tikopia, values ranged from 2.2 (least diverse) to 7.2. Most D.I. values averaged around 5.5 and suggest that shellfish gathering was always fairly generalized, without dominant emphasis on only a few preferred species.

I calculated the diversity index for the twenty sites tabulated by Takamiya (1997, 252–262) (Table 5.2). Most of the sites of the Late Jōmon Period (Middle Shellmound Period) show a very low index, which indicates selection of very few species. Inhabitants of these sites appear to have harvested large colonies of particular species to use in soups or side dishes. These assemblages are composed of many species of shells that occur in very low frequencies (less than 1 percent), suggesting that collectors gathered up shells indiscriminately while gathering the main target species. The exception is the Takamine Site, in which three species are in second place, behind the predominant, freshwater shell, *Semisulcospira libertina.* This site appears to occupy a specialized local environment. Sites of the Late Shellmound Period display a higher index of diversity, indicating that a wider range of species was exploited. Such a trend could indicate less dependence of small bivalves, but, still, the total percentage of larger, heavier shellfish is not very high.

As mentioned above, rough data collected for the Kitahara Site, Kumejima, was analyzed for each spit or sublayer within one cultural layer (Pearson 1994; 1997a). A similar trend was found with Layer III of the Kitahara Site, ranging from 2.55 for Level 8, to 7.46 for Level 1, indicating a trend toward diversification of shellfish use in the first millennium AD. This trend could be interpreted as showing increased pressure on reef resources in the form of more diversified shell collecting.

TABLE 5.2 Shell Data and Index of Diversity for Twenty Sites Tabulated by Takamiya

Site	*Total Shell MNI*	*MNI of Top Ten Species*	*No. of Identified Species*	*Diversity Index*	*General Collecting Environment*
LATE JŌMON (MIDDLE SMP)					
1. Kogachibaru	126,891	117,950	106	1.32	mangrove, muddy, intertidal
2. Kigahama	4,115	3,396	74	1.50	lagoon, intertidal
3. Furuzamami Area II	49,187*	29,343	103	1.80	intertidal, low tide
4. Hyakuna No. 2	17,153	4,187	96	1.76	mangrove, rubble
5. Fukidashibaru	1,416	357	56	1.90	intertidal, lagoon, mangrove
6. Shinugudō	2,996	343	67	6.02	lower tidal zone, lagoon
7. Chiarabaru	197,407	106	182,193	1.86	mangrove, tidal
8. Furuzamami Area I	49,187*	106	2,287	3.56	tidal, intertidal, lagoon
9. Takamine	6,941	123	1,755	17.24	freshwater, intertidal
10. Kōribaru	3,579	ca. 200	2,097	6.49	reef, lagoon
YAYOI (LATE SMP)					
11. Bise	18,209	8,173	152	5.03	reef, outer reef slope
12. Chijifuchā Cave	1,817	1,536	72	4.38	
13. Uzahama B	1,810	1,292	77	5.78	
14. Kijoka	—	7, 406	194	7.30	
15. Uken	23,175	21,374	72	1.33	mangrove, lagoon
16. Akajangā	—	35,175	71	1.72	mangrove, lagoon
17. Kajō	14,806	19,819	183	7.87	rocky shores
18. Ara	8,999	2,742	97	3.86	lagoon rocky outer slope
19. Furuzamami Area III	49,187	1,781	103	5.26	lagoon, plus
20. Shimizu	50,402	36,983	123	4.10	lagoon, rocky outer slope

Source: Takamiya Hiroto 1997, 252–262.
*MNI for entire site.

Kurozumi (2011, 96, 97) has observed that substantial percentages of large gastropod shells such as *Tricornis* show marks on their apertures that indicate that they have been inhabited by animals such as hermit crabs, which can only take possession of the shell as their habitation after the death of the *Tricornis.* He postulated that these dead shells, which were not originally gathered for food, accumulated in channels in the reef that are flushed in tidal activity. In the absence of other shellfish from the sloping outer edge of the reef such as *Chicoreus ramosus* (branched murex) in site assemblages, he questions whether diving to depths of 10 m or more to harvest these creatures was a common practice. In ethnoarchaeological studies of the Gilbertese Islanders, Thomas (2002) found that very large shellfish were processed near their place of capture, and the shells were discarded in the reef rather than being carried back to the home base, because they are very heavy. Therefore, it seems probable that very large gastropods were harvested, disposed of in the reef, and later harvested as dead shells for processing into artifacts. (Such artifacts are discussed in Chapter 6.) Judging from the distribution of *Tridacna* on accessible reef flats in the Gilbert Islands (Thomas 2002) and in French Polynesia (Gilbert et al. 2006), it is likely that they may have been easier to collect in the Ryukyus in prehistory than at present since now they are found only on the dangerous outer slope of the reef in deep water. On the island of Rotuma, Polynesia, T. Ladefoged reported that immature live *Tridacna* are gathered from the reef and raised in a convenient location near the houses of villagers until they are mature (personal communication).

Kurozumi (2011, 100) states that the number of large shells decreases with the decline of the shell exchange (discussed in Chapter 6), indicating that the shells found in archaeological sites were collected for making artifacts rather than for subsistence.

Patterning of Fish Bones

Tōizumi (2002, 64) concluded that he could not detect major changes in fishing patterns from the beginning of the Shellmound Period to the present. He tabulated fish remains from thirty-six components of thirty-six sites in the Amami and Okinawa Islands, from virtually all Holocene archaeological periods (Tōizumi 2006, 106–107; 2007a, 533–534). His analyses show that three species of bony reef fish (parrot fish, wrasses, and emperor fish, in order of abundance), generally about 50 cm in length, dominate virtually every assemblage. Puffer fish are ranked fourth (from 10 to 20 percent). Shallow bays seem to favor wrasses, while reef lagoons favor parrot fish. In a few sites, up to 10 percent of the fish assemblage was composed of fish from outside the reef. Tōizumi's analysis is based on "pickup" samples collected during excavations. This type of analysis may favor larger specimens. In a cluster analysis of twenty-eight fish species from thirty sites of the Early and Late Shellmound Period, Najima (2003) found that species clustered according to general environment rather than according to temporal subperiod, indicating an absence of change in each particular environment. She found three major clusters: A, composed of species living on the outer slopes of the reef (*hishi*); B, species from the lagoon (*ino*); and C, unusual cases from sites near rocky foreshores of the Kasari Peninsula of Amami Ōshima. The latter contained a high percentage of bones of groupers (*hata*), which prefer this environment.

Recent research shows that fishing techniques from the Early Shellmound Period (Late Jōmon) were more diverse than previously known. Water screening of remains from Sumiyoshi on Okinoerabujima has yielded small fish bones indicative of net fishing. Clupeidae (herring) and Exoceitidae (flying fish) have also been recovered (Tōizumi 2008). Common Ryukyu reef fish are illustrated in Figure 5.2 and described in Table 5.3. In the Late Shellmound Period, net fishing of small fish developed, judging from the increase in shell net weights.

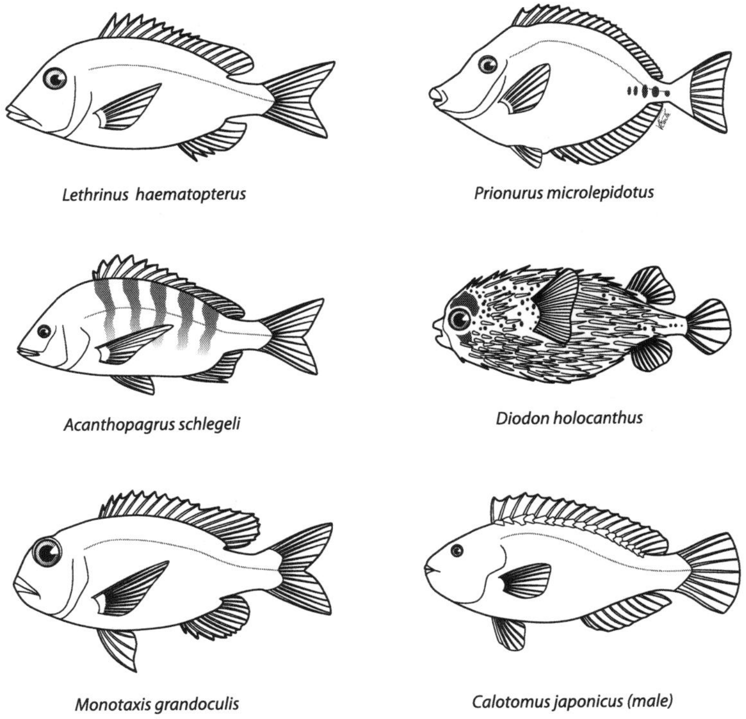

Figure 5.2. Major types of reef fish recovered from sites in the Central and Southern Ryukyus. Fish images redrawn from various sources.

TABLE 5.3 Major Reef Fish Species Found in Archaeological Sites in the Ryukyus

Genus and Species	*Family*	*English Common Name*	*Japanese Common Name*	*Maximum Size*	*Habitat, Diet, Fishing Method*
no single genus	Lutjanidae	snapper	*fuedai*	50 cm	reef, adjacent areas
Lethrinus haematopterus	Lethrinidae	emperor fish	*fuefukidai*	50 cm	reef
Monotaxis grandoculis	Lethrinidae	emperor fish	*yokotsu magurodai*	50 cm	angling, drive in net
Acanthopagrus schlegeli	Sparidae	porgie	*kurodai*	30 cm	sandy bottom, grass beds, brackish water
no single genus	Synodontidae	lizard fish	*ei*	30–50 cm	coral reef, coral rubble, sandy, muddy bottom
several genera including *Balistes* and *Balistoides*	Balistidae	trigger fish	*mongara, kaohagi*	variable	diet of benthic animals
Choerodon sp.	Labridae	wrasse	*bera*	30–100 cm	coral reef, reef, handline, drive in net
many species	Chrondrichthyes	shark	*same*	variable	free roaming, reef and deep sea
Diodon holocanthus	Diodontidae	porcupine fish	*harisenbon*	40 cm	juveniles pelagic, adults inhabit reefs, hand net, poisonous unless prepared correctly
Calotomus sp.	Scaridae	parrot fish	*budai*	35–70 cm	reef, lagoon

Source: Shiro 2010.

With the adoption of water screening of midden samples, many bones of small fish have been recovered, whereas previously hand picking up of fish bones while digging favored large fish. Analysis of fish bones alone does not support a trend to increased catching of small fish in nets because there are not yet enough comparable samples.

Ethnoarchaeological research by Ono Rintaro (2009) on reef fishing of the Sama people of Sabah sheds light on prehistoric reef fishing of the Ryukyus. All of the fishing of the Sama people was carried out in shallow reef conditions, using small boats, some with small engines (up to 60 horsepower). As in the Ryukyus, the predominant catch was Serranidae (grouper), Lethrinidae (emperor fish), and Scaridae (parrot fish). These three genera comprised 98 percent of the total. Most of the fish were taken in gill nets, but some were taken in seine nets, and larger specimens were caught on hook and line. Net fishing was by far the most efficient method, measured by the weight of the catch per person per hour. Ono cautioned that the size of the fish in addition to the MNI must be considered and that many of the fish are under 20 cm in length. Large quantities of small fish provide substantial protein, which the Maritime Sama traditionally exchanged for cultivated produce. This method of securing protein is low risk and highly efficient; gill netting yields 1.84 kg of catch per person per hour, compared to 0.4 kg per hour for shellfish gathering (exclusive of the weight of the shells) (Ono 2009, 85). The ethnoarchaeology shows that small fish are very important in reef fishing as a source of protein and that the size of fish is important as well as counts of individuals.

Environmental Changes and Subsistence

Finally, it is important to review environmental changes that might have affected subsistence patterns. Attention has recently been devoted to the formation of the reef environment, which was governed by rising Holocene sea level and sea surface temperatures among other factors such as hydro-isostasis, discussed in Chapter 2. Kawana (2011) has matched calibrated radiocarbon dates with stages of reef development. Generally he found that from 7900 to 7000 cal BP reefs on the west coast of central Okinawa Island were not yet well developed, and strong waves could reach the shoreline. From 6200 to 5500 cal BP, the time period of Sobata Type pottery, reefs were in an early stage of development, and reef resources would have been restricted. Tōizumi (2011) noted bones of large shark and mackerel (Japanese *aji,* Carangidae) in sites of these two time periods but not in later sites. From the time period of the Iha and Ogidō Types (Early Shellmound Period IV and V), the reefs were well developed and would have been rich sources of food. However, as noted by Kan (2010), the lower layers of sites such as Aragusuku Shichabaru contain reef species. The most likely explanation for this is that restricted areas of shallow, calm water must have existed in early times, but the relative area of the lagoon increased dramatically as the fringing reefs became complete.

Periods of cool climate at 4200 to 4000 BP, 1700 to 1250 BP, and 650 to 480 BP as well as warm periods at 7500 to 5000 BP (Mid-Holocene Optimum) and 1200 to 700 BP (Mediaeval Warm Period) must have affected the Ryukyus. The first cool period may have been a factor in the shift of settlement to higher locations as well as the occurrence of large tsunami. The lack of radiocarbon dates from this period is significant and could indicate low population. The Kofun Cool Period, 1700 to 1250 BP, may have had a delaying effect on the adoption of cultivation, with a strong winter monsoon retarding growth and a weak summer monsoon creating drought. The Mediaeval Warm Period with its strong summer monsoon may have been important in the adoption of cultivation of rice and millet, summer crops that rely on adequate moisture. The Ryukyus have been difficult places for palynological studies because of the lack of freshwater lakes and acidic bogs; however, coring of marine sediments from inshore locations may provide important climatic data in the future.

Prehistoric Island Adaptation

Prehistoric Population Trends in the Ryukyus and Their Consequences

At present archaeologists know roughly how long people have inhabited the Ryukyus and their basic subsistence practices but are still uncertain about the intensity and continuity of occupation. For the Northern and Central Ryukyus archaeologists have described the development of different pottery types including types of local origin, indicating the presence of a population that grew independently in the islands, as described in Chapter 3. Was local population growth sustainable, and what conditions and practices supported it?

Hunter-gatherers who lived throughout the Ryukyus from the time of initial colonization in the Holocene until the adoption of cereal cultivation lived in relatively low population densities. In Sakishima the Shimotabaru Period population appears to have died out, to be replaced roughly 1,100 years later by people with a distinctive artifact assemblage that lacked pottery (Non-Ceramic Period). The small communities of the Earliest Shellmound Period on Okinawa may have been unable to sustain their populations because of small community size rather than failure to secure enough food. Small populations are inherently unstable because of imbalances in the sex ratio and can avoid extinction only by means of high migratory inflow, determined to be in the range of 7 percent for 50 individuals and 3 percent for populations of 350 to 400 individuals (Bocquet-

TABLE 5.4 Takamiya Hiroto's Interpretive Framework for Human Subsistence Adaptation to the Okinawa Islands

Palaeolithic Period	Habitation of large islands or part of mainland. The Ryukyus became islands, people migrated out or became extinct.
Jōmon Period	Up to the middle of Middle Jōmon, unsuccessful colonization; population could not adapt to island environment. From latter half of Middle Jōmon, successful adaptation to island environment, establishment of subsistence system based on reef fish. Latest Jomon, system collapse, search for new system.
Yayoi-Heian Period	Early half, fifth to eighth centuries? Establishment of new system, could not overcome food stress. Late half, 1-1, eighth to ninth centuries AD? Cultivating colonists, beginning of cultivation. 1-2, tenth to twelfth centuries? Development of cultivation. *or* 2-1, eighth/ninth to tenth centuries AD. Immediate beginning of cultivation. 2-2, gap? Later colonization by cultivators.
Gusuku Period	Period of intensive cultivation.

Source: Takamiya Hiroto 2005, 204.

Appel 1985). Small groups on Okinawa who lost contact with Kyushu may not have been able to sustain their numbers. The same process may have occurred in Sakishima, creating the gap of roughly 1,100 years between the Shimotabaru and Non-Ceramic Periods.

Takamiya Hiroto (2006b) has proposed that it was not until the Late Jōmon, around 1500 BC, that settlements in the central Ryukyus show a strong population increase and what Takamiya terms "successful colonization." This was achieved in the Late Jōmon through a combination of reef fishing, collecting shellfish from the lagoon, gathering nuts and other plant foods, and hunting wild boar. The subsistence pattern of the late part of the Early Shellmound Period, Late and Final Jōmon, shows adaptation to reef resources, but Takamiya has proposed that this was not sustainable and collapsed in the late first millennium BC, at the end of the Early Shellmound Period (Table 5.4). Itō Shinji (2011b, 48) notes that a demographic crash is also postulated in the Japanese main islands in the Late and Final Jōmon, when population is thought to have overshot available resources.

"Successful colonization" has been measured by an increase in sites per century, grouped into the periods of the Japanese chronology (six subperiods of Jōmon, Yayoi-Heian) (Takamiya Hiroto 1997; 2006a, b). Itō (2006, 11) has criticized this method of measuring population because of the difficulty of dating the time span of occupation of each site and correlating the Okinawan chronology of periods and pottery types with the chronological divisions of the Japanese main islands.

Takamiya has also noted an increase in suid bones in some sites of the Late Shellmound Period. At this time the proportion of suid bones in the tabulation of vertebrates for each site also increased. Takamiya states that hunting wild boar is dangerous and time consuming; therefore this pattern indicates food stress and that suids constitute a costly system for getting food (Takamiya 2007). However, it should be noted that the matter of suid consumption in the Late Shellmound Period is complicated since the islanders seem to have been receiving pigs from the Japanese main islands and releasing them for later hunting. There is also tantalizing evidence from the Kogachibaru Site that dogs may have been eaten to provide protein. Hudson and Takamiya (2001) propose that an increase in human dental hypoplasia (imperfect formation of tooth enamel before maturity) in the first half of the Late Shellmound Period supports the interpretation of food stress. While it seems quite possible that this trend of hypoplasia may be linked to diet, as Hudson and Takamiya indicate, the condition can also be caused by childhood disease and infection, or genetic predisposition (Hillson 1992). As pointed out by Mark Hudson (personal communication), childhood disease and infection are not inconsistent with food stress. However, they could occur independently of food stress. Environmental changes such as cycles of severe climate should also be considered. Future research on this problem will be very interesting. Temple (2010) found a relatively high incidence of dental hypoplasia in Jōmon populations of western Japan compared with Jōmon populations of eastern Japan, who had a richer range of plant foods and game, and Yayoi populations, who adopted irrigated and dryland cultivation. While the concept of food stress in the Late Shellmound Period has not been discussed by other Okinawan researchers, Tōizumi (2002) noted that there is an increase in bones of suids from the Early to Middle Shellmound Period, but he was not sure whether this was a general trend or was localized in specific conditions. The Ryukyu islanders did prepare for times of food shortages. Food processing techniques to remove the toxin cycasin from the seeds and pithy trunk of the cycad palm (*Cycas revoluta*) have been documented by Ankei Takako (2011), who proposes that simpler techniques were similar to those used locally for acorns, but more elaborate processes of fermentation may have come from China. Ankei also found evidence that less toxic varieties of *Cycas,* with distinctive foliage, were exchanged within the Ryukyus.

Takamiya (1997, 206–227) analyzed stable carbon and nitrogen isotopes in bones from the Azamabaru Sites, concluding that the individuals consumed slightly more terrestrial C3 plants than marine resources and did not consume C4 plants. In the absence of cultivated cereals from sites of this period, he concluded that the C3 plants must be wild roots and nuts, and that the population was nonagricultural. Similar results were published by Yoneda (2010).

Takamiya (1996; 2005) measured the Okinawan case against a model of successful island colonization, indicated by long-term reproductive success manifested in a logistical pattern of population increase (Takamiya 2004) up to the limits of carrying capacity. Kirch (1984) used this model to compare growth rates among Polynesian cultivators. Like any optimizing model, it may provide a grid for comparing the Okinawan case with island cultivators, but it may not explain much about expected and observed rates of population growth among hunter-gatherers. Athens (2007, 269–276) notes that, even among cultivators in Kosrae, eastern Micronesia, prehistoric populations experienced relatively low rates of population growth despite a rich environment and absence of major diseases.

As indicated above, re-creating prehistoric population trends by counting the number of sites in each archaeological period is subject to inaccuracies created by the impressionistic typology and imprecise time periods. A different method, utilizing radiocarbon dates as proxies for population trends (Rick 1987), has been used in the Hawaiian Islands (Dye and Komori 1992). Its underlying premise is that if prehistoric people all contributed a known equal amount of carbon each year, and it was perfectly preserved, this amount could be sampled to determine the past population of a given region. If the actual population were known for one time period, it would be possible to estimate a population curve by plotting the relative amounts of carbon sampled for other periods. For a frequency distribution of 14C age determinations to be isomorphic to a population growth curve, three conditions must be met: (1) the 14C age determination sample is representative of the archaeological carbon deposit, (2) the extant archaeological carbon deposit is representative of the original carbon deposit, and (3) the amount of carbon added to the original deposit per capita per unit of time is constant over the period of interest. In cases where these conditions are not met, Rick identified three biases: investigation biases, preservation biases, and creation biases (1987, 56).

In the case of Okinawa and Sakishima, Najima et al. (2008) have provided tabulation of radiocarbon dates that they consider to be the most reliable, based on the nature of the sample, method of analysis, and documentation. I selected only AMS dates from their most reliable group and chose the midpoint of the two-sigma range of dates that they presented. The distribution of the 14C dates is shown in Figure 5.3 (a), (b), and (c). Figure 5.3 (a) shows the earliest dates for

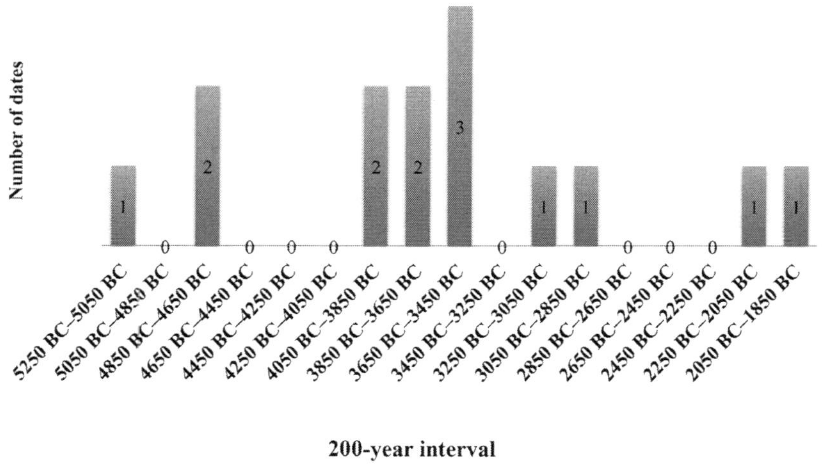

Figure 5.3 (a). Number of calibrated AMS 14C dates per two-hundred-year interval, Okinawa Islands, 5250 BC to 1850 BC, n = 14

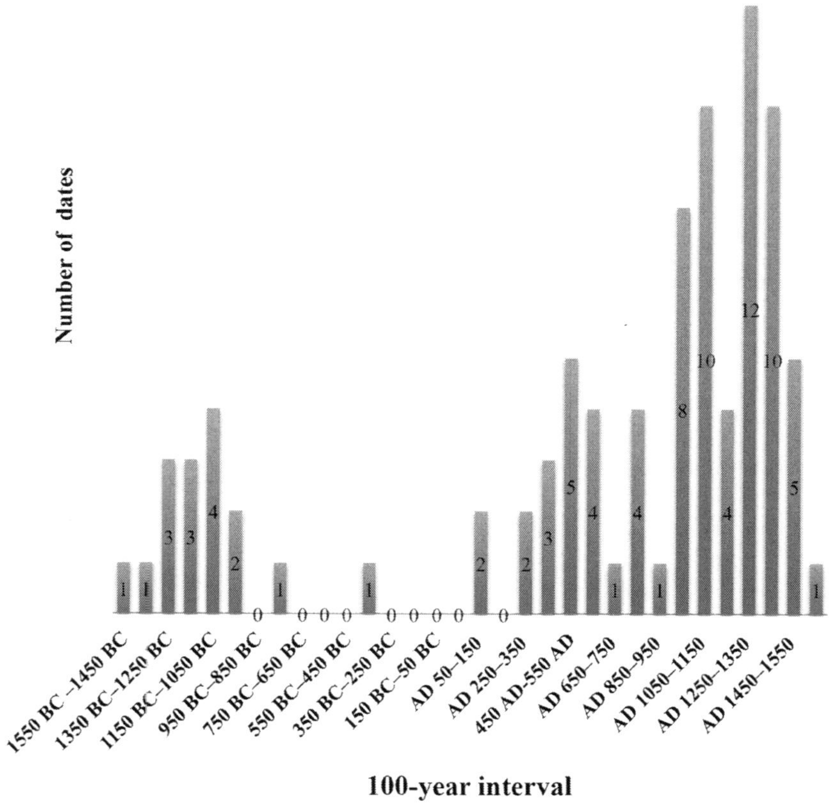

Figure 5.3 (b). Number of calibrated AMS 14C dates per one-hundred-year interval, Okinawa Islands, 1550 BC to AD 1650, n = 89

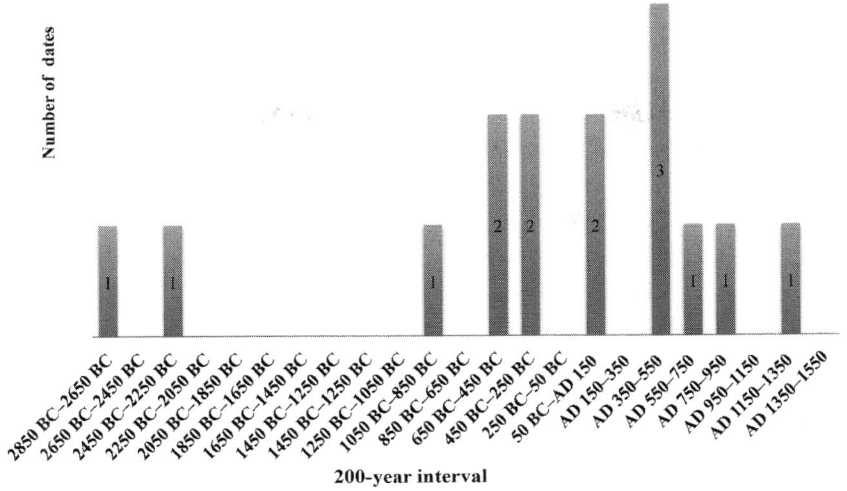

Figure 5.3 (c). Number of calibrated AMS 14C dates per two-hundred-year interval, Sakishima Islands, 2850 BC to AD 1550, n = 15

Okinawajima from cal 5250 BC to cal 1850 BC. The number of dates is low and the distribution discontinuous. It is possible that this distribution is the result of the overall small number of dates. However, it raises the question of a discontinuous population history, first raised by Takamiya Hiroto (1996). Two gaps of six hundred years occur, suggesting that population was low and communities died out. This is a hypothesis that could be tested by the selection of appropriate data with greater precision than the plotting of sites by period. It should be noted that the sites are grouped in two-hundred-year intervals because of the low sample size and the long time span being considered. In Figure 5.3 (b), which shows dates from cal 1550 BC to cal AD 1650, the dates show puzzling discontinuities in the first millennium BC after a substantial rise in the latter half of the second millennium BC, which may coincide with Takamiya's period of adaptation to reefs (2005, 189). From the beginning of the Common Era there is a substantial increase, peaking in the fifth century AD, followed by fluctuation until AD 950 to 1050, which coincides with the proposed population increase following the adoption of cereal cultivation. The patterning of dates per one-hundred-year interval seems unlikely to be produced completely by investigative bias. The rise in the first half of the first millennium AD requires explanation. It may be related to subsistence experiments and/or the introduction of pigs from Kyushu, and it does not seem to indicate food stress. Or the date of the beginning of cereal cultivation may be earlier than current data indicate.

What appear to be breaks in the occupation sequence, in both Okinawajima and Sakishima, imply that, before the advent of cereal cultivation, communities in both the Central and Southern Ryukyus may not have been continuously sustainable and died out, to be replaced by new arrivals. In the Sakishima Islands a plot of fifteen calibrated AMS dates from Najima et al. (2008, 45) in Figure 5.3 (c) confirms the gap of roughly 1,100 years between the Shimotabaru and Non-Ceramic Periods. It also appears that population was lower from AD 550 to around AD 1000.

It could be claimed that until recently Okinawan investigators have shown little interest in building a systematic radiocarbon chronology; therefore, the dates show too much investigative bias to be useful. The tabulation of Najima et al. (2008) seems to refute this point since the sample of reliable dates is larger than anticipated and seems to include a range of different time periods. In general, both the Central and Southern Ryukyu Island groups seem to have experienced long periods of very low population and almost continuous population replacement. Although I would not propose that we use these trends to estimate actual population numbers, I think they may be useful in detecting relative changes in population. As more reliable, fully documented dates become available, the trends indicated in this preliminary analysis can be tested.

As we should expect, Ryukyu subtropical island hunter-gatherers sustained low populations, probably dying out in the Sakishima Islands. Takamiya Hiroto proposes that it was reef resources and nuts that allowed them to survive (2006b), but it could also be that yams were cultivated and suids were tended as well, contributing to the total broad spectrum diet. In both the Ryukyus and, a close analogy, the islands of the Caribbean, low hunter-gatherer populations were overtaken by agricultural immigrants with expanding populations.

Why Did Islanders Adopt Cultivation at Such a Late Date?

Bellwood (2005, 34, 42) describes many situations in which hunter-gatherers maintained contact with farmers in adjacent regions but did not adopt agriculture. The adoption of cultivation involves a fundamental reorganization of social relations from collective sharing to a household mode of production as well as a heavy cost of labor and a delayed return. Since the shift does not lead to an immediate increase in productivity, social and demographic aspects must be the prime movers in its adoption (Barker 2011; Bowles 2011). Food stress is not a sufficient cause for the shift.

If pig tending and root crop cultivation are indeed confirmed, we can expect them to have been supplementary rather than mainstays. Pig raising may have been related to ritual exchange and occasional collective feasting.

None of the cereal crops that the islanders finally adopted is native to the islands. Irrigated wet rice, grown in Kyushu since the late first millennium BC, can only be grown on a small percentage of the island land mass, given the lack of extensive alluvium and the predominance of mountainous or thin limestone coral soils. Summer storms drastically affect the harvesting of summer crops. Currently it is thought that only with substantial migration from the Japanese main islands were Okinawans pushed into cereal cultivation. Were the islanders pushed aside by incoming farmers, or did they imitate the new immigrants whose presence is confirmed by skeletal similarities of Gusuku Period populations to main island Japanese?

How did they adapt their cultivation systems to the subtropical islands and coral-derived soils? Is it possible that some aspects of the agricultural systems are in fact Chinese? In Chapters 6 and 8 the evidence for early direct trade with south China is discussed.

Although we may know the dates of occurrence of cultivated cereals in some sites in the Ryukyus, we still have little information concerning the processes of adoption. How long was the period of investment in land clearance and stabilization of the cultivation systems? Can stages in the adoption be seen in temporal spreads of dates on different sites, and can the arrival of groups from the Japanese main islands be discerned in diverse artifact assemblages or settlement types? What is the relationship of cultivation to the raising of livestock in addition to pigs, such as cattle, horses, and domesticated fowl?

Ryukyu islanders lived in low population densities on gathered and processed resources for a long time, as did other islanders, as described in Chapter 10. The cultivation systems of the Ryukyus were the composite and changing outcomes of inputs from various sources and local adaptive processes. In Chapter 7, the fundamental changes brought about by the adoption of cultivation are discussed.

Chapter 6

Exchange Networks and the Lure of Tropical Shells

In the previous two chapters I have discussed the arrival of Holocene populations in the Ryukyus and the subsistence patterns of the Shellmound Period. In this chapter I discuss another aspect of Ryukyu prehistory, the development of exchange systems in the Amami and Okinawa Islands. This is a topic of general interest in island archaeology. The exchange systems discussed here occurred from about 2,600 years ago to as late as 700 years ago.

In the first millennium BC islanders retained their subsistence pattern of hunting and gathering, while huge changes occurred in Kyushu and the other main islands of Japan. Immigrants from the Korean Peninsula to Kyushu introduced the Yayoi Culture (1000 BC to AD 250), a new way of life based on intensive rice cultivation, along with radically different styles of artifacts. Yayoi immigrants are thought to have brought the ancestral form of the Japanese language to the Japanese islands (Hudson 1999, 83–93). In northern Kyushu Yayoi people lived in fortified villages, dominated by chiefs who were buried in separate cemeteries with rare grave goods including bronze mirrors and weapons, and glass beads. The site of Yoshinogari, Saga Prefecture, is a good example of a Yayoi center in Kyushu (Hudson and Barnes 1991). The Yayoi Period was succeeded by the Kofun Period (AD 250 to 600), during which society became more hierarchical and approached the level of state organization. Although the Ryukyu islanders lived in a world largely unaffected by these fundamental changes, they were in constant contact with the Japanese main islands through systems of exchange discussed in this chapter, and their simple hand-built pottery shows Yayoi influences in the constricted foot and rim decoration. A set of pottery types found in the Amami and Okinawa Islands, which parallels the pottery types of the Yayoi and Kofun Periods, has been worked out by Shinzato Takayuki (1999).

Since tropical shells were a dramatic part of these exchange systems, they will be discussed first, followed by pottery and other artifacts. It is important to note that the exchange systems were much broader in their scope than simply the movement of shells.

Stages of Shell Exchange

The coral reefs of the Okinawa and Amami Islands produce a variety of tropical shells that were prized items in the Japanese main islands and parts of East Asia from about 600 BC to at least AD 1200. The shell exchange tied together dynamically changing communities of trading partners. The shell species that were exchanged and the communities that received them as well as the uses of the shells and their social context constantly changed. The exchange joined different temperate and subtropical ecological zones, each with distinctive resources desired by the other (Kinoshita 2005). The shells that were traded were mostly large gastropods with unusual white or orange coloring. To the elite of Kyushu, they may have embodied a relationship with a southern, tropical, "other."

Kinoshita Naoko (2009a) has proposed four stages of exchange of Ryukyu shells. In 2003 she organized an international research team to explore the use of shell ornaments in China and to test the hypothesis of an even earlier stage of exchange (Kinoshita 2003a), but the hypothesis was not supported by malacological data. At that time she hypothesized that abundant cowrie shells, particularly *Cypraea moneta,* especially abundant in the Shang dynasty of north China but also found in sites from various time periods, were collected from the Ryukyus by traders from China. Such contact would explain the development of Okinawan bone ornaments decorated with bilaterally symmetrical motifs not found in the Jōmon or Yayoi cultures of the Japanese main islands. Dating to the first and second millennia BC, these artifacts have always been a puzzle in Okinawan archaeology. However, in a detailed review of the types of shells found in Chinese sites and the most common types found in the reefs of the Ryukyus, Kurozumi (2003, 20) concluded that the Ryukyus were not the source for these shells. He found that several *Cypraea* species very common in the Ryukyus are completely absent from the Chinese sites, whereas others that are rare in the Ryukyus are much more common in areas such as southern China, mainland Southeast Asia, or the Penghu Islands of the Taiwan Strait. These are the most likely sources for the cowrie shells that were prized as currency and ornaments in ancient China. There is no conclusive artifactual evidence of direct contact between China and the Ryukyus in the second and first millennia BC, and the origins of Okinawan zoomorphic ornaments are still unclear.

TABLE 6.1 Four Stages of Shell Exchange

Stage	*Main Shells for Trade*	*Use*	*Major Consumer*	*Major Supplier*	*Traders*
first stage: Yayoi Period, sixth century BC to third century AD	broad Pacific conch (*Strombus latissimus*), *Strombus therites,* and lettered cone (*Conus litteratus*)	bracelets	main islands of Japan	Okinawa Islands	coastal people of Kyushu and Amami islanders
second stage: Kofun Period, third to seventh centuries AD	*Strombus therites*, Chiragra spider conch (*Harpago chiragra*), and *Conus litteratus*	prestige goods, horse trappings	main islands of Japan, Korean Peninsula	Okinawa Islands	coastal people of Kyushu and Amami islanders
third stage: Ancient (*kodai*) Period, seventh to ninth centuries AD	great green turban (*Turbo marmoratus*)	material for mother-of-pearl inlay	main islands of Japan or China	Amami and Okinawa Islands	Kyushu traders? Amami islanders? Chinese traders?
fourth stage: Ancient and Mediaeval Periods, ninth to fifteenth centuries AD	*Turbo marmoratus*, conch shells	material for mother-of-pearl inlay and conch shell trumpets	main islands of Japan	Amami and Okinawa Islands	Japanese traders

Source: After Kinoshita 2009a, 34.

Although an early exchange of cowrie shells could not be confirmed, the evidence for four stages of active exchange of shells between the Okinawa and Amami Islands and Japan, Korea, and China is extensive (Kinoshita 1996; 2005; 2009a, 34) (Table 6.1). Since Kinoshita has recently summarized her findings in English (Kinoshita 2009a), my treatment will focus only on the major points. It is important to note that the dating of the Yayoi Period has recently been revised to match calibrated AMS dates (Ōnuki 2005). Although some archaeologists still have questions about the revised chronology, Kinoshita has adopted it: (Earliest Yayoi, 1000 to 800 BC; Early Yayoi, 800 to 450 BC; Middle Yayoi, 450 BC to AD 50; Late Yayoi, AD 50 AD to 250).

What was the role of the Ryukyu islanders in the shell exchange? Caches of shells, some of which had been perforated both for stringing and for the initial stages of bracelet making, have been found in sites such as Ohara Locality A, Kumejima, and Furuzamami and Atta II, Okinawa Island. Judging from the absence of Ryukyu pottery or stone tools in Kyushu, it seems clear that traders from Kyushu traveled to the Central Ryukyus to secure the shells and finished the production of bracelets in Kyushu.

Stage 1: Yayoi Period

While the Yayoi Period lasted from the tenth century BC to the third century AD, the exchange began around the sixth century BC. Yayoi Period trading partners were people of northern Kyushu, and bracelets were produced from broad Pacific conch (*Tricornis latissimus*, also known as *Strombus latissimus*), lettered cone (*Conus litteratus*), and true limpet (*Penepatella* sp.) (Figure 6.1). Although some bracelets of limpets from the cooler waters of the northern Ryukyus were used by Jōmon populations, it can be said that the use in Japan of tropical shells from the Ryukyus began in the Yayoi Period.

As indicated in Chapter 4, the presence of Kyushu obsidian and Ichiki Type pottery in Okinawan sites of the Final Jōmon Period indicates contact between Kyushu and the Ryukyus. Kinoshita proposes that such contact led to familiarity with the tropical shells of the Ryukyus among the people of Kyushu and that beginning in the Yayoi Period these shells were fashioned into bracelets to imitate continental bronze and jade bracelets used by elites in sites such as the Lelang commandery near Pyongyang, North Korea (2009a, 19). Kinoshita notes that the hard, dense white shell from the large gastropods resembled white jade, prized in China (1996, 533–539). While the islanders may have wished to imitate jade, I also think it is likely that Kyushu and Ryukyu peoples adopted distinctive materials and motifs to distinguish themselves from their continental contemporaries. Kinoshita (2009a, 22) states that at present there

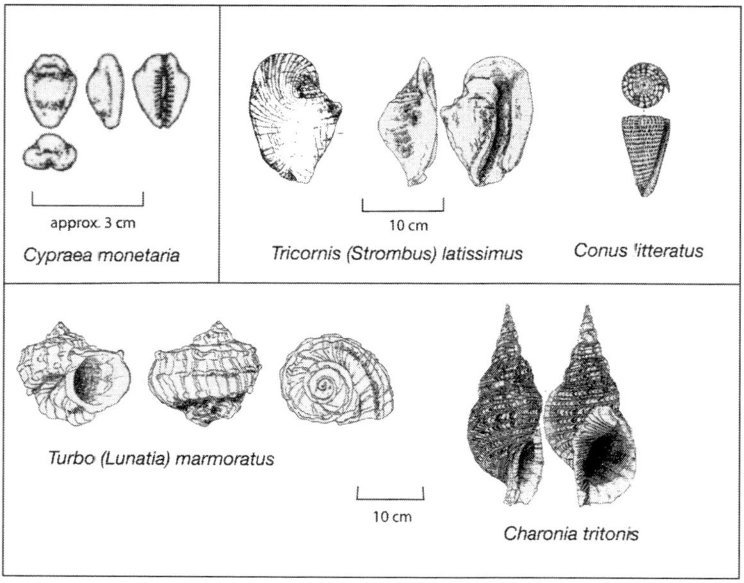

Figure 6.1. Shells of the Central Ryukyus important in exchange systems. Adapted from Kinoshita 2003a. Courtesy of Kinoshita Naoko.

are records of fifty-five sites containing 671 tropical shell bracelets from the Yayoi Period. From a small sample of Yayoi burials examined in 1990, I found that, in general, grave goods of any sort are quite rare. A small group of elite persons were buried with shell bracelets, and within this group a small group also had bronze daggers, Chinese Han dynasty bronze mirrors, iron halberds, or glass beads (Pearson 1990).

Although bracelets of univalve shells were used occasionally by Jōmon people, the first Yayoi people to use them were the semiagricultural inhabitants of the Gotō Islands near Kyushu, who used bracelets of univalve limpets as grave goods in their Korean-style cist graves (Kinoshita 2010, 69). The bracelets are an important aspect of social interaction extending from the Korean Peninsula to Kyushu and the Ryukyus. In the Early Yayoi Period the use of bracelets spread from the coastal inhabitants of north Kyushu to agricultural people on the alluvial plains. It has been proposed by Takakura (1981) that bronze weapons and mirrors in Yayoi burials signified persons with political prestige, while shell bracelets were worn by religious practitioners. In northern and central Kyushu different styles of *Tricornis* bracelets were produced (Figure 6.2).

The basic method of manufacture was to slice a bracelet blank from the bulging dorsal side of the shell. In the Kanenokuma and Doigahama Types of the

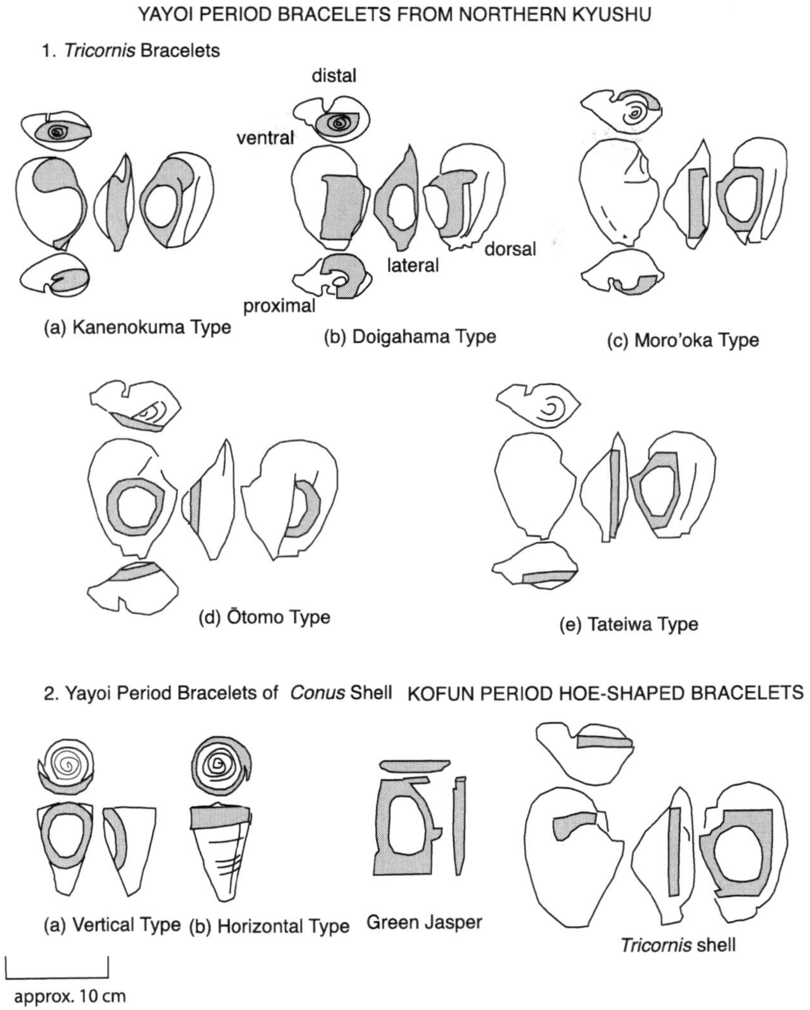

Figure 6.2. Types of bracelets, fashioned from Ryukyu shells, recovered from Kyushu sites. The shaded area indicates the finished bracelet after it was cut from the original shell. Redrawn from Kinoshita 1996, 34, 35, 255, 257. Courtesy of Kinoshita Naoko.

Early Yayoi Period, the bracelets are thick and three-dimensional. In the former, a substantial portion of the shell was retained, to make a spoonlike protuberance. In later types such as Moro'oka and Ōtomo, the bracelet was flatter. In the Tateiwa Type, a flat, angular shape was created by trimming away more of the shell and retaining a hooklike projection of the shell spiral. The flatter bracelets could be worn in greater numbers, the maximum being fourteen on the forearm of a male buried in Burial No. 34 of the Tateiwa Site, Fukuoka (Tateiwa Iseki Chōsa Iinkai 1977, 77). *Conus* shells could be cut vertically or sliced horizontally to produce bracelets (Okinawa Ken 2001, 18–19).

In the Middle Yayoi Period, the people of the Okinawa Islands no longer exported unprocessed raw shells but produced semiprocessed shell bracelets, made by piercing a hole in the surface of the broad Pacific conch, which could be enlarged to fit the wrist of the wearer. The bracelets were finished in Kyushu. There are many questions regarding the nature of the goods offered in exchange by people from Kyushu. Kinoshita notes that small quantities of continental metal artifacts (sometimes fragmentary), glass beads, jade ornaments, and even several Goshusen (Chinese Wushuqian) coins have been found in the Ryukyus. These coins were minted around the beginning of the Common Era and again in the Sui dynasty (AD 581 to 618). Although it has been proposed that the Ryukyu finds are of the latter type (Zaidan 2003, 227–230), more research is needed on this point. They have been found in several sites on Kumejima and also on the Yomitan Peninsula of Okinawajima. Yayoi pottery, primarily storage vessels from both northern and southern Kyushu, appear to be the chief items of exchange. These probably contained rice and beans and special kinds of rice wine. Such food materials must have been ceremonial offerings since generally, in exchange systems, valuables are exchanged for valuables rather than staples. Knife-shaped coins termed Meitōsen (Chinese Mingdaoqian) of the Chinese Yan Kingdom of northeast China, which flourished in the Warring States Period (403 to 221 BC), have been found in the Gusukudake Shellmound, Naha, and in a cave deposit near the Gushichan Gusuku Site, southern Okinawajima (Tōma Shi'ichi 1997). Early coins discussed in this section are shown in Figure 6.3.

Stone cist graves, similar to the type used by coastal Yayoi people of Kyushu, have been found on Tokarajima, Tokunoshima, and Okinawajima. At the Momenbaru Site, Okinawajima, seven cist coffins made of coral slabs with coral rubble spread in the bottom contained dorsal, extended burials. In four coffins there were thirteen individuals (Takemoto and Asato 1993, 121), buried serially. A single *Tridacna* shell was placed at the head of one individual and at the foot of another. Other grave goods were jade beads. Offerings of Yayoi pottery from Kyushu, dating from the end of Early Yayoi to Middle Yayoi, were placed outside the coffins. Those who were buried in stone cists made of coral showed physical characteristics of both Ryukyu islanders and Yayoi coastal people (Matsushita 2003). Recently a similar cistlike coffin was found in the Bugeidō Cave, Nanjō City, southern Okinawajima (Okinawa Kenritsu Hakubutsukan 2010).

At the Tomachin Site on the southern coast of Tokunoshima, another burial site apparently used for several generations consisted of cist burials fashioned from coral with later burials placed on top of them. They date from Latest Jōmon

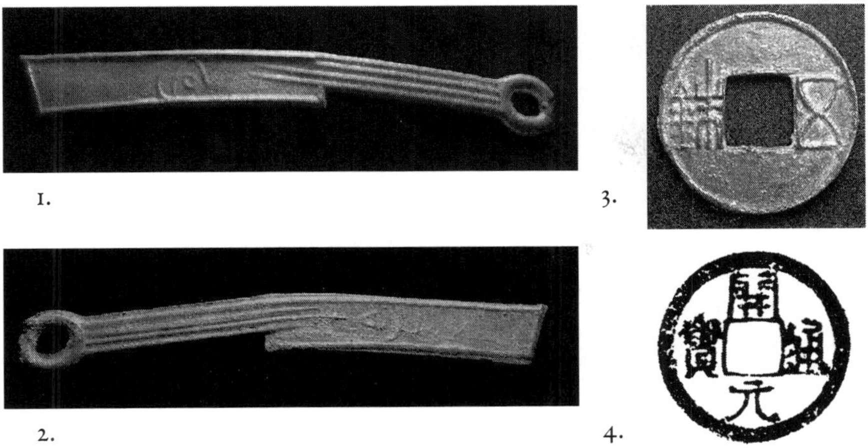

Figure 6.3. Examples of the earliest types of Chinese coins found in Ryukyu sites. (1, 2) *Meitōsen* knife-shaped coin (private collection, not from Okinawa, photo R. Pearson), converse, obverse. (3) Goshu coin (private collection, not from Okinawa, R. Pearson photo). (4) Kaigen Tsūhō coin from the Sakieda Akasaki Site, Ishigakijima. Diameter approximately 2.5 cm. From Ishigaki Shi Kyōiku Iinkai 1987, 63. Courtesy of Ishigaki Shi Kyōiku Iinkai.

to Early Yayoi. Grave goods in the upper portion of one of the burials consisted of jade beads from Itoigawa, Niigata Prefecture, Japanese main islands; *Tricornis* shell bracelets; a pointed tool of *Charonia* shell; fossil gastropods; and fragments of *Turbo* shell. They may have constituted a collective offering (Shinzato Takayuki 2007; 2008a; 2011; 2012).

Kinoshita states that Yayoi coastal people voyaged to Okinawa, selected and stored shells, and brought the shells back to northern Kyushu, stopping at transit villages on the Satsuma Peninsula of southern Kyushu. They intermarried with Okinawan villagers (2009a, 28). She divides Yayoi shell bracelet exchange into two substages, 1 and 2. In substage 1 coastal people of northern Kyushu conducted the exchange, whereas in substage 2 people conducting the exchange lived near the bays of Ariake and Yatsushiro and in southern Kyushu, as indicated by the types of pottery found in Okinawa, which were from the latter area. In addition, the presence of ceramics from the Amami Islands suggests that Amami islanders were transporting shells within the Ryukyus.

A study of trade goods including pottery from Kyushu and the Amami Islands, bronze arrowheads and mirrors, iron adzes, glass beads, Goshu Chinese coins, iron ore, Yayoi-type flat stone adzes, and an iron awl, along with features such as shell caches and stone cist burials, shows that the shell exchange is part of a larger system (Shinzato Takayuki 2001). Although the Goshu coins may date to the sixth century AD, as mentioned previously, the other artifacts show important trends. Shinzato Takayuki tabulated the presence/absence and mapped the distribution of these artifacts from sixty-seven sites in the Okinawa Islands (2001, 57–58). He found that pottery from southern Kyushu peaked in the Okinawa Islands at the time of the Middle Yayoi Period (450 BC to AD 50), whereas Amami types of pottery peaked in the time period of the Late Yayoi Period (AD 50 to 250), suggesting that first Kyushu people and later Amami people participated in the exchange. The predominance of wide- and narrow-mouth jars (containers) suggests that Yayoi and Amami people may have brought goods and stayed in central villages, perhaps seasonally. A few sites on Okinawa-jima, Kumejima, and Iejima have yielded most of the exotic artifacts, along with shell caches and stone cist burials.

Takayuki Shinzato's study (2003) of the distribution of Okinawan sites in the time period 300 BC to AD 300 shows that goods from Japan and Kyushu including Yayoi pottery cluster in distribution centers. These distribution centers, termed Rank I settlements, are regularly spaced and located at places advantageous to trading communication routes. Cist graves occur in these centers, indicating the presence of people with special social status. Rank II settlements have substantial amounts of exotic ceramics, suggesting that they were also involved in the exchange, whereas Rank III settlements have few imported objects. Shinzato concluded that "powerful local groups based in Rank I settlements collected and processed large shells at surrounding Rank III settlements and then conducted trade at Rank II settlements with shells exchanged for cereals in pots, rice wine, and nonceramic items" (Takayuki Shinzato 2003, 79). Major centers occurred in the Motobu area and Iejima (Ufudōbaru, Gushiken, and Gushibaru Sites), Yomitan (Nakagawabaru and Momenbaru), Uken (Uken Site) and Kumejima (Ōhara and Shimizu Sites). It seems most likely that there was an exchange system among the Ryukyu sites themselves (Shinzato Takayuki 1999). Caches of *Conus* and *Tricornis* shells have been found in some thirty-two sites in the Okinawa Islands. The shells were probably buried until the dead animal inhabiting the shell decomposed and the shells could be assembled for transport. Kinoshita's scenario that the shells were gathered and stored by outsiders seems unlikely in the light of the wide distribution of buried caches in many small sites, as shown in Shinzato's analysis.

Stage 2: Kofun Period

Ryukyu shells were important prestige items in the Kofun Period (AD 250 to 600 AD), and in the Late Kofun Period (AD 500 to 600 AD) the circular portion of the lettered cone shell (*Conus litteratus*) was used to make disk-shaped ornaments for saddles and horse trappings in both western Japan and Korea, and also for shell decorations in the Northern Ryukyus. Bracelets were also made from *Tricornis*. A stylized type with the shape of a stone hoe (*kuwa*) has been termed the hoe-shaped bracelet. Highly polished stone versions of green jasper are found in western Honshu (see Figure 6.2 above). The Chiragra spider conch (*Lambis*), native to the Ryukyus, was used for bracelets in the Kanto area and is the prototype of the *tomoegata* bronze whorl-shape decoration found in the Yayoi and Kofun Periods (Pearson 1990, fig. 2). The protuberances of this shell were used as chisels by prehistoric people in the Central and Southern Ryukyus (Katō 2010).

THE HIROTA SITE, TANEGASHIMA

The Hirota Site, Tanegashima, the center for production of shell ornaments sewn on garments and placed on burials, dates from the Late Yayoi to the Kofun Period (third to seventh centuries AD) (Hirota Iseki 2003). The dating of the site is extremely important since it is too late for its occupants to have played a role in Stage 1 exchange, as I proposed in 1990 (Pearson 1990), before the publication of the final site report. The exact role of Tanegashima in Ryukyu exchange systems deserves further research. The site is situated at the extreme northern boundary of the coral reef zone. A total of ninety burials containing 157 individuals were recovered from sand dunes formed in the Yayoi Period and later. They were exposed in a typhoon in 1955, and excavations took place from 1957 to 1959. Survey in 2005 and 2006 revealed more burial areas within the dune (Ishidō and Tokuda 2007). Osteological analysis showed that the population of the Hirota site had slender limbs and low stature, and was close to Jōmon and divergent from Kyushu Yayoi populations. Tooth extraction, the artificial removal of maxillary incisors and canines, was practiced by 85 percent of the individuals.

The Hirota Site is unique for the large quantity of shell bracelets, plaques, and beads. Ishidō and Tokuda (2007) set the total at over 44,000 objects. Kinoshita (2003d) grouped the shell ornaments into two classes: A (termed the Lower Layer Type), perforated, and B (termed the Upper Layer Type), unperforated. A Type artifacts were worn singly or in groups and appear to have been applied to garments. They are almost exclusively found in the lower layer. B Type ornaments were placed on the corpse. They are almost exclusively found in the upper layer. Of the total of 550 plaques from the Hirota Site, A Type comprised 20 percent; B Type, 79 percent; and others, 1 percent. In the lower layer, A Type comprises 96 percent of all plaques. Shell bracelets were the most common shell artifact in the lower layer, whereas shell plaques predominate in the upper layer. Some Hirota shell bracelets from the upper layer are very thick, utilizing the whole *Tricornis* shell, with the dorsal bulge and ventral lip areas removed. The steep sides of the shell are incised with symmetrical patterns. The majority, however, are relatively flat and circular. The shell plaques were made of lettered cone shell, either from the round, flat "end" or from the side of the shell.

Within the lower-layer burials there are older (Late Yayoi to Early Kofun) and younger (Middle Kofun, fifth century AD) stages. Some of the burials of the lower layer were marked by coral chunks above the grave pit; others had a horseshoe-shaped arc of coral chunks around part of the pit; and the remainder were unmarked. Burial 2 in Area DIII, an adult male, an example of a lower-layer burial, is set in an enclosure of stones, in dorsal position, with legs crossed and arms crossed over the chest (Hirota Iseki 2003, 180) (Figure 6.4a). The body was covered with beads fashioned from *Conus* shells and several species of slender, pointed *Dentalium*. Type A shell plaques, which are distinguished by their perforation, and dragon pendants were placed near the head and waist, and a group of seven large *Dentalium* beads were placed near the top of the head. There were a total of 9 shell plaques, 24 dragon pendants, 115 beads of shells such as *Dentalium* and *Pusiostoma,* and 6,000 *Conus* beads. A unique aspect of Ryukyu shell beads is the utilization of the column of gastropods such as small cone shells, cutting them laterally, to make use of the natural hole in the center of the column. The cone shells are often degraded by wave action so that only the column remains (Kinoshita 2003c, 238).

The upper layers, dating to the sixth and seventh centuries AD, contained burned bones and groups of bones in secondary burials. Secondary burials, each consisting of two or more individuals buried together, were found within stone enclosures approximately 7 m long. Cranial and long bones were carefully arranged, along with shell bracelets, plaques, and pendants as grave goods. Below these groups of bones there was a layer of bones 20 to 30 cm thick, lying on a layer of stones. In a middle layer that did not extend through the whole site, and also in the lower layer, there were individual burials in pits. Burial 15, Area D, is an example of a secondary burial of the upper layer (Hirota Iseki 2003, 110–112) (Figure 6.4b). The cranium faces northwest. At the left hand there are thirteen Upper Layer Type (unperforated) plaques; at the head, a glass bead; and at the left hand, one glass bead. One shell bracelet was found separated from the body, and in the area of the upper body there were five beads of *Conus* shell.

Although Hirota-type shell plaques, pendants, and bracelets have been found in a total of thirty-six sites from Tanegashima to Okinawajima, for every type of artifact, 88 percent or more of the total sample is found in the Hirota Site. In no other site are the artifacts associated with burials, their quantity and context being completely different from the Hirota situation. Within the Hirota Site, Kinoshita (2003c, 354) found that the type of shell material used for artifacts

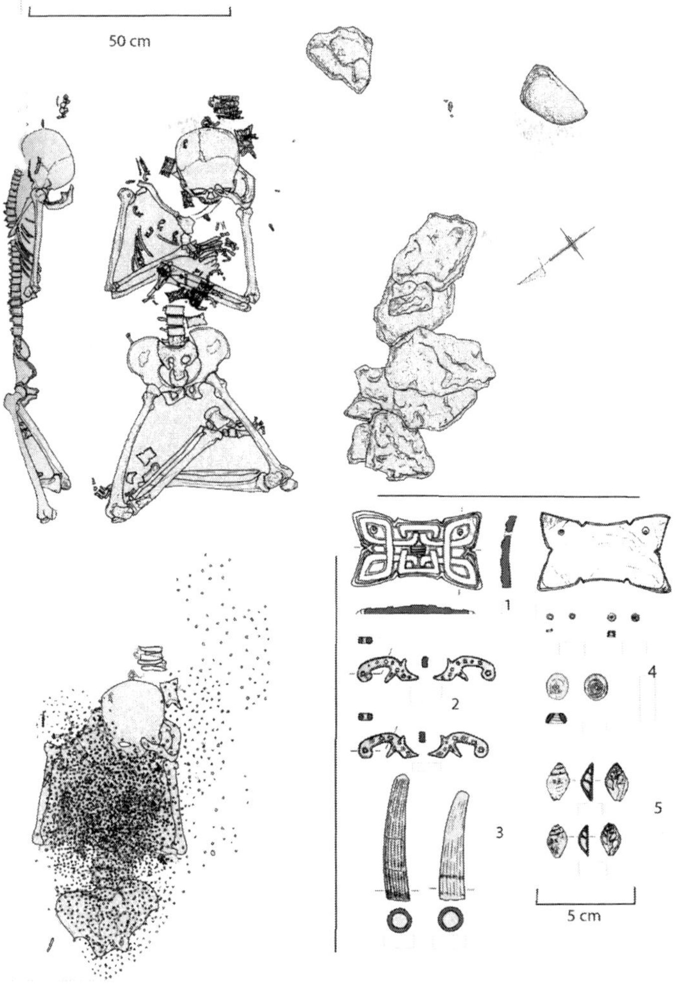

Figure 6.4 (a). Burial DIII2, Hirota Site: Early Period. Rectangular shell plaques (1) of the Early Type can be seen in the area of the head and chest. Shell dragon-shape pendants (2) appear around the upper body. *Dentalium* shells (3) were placed above the head. The burial was covered with shell beads (4, 5). Adapted from Hirota Iseki 2003, 181 (figure 108). Courtesy of Professor Kanaseki Hiroshi and Kagoshima Kenritsu Rekishi Shiryō Sentā Reimeikan.

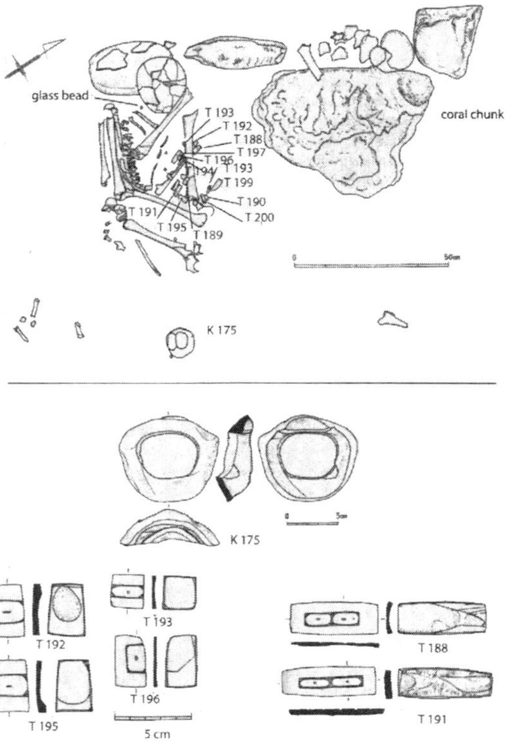

Figure 6.4 (b). Burial D15, Hirota Site: Late Period. Artifacts T188–T200 are Late Type shell plaques. T188–T193 are illustrated. K175 is a *Tricornis* shell bracelet. Adapted from Hirota Iseki 2003, 111 (figure 61). Courtesy of Kanaseki Hiroshi and Kagoshima Kenritsu Rekishi Shiryō Sentā Reimeikan.

changed from the lower layer to the upper layer. In the lower layer, earlier stage, the shells that were used came predominantly from Amami Ōshima and the islands to the north, whereas in the lower layer shell materials from Okinawajima increase, indicating a deepening relation with the Central Ryukyus (ibid.). The bilaterally symmetrical form of the decoration as well as the arrangement of the motifs inside a lozenge pattern are not found in Jōmon or Yayoi decoration, suggesting to earlier writers that there must have been contact with coastal China. Kokubu proposed that the motifs on the shell plaques were derived from Chinese jades and bronzes (1972, 371–385). These plaques along with the butterfly-shape objects from sites such as Sachihijah and animal forms were thought to be part of a Nanyō Suijin Shakai (Southern Maritime Society) derived from coastal south China. Parallels with Han dynasty decorative pieces may occur, but these have not yet been worked out.

Up to 2003 shell plaques were known from a total of thirty-six sites in the Ryukyu Islands, including Hirota. Shell plaques of the Upper Layer Type are more frequent than plaques of the Lower Layer Type. The northern limit of distribution is Tanegashima, while the southern limit is Kumejima. The Hirota people received shells from the Amami and Okinawa regions, since the seas surrounding Tanegashima were not warm enough to support the preferred species. They may have had their own collecting areas, such as Iejima and Kumejima, which were separate from the main routes to Kyushu, judging from finds of Hirota-style shell plaques on these islands (Kinoshita 1996, 537). In addition, they made thin, circular bracelets of the limpet shell (*Penepatella* sp.), which was available locally. Hashimoto found that the production of raw and semiprocessed shells in Okinawa increased after the consumption of bracelets in northern Kyushu declined, as Okinawans shifted their production to other consumers, such as the people of Tanegashima (Hashimoto Mika, 2010).

Stage 3

In Stage 3 (seventh to ninth centuries AD) exchange focused on a different species, the great green turban shell, *Turbo marmoratus*. The *Turbo* shell was used in at least four different ways. Their stonelike "lid" (operculum), the thick disklike cover for the aperture, was chipped along its edges to make a scraping tool. The meat was eaten, judging from disposal patterns on some sites. The shell was used to fashion ladlelike spoons, which are found in the Amami and Okinawa Islands, and *Turbo* shell was used for shell inlay in China and Japan.

Turbo shells were traded for iron goods (Takanashi 2005). Kinoshita dates this trade to the seventh to ninth centuries, stating that at this time exchange with Yamato was declining. According to Kinoshita (2009a), the motive of tributary delegations to Yamato in the eighth century was to request increased exchange. Yamazato (2010) states that the delegation of some two hundred members probably went to Dazaifu, as the official port of Yamato.

Historical and archaeological materials give different impressions of the ancient society of the Ryukyus at the time of the *Turbo* trade. The historical sources mention delegations from the Northern Ryukyus and their submission of tribute to Yamato, implying a relatively high level of social complexity, while the archaeological sources give the impression of simple hunting and gathering societies of the Late Shellmound Period (Nakayama 2008). The archaeological picture seems like a "black box" in which there is little detailed information on the social and political life of the islanders. Asato Susumu (2010) has proposed that the *Turbo* shell trade was regulated by chiefs who were linked in a regional network that was above the level of villages. He concluded that because there are two clusters of *Turbo* shell processing sites, with five sites in northern Amami Ōshima and two sites on Kumejima, the shell material was traded to both Japan and China, not just to Japan. He proposes that traders from Fujian, particularly the Quanzhou area, may have been involved in shell trade to secure mother-of-pearl in the Tang period (AD 618 to 906). As mentioned in Chapter 5, Watanobe et al. (2002, 230) discovered a subgroup of suid bones on Kumejima that may have been introduced from the Asian continent.

The external trade in *Turbo* shell probably linked the Ryukyus and China in the seventh to ninth centuries AD (Kinoshita 2006), judging from the distribution of Tang dynasty Kaigen Tsūhō coins in the Ryukyus without Japanese coins, which should have been present if Japan was linked at the same time period. A total of 36 coins have been found in eight sites in the Okinawa Islands, and 28 coins have been found in two sites in Yaeyama. The Sakieda Akasaki Site of Ishigakijima yielded a cache of 27 coins (Ishigaki Shi 1987; Zaidan 2003, 229). (The same disturbed layer yielded a substantial sample of large stone adzes.) While some authors believe that the coins were brought by traders from south China, others believe that they were brought from Hakata. It has also been suggested that they might have been brought on ships of the *kentōshi* tribute missions from Yamato to China (Zaidan 2003, 230). The earliest date of minting of the type of Kaigen Tsūhō found in the Sakieda Akasaki Site is AD 713 (Ishigaki Shi 1987, 12).

Takanashi (2005; 2010) stresses the northward trade from Amami to the Japanese main islands. Contending that since Japan did not use *Turbo* shell for inlay until the ninth century AD, Yoshinari (2010) states the processing sites dated to the seventh and eighth centuries must have been for the production of shell spoons for local consumption. The collection of *Turbo* shells in Stage 3 appears to have been centered on the Amami Islands. Many aspects of this exchange system remain unclear. The production of spoons from *Turbo* shells was directed to internal consumption within the Ryukyus, with few exceptions. How did this exchange operate? What was the function of these shells in Ryukyu society? If the working of *Turbo* shell for mother-of-pearl inlay in Japan did not begin until the late eighth century AD, how was earlier exchange with China conducted?

Stage 4

Later, in Stage 4 (ninth to fifteenth centuries AD), direct exchange of *Turbo* shell with Japan began when the use of mother-of-pearl for decoration developed in Japan (Yoshinari 2010; Takanashi 2010). In the final years of the eighth century, Japanese adopted Chinese shell inlay techniques and began to produce their own objects. Immediately before that time they imported large *Turbo* shells and objects inlaid with *Turbo* mother-of-pearl from China. According to Kinoshita (2009b), the spread of the new techniques and a deepened appreciation for inlay is associated with the enormous artistic production surrounding the festivities at the Tōdaiji Temple, Nara, in AD 752. The Gusuku Site Group of Kikaigashima must have been involved in *Turbo* trade, although it is difficult to determine its exact role from available evidence. It is discussed in Chapter 7. The *Turbo* trade had a huge impact on the trade systems of the Early Gusuku Period because it was their immediate antecedent (Asato Susumu 2003b; 2010).

The Matsunoto Site, a sand dune site adjacent to the seashore on the Kasari Peninsula of Amami Ōshima (Nakayama 2008; Kasari Chō Kyōiku Iinkai 2006), is a typical shell processing site of Stage 4. It has been dated through stylistic analysis of Kaneku Type pottery. Worked and natural *Turbo* shells are abundant. Huge amounts of shells must have been carried away for inlay material, the remaining shells being the remains of manufacture of shell spoons and consumption of meat for food. Large shells were cut for making shell spoons, while the animals of smaller shells were eaten for food. Iron and copper tools as well as red earthenware from Kyushu *(hajiki)* were found.

Trading networks along the Japan Sea have existed for several millennia, judging from finds in Okinawa of Itoigawa jade from Niigata mentioned in Chapter 4 and objects made of Ryukyu shells found in the Usu Moshiri site of Hokkaido, dating to the first few centuries AD (Zaidan 2003, 220). In November 2011 I observed that *Turbo* shell inlay was used for the base of the main Amida figure in the Byōdōin, Uji, Kyoto, and cut shell was used in ornaments suspended from the ceiling above the figure, now in the Byōdōin Museum. Many examples of *Turbo* inlay appear on Heian artifacts such as saddles, chests, and mirrors. The decoration of the twelfth century AD mortuary temple of the Ōshū Fujiwara clan, the Konjikidō of Hiraizumi, northern Japan, required huge amounts of mother-of-pearl (Yiengpruksawan 1998), which must have come from the Ryukyus. Only one small portion of each shell could be used for inlay (Takanashi 2008c, 220); therefore, the extensive decoration found in the Konjikidō must have required many shells. At the same time, triton shell, *Charonia tritonis,* was used for trumpets in Buddhist temples. In the thirteenth to fourteenth centuries AD, abalone shell from cold northern waters superseded *Turbo* for inlay in Japan, but some shell was still employed. Advanced techniques used much thinner pieces than previously (Nakazato 1995; Takanashi 2008c, 220). While Song dynasty Chinese and Koryo Korean artisans adopted the use of abalone, I believe that the opaque creamy quality of *Turbo* inlay, which is different from the bluish iridescent glitter of abalone, can be seen in some Chinese Yuan dynasty pieces in Western museums.

Conclusions

In the prehistoric exchange systems linking Kyushu, Amami, and Okinawa, raw materials, semiprocessed ornaments, and finished goods were circulated. Exchange systems spanning several millennia began as infrequent down-the-line exchange of obsidian and nephrite. Intensive research on the archaeology of the shell route has revealed a complex pattern of social networks linking the Amami and Okinawa Islands to several parts of Kyushu and to China (in the exchange of *Turbo* shell). Networks within the Northern and Central Ryukyus were employed in the harvesting and distribution of shells for exchange. Kinoshita's research indicates that groups came not only from the center of Yayoi power in northern Kyushu, but also from the Ariake area. Judging from the diffusion of the practice of Yayoi cist coffin burial from northern Kyushu and anthropometric data, some people from Kyushu lived in Okinawa. The Kyushu trading groups who transported the shells built up navigational expertise based on the voyaging of Jōmon peoples. Shinzato's work on site multifunctionality cited above (Shinzato Takayuki 2003) confirms that Ryukyu islanders played an active role in the exchange, harvesting the shells, cleaning and storing them, and perforating the shells for stringing and initial bracelet manufacture. Pottery styles of Amami were influenced by those of southern Kyushu, whereas Okinawan styles were not greatly affected (Kinoshita 2005). Amami people may have been intermediaries in the exchange since their northerly reefs were less productive than the reefs of Okinawa. Kinoshita has noted that the shell exchange was important for bringing iron goods to Okinawa. A hierarchy of sites in distribution networks and preferential burial treatment indicates the presence of social ranking. The shell exchange systems involved goods transported in distinctive social arrangements. While shell bracelets moved north and Yayoi pottery moved south in Stage 1, it is not clear that they were part of a reciprocal exchange; Shinzato Takayuki states that they are types from southern Kyushu, rather than northern Kyushu, the destination of most of the bracelets. Nevertheless, they are considered to be containers for imported goods (Shinzato 2003) such as wine or food. The longest distances were covered by the Yayoi traders of Kinoshita's Stage 1, who traveled from northern Kyushu to Okinawa to secure *Tricornis* shells, said to be more abundant in Okinawa, where the reefs are wider and the large gastropods are more abundant than in Amami. Yayoi pottery is much more abundant in the Okinawa Islands than in the Amami Islands. It should be noted that the latter have undergone fewer excavations. Nevertheless, the center of gravity for the trade of *Turbo* shell appears to be the Amami Islands. Later trade of *Turbo* and *Charonia* shells probably involved government agents resident on Kikaigashima, as mentioned in Chapter 7.

Unlike some islanders of western Melanesia who occupied coastal or offshore islands that are extremely marginal (Kirch 1991, 155), Ryukyu traders do not seem to have become dependent on exchange for food products. However, once again the introduction of domesticated pigs from Kyushu into the Amami and

Okinawa Islands must be considered. They may have been an important item in the "Shell Route."

In the Late Yayoi and Early Kofun Periods (Stage 2), when cone shells were used for decorative plaques, the Hirota area of Tanegashima, in the Northern Ryukyus, became a center for the production of the distinctive shell ornaments. The Hirota Site is a cemetery; the workshop for ornament production has not yet been found. Hirota shell ornaments have been found in some sites in the Okinawa Islands but not in burials. Hirota clearly occupies a special place as a kind of ritual center and was probably important as a link in the shipment of shells along the eastern coast of Kyushu, to the Inland Sea and beyond. While the report of the Hirota burial site excavations of the 1950s was finally published in 2003 (Hirota Iseki 2003), the reporting was concerned with preserving the record of the complex stratigraphy of the site. We know nothing about the subsistence or social life of its inhabitants. Did the people of Hirota constitute an enclave isolated from the major exchange routes extending from northern Kyushu to Okinawa? Why did they produce such distinctive ornaments, and why in the sixth and seventh centuries AD did their unique shell burial plaques circulate in the central Ryukyus? Was their mortuary culture, which lasted for some five hundred years, a sign of a ritual center? There is much more to be learned about Hirota communities on Tanegashima.

Centers of *Turbo* processing in Amami and Kumejima indicate specialized trading circuits. If shell material was traded to China and Kaigen Tsūhō coins were linked to this trade, we have evidence of the "filling in" of social relations in the East China Sea region. The East China Sea became a zone of intense cultural interaction, in the same manner that the Mediterranean Sea was transformed into a cultural world (Broodbank 2006).

The shell trade of Kinoshita's Stage 4 leads into the topic of full-time traders of the East China Sea, based on the China coast and in Hakata, north Kyushu. In Chapter 7 the role of the maritime trading community is shown to be essential for the rise of local polities in the Gusuku Period. In the following chapters we will see how exchange systems expanded to include a wide variety of products and social networks, forming the basis of traditional Ryukyu culture and political organization.

In this account I have introduced production, distribution, and consumption in the Ryukyu Islands rather than in the total shell exchange system, which includes Kyushu and other parts of Japan as well as Korea (Kinoshita 1996). Many different modes of exchange can be seen in this zone of interaction, beginning with down-the-line transaction in the Early Shellmound Period. Shinzato Takayuki's findings of concentrations of exotic artifacts and centers for the collection of shell material indicate the rise of social complexity in the late first millennium BC. Social ranking is also indicated at Tomachin, Tokunoshima, where a permanent burial facility was used for several sequential interments.

We need to learn more about the harvesting and distribution of *Turbo* shells and the role of Japanese and Chinese traders. From at least the eleventh century, Song traders appear to have been active not only in the East China Sea, but also in the Inland Sea. They seem to have fascinated Heian leaders of the twelfth century AD such as Taira no Kiyomori (Takahashi Masa'aki 2011). While much has been learned by archaeological and historical research in the past decade concerning Kikaigashima (Chapter 7), there is much more exciting work ahead.

Chapter 7

The Gusuku Period (AD 1050 to 1429)

A New Order

Following a period of over eight thousand years during which small-scale societies lived by hunting and gathering, very rapid cultural and social change began in the eleventh century AD. In this chapter I first outline these changes, which are best known for the Okinawa Islands, and then describe briefly the important changes that took place on other islands, such as the development of the Gusuku Site Group of Kikaigashima and the grayware kiln sites of Kamuiyaki on Tokunoshima. (Kamuiyaki is a locality where grayware termed *kamuiyaki* was produced.) In the final section I present two case studies of the famous Okinawan *gusuku* sites Urasoe and Nakijin. (In Chapter 9, I describe Shuri, the primary *gusuku* site of the Ryukyus.) These are huge excavations that deserve separate attention.

The period is named after the Okinawan term for a stone-walled enclosure. Although this term can be written with the Sino-Japanese character for castle (*shiro*), the Okinawan term *gusuku* has a deep religious significance that includes sacred rock outcrops and shrines. They are more than castles, having deep connections to the veneration of nature. The entire surfaces of some enclosures were scraped and leveled, while in others rocky crags and groves were often protected or enhanced to become areas for worship. These areas are often venerated today. Archaelogists have emphasized the physical aspects of the defensive enclosures, whereas folklore and religious specialists have stressed the religious aspects (Asato Susumu 2003a). The highest and most inaccessible section of the *gusuku* was a sacred area, and *gusuku* sites contain *utaki* (shrines) dating from the seventeenth century or later. Villagers see *gusuku* sites as a place for worshipping nature and ancestors. At first it was thought that the period began as late as AD 1200 and that *gusuku* construction started around that time. However, now it is real-

Historical Period			Events, Trends	
China	Japan	Okinawa	Okinawa Islands	Year (AD)
Northern Song AD 960 to 1126	Heian AD 794 to 1185	Late Shellmound Period 300 BC to AD 1050		1000
Southern Song AD 1127 to 1279	Kamakura AD 1185 to 1333	Gusuku Period AD 1050 to 1422	Beginning of agricultural society, Chinese porcelain, *kamuiyaki*, steatite cauldrons, trade goods widespread.	13th century
Yuan AD 1260 to 1368			From this time on, large fortified castles, construction of Gokurakuji at Urasoe.	1265-1278
		(Sanzan Period AD 1300 to 1422)		1372
			King Satto sent tribute to Ming.	1390
Ming AD 1368 to 1644	Muromachi AD 1336 to 1573	(First Shō Dynasty AD 1406 to 1469) Early Ryukyu Kingdom Period (Second Shō Dynasty) (Early) AD 1469 to 1609	Miyako, Yaeyama, sent tribute to Ryukyu Kingdom.	
			ca. 15th century, peak of export of Chinese trade ceramics to Ryukyu, unification of Okinawajima under Shō Hashi (1422 or 1429).	1472
				1453
			Shiro Furi Struggle, burning of Shuri Castle, Kanemaro began Second Shō Dynasty. Construction of Enkakuji.	1470
				1492
	Momoyama AD 1568 to 1603		Construction of Shurei Gate.	1529
			Satsuma invasion of Ryukyu.	1609
		Second Sho Dynasty (Late) AD 1609 to1879		1616
			Wakuta adopted Korean ceramic methods. First Kurosato sugar production. Consolidation of Tsuboya kilns.	1623
Qing AD 1644 to 1912	Edo AD 1603 to 1868			1689
			Shuri Castle fire.	1709
	Meiji AD 1868 to 1912			

Figure 7.1. Chronology of the Gusuku Period

ized that changes in subsistence and social organization started as early as AD 1050 and that building of the *gusuku* began around AD 1250 (Figure 7.1).

Following Asato Susumu (2006) I have restricted the Gusuku Period to the rapid social change, trade, and warfare beginning around AD 1050 and leading up to the consolidation of power of the Chūzan Kingdom in AD 1429. I have termed the period from AD 1429 to 1609 the Early Ryukyu Kingdom to mark the distinctive character of the independent Ryukyu Kingdom. Economic changes are visible from around AD 1050. However, construction of *gusuku* began in the thirteenth century AD, and particularly large *gusuku* were constructed in the thirteenth and fourteenth centuries AD (Asato Susumu 1996; 2006). I use Chūzan to refer to the kingdom before unification and Ryukyu to refer to the kingdom after unification. I have divided the period into Early Gusuku Period (AD 1050 to 1250) and Late Gusuku (AD 1250 to 1429) to separate early changes in agriculture and settlement from the later period of heightened competition and extensive construction, and the emergence of the Chūzan Kingdom as seen at the site of Urasoe. The location of major sites of the Gusuku and Early Ryukyu Kingdom Periods mentioned in the text are given in Figure 7.2.

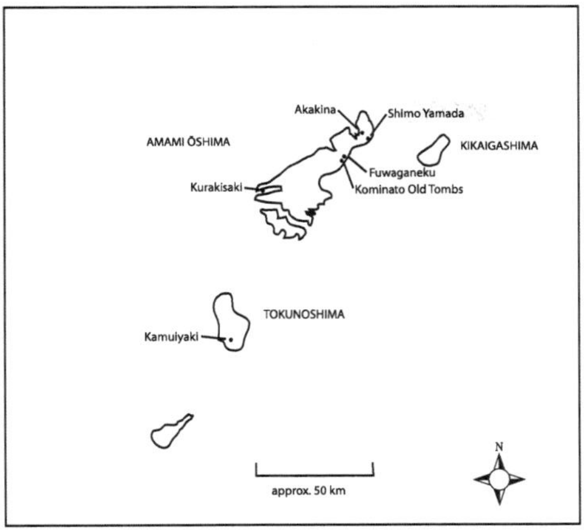

a.

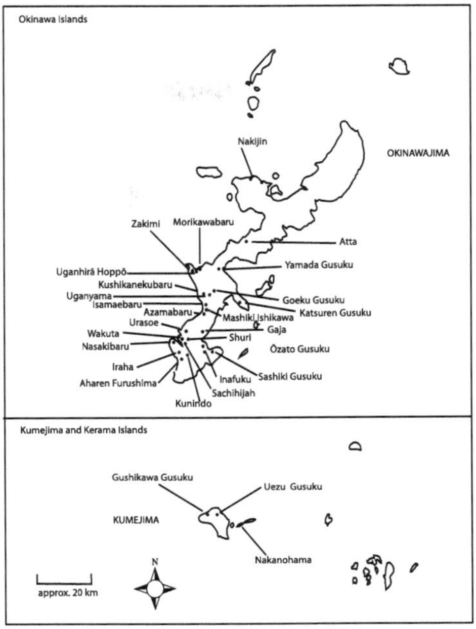

b.

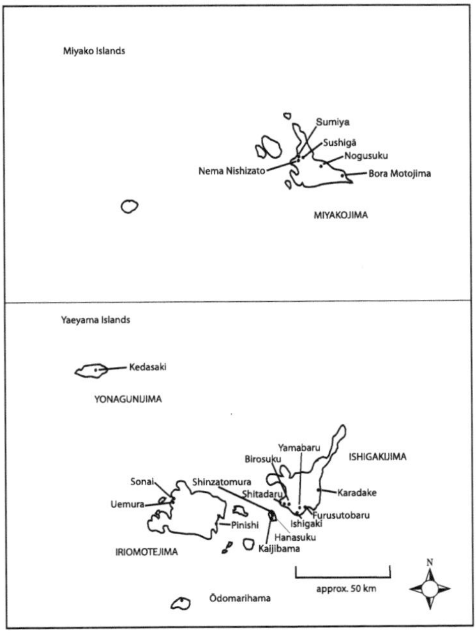

c.

Figure 7.2. Location of major sites of the Gusuku and Early Ryukyu Kingdom Periods mentioned in the text. (a) Amami Islands, (b) Okinawa Islands, (c) Sakishima Islands.

In the Gusuku Period, a shift from prehistoric to protohistoric society took place. By protohistoric we mean that, although the Ryukyuans were not writing their own historical accounts, others wrote about them. For instance, Chinese dynastic accounts such as the *Ming shilu* (Veritable records of the Ming) describe missions from Okinawan polities in the late fourteenth and early fifteenth centuries AD that competed for tributary status. In the seventeenth century AD, officials of the Ryukyu Kingdom wrote their own history, the *Chūzan seikan* (Haneji 1983). From this and other documents historians have pieced together a history that goes back to the mid-thirteenth century AD reign of King Eiso—traditionally dated to AD 1260 to 1299—who is thought to have unified parts of southern and central Okinawa and established the capital of the Chūzan Kingdom at Urasoe (Asato Susumu 2006; 2009). Rulers before this date are generally thought to be legendary.

In the fourteenth century AD, Chūzan moved its capital from Urasoe to Shuri. In the fourteenth century there were three major contending small states: Chūzan, centered on Shuri; Sanzan, centered at Ōzato in southern Okinawa; and Sanhoku, centered at Nakijin in northern Okinawa. Urasoe and Nakijin are described here because these sites have yielded more extensive archaeological material than Ōzato. In the early fifteenth century Chūzan defeated both Sanzan and Sanhoku. The Ryukyu Kingdom expanded to Amami and the Sakishima Islands in the fifteenth and sixteenth centuries, establishing administrative outposts and extracting tribute. The Early Ryukyu Kingdom and its expansion are described in Chapter 9.

The Gusuku Period marks a fundamental change in the life of the Ryukyu islanders, a transformation from hunting and gathering to cultivation and to small states within a span of a few centuries. Ironworking, which was first introduced into the Amami Islands around AD 500 (Kamimura 1999), became widespread throughout the Ryukyus. In this period, a new magnitude of extensive trade links connected the island communities to the surrounding regions of East Asia. As seen in the previous chapter, more than a millennium of prior experience in the trade of various tropical marine shells to Japan as far north as Hokkaido, and to China and Korea, allowed the people of the Ryukyus to use the knowledge, capital, and economic expertise that flowed into the islands to achieve new forms of political and social organization. In the tenth and eleventh centuries AD, the Ryukyu Islands became "Japanized," to use a term coined by Asato Susumu (2002; 2003b, 102–104; Asato and Doi 1999). Moreover, by the end of the Gusuku Period, the islanders were drawn into the Chinese world order through the establishment of tributary relations in AD 1372. The start of the Gusuku Period, around AD 1050, marks the beginning of the development of the Ryukyu world, the historical culture of the Ryukyu Kingdom and one of the cultural blocks of East Asia (China, Korea, Japan, Ryukyu), which was a complete change from the Epi-Jōmon World that preceded it (Asato Susumu 1992). In this period, the two different cultures of the Northern and Central Ryukyus and Sakishima came together in a single zone of trade, with the circulation throughout the islands of *kamuiyaki* (gray stoneware produced on Tokunoshima), and steatite cooking vessels and Chinese hard-fired white trade wares

(Asato 1992). It is important to note that *kamuiyaki* was a local product with antecedents in Japan, and steatite cooking vessels came from Nagasaki Prefecture. This shows that, although Chinese trade goods predominated in the late thirteenth century AD, the original trade systems had strong links to Japan. The Gusuku Period is first and foremost a period of stimulated interaction with Japan, in the broader sphere of increased interaction throughout East Asia. Trade was the strongest stimulus for social change in the Gusuku and Early Ryukyu Kingdom Periods. Trade ceramics comprise a huge proportion of the archaeological finds and take up the bulk of archaeological reports. They are very useful for establishing chronologies and reconstructing social relations. This chapter deals with subsistence, settlement, local economy, and important sites of the Gusuku Period. I have placed the discussion of trade, with historical background and chronological studies, in Chapter 8 and Appendix 1.

From about the middle of the thirteenth century AD, there is evidence of large-scale construction, including the building of the royal capital of Urasoe. In the Early Gusuku Period, the Gusuku Site Group of Kikaigashima and the grayware kiln sites of Kamuiyaki indicate rapid social and economic change particularly in the Amami Islands, which were the economic center of the Ryukyus. In the Late Gusuku Period, the center shifted to Okinawa Island, with the development of historic kingdoms.

In Sakishima, similar shifts to cultivation and the use of iron began roughly around the same time, and the term Suku Period is used for this period by Ōhama (1999). The regional distinctiveness of this period in Sakishima is discussed in a separate section below.

Why did such rapid changes occur at this time? The Gusuku Period must be seen in light of trends occurring in East Asia and Japan. The rise of commercialism and international trade in the Song dynasty led to the expansion of trade networks in the region, profoundly affecting Japan, both economically and culturally. At the same time, the prolonged wars of the late twelfth century AD in Japan pushed refugees to all parts of Japan and the Ryukyus. While trade goods from the Japanese main islands have been noted in the Ryukyus, it is only recently that the broader implications of the archaeological and osteological information have been realized. While it had been expected that prehistoric and early historic Okinawan populations should show resemblances to Jōmon or Ainu populations, with longer crania and narrower faces, it has been found by Doi (Doi et al. 1997) that, from the late first millennium AD, Okinawans show close similarities with modern Japanese, with rounder crania and shorter faces, suggesting an influx of migrants, including traders, settlers, and craftsmen. There was a movement of people and things from the Japanese main islands, major changes in production, and also changes in the physical type of Okinawans, who came to resemble more closely modern Japanese; these changes were accompanied by a tenfold increase in archaeological sites (Asato Susumu 2003b, 103). Miyagi (2011, 221) reported that in a total of 1,847 sites belonging to the Gusuku and Shellmound Periods from the Amami and Okinawa Islands, 64 percent (1,254 sites) belong to the Gusuku Period, 30 percent (593 sites) belong to the Shellmound Period, and 6 percent belong to both periods. Note that the Shellmound Period is much longer than the Gusuku Period so that the number of sites inhabited at any given time was quite low.

Chronology

Changes in trade ceramics provide a chronology for this period. The spread of new wares, such as Tokunoshima *kamuiyaki* stoneware, steatite cauldrons, and Chinese whitewares, indicates increased interaction and a sense of community throughout the Ryukyus. Different groups of traders were active in addition to local islanders. These included Song Chinese and Hakata traders as well as traders from Kikaigashima (see below) (Morimoto 2008, 279; Pearson 2007). In the eleventh century AD, locally made flat-bottom earthenware termed Gusuku Type pottery appears throughout the Ryukyus. It shows strong influence from various wares used in the Japanese main islands, such as steatite cauldrons, reddish *hajiki* ware, and soft gray pottery. Gusuku Type pottery not only imitated the external lug handles of steatite cauldrons; some of it was tempered with ground steatite from broken steatite cauldrons (Ōshiro 1997, 17). Its shapes fall within the total range of shapes of mediaeval ceramics of the Japanese Islands, indicating strong cultural continuities between the main islands and the archipelago. In the eleventh to twelfth centuries, this flat-bottom local type of utilitarian ware appears together with gray stoneware and Song Chinese white porcelain in sites such as the Kominato Old Tomb Group (Amami), Fuwaganeku (Amami Ōshima), Kushikanekubaru and Iraha Higashi (Okinawajima), and Ōdomaribama (Haterumajima) (Morimoto 2008, 266). The next step is marked by Chinese Longquan bowls of Type I and Tong'an celadon (Jukō celadon) and later types of whiteware, found in sites such as the shipwrecks of Kurakisaki (Amami Ōshima) and Nakanohama (Kumejima). Kin (1998) has subdivided the Gusuku Period into three subperiods. Period I extends from the tenth to twelfth centuries AD. It can be seen in the classic site of Atta, which spans the transition between the Late Shellmound Period and the Gusuku Period. The earliest components of the site, dating to the tenth century AD, yielded artifacts of the Late Shellmound Period but no Chinese ceramics or *kamuiyaki* (see below). Later components have abundant flat-bottom local pottery termed Gusuku pottery and an iron knife, while the latest component has Song dynasty whiteware and soapstone cauldron fragments dating to the twelfth century. Kin's Period II, late twelfth and thirteenth centuries AD, features Chinese celadon bowls with incised lotus petal decoration, whitewares with comb decoration or unglazed lip, whitewares with concave inner lips (the Birosuku Type, not found in the main Japanese Islands and thought to have come directly from China) (Kin 2007b; Shinzato Akito 2003, 90), bluish white glaze (*seihakuji* in Japanese, *qingbai* in Chinese) bowls, and Tong'an celadon bowls from the Quanzhou region of Fujian Province. Period III begins in the thirteenth century and extends to the early fifteenth century AD, the time of consolidation of the power of Shuri and the beginning of the Ryukyu Kingdom (AD 1429–1609). Major ceramics include Longquan and Longquan-related celadons from Zhejiang and Fujian, and small quantities of Vietnamese, Thai, and Korean wares.

The study of thirty-nine sites bearing twelfth-century AD gray stoneware, iron artifacts, and artifacts for iron production by Tezuka (2000) showed that fourteen sites (36 percent) were *gusuku* and twenty-five (64 percent) were village sites. Twenty-one sites (54 percent) contained Fensa Lower Layer pottery, thought to date to the tenth and eleventh centuries. Thus, gray stoneware is an important marker of the transition from the earlier Shellmound Period to the later Gusuku Period, which is characterized by widespread trade, cultivation, and the construction of fortified sites.

Gusuku Period Cultivation

In the previous chapter I reviewed the arguments based on archaeological features, site location, and malacological trends for the presence of cultivation in the Early Shellmound Period. Takamiya Hiroto has concluded that the earliest evidence of cultivation are the flotation samples and archaeological features at the Nazakibaru Site, Okinawa Island, dating to the eighth to tenth centuries AD (Takamiya 2007, 167). Seeds of cultivated rice, barley, wheat, foxtail millet, and possibly domesticated beans were found in flotation samples. The site also yielded ancient hoe marks and two possible drainage ditches, visible as dark material from the cultural or humus layer cut into the subsoil. Recently the possibility of cultivation in the Okinawa Islands as early as AD 800 has been entertained (Takamiya Hiroto et al. 2011). However, Takamiya estimates that the cultivation system was not fully established until the tenth to twelfth centuries AD at sites such as Morikawabaru. There appears to have been a period of about one hundred to two hundred years between the beginning of cultivation and the appearance of the earliest whitewares, steatite cauldrons, *kamuiyaki,* and Gusuku Type earthenware pottery (Morimoto 2008, 270). Postulating food stress and population decline from AD 500 to roughly AD 1000, Takamiya (2007) concluded that it was the arrival of substantial numbers of immigrants from Japan that pushed the subsistence system to full cultivation. The introduction of cultivation led to a huge increase in the number of sites and competition for land. Cultivation in the Ryukyus might seem easy because the climate is subtropical; however, it is hampered by summer and autumn typhoons and winter drought as well as thin soils.

Shiroma and Ueda (2007) reviewed the evidence from twenty-seven sites on Okinawa Island that show traces of cultivation. Some show traces of ridges and hoe marks, whereas others show lines of small pits roughly 30 cm in diameter and 30 cm deep. Plant silica analysis shows small quantities of stems and leaves of rice, wheat, and barley, and dating of the sites ranges from 500 to 1,100 years ago. Shiroma and Ueda found that the sites were generally on sloping ground and that the earliest sites were on low-lying alluvium, whereas later cultivation sites were on higher slopes. Dryland rice cultivation was recorded by Korean castaways in the late fifteenth century AD. Takamiya Hiroto (2007) found that flotation samples from central Okinawajima yielded little rice and a predominance of wheat and barley, while sites in northern Okinawajima and Amami Ōshima yielded mostly rice. It appears that originally a single rice crop was grown in the winter, to avoid damaging typhoons, but that from the time of the First Shō Dynasty, around AD 1406, two crops were grown on Okinawajima.

Contemporary rice cultivation in the Central and Southern Ryukyus is based on two cycles, December to July and August to December. Two types of rice are grown. In the first cycle, the Japanese main islands type *Oryza japonica* blooms on a lengthening day length, being harvested in June of the lunar calendar, whereas in the second cycle, the type termed tropical *Oryza sativa* blooms on a shortening day length, being harvested in October of the lunar calendar (Asato Susumu 1998, 61). The tropical *O. sativa* is close to the form found in Taiwan and the Philippines, which has hairy stems and leaves (Satō 2010). The Ryukyu system appears to be composite, but its evolution is not well understood. It seems likely that Japanese *O. sativa* was introduced from the Japanese main islands around AD 800, and tropical *O. sativa* arrived later through trade with China and Southeast Asia, perhaps as early as the First Shō Dynasty, as mentioned above.

The relationship of Gusuku Period settlements to soil types was explored by Ladefoged and Pearson (2000, 408), who found that Okinawan *gusuku* were situated in locations with access to more than one soil type: even in southern Okinawa, where upland weathered clay soil zones are extensive, there was a preference to locate sites at the edge of a soil zone. Asato Susumu (1998, 35) noted that Gusuku Period villages clustered in regions such as Ginowan, where there is a combination of small alluvial valleys and upland limestone, permitting both irrigated and dryland crops. He concluded that these areas were superior to areas with larger areas of potential paddy land, such as Sashiki in southeastern Okinawajima, which were subject to flooding and high tides (1998, 57).

Although archaeological features and carbonized seeds have been found, the nature of agricultural systems and their role in the rapid rise of social complexity are not clear. For instance, the degree of reliance on draft animals and the general role of livestock such as pigs are not clear. Except for a small iron sickle, iron agricultural tools are rare or absent from sites, and wooden tools are rarely found. Asato (1998, 28) states that Korean castaways of the mid-fifteenth century AD reported that only a wooden spatula-like tool was used, and plows and hoes were absent. In the Early Gusuku Period population increased and the proliferation of *gusuku* appears to indicate pressure on land. Much of Okinawajima's limited wet rice land is restricted to military bases. When this land is released, research on wet field systems and their intensification may develop quickly. Also it is important to remember that sweet potatoes and sugarcane, mainstays of modern Ryukyu agriculture, were not introduced into the Ryukyus until the early seventeenth century AD.

Research in the Hawaiian Islands has shown that irrigated cultivation on geologically older islands such as Kaua`i and Oahu was combined with upland dry field cultivation on geologically younger islands such as Maui and Hawai'i, to create agricultural surpluses that fueled the shift from chiefdom to kingdom (Kirch 2010). In a similar fashion the fertile yet limited areas of wetland cultivation in the Ginowan area may have given the rulers of Urasoe higher yields and more political power. Strategies for exploring processes of agricultural change beyond the dating of plant macrofossils are needed. In the Hawaiian case, warfare and social competition arose when the limits of available cultivable land were reached. It is tempting to suggest that the rise of construction of fortified enclosures in Okinawa around AD 1250 was the result of competition for suitable land and population pressure as well as competition for trade. Finer resolution of the chronology of agricultural and residential sites would elucidate changes in this period.

Gusuku Period Settlements

Huge changes took place in the span of four hundred years from the Late Shellmound Period around AD 1000 to the end of the 1300s. In the Gusuku Period new forms of communities appeared as a result of the influx of people from the Japanese main islands, contacts with China, and the emergence of social hierarchy. The style of buildings and their construction techniques rapidly diversified. Elite forms of construction required increasing technical knowledge and the recruitment of labor. From the latter half of the thirteenth century, the hallmark of the period, fortified stone structures (*gusuku*), were constructed.

Villages of the eleventh to thirteenth centuries AD usually consisted of sets of elevated main houses and storehouses, set on stout posts dug into the ground. This pattern must have been adopted from the Gusuku Site Group of Kikaigashima. Archaeological reconstructions are based on patterns of post molds (Nakasone 2004; Miyagi 2007; Yamamoto Masa'aki 2007). The smaller structures are termed elevated storehouses (*takakura*) by some authors or simply associated buildings by others. Such storehouses are well known from the ethnographic accounts and existed in the Ryukyus well into the twentieth century AD. They are 10 to 15 m distant from the main buildings, usually to the southwest, in order to receive sunlight and ventilation. Burials were earth interments in pits, within the village site. At the Kushikanekubaru Site, Chatan, Okinawajima (Nakasone 2004, 274), there were three pits for storage of iron sand for the production of iron artifacts. Some sites yielded iron-working hearths and clay bellows valves (tuyeres). The largest houses had two internal hearths. The standard distance between pillars in the houses (termed a bay or *ken*) was about 100 cm in Okinawa. This is smaller than the unit in the Japanese main islands, which probably reflects the nature of local building materials (Nakasone 2004). The posts for large houses had diameters of 50 cm or more. Typical sites of this period, the eleventh to thirteenth centuries AD, before the construction of *gusuku* include Uganhirā Hoppō (Yomitan) (Figure 7.3), Isamaebaru (Okinawa Kenritsu Maizō 2001a), Kushikanekubaru, Mashiki Ishikawa (Ginowan), and Shimo Yamada III (Amami Ōshima).

Yamamoto Masa'aki (2007) proposed that in the thirteenth century AD there was a trend to locate villages in defensive locations and surround them with palisades. Before the construction of completely fortified *gusuku,* there were partially walled sites that contained commoners' residences. Within these early *gusuku* were elite residences, commoners' residences, and *utaki*. Outside these major sites were dependent villages. From the fourteenth century AD, the *gusuku* became larger and more specialized, and elites and commoners lived in separate settlements. Generally, villages of the Gusuku and Early Ryukyu Kingdom Periods looked different from present-day villages, which have walled individual house compounds often marked by rows of tall, dense trees.

At the end of the Late Shellmound Period, pit houses showed little variation in size or facilities. Within a century new forms of houses had posts dug into the ground, which supported the roof, and some large examples had interior posts. In the late thirteenth century the islanders began to employ stone-wall construction, which reached spectacular levels in the fourteenth and fifteenth centuries. *Gusuku,* often located in defensive positions, had massive stone walls and inter-

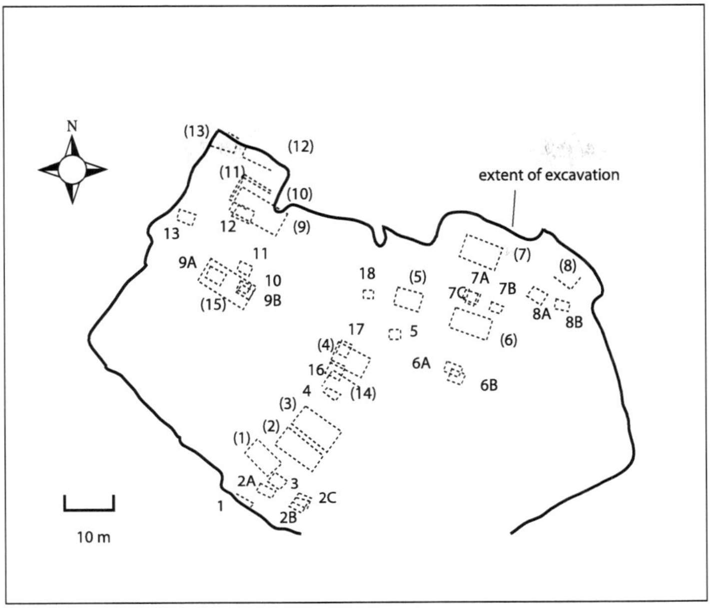

Figure 7.3. Plan of main and attached houses at the Uganhirā Hoppō Site, Yomitan, Okinawajima. Main houses are indicated by numbers in parentheses. Redrawn from Nakasone 2004, 272–273. Courtesy of Nakasone Motomu.

nal enclosures. In general they contained an elite residence facing an open plaza, an enclosed shrine, and storage and work areas. The shrine was usually adjacent to the elite residence and was usually in the highest and most protected location. The elite residence took on the function of administrative center. The plaza was sometimes flanked by two buildings situated perpendicular to the residence. The total area of the *gusuku* ranges from a few hundred sq m to about 40,000 sq m. A total of 192 *gusuku* sites have been recorded for Okinawajima alone. The *gusuku* sites show substantial variation in form. Although the typical form of central Okinawa has walls of natural coral limestone cobbles, which were replaced in the fifteenth century AD with walls of pieces of coral limestone that were carefully cut and fitted, there are exceptions, such as Kunindō in southern Okinawajima, which are constructed of earth ramparts and palisades. Those of the Amami Islands were built for mountain defense, with small enclosures protected by large ditches cut across narrow ridges. There is some indication in the Kasari area of Amami Ōshima that fortifications on headlands show influence from Okinawa, being constructed of limestone coral walls. The *gusuku* are often located within sight of each other, and their construction must have created fierce competition for labor. In Sakishima walled enclosures are also found, although they tend to be smaller and simpler.

Although there are still chronological problems to be resolved, *gusuku* building occurred from the mid-thirteenth century to the early fifteenth century AD (Late Gusuku Period). After the unification of Okinawa by the Ryukyu Kingdom in AD 1429, construction was limited to a few sites and the expansion of Shuri (see below). The *gusuku* sites show spatial clustering that reflects political groupings (Ladefoged and Pearson 2000). In the latter half of the thirteenth century AD, Urasoe Gusuku dominated central and southern Okinawa Island as a royal capital (Asato Susumu 2009). In the fourteenth century AD three powerful centers are known from historical sources such as Chinese dynastic and Okinawan seventeenth century AD histories. Many important *gusuku* have been excavated intensively, with spectacular finds of stone architecture and trade ceramics. These include Katsuren (Pearson 1999, 288–293), Nakagusuku (Toguchi 2000a–c), and Zakimi on Okinawajima; and Gushikawa and Uegusuku on Kumejima. Several were occupied by important leaders (Kin et al. 1988; Okada and Kuniyoshi 2000). In the early fifteenth century AD the Chūzan Kingdom, with its capital at Shuri, unified the Okinawa Islands and later expanded to the Amami and Sakishima Islands.

The Gusuku Period in the Amami Islands

Although the Gusuku Period is a term generally used in the Central Ryukyus (Okinawa Islands), I have expanded its use to include the Amami and Sakishima Islands, where similar but not identical developments occurred.

In the Amami Islands, which are closer to the Japanese main islands and in intensive contact with Kyushu earlier than Okinawa, the boundary of the Gusuku Period is difficult to establish. Dramatic new discoveries on Kikaigashima and Mottaimatsu, southern Kyushu, show that the central Yamato government of the Nara Basin was in contact directly, and through Dazaifu, with southern Kyushu and Amami by the eighth century AD. These new trading communities stimulated social change in the region. Distinctive architectural and artifactual remains and burial patterns show the existence of a separate community of administrators and officials whose life was different from life in the surrounding islands.

In addition to trade in shells and plant materials, sulfur from Tokara Iōjima, northwest of the Amami Islands, was probably an important trade item. It was used for torches, medicine, and gunpowder. Historical sources discussed by Yamauchi (2009, 12) mention that sulfur was sent by Japan to Song China. Although there appears to be no specific historical description of export from

Iōjima itself, the proximity of the island to China and navigation routes in the East China Sea make it likely that the island was an important supplier at the time of the height of activity on Kikaigashima (eighth to thirteenth centuries AD). It seems probable that administrators stationed on Kikaigashima supervised its extraction and export.

Recent surveys in the central and northern part of Amami Ōshima, in the present administrative unit of Amami City, confirm that *gusuku* sites exist on virtually every ridge and headland, protecting deep bays and river mouths (Amami Shi 2008; 2009b). Excavations of Akakina Gusuku, which overlooks the small town of Akakina on the west coast of the Kasari Peninsula, Amami Island, give a preliminary picture of a *gusuku* site of the Amami Islands. Akakina Town was an important administrative center and port in the seventeenth to nineteenth centuries AD; the extensive Akakina Gusuku Site confirms that it was also important in earlier times. Although it is on the west coast of the Kasari Peninsula, not facing toward Kikaigashima, it faced a protected bay and substantial river mouth. The site consists of two flat areas surrounded by defensive ditches and smaller flat areas (Figure 7.4). The main enclosure in the upper area, Group A, is 22 m × 13 m, while the lower area, Group B, contains two en-

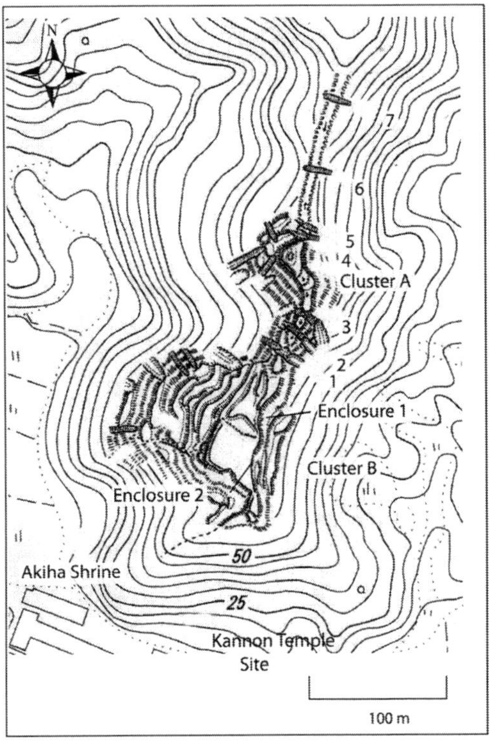

Figure 7.4. Plan of Akakina Gusuku, Amami Ōshima. Numbers 1 to 7 indicate defensive ditches. Contours are in meters. Adapted from Amami Shi 2009b, 26. Courtesy of Amami Shi Kyōiku Iinkai.

closures, 30 m × 40 m and 10 m × 30 m. The two areas are separated by three ditches cut across the spine of the ridge. The enclosures are surrounded by earth ramparts rather than stone walls. There is no mention of internal platforms or structures. Ceramics excavated from the site included bead rim whitewares and *kamuiyaki* dating to the twelfth to thirteenth centuries AD. Trade ceramics of the fourteenth century AD are absent, which is surprising, since this is the peak period for trade ceramics in this area. However, Longquan celadon bowls with *raimontai* (thunder-pattern band) dating to the fifteenth century AD are relatively abundant (Amami Shi 2009a; Nakayama 2009, 73). The site was also active in the seventeenth century AD.

The Gusuku Site Group, Kikaigashima

Recent wide area excavations of seven sites in the Gusuku Site Group on Kikaigashima have transformed our comprehension of the Late Shellmound Period and the emergence of complex society in the Ryukyus. These sites date to both the Late Shellmound Period and the Early Gusuku Period, and are also related to the trade in *Turbo* shells discussed in the previous chapter. In this case, "Gusuku" is used as a place-name rather than as a term for "castle." Heretofore the period from the eighth to twelfth centuries AD has been poorly comprehended; however, discoveries from Amami and Kikaigashima are filling the gaps and show increasing social complexity spanning several centuries. Kikaigashima is 56.9 sq km in area. It is located 380 km from the Kagoshima mainland and 25 km from Amami Ōshima. The total area of excavations at the Gusuku Site Group is 13,000 sq m. The large scale of the villages is remarkable for the Ryukyus in this time period. A total of about 150 raised buildings, 40 burials, 50 hearths, 30 iron-working hearths, and one paved area were found. Goods made outside of Kikaigashima accounted for 70 percent of the assemblage (Sumida 2008).

In the second half of the first millennium AD, an area of intense activity existed in the northern Kasari Peninsula of Amami Ōshima and Kikaigashima, as noted in Chapter 6. The Kasari Peninsula, with extensive reefs, broad foreshore, terraces, and sand dunes, was extensively occupied in prehistory, while the rest of Amami Ōshima, with steep mountains, dense forests and narrow foreshores, was sparsely populated. It provided timber, water, stone materials for tools, and forest products for the densely settled raised coral island of Kikaigashima, which has five marine terraces, sloping in the direction of Amami Island. Although raised limestone islands have good drainage and level areas for cultivation, water sources are limited, coming from springs in caves, and there was a dearth of trees suitable for house construction. The high and low islands existed in a symbiotic relationship.

Sites of the Jōmon, Yayoi, and Kofun Periods have been found on Kikaigashima as well as Amami Ōshima (Ikeda 2008). In addition, there are many sites on the northern end of the island dating to the twelfth to thirteenth centuries AD, and there are many traditions concerning the flight of the Genji, one of the warring factions in the Japanese main islands, to this island in the late twelfth century AD.

The Gusuku sites in general have yielded a distinctive assemblage of artifacts not found on other sites in the Ryukyus (Sumida 2008). Local earthenware of the Kaneku Type found on Amami is rare or absent, replaced by *hajiki* (red earthenware) and *sueki* from regions such as Higo and Sanuki in Kyushu. Gray-glazed ware from the Tōkai region was also found. Koryo celadon of the late eleventh and early twelfth centuries AD is similar to that found in Daizaifu and different from the type found in the Ryukyus, which dates to the fourteenth century AD. The artifacts mentioned above indicate that wares for daily use were imported from the Japanese main islands and that there was a strong connection to Dazaifu. The sites also produced an unusually large number of steatite cauldrons and very old, high-quality Chinese trade wares such as *yue* ware, a kind of proto-celadon dated to the eighth and ninth centuries AD.

In a review of historical documents concerning the Amami Islands, Suzuki Yasutami (2008, 18) found records that groups of islanders from Amami Ōshima and Yakushima took tribute, including *akagi* (*Bischoffia javanica*), used for red dye, and *Turbo* shells, to the Yamato court in AD 683 and 698. Large delegations of people from Amami are recorded in AD 710 and 727. Wooden slips bearing the names Amami and Okinoerabujima, thought to be tags for tributary goods, have been recovered from Dazaifu. Suzuki (2008, 23) and Yamauchi (2009) cite Song dynasty records of tribute including utensils decorated with mother-of-pearl (in this case *Turbo* shell) and sulfur products from the Amami region being sent from Japan to China in the tenth century AD. Most goods sent from Amami to Yamato passed through Dazaifu. The Gusuku Site Group was a collecting point for local resources, shared by Heian officials and associated private traders.

Major Sites

YAMADA NAKANISHI

At Yamada Nakanishi (Sumida and Nozaki 2008, 156; Takanashi 2008a, 124; Kikai Chō 2006; 2008), an excavation of 6,000 sq m in total yielded the remains of 10 houses with dug posts, 9 earth pit graves, and 10 pits. The buildings had elevated floors supported by stout posts dug deep into the ground. In Japanese the posts are termed *hottate bashira*. The buildings are rectangular in plan, the smallest being elevated storehouses set on four posts about 2.5 m apart; larger buildings were set on rows of posts up to 6 m long. This variety of building types, including large examples, is unknown in the Ryukyus at this time. Often diagnostic artifacts were found in the fill of the postholes, making future relative dating possible. Further research is required to gain a clear picture of the nature of changes in the function of the buildings on the site. From the available reports, the first occupation was in the ninth to tenth centuries AD. The peak of occupation was in the eleventh to twelfth centuries, and the site declined in the thirteenth century AD. The artifacts recovered include *hajiki, sueki, yue* celadon, whiteware, Koryo celadon, steatite cauldrons, pottery with steatite temper, Korean-type unglazed ceramic, *kamuiyaki,* iron knives, tuyeres, slag, and stone tools. *Haji* or *hajiki* (red earthenware) and *sue* or *sueki* (gray stoneware) are ceramics produced in the Japanese main islands. *Yue* ware is an early form of Chinese celadon. The buildings are one bay by two bays with dug posts and are surrounded by a line of fence posts set in the ground. The carbonized wood from these posts has been identified as *Castanopsis* and *Cinnamomum camphora,* tall broadleaf evergreen trees, and has given an AMS date of 1074 ±20 BP. Eight earth pits with cremated bones and one simple interment were found. The cremation burials yielded several *kamuiyaki tsubo* (narrow-necked jar), one knife, and one bead. The burned bones were placed in a round or rectangular pit. Burials show variation in shape and arrangement.

The occurrence of cremation burials is a distinct feature of the Kikaigashima sites. The custom of cremation was limited to elite persons in Japan at this time and was present, but uncommon, in the Ryukyus. Burned bone fragments were discovered at the Hirota Site, described in Chapter 6. At the Yamada Nakanishi and Kohane Sites, remains that appear to be secondary cremation burials were recorded. A deposit of burned bones and grave goods was found in the grave fill of a pit of sufficient length to accommodate an extended burial. The deposit was situated a few centimeters above the original floor of the grave pit. It appears that the individuals were first buried in an extended position, then, after the flesh had decomposed, the bones were exhumed and cremated, and reburied, sometimes with objects such as glass beads. In two cases *kamuiyaki* vessels with inverted whiteware bowls as lids were placed with the departed.

Katagiri et al. (2007) reported cremation burials from the Shītachi Site on Gushikawa Island, in the Iheya-Izena Islands, which lie slightly to the north of Okinawa Island. Disarticulated burials of some sixty-two individuals dating to the Early and Middle Shellmound Period were found in a sand dune below a rock shelter facing the ocean. Some of the burials show signs of drying from exposure to the wind before burning, whereas others were cremated immediately after death. The practice of delayed cremation seems similar to some of the Yamada Nakanishi burials, suggesting that this unusual custom may have old roots in the Ryukyus.

MAEHATA SITE

The Maehata Site (Sumida and Nozaki 2008, 161; Takanashi 2008a, 126) dates to the eighth to twelfth centuries AD. From an excavation of 7,000 sq m, four thousand post molds were recorded. These have been interpreted as belonging to nineteen buildings with posts dug into the ground. This site has the same artifact inventory as the sites described above but also has a small amount of local Kaneku Type pottery. Of particular importance is the discovery of iron sand in the cultural layer. It was also found in the Ōufu Site mentioned below. A substantial number of small buildings of four posts (one bay by one bay) were found. There were also two irregular burial pits, 200 cm in diameter. In one of these there were two extended burials—the first instance of extended burials in the Gusuku Site Group. In the site there was an area paved with limestone fragments forming two separate surfaces, making a flattened area on a natural slope. The pavement seemed to mark the edge of a dry field, as if the paved area cut into the dry field area. Perhaps it was a threshing area. This site yielded many tuyeres, and, in the extreme eastern edge, there was a large amount of slag.

YAMADA HANTA SITE

From an excavation of 22,000 sq m in area at the Yamada Hanta Site (Sumida and Nozaki 2008, 159; Takanashi 2008a, 125; Kikai Chō 2009) (Figures 7.5 and 7.6), remains of fifty buildings with dug posts were interpreted from four thousand post molds. The major use of this site was in the latter eleventh to twelfth centuries AD. At this time the site served as the center of the Gusuku Site Group. Five earth burials, two hearths, sixteen pits, and one ditch were mapped, and *hajiki, sueki, yue*-type celadons, fabric-impressed pottery (used for salt making), gray-glazed pottery, whiteware, celadon, early Koryo celadon, steatite cauldrons, *kamuiyaki,* iron artifacts, and stone tools were found. The early type of *yue* ware found on this site is the same as the type found at Dazaifu and Heian Kyō (Kyoto). This type is not found in other sites in Kagoshima Prefecture (Kikai Chō 2009, 227–230). Several types of buildings were encountered. Some were

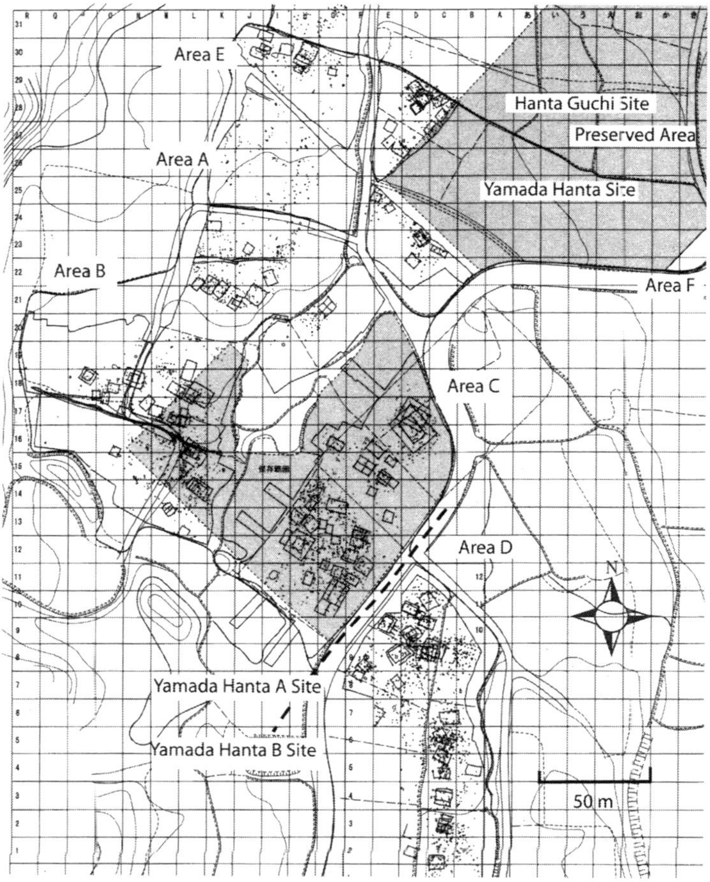

Figure 7.5. Plan of the Yamada Hanta Site, Gusuku Site Group, Kikaigashima. From Kikai Chō 2009, 14. Courtesy of Kikai Chō Kyōiku Iinkai.

of one bay by one bay, sturdy buildings sitting on very large posts, 1.2 m in diameter. Some were of one bay by two bays. One of these had thirty postholes surrounding the main building, while another had thirty-four posts. Two of the largest buildings have one rectangle of posts set inside another, with very large posts in the central area, as if they supported a raised storehouse with surrounding platform. Flotation analysis of soil samples taken from pits, areas of burned earth, and burials yielded remains of rice, wheat, barley, and millet, and confirmed that the inhabitants practiced dry field cultivation. The extent of cultivation is not yet known, and the plant materials will be dated in the future (Takamiya Hiroto 2009, 180).

Figure 7.6. Aerial photo of excavations of the Yamada Hanta Site, Gusuku Site Group, Kikaigashima. From Kikai Chō 2009, 233. Courtesy of Kikai Chō Kyōiku Iinkai.

HANTA SITE

The Hanta Site (Sumida and Nozaki 2008, 165) yielded various types of features including six earth pit burials, pits, ditches, and postholes. The six earth pit burials yielded nine secondary burials. The ceramics included *yue* ware, Kaneku Type pottery, whitewares, celadon, blue and white, steatite cauldrons, *kamuiyaki,* and glass beads. However, there were no clear indications of grave goods. One of the burials showed sequential interment of two individuals into the same pit.

ŌUFU SITE

From an excavation of 2,000 sq m at the Ōufu Site (Sumida and Nozaki 2008, 235–256), ten buildings were recognized as well as thirty pit burials and some thirty areas of burned soil. These are most likely areas of metalworking. There were also pits containing iron sand, which was heated to derive iron. The range of artifacts was similar to those found in the sites above. Some burials seem to be deposits of cremated bones in round pits, while one burial contained the remains of a wooden coffin containing human bones, a whiteware small bowl, a *kamuiyaki* jar, and glass beads. This burial cut through an area of postholes and blacksmith hearth, indicating that it was more recent than the other features.

Unusual Features of the Kikaigashima Sites

The Gusuku Site Group shows a number of remarkably unusual features.

1. There is a paucity of Kaneku Type pottery, the predominant type in the late first millennium AD (Kinoshita 2002; Takanashi 2007; 2008a), coupled with a predominance of utilitarian wares imported from the Japanese main islands. This indicates different cultural affiliations from Amami Ōshima, despite its proximity (Ikehata 2008, 249).
2. The finding of *yue* wares of the eighth to tenth centuries AD in Kikai sites where Kaneku Type pottery is abundant and the recording of two spouted *yue* ware heirloom vessels at Onotsu, Kikaigashima, extends the southern limit of the distribution of these wares from Tanegashima to Kikaigashima (Kamei 2007). In the Japanese main islands these wares are found in administrative sites, temples, shrines, and elite residences and burials. Early Koryo (Korean) celadon, of the type found in Dazaifu, also indicates a link between the Gusuku Site Group and administrative sites in Japan. While Korean unglazed ware has been found in Dazaifu and in Mottaimatsu in Kyushu, its occurrence here is the first recorded instance in the Ryukyus. The sherds are primarily the rims of large jars, indicating shipping containers rather than food serving vessels.
3. Large residences and storehouses appear in the Yamada Nakanishi, Yamada Hanta, and Kohane sites. Sites on a lower terrace, Maehata and Ōufu, have concentrations of metalworking sites.
4. From a total sample of forty-four mediaeval sites surveyed on Kikaigashima, all contained ceramic sherds from the eleventh to twelfth centuries AD; about 64 percent of the sites contained ceramics from the thirteenth century AD, 21 percent contained ceramics of the fourteenth to fifteenth centuries AD, and 21 percent contained ceramics of the sixteenth century (Ikehata 2008, 253). This distribution contrasts with the predominance of twelfth to fourteenth century AD ceramics found generally throughout the Ryukyus, discussed in Chapter 8, and shows the importance of Kikaigashima in the trade of the Early Gusuku Period, at the height of the *Turbo* trade.

The Significance of the Gusuku Site Group

Takanashi (2007, 66) concluded that the Gusuku Site Group must have been the locus of political authority connected to Yamato. In layout, the site resembles contemporary government office sites (*kanga*) on the main islands of Japan. Finds of high-quality *yue* ceramics of the eighth to tenth centuries AD at the Yamada Nakanishi and Yamada Hanta sites are unique in the Ryukyus. The very large buildings with raised floors and excavated post construction, and the unusually large quantities of soapstone vessels suggest an official site. The adoption on Okinawajima of the settlement plan of the Gusuku Site Group, with large buildings and accompanying storehouses, indicates emulation of and interaction with the elites from Heian Japan. The nature of this interaction is not fully comprehended; this will come with a fuller analysis of the recently excavated finds.

From the eighth to tenth centuries AD, the local pottery of the Amami Islands, termed the Kaneku Type, consisted mostly of wide-mouthed jars (*kame* and *hachi*) that had a collar decorated with applied clay strips and incision. The small flat foot was constricted, and there are usually leaf imprints on its bottom. Takanashi (2007) has examined all of the known sites of this time period and has found three groups: (1) sites with Kaneku pottery and no other types, (2) sites with Kaneku Type pottery plus small quantities of *hajiki* and *sueki* (presumably made in Kyushu), and (3) sites with no local Kaneku Type pottery and exclusively *hajiki* and *sueki*. The sites with almost no local pottery are concentrated on Kikaigashima. They appear to be trading sites where main island Japanese were part of the community. Judging from similarities in artifact types, these sites had close relations with Dazaifu, the Yamato government's administrative center in northern Kyushu and the gateway to continental Asia in northern Kyushu of the central Yamato government in the eighth to eleventh centuries AD. Sites with Kaneku Type local pottery and small quantities of *hajiki/sueki* have large quantities of *Turbo* shells and iron; they appear to be sites where local goods such as *Turbo* shells, used for mother-of-pearl decoration, were exchanged for goods such as iron implements. Sites with only Kaneku Type pottery appear to be local islanders' habitation sites.

Kamuiyaki Kilns

An important step in the formation of the Ryukyu world occurred with the production of gray stoneware at the kiln group located in the Kamuiyaki locality in southern Tokunoshima in the eleventh century AD. The gray stoneware manufactured in these kilns, called *kamuiyaki,* gave its name to the locality. It could

Figure 7.7. Kamuiyaki ceramics, showing vessel shapes and surface treatments. From Shogakukan, ed., *Kokogaku shiryo taikan,* vol. 12 (Tokyo: Shogakukan, 2004). Original photo by Oda Kikuo. Property of Isen Chō Kyōiku Iinkai. Courtesy of Shogakukan Publishers and Isen Chō Kyōiku Iinkai.

be considered a distinctive, late, local variant of the *sueki* of the Japanese main islands. Whereas many exchange networks of smaller scale and based on various products were common in earlier times, for the first time a product was manufactured for exchange throughout the entire archipelago (Shinzato Akito 2003; 2009; Pearson 2007). Over one hundred kilns spanning a period from the eleventh to thirteenth centuries AD have been found. Throughout the span of production, most of the wares consisted of jars, some with narrow necks (*tsubo*) and others with wider mouths (*hachi*) (Figure 7.7). In addition, bowls, cups, and pouring vessels were produced in the thirteenth century AD to compete with Chinese trade ceramics. However, in the fourteenth century AD the kilns finally stopped production.

The methods of production were a blend of Japanese and Korean techniques with local innovations. Hakata traders along with local intermediaries probably transported the wares throughout the Ryukyus, along with Chinese whitewares and steatite cauldrons, in exchange for shells and other products such as *akagi* (*Bischoffia javanica*), used for red dye in the Japanese main islands.

The regional exchange system of *kamuiyaki* is evidence of commercial communication throughout the islands from the Northern Ryukyus to the southernmost islands of Sakishima and can be seen as a prelude to the emergence of regional political unity. Before the Gusuku Period, the Sakishima Islands were isolated from the Central and Northern Ryukyus by the Kerama Gap. A sense of regional Ryukyu identity was created through the circulation of local products to every corner of the archipelago.

The survey and excavation of the kiln sites has been a substantial project. It is hoped that in the future villages occupied by the craftspeople who worked in the kilns will be found and excavated since the social and economic context of the relatively large scale production remains completely unknown. With the discoveries of the kilns at Kamuiyaki, the port site of Mottaimatsu (see Chapter 8), and the Gusuku Site Group of Kikaigashima in the past two decades, each discovery affects the interpretation of the others. Despite a dearth of relevant historical sources, it seems probable that the community on Kikaigashima was involved in the establishment of the kilns and in their administration (Yoshinari 2010, 25). *Kamuiyaki* wares are abundant in the Kikaigashima sites. Private traders and Yamato officials must have been involved in the organization of production in Kamuiyaki. Perhaps the kilns were semiofficial, with a mixed group of traders carrying the wares throughout the islands. It appears that the kilns were ultimately unable to compete with the flood of Chinese imports in the fourteenth century AD and ceased production.

The Gusuku Period in the Sakishima Islands

At about the same time as the beginning of the Gusuku Period, in the eleventh century AD, interaction between Sakishima and the Northern and Central Ryukyus is indicated by the appearance of steatite cauldrons, Chinese whitewares, *kamuiyaki,* and iron trade goods in Sakishima sites.

Ōhama has termed this period the Suku Period of Yaeyama, and the term can be extended to the Miyako Islands. Ōhama (1999; 2008) divides the Suku Period into Early Suku (eleventh to fourteenth centuries AD) and Late Suku (fourteenth to sixteenth centuries AD). Early Suku Period sites are marked by the presence of Chinese whitewares with beaded lip and unglazed rim, brownwares, celadon bowls with ridged lotus petal decoration, and the presence of tuyeres for ironworking. Ōhama's Suku Period is useful for our discussion because it is comparable to the Gusuku period of Okinawa and Amami, and this comparability makes it easy to discuss trends within the region. A more detailed chronology has been proposed by Kin (Ishigaki Shi Sōmubu 2008a, 2–3; 2008b, 2–4). It is based on changes in the distinctive thick, reddish flat-bottom earthenware of the Yaeyama Islands. Two periods are proposed: the Shinzatomura Period (twelfth to thirteenth centuries AD) and the Nakamori Period (thirteenth to seventeenth centuries AD). While this pottery copied the external lugs and flat bottom of steatite cauldrons from Kyushu, it is distinctive from other wares because of its thickness and distinctive paste. Unlike the Gusuku Period earthenware of the Northern and Central Ryukyus, which died out in the fifteenth century because of competition from imported ceramics and ironwares, the earthenware of Sakishima persisted until the seventeenth to nineteenth centuries AD, when it was used for ritual and burial containers. This period is referred to as the Panari Period, *panari* being the local name for the coarse earthenware that typifies this period (Kin 1994, 85).

The earliest finds of rice and millet in Sakishima are dated to the twelfth to thirteenth centuries AD (Ōhama 2008, 350). Ōhama proposes that cultivation was carried out on hillocks of limestone, 2 to 3 km inland from the sea. Ōhama's surface surveys have located a number of inland sites near small rivers, which may have been suitable for early cultivation. The Late Suku Period, particularly the fifteenth century AD, was a time of prosperity for Sakishima, before the islands came under the tight political control of the Chūzan Kingdom (discussed in Chapter 9). Private Chinese traders as well as traders from the north came to the islands. Alliances were formed among local chiefs (Pearson 2003). On the Miyako Islands a substantial number of sites dating to the twelfth and thirteenth centuries AD yield soapstone cauldrons, Chinese whitewares with bead lip and unglazed rim types, celadon bowls with incised floral decoration or ridged lotus petal decoration, Tong'an ware incised bowls, and bluish white-glazed (*seihakuji*) bowls of Song/Yuan date from Fujian. The Chinese trade ceramics occur in small quantities. The earthenware of the Miyako Islands generally resembles that of Yaeyama, but local archaeologists employ their own typology.

An entry in the historical records of the city of Wenzhou in coastal Zhejiang, the *Wenzhou fuzhi,* records the rescue of people thought to be Miyako Islanders from "Bora," thought to be Boranomotojima (Kaneko and Melichar 1972, 15), in AD 1317. It was first noted by the Japanese scholar Fujita in 1917 (Shimoji Kazuhiro 2008, 336). According to Fujita, the entry stated that a group of sixty people embarked in two ships for Melaka, but were ship wrecked on their way. If this account is accurate, it indicates that by the early fourteenth century AD Miyako islanders were sufficiently proficient voyagers to undertake long trips to Southeast Asia. Although the entry states that they were from Bora, Shimoji believes that such a large group must have been assembled from several villages.

Several sites on Miyakojima show substantial communities involved with trade with China and Southeast Asia. The Sumiya Site contains material from the Late Gusuku Period and the Early Ryukyu Kingdom Period. It is discussed in Chapter 9. Adjacent to the Sumiya Site is the Nema Nishizato Site (Miyakojima Shi 2006); judging from the finding of Thai clay lids for large jars (*hannera*) dated to the late fourteenth century AD and late thirteenth century AD Chinese trade ceramics, it must date from the thirteenth to fifteenth centuries AD, although materials from later periods up to the twentieth century were also found. Abundant evidence of ironworking and traces of brass in a crucible indicate that it was a metalworking site. Reworking of scrap iron cauldrons and smelting of iron sand, thought to be brought from Kagoshima, took place. It is also possible that raw materials for ironworking were coming from the China mainland or Southeast Asia. Since copper and zinc slag were also recovered, Ōzawa (2006) concluded that the inhabitants were working a variety of metals. However, because the site was heavily disturbed by the laying of water pipes and electrical conduits, the dating of these metals is uncertain. Another site close to Sumiya, Sushigā, may have been a fortified site occupied during local battles in the fourteenth and fifteenth centuries AD (Hirara Shi 2003). Iron sand, iron artifacts, and evidence of ironworking (crucibles, slag, and burned areas) were recovered.

The Shinzatomura Period of Yaeyama

The Shinzatomura Period dates to the twelfth and thirteenth centuries (Ishigaki Shi Sōmubu 2009a), roughly the same period as the beginning of the Late Gusuku Period in Okinawa. In this period a Ryukyu Island–wide community, linked by trade and migration, was realized. The number of sites of this period is small; they occur on Ishigakijima, Birosuku, and Karadake Higashi, and on Taketomijima, Shinzatomura East, and Kaijibama. These sites yield beaded-lip whitewares and *kamuiyaki*. People also used steatite cauldrons, and they made pottery versions of these, called the Shinzatomura Type. There are fragments of steatite cauldrons in Ōdomaribama Layer IV, Hateruma. This site has been dated to the twelfth century AD at the end of the Non-Ceramic Period.

The use of pottery was an important change, allowing the preparation of different kinds of food. On the exterior of the rim of the Shinzatomura Type pottery there are four lugs that imitate the lugs of steatite cooking vessels. The vessels have flat bottoms and are tempered with steatite, recycled from broken cauldrons. The end of the Non-Ceramic Period must be around the end of the eleventh century to early twelfth century. Twelfth-century dating is confirmed by the presence of Song dynasty types of imported whiteware of the thickened lip and everted lip types. Following the Shinzatomura Type was the Nakamori Type, which had a diversity of forms, including bowls and wide-mouthed jars.

In the Nakamori Period pottery was abundant; this was the peak of local earthenware production.

SITES AND SUBSISTENCE

Generally, in the Shinzatomura Period, houses were not enclosed by stone walls and were square with dug posts, but in the Shinzatomura East Site there were a palisade and surrounding wall (Ishigaki Shi Sōmubu 2009a, 9). The site was situated on a slope, with a rough stone wall along the lower portion. Remains of charred rice and plant opals of rice and millet were recovered from the site. Shellfish found in sites of this period were collected from the lagoon, estuaries, and mangroves. Bones of Scaridae (parrot fish, *budai*), which inhabit the shallow waters of the reef, are found in all sites as well as cow bones from Shinzatomura East, indicating the raising of cattle. Red earthenware was of the Birosuku Type, with short outflaring rim and no lugs (possibly in imitation of Kyushu *hajiki* earthenware) in addition to the lugged Shinzatomura Type. Both appear in the Shinzatomura Period. The Shinzatomura West Site is dated to the subsequent Nakamori Period and is similar to the Furusutobaru Site, mentioned in Chapter 9.

Important Gusuku Sites on Okinawa

In the Late Gusuku Period (AD 1250 to 1429), regional centers of power emerged. In this section I describe Urasoe, in central Okinawajima, and Nakijin in northern Okinawajima.

Urasoe Gusuku

Urasoe was the residence of the rulers Shunten, Eiso, and Satto (Takemoto and Asato 1993, 69). It was the capital of Chūzan before the ascendancy of Shuri and was the largest of the Okinawan castles in the early fourteenth century AD. It is located near the west-central coast of Okinawajima, on the northern edge of Naha City and inland from Urasoe City. In this area the ridges of Ryukyu limestone are low and gradual, the highest in the entire central region of Okinawa (Nakagami) being 220 m in elevation. The site lies behind Urasoe City at an elevation of 130 to 140 m. At the foot of the northern edge of this escarpment is the Machiminato River, at the mouth of which was a small port, Machiminato. The main port for the castle was Tomari, which has a deeper harbor and is located a few kilometers to the south.

Lying in a northwest-southeasterly direction, the site's maximum length is

380 m. It is 60 to 70 m wide, on a northeast-southwest axis. This alignment is similar to that of Shuri Gusuku (see below). On the shortest day of the year, the sun rises over the sacred island of Kudakajima and lines up with the eastern tip of Urasoe Gusuku (Asato Susumu 2006, 55). Unlike Nakijin or Katsuren, other prominent castle sites, its walls and pavements have been extensively damaged both in the past and in more recent times, so that it is almost impossible to determine the outline of the structures, except to say that lying in a general east-west direction there were a series of adjoining enclosures. The high, eastern area is called the Kogusuku (lit. old castle), while the western, lower area is called the Migusuku. There is a local tradition that the residential area moved from the Kogusuku to the Migusuku (Urasoe Shi Shishi Henshū Iinkai 1986), and there is also a tradition that building materials were carried away from the site for the enlargement of Shuri Castle in the early sixteenth century AD (Takemoto and Asato 1993, 98). In AD 1509, when the son of King Shō Shin, Shō Iko, moved from Shuri to Urasoe, it is said that Urasoe was in ruins and was refurbished (Urasoe Shi Shishi Henshū Iinkai 1986). In AD 1609, at the time of the invasion by the Satsuma Fiefdom of Kyushu, the castle was burned, along with the Ryūfukuji Temple, which was situated below it.

The north side of the castle, protected by steep cliffs, may have lacked a wall or ramparts, whereas the south side, which is more gradual, was protected by four separate ramparts with palisades and a moat that has been dated to the latter half of the fourteenth century and the first half of the fifteenth century AD (Asato Susumu 1997). There are also local shrines and sacred places, including two Buddhist temples, the Gokurakuji and the Ryūfukuji, the oldest Buddhist temples in Okinawa. Near the northwest cliff of the castle is Urasoe Yōdore, the mausoleum of King Eiso (r. AD 1260–1299), who must have built the castle, and King Shō Nei, sovereign at the time of the Satsuma takeover in AD 1609. The two mausoleum chambers, excavated into the cliff, were flanked by two small oblong enclosures paralleling the cliff, which were reached by a ceremonial path descending from the castle along the cliff face (Urasoe Shi 1996). On the western side of the castle was a large artificial pond, discovered in the 1990s (Figure 7.8).

Three excavations in 1982–1984 were undertaken by the Urasoe City Board of Education, uncovering a total area of 1,900 sq m (Urasoe Shi Shishi Henshū Iinkai 1986, 171). Some 30,000 artifacts were recovered from the excavations, including architectural items and ceramic utensils, weapons, ornaments, and food remains (Kinjō Kamenobu 1999, 258–259).

Excavations of 1993 showed that outside of the later castle wall there was a small palace along the southern side, bordered by a deep ditch, 15 m wide and 3 m deep (Asato Susumu 2006, 22–25). It is thought to have been built in the early

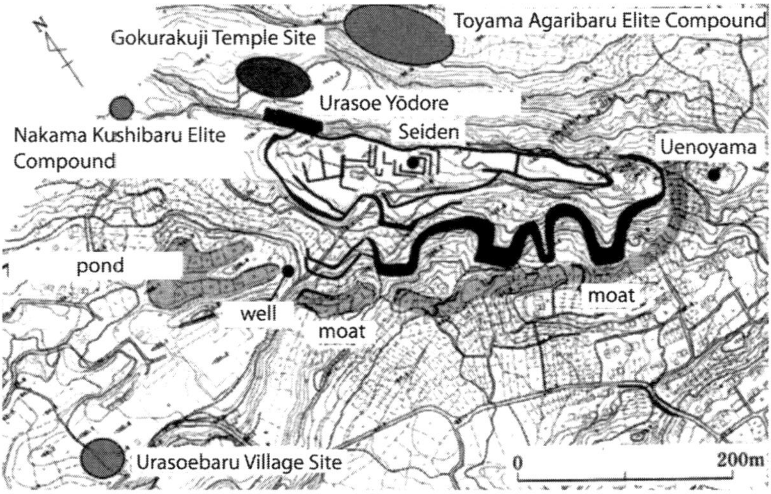

Figure 7.8. Map of the Urasoe Gusuku area. Adapted, with permission, from Asato 2006, 27. Courtesy of Asato Susumu.

thirteenth century, and it contains artifacts as early as the eleventh and twelfth centuries AD. Its area was 20, 000 sq m. In the late thirteenth century a castle of some 40,000 sq m of cut-stone construction, with a main palace (Seiden) with a tiled roof, was built. To the north of the castle were the royal mausoleum, temples, and elite residences. The Gokurakuji, the first temple in the Ryukyus, is thought to be in an area to the north of Urasoe Gusuku that was completely destroyed after World War II. It has been suggested that the mausoleum itself was also referred to as Gokurakuji. An elite residential site, Tōyama Agaribaru, contained a large elevated storehouse with posts set on stone bases. The space between the posts was almost 3 m (Asato 2006, 26–29). Ceramics found in the site were dated to the fourteenth to sixteenth centuries AD and included blue and white, and South Chinese Three-Color Ware (Japanese Kōnan Santsai, Chinese Huanan Sancai) used in rituals (Chapter 9 and Appendix 1). Gilt bronze fittings were also recovered. Nearby, a clay mold that may have been used for producing copies of Ming dynasty Hongwu (AD 1368 to 1398) coins was found. The presence of an elaborate storehouse plus the array of high-status ceramics and remains of metalworking indicate that this was the residence of a vassal of Urasoe when Urasoe was no longer capital of Chūzan. Village sites, Nakama Kushibaru on the west side, and Urasoebaru on the south side, were partially excavated. The Nakama Kushibaru Site yielded thirteenth to fourteenth century AD postholes and sherds of steatite cauldrons, whiteware bowls with beaded lip, and earthenware (Shimoji Yasuhiro 2004).

Urasoe Yōdore

The burial area called Urasoe Yōdore lies below the precipitous north face of the limestone ridge on which Urasoe castle is situated. It was used from the time of King Eiso up to the time of King Satto (Asato Susumu, Miyazato, et al. 2001, 119) (Appendix 2). It was very badly damaged at the end of World War II, when the structures in front of its burial caves were obliterated and the sarcophagi that they protected were exposed to the elements. After World War II the Ryukyu government replaced the broken front walls of the burial caves, and from AD 1997 to 2005 excavations and reconstruction took place. The development of the mausoleum took place in three major time periods in the late thirteenth century AD, the early fifteenth century AD, and the seventeenth to nineteenth centuries AD. The first two are discussed in detail here.

Since the mausoleum can be seen from the river port of Machiminato, it would have been an important symbol of local power at the time of its construction. Momojanabaka, a similar cave type of burial area, with wooden coffins and enclosing front walls of wood, overlooks the harbor of Unten, near Nakijin Gusuku, described below. In the late thirteenth century AD two artificial caves were carved into the limestone cliff face. In their present form they are each about 500 cubic m in volume. The floor area of the west cave is 123 sq m, and its height is 3.6 m. In the late thirteenth century AD the front of the caves was open to public view. Inside the caves were wooden structures consisting of a roof covered with Korean-type roof tiles and supporting posts set on pillar bases (Urasoe Shi 2001). Korean-style roof tiles were used in very high status buildings at Urasoe, Shuri, and a few other sites such as Katsuren. These structures each housed a wooden Chinese-style chest (*karabitsu*) with elevated legs, which was painted with red lacquer and had gilt bronze fittings. This type of chest has a very long tradition in Japan, being used to store treasures, clothing, or books.

The Urasoe wooden caskets were lacquered and had diamond-shaped metal fittings, some of which were found in the debris from the renovation of the early fifteenth century AD (Urasoe Shi 2005a). They are of the same type as the gilt bronze fittings on a palace-shaped receptacle in the Saidaiji Temple (Nara), which is dated to the thirteenth century AD (Kubo 2003). As mentioned above, the Urasoe wooden structures housing the caskets had stone pillar bases supporting posts and roofs tiled with Koryo-type tiles. The motif on the end of the circular tile ends is a lotus flower (Type 1B) such as those on the Koryo tiles found on Chindo, Korea, at the Yongjang Castle (Eight-Petal Lotus Flower B). Yongjang Castle was a palace used for a short period between 1270 and 1273 AD (Mokpo Taehakkyo Panmulgwan 1990). The Urasoe Yōdore Lotus Flower Type 1B tiles are found together as part of a set with flat tiles with the stamped in-

Figure 7.9 (a). Stone coffin from Urasoe Yōdore, early fifteenth century AD. Coffin No. 1. From Urasoe Shi 2005b, 56, 58. Courtesy of Shi Kyōiku Iinkai.

scription "Mizunoto Tori Doshi Kōraigasho Tsukuru" (Koryo Tile Made in the Year Mizunoto Tori) (Urasoe Shi Shishi Henshū Iinkai 1986; Asato Susumu 2009, 58). There are various interpretations debating which sixty-year cycle is correct. Considering the date of the Yongjang Castle, there is a high probability that Mizunoto Tori must be AD 1273. Radiocarbon determinations also support the date of AD 1273, the ninth year of the Southern Song Xianchun reign.

In the first half of the fifteenth century AD, a major renovation occurred in which the roofed structures and wooden sarcophagi were replaced with imposing carved, lidded stone sarcophagi of green tuff from Quanzhou, Fujian (Figure

Figure 7.9 (b). Stone coffin from Urasoe Yōdore, early fifteenth century AD. Coffin No. 4. From Urasoe Shi 2005b, 56, 58. Courtesy of Shi Kyōiku Iinkai.

7.9), and the caves were closed in with walls and entry doors (Urasoe Shi 2001; 2005b). In front of these a forecourt was created and enclosed by a wall protecting the cave entrances from public view. The forecourt was entered through an arch connecting it to a small outer terrace. A portion of the pathway leading down to the outer court from the castle was enclosed by extending a wall up to a natural overhang to create an artificial tunnel leading to the mausoleum. When further renovations took place some time after the burial of King Shō Nei and his family in the early seventeenth century AD, the outer walls were made higher and a wide terrace was added below the walled forecourt.

How is it known that the first renovation of the Yōdore Mausoleum occurred in the first half of the fifteenth century? The method of constructing the stone wall is termed *nunozumi*. The vertical edges between the stones in each alternating horizontal row line up above and below each other, creating a broken line down the wall, like a vertical warp in cloth, which passes over and under the weft. According to Tōma Shi'ichi (1988), the use of this method dates from the fourteenth century to the early fifteenth century AD. The first renovation can thus be dated to the first half of the fifteenth century AD. A large quantity of ceramics dating to the first half of the fifteenth century AD were found, and the radiocarbon dates also cluster around the early fifteenth century AD. Decoration on the four sides of the stone sarcophagi consists of birds and flowers, deer, lion dogs, and Buddhist figures and treasures. The lids are carved to imitate tiled roofs with finials, and the tile ends have motifs of dragons and phoenixes. From the style of the imitation roof tiles, the date of manufacture must be in the early fifteenth century AD, since the female tiles have a triangular flap that was unknown before that time (Education Commission 1975, 38).

A total of twelve elite coffins of stone imported from Fujian are known in Okinawa (Seto 2009b, 136). They all take the shape of a "palace" with tile roof, and they are often decorated with Buddhist motifs.

Walling up of the burial caves removed the burials from public view and rendered them enclosed and secret. The interiors of the burial chambers, including the floors, were painted white. The stone sarcophagi were arranged in an L shape, to imitate the Seiden and two flanking buildings, as in an actual large *gusuku*. These changes are thought to reflect the development of the sun god ideology of the Ryukyu Kingdom, in which the rulers were thought to be descendants of the sun god (Asato Susumu 2009; Hokama 1986). As early as the mid-fourteenth century at Nakijin and the mid-fifteenth century AD at Shuri, the orientation of the Seiden shifted from south facing to west facing, reflecting a shift from Chinese to local ideology and orientation to the sun.

The bones in the large stone sarcophagi Nos. 1 and 4, installed in the first renovation of Yōdore, belong to the Initial Period, whereas the individuals buried in Nos. 2 and 3 belong to the First Shō Dynasty (AD 1429 to 1469). Analysis of mitochondrial DNA on the skeletons from No. 4 showed that both have Haplotype F (Shinoda 2005), common in south China and Southeast Asia. At this time Ryukyu overseas trade with Southeast Asia was not yet fully developed. Thus, the mtDNA appears to be related to south China and the center of Quanzhou. Since mtDNA is transmitted through the mother, the most likely explanation for the presence of the mtDNA is that one of the wives of King Eiso must have been Chinese, from Quanzhou. The clay analysis of the roof tiles from Urasoe Yōdore showed that both the Koryo and Yamato types were produced in Okinawa (Urasoe Shi 2005a), indicating that although the manufacturing techniques were imported, the tiles were made locally. A male cranium from Sarcophagus No. 2 was typical of the Japanese mediaeval population (Doi 2005). The average height of skeletons from Yōdore was 157 to 163 cm for males and 146 to 148 cm for females (ibid.), while the averages for individuals from the Shuri Tama Udun Mausoleum of the Second Shō Dynasty (AD 1470 to 1879) were 155.6 cm (males) and 144.8 cm (females) (ibid.), some 4 to 5 cm shorter than the average of the former population. The taller individuals were probably recent immigrants. It appears that the flesh was removed from the bones with the aid of small cutting implements, since cut marks on the bones have been observed (Tamaki 2010). From historical sources, Tamaki Nobuhiko reconstructed the distinctive royal burial ritual of the fifteenth century AD. The king's body was first placed in a wooden receptacle and later defleshed, and the bones were washed. Then the bones were placed in a temporary stone sarcophagus, which was replaced after three years by a permanent stone sarcophagus. This study would suggest that the early wooden chest later became a stage in the royal burial ritual.

The Amida Triad motif on the sarcophagus has been interpreted by China Teikan (2005) to mean that the royal family embraced Jōdo Shinshū Pure Land Buddhism, while the bird motifs indicate local Chinese religion). The form of the sarcophagus base shares features with Islamic and Christian tombstone bases from Quanzhou. In addition, the location and structure of the Yōdore tomb shows belief in local Okinawan concepts of the other world of Nirai Kanai (Asato Susumu 2009). In the twelfth to fourteenth centuries AD, commoners in most parts of the Ryukyus were buried in rectangular graves in the ground, usually but not always in wooden coffins. This pattern reflects influence from the Japanese main islands. In the fifteenth to sixteenth centuries there was a shift to burial in areas protected by cliffs, in which the body was first exposed to the elements, and later the bones were placed in a wooden coffin. In the seventeenth century AD ceramic burial jars came into use (Seto 2009b). (The unusual "turtle-back" (*kamekobaka*) tombs of "traditional Okinawa" did not appear until the seventeenth and eighteenth centuries AD.)

Metalworking Sites

Three pits with remains of metalworking were found during excavation of the flat area below the walled enclosure in front of the burial caves (Urasoe Shi 2007; Asato Susumu 2009). A separate oblong pit yielded discarded roof tiles, burned wood, and metal fittings, from the renovation of the early fifteenth century AD. One of the pits yielded two sherds of whiteware dating to the late thirteenth century AD, and a gilt bronze fitting from the wooden burial chest and celadon sherds dating to the late fourteenth and fifteenth centuries AD.

Three radiocarbon dates from an earth pit in Locality C gave dates in the thirteenth century. Although no molds or mold fragments were recovered, since the excavators found fragments of crucibles used for melting copper as well as pieces of melted copper, they concluded that the area was probably used for casting. In Area C a small quantity of gold used in gilding was found in a crucible. Tuyere valves and abrading stones were also found (Urasoe Shi 2007). The writers of the site report (Urasoe Shi 2007, 60) concluded that the stratigraphic relationships among these features were not clear. Asato Susumu (2009) has concluded that these pits represent two distinct periods of metalworking, the first dating to the latter thirteenth century AD and the second to the beginning of the fifteenth century AD, on the basis of combined evidence, including the associated artifacts.

Urasoe and the Emergence of Royal Power

Asato has concluded that the elaborate and formalized construction of Urasoe in the thirteenth century AD indicates that it was the center of power in southern and central Okinawajima by that time. To excavate the caves of Urasoe Yōdore required a large quantity of iron tools and a large labor input. The structures inside the caves had tile roofs as mentioned above; analysis of the tiles shows that they were made in the Ryukyus. The lacquer used to paint the caskets and the gilded metal fittings show the use of particular Ryukyu techniques (Kubo 2003; Yotsuyanagi 2006). Also, the metal tools and gilded objects required for the project were made locally, judging from archaeological features, which show manufacturing on site. In the construction of the burial facilities various craftsmen were mobilized: carpenters, roof-tile makers, fine woodworkers, and specialists in lacquering, metal casting, forging, metalworking, and gilding. These craftsmen would have worked on the construction of the castle. In order to sustain royal power, their skills and labor would also have been required for the maintenance of the castle and mausoleum. Yōdore surpassed the tombs of other local chiefs in scale, content, construction, labor, and craft organization required, and the quantity of iron tools. All of these support the notion of Eiso's royal power. Generally it has been thought that in the twelfth and thirteenth centuries AD, three centers in northern, central, and southern Okinawa emerged from a large group of small contending confederacies, to be unified by the Chūzan Kingdom, based at Shuri Castle, in the early fifteenth century. The evidence from Urasoe indicates a different process in which large portions of Okinawa Island were unified in the thirteenth century AD but split into three polities in the early fourteenth century AD, to be unified in the fifteenth century by Chūzan (Asato 2006; Kreiner 2008). Asato proposes that a top tier emerged in the thirteenth century AD at Urasoe, the predecessor of Shuri, that Urasoe provided a set pattern for a royal capital, consisting of palace, plaza, pond, mausoleum, and Buddhist temples, and that this pattern was rigidly maintained in other large castles (Asato 2006).

Urasoe Yōdore and International Relations

The people buried in Yōdore, from their physical morphology and DNA as well as their religious beliefs, had deep relations with the people of south China, Japan, and Koryo. The emergence of Ryukyu royal authority was based not only on Okinawan internal social development, but also on foreign interaction including intermarriage (Asato Susumu 2009). Judging from the Koryo-type roof tiles and mtDNA, the Mongol invasions of East Asia emerge as an important factor. As mentioned above the Yōdore roof tiles are the same type as those found at the Yongjang Fortified Site, dated to some time around AD 1270, on Jin Island (Chindo). It was a palace of the state of Sambyeolcho, a polity derived from the military of Koryo, which briefly became independent in a rebellion against Koryo. In AD 1273 Sambyeolcho was pushed from Jin Island to Jeju Island (Chejudo), where its forces were defeated by Koryo and Mongol forces. There is a strong possibility that not only did techniques such as roof tile making go to Okinawa, but some of the people of Sambyeolcho also went to Okinawa and contributed to the rise of the royal power of Eiso. The appearance of Haplotype F mtDNA in Okinawa indicates intermarriage between the Ryukyu royal family and overseas Chinese from Quanzhou at the time of Initial Yōdore and predates the arrival of the "Thirty-Six Families" from south China at the time of King Satto at the end of the fourteenth century AD. It is thought that the reason for the arrival of the south Chinese was to promote smooth trade relations, but the fall of Quanzhou in AD 1277 and the end of the Song dynasty in AD 1279 must have been important factors as well. At the time of the appearance of Eiso, the Mongols invaded East Asia and claimed the allegiance of Koryo, the Southern Song had collapsed, and even Japan experienced turbulence. The Ryukyus were connected to continental events at this time, including the fall of the Song dynasty and the Mongol occupation (Asato Susumu 2009).

Nakijin Gusuku

Nakijin Castle is located on the Motobu Peninsula in northern Okinawa, some 85 km north of Shuri (Nakijin Village 2008). Its sphere of power extended from

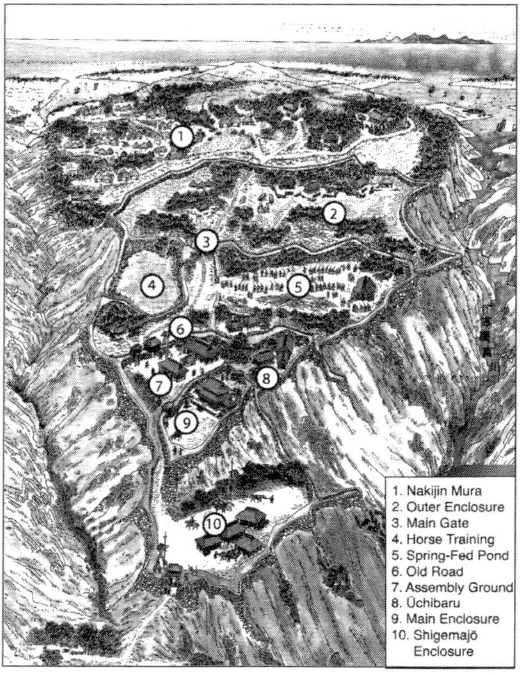

Figure 7.10. Reconstruction of Nakijin Gusuku in the late fourteenth and early fifteenth centuries AD. Reproduced with permission from the pamphlet *Sekai Isan Nakijin Jōato* (World Heritage Site Nakijin Castle), published by Nakijin Son Rekishi Bunka Sentā (no date). Courtesy of Nakijin Son Kyōiku Iinkai.

central Okinawa to the Amami Islands. It covers an area of 78,000 sq m and is located 90 to 100 m above sea level. The site commands a view to the north, which includes the islands of Izena, Iheya, and, in clear weather, Yoronjima. On its east side is the deep valley of the Shigema River. It is located on Palaeozoic, not Pleistocene, limestone, and its walls are dark in color, in contrast to the castles of southern Okinawa. The thickness of the walls varies from 2 to 6 m, and they have a circumference of about 1.5 km, with a total of ten enclosures. The rulers of Nakijin sent many tribute missions to the Ming court over a period of thirty-three years from AD 1383 to 1415. Nakijin was defeated in AD 1416 (or AD 1422 in some accounts) by Chūzan, who installed a military governor to pacify and secure the region. The village site of Shīnagusuku is traditionally thought to be a precursor of the walled site of Nakijin Gusuku. It is located 5 km inland from Nakijin Gusuku, on a hilltop some 90 m above sea level. It has two simple enclosures, which have yielded trade ceramics from the latter half of the thirteenth century AD as well as a large quantity of local earthenware (Nakijin Son 2005, 176). There is a tradition that the ruler of this small castle moved to Nakijin Gusuku, where water was more abundant (Kin 2004, 172). Nakijin Gusuku's ten enclosures include the Main Enclosure for the Palace (Seiden), a pond, a residence for female officials (Ouchibaru), and a plaza (Unā). There is also an enclosure, termed the Shigemajō Enclosure, to the south (inland) side of the Main Enclosure, which was used by retainers who serviced the palace. The largest enclosure seems to have been used for raising and training horses. In recent years substantial excavations have occurred in the northernmost large enclosure and at a village site outside of the walls on the northern side, named Nakijin Mura. Since sites in the countryside around the *gusuku* have not been covered over by the urbanization surrounding southern sites such as Shuri and Urasoe, the regional pattern is more visible. Satellite villages included Oyadomari Village to the north and Shigema village to the south. Miyagi (2007) proposed that four social classes lived in Nakijin and its surroundings: the ruling class (*aji*), retainers, castle townspeople who lived in the Northern Enclosure and Nakijin Mura, and outlying villagers (Figure 7.10).

MAIN ENCLOSURE

The stratigraphy of the Main Enclosure (Figure 7.11) has been very useful in comprehending the building sequences of Nakijin (Kin 2004). Nine layers show the preconstruction preparation and four periods of building. Layer IX is a deposit on the original surface left by a community that may have been engaged in preparing the site for later construction. It is 2 to 20 cm thick, and black in color, containing fish and wild boar/pig bones and ceramics from the end of the thirteenth century AD. Because of the irregular, hard rock surface, post construction was not possible, and settlement was impermanent. The main settlement at this time appears to be in the area of Nakijin Mura, to the north of the present castle site. The ceramics include *kamuiyaki,* local earthenware, celadon bowls with ridged lotus petal decoration dating to the thirteenth century AD, and the Nakijin Type whiteware bowl with straight rim (Kin 2007a). Similar ceramics were found at the Shīnagusuku Site, some 5 km west of Nakijin.

BUILDING PERIOD I

In Building Period I (Layer VII, end of thirteenth century AD–early fourteenth century AD), site preparation included cutting and leveling a north-south ridge and spreading the fill east to west. Linear piles as high as 1.5 m were created. Following this the builders laid down up to twenty layers of stamped earth (*hanchiku*) of red, yellow, or black soil to create a flat surface. Among the Okinawan castles investigated so far, only Nakijin has shown this refined style of stamped earth construction. On the north side of the area, facing an open plaza to the south, a large building (Seiden) was constructed. It was raised on posts. Judging from the posts, the building had four bays north-south and six bays east-west. As in Periods II, III, and IV, since no roof tiles have been found, it is

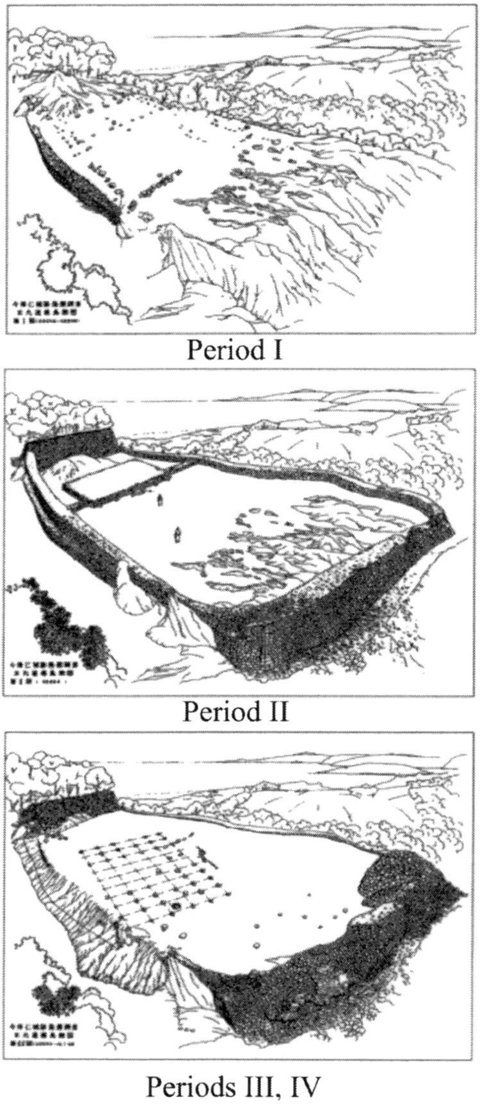

Figure 7.11. Reconstruction of the building sequence of the Main Enclosure, Nakijin Gusuku. From Miyagi 2006a, 29. Courtesy of Miyagi Hiroki and Nakijin Son Kyōiku Iinkai.

assumed that it had a wooden shingle or reed roof. A row of palisades was placed on the east (15 posts), north (3 posts), and west (15 posts). The entrance to the palisaded area was on the west, by a narrow stone path. Similar kinds of palisades can be seen at the Makubaru and Katsuren Sites. Although stone walls are thought to be typical of *gusuku* sites, these sites show that, before stone walls, wooden palisades were used. In comparison with Layer IX, ceramics are more abundant. In addition to the types found in Layer IX, new types of celadon and whiteware appear. The celadon includes bowls with an exterior horizontal line below the lip and presentation bottles. The whitewares include bowls and plates with unglazed rims and are of the Birosuku Type as well as the Nakijin Type. The former is now known to have been produced in the Pukou kilns of the Lianjiang area, Fujian. Miyagi dates the Nakijin Type to the thirteenth to fourteenth centuries AD and the Birosuku Type, with three subtypes, to the fourteenth century AD (2011, 222).

BUILDING PERIOD II

Layer VI of Building Period II (mid-fourteenth century AD) is a layer of fill, which provides the base for the period's cultural layer, Layer V. This is the period of major wall building. The present total length of the surrounding wall is 1.5 km, and the maximum height is 6 m, while the average height is more than 3 m and the thickness 1.5 to 4 m. The walls surround the ten enclosures. The plaza area was expanded and raised by a layer 5 to 30 cm thick. The main building (Seiden) was transformed from a dug post building, supported by posts dug into the ground, to a building sitting on a stone platform (*kidan*) some 90 cm high. The posts of the building sat on stone pillar bases, and the building faced south. Two winglike extensions were supported by pillars set on stone bases. This is a radical change in architectural style from a Japanese-style building with elevated floor to the use of a Chinese-style building on a raised stone platform.

In comparison to Layer I, earlier ceramic types such as local earthenware, *kamuiyaki,* and celadon with ridged lotus petal decoration decrease, while the Birosuku Type whiteware and whitewares with unglazed rims remain relatively constant. Celadon bowls with horizontal linear band and plain bowls with everted lips increase. An octagonal small Koryo inlaid celadon jar was also found. This is the oldest type of Korean celadon found in Okinawa; the same type has also been found in Dazaifu, dated thirteenth to fourteenth centuries AD. An unusual group of six celadon bowls and one plate was found buried in a small pit. It has been interpreted as a votive offering (Kin 2007a, 185).

BUILDING PERIOD III

Building Period III (Layer II, fourteenth to early fifteenth century AD) marks the height of prosperity of Nakijin. Low areas were filled in, and the whole area of the Main Enclosure was covered with new fill. Fist-size rocks were spread, and yellow soil was put over them. The construction style changed to posts set on stone bases, instead of the stone platform, which was buried. It was thought that there were two buildings, north and south. The post bases of the north building were removed in Period IV; therefore, its size is not clear. Orientation of the building in Period III is difficult to determine. Asato Susumu states that it is east-west (2006, 91), a radical change from the north-south orientation of earlier buildings.

The size of the main building remained four by five bays. An enormous quantity of ceramics was recovered. Kin believes that the ceramics were received during the eighteen tribute missions to China between AD 1383 and 1415. In contrast to smaller vessel forms of celadon and whiteware in Periods I and II, there were large pieces, flower vases, and wine presentation bottles. There were also Yuan blue and white and Ming blue and white wares, celadon ridgeless lotus petal celadon bowls, bowls with thunder pattern (*raimontai*) decoration, and plain whiteware everted rim bowls (Kin 2009). The two earlier types of whiteware, Nakijin and Birosuku Types, were absent. Of particular note are blue and white jars with dragon motif. The dragons have three and four claws, not the five claws of the highest ranked wares. These are most likely tributary gifts from China. All of Layer II belongs to Period III. The upper part of Layer II is mixed with Layer I, but there is a substantial portion, 50 to 100 cm thick, that is not disturbed (Kin 2007a, 185).

BUILDING PERIOD IV

Building Period IV (AD 1416 [1422?] to 1655?) dates to the years following the defeat of Nakijin by Chūzan, dated to AD 1416 or 1422 AD, when Nakijin was occupied by a governor who in early times was a close relative of the king of Ryukyu. From the mid-fifteenth century AD the governorship passed from father to son. The governorship lasted until 1665 AD, after which the castle was not occupied but became the locus of a group of important shrines (*utaki*). In the Main Enclosure a large building set on posts on stone bases was built to face west onto the plaza. The total dimensions were 12.2 m by 19.5 m. From the pattern of the pillar bases, it is possible that instead of one large building there were two smaller buildings. Since no roof tiles were found in association with this building, it is thought that the roof was made of wooden slats or reeds.

Sherds of Chinese, Thai, Vietnamese, and Korean wares were found; however, the large Chinese vessels of Period III are absent. The most common types of celadon are bowls with the thunder pattern (*raimontai*) on the exterior rim, bowls decorated with thin lotus petals, and plates with a petal form rim. Plates with chrysanthemum decoration and small white plates with straight rims were also found. Some fifty specimens of whiteware dish-shaped lamps were also found. The Thai ceramics included boxes, *kendi* spouted pouring vessels, and ewers, as well as large- and medium-size brownware narrow-necked jars (*tsubo*) with clay lids. These were used for the transport of Thai wine. A large stock of these jars was found in the Kyōnouchi area of Shuri Gusuku (Kin 2007a, 186). The Vietnamese ceramics include celadon bowls with ridged petal decoration as well as whiteware bowls, celadon jars and bottles, and enamel decorated boxes. Korean inlaid celadon sherds were also found as well as Japanese Bizen ware shredding bowls (*suribachi*).

SHIGEMAJŌ ENCLOSURE

On the southern (inland) side of the Main Enclosure, near the back gate of the castle (Shigema Gate) and overlooking the gorge of the Shigema River, is an enclosure occupied by Period III (Kin 2007a, 188). It was terraced in five levels, and on Terraces 2, 3, and 4 there were remains of four houses with internal round hearths. The dimensions were 6 × 4 m, 7 × 6 m, 6 × 6 m, and 5 × 5 m. This enclosure is thought to have been a service area that included kitchens and storage facilities, occupied by retainers who served the rulers who occupied the Main and Ouchibaru Enclosures.

CERAMICS FROM THE SHIGEMAJŌ ENCLOSURE

Data from the four buildings and two other areas within the enclosure allow us to explore the functions and styles of ceramics in an elite residential area (Okinawa Ken Nakijin Son 1983). The total area of the enclosure is 1,700 sq m. Area 1 is a paved area leading to the adjacent Main Enclosure. Areas 2 to 4 were residential areas. One rectangular dwelling, marked by postholes, was found in each of Areas 2 and 3, and two dwellings were found in Area 4. Area 5, the lowest part of the Shigemajō Enclosure, is an area of soil deposition from higher areas, some 130 cm deep, containing abundant artifacts, carbonized grains of rice and wheat/barley, and fish and animal bones, recovered by water screening. Another area, Area 6, on a slope immediately below the Main Enclosure, was not a living surface, but yielded Yuan blue and white and other ceramics thrown away from the Main Enclosure. It appears that it was used previously for dwellings and was later terraced to improve drainage by cutting into the slope and erecting retaining walls. In Area 2 there were post molds under the fill and retaining wall and in Areas 2 and 4, artifacts from the early to mid-fourteenth century AD.

The excavation technique consisted of the removal of the surface humus layer of about 20 cm, followed by excavation in 5 cm spits. The excavators found that the stratigraphy, created by the discarding of artifacts from the Main Enclosure, was disturbed by building episodes and tree falls. Only in the deeper portions of Areas 4 and 5 was the stratigraphy thought to be intact.

In Areas 3, 4, and 5, it seems likely that the houses date to the late fourteenth and early fifteenth centuries AD, judging from the finds of Ming blue and white bowls and celadon bowls with narrow chrysanthemum petals. Judging from the virtual absence of tile fragments in the deposits, the houses did not have tile roofs. They appear to have had the same kinds of open central hearths as houses in northern Okinawa in prewar times. From the entire Shigemajō Enclosure, only 195 sherds of local earthenware were recovered (Okinawa Ken Nakijin Son 1983, 95). Although the sherds are very small, they appear to belong to narrow-necked jars (*tsubo*). In this discussion I rely on the typology and analysis carried out by the authors of the Nakijin report, Kin Seiki and Miyazato Suehiro (Okinawa Ken Nakijin Son 1983). Ceramics are not distributed evenly in the five areas of the enclosure. In all cases celadon is the most common ware, followed by whitewares and Ming blue and white. Yuan blue and white is very rare. The percentage of the three most common functional types, bowls, plates, and chargers, is very uniform across the five areas, suggesting that there might be a particular ratio that could be related to elite status. Large chargers are relatively frequent, perhaps indicating a style of eating or display of food. Both cups and tripod incense burners, while very rare, were recovered from virtually every area, suggesting that they may have been part of each household set. The outcurving lip type of celadon bowl predominates, followed by bowls with thickened rims or narrow lotus petal exterior decoration. The thunder pattern, common from the late fourteenth century into the Ming period, occurs in all the deposits. In the category of celadon plates, the most common stylistic type has an everted lip. Platters with bent and grooved rim were next. Other vessel types, such as incense burners, covered jars, ewers, bottles, and Buddhist figures, are very rare. In the distribution of functional types of whitewares, bowls predominate, followed by plates. Within the functional type of whiteware bowls, the bowls with a flat bottom or stamped decoration in this area predominated along with plates with everted rim. The functional types of the rare Yuan blue and white were various: jarlets, narrow-mouth jars, bottles, containers, and large plates or platters. Bowls were also the most common functional type of the Ming blue and white, although a substantial amount of the Ming blue and white could not be assigned to stylistic types. Yuan blue and white may have been "curated" or retained in houses as precious objects rather than discarded in the refuse dump.

LARGE NORTHERN OUTER ENCLOSURE

The largest outer enclosure has an area of some 20,000 sq m. Excavation of Areas III and IV within the Northern Outer Enclosure (Okinawa Ken Nakijin Son 2009, 239) yielded two main cultural layers, the first dating to the latter half of the thirteenth century to the middle of the fourteenth century, and the second to the first half of the fifteenth century AD. Since the stone walls in this area sit on top of a layer containing Gusuku Type pottery and early types of Fujian whitewares and Longquan celadon, one can conclude that the area was first a small open village and was later surrounded by a wall and attached to the castle. This sequence is similar to that of the Main Enclosure, where the walls were built after an early occupation. The enclosing walls were built around the mid-fourteenth century AD, and in the same time span as Period III in the Main Enclosure, the occupants built large houses and elevated storehouses. There were virtually no artifacts from the latter half of the fifteenth century. This suggests that the site declined in size after it was taken over by the Chūzan Kingdom.

NAKIJIN MURA SITE

The Nakijin Mura Site, consisting of some 40,000 sq m outside the Nakijin Gusuku northern walls, has been divided into five elite residential sites, numbered I to V. About 10 percent of the area was sampled. Investigation was carried out in preparation for building a parking lot after Nakijin Gusuku became a World Heritage Site in 2000.

Two main cultural layers, II and IV, were identified. Since Layer IV yielded *kamuiyaki* and early whitewares, it was dated to before the twelfth to thirteenth centuries AD. This area, which is flatter and more amenable to construction, was a village site at the time of the clearing of the castle site for construction (Kin 2007a, 182). However, the nature of the occupation is not clear, since the excavators could not discern clear-cut features in this layer.

Layer II dates to the latter half of the fourteenth to the sixteenth centuries AD. Most of the features were post molds of dug posts, as well as pits, left from the construction of a variety of large and small houses and elevated storehouses. Three elite residential areas (*yashikichi*) were excavated. Each consisted of the remains of a residence, marked by post molds from supporting posts, and the post molds from one to four elevated storehouses (Okinawa Ken Nakijin Son 2005).

Hearths, crucibles, and iron artifacts indicate the presence of ironworking. As in the Main and Shigemajō Enclosures, more than 90 percent of all the finds were Chinese ceramics. They were also of similar types and frequencies, including high-quality types such as Yuan blue and white bottles and wine jars (*shukai tsubo*). Thai ceramics were also found as well as beads and coins. Food remains included carbonized rice, millet, wheat, and barley. The prestigious types of ceramics plus substantial amounts of rice indicate that this was an elite area with close connections to the rulers who lived in the Main Enclosure (Okinawa Ken Nakijin Son 2008, 80–82).

FAUNAL AND FLORAL ANALYSES

Analysis of samples obtained by flotation and pickup methods was undertaken by Tōizumi (2007b) from a number of locations in the entire Nakijin site. The samples from Area IIIb, Residential Area No. 2, in Nakijin Mura included remains of reef fish—Labridae (*bera,* wrass), Scaridae (*budai,* parrot fish), Lethrinidae (*fuefukidai,* emperor bream)—and also small migrant, inshore fish such as *Siganus* (*aigo,* rabbit fish). Remains of dugong and sea turtles were not found in these samples, and there were virtually no remains of chickens. Bones of domesticated pig, horse, and cow were found, the cow bones showing butchering marks. There seem to be differences between houses within the elite residential areas in the relative frequency of horses and pigs. Houses with relatively high numbers of pig bones had relatively few bones of horses, and vice versa. In the Shigemajō area there were dugong and seal bones, and fish bones occurred in higher frequencies than in other residential areas. In the Main Enclosure there were bones of a wide variety of fish, plus chickens. Tōizumi found that there was a general correspondence to Miyagi's model of four strata for the Nakijin area: Class 1 (rulers, *aji*) in the Main Enclosure; Class II, retainers, in the Shigemajō Enclosure; Class III ("castle town," *jōkamachi*), Nakijin Mura; and Class IV, general villagers or commoners, in outlying sites. The general pattern seems to show that the occupants of the Main Enclosure ate chickens, fish, and wild boar/pig, and those in the residential area outside the walls, in Nakijin Mura, consumed cow and horse, agricultural animals that were eaten only at the end of their working life. The Shigemajō occupants consumed fish and dugong as well as cow, showing an intermediate position between the Main Enclosure and Nakijin Mura. One house site, No. 2, in Nakijin Mura, seemed to have higher frequencies of fish and wild boar. Tōizumi noted that fish remains from inside the castle are of larger individual fish but cautioned that this trend needs to be confirmed with further research (Tōizumi 2007b, 262). He found that fishing gear occurred both in the Shigemajō Enclosure and in one house in Nakijin Mura, suggesting that it may have been shared by different groups. Tōizumi concluded that boar/pig is more common in elite sites, while cow is found in sites thought to belong to people of lower status. The high social value of boar/pigs may reflect acculturation to China. A tiger claw found in the Main Enclosure may have come from a tiger skin, which was a symbol of very high status (ibid., 263).

Analysis of plant remains undertaken by Takamiya Hiroto (2007) indicated that rice was most common in screened samples from the main enclosures of Nakijin Gusuku, but in the residential areas outside the castle walls other kinds of dry crops were more abundant than rice. These include barley (*Hordeum vul-*

gare, ōmugi), wheat (*Triticum aestivum, komugi*), broomcorn millet (*Panicum miliaceum, kibi*), and foxtail millet (*Setaria italica, awa*).

Gusuku Period Communities

In the span of a few centuries, the societies and landscapes of the Ryukyus were completely transformed. Virtually all of our knowledge comes from recent excavations, although the full implications of the excavations are still being assessed.

The Gusuku Site Group Community

The earliest community is represented by the Gusuku Site Group of Kikaigashima, thought to be a Yamato government outpost. While its beginning actually precedes the Gusuku Period, it is best discussed with this period since it had important consequences for life at this time. The sites span the Kodai (Ancient) and Chūsei (Mediaeval) periods of Japanese history. As the Kodai Period gave way to the Chūsei Period, a shift from government-controlled trade to private commerce took place. The imposing size, methods of construction, and style of buildings as well as the artifact assemblages show that the community was composed of outsiders from the Japanese main islands. The inland location of the raised terraces of Kikaigashima indicates that defense must have been important. Some of the large buildings appear to have been warehouses used for storage, perhaps for supplies, since it seems that the community was not self-sufficient. It must have consisted of official and traders, involved in the securing and transport of local products such as shells and sulfur. The community must have been established to regulate commerce on the southern boundary of Yamato and to establish loose political control over the area. Elite Chinese *yue* ceramics show links to Dazaifu, the official Yamato center for interaction with continental Asia. Ironworking remains at the sites of Ōufu and Maehata may have been devoted to the needs of the outpost, but it seems likely that the Gusuku Site Group served as a point of distribution to the Amami Islands for iron goods coming from the Japanese main islands.

The Kikaigashima community must have played a role in the establishment and operation of the Kamuiyaki kilns on Tokunoshima. *Kamuiyaki* sherds are abundant in the sites, and Kikaigashima and Tokunoshima are within sight of each other. The nature of their relationship requires further investigation. Although Kikaigashima is mentioned as a place of exile in the twelfth century AD, no historical documents describe the island before that date.

It has been proposed that the very large quantity of steatite cauldron fragments indicates that Hakata traders may have been part of the community, since they are known to be associated with their trade and use. The Gusuku Site Group represents different communities serving different purposes, at different time periods. As the centralized government control of trade declined in Japanese main islands centers such as Dazaifu in the eleventh century AD, a similar shift to private trade must have taken place on Kikaigashima. The decline of the sites by the thirteenth century AD must be related to political instability in the Yamato center and the rise of power in the Okinawa Islands.

The Kamuiyaki Pottery Community

A community of skilled potters lived and worked on southern Tokunoshima from the tenth to fourteenth centuries. Although over one hundred kilns have been recovered, and sherds of *kamuiyaki* are found on more than four hundred sites throughout the Ryukyus, the number of kilns operating at any one time during such a long period must have been small. In fact, one wonders if production could even have been continuous. However, the community maintained its identity for several centuries. The complexities of manufacturing stoneware in a region that had previously produced only earthenware and the wide distribution of vessels throughout the Ryukyus required expertise, capital, and organization from sources outside the archipelago. Entrepreneurial expertise must have shifted to meet changing conditions within the region. At present there seems to be no information about the life of the potters.

Traders' Communities

Circulating through the Ryukyus were communities of traders, who can be identified in part by their wares. Their relationship to officials living in the Gusuku Site Group needs to be explored in future. Hakata traders, closely linked to Chinese Song dynasty networks that brought Chinese commerce to Hakata, carried Song white ceramic wares, along with soapstone cauldrons and *kamuiyaki*. Although no sunken ships have been found with this combined cargo, the combination of Chinese and Japanese wares on most living sites is interpreted as evidence that these wares were carried together from Kyushu. Twelfth century AD underwater sites at Kurakisaki, Amami Island, and Nakanohama, Kumejima, consist solely of Chinese ceramic wares, confirming the existence of a route from the China coast to Kyushu through the Ryukyus, which is discussed in Chapter 8. Independent traders from Fujian also brought local wares to Sakishima in the twelfth to fifteenth centuries AD (Ōhama 2008).

Local Communities

The islands were dotted with small agricultural coastal and inland villages consisting of groups of houses with elevated floors, set on substantial posts (*hottate bashira*), and elevated storehouses. This type of construction, originating in the Japanese main islands, persisted up to the twentieth century. Throughout the Ryukyus there are variations in village plans, but all share a common set of artifacts including iron tools and the ubiquitous triad of trade wares: whitewares, *kamuiyaki,* and steatite cauldrons. In the Gusuku Period most villages were unfortified, but in the subsequent Early Ryukyu Kingdom Period, villages in Yaeyama were often walled. Remains of ironworking have been found in many villages. In southern and central Okinawajima, Asato Susumu (1990) found that spatial groupings of villages shared similar types of temper in their pottery, indicating that they were social groups. These groups were similar to later political groupings of *gusuku* sites based on spatial proximity (Ladefoged and Pearson 2000) and to the *magiri* political units of the seventeenth century AD and later. As mentioned earlier, dryland crops such as millet, barley, wheat, and barnyard grass were common in central and southern Okinawa, whereas rice cultivation was more common in northern Okinawajima and Amami Ōshima.

Small Port Communities

A survey of sites on Kikaigashima revealed many small natural ports bearing names ending in *tsu*, meaning "port" (Ikehata 2008). The same term is found throughout the Japanese main islands. Small ports were often attached to *gusuku* sites, such as the port sites attached to large sites such as Urasoe and Katsuren. In addition, throughout the islands there are beaches where sherds of trade ceramics can be found in abundance. Such places must have been small ports for local trade, and nearby settlements must have been somewhat different from inland agricultural communities. There were probably also local fishing enclaves, although these have not yet been identified from excavations or survey.

Communities Living in Gusuku

The walled structures of the Late Gusuku Period are the most distinctive features of Ryukyu archaeology. Who lived in them, and how did they actually function? The artifactual assemblages and architectural features support later historical accounts that they were the residences of elites (*aji*) who competed for

TABLE 7.1 Changes in Subsistence, Commerce, Politics, and Ethnicity in Ryukyu Secondary State Formation

Approximate Date	*Chronological Indicator*	*Subsistence*	*Commerce*	*Politics*	*Ethnicity*
Late Shellmound AD 600 to 800	Kaigen Tsūhō, *Turbo* trade sites	adoption of cereal cultivation plus root crop cultivation?	*Turbo* trade	not clear	migration from Yamato (Japan main islands) begins
Late Shellmound AD 800 to 1050	Chinese *yue* wares (rare)		*Turbo* trade	Yamato presence in Kikaigashima	
Early Gusuku AD 1050 to 1250	*kamuiyaki*, steatite cauldrons, whitewares	combination of wet/dry, cattle, horses	Song, Hakata traders, iron goods distri-bution, ceramics, *kamuiyaki*, steatite	Yamato village plan in Okinawa	migration from Yamato
Late Gusuku AD 1250 to 1300	Chinese ridged lotus petal celadon bowl			fortified *gusuku*, rise of Urasoe confederation	refugees from Korea, Southern Song?
Late Gusuku AD 1300 to 1350	Chinese plain celadon bowl		Southeast Asian trade begins (sappanwood)	power consolidation, Shuri construction, changes in Nakijin Seiden	
Late Gusuku AD 1350 to 1422	Chinese *raimontai* celadon, Yuan blue and white	two rice crops annually (Okinawa)	establishment of tributary trade, expatriate Chinese involvement	three contenders, unification, defeat of Nakijin and Ōzato	fall of Yuan, some Chinese traders move to Okinawa

trade in iron and ceramics. Weapons and fragments of iron armor of the general types found in the Japanese main islands have been recovered from *gusuku* sites, but ironworking was carried out in village sites. In the Late Gusuku Period a third tier of elites, above commoners and local chiefs, assumed royal authority under King Eiso at Urasoe. The consolidation of their power was expressed in the daily life and architecture of Urasoe and subsequently Shuri, both of which housed retainers, artisans, administrators, and religious officials.

Processes of Secondary State Formation and Increasing Social Complexity

As a summary for this chapter, I present a scenario for further testing, illustrated in Table 7.1. The Ryukyu Kingdom is a good example of a secondary state. Unlike pristine states that arose in a few places without significant contact from other states, secondary states arose on the edge of established states through trade, political domination, and migration. At least four sets of factors were involved in the development of the Ryukyu Kingdom over some eight hundred years. A tentative chronology based on trade ceramics gives a rough idea of the sequence of changes. The Northern and Central Ryukyus were in contact with Japan and probably with China for much of the period under consideration. However, political and economic changes depended on population levels, environmental factors, and strategies chosen by the islanders. Sequential processes involved in secondary state formation involved cultivation and economic circulation, immigration and emulation of the immigrants, competition, unification, and centralization. The last two processes are introduced in Chapter 9.

Chapter 8

Ryukyu Trade in the Gusuku and Early Ryukyu Kingdom Periods

In this chapter I break the chronological sequence of Chapters 7 and 9 to focus on the development of trade and the growth of the Ryukyu maritime entrepôt. This chapter provides background for both Chapters 7 and 9 on particular features of regional exchange and trade, and the ways in which they created and supported various communities in the rise of the Ryukyu Kingdom. Trade was a key factor for the island political economy of the Ryukyus. To better understand the context of trade, I cover major milestones in the history of relations between the Ryukyus, Japan, Korea, and China. The final section of the chapter shows the use of trade ceramics in exploring social relations.

Figure 8.1 is a map of major trading centers in contact with the Ryukyus, particularly in the Early Ryukyu Kingdom Period. I have incorporated material from a number of my earlier publications into this discussion. The description of Mottaimatsu, the early trading center in southern Kyushu, is based on Pearson 2007 (139–140), while the outline of the trading port of Quanzhou in Fujian Province of coastal China is derived from Pearson et al. 2002. The quoted sections on diplomatic exchange of the Ryukyu Kingdom, from the translated *Rekidai hōan* (Kobata and Matsuda 1969), were included in Pearson 1997b, and the discussion of the distribution of trade ceramics from Okinawan sites was first published in Pearson 2001. The *Rekidai hōan* (literally, *Valuable Records of Successive Generations*) is a collection 269 volumes of diplomatic documents written in Chinese and dated from AD 1424 to 1867 (Okinawa Kenritsu Toshokan 1992).

Mediaeval Ryukyu trade developed in a very particular geographic region. The Ryukyu Islands lie to the east of the Asian continent in the East China Sea, part of an inner sea running from the far north to the tropics in a zone of com-

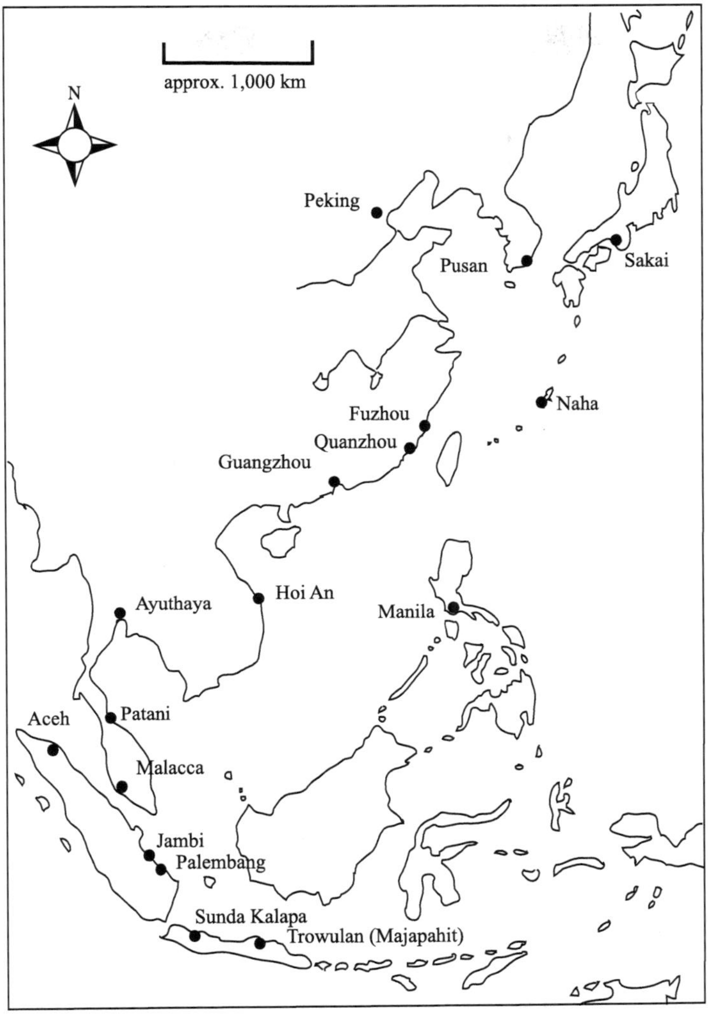

Figure 8.1. Major Asian trading centers in contact with the Ryukyu Islands in the Late Gusuku Period (AD 1250–1429) and Early Ryukyu Kingdom Period (AD 1429–1609)

plex trading relationships. In the rise of the Ryukyu Kingdom as a maritime entrepôt, trade and cultural complexity had a mutual effect on each other, trade stimulating competition, consumption, and display. As the kingdom emerged, its expanded hierarchy and political control created new motivation for long-distance trade as a kind of feedback. It is important to introduce historical, economic, and social aspects of the trade in order to comprehend recent archaeological discoveries, since the archaeological record is a palimpsest of the activities of daily life in which things move through various social settings and finally come to rest in the ground. Robb and Farr state that "in many, or most forms of exchange, the item itself is often less important than the social relationships it creates or signifies" (2005, 24). Many kinds of trade goods were perishable, and even the sites where goods were exchanged may be marked by few archaeologically visible traces. In order to fully understand the impact of trade, we need to explore linkages among all kinds of traded commodities, not only those preserved in archaeological sites, using historical sources as well as excavated materials. At the same time, archaeological data can extend interpretation beyond the range of historical sources (Gotō 2008, 19). Trade provided the information flows for the formation of identity, and the creation of culture and material goods for prosperity. It must be viewed as multilayered and reticulated, rather than looking at trade between Ryukyu and Ming independently, for example. One must examine regional differences within the Ryukyus as well: for example, the Amami region.

Two classes of goods were traded: those of local origin and those that were transshipped or relayed. In addition, some trading ships secured fresh water and local provisions from ports. Products from the Ryukyu Islands included sulfur, native horses, mother-of-pearl, textiles, and red dye from the *akagi* tree (*Bischoffia javanica*); transshipped goods included Japanese swords, fans, silver, Chinese ceramics of all kinds, food and wine in containers, textiles, coinage, and iron goods. Of great importance were Chinese cultural objects, including antiques, scrolls, books, and ceramics, some of which were retained in the Ryukyus. Southeast Asian goods included sappanwood, ceramics, incense, pepper, and other spices.

The trade artifacts surviving in archaeological sites usually consist of ceramics and metal objects such as iron tools. The ceramics include various kinds of serving vessels, such as plates, bowls, and cups, as well as vessels for processing food such as ceramic grating bowls (*suribachi*). There are also containers for wine, processed food, medicinal materials, and small valuables. Some were used as containers for cosmetics or other luxury goods or as lamps. Particular vessel forms such as incense burners and burial jars may indicate ritual and social activities. Trade ceramics constitute one of the most abundant artifact classes. Whereas other trade goods may be totally consumed or may decompose after discard, hard-fired ceramics in particular remain as durable parts of systems that might otherwise not be detectable archaeologically. Chinese ceramics are often used as chronological indicators, based on their stratigraphic position and association with dated coins or inscriptions. Sometimes they are referred to in historical documents. They may indicate interaction between the islanders and different production centers in China and Japan. Their geographical distribution may provide clues as to the agents who circulated them. Underwater sites provide information on navigation routes and may be useful for dating because they indicate which goods were shipped together. Ceramics might be considered useful for studying trade systems only because they are ubiquitous and durable, the only alternative when perishable items, more central to trade systems are not available. However, information in this chapter shows that ceramics were "primers of the pump" for trade systems and were essential to their functioning. Ceramics constitute a durable, material component of complex trade systems that transmitted goods, information, and services. We need to understand trade systems as well as trade goods.

The frequency of ceramics in sites is not simply a function of the time and rate of production of the appropriate kilns. Complex social, political, historical factors affect production, distribution, consumption of ceramics, and their distribution in archaeological sites may also be affected by geomorphological processes. Readers familiar with debates on the active role of material objects in cultural negotiations and practice will recognize that the actual ceramics, as food servers, containers, gifts, burial goods, ritual objects, and objects of prestige, were at the center of the formation of evolving and dynamic island communities.

Historical Background

As described in Chapters 6 and 7, in the latter stages of shell exchange, new phases of trade began in the eighth century AD, when islanders from Amami and the Northern Ryukyus sent tribute missions to the court at Nara. Kinoshita (2009a, 30) has described these missions of several hundred people as attempts to stimulate declining relations with the Yamato state. As mentioned in Chapter 7, excavations in Amami Ōshima and Kikaigashima in the past decade have revealed evidence of trade in *Turbo* shell as well as the remains of an outpost of the Yamato government dating from the eighth to eleventh centuries AD. In the eleventh century kilns for the production of gray stoneware, which was traded throughout the Ryukyus up to the fourteenth century AD, were established on Tokunoshima. These wares, termed *kamuiyaki,* were distributed by traders from Hakata and the southern Satsuma Peninsula, who sailed the length of the Ryukyu Archipelago. Together with the stoneware, new types of Chinese whitewares and steatite cooking pots or cauldrons from southern Kyushu were traded. In the twelfth century AD substantial quantities of celadon and brownwares from the Longquan kilns of Zhejiang Province and kilns in Fujian were also shipped into the islands by Chinese traders resident in Hakata. From the latter half of the thirteenth century AD, a major shift in trade partners, from Japan to China, occurred, with ceramics being traded to the Ryukyus from Fujian. In particular, rough whitewares were important (Miyagi 2006b). From the fourteenth century AD Okinawa became a distribution center for Chinese ceramics, and from the fourteenth to fifteenth centuries, new wares from Japan and Southeast Asia also appeared. In addition, the Chinese ceramic repertoire expanded to include wares from Jiangxi Province and the production center of Jingdezhen.

Of particular importance for the Ryukyus was the Ming Maritime Trade Ban (Chinese Ming Haijin), which prohibited all private maritime trade with China, permitting only official trade. (For convenience I refer to it hereafter as the Ming Ban.) This system, in which coastal populations were forced to move inland, was applied from as early as the beginning of the Ming dynasty. The stringency of restrictions varied throughout the Ming Ban. The polities of Chūzan, Sanhoku, and Sannan were granted tribute status from about AD 1372 and were able to trade officially with China; after unification in AD 1429, the Ryukyu Kingdom was the sole power in the Ryukyus to retain tributary status with the Ming government. It relayed goods to other polities who had more restricted access to China, such as Japan. The Ming Ban was a factor in the prosperous trade of the Ryukyu Kingdom until AD 1567, when it was lifted. The purpose of the ban was not only to control piracy and tax evasion along the coast, but also to curb commercial power. Further details are given in the section of this chapter devoted to trade with China.

Throughout the period under discussion, much of the trade was in the hands of private traders. From AD 1372, tributary trade with China commenced. Since it figures prominently in official historical records, it catches our attention. Although tributary trade was officially the only type of trade permitted with China under the Ming Ban, private trade actually continued. With its lifting in AD 1567, private trade again took the lead, but tribute missions to China from the Ryukyus continued until the mid-nineteenth century AD. Diplomatic exchange was most active in the heyday of the Ryukyu Kingdom in the fifteenth century AD.

I have attempted to separate the general background of historical relations with Japan, China, and Korea from the dynamics of various types of trade; however, the reader may find overlap between these two topics.

Trade Relations with Japan

Although the archaeological record shows a preponderance of Chinese trade ceramics and the sheer quantity of historical sources on tributary trade and diplomatic relations with China is overwhelming, one must not lose sight of the profound significance of relations with Japan. New discoveries from Kikaigashima and the Satsuma Peninsula of southern Kyushu have changed our notion that the Ryukyus were isolated from Japan in the latter half of the first millennium.

The nature of historical documentation of relations with the Japanese main islands is very different in its quantity and nature from the entries in the official Chinese histories. Japan played a far greater role in Ryukyu's early development than has been appreciated. The relative scarcity of studies on the role of Japan can be explained by the incomplete nature of the surviving historical sources (Nelson 2006).

In addition to trade between the Ryukyus and Japan, tribute missions from Japan to China appear to have passed through the Ryukyus for a short period. Official tribute missions from the Yamato court to China (*kentōshi*) followed a southerly route from the Gotō Islands to the mouth of the Yangtze in the eighth century AD. These were large delegations of five hundred people in four ships, which often became lost from each other during the voyage. Two ships are recorded to have made landfall on Tanegashima in AD 734 and Okinawa in AD 753 (Fuqua 2004). From these ships as well as from Chinese traders, Tang dynasty Kaigen Tsūhō coins may have been introduced into the Ryukyus.

Mottaimatsu, Southern Kyushu

Although Mottaimatsu is in southern Kyushu and not in the Ryukyu Islands proper, it is essential for understanding the Ryukyus. I have included it in this chapter as background material.

In the eleventh century AD, Japanese and Chinese merchants from Hakata, the commercial trading port that superseded the official government-controlled trading facilities of the Korokan attached to Dazaifu, began to venture into the Ryukyus. They played a critical role in Ryukyu trade and economic development. In addition to Hakata, new discoveries have been made in northern Kyushu. Early Ryukyu trade with the Japanese main islands should be considered part of the broad subject of trade between Song dynasty China and Japan. Song trade was a key factor in Japan's mediaeval transformation.

Recent excavations have revealed an important trading center at the mouth of the Manose River in southern Kagoshima Prefecture and in the nearby Bōnotsu area (Kinpo Chō 1998; Kinpo Chō Rekishi Shinpojiumu Jikkōinkai 1999; Miyashita 1998). This area holds a key to understanding sites in Amami Ōshima and Tokunoshima. Sunken ships also attest to commercial activity in the area, and historical documents shed some light on the structure of local power and its influence. Excavations at the Mottaimatsu Site uncovered layers from the Yayoi to Mediaeval Periods (Kinpo Chō 1998; Yamamoto Nobuo 1997; 2003), the Chinese ceramics from Mottaimatsu dating from the latter half of the eleventh century AD to the beginning of the fourteenth century AD. In Mottaimatsu Period I (AD 1050 to 1150), the ceramics were mostly white-wares. The peak of trade was reached in Period II (AD 1150 to 1200), when trade wares were mostly from Tong'an (Fujian) and Longquan (Zhejiang) (Yanagihara 1999; 2003).

Since no other sites with such abundant remains of early trade have been discovered thus far in Kagoshima Prefecture, the site is very important in the study of early mediaeval trade (Yamamoto Nobuo 2003). Chinese wares from the twelfth century AD included unusual types such as Cizhou wares, yellow-glazed basins painted with iron glaze from Quanzhou, and whiteware bowls and small green jars from the Fujian area. Large earthenware vessels of forms that have been found only at Dazaifu, the regional government center near Hakata in north Kyushu; ceramics from Izumi (near Ōsaka), and older low-fired (*kawarake*) pottery from the Kinai region; as well as wares from many different parts of Japan including gray stoneware (*sueki*) were found. The time span of the ceramics extends from the late eleventh century AD to the early thirteenth century AD (Yamamoto Nobuo 2003). Some Chinese trade ceramics from the 1981 excavation of the Ichijōin Temple in Bōnotsu and surface collections from nearby Tomarihama date to the twelfth century AD, corroborating the early mediaeval activity seen at Mottaimatsu (Hashiguchi 2004).

The general area of Mottaimatsu consisted of an administrative center, temples and shrines, a Chinese community, and a market. Near Mottaimatsu is the Kozono Site, an important local center on the western slopes of Mt. Kinpo, a religious mountain sharing many features with Mount Kinpo to the south of Nara. It yielded high-quality trade ceramics similar in type and date to those from Mottaimatsu (Kinpo Chō 2000), suggesting that it was an elite administrative center (Miyashita 1998). Twenty sherds of *kamuiyaki* gray stoneware were found in the site. Mottaimatsu and Kozono were part of a network of sites including a temple site to the deity Kannon (Miyashita 2003; Yanagihara 2003), in the region of Mount Kinpo. Several of these sites have produced incense burners, *tenmoku* (oil-spot glaze) bowls, and soapstone Buddhist images. These sites are a northern anchor point for the *kamuiyaki* trade network and must have played some role in the development of the kilns.

In the twelfth century AD commercial activity in the Inland Sea of Japan increased. Taira no Kiyomori, a samurai who gained control of the court in Kyoto, had aspirations to expand trade with the Song dynasty and to bring Song ships into the Inland Sea, beyond the control of Hakata. Excavations at the port site of Ōwada Tomari, later called Hyōgo Tsu, have yielded abundant twelfth-century Chinese celadons. Kiyomori died in AD 1181, and events in Japan and China cut short Japan's relations with Song. However, I expect that future research will show that twelfth-century Heian networks were active far to the south in the Ryukyus, in the Northern and Central Ryukyus. The trade of *Turbo* shell for decoration of monuments such as the Byōdōin, in Uji, and the Konjikidō, in Hiraizumi, are part of a picture of expansive political and economic relations.

Later Trade

Trading links between Japan and Ryukyu were not as closely monitored or restricted by the central authorities as they were in China. From the end of the fifteenth century AD, there was no single unified administration in Japan with which Ryukyu islanders had to deal. As one might expect from the turbulent heterarchical political landscape of Japan in the fourteenth to sixteenth centuries AD, relations with Japanese trading factions were complicated and unstable. At least six factions received goods and sent ships: the Ashikaga shōguns; the Hosokawa, Ōuchi, and Shimazu clans; and the Hakata and Sakai merchants (Kōji Ito 2008). The complicated interplay of these powers affected the distribution of Japanese goods in the Ryukyus in ways that are not yet completely understood.

Whereas Ryukyu was influenced by the Ming state, it was influenced by Japan as a cultural entity (Nelson 2006, 370). A period of intense trade between Japan and Ryukyu occurred in the late fourteenth and fifteenth centuries AD. Since direct trade between Japan and China was restricted during the Ming Ban, relaying trade between Ryukyu and Japan accelerated. Ryukyu ships brought goods from China and Southeast Asia to Hakata and to the port of Hyōgo Tsu (Kobe). The most active period was from AD 1429 to 1440, but between AD 1403 and 1466 there were fifteen voyages from the Ryukyu Kingdom to the Muromachi Bakufu (Tsuzuki 2011b, 97). At this time Thai and Vietnamese wares appeared in the site of Sakai, Osaka. Documentary evidence shows that Naha functioned not only as an official port for trade with China, but also as a port for private and official trade with regions such as Kagoshima and the Inland Sea (Niijima 2005). Yogi (1995, 7) reports that in 1433 the Chinese envoy Li Shan brought two thousand strings of cash with him and purchased some thirty-two luxury swords as well as sulfur. While such swords could have been produced in Ryukyu, it seems more plausible that they were relayed from Japan. The swords were decorated with gold, silver, lacquer, and shell inlay. Although it should be noted that Ming trade regulations prohibited the export of arms or coinage from China, private trade in weapons may have been more important than previously recognized. Hand-held cast iron bazooka-like fire cannons, produced in China in the Yongle period (AD 1403 to 1424), were displayed by the Ryukyu envoy to Kyoto in 1466 (Yogi 1995; Uezato 2002).

Merchants from the port of Sakai played an important role in the managing of relations between Japan and the Ryukyus. They became particularly active from the latter part of the fifteenth century AD, traveling on their own route, which avoided the Inland Sea and followed the Pacific coast of Shikoku and Kyushu to Kagoshima and Okinawajima, and on to the Fujian coast and Quanzhou (Morimura 2007a, b; 2009; Tsuzuki 2011a, b; 2012). The route was taken on the return of the tributary mission from the shogun to Ming China in AD 1469 because of danger in the Inland Sea caused by the Ōnin Disturbances. Finds of Thai black-glazed jars with four ears and Chinese brownwares in Sakai and ports along this route including the Ryukyus confirm documentary evidence of its existence.

Powerful Zen temples in Kyoto and Sakai merchants sponsored this trade route. Collcutt states that when the great "Five Mountain" temples of the Rinzai Sect of Zen were deprived of the landholdings in the latter fifteenth and early sixteenth centuries, they turned to the China trade to earn revenue (1981, 253–284). On most of the trade missions sent by various Kyoto powers from AD 1401 to AD 1547, Zen monks were the chief envoys and often traders as well. Kai'in Shōko, who belonged to the Nanzenji Zen temple of Kyoto, was a founder of the Enkakuji temple of Shuri described in Chapter 9. He not only served as a cleric, but also acted as political envoy of the King of Ryukyu (Murai 1994). In AD 1527, the priest Ankei, former abbot of both Tennoji and Enkakuji in Okinawa, was sent to negotiate the restoration of relations between Japan and Ming, which were suspended by China after the Ningbo Incident of AD 1523 (Murai 1994, 194).

This network of Zen temples stimulated trade and consumption of luxury items such as ceramics, incense, textiles, shells, and medicinal products as well as other craft products. Tea drinking was particularly important, acting as a stimulant for all kinds of cultural exchange. Excavations in Sakai and the Ryukyus have shown that huge quantities of ceramics were required for the consumption of tea and its associated rituals (Morimura 2007b, 2009). Morimura proposes that the spread of Bizen wares to Kagoshima and the Ryukyus was in part related to new forms of Zen vegetarian cuisine, which required shredding bowls, and that several important Bizen shapes were copied from Vietnamese trade ware brought to Sakai in the late sixteenth century (Morimura 2006). Thus Zen Buddhism, tea practice, and luxury trade linked the Kyoto Sakai area to Kagoshima, Ryukyu, and Fujian. Through this route all kinds of Chinese and Southeast Asian raw materials and finished goods flowed into the

Ryukyus. The ceramics included tea bowls, tea containers, braziers, boxes, and incense burners (Arakaki 2007).

Uezato lists twelve Buddhist temples in different parts of Naha. These were devoted to the needs of Japanese residents and were considered foreign religious institutions by the Okinawans. Records of family genealogies of immigrant Japanese families from the fifteenth century AD show connections to the Kinai (including Sakai), Hokuriku (Echizen), and Tokara Islands. He also lists nine Shintō shrines located in Naha (6), Shuri (2), and Nakagusuku (1) (2005, 5, 6). They were primarily of the Kumano Gongen Sect. There is mention of the Nihon Kan warehouse, residence, and financial facilities. Japanese also traded silver to Ryukyu. Merchants made congratulatory presents of silver at the time of accession of a new Ryukyu ruler to gain favor (Uezato 2008).

The first appearance in the Ryukyus of mediaeval ceramics from mainland Japan seems to occur in the mid-fourteenth century AD with the import of gray tileware braziers and shallow bowls (*gashitsu doki*) (Seto 2007, 226). This type of pottery has been labeled *hondo kei* (Japanese main islands type) *doki*. It is a smooth dense grayware, softer than stoneware, decorated with rows of stamped chrysanthemum flowers below the rims. The vessels date mostly to the fifteenth and sixteenth centuries AD, are found in *gusuku* sites and temples, and may have circulated through networks among Zen Buddhist temples. These wares are common in Dazaifu and Hakata. Okinawan examples are not identical although, from the analysis of the clay body, which contains volcanic glass, they were made in the Japanese main islands (Seto 2009a, 169). Some braziers are red, low-fired *hajiki* ware that may come from another area of Japan. As noted above, Bizen wares have been found (Ikeda 2007b). They are limited to Shuri, Sashiki, Nakijin, Urasoe, the Wakuta kilns, and a few other sites from the time period of the end of the fourteenth century to the beginning of the sixteenth century AD. They are mostly concentrated around Shuri and related sites. In the seventeenth century the Wakuta kilns of Okinawa made local *suribachi* when demand increased as well as gray tileware items.

Further evidence of connections with Japan is the casting of twenty-nine bells in the fifteenth (28 bells) and sixteenth (1 bell) centuries. Twenty-three of these were cast within one decade, the 1450s (Nelson 2006, 391). In the *Ryukyu koku yuraiki,* written in AD 1713 (Hokama and Hateruma 1997), there is a list of all of the large temple bells in Ryukyu at the time, together with the date they were cast, the name of the priest who composed the inscription on each bell, and the name of the bell caster. Most bells were cast between AD 1456 and 1459, in the reign of Shō Toku. There is a debate about whether they were cast in Kyushu or Okinawa. Wang Zhongshu (2001) concluded that they were cast in Ryukyu, since it would have been impossible to bring so many bells from Kyushu in a short period. Judging from their style, many of them were cast by specialists from north Kyushu (Kōji Itō 2008, 88). The source of metal for bell casting appears to have been Chinese copper coins.

There was a steady demand from elites of the Japanese main islands for Chinese scholarly accoutrements and antiques (Japanese *karamono*) even as early as the twelfth century (Taniguchi 2009). During the Ming Ban these could only be secured through offshore ports such as Naha. Members of the Shimazu Clan of southern Kyushu and the Ōuchi Clan of northern Kyushu approached Ryukyu to secure *karamono* (Chinese luxury goods) for exchange with the courtiers and shōgun in Kyoto (Uezato 2005, 18). In order to trade, they arrived at the same time as the Chinese missions. Ships also came from other areas of Japan in search of Chinese luxury items such as paintings, ceramics, and utensils, prized by the literati (ibid., 18). These goods were purchased from the Chinese embassies traveling to the Ryukyus to confirm the Ryukyu kings' investiture.

From the fourteenth to sixteenth centuries AD, there were constant problems with Wakō, a very powerful multiethnic group of maritime pirates or smugglers, who preyed on coastal communities and shipping (Schottenhammer 2007, 58–60). Although the Ryukyu Kingdom attempted to protect itself from their influence, it seems that members of Wakō groups must have frequented the port of Naha from time to time (Uezato 2009). The Wakō were probably trading in slaves in addition to arms and other goods.

From the 1530s Japan saw an expanded growth in the production of gold and especially silver. In AD 1534 a rich silver deposit was found at Ikuno in Tajima, and in AD 1546 another silver mine was discovered at Ōmori, Iwami. Silver was transshipped through the Ryukyus to Manila.

In the late sixteenth century AD, trade in the East China Sea was transformed by the arrival of the Europeans and trade of large quantities of Japanese silver (Kanyang Li 2007, 125–128; Uezato 2005, 22). At this time Japanese traveled via Ryukyu to Luzon, Fujian, and Southeast Asia. Although the last voyage to Siam recorded in the *Rekidai hōan* was in 1570, trade of silver through Luzon continued for a substantial period beyond that date. This trade with Southeast Asia was distinctive from tributary trade. Naha became an important point in the Japanese network in Southeast Asia, and the Japanese community in Naha was similar to Japanese enclaves in Southeast Asia; the network was comparable to the Chinese trading network in Southeast Asia. As tributary trade sponsored by the Ryukyu government declined from the sixteenth century AD, in the sixteenth and seventeenth centuries trade in East Asia developed around the exchange of silver for raw silk among traders in Fujian, Manila, Ryukyu, and Japan. The Ryukyu government traded with private merchants. Naha became a link between Japan and Southeast Asia (Uezato 2008, 70). After 1570 AD, the Macao-Nagasaki route bypassed Naha, and Luzon-Nagasaki routes were used for the silk trade. The use of these direct routes led to a decline in Naha's role in relaying trade.

Trade Relations with China

The change of sea routes between Japan and China in the thirteenth century AD stimulated the growth of Naha. The route from Hakata to Mingzhou (Ningbo) was replaced by the safer southern route from Takase in Higo, southern Kyushu, to Fuijian via Satsuma and Ryukyu (Uezato 2008, 58).

The peculiar characteristics of the China trade were of crucial significance to Okinawan political and social development. Three kinds of trade existed—private trade, official tributary trade, and relaying or transshipping trade—with goods flowing from one type of trading arrangement into another. Vigorous Chinese maritime trade can be traced to the Song dynasty (AD 960 to 1279), when Chinese merchants began to appear in the South China Sea and Indian Ocean. Arabs and Malays had previously been the chief traders in the region. With the exception of territorially contiguous polities such as Korea and Vietnam, which were invaded by China, the relationship between China and its tributary subordinates was unusual in that the flag did not follow trade. Outlying regions were not annexed or even defended when threatened or overcome by foreign powers. Gungwu Wang (1993) calls Chinese traders "merchants without empire," who were at the bottom of the Chinese social scale. After the tenth century, even though they experienced new roles with the expanding trade of the Song, they were not employed for imperial expansion. Unfortunately, although trade generated great wealth, contemporary records are not very helpful (G. Wang 1993, 402).

In the late eleventh to early twelfth centuries AD, Song traders became active in the East China Sea bringing ceramics and other goods to Hakata in northern Kyushu. Hakata traders carried some of these goods to the Ryukyus, particularly early whitewares. Shipwreck sites such as Kurakisaki, Amami Ōshima, and Nakanohama, Kumejima, dating to the twelfth to thirteenth centuries AD, show that a direct route from Zhejiang or Fujian to Kyushu was being used (Kanazawa 2004), although it is thought that most traders were based in Hakata. Subsequently, from the Yuan dynasty (AD 1276 to 1368), traders used a direct route from China instead of Kyushu.

Chinese Coinage

In addition to ceramics, Chinese traders brought copper coins to Japan in vast numbers. The tabulation of coins from excavation, in search of chronological trends, is complicated by the fact that many coins have illegible reign dates, and a substantial quantity of coins were old before they were exported. From the eleventh century AD to the end of the mediaeval period around AD 1600, the Japanese civil authority did not mint its own official coinage but depended almost entirely on imported Chinese coins, along with some plain coins and counterfeit Chinese coins produced in Japan. A few types of coins may have been minted in Okinawa in the fifteenth century, as noted in Chapter 9. The total quantities of Chinese coins in the Ryukyus are generally much smaller than those from parts of the Japanese main islands. An exception is a cache of 6,215 Chinese coins, from Kaigen Tsūhō (seventh to eighth centuries) to Ming Xuande (AD 1426 to 1435) recovered in Amagi Chō, Tokunoshima (Itō Shinji 2011a, 299).

Suzuki Kimio (1999) compiled a study of 275 sites in Japan yielding 3.5 million coins, finding that 77 percent of all coins were of Northern Song (AD 960 to 1127) date, while 2 percent were of Southern Song (AD 1127 to 1279) date. He concluded that they were all probably imported into Japan in the first half of the thirteenth century AD and buried in the fourteenth and fifteenth centuries AD. From the Hakata sites of northern Kyushu, Ōta found a similar peak of buried Song coins in sites dating to the latter thirteenth to early fourteenth centuries AD (2009, 16). Miyagi (2010) found that 84 percent of the mediaeval Chinese coins found in the Japanese main islands are from Northern Song, and 9 percent are from the Ming (AD 1368 to 1644); whereas in the Central and Southern Ryukyus, 44.7 percent are from the Northern Song and 46.6 percent are from the Ming, showing the close access of the Ryukyus to Ming trade (Miyagi 2010).

Tabulation of two hundred Chinese coins from twelve sites in the Ryukyus showed a ratio of 12:1 of Northern versus Southern Song coins (Pearson et al. 2001, 226). After the Northern Song, the next period of abundance is the early Ming dynasty, in the reign of Yongle (Japanese Eiraku) (AD 1403 to 1424) (Hashimoto Yū 2009). These coins appear in the Shuri and Nakijin Gusuku sites, described in Chapters 7 and 9. Of a total of 707 identified coins from some fifteen reports of Shuri excavations, Tang dynasty Kaigen Tsūhō (59), Kōbu (Chinese Hongwu) Tsūhō (217), and plain coins (285) were tabulated by Nagahama (2006), who noted that similar quantities, in roughly the same pattern of distribution, were found in Nakijin. The Kaigen Tsūhō coins, either antiques or later copies, were sometimes used as votive offerings at ritual sites in the Ryukyus. By way of comparison, these quantities of coins are small compared to the eight tons of Chinese copper coinage carried on the Sinan ship that sank near Mokpo, Chŏlla Namdo, Korea, around AD 1323 (Information Section 1984), or the huge hoards found in various parts of Japan (Suzuki Kimio 1999; 2002). One source of metal for casting bells was Chinese coinage. Uezato mentioned that around AD 1471 coinage was shipped from Sakai to Naha. Earlier in this chapter, it was mentioned that a Ming envoy bought swords with strings of cash. Atwell (2002, 86) mentions that in AD 1407 and 1434 the Ming court sent Japanese leaders gifts of 15 million and 30 million coins respectively. Some of these may have found their way to Ryukyu, and they may have been used for bronze casting rather than finding their way into archaeological sites as old coins. Of some 11,332 coins tabulated by Miyagi (2010, 531) from the Central and Southern Ryukyus, 7,003 are from the Naha/Shuri area and 1,580 are from Nakijin. In these elite areas coinage may have been used in everyday transactions. Miyagi concluded that in the sixteenth century AD coinage may also have been used in villages for limited transactions (ibid., 538).

The Ming Maritime Trade Ban

The Ming Maritime Trade Ban, in effect from AD 1368 to 1567, made maritime trade with foreigners illegal except for trade conducted by tributary and investiture missions. The Kingdom of Ryukyu was given extremely favorable conditions for tributary trade from AD 1372. The ban forced trade through government channels to reduce losses of uncollected taxes. Under its provisions, private citizens were forbidden to sail overseas, and foreigners could enter China only on tribute missions. Tributary trade necessitated large gifts from China to tributary vassals and drew hundreds of participants on tributary missions who had to be fed and housed, while grasping all occasions to carry out their own unregulated private trade.

Despite restrictive government regulations, the south Fujianese, in the second half of the Ming, embarked on an unprecedented participation in maritime business (Ng 1971, 81). Seagoing trade yielded a tenfold profit, since the Ming Maritime Trade Ban was largely ineffective. Smuggling became a major part of the economic, social, and political life for inhabitants of Fujian and Zhejiang Provinces in the fifteenth and sixteenth centuries. Chinese, Japanese, and Southeast Asian seafarers were used by prominent mainland lineages to bring goods into Fujian. There was even a maritime quasikingdom in the 1540s. The Ming government tried unsuccessfully to subdue the smugglers for several decades—indeed, the pirates had grown so bold that four thousand of them attacked two towns in southern Fujian in AD 1562 but were beaten back (Pin-Tsun Chang 1983, 60, 242).

By 1517 AD, because of falling revenues, the Ming government prepared to relax the prohibitions. Ng (1971, 100) describes groups with opposed opinions: the traditionalists (opposed to smuggling and foreign trade in general), the profiteers (in favor of opening trade), and the pragmatists (in favor of legalizing trade as a way to reduce piracy). Ng argues that the government's restrictive policy destroyed the development of a great maritime enterprise and failed to prevent substantial emigration. With a more favorable policy, the Fujian trade could have grown to the scale of Western maritime ventures instead of remaining a peddling trade.

Although the Ming Ban was lifted in AD 1567, the prohibition against trade with Japan remained in force; therefore, the Japan-China trade was carried by the Portuguese from Kyushu to Macao. Ryukyu, which still carried out tributary trade with China, remained a coveted source of Chinese goods. A total of eighty-eight licenses were given in AD 1589 from the ports of Fujian. In two tax lists from this licensed trade, written in AD 1589 and 1615 and covering 115 commodities, items obtained from Ryukyu were unripe pepper seeds, sulfur, two varieties of conch shells, horse tails, ox and horse skins, and copper (S. T. Chang 1992, 164–186). The pepper and copper were surely transshipped goods. Atwell (1977, 25) has noted two peaks of Ming prosperity that may be relevant to understanding political events and periods of intense construction activities in Okinawa. The first, which occurred in the early fifteenth century AD, was a peak in the domestic mining of silver, and the second, in the late sixteenth and early seventeenth centuries AD, was marked by the large-scale importation of silver. Okinawa's first appearance as a Chinese tributary state coincides with the first peak of prosperity, and its subjugation by Satsuma and demise as an independent entrepôt coincide with the second peak of prosperity. During the latter period, Okinawa was invaded by Satsuma, and its political independence came to an end. Japanese trading interests, formally shut out of China, became particularly anxious to gain access to trade with China at the time of the second peak. Thus Ryukyu trade can be seen as a loop in a larger system linking China to the world economy.

During the Ming dynasty, Takara estimates, 100,000 people from Ryukyu traveled between Ryukyu and China, while 32,000 people traveled to China from Southeast Asia (1987, 379). Although he does not provide the basis for his calculation, I expect that it is based on the historical records of the frequency of tribute missions, the size of the ships, and the number of voyagers.

Ryukyu and Quanzhou

Ryukyu's relationship to the Quannan region of Fujian Province had a special effect on its early development, and tangible evidence of close connections has been found at sites such as Urasoe Gusuku and Shuri Gusuku in the form of carved stone coffins. The region was isolated from Chinese Han culture until the late Tang (AD 618 to 960), but during the tenth and eleventh centuries AD its economy expanded rapidly with the expansion of trade from Guangzhou to Quanzhou. The city of Quanzhou (Zayton) was the center of Fujianese maritime trade from the ninth century to the fifteenth century AD (Ng 1971). Although it had commercial ties with Korea and Japan throughout the Tang dynasty, it was only toward the end of that period that a large portion of the southern sea trade was directed to Quanzhou from Canton, primarily because Quanzhou could supply products from Korea and Japan more easily than Canton.

Quanzhou also had its own porcelain kilns, located outside the east gate of the city and dating from the Song dynasty, which produced a variety of green and white wares as well as bluish white wares (*seihakuji* in Japanese, *qingbai* in Chinese), which have been found in archaeological sites on the main islands of Japan, Okinawa, and Southeast Asia. Other kilns in Fujian and Guangdong Provinces supplemented the production of the well-known Longquan kilns of Zhejiang during the Song and Ming dynasties (Pearson et al. 2002).

At the time of the change from the Northern to Southern Song dynasty (AD 1126) a substantial push to increase trade and tax revenue took place. In hopes of alleviating government financial crises and in order to provide for the needs of the royal families of the Southern Song, the court invested a large sum in the sea trade and permitted the port of Quanzhou to implement favorable trade policies (Fu 1992). Encouragement was also given to private trade through registration of ships and households, to allow ships and crews to take turns going abroad (ibid.).

In AD 1132, when the office of the Fujian Maritime Trade Supervisor was established in Quanzhou, incentives were given to those who generated trade and related tax revenues. There was strong motivation to contact very small markets as well as very large ones because of fierce competition among numerous merchants (Chen Xiyu 1991, 53). Private traders such as Li Chong (who sailed in AD 1105) are recorded to have sailed from Zayton to Japan to trade fabrics and ceramics (Fu 1992, 336). There was a very large increase in the volume and diversity of trade. Fu reports that the number of different kinds of goods arriving in Quanzhou expanded from forty-five at the end of the eleventh century to four hundred in AD 1141 (1992, 339). In the early twelfth century AD the foreign community was particularly vigorous: a foreign school was opened in Quanzhou, and foreign residential areas were established near the south gate. These trends seem to coincide with the trade in white and brown wares as well as Tong'an celadon, which appears in the Ryukyus.

By early in the eleventh century AD, unofficial trade in and out of Quanzhou had become substantial, and no revenue was collected by the state. Transshipment of goods from Southeast Asia made up a substantial part of this trade. Clark (1991, 175) notes a substantial drop in trade passing through the Quanzhou Trade Superintendency during the thirteenth century AD, occasioned by a variety of factors—piracy, corruption, and the enormous cost of supporting the Southern Branch of the Chinese imperial clan in Quanzhou and the Western Branch in Fuzhou. Indeed, support of the court was an enormous drain on the economy in general. Clark thinks that some of the trade may have been diverted to local smuggling, in which case it would disappear from official statistics but not from the local economy. If this were the situation in Quanzhou, it is possible that the trade moved offshore—perhaps to places like Okinawa.

How did conditions in Quanzhou in the Yuan (AD 1279 to 1368) affect trade with the Ryukyus? It was at this time that the volume of trade increased dramatically, and celadon wares came to the Ryukyus in abundance.

The powerful trader Pu Shougeng led the city of Quanzhou to surrender to the Yuan after the fall of the Song (Kuwabara 1989). In return for this action, the port areas were given favored status in the late thirteenth century AD. The Quanzhou Maritime Trade Superintendency was the first port to be reestablished in the Yuan and to remain intact despite the merging and disbanding of other trading ports. In the early years of the Yuan, trade routes expanded deep into the Indian Ocean.

Two trends in the late Yuan were significant. The policy of long-distance direct trade voyaging was replaced by a system of transhipping, whereby Quanzhou merchants took their goods to intermediate ports, from which other merchants carried them to their destination. This system allowed the Chinese to realize greater profits on shorter distances. In addition, the nature of the cargoes changed, with preference for less expensive textiles and iron and copper tools for cutting, plowing, and hunting (Fu 1992, 338). Occasional attempts were made to prohibit private trade in the Song and Yuan, but these moves lasted only three to five years (Chen Xiyu 1991, 53).

What conditions in Quanzhou favored the development of Ryukyu's particular position as transshippers in the Ming dynasty? As mentioned above, the Ming Trade Ban was instrumental in closing down private trade and transforming it into smuggling. Chen Xiyu (1991, 98) notes that in the early Ming dynasty, the Ryukyus served as go-between for the merchants of Japan and Southeast Asia. This position was reinforced by the changes occurring after the Zheng He voyages in the early fifteenth century AD. Ships became smaller, and less suitable for long-distance voyaging. Europeans began to compete with Chinese traders, who preferred the trade with Japan and Luzon because distances were short and profits were high (ibid., 84). From mid-Ming, smuggling became the main form of trade. Foreign trade needed ships and capital; only local wealthy officials could defy the law and become large-scale smugglers.

The Ming Ban affected Quanzhou very seriously. Quanzhou and other Fujian ports became imperial garrisons, with walled fortifications and flotillas of ships that controlled illegal shipping and piracy, whether by Chinese or by foreigners.

Fujian traders traveled along the coast, engaging in domestic trade and escaping to foreign ports whenever they encountered a chance to evade government surveillance (G. Wang 1993, 406–408). It was economic growth in the coastal region as well as constant harassment from pirates and illegal traders, however, that led to the end of the Ming Ban in AD 1567. I believe that the most favored tributary status, which Ryukyu enjoyed during the Ming Ban, was instituted to serve Fujian interests. Fujian officials profited from it and participated in its operation both in Ryukyu and in Fujian. The role of Fujian expatriates in setting up the tribute system is confirmed by Smits (2010), who notes that before unification the three states of Sanhoku, Chūzan, and Sannan conducted their tributary relations through a quasi-independent office in Chūzan, staffed by Chinese expatriates.

Late in the fifteenth century, Yuegang in Zhangzhou County began to replace Quanzhou as a center of trading importance. An important smuggling port, it was renamed Haicheng in AD 1567 and made an administrative seat—principally to control the trade. The Zhangzhou area was known for its silk, crude porcelain, lacquered boxes, fans, salt, and iron pots and utensils, which were traded to Japan, the Ryukyus, and the Philippines. Ng (1971) reports that prominent Fujian families were able to monopolize the trade and minimize risk by including servants and managing partners in their ships' crews so that all aspects of the trade were under the control of the family and its trusted employees. They also adopted children to establish trading partnerships.

After the takeover of Okinawa by the Satsuma Fiefdom of Kagoshima Japan in AD 1609, the Ming government was reluctant to engage in Ryukyu tributary trade because it compromised the ban on trade with Japan.

Trade Relations with Korea

The Korean Peninsula and the Ryukyus might seem to be remote, judging from topography and ocean currents. However, winter winds generated by the high pressure systems of continental Asia are very strong, transporting dust from north China to the Ryukyus every winter and pushing voyagers traveling along the southern Korean coasts down into the Ryukyus. As seen in Chapter 4, the spread of Sobata Type pottery from the Korean Peninsula to western Kyushu and the Ryukyus is evidence of some kind of population movement in the Early Jōmon Period. Ryukyu shells were traded to Korea, via Japan, in the middle of the first millennium AD. The mixture of Korean and Japanese techniques in the manufacture of *kamuiyaki* stoneware of Tokunoshima is also important. Thirteenth century AD roof tiles from the Urasoe Yōdore Mausoleum are of the same type as those from the Sambyeol, Chindo (Asato Susumu 2009), and the widespread use of Korean-style roof tiles in several palace buildings of the highest elite in the fourteenth century AD are also important sources of evidence. The sojourn of several months in Korea of the *aji* of Sannan in the late fourteenth century AD indicates that mediaeval 8.2 connections were maintained (Kin et al. 1988, 86), and requests from the Ryukyu Kingdom to the Choson court for sets of Buddhist sutras in the fifteenth century AD show that official connections were important.

The late fourteenth and early fifteenth centuries AD were a time of intensive interaction. Japanese raiders along the Korean and Chinese coasts took captives who may have been traded as slaves in Naha from the mid-fourteenth century AD (Robinson 2000, 112). The Chōson court retrieved Koreans from Japan and the Ryukyus with the assistance of the Kyushu deputy, who was deeply involved in repatriation and trade; in AD 1394 and 1395 two officials escorted more than one thousand men and women. In an official embassy to repatriate Koreans in 1453 AD, the Japanese monk Dō'an represented the King of Ryukyu as an envoy. From the 1450s Japanese serving in Hakata began serving as the king's envoys (Robinson 2000, 112; Hong-Schunka 2005, 140). In the late fourteenth and early fifteenth centuries AD the Ryukyuans made a number of attempts to establish direct diplomatic links with Korea (Nelson 2006, 377). On at least one occasion, Japanese imposter envoys, unsuccessfully using the names of dead Ryukyu kings, posed as royal envoys of Ryukyu kings on forged state documents but were rejected. Sets of block-printed Buddhist scriptures (including the Koryo Tripitaka) were given to high-ranking persons such as the Ashikaga shōguns and the kings of Ryukyu in the mid-fifteenth century AD (Robinson 2000, 116). The acquisition of Buddhist sutras was a major motive for trade with Korea (Kobata and Matsuda 1969, 6). Korean cotton cloth was particularly favored by Japanese and Ryukyuans (Hong-Schunka 2005, 137). In 1467 the Korean court sent 10,000 bolts to Chūzan as part of a substantial diplomatic gift (Kobata and Matsuda 1969, 15). In AD 1500 the first embassy staffed by Ryukyuans in forty years arrived in Korea. There were 470 men in four ships, a substantial undertaking (Robinson 2000, 119). Goods moving from Japan to Ryukyu included copper and iron artifacts. Japanese secured pepper from Ryukyu or Southeast Asia to trade to Korea in the mid-sixteenth century AD. However, shortly after that the Japanese concentrated on the export of silver (Nelson 2006, 380). Sappanwood, one of the most important items to be transported by Ryukyu from Southeast Asia to China as tribute, was also transshipped to Korea along with spices by Japanese traders, who purchased them in Ryukyu (ibid.).

Varieties of Trade

Table 8.1 illustrates the major varieties of trade from early prehistory to AD 1609.

TABLE 8.1 Summary of Major Types of Trade, from Early Prehistory to AD 1609

1. Jōmon lithics exchange: chert, nephrite, obsidian. Also pottery exchange (reciprocal).

   (ca. 4000 to 1000 BC)

2. Yayoi-Kofun exchange: pottery, shell bracelets, prestige goods (reciprocal, redistribution).

   (ca. 500 BC to seventh century AD)

3. *Turbo* shell (linked to Kaigen Tsūhō coins?) (regulated through Kikaigashima?).

   (seventh to twelfth centuries AD)

4. Early private trade: Chinese whitewares, iron goods, steatite cauldrons.

   (eleventh to thirteenth centuries AD)

5. Large volume private trade: celadon, Southeast Asian goods (sappanwood), iron goods. Coinage still in limited use.

   (thirteenth to fourteenth centuries AD)

6. Tributary trade with China: Chinese goods (ceramics and coins) and Ryukyu local goods such as sulfur and horses.

   (from AD 1372)

7. Ryukyu Kingdom relaying trade (i.e., with Japan): Japanese goods, relayed goods from China and Southeast Asia.

   (fourteenth to seventeenth centuries AD)

8. Diplomatic exchange: elite goods to and from Southeast Asia.

   (fourteenth to seventeenth centuries AD)

Private Trade

Although it is certain that the Northern and Central Ryukyu islanders traded *Turbo* shells with Japan in the eighth to tenth centuries AD, it is possible that Chinese traders were also active in the area, judging from the presence of Kaigen Tsūhō coins (Kinoshita 2000; Takamiya Hiroe 1995; 1997). Sulfur was traded to the Southern Song in the eleventh century AD for the production of gunpowder needed for their conflict with the Xixia people of northern China (Ikeda 2007b, 7) and for other military purposes (Yamauchi 2009, 18).

Private or nonofficial trade accounts for all of the trade from the eleventh to late fourteenth centuries AD, at which time official tributary trade with the Ming began in AD 1372. In the expansion of private trade, different communities all played important roles. Asato Susumu (1996) stresses the active role of the Ryukyu islanders, whereas Kamei (1993) places more stress on Hakata and Song traders, and Takanashi (2005) emphasizes trade carried out by Amami islanders.

In the fourteenth to sixteenth centuries AD, private trade as well as smuggling coexisted along with the official tributary system. Following the tributary gift (described below), permission was granted for private trade. In addition, private traders visited the Sakishima Islands from the twelfth to fifteenth centuries AD, bringing ceramics for local use and trade. Chinese ceramics and other goods could be traded to Southeast Asia, exchanged with Japanese traders in Naha, or carried north to small ports in Japan.

The enormous number of traded ceramics found on Okinawa—and even greater number on Southeast Asian sites—cannot be accounted for by tributary trade alone (Gotō 2008). Some must derive from the private, unofficial trade and smuggling that proliferated (P. Chang 1983, 225–250).

Through its trade with China, Okinawa also entered into the Chinese diaspora, socially interdependent and spatially linked communities joined by kinship links and sharing Confucian cultural and political values. The diaspora consisted of permanently settled individuals as well as those who stayed for short periods or traveled on the junks. Tradition states that in the late fourteenth century AD a group of Chinese families from Fujian were sent by the Ming government to live in Okinawa. They and their descendants were employed by the Chūzan rulers to establish and sustain maritime trade and a market network in East Asia. They were known as the Thirty-Six Families of Min (Miyazato and Kadena 1968, 15). The tradition of the founding of the Chinese settlement at Kumemura by the thirty-six families from Min is probably a kind of rationalization, since the Chinese were present in Okinawa before AD 1392. (Thirty-six is an auspicious Chinese number often used as a metaphor.) However, the Fujianese may have been authorized to engage in tributary activities within the port of Naha (Okamoto 2008). I would imagine that they were involved in the preparations and negotiations leading to the consolidation of tributary status. A network of private traders linked virtually every part of the Japanese main islands to the Ryukyus, including merchants from Hakata and Sakai and representatives of the great temples of Kyoto.

It is difficult to quantify the volume of goods carried in nonofficial trade. For instance, Kamei calculates the number of ceramic vessels carried on official Ming tribute missions over 270 years (111 missions out of 270 carried cargo), each ship carrying about 70,000 ceramic vessels. He proposes that out of some 7.7 million items that flowed into Okinawa about 3 million stayed in Okinawa (roughly based on sherd counts from sites) and 4.77 million were transshipped to Southeast Asia and Japan (Kamei 1997). His calculations do not allow for an undetermined quantity of ceramics that arrived in Okinawa through unofficial trade. When traders went to the Chinese ports, they contacted Chinese agents who brought ceramics from inland kilns (Kamei 1997, 41–47). Although some ceramics came from Fujian or Guangdong, most came from the Longquan area of Zhejiang.

Tributary Trade

BACKGROUND

Official tributary trade required that states surrounding China pay homage to the emperor, with appropriate ritualized recognition of Chinese superiority and the presentation of tribute, in return for which China provided lavish gifts. This exchange was the required basis for trade. Tributary states were given privileges to trade at certain ports, and some goods given as gifts by the emperor to the representatives of the tributary rulers were carried home to be sold or distributed to political allies. At the level of state interaction, tributary trade was the official means of commerce. It legitimized and supported the Okinawan state and provided financing for public projects and maintenance of the royal family. Ryukyu was the last polity to enter the Chinese tributary system, which it did in the first years of the Ming dynasty. Other states from Southeast Asia had been sending tribute to China for centuries. The Chinese system offered little or no military protection to tributary states, but neither did it interfere in their domestic affairs. The Ming tributary system served to legitimize the rule of the Chūzan and later Ryukyu Kingdom and brought with it substantial cultural exchange, such as the education of foreign students. The trade aspects of the tributary system presented in this chapter are only a fraction of a much bigger topic (F. Zhang 2009).

Strictly speaking, only during the first half of the Ming dynasty (from AD 1368 to 1550) did a unified tribute system provide the matrix for all of China's foreign relations (Schottenhammer 2007, 8). Before the Ming this tribute system often constituted more of a political claim than a reality, and by the second half of the Ming it weakened again. The first Ming emperor, Hongwu, sought to reestablish the agrarian sector as the foundation of a Confucian hierarchical society in which commercial activity would be reduced and the accumulation of large profits was considered a danger to society (ibid., 13). Hongwu intended to establish a society based on agriculture and equal land distribution, relieving the rich, including officials, aristocrats, monasteries, and wealthy merchants, of most of their wealth and landed property. Production of commodities largely took place in state-owned factories, and land taxes and labor services were the main pillars of state income. Trade and production of commodities for sale in markets were reduced to a minimum. As early as the second half of the fifteenth century AD, however, it became apparent that these economic institutions and principles did not serve their purpose. Wealth from landholdings once again became concentrated in the hands of the rich, state factories went bankrupt, and private trade through illegal channels became essential. By the early sixteenth century AD the traditional Ming tribute system had already eroded, and many merchant ships came to China to trade. In the course of the sixteenth century, the strict maritime trade proscription gradually gave way to a new political line that considered foreign trade as a source to be tapped but without abandoning the original idea of a tribute system. An attempt was made to maintain the tribute system and the political ideology of Hongwu, while at the same time seeking to obtain money from the taxation of maritime trade (ibid., 16–24).

Tribute goods were divided into "official tribute goods" and "private commodities" (Schottenammer 2007, 15). The official goods had to be sent to the emperor, whereas, after a commission was paid, part of the private cargo could be sold at the port of entry. As a rule 60 percent of the cargo was bartered by the Shibosi (Trade Superintendent in Quanzhou or Fuzhou). It is important to note that the Ming rulers permitted a certain quantity of business or trade for profit by private merchants during the phases of strict overseas trade prohibition (Schottenhammer 2007).

Tributary trade was part of a policy of trade and foreign relations that included the Ming Ban, which was in partial or full operation from AD 1370 to 1567. Preferential treatment was extended to Ryukyu by the Ming. The Ming court accepted Ryukyu tribute whenever it was offered. Ryukyu was given the monopoly to trade at Quanzhou and Fuzhou during the Ming Ban, whereas the Japanese traded at Ningbo until AD 1523, when they were excluded after disturbances caused by competing Japanese tribute missions. My opinion is that the goal of Fujian merchants and producers themselves, was to have an offshore base in Ryukyu to maintain the flow of foreign trade without punitive taxes and maritime restrictions.

THE PRACTICE OF TRIBUTARY TRADE

With the establishment of the Ming dynasty in AD 1368 AD, goods flowing to the Ryukyus flowed through the channel created by tributary trade. On the establishment of the tribute relationship with Ming, Chūzan received from the Chinese court a gift of 1,000 ceramic vessels, fine silk, and 10 iron kettles. In addition, the Ming emissary took 50 bolts of fine silk, 69,500 ceramic vessels, and 990 kettles to trade for horses (Wada 1975, 20). According to Wada this occurred in AD 1375, and in AD 1376 the emissary returned to China from the Ryukyus with 40 horses and 5,000 *jin* (1 *jin* equals 596.8 grams) of sulfur. This pattern of receiving ceramics for sulfur and horses continued into the fifteenth century (Okamoto 2008; Kamei 2008). The ceramics were transported to Southeast Asia to buy sappanwood and pepper, which was traded to China. Before 1475, annual tribute missions from Ryukyu often consisted of more than two hundred persons who waited for months in Fujian while a small group proceeded to Peking. For each investiture mission in the Hongwu period (AD 1368–1398), five hundred Chinese visited Okinawa, most carrying goods for private trading. The polities of Sanhoku and Sannan both sent tribute missions to China in the late fourteenth and early fifteenth centuries AD before their defeat by Chūzan in AD 1422 and 1429 respectively. Whether the subsequent political centralization under the power of the Chūzan Kingdom in AD 1429 constricted the flow of goods from a multichanneled, dispersed pattern to a single-channeled, constricted pattern of entry to Okinawa, followed by a dispersal to vassals, is not clear.

In his study of the tributary trade system between Ryukyu and China of the early Ming Period, Kinjō Seitoku (1971) provides expanded lists of items that circulated through tributary trade. He notes two classes of tributary goods—luxury items and military items. Secret trade of military material was severely punished (Kinjō 1971, 8). Native Ryukyu products sent as tribute were horses, sulfur, safflower dye, native silk floss padding, linen cloth, banana fiber, ramie, fans, white paper, and whetstones. Substantial numbers of shells were sent to Ming China in the AD 1430s: in 1434, 8,500 *Turbo* shells and 5.5 million cowries were sent (Maehira 2004, 199). Shark skin, used for sword scabbards, was also exported (Yogi 1995). Japanese products included short and long swords, spears, armor, gloves, shoulder and leg covers, helmets, horse armor and head protection for horses, saddles, bridles, shields, fans, fruit boxes, small boxes, preserved plums, incense burners, vessels of gold and silver, lacquer objects, gold, and copper. Products from Southeast Asia included pepper, sandalwood, tin, ivory, sappanwood, incense wood, cloves, putchuk (a root used for seasoning), incense, aloewood, rhinoceros horns, and sea otter skins. Sappanwood was a particularly important item. The wood of this tropical tree, *Caesalpina sappan*, has medicinal, antibacterial, and coagulant properties and also yields a red dye termed "brazilin." Ryukyu officials bought it for submission as a tribute item to China, and it was in high demand in Japan and Korea.

To obtain goods for tributary trade and transshipment, Ryukyu ships went regularly to Japan and Southeast Asia carrying Chinese goods such as ceramics (P. Chang 1983, 172–173). From 1390 AD, Ryukyu tribute goods sent to China included Siamese goods (Kobata and Matsuda 1969, 53). In addition to the ceramics that the Okinawans carried to Southeast Asia, Ryukyu traders also purchased goods for trade in Southeast Asia in China with coinage or paper money as well as with Chinese ceramics (Kamei 2008, 30). Sino-Ryukyu tribute trade was most active in the fourteenth and fifteenth centuries.

Okamoto observed a number of trends in Ryukyu trade. There was a rapid increase in tribute missions from once every two years in the AD 1370s to forty-three missions in fifteen years from AD 1384 to 1399. Thereafter until the 1430s missions were sent regularly three times per year from the Ryukyus as a whole. In the Hongwu and Yongle (AD 1403 to 1424) eras Ryukyu had as many as thirty seagoing ships, but in AD 1439 the number had fallen to seven (Okamoto 2008, 49). The golden age of tributary trade between Ryukyu and Ming must have been before the AD 1440s. From AD 1385 to 1547, Ryukyu used Fujian-built ships for navigation not only to China, but also to Japan and Southeast Asia (P. Chang 1983, 185). Chang has calculated that, during the peak of tributary trading activity with Ryukyu, an average of 1.58 ships per year traveled to China. Although there are no documents in the *Rekidai hōan* for the AD 1440s or 1450s, the *Rekidai hōan* shows a decline in the frequency of ships to once every two years in the 1480s. The number of ships declined further during the Jiajing period (AD 1522–1566), when smuggling and piracy were at their peak on the Fujian coast.

Okinawans needed gifts of high prestige as well as local raw materials to present to the Ming authorities. To gain favor, these gifts had to appeal to the Chinese elite, necessitating the importation of new technology to Okinawa. The making of high-quality lacquer utensils and containers in Ryukyu for use as tribute gifts is an interesting example of elite sponsorship of craft production. Brumfiel (1992) notes that although elites presumably are able to impose their will on subordinates and to extract revenues from them for support of political superstructures, it is often the case that elites are unsuccessful in collecting taxes from kin-ordered commoner classes. In such cases, they often establish enterprises to generate income, using the labor of individuals who are separated from the protection of kinship groups. Okinawan lacquer production is a good example of this type of enterprise. It began in the fourteenth century, based on techniques imported from Fujian Province (Watt and Ford 1991, 330) and was sponsored by the Shuri court for tributary exchange with China. Most—if not all—of the raw materials were imported, since lacquer-producing trees grow poorly in the typhoon-prone climate of Okinawa (Ryūkyū Shikki Jigyō Kyōdō Kumiai 1991, 30).

An integral part of the tributary system in the South China Sea and Indian Ocean were the great voyages of Admiral Zheng He, from AD 1405 to 1433. These were diplomatic endeavors to establish China at the apex of regional relations. They had little direct impact on the Ryukyus or the East China Sea.

Relaying Trade

The Ming Maritime Trade Ban from 1368 to 1567 AD, followed by the granting of tributary status to the Chūzan Kingdom in 1372 AD, created a unique opportunity for Ryukyu trade and prosperity. Japan, which had restricted access to China, depended on Ryukyu to relay goods to Naha, where Japanese could buy them. With Chinese ports closed to private trade, Naha and Vietnamese ports such as Hoi An prospered. Although the Ming Ban was meant to control unregulated trade along the coast, it imposed great hardship and did not alleviate the problem of pirates such as the Wako, a powerful group said to be Japanese but in fact multiethnic. The Chūzan and later Ryukyu kingdom also transshipped goods across East and Southeast Asia.

Ryukyu's transshipment trade was particularly active in the fifteenth century AD. At that time, ships sent from Japan by the Muromachi government and powerful families and temples could only go to China every ten years, whereas ships from Ryukyu went annually. From AD 1413 to the 1460s Ryukyu ships sailed to the Kinai/Kyoto region every three or four years, via Kyushu and the Inland Sea. The ship that sailed from Sakai for China in AD 1451 carried five times as much sappanwood as the previous ship. This wood was received from Southeast Asia via Ryukyu. Sakai merchants expanded their network beyond Tosa and Satsuma, and the Shimazu family of Satsuma had a deep relationship with the Konoe family of Sakai (Sakai Shi Hakubutsukan 1993, 106–107). After the recall of the Ming Ban in AD 1567, the relay trade of Ryukyu declined, and new direct trade routes were created. One route extended from Zhangzhou Fujian, to Taiwan, Ryukyu, Bōnotsu (southern Kagoshima), and Sakai. It carried inexpensive blue and white ceramics produced in the Zhangzhou area (Morimura 1999).

Diplomatic Exchange

Transshipment of rare elite goods is also well documented in the *Rekidai hōan*, which provides an unusual glimpse into Okinawa's interaction with other Asian polities and the transshipping trade. As in tributary trade, a substantial gift of precious materials to the ruler opened the way for private or commercial trade. Local rulers would keep a portion of the presents and use the rest as gifts to retainers or goods for sale (Kobata and Matsuda 1969). In their *Ryukyuan Relations with Korea and South Sea Countries,* Kobata and Matsuda translate and extensively annotate entries from the *Rekidai hōan*. I have chosen a number of dispatches of different countries to show the kinds and quantities of materials that were sent. In addition to the gifts described in the diplomatic dispatches, large quantities of goods such as ceramics were sent for private sale. (I have replaced "vase" with "charger plate" or "plate" after checking the text from which the translation was made. For "blue" I have substituted "green," since the vessels in question were celadon).

DISPATCH TO THE COUNTRY OF CHŌSON (KOREA)
CHENGHUA 6/4/L (MAY 1, AD 1470)

Accompanying material:

wide cotton cloth 2 bolts, color patterned cotton cloth 2 bolts, checkered handkerchiefs in different colors 2 bolts, color patterned handkerchiefs 2 bolts, dyed cotton handkerchiefs 2 bolts, long tapestries for brick steps or dais 2 bolts, blue brocade with peacock feathers woven into it 2 bolts, folding fans with black frame 20, rhinoceros horns 6, buffalo horns 20, glass vases 2, blue and white bowls 20, large green bowls 50, incense wood 50 chin [*jin*] sandal wood 50 chin, cloves 50 chin, nutmegs 20 chin, sappanwood 200 chin, barbarian tin 200 chin, long swords 2 complete sets, parrot 1, white pigeon 1, ivory 4 pieces 100 chin, peacock tail plumes 300 pieces, blue and white plates 20, green charger plates 20, small green bowls 100, lakawood 100 chin, putchuk 20 chin, bean sprouts ? 20 chin, ebony 100 chin, pepper 2000 chin, mynah bird l, Indian wine l jar. (Kobata and Matsuda 1969, 19; 1 chin [*jin* in pinyin] = about 600 grams)

TO SIAM
XUANDE (3) 9/2 (OCTOBER 10, AD 1428)

white satin 20 bolts, small green plates 400, sulfur 3,000 chin (Chin-pao 2,500 chin) folding paper fans 30, superior quality satin 5 bolts, large green charger plates 20, small green bowls 2,000, swords 5. (ibid., 61)

TO MALACCA
CHENGHUA 6/?/? (AD 1470)

dyed satin 5 bolts, swords 5, large green charger plates 20, green bowls 2,000, blue satin 20 bolts, fans 30, small green plates 400. (ibid., 114)

TO JAVA

XUANDE 5/LO/L8 (NOVEMBER 3, 1430 AD)

> gold satin 2 bolts, white satin 20 bolts, large green charger plates 20, small green bowls 2,000, golden gauze 3 bolts, swords 5, small green plates 400. (ibid., 156)

A number of points can be derived from these lists. Many of the items sent to Korea were not originally from the Ryukyus but were transhipped from Southeast Asia and China. The objects from Ryukyu itself include cow hides and sulfur, horses, and perhaps small quantities of subtropical woods. It should be noted that only a token gift of celadons traveled to Korea, which had its own highly sophisticated ceramic production, compared to the substantial quantities that were sent to Southeast Asia. From the documents at hand, it appears that no ceramics were sent to Palembang (Kobata and Matsuda 1969, 113–146) or Annam (ibid., 183–186). These countries received primarily textiles.

Relations between Siam and the Ryukyu Kingdom are covered in twenty-eight documents sent from Ryukyu to Siam between AD 1425 and 1469, six documents from Siam to Chūzan, and some twenty-three voyage certificates or licenses for official Ryukyuan missions to travel to Siam. The major items that were carried from Siam to Okinawa were cloth, sappanwood, wine, and sulfur. The wine was carried in jars, and these jars were probably the Sawankhalok or "nanban" vessels sherds of which are found in a number of Okinawan sites along with earthenware (*hannera*) lids. These were transshipped to Japan, particularly Sakai. Kobata and Matsuda believe that Siamese relations with Ryukyu must have begun at about the same time as relations with Japan and Korea—the fourteenth century AD—and that the trade began on the initiative of Chinese merchants living in Siam (1969, 54).

The kinds of goods sent to Siam and their relative quantities remained virtually the same in twenty-six shipments between AD 1425 and 1469: five bolts of woven-gold satin, twenty bolts of white satin, three thousand *jin* of sulfur, five swords, thirty folding paper fans, twenty large green charger plates, four hundred small green plates, and two thousand small green bowls (Morimura 1998).

It is interesting that the Okinawans appear to have carried only celadon, and not Ming blue and white, to Siam. These ceramics served both as gifts (*reimotsu*) and as objects for private sale. Recent excavations in Shuri Gusuku have yielded concentrations of rare Yuan blue and white (Kamei 2009) and South Chinese Three-Color vessels that may have been part of an exchange system among elites in Southeast Asia, as proposed by Kamei (1986b, 335–374; 2009). These finds are discussed in Chapter 9.

Maritime Archaeology and the Trade

Although the seas around the Ryukyus have not yet yielded the actual remains of sunken ships, scattered ceramics and large stone cross-piece weights of Chinese anchors have been found in several locations. Miyagi et al. (2004) recorded twelve sites dating from the twelfth to fifteenth centuries AD. Some sites consist of the cargoes of wrecked ships, and others are the remains of small ports such as Imadomari, Nakijin, and the mouth of the Shirase River on Kume, marked by scatters of ceramic sherds. Hatenohama, Kumejima (Tezuka 2004; Kanazawa 2004), yielded Tong'an and Longquan celadon dating to the twelfth and thirteenth centuries AD. The Kurakisaki Underwater Site near Uken, southwestern Amami Ōshima, has yielded twelfth to thirteenth century AD Chinese ceramics (Longquan-type celadon, brownwares, Tong'an celadon, whitewares, and *qingbai* wares) in a depth of 2 to 3 meters of water. Although no ship remains have been found in the coral reef site, Chinese-style stone anchor weights were recovered long ago (Kagoshima Ken 1998). They confirm the existence of a trade route from the coast of Fujian through the Ryukyus from the twelfth century AD.

Analysis of Ceramic Assemblages

In this section I describe some of the general trends in production and distribution of trade ceramics seen from archaeological analysis. Shinzato Akito's review (2009), based on tabulation of hundreds of sites in Kyushu and the Ryukyus, examined changes in the number of sites with ceramics dated to fifty-year time periods. It is important to note that Shinzato compared the number of sites with ceramics of a certain time period, not the actual number of sherds present on each site. In Kyushu and the Ryukyus, the greatest number of sites occurs from the middle to the latter half of the twelfth century AD, and the number remains high through the first half of the thirteenth century AD. In Kyushu the peak of consumption occurred between 1150 and 1200 AD, based on site counts (Shinzato Akito 2009, 52). In Kyushu the number of sites drops to half from the mid-thirteenth century to the beginning of the fourteenth century AD, with a sharp decrease in the fourteenth century, but in the Ryukyus the number of sites increases up to the latter half of the fourteenth century AD. Shinzato's data, limited to AD 1050 to 1350, show a peak in the number of sites with Chinese ceramics in the thirteenth century AD, long before the advent of tributary trade in the late fourteenth century AD. Kamei (2008) measured trends in the trade using different data. He based his generalizations on the increase or decrease in ceramics found in key sites. From Nakijin he found that after the second half of the fourteenth century there is a very sharp increase compared to the amount found in earlier strata (2008, 23). The number of sites appears to decrease, but in some sites the number of ceramics increases, indicating concentration in fewer sites.

Access to Trade Ceramics

Who had access to the different kinds of ceramics found in Ryukyu sites? Some types, such as Yuan blue and white, are found only in sites of the highest social strata, whereas other types are distributed very widely.

Using the typology built up by a number of scholars, we need to look at variability in archaeological context. On some large excavations, the degree of archaeological resolution employed in the excavation and recording is insufficient to determine the exact position of each find, and ceramics have been grouped into very broad time periods, such as late fourteenth to early fifteenth centuries AD. Therefore, the chronology employed here is very broad (Ikeda 2004, 23).

Sakamaki (1964) has suggested that Shuri gradually assumed control of exacting tribute from Okinawan communities, achieving, at the same time, a monopoly over the trade with China. However, a complete monopoly is not substantiated by the archaeological assemblages, which indicate that centers such as Nakijin Gusuku and Katsuren Gusuku had their own supplies of fine ceramics. The pattern of an upward movement of surpluses and a downward movement of trade goods seems to be far from perfect (cf. Wolf 1982, 82), and it appears that during the Gusuku Period no single political entity in Okinawa controlled the flow of goods from China. One might expect, given the processes of centralization and monopolization that are postulated to occur in state emergence (Flannery 1972), that access to trade goods would become increasingly restricted. However, resistance to centralized control in the form of smuggling is known to have been prevalent. Different distribution patterns of trade goods may be created by different degrees of control. I investigated these patterns of distribution in sites of different types, postulating that rare and precious ceramics might be concentrated in large fortified sites rather than in smaller or unfortified sites. The distribution of ceramics in ten sites representing different social groups in the Gusuku Period is presented in Tables 8.2 and 8.3. In these figures I indicate the local term for the ceramics, to avoid ambiguity, and the sources of manufacture. An assumption is that ceramics from distant sources such as Jiangxi, Thailand, and Vietnam are more precious than local ceramics because of the greater cost of securing them. Background information on the sites compared in Tables 8.2 and 8.3 is presented in Table 8.4. The data have been taken from archaeological reports and regrouped in some cases to make comparable categories. For Table 8.2, I have not given percentages since not all data are available in the same format. Table 8.2 shows the distribution of wares in unfortified, fortified, and fortified capital sites.

TABLE 8.2 Comparison of Trade Wares from Ten Ryukyu Sites

			UNFORTIFIED			
Ware	*Term*	*Source*	Inafuku	H. Tōbaru	Kunindō	Ahagon
MAJOR CHINESE WARES						
Brown-Glazed	*katsuyū*	Fujian, Guangdong	some		many	842
Celadon	*seiji*	Zhejiang, Fujian	284	30	128	1,632
Whiteware	*hakuji*	Fujian	many	20	152	315
Blue and White	*sometsuke*	Jiangxi, Fujian		27	290	
Black-Glazed	*kokuyū*	Fujian				
Red-Glazed	*kōyū*	Jiangxi				
MINOR CHINESE WARES						
Qingbai	*seihakuji*	Fujian	some			
Oil Spot	*tenmoku*	Fujian				
Tea Container	*chaire*	Fujian				
Green-Glazed	*rokuyū*	Fujian?		1	4	17
Three-Color	*sansai*	Fujian?				4
South Chinese Three-Color	*kōnan sansai*	Fujian?				
Jade Color Glazed	*hisuiyū*	Fujian?				
Red Overglaze Enamel	*akae*	Jiangxi			1	
Overglaze Enamel	*iroe*	Jiangxi				
Dark Blue Purple	*ruriyū*	south China			2	5
Five-Color	*gosai*	Jiangxi?				
Jizhou	Kisshū	Jiangxi	1			
JAPANESE WARES						
Imari Blue and White (b)	Imari	Kyushu		1	many	746
Tilelike Gray	*gashitsu*	Japan				37
Inlaid Stoneware	*zōgan toshitsu*	Kyushu				
Karatsu (b)	Karatsu	Kyushu			2	10
Bizen (c)	Bizen	Honshu			2	
OTHER ASIAN WARES						
Inlaid Celadon (Koryo)	*zōgan seiji*	Korea				
Thai Earthenware	*hannera*	Thailand				
Iron Painted (Thai)	Sunkuroku	Thailand			2	4
Thai Brownware	*Tai katsuyū*	Thailand			2	
Vietnam	Betunamu	Vietnam				

(a) min. no. of vessels, not sherd counts; (b)17th–18th century; (c) *suribachi,* mortar with interior incised; (x) total not given, only typical sherd described; (xx) sherd count, only for Thai Brownware

Site						
FORTIFIED				CAPITAL FORTIFIED		
Itokazu	Goeku	Kats. Enc. 2	Kats. Enc. 1	Urasoe	Shigemajō	Kyōnouchi (a)
199	26	660	2,520	11,276	10(x)	179
3,802	200	604	1,528	6,741	7,490	609
427	68	91	130	494	2,034	75
50	21	51	172	333	1,649	116
6	3	2	11	569	7(x)	4
						1
6						20
		1				7
12				4	10	
				1		
					9	
				1	42	
		4	4	1		
				13	14	2
					1	
2	1					
4				35	7	
				1	1(x)	
						1
					4(x)	
				12	39	
6						84
				7	1(x)	
			18			361(xx)
					1(x)	3

TABLE 8.3 Percentage of Functional Types of Celadon Vessels from Ten Ryukyu Sites

		UNFORTIFIED			
Functional Type	*Term*	Inafuku	H. Tōbaru	Kunindō	Ahagon
		n=284	n=30	n=118	n=1,632
Bowl	*wan*	85%	7%	52%	23%
Dish	*sara*	7%	3%		29%
Plate (charger)	*ban*	6%	7%	5%	1%
Deep bowl, jar	*hachi*			1%	
Cup	*hai*		3%		
Bottle	*hei*				0%
Wine presentation jar	*shukai tsubo*			1%	
Presentation jar lid	*futa*				
Narrow-necked jar	*tsubo*				0%
Jade spring bottle	*yuhucun* (Chin.)				
Lidded container	*fukuromono*				
Incense burner	*kōro*	1%		1%	
Pouring vessel ewer	*suichū*	0%			
Small box	*gōsu*	1%			
Large box	*dai gōsu*				
Stirrup cup	*bajōhai*				
Mortar	*suribachi*				
Flower vase	*meipin*				
Bottle	*bin*			1%	
Lid	*futa*				
Handle	*mimi*				
Unidentified			80%	40%	45%
Total percent		100%	100%	100%	100%

Note: Sherd counts except Kyōnouchi, where count is number of vessels (0% = less than 1%).

The unfortified sites are thought to be agricultural villages where common people lived. The fortified sites are the residential sites of elites. From Katsuren Gusuku, ceramics from the ritual area (Enclosure 1) and the residential area, the site of a tiled roof structure (Enclosure 2), are presented. The following trends can be seen.

1. All three types of sites used local earthenware, although the ratio of earthenware to trade ceramics was lower in the fortified and capital sites. It appears that the local earthenware was used more extensively in the thirteenth

Site						
FORTIFIED				FORTIFIED CAPITAL		
Itokazu	Goeku	Kats. Enc. 1	Kats. Enc. 2	Urasoe	Shigemajō	Kyōnouchi
n=3,802	n=201	n=1,528	n=608	n=1,575	n=7,490	n=609
65%	58%	59%	23%	43%	71%	33%
13%	22%	13%	3%	12%	14%	44%
9%	12%			17%	14%	17%
		17%	4%			1%
0%				0%	0%	
0%						1%
1%	1%			0%		
0%				1%		
		1%	1%	0%		3%
					0%	
				0%		
0%		3%		0%	0%	0%
	0%				0%	0%
						0%
						0%
0%		1%				
		0%			0%	
	1%	4%				
		1%				
11%	4%		69%	26%		
100%	100%	100%	100%	100%	100%	100%

and fourteenth centuries, and declined and disappeared in the fifteenth century AD.

2. Celadon, whitewares, and brownwares were used in all three types of sites. The brownware jars are difficult to identify from very small sherds. Probably the majority of the brownware jars are of south Chinese manufacture, but a substantial number may be Southeast Asian. Beyond these types, the rarer Chinese wares, such as green-glazed, three-color, red-overglaze and dark blue, occur in traces in all three types of sites.

TABLE 8.4 Site Information for Tables 8.2 and 8.3

Site	*Date* (AD)	*Description*	*Source*
Inafuku	thirteenth century	Inland agricultural community, cluster of 5 houses, population from 10 to 25.	Okinawa Ken Kyōiku Iinkai 1983
Heshikiya Tōbaru		Coastal site, overlapping occupations.	Okinawa Ken Kyōiku Iinkai 1996
Kunindō	twelfth to sixteenth centuries	Inland site on three flat-topped hills, no stone outer walls or enclosures but defensive ditch, palisades, earth banks, postholes, house remains.	Okinawa Ken Haebaru Chō 1996
Ahagon	fourteenth to sixteenth centuries	A satellite of Ahagon Castle (immediately adjacent), rock concentrations, rectangular pavement stone alignments.	Okinawa Ken Kyōiku Iinkai 1990a
Itokazu	twelfth to sixteenth centuries	Large site with extensive fortifications.	Okinawa Ken Tamagusuku Son 1991
Goeku	fourteenth to sixteenth centuries	Heavily damaged by construction, important regional center, residence of Shō Taikyū before he was king.	Okinawa Shi Kyōiku Iinkai 1988
Urasoe	twelfth to sixteenth centuries	See description in Chapter 7 for details.	Okinawa Ken Urasoe Shi 1985

Katsuren	twelfth to sixteenth centuries	Major site with five or more enclosures, extremely impressive fortifications, east coast. The seat of Amawari. Strategic for controlling northward trade routes. Enclosure 1 is innermost, sacred area, Enclosure 2 is location of palace (Seiden).	Kamei, 1984, Katsuren Chō 1984, Katsuren Chō 1988
Nakijin, Shigemajō Area	thirteenth to sixteenth centuries	Shigemamon Area is elite residential area adjacant to ruler's living area in Nakijin, capital of Sanhoku Kingdom subjugated by Shuri.	Okinawa Ken Nakijin Son 1983
Kyōnouchi (Shuri)	fourteenth to fifteenth centuries	Sacred area of Shuri	Okinawa Ken Kyōiku Iinkai 1998

3. Chinese blue and white occurs in all three types of sites. In some sites some Yuan blue and white has been identified. Other sherds are difficult to date because of their extremely small size.
4. Korean wares occur exclusively in the fortified capital sites. It is possible their low frequency is peculiar to this sample. It is also possible that connections with Korea were limited to a few important centers.
5. Japanese wares are found in the three site types, but they date from the seventeenth and eighteenth centuries AD.

Can restricted access to trade goods be seen in the distribution of functional or use types of vessels within the same ware, such as celadon? Celadon distribution by use type is shown in Table 8.3. The following trends can be noted.

1. In some sites such as Heshikiya Tōbaru and Katsuren, the functional vessel type of a high percentage of sherds could not be determined. This skews the percentages of vessel types. In all the sites, however, bowls, flat dishes, and concave plates are the staple types.
2. Other functional types occur as traces throughout different types of sites, suggesting that they were not restricted to the most elite types of sites but were always present in very small numbers. Of particular interest is the role of incense burners, which are very widespread, but always rare. Rokkum states that on the island of Yonagunijima, they are owned by many elderly women as precious items for worship, having been initiated during visits to freshwater springs. Young female helpers receive ashes from their seniors' incense burners. They are ubiquitous in local ancestral shrines today and appear to have been important religious artifacts for many centuries (Rokkum 1998, 114).

Tables 8.2 and 8.3 show that, in general, access to imported ceramics was not restricted by ware or vessel type and that access to the overseas trade goods was somewhat free or heterarchical. I expect that the abundance of trade goods was created by unofficial trade. At the same time, tributary trade brought rare and valuable items to the court in the fourteenth and fifteenth centuries AD. The overall impression is one of some hierarchy and control in the trade created by tributary exchange of precious items, mitigated by heterarchy created by the flow of goods through channels beyond central control.

A comparison of the relative abundance of trade ceramics and local earthenware in Katsuren Gusuku and the Inafuku Site from the thirteenth to fifteenth centuries AD showed that, although trade ceramics were available to occupants of both sites, in Katsuren Gusuku they became much more abundant relative to local earthenware as time progressed, indicating more social separation of villagers from the *aji* class (Asato Susumu 1998, 91).

Conclusions: Trade and Ryukyu Island Communities

In this chapter, various types of trade and exchange that linked the Ryukyu Islands to each other and to surrounding areas have been explored. The term "exchange" often refers to services or obligations in which payment is not involved, whereas trade is considered to involve markets or payment. An exclusive temporal division between these two forms is not clear in the long span of Ryukyu culture history. Early lithic materials and pottery of the Early Shellmound Period must have been exchanged reciprocally, obsidian and jade being passed down the line from their sources in the Japanese main islands. Some types of Early Shellmound Period pottery must have been brought with migrants, while other less abundant types may have been given or exchanged. The shell exchange of the Yayoi and Kofun Periods has been interpreted as a kind of barter, in which shell objects or raw material was exchanged for iron goods, pottery vessels, or other prestige items. Chinese coins, including Kaigen Tsūhō, are too few to have circulated as currency but may have functioned as valuables or as currency in transactions with foreigners. *Turbo* shells were exchanged for iron goods.

What was the mechanism of exchange for Chinese ceramics of the eleventh and twelfth centuries AD, when quantities were small? Informal exchange for local products seems to have been the way in which private trade in the Gusuku Period functioned. How did ceramics become distributed throughout the Ryukyu Islands at the height of the trade, when an enormous quantity of ceramics reached every corner of the islands? Were local people given ceramics as payment for labor such as castle building? Most of the foreign ceramics were small bowls and plates used for serving food, or storage vessels. A very small quantity were large vessels for display, and these are generally found in sites with substantial architecture. Were ceramics circulated by local traders? Were workers paid with coins? Ono Masatoshi describes the use of cash and the purchase of ceramics in Ichijōdani, a large sixteenth-century site in central Honshu (1997b, 191). However, it seems unlikely that such extensive use of cash occurred in the Ryukyus in the twelfth to sixteenth centuries AD. Since there are few large hordes comparable to those found in the Japanese main islands, coinage must have been used in a limited range of formal transactions. In the case of tributary trade, we know that ceramics given to the Chūzan and later Ryukyu Kingdom by the Ming government were exchanged for Southeast Asian and Japanese products.

With regard to the social linkages created by trade, a pattern of shifting relations with dynamic boundaries can be seen. From the beginning of the Early Gusuku Period (AD 1050 to 1250), a quantum increase in the diversity of goods and the size of cargoes was achieved. The interplay of relations with various parts of China, Korea, and Japan, stimulated the flow of relations in the East China Sea. Old trade routes extending from northern Kyushu and the China coast were followed; in fact, they were linked by a direct trade route through the Ryukyus to Kyushu, used from the twelfth century AD. Private trade by Song, Hakata, and Sakai merchants can be seen as the evolution of the trade of shell bracelets with elites in northern Kyushu. At the same time, private trade from the China coast may have followed earlier trading links based on sulfur and shells. Improved navigational technology made it possible to cross the Kerama Gap, between the Okinawa Islands and Sakishima. With vigorous private trade came the establishment of commercial communities of Chinese, Japanese, and probably Southeast Asians in Naha. Communities engaged in private trade, tributary trade, relaying trade, and diplomatic exchange depended on each other for access to new markets in new locations.

With the development of tributary trade in the late fourteenth century AD, the Chūzan Kingdom was linked to a vast network of Chinese tributary states, which made it a member of a huge political and economic community. Links to Fujian were later expanded to include officials involved in maintaining diplomatic and tributary ties as well as traders.

However, the trade declined in the later sixteenth century AD for the following reasons: (1) the advent of Europeans and their violent trading activity, (2) the ineffectiveness of the Ming Ban and increasing activity of Chinese merchants, and (3) the advance of Japanese merchants into Southeast Asian trade whereby Ryukyu lost its advantage in relaying trade.

Although the Ryukyus were the last polity to be included in the Chinese tributary system, their contacts with China and the appearance of the first Chinese trade ceramics follow the general pattern found in Southeast Asia. Surveys by Guy (1989) and Aoyagi (1991) indicate that the earliest ceramics in most of the East and Southeast Asian region are Persian ceramics found with Chinese ninth century AD assemblages in some parts of Southeast Asia and coastal China (Yangzhou and sites in Fujian); they have not yet been found in the Ryukyus.

Data from Okinawa elucidate the broader picture of pre-European trade described by writers such as Abu Lughod (1989), who speaks of the emergence of a world trade system extending from Europe to East Asia in the thirteenth century AD. However, Abu Lughod's Zone VII, East Asia, is mistakenly abbreviated. She describes Japan as a "borderline outreach" (1989, 37), when in fact it was tightly integrated into Chinese trade networks. She omits Japan, Korea, Ryukyu, the central and southern Philippines, Sulawesi, and even Java, all of which enjoyed vigorous commercial relations with China.

For the general reader, it is significant to note peaceful trade was carried out in the Ryukyu and East Asian region for many centuries before the arrival of the Europeans in the sixteenth century AD. In particular, vigorous private trade flourished for over three hundred years before formal tributary trade with China was initiated in AD 1372. The new discoveries of the Gusuku Site Group indicate that even before the rise of private trade, the Japanese Heian government had a presence in the Amami region, which was almost unknown until recently. It is exciting that much of this new information has been generated by field archaeology!

Chapter 9

The Early Ryukyu Kingdom (AD 1429 to 1609)

This chapter is concerned with the archaeology of the Ryukyu Kingdom from the time of the defeat of its rivals in the early fifteenth century AD to its subjugation by Satsuma in AD 1609. It covers the archaeology of the capital, Shuri Gusuku, the port town of Naha, and the expansion of the kingdom to the surrounding islands of the Ryukyus.

In this period the newly unified Ryukyu Kingdom, consisting of Chūzan and its defeated rivals of Sanhoku and Sannan, reached its full development. It interacted on several levels with communities of all types, from royal courts to small traders and pirates, throughout East and Southeast Asia. Within the Ryukyus a distinctive high culture was created. While old connections with the Japanese main islands took on a new form, an entirely new status as tributary state was consolidated with China. In turn, the kingdom established its own internal tributary system by subjugating nearby islands and extracting tribute. The building of a royal capital, linked to a substantial port for transshipment, created a unique islandscape within East Asia.

Asato Susumu (2006) has concluded that by the thirteenth century AD, the rulers of Urasoe already controlled central and southern Okinawajima. In the fourteenth century AD their power was contested by Sanhoku in the north, with its capital at Nakijin, and Sannan in the south, with its capital at Ōzato, as described in Chapter 7. Spatial analysis of *gusuku* sites shows three clusters, which coincide with the historically known political units (Ladefoged and Pearson 2000). The castles within each of the three political units form subgroupings that often coincide with historically known political factions. This would suggest that at one time the three polities consisted of several smaller political factions that go back to the Late Shellmound Period (300 BC to AD 1050) as proposed by Asato (1990).

Two types of historical records allow us to reconstruct some of the struggles and victories that took place on sites that are now being excavated. There are local histories, surviving versions of which date from the seventeenth century AD, and official dynastic annals of China and Korea, which record diplomatic missions and sometimes describe the nature of political units. The diplomatic documents collected in *Rekidai hōan,* mentioned in Chapter 8, are dated from AD 1424 to 1867 (Okinawa Kenritsu Toshokan 1992). Murai (2000) states that the only original copy of this huge set of documents was destroyed in the Kanto Earthquake in Tokyo and the Battle of Okinawa, and that the surviving photocopies are not clear in some parts, and some passages are difficult to interpret because of unusual Chinese character forms. Beginning in the late fourteenth century AD, there are also Chinese and Korean official histories (Chinese *zhengshi,* Korean *chŏngsa*) and veritable records (Chinese *shilu,* Korean *sillok*) of the Ming, Qing, Koryo, and Chŏson; correspondence with Japan's Shimazu family and the Muromachi Bakufu (military government); historical sources pertaining to Japan's Zen sects; the *Omoro soshi* songs of the Shuri court; and official warrants or licenses of the Ryukyu Kingdom (*jireisho*) (Murai 2008, v).

In the thirteenth century AD parts of Okinawa Island were controlled by King Eiso from his political center of Urasoe. In the fourteenth century AD, competing polities in the north, central, and southern regions of Okinawa Island controlled regional confederacies. Unification under the central Chūzan Kingdom with its capital at Shuri took place in 1429 AD. The victorious Ryukyu Kingdom compiled the *Chūzan seikan* as its history in the seventeenth century AD, outlining a succession of three early dynasties (Haneji 1983). These were the Tenson Dynasty, the Eiso Dynasty (AD 1260 to 1349), and the Satto Dynasty (AD 1350 to 1405) (Appendix 2). From its beginning in legend, the first (Tenson) dynasty is said to have continued for twenty-five generations, finally to be defeated by a local lord, Shunten, said to be the son of the daughter of the Lord of Ōzato and a Japanese prince, Minamoto Tametomo, who drifted to the Ryukyus after the defeat of the Minamoto Clan by the Taira Clan in the late twelfth century AD (Kerr 1958, 58). The link to Japanese rulers, through Minamoto Tametomo, a descendant of the Japanese emperor Seiwa (reigned AD 858–876), is thought by some scholars to be a creation of the seventeenth century AD, to rationalize the Japanese subjugation of the Ryukyus after AD 1609. Kerr notes that the author of the *Chūzan seikan,* Haneji Chōshū, was "a regent whose policy centered in the need to reconcile and accommodate Okinawan interests and interests of the Japanese" (Kerr 1958, 46). In addition to this early history of the Chūzan ancestors, other sources give glimpses of local rulers in the north (Nakijin) and the south (Ōzato) as well as lesser centers (Pearson 2001, 248–249).

In the late fourteenth century AD all three powerful polities sent diplomatic missions to China, and Chūzan and Sannan established relations with Korea as well. These are recorded in the Chinese and Korean official histories. Following the collapse of the Chinese Yuan dynasty in AD 1367, the first Ming emperor, Hongwu, sent missions throughout East and Southeast Asia to proclaim the dynasty's legitimacy. Chūzan, Sanhoku, and Sannan each sent their diplomatic missions, with Satto, ruler of Urasoe, being the first Okinawan ruler to be recorded in the Chinese records as a tribute sender (Takara 1993, 53). After him all of the Chūzan rulers are mentioned in the Ming dynasty records with the exception of Shō Sen-i, who ruled for only a year in 1477 AD. Rulers before Satto are not mentioned in the Chinese records of either the Song or Ming dynasties, casting some doubt on early Okinawan documents such as the *Chūzan seikan* (which were not written as modern historical chronicles). The period of the three contending polities lasted from the early fourteenth century until AD 1422, according to Wada (2006), or 1429 according to Takara (1987, 15).

There was also an important increase in agricultural productivity from the time of the beginning of the First Shō Dynasty, around the beginning of the fifteenth century AD, when two crops of rice were planted annually (Asato Susumu 1998, 58). This innovation came from Fujian with the early tribute missions and was restricted to Okinawajima, according to Korean castaways' accounts. In the Amami and Sakishima Islands two harvests were obtained from one planting, the plants being semiperennial.

Following the unification, there was a period of very active commerce and international contacts, coupled with a rapid succession of rulers. After the death of Shō Hashi in AD 1439, from 1440 to 1469, there were five rulers in twenty-nine years and two power struggles in the 1450s. This period of instability contrasts with the succeeding fifty-year reign of Shō Shin, from AD 1471 to 1526. Takara describes this as a period of consolidation of the kingdom, in which Shō Shin achieved increased centralization and regional control (Takara 1987, 17).

In the 1450s, fierce competition for the throne between Shiro, son of King Kinpuku, and his uncle, Furi, led to the death of both incumbents and the burning of Shuri Castle. This fire of AD 1453 is of great archaeological significance and is described below. A second fire broke out in AD 1459 at the time of struggles involving the powerful chiefs Gosamaru and Amawari.

The Second Shō Dynasty began in 1469 AD. The reign of Shō Shin (AD 1477 to 1526) was a period of great prosperity for Chūzan. It was Shō Shin who fully established the kingdom's system of rule (Okamoto 2008, 55). During his reign, all *aji* were made to reside in Shuri, and their estates were put in the hands of stewards (Sakihara 1987, 175). Until that time, most of the *aji* lived on their own hereditary estates (Kerr 1958, 106), and the change in policy effectively separated them from the rural communities that had been their bases of power. Another effect of coercing the *aji* to move to the capital was to reinforce the divisions of social class over local kin groups. The Second Shō Dynasty could be seen to be the threshold of true state organization. In this case, the earlier polities of the thirteenth to mid-fifteenth centuries would be considered well-developed chiefdoms.

The Okinawan policy was more radical than that of the Japanese Tokugawa during the eighteenth and nineteenth centuries AD, for Japanese lords were allowed to reside in their own fiefs in alternate years. Weapons were gathered in the capital, and a system of administrative units, *magiri* and *shima,* was established (Asato Susumu 2003b). Okamoto is of the opinion that the decline of Ming tributary trade was a factor in the centralization of the Ryukyu Kingdom, in which the state acted as a trader while there was a decline in private trade (Okamoto 2008, 55).

Shō Shin made a concerted effort to develop centralizing cultural institutions, including the hierarchy of state-sanctioned female religious practitioners (*noro*) who were located throughout the realm (Uezato 2010, 90). From the late fifteenth century the production of luxury goods and ornaments including curved pendants (*magatama*) for the *noro* and gold casting as well as lacquer production were centralized under state control. Shō Shin sponsored impressive Buddhist temples such as the Enkakuji as a memorial temple for his ancestors (see below) and erected inscribed monuments around the capital to create a landscape of power (Takara 1987, 84–85). Many concepts of the classical Chinese *jinei* (Japanese *kinai*) system that had been adopted by Yamato in the seventh century AD can be found in the Ryukyu Kingdom, particularly during the reign of Shō Shin. These include the designation of three inner *magiri* (administrative districts) (Nishihara, Mawashi, and Haebaru) to form the heartland (*kinai*) ssurrounding the Shuri capital (Makishi 2012).

Within the aristocracy residing in Shuri, court status distinctions based on six colors for clothing and accessories were introduced in AD 1506, apparently to rationalize the positions of various outlying local aristocrats into one unambiguous system at the center. Three years later, sumptuary rules were instituted, regulating dress and other manifestations of rank in Shuri (Kerr 1958, 110).

Rebellions occurred in the outlying islands from about the middle of the reign of Shō Shin, perhaps precipitated by harsh exploitation by the Shuri government as it became overextended. The Yaeyama Islands, located some 370 km southwest of Okinawa, stopped sending tribute to Okinawa in AD 1496 or 1497. They were punished in AD 1500 by a force of three thousand soldiers in forty-six ships organized by Shuri, who annexed the islands and began to extract tribute shortly thereafter (Sakihara 1987, 185; Pearson 2003; Ōhama 2005).

Shō Shin also reorganized elites into units called *hiki,* which supervised defense, internal security, and the administration of trade, including the security of official ships that were armed against pirates (Smits 2010; Takara 1987, 102–122). In AD 1546, Shuri Castle was enlarged and strengthened. By this time, the only functioning castles remaining besides Shuri were Nakijin Gusuku, which protected the north under a governor appointed from Shuri, and the defensive castles for Naha Harbor, Yarazamori Gusuku and Mie Gusuku, both built in AD 1554. A further development in 1556 was the creation of a Council of Three (Sanshikan), which developed out of a council of regents. Its members were powerful scholar aristocrats who worked with the king to direct the heads of different government bureaus.

The conquest of Okinawa by Satsuma in AD 1609 brought the end of independence. Although the ruling Shimazu family of the fiefdom of Satsuma held a nominal title, Lord of the Southern Islands, conferred by the Kamakura Bakufu in AD 1206, it had never been able to exercise any de facto control. Ryukyu refused to contribute soldiers to General Hideyoshi's campaigns in Korea in the 1590s, finally making a delayed contribution of supplies. Following the victory of the Tokugawa Clan in AD 1600, Satsuma repaired its relationship with the first Tokugawa ruler, Tokugawa Ieyasu, who confirmed the hereditary titles of the Shimazu Clan (Kerr 1958, 154–168). In AD 1609 Satsuma invaded Ryukyu and removed King Shō Nei to Japan for three years, extracting an agreement that Satsuma would control Ryukyu and appropriating all islands from Yoronjima to the Amami Islands. Ryukyu was to continue its tributary status with China, giving Satsuma access to China and creating a relation of dual subordination by both China and Japan.

In 1997 I proposed that, in the period of its prosperity and independence (Early Ryukyu Kingdom Period, AD 1429 to 1609), the Ryukyu Kingdom displayed some characteristics of a city-state (Pearson 1997b). Griffeth and Thomas (1981) described the following defining attributes. These states have a defined core, usually enclosed by walls or surrounded by water, and they are economically self-sufficient, often through the acquisition of an immediate and productive hinterland. They are also politically independent and self-governed. They seem to develop when polities in surrounding areas are relatively weak. In the fourteenth to sixteenth centuries AD, central authority in the main islands of Japan was relatively weak, and China had little interest in conquest of such small islands. When power in the Japanese main islands was consolidated and centralized in the early seventeenth century AD under the control of the Tokugawa

Shōgunate, the Ryukyu Kingdom was subjugated by a Tokugawa vassal, the Shimazu Clan, and lost its independence.

Is it heuristic to think of the Ryukyu Kingdom in terms of a city-state? Comparison of the Ryukyu case with city-states emphasizes its mercantile nature, small scale and hinterland, centralized administration, and opportunistic rise and decline. It was also self-sufficient for food but not for raw materials such as metal. Unlike Mediterranean city-states, it did not have a democratically organized citizen class (*polis*) or slaves, nor was it ruled by a council of merchants, in the manner of Sakai, Osaka, in the fifteenth and sixteenth centuries AD. In addition, the degree of urbanization in the region of Naha and Shuri in the fifteenth to seventeenth centuries AD was probably low. European and Mediterranean city-states usually occur in competing groups, which is not the case in the East China Sea. However, the Mediterranean city-states are not considered to be the only form of city-state (Charlton and Nichols 1997, 4). In contrast to territorial states, which integrate large areas through a hierarchy of administrative centers, the Ryukyu Kingdom was highly centralized, although there were regional centers for the collection of tribute in Ishigakijima, Miyakojima, Kumejima, and Amami Ōshima, from the sixteenth century AD. Despite its diminutive size, it relied on a relatively large peasant class for agricultural produce (Asato 1998, 137–238). Exploring diversity among small commercial entrepôts in Asia and other areas may lead us to understand the varied processes of their development. Probably the label "city-state" is not heuristic.

The Configuration of the Shuri Capital

In this discussion I refer to the Shuri capital as Shuri Gusuku, to emphasize its Okinawan features, such as type of construction and religious significance, which are distinctive from those of Japanese or European castles. The castle is situated on a ridge of limestone some 100 to 135 m in elevation, lying inland and to the west of the port of Naha. It commands a view over much of the southern part of the island, including the earlier capital of Urasoe to the north and the trading port of Naha to the west, as well as important offlying islands. Its dimensions are 400 m east to west and 270 m north to south, with a total area of 42,000 sq m (Fujimoto and Naka 1980, 288). Beginning with the First Shō Dynasty, it was the castle site of the king of Ryukyu. The oldest inscribed stela in Okinawa, the Ankokuzan Jukaboku no Kihi, was erected by King Shō Hashi in AD 1427 (Shimajiri 1983) to the north of the Sonohyan Utaki near the first gate (Shurei no Mon) of the Shuri Castle. It confirms that the castle was built at least by the early fifteenth century AD. It records the planting of trees and flowers

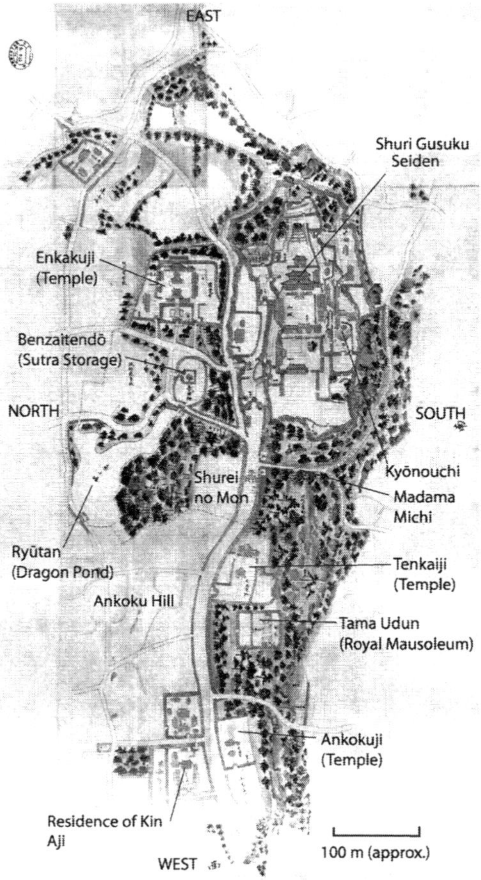

Figure 9.1. Map of the Shuri royal capital area, showing Shuri Gusuku, adjacent temples, and the Royal Mausoleum (Tama Udun). From a map in the Okinawa Prefectural Library, titled "Shurijō no fukin no zu" (Map of vicinity of Shuri Gusuku), published in Shurijō Fukugen Kiseikai, *Shashinshu Shuri Jō* (Collection of photographs of Shuri Castle) (Naha: Naha Shuppansha, 1987), p. 40 (figure 48). Courtesy of Okinawa Kenritsu Toshokan and Naha Shuppansha.

on Ankoku Hill, created with fill from digging the adjacent Dragon Pond (Ryūtan), as well as the political ascendancy of Chūzan and the establishment of tributary relations with the Ming dynasty (Figure 9.1).

The earliest phases of occupation and the initial phases of castle construction are not clear, and recent reconstruction of some of the buildings may make it impossible for archaeologists to expose large areas of earlier strata. The castle itself may date from the reign of Satto (AD 1350–1395), but less complex elite residences probably preceded it. It is likely that Shuri was not the center of Chūzan when it was first built. At that time Urasoe was still the capital. The transfer of the capital from Urasoe to Shuri took place during the reign of King Satto (Sakihara 1987, 105). The finding of very valuable Chinese ceramics, which must have been part of the gifts given by the Ming emperor Hongwu to Satto in AD 1374, in at least two areas of Shuri, means that by the late fourteenth century Shuri must have been the capital, not Urasoe (Kin 2008a, 42). Along the outer periphery wall were four outer gates, and nine interior gates gave access to different divisions within the palace. Most of the inner walls were of cut limestone, 6 to 12 m high, surmounted by wooden structures. The arched construction of the gates is of Chinese style. Administrative functions were carried out in three large buildings arranged around an open space (Unā), which was used for state occasions. These are the Seiden (administrative palace), Nanden, and Hokuden. To the east were two residential buildings for the king and queen.

Shuri Gusuku was surrounded by the residences of royal relatives and retainers, temples, and administrative offices (Seto 2010b). To the immediate north was the Enkakuji temple. Outside the eastern edge of Shuri Castle was the Sakiyama Utaki and to the west, the Tenkaiji temple and the Royal Mausoleum (Tama Udun) (Zaidan 2003, 274–277). In the Early Gusuku Period, *gusuku* were separated from villages, but in the Late Gusuku Period, in the Chūzan area, the *gusuku* became the nucleus of a walled town. At the time of the First Shō Dynasty (AD 1406 to 1469), additional buildings already occurred inside the walls. In the reign of Shō Shin (AD 1477 to 1526) storehouses for containing the arms that were relinquished by the local *aji* and residences for the elite were built. To strengthen its fortifications, walls were added in the middle of the fourteenth century AD, during the reign of Shō Hashi. During the reigns of Shō Shin and Shō Sei (reigned AD 1527 to 1555) in the Second Shō Dynasty, the stone walls on the north and east sides were doubled in length during a major enlargement and reorganization (Asato Susumu 1998, 47), achieving a form that remained unchanged until the total destruction of the site in the Battle of Okinawa in AD 1945. Detailed maps of the surrounding area have survived from the nineteenth century, and exploratory excavations are ongoing. An example is the residence of the crown prince, the Nakagusuku Udun, which was built in AD 1621. It has yielded trade ceramics from the late fourteenth and early fifteenth centuries AD. Destroyed in World War II, it became the site of the Okinawa Prefectural Museum from 1966 to 2007, before the opening of the new museum in its new location in Shintoshin, Naha (the former residential area of high-ranking American military officials) (Okinawa Kenritsu Maizō 2010).

In the centuries following its first construction in the early fourteenth century AD, Shuri Gusuku was burned four times, and a portion was rebuilt in AD 1992. The buildings that were standing in early AD 1945 had been rebuilt in AD 1712–1715, and their partial reconstuction in 1992 was based on the eighteenth- to nineteenth-century version. Before the eighteenth century AD it certainly was not exactly the same as later versions. From excavations of the

Kyōnouchi, one can see pits dug into the coral limestone and can find Korean-type roof tiles, which appear to be associated with the buildings of the fourteenth to fifteenth centuries AD. Roof tiles of three distinctive types, Korean, Yamato, and Chinese, have been found in Shuri. Although it was previously thought that the so-called Korean-style tiles were made in Korea and shipped to Okinawa, petrographic analysis has shown that the three types were all made with the same clay, which contains coral inclusions and matches clay samples from the western part of Nago City, Okinawa (Yamamoto Masa'aki et al. 2007). These three types, as well as soft gray pottery and floor tiles from Shuri Gusuku, have the same petrographic signature and were all produced in Okinawa. The paste has chert inclusions from the Nago Geological Layer of the Motobu region of northern Okinawa. The Korean-style tiles share some motifs with the Yamato Type, indicating that, after the adoption of Korean manufacturing methods, there was local innovation. Uehara (2004) proposed that either Yamato craftsmen came to Okinawa or Okinawans learned tile production in Japan.

Spatial Organization of Shuri Castle

Different buildings and areas of Shuri Castle served a number of functions in the administration of the kingdom, judging from the prewar plans of the last stage of Shuri, rebuilt in AD 1712–1715 (Figure 9.2).

At least four buildings set around a large forecourt were devoted to record keeping, administration of sacred places, foreign relations, and records of births and deaths. Shuri Gusuku contained the residences of the king and queen as well as the seat of administration (Seiden). The plaza in front of the administrative palace was an area for state functions and assemblies. The administrative palace faced to the west instead of the south as it did in Urasoe (Asato Susumu 2006, 91). This shift in orientation followed Ryukyuan ideology of the king as the child of the sun (*tedako*), which came to take precedence over Chinese rules of north-south orientation in the early fifteenth century AD (Asato Susumu 2009). On the north and south sides of the plaza were the Hokuden and Nanden, reception halls for Chinese and Japanese delegations respectively. Spaces for ritual activities were dispersed. The largest of these, the Kyōnouchi, was located in the southern portion of the western half of the castle, while the king's private shrine, the Shinbyōden, was at the extreme east. An important shrine, the Sonohyan Utaki, was located outside of the castle walls on the west, inside the ceremonial gate (Shurei no Mon) and near the juncture of roads leading from the castle to the port of Naha. A watch tower, bell tower, and craft workshop area were situated on the extreme western side. Below the castle walls, on the north side, were the Ryūtan Pond and the largest Buddhist temple in the

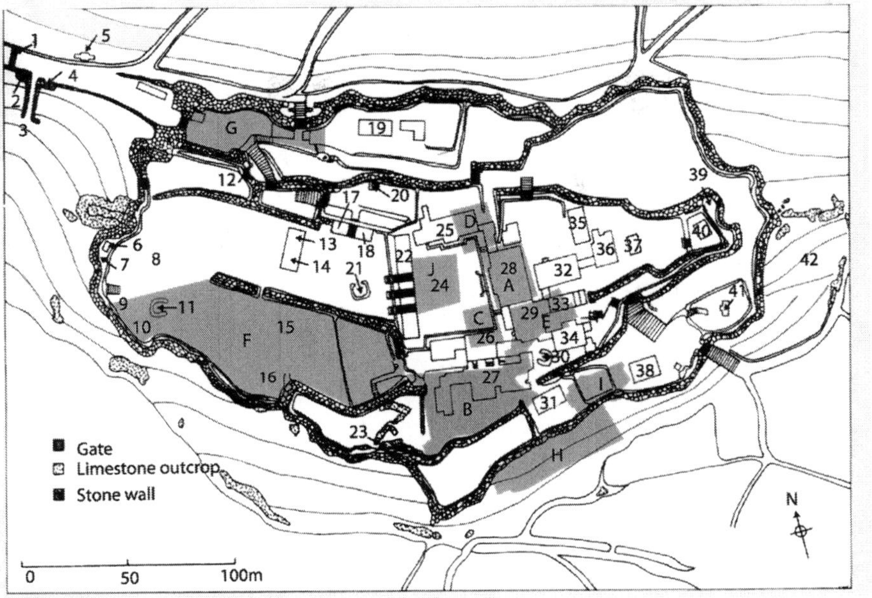

Figure 9.2. Plan of Shuri Gusuku, late nineteenth century AD. Major excavated areas indicated by shading. Redrawn from "Shurijō yōzu" (Rough map of Shuri Gusuku), in Shurijō Fukugen Kiseikai 1987, 52–53 (figure 59).

1. Ceremonial Gate (Shurei no Mon), first erected AD 1529
2. Monument marking beginning of stone paved road to Shikina Summer Residence (Madamaminato Himon), first erected AD 1522
3. Start of Madama Road
4. Monument dedicated to Sixth Abbott, Enkakuji temple, erected AD 1522
5. Shrine (Sonohyan Utaki)
6. Bell Tower
7. Western Parapet
8. Iri no Azana Area
9. Cave
10. Takayosōridun Area
11. Shrine (Madamamori Utaki)
12. Dragon Watercourse
13. Royal Records (Keizuza)
14. Foreign Relations Records, Protocol (Yubutsuza)
15. Royal Storehouse (SK01)
16. Administration of Sacred Places (Jiinza)
17. Registry of Births, Deaths, and so forth (Daiyoza)
18. Warehouse for Ritual Objects (Zenigura)
19. Sundial Clock
20. Shrine (Shurimori Utaki)
21. Storage of Medicine, Tobacco (Naden)
22. Watch Tower
23. Plaza
24. Reception Hall for Chinese Envoys (Hokuden)
25. Reception Hall for Satsuma Japanese Envoys (Nanden)
26. Royal Residence (Shoin)
27. Administrative Palace (Seiden)
28. Sitting Rooms for King, Queen
29. Shrine (Kaimei Utaki)
30. Hall for King's Succession Rituals (Yobokoridun)
31. Queen's Residence (Ōgon Odon)
32. Royal Refectory (Sakiman?)
33. King's Residence (Nikaiden)
34. Sitting Rooms for Court Ladies
35. Kitchen
36. Residence of Queen Mother, Court Ladies (Yosoidun)
37. Kitchen Storage
38. East Parapet
39. King's Shrine (Shinbyōden)
40. Sashiki Palace (for Queen's Administrators)
41. Kuninaka Utaki

Excavation areas (approximate scale):

A. Seiden	F. Kyōnouchi
B. Shoin	G. Kankai Mon area
C. Nanden	H. Outside South Wall
D. Hokuden	I. Administrative Road Area
E. Nikaiden	J. Unā

kingdom, the Enkakuji. When King Shō Shin forced the local lords to relinquish their arms and move to the capital, storehouses for weapons were built inside the castle, presumably in one of the outer enclosures.

The Seiden

The central administrative building, the Seiden, 16 m high in its present form, was the largest structure on Okinawa in its time. By at least AD 1450, it was two stories high. In front of the Seiden were two carved stone dragon pillars erected in AD 1508. In contrast to palaces in Kyoto, which were raised on wooden pillars, the Seiden and other official buildings were set on stone platforms about 90 cm high. They had tile roofs, wooden walls, and round pillars.

Excavations in the 1980s, at the time the Seiden was reconstructed, revealed five different construction periods, but the actual forms of earlier buildings were not clear. Period I, known from only a small excavation sample, was marked by a brown soil layer. Roof tiles of Yamato (Japanese) Type were recovered and are thought to be from a building preceding the Seiden. In Period II, a layer of cut stones was laid down, and its surface shows evidence of burning, perhaps from the disturbance of AD 1453. On top of the cut stones was a building 16.36 m × 9.09 m (Kin et al. 1988, 45–46). The western (front) portion of this building contained burned sherds of trade ceramics, armor slats, metal fittings, and fragments of burned charcoal, suggesting that the structure had suffered extensive burning. In Period III, the stone cutting and paving became extremely rough, as if refacing of the platform was done in a great hurry, perhaps because of some major event that occurred at this time. At least two more refacings occurred, in Periods IV and V, with the facing from Period V remaining until twentieth century AD. The stratigraphy of the base platform of the Seiden has not been tightly correlated to historical events (Zaidan 2003, 276; Ijū 2010).

The Shoin Area

In the area of the guard station (Tsumesho), there was an unusual feature consisting of a pavement of large ridged clamlike shells, *hirejako* (*Tridacna squamosa*), placed with the exterior of the shell upward (Okinawa Kenritsu Maizō 2005b, 212). This kind of feature has not been found in elsewhere in Shuri Castle. Beneath this pavement is a layer containing artifacts, the most recent of which is a Ming dynasty Yongle coin dated AD 1408. In the sand and gravel layer covering the pavement there were ceramics dating to the fifteenth to sixteenth centuries AD. About 30 cm above the shell pavement layer was stone pavement no. 2, which resembles the paved walkways in other parts of the castle. It would be difficult to walk on the shell pavement; therefore its meaning and purpose are not clear.

The Nanden (Southern Palace) and Hokuden (Northern Palace)

The Nanden and Hokuden flanked the Seiden, at right angles, forming two sides of the main plaza. The fourth side of the plaza was formed by the Hōshin Gate. In the period from AD 1609 to 1879, the Hokuden housed visiting Chinese envoys, while the Nanden housed visiting Satsuma envoys, so that the configuration reflected the dual sovereignty of China and Satsuma in relation to the Ryukyu Kingdom. The Hokuden was constructed in Chinese Ming style. Associated artifacts and stratigraphy confirm that the configuration of the three buildings was in existence from the mid-fifteenth century AD.

Six building periods of the Nanden were discerned from excavation (Okinawa Ken 1995b, 173). Nanden Period VI appears to be the building of the Satsuma Period, after AD 1609. The excavation reporters mention that there is a reference in the *Ryūkyū koku yuraiki* (Hokama and Hateruma 1997) to a building called the Gusuku Udun, which may be one or all of Nanden I to VI. Nanden Period I is correlated with Seiden Period II. It was built on a leveled outcrop of Ryukyu limestone. The east corner of the *kidan* platform remains. It was constructed of carefully cut limestone blocks, set in the *nunozumi* style. The surface of the corner has been reddened by strong heat, which is thought to be from the fire of AD 1453. Nothing above the stone base remains. The remains of Nanden Periods II, III, IV, and V appear to be contemporary with Seiden Periods III, IV, V, and VI.

The building sequences of the Hokuden are not clear, but there seems to have been a building on the site at the time of Seiden Period II. Artifacts recovered from this area confirm that the three buildings were in place by the mid-fifteenth century or slightly earlier. Although some stone adzes found at the site of the Hokuden may be specimens belonging to a museum housed in the Hokuden before World War II, most artifacts recovered are from the fourteenth to fifteenth centuries AD, Chinese celadon comprising 50 percent of the materials. East of the Nanden was the Ouchibaru Shoin, a residence of the king and queen that was connected to the Seiden. Behind this was the Shoin, a Japanese-style reception building with a tiled roof.

The Royal Residential Area

In an area to the immediate south of the Seiden, in the space between the Seiden and the Nikaiden, were several small buildings that were the living quarters of the royal family. There are no existing photos or historical records of these buildings. Some stone alignments and pillar bases have been found as well as artifacts from the fourteenth to nineteenth centuries AD including ceramics, roof and floor tile fragments, metal fittings, and beads (Okinawa Kenritsu Maizō 2007b). The first building, the Yoseman, a kitchen and bathing area for the king and queen, could not be conclusively located. The second building, the Ōgon Odon (Yellow Gold Palace), contained the sleeping quarters for the king and queen. Although the date of construction is unknown, there are records that it burned in AD 1660 and 1709 (ibid., 206–210). No features can be conclusively dated to the period before AD 1609. It is thought to have had a tile roof similar to that of the Nikaiden. A substantial number of artifacts, including roof tiles, floor tiles, Chinese celadons, brownwares, and Okinawan ceramics as well as Thai, Vietnamese, Bizen, and other Japanese main islands wares were found in this area. In particular, sherds of large Chinese vessels were recovered, dating to the fourteenth to nineteenth centuries AD, with the majority dating to the fifteenth century AD. The remains of a third building, a kind of side room for the ruler's personal assistants such as administrators and scribes, the Kinju Tsumesho, is located to the southwest of the Yellow Gold Palace (Ōgon Odon). Its paved floor and pillar bases were located in the excavations. In the space between the Kinju Tsumesho and the Ōgon Odon there was a room called the Suzuhiki no Ma (lit. Bell-Pulling Room) where female officials could summon attendants to the ruling family. As with other buildings in this area, there are no detailed written records.

The Nikaiden (Main Royal Residence)

The Nikaiden, now reconstructed, is located on the south corner of the Seiden. Historical records date its present form to the eighteenth century AD (Okinawa Kenritsu Maizō 2005e, 93). On the west a staircase connected it to the Seiden, and there was also an eastern staircase that gave access to the outside.

Although historical records pertaining to this area of the castle do not extend back beyond the eighteenth century AD, excavations have yielded a stratigraphic record extending back to the late thirteenth century AD. Layer I contained postwar debris, mixed with disturbed material that included ceramics of the Gusuku Period. Layer II belongs to the construction period of the Nikaiden and includes its stone base. Below the stone base is an unconsolidated deposit of sherds. It contains burned ceramics, particularly celadon sherds, which date to the fourteenth and fifteenth centuries AD. This dumped deposit, consisting of ceramics, coins, metal objects, and beads, appears to have been transported and dumped as fill (*ochikomi*). Thus it is not clear that the contents were originally associated with a royal residence, but it seems likely that they were not transported very far. The contents are described below.

NIKAIDEN DUMPED DEPOSIT: ARCHAEOLOGICAL FEATURES SR11, SR12, SR24, SR32, SR33

In the Nikaiden Dumped Deposit a group of ceramics comprising blue and white, celadon, and whiteware is particularly notable. The celadons and whitewares are comparable to those found in the Sinan sunken ship found near Mokpo, Korea, dating to the 1320s AD. The Chinese blue and white wares fall into two groups, dated to the Yuan and Ming periods. The Yuan blue and white sherds are particularly large and come from large specimens. The total sherd count is 18, and the minimum number of vessels is 10, while the total count of Ming sherds was 370 and the minimum number of vessels was 71 (Okinawa Kenritsu Maizō 2005e, 55). Some of the Yuan blue and white finds from the Nikaiden are unique in Okinawa Prefecture. These include blue and white jars (*tsubo*) with a lotus pond motif as well as a tree peony and arabesque motifs, a bottle (usually referred to by the Chinese *yuhucun*) with dragon and pearl motif, and a small rectangular stand with open work. Also unique is a whiteware bowl of the Chinese Shufu Type. How did these particularly unusual ceramics reach Shuri? Were they actually traded during the Yuan period, or were they tributary items that were already antiques when they reached Okinawa? Kamei (2008; 2009) emphasizes that a substantial number of Zhizheng Type finely painted specimens, which are different from crudely painted small containers found in Southeast Asia, have been found in Shuri and that their quantity is comparable to the numbers found in Southwest Asia and China. Were the Yuan blue and white ceramics of the Nikaiden part of a separate exchange system in which Shuri was a major player? Shuri Gusuku has yielded 79 Yuan blue and white vessels, 72 percent of a total of 109 from seven sites in Okinawa. Of the 459 total specimens of Yuan blue and white vessels recorded in a comprehensive survey by Kamei from China, Korea, Japan, Ryukyu, and South and West Asia, 109 come from Ryukyu and 179 from South and West Asia (Kamei 2009, 66). Kamei believes this distribution implies that the Ryukyus were an important center for the distribution of these ceramics, which have often been considered diplomatic gifts produced for distribution in South and West Asia. The pieces are particularly large and impressive. Kin (2008a) has suggested that they may have been part of the initial tributary gift from the Ming rulers. The large finely painted pieces are similar in type and quantity to those found in the Majapahit capital of Trowulan, Java (Dupoizat and Harkantiningsik 2007, 57–64)

Two small brown-glazed jars of a type not often found in other parts of Shuri or Okinawa Prefecture have been identified as products of the Cizao kiln, Quanzhou, Fujian. This type has also been found in the Hakata Site Group and in Dazaifu, and is dated to the twelfth to thirteenth centuries AD. Early connections with Quanzhou are particularly interesting in light of the discoveries from Urasoe (described in Chapter 7). Two other wares are thought to be products of kilns in the lower Min River area of Fujian: a brown-glazed jar and a white-glazed jar (Okinawa Kenritsu Maizō 2005e, 96).

The deposit contained 532 base sherds of bowls, with black oil spot glaze termed *tenmoku* in Japanese, on a light gray body and a sharply trimmed foot rim, made in Nanping City and other kilns in the area of Fuzhou, Fujian Province. They are of the most common type found in Okinawa Prefecture. There are also sherds of tea containers (caddies). They are dated to the fourteenth century, estimated to be from a relatively short period. Could they represent a single tribute gift, shipped from Fujian? These bowls confirm the consumption of tea, in Chinese style, by the Ryukyu court. Alternatively they could have been reserved for shipment for Japan (Seto 2004, 146).

Vietnamese wares dating to the fourteenth and fifteenth centuries AD were far more numerous in this site than in other Okinawan or Japanese sites. A total of 545 sherds or a minimum number of 105 pieces was recovered, comprising 4 percent of the total sherds from the Nikaiden. Blue and white pieces, such as bowls with an unglazed base with chocolate-colored interior ring, were particularly numerous. The bowls are of two types, with different dating (Okinawa Kenritsu Maizō 2005e, 94). Type I is a deep bowl with everted lip. The white glaze is close in tone to that of Yuan blue and white. By comparison with specimens from the Dazaifu Site in northern Kyushu, it is dated to the mid-fourteenth century AD. Type II is dated to the late fourteenth to mid-fifteenth centuries AD. The Thai wares, which also comprised about 4 percent, were primarily sherds from large brownware jars, but there were a few sherds from earthenware jars with Chinese characters stamped on the shoulder, which may have been produced in Laos in the fifteenth century AD (Okinawa Kenritsu Maizō 2005e, 96).

Finally, there are a few sherds of soft grayware unfired braziers (late fourteenth to early fifteenth century AD), which appear to have been made in a site on the Inland Sea coast of Kyushu. Similar wares have been found in Ichijōdani and Tosaminato (Okinawa Kenritsu Maizō 2005e, 96).

The ceramic deposits of the Nikaiden define an archaeological space that would otherwise provide few clues as to its function or program. The Yuan blue and white ceramics indicate the privileged role of the Ryukyu kings in the Chinese tributary system and also show their power to conduct exchange with peers in East and Southeast Asia. The Fujian tea bowls indicate the adoption of tea drinking that they shared with other elites in East Asia. In addition to *tenmoku* tea bowls, tea containers (*cha tsubo*) are found not only in *gusuku* sites but also in large villages (Arakaki 2004; 2007). Tea drinking is not only closely associated with China and Buddhism, but is also linked to mediaeval Japanese samurai culture. The ceramics from Thailand and Vietnam support the accounts of elite exchange in the records of the *Rekidai hōan* (Okinawa Kenritsu Toshokan 1992).

NIKAIDEN, SB04

In a layer termed SB Lower Layer, found under a stone pavement in the Nikaiden area, another accumulation of ceramics yielded a minimum number of seventy-seven vessels, mostly celadon, with a few *tenmoku* and whitewares, dating from the fourteenth to fifteenth centuries AD. The celadons are largely plain with everted rims, and others have broad, unridged lotus petal motifs on the exterior, as well as "lama-style" lotus petals. Six *tenmoku* bowls were stuck together with a calcareous deposit from limestone; they may have been redeposited from another area of the castle site. Many of the ceramics appear to have been exposed to strong heating. They may have gone through the same fire as the *ochikomi* material and the Kyōnouchi artifacts (described below), and may actually belong to a shorter time span than the others.

The Kyōnouchi

The Kyōnouchi was a ritual space of the mid-fifteenth century AD (Okinawa Ken 1998; Okinawa Kenritsu Maizō 2009b). Its name means "sacred area with spiritual power" (Okinawa Ken 1998, 15). Archival evidence suggests that there were originally five *utaki* (shrines) in the area. Of the total area of 5,000 sq m, 2,000 sq m have been excavated. A substantial number of features, including walls, alignments, pavements, ditches, pits, building foundations, and a staircase have been excavated. From the complex configuration of features, six periods of construction were determined (Okinawa Ken 1998, 26) (see Figure 9.2). An investigation of the features from this oldest part of Shuri Castle yielded earlier features dating to the first half of the fourteenth century AD, including stone building material, pillar bases, and drainage ditches. Roof tiles of the same types as those found in Urasoe have been found in this area. The Kyōnouchi was referred to as the old *gusuku* (Kogusuku). Tawada has proposed that the oldest buildings were built in the Kyōnouchi area at the time of the move of the capital from Urasoe to Shuri in the fourteenth century AD (Tawada 1980; Kinjō Kamenobu 2001, 72–73). The area where these early structures are located is termed the Takayosōridun. In that area, the remains of a multistoried building thought to be the Takayosōridun itself was found in excavations, but it was heavily disturbed. According to Kinjō Kamenobu (2001), after the Takayosōridun burned, the Kyōnouchi assumed a religious function. It was separated from the structures with primary political functions such as the Main Palace, South Palace, North Palace, and Hōshin Gate by stone walls 3 to 7 m in height. Located at one of the highest points within the castle, it had a lookout from which Kudakajima and Kumejima as well as Zakimi on Okinawa Island could be seen.

EARLY FEATURES (SA24, SA03)

On the south edge of the Kyōnouchi, there are low walls and pits that contain sherds of Chinese whitewares and *tenmoku* dating to the early and mid-fourteenth century AD (Okinawa Ken 1998, 29). These indicate that there were substantial buildings within Shuri Gusuku before the unification by Chūzan and the establishment of the Ryukyu Kingdom. These finds confirm Tawada's hypothesis mentioned above.

CAVE SX01

A cave feature had cut stones at the entrance and a floor of sandstone overlain by gray tiles. The main use of the cave appears to have been in the sixteenth and seventeenth centuries AD. In the lowest layer of the cave floor, a sherd of Vietnamese blue and white porcelain was found (Okinawa Ken 1998, 25–26).

SACRIFICIAL PITS

Features B13, B14, C15, C16, D15, and D16 were six fourteenth century AD pits, with a depth of about 30 to 40 cm and a diameter of 40 to 50 cm, that contained cow crania and hooves thought to be the remains of some kind of ritual (Okinawa Ken 1998, 27). A similar group of pits has been recovered at the Nakamamura Site, Haebaru Chō, Okinawajima, a thirteenth century AD site yielding the lower mandibles of five cows lined up next to the remains of a *kuba* tree (*Livistona chinensis*). These are also thought to be the remains of an agricultural ritual (Kinjō Kamenobu 2001, 78). The *kuba,* or Chinese fan palm, is still believed by Okinawans to be a resting place for spirits, and groves of this tree often surround shrines (*utaki*), religious sites sometimes sheltered in a small structure, marked by an incense burner and small porcelain bottles for flowers or water. Further ethnographic research is required to determine the significance of this ritual and its location within the Kyōnouchi.

ROYAL STOREHOUSE (FEATURE SK01)

The most important feature excavated in the Kyōnouchi is the remains of the Royal Storehouse (*sōko*), thought to have been burned in AD 1459. A portion of the storehouse consisting of a rectangular pit or basement 3 m × 4 m and 0.5 m deep, with three steps, shows signs of burning. Nonceramic artifacts include armor, a sword, bead ornaments, and a metal lock (Okinawa Ken 1998, 255–258). The *Omoro sōshi* songs (Hokama and Saigo 1972) mention the ritual significance of the sword and armor. The beads may have decorated bottles of a type seen in later heirlooms.

The major contents of the storehouse are ceramics, including some very fine specimens (see frontispiece). The contents of the storehouse are thought to have come from two main sources. First, an important collection was received from the Chinese court in AD 1459, and, second, ceramics were received in trade with various countries in the mid-fifteenth century AD. A fire destroyed the Royal Storehouse in AD 1453 at the time of the Shiro-Furi Rebellion, a succession struggle between Shiro, the son of King Kinpuku, and his uncle Furi, the sixth son of the previous ruler, Shō Hashi. To replace the ceramics stored there, King Shō Taikyu received a new collection from the Ming court, in exchange for copper coins, rather than the usual gift of sappanwood from Southeast Asia. Sixty percent, by value, of the goods from China came from the Peking Treasury, and 40 percent came from Fujian in the form of a special kind of woven silk and locally made celadon and blue and white ceramics. Since the 6:4 division took account of the value of the objects, the actual number of pieces from Peking was relatively small (Kinjō Kamenobu 2001, 78; Okinawa Ken 1998, 256). Thus, the collection contains some dramatic treasures of the highest quality along with large numbers of ordinary objects such as celadon bowls (Okinawa Kenritsu Maizō 2001c). In the frontispiece, celadon vessels are grouped on the right. They consist of jars, ewer, stemmed cup, dishes, and a large baluster vase *(rear),* dating to the early fifteenth century AD. On the left are blue and white vessels. The vases and large jar *(rear)* are dated to the fifteenth century AD, whereas the large covered box and stemmed cup are dated to the fourteenth century AD (end of the Yuan dynasty). The overglaze enamel bowl in the center foreground is dated to the early fifteenth century, and the red-glazed ewer *(center)* is dated to the fourteenth century.

Spectacular pieces of the royal collection include a whiteware bowl referred to as the Shufu Type, a Ding Ware white lotus shaped cup, a red-glazed Yuan ewer, a *ruri-*(brilliant blue) glazed ewer, a dragon pattern blue and white stirrup cup (*bajōhai*), an exceptionally large Yuan blue and white covered box (Kamei 2002a, b, and a celadon bottle with tree peony and arabesque (Japanese *kara-*

kusa) decoration. Examples of several of these are previously unknown in Japan. The red-glazed ewer is thought to be unique worldwide; and the white stirrup cup with stamped dragon pattern, thought to have been presented by the Ming court to legitimize the authority of surrounding vassal states, is one of twenty specimens known worldwide. Many of the Yuan and early Ming celadons are of exceptional quality.

In the period between the rebuilding of the warehouse after the 1453 fire and the second fire in AD 1459, ceramics were received from Siam, Vietnam, and Japan, and this mixed collection was burned in the second fire. Thai earthenware, in the form of sixty-seven lids and four vessel sherds, was recovered. The lids are thought to have been used for large brown-glazed four-eared jars. Some may be of Okinawan manufacture (Okinawa Ken 1998, 61). Kin's explanation is that large brown- and black-glazed Thai jars with earthenware lids contained special Siamese liquor served to Chinese envoys (Kin 1993; 1999; 2000). Mukai (2002, 79) suggests that they may also have been used as containers for other products from different parts of Southeast Asia such as food or dyes. Kin (2000) proposed that, since most of the Kyōnouchi ceramics are food-serving vessels of Chinese manufacture, they must have been used for serving Chinese envoys who arrived in the tribute missions or in palace rituals such as succession ceremonies. Kinjō Kamenobu proposed that some of the pouring vessels could have been used in religious ceremonies associated with local shrines (*utaki*) (2001, 78). Kin (2008a) notes that the finest ceramic pieces in both the Kyōnouchi Royal Storehouse and the Nikaiden Deposit cover a time span from the mid-fourteenth to mid-fifteenth century AD. He proposes that the late Yuan pieces were part of the gift of ceramics given to King Satto in AD 1374 by the Ming emperor Hongwu. In both interpretations the finest wares were presented by the Ming court.

Fragments of royal armor, including helmet ornaments, were found in the Royal Storehouse. These are important for showing the construction of a distinctive Ryukyu style in the first half of the fifteenth century AD. Yamamoto and Uezato (2004) state that, although many finds of metal armor are yet to be systematically studied, current finds show that Ryukyu armor is generally of Japanese style. The general form of the armor follows that of the Japanese main islands, but some of the decoration is distinctive. The helmet ornament (*tatemono*) (Figure 9.3) has a main column, and two hoe-shaped wings. The shape, unique to Ryukyu, consists of sun, moon, and stars. This motif is termed the motif of auspicious clouds, moon, sun, and stars (*zuiun hitsuki sei mon*). Fragments of similar helmet ornaments have been found in the Nanden and the Hokuden. The metal helmet in Japanese armor is not a single cap but is composed of metal-like strips fastened together. Examples from Shuri show a distinctive Ryukyu feature in which the helmet was composed of an underlying set

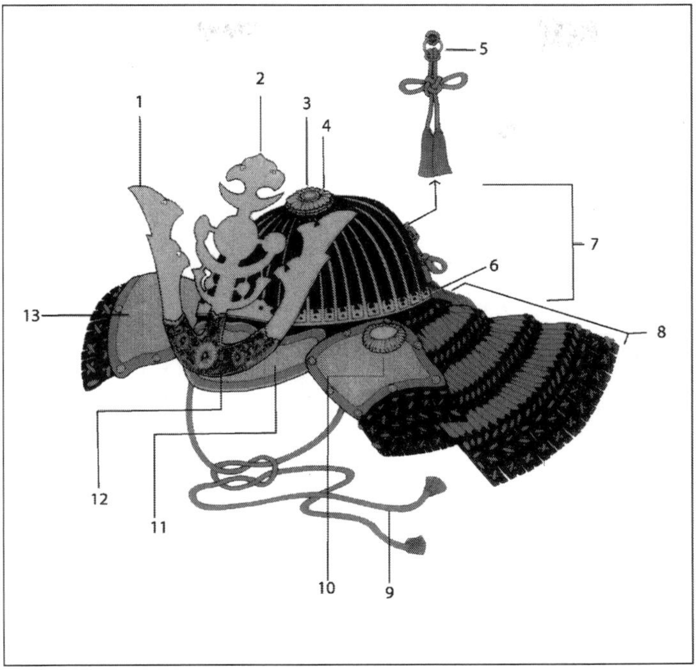

Figure 9.3. Reconstruction of a helmet found in the Royal Storehouse of the Kyōnouchi. From Okinawa Kenritsu Maizō 2009b, frontispiece plate 13. Courtesy of Kinjō Kamenobu and Okinawa Kenritsu Maizō Bunkazai Sentā.

1. Deer-antler-shaped uprights (The Japanese term describes them as hoe-shaped, *kuwagata*). 2. Main upright decoration (*tatemono*) with Ryukyu motif of clouds, sun, and moon. 3. Top of helmet (*tehen*) with hole where metal slats meet. 4. Chrysanthemum-shaped metal fitting covering hole. 5. Tassel held in riveted ring. 6. Decorative band in shape of sacred boundary fence (*ikaki*). 7. Helmet (*hachi*) composed of metal strips. 8. Skirt of lamellar pieces for protection of neck. 9. Fastening cord. 10. Ornament with sawtoothlike edge (*kyomon kanamono*). 11. Visor (*mabisashi*). 12. Ornamental socket for upright ornament. 13. Protective flange (*fukikaeshi*).

of iron strips overlain by a layer of bronze strips, which were probably gilded. The creation of unique forms of armor of Japanese style confirmed the status of the king of Ryukyu as a paramount among Japanese equals at official functions with Okinawan confederates or Japanese envoys, in a similar manner to the use of Chinese-style royal regalia of appropriate rank in ceremonies for the Ming envoys. The unique symbolism of the helmet ornament reflects Okinawan political identity and cosmology.

SHURIMORI UTAKI

The Shurimori Utaki was situated to the west of the other *utaki* in its own walled enclosure entered through an arched gate (Kinjō Kamenobu 2001, 74, 79). It was devoted to the worship of the legendary founding people of Okinawa, the Amamikyo, and was one of the most sacred shrines within the castle. Its general location is known from eighteenth-century maps. Excavations were undertaken in hopes of finding remains that would be useful for its reconstruction; however, nothing could be found except a portion of a wall from the rebuilding of AD 1712. While the *utaki* is mentioned in the early sacred song collection *Omoro sōshi* (AD 1531–1623) (Hokama and Saigo 1972) and the first Okinawan history, the *Chūzan seikan,* written about AD 1650 (Haneji 1983), and appears on early-nineteenth-century maps as a C-shaped enclosure (Okinawa Kenritsu Maizō 2008b, 107–108), it disappeared from maps between AD 1881 and 1893. Its complete disappearance "is thought to have some relation to the dissolution of the monarchy" (ibid., 108), suggesting to me that it may have been intentionally destroyed to extinguish Okinawan state religion. Most of the finds, which consist of sherds of ceramics and roof tiles, and Chinese, Thai, and Vietnamese ceramics, came from disturbed layers. It now seems likely that some of the Yuan types of wares were made in the first decades of the Ming dynasty (Lam 2012).

RITUAL CERAMICS FROM THE KYŌNOUCHI

In AD 1936 Itō Chuta and Kamakura Yoshitarō made small excavations in two locations on the northwestern side of the Kyōnouchi (Itō and Kamakura 1937, 43–48; Kamei 1986b, 368). They found several hundred sherds of water droppers, jars, and other utensils of South Chinese Three-Color Ware, which comprised half of the entire sample of two test pits, suggesting a high concentration of this ware. In recent excavations in the area thought to be the location of the Shurimori Utaki, a total of thirty-nine sherds of the same ware were recovered. The concentration of this ware in the ritual area of the Kyōnouchi rather than in administrative buildings confirms its importance in state religion and religious networks in the fifteenth to sixteenth centuries AD (Kamei 1986b, 368). These wares have been found in other Okinawan sites such as Nakijin and the northern island of Akusekijima; Kamei proposes that since the center of distribution of these wares is Shuri in Okinawa, these objects had an elite ritual function in the Ryukyus and were exchanged in Ryukyu official voyages.

A product of kilns in the Quanzhou region of Fujian Province, the ware was decorated with unusual combinations of lead glazes, such as brown, yellow, and green, as well as other colors (see Appendix 1). Many of the objects are small water droppers, used for diluting ink in painting or calligraphy. The mold-made forms take eccentric shapes, such as those of birds, crayfish, small boxes, and plates. Small spouted pouring vessels are also found (Kamei 1986b, 355–374). From the context of these objects in Okinawan sites and sites on the main islands of Japan, Kamei dates them to the fifteenth and sixteenth centuries AD. Although the actual kiln sites producing water droppers are not known, covered boxes with similar glaze, termed Cochin glaze, from excavations of the Hangdian kiln, near Pinghe, Zhangzhou, Fujian, are dated to the later sixteenth and early seventeenth centuries AD (Chado Shiryōkan 1998).

THE IRI NO AZANA METALWORKING AREA OF THE KYŌNOUCHI

In the extreme western area of Shuri Castle, abundant evidence of metalworking dating to the fifteenth to sixteenth centuries AD has been found (Okinawa Kenritsu Maizō 2009b; Uehara 2009a, 40–49; 2009b). The finds include the remains of a furnace for extracting metal that was connected to a shallow trench, crucibles, tuyeres (bellows valves), large amounts of iron and bronze filings, molds for the production of temple bells, and other metal objects. The finding of the stem and branch of a multiple-coin mold, but not the actual coin mold, raises the possibility that three types of coins bearing characters of Okinawan reigns could have been manufactured here. The stem and branch are of the same type of mold as those found in mediaeval sites in the Japanese main islands. Uehara notes that copper slag with the same composition as the material in Ryukyu coins has been recovered. These types of coins, Taisei Tsūhō, Sekō Tsūhō, and Kinen Sehō, have been attributed to the Ryukyu Kingdom around AD 1450, on slim evidence, since they have cast characters that match with posthumous names of three Okinawan rulers, Shō Taikyū (AD 1454 to 1460), Shō Toku (AD 1461 to 1469), and Shō En (Kanemaro) (AD 1470 to 1476). A fourth type, Chūzan Tsūhō, is said to have been minted in the reign of King Satto (Miyagi 2009). Of the 3.5 million mediaeval coins found in all of Japan, Miyagi reports that only 210 specimens of these Ryukyu coins have been reported. They appear to have been made by reworking an old Chinese coin (Eiraku Tsūhō) of the Ming Yongle era (AD 1403–1424) to make a master or by making a new master from which a mold could be produced (Smits 2008; Uehara 2009a). Jones (2007, 85–94) concluded that they were produced somewhere in Kyushu as counterfeit. However, without the actual mold of the coin such casting cannot be proven. Like mediaeval Japan, Ryukyu did not mint its own official inscribed currency until after the seventeenth century AD, with a possible exception of the four types mentioned above. Until the recently reported excavations of the Iri no Azana, no evidence for the production of these four coin types had been recovered from the Ryukyus. If local production can be confirmed, it would appear that manufacture of an independent currency for external use was meant to confirm and legitimize Ryukyu as an independent state. Further research on this topic will add a new dimension to the understanding of the political economy of the kingdom and the use of the extreme western portion of the castle.

Other cast objects include a temple gong (*unpan*) and metal *sake* bottle. It is thought that the furnace technology for casting these objects came from mediaeval Japan, although there are some similarities with Song Chinese furnaces. From the finding of the outer portions of molds with raised nipples and horizontal bands, it can be concluded that large temple bells were cast in the Iri no Azana under royal control. Crucibles have been found in other parts of Shuri Castle including the Shurimori Utaki (Uehara 2009a, 49). A separate report (Uehara 2009b) describes in greater detail the evidence for metal casting in the Kyōnouchi. Some 1,670 metal fragments were found, including tools such as handles, ornaments such as decorative pieces, ritual items such as small jingle bells, mirrors, incense burners, a long-handled dipper, vases, and utilitarian items such as cauldrons. Many glass beads of various types were also noted. The small bells may have been used along with mirrors and incense burners, since they have been found together in the Shigemajō Enclosure of Nakijin and in the Tenkaiji Temple Site (Okinawa Kenritsu Maizō 2009a, 253). A total of twenty-two Chinese coins dating from AD 1078 to 1205, and AD 1368 to 1408 were also found.

Armor and related ornamental fittings were cast in the Iri no Azana area. These consist of pieces of perforated armor platelets, fragments of chain mail, and cast bronze fittings and ornaments for helmets, which have been found in several localities of Shuri Gusuku, including the distinctive pieces from the Royal Storehouse in the Kyōnouchi area.

The casting of iron and nonferrous metals shows separate patterns of development in Okinawa (Uehara 2009a, b). Ironworking began in the latter half of the twelfth century AD at the latest. Ironworking sites are not in *gusuku* but in village sites; 150 sites are recorded. Weapons, armor, agricultural tools, fishing tools, building tools, knives, and iron cauldrons were produced. Iron objects that could not be produced locally were imported in the same manner as foreign ceramics. The working of nonferrous metals began in the thirteenth or early fourteenth century AD. Workshops for nonferrous metals also worked iron, making religious objects as well as ornaments for armor. Many of the copper or bronze objects are ritual objects the casting of which was under the tight control of royal castles (Urasoe and Shuri). Nonferrous metal production can be divided into two periods, thirteenth to fourteenth centuries and fifteenth to sixteenth centuries AD. In the former period it was small in scale and limited to very large castles; in the latter, although there are no historical documents, it is clear that bells were cast. More specialized production began in the seventeenth century AD.

The casting of bells for the Shuri Gusuku and surrounding Buddhist temples involved the recruitment of specialists from the main islands of Japan and the marshaling of knowledge and resources. Some scholars have proposed that this kind of metallurgical enterprise could not have been accomplished on Okinawa, and the bells were imported. However, the quantity of bells cast around AD 1450 seems to be too great for them to have been imported, and the finding of fragments of bell molds confirms their local manufacture. Control by the king of the casting of temple bells, a symbolic hallmark of Buddhist temples, may indicate the king's control of the production of Buddhist spaces. The fact that the bells were produced in an old, sacred area of Shuri shows the power of local religion over Buddhist institutions in Okinawa. At the same time, it seems puzzling that an activity as dangerous as casting bells would have been undertaken inside the confines of a royal capital, with the danger of spreading fire and toxic fumes. Could some of the bells have been brought from the Ōsaka region, on the ships of Sakai merchants?

Along the steep southern face of Shuri Gusuku below the Kyōnouchi area, excavations in 2001 and 2002 yielded a number of old tombs, stone stairs, alignments, and pavements (Okinawa Kenritsu Maizō 2004). Three substantial old tombs were recovered. No. 2 resembles the cliffside mausoleum of Urasoe Yōdore in its side location and constructed access. Judging from its location, it must be an official tomb; however, rulers of fourteenth- and fifteenth-century Shuri were not buried here but were buried in separate locations within the Shuri region. There is also a cave that appears to connect to the Kyōnouchi. This feature is known as Kundagusuku and is thought to date to the fifteenth and sixteenth centuries, since a bronze mirror recovered from it dates to that time period.

The Area between the Kankai and Kyūkei Gates

The area between the Kankai and Kyūkei Gates is thought originally to have been outside the castle walls but to have become part of the castle after the expansion under Kings Shō Sei and Shō Shin in the latter half of the fifteenth century to the first half of the sixteenth century AD (Okinawa Ken 1988, 139). However, the excavators reported that no fifteenth to sixteenth century artifacts that would confirm this dating were found; instead fourteenth century AD trade ceramics were recovered, suggesting that the dating of this construction should be reconsidered. Evidence of bombing in World War II was found in several places.

A tank and conduits from the spring that gives rise to the Kansuigawa (River of Water of the Cold Season) were found. It flowed through a dragon-head-shaped pipe similar to the one in front of the Zuisen Gate, into a tank, and on to the two ponds on the north edge of Shuri Castle, the Enkan (Circular Mirror) and Ryūtan (Dragon Pond). Stone drains around the Zuisen Gate, on one side of the expanded enclosure, were found to be made of volcanic tuff, which is not found locally and must have been brought from Kagoshima (Okinawa Ken 1988, 145–147). Several stelae were erected in this area and in front of the Zuisen Gate. Some fragments of these have been found. Ceramics found in this area include blue and white, whiteware, Koryo celadon, and Yamato Type roof tiles and Meiji Period artifacts including Okinawan ceramics. Gaming pieces or counters, made by shaping broken ceramics into round disks, were found in this area as well as other areas of the castle site. Their diameter ranges from 3 cm to 7 cm, and they were made of roof tile fragments as well as old ceramic sherds. From their wide distribution they are thought to have been used by both adults and children. They were not found in association with any particular features.

Kobiki Mon Area

A small number of *hajiki* (red earthenware) shallow dishes that look like oil lamps from southern Kagoshima, thought to have a ritual function, were found in the Kobiki Mon area. Their temper may be of local origin, raising the possibility that they are locally made, following a prototype from Kagoshima. They look like a miniature frying pan with a short handle (Seto 2005).

Excavations outside the Walls, Southern Side

In preparation for an access road extending into the castle from the southeast side, an area of sloping terrain, in which mixed cultural material from the castle has accumulated in depressions, was excavated (Okinawa Kenritsu Maizō 2001b, 208). A wide variety of Chinese, Thai, Vietnamese, Okinawan, soft gray, and Japanese main islands ceramics were recovered. The most common group of Chinese wares was Longquan celadon dating from the fifteenth to seventeenth centuries AD. Other Chinese ceramics included white, blue and white, glazed red enamel, black (*tenmoku*) wares, as well as South Chinese Three-Color Wares from the Quanzhou area of southern Fujian. The most common forms of this ware were a greenware wine bottle (*shukai tsubo*), incense burners, and wide-mouth jars. Seventeenth-century Japanese wares included Nabeshima, Hasami, Bizen Type, Seto, Minō, Kyōyaki, Shigaraki, and Satsuma. These wares as well as later ceramics from south China and Okinawa show the continuing vitality of the castle after the Satsuma Invasion, a period that is beyond the scope of this book.

The Madama Road

In AD 1552 a military road called the Madama Road was built from the Shurei Mon to the Yarazamori Castle in Naha Port, a distance of 10 km. The road complements the earlier road system running from Shuri Castle downward through Asato to the north side of the Naha port. It was important for the defense of the port against Wakō pirates and for the conveyance of tributary goods to Shuri from the port. At the point of departure from Shuri Castle, on the southeast side of Shurei Mon, a monument indicating the military importance of the road and describing its route was erected. A socket for the base of this monument was cut into the limestone bedrock. Some small fragments of the original monument, severely damaged in the war, were found in excavations (Okinawa Kenritsu Maizō 2005b; 2007a, 69, 77; 2008a). The immediate area surrounding the monument was paved, and, in the disturbed soil, Chinese, Japanese, and Southeast Asian ceramics, mostly postdating the erection of the monument, have been found (Okinawa Kenritsu Maizō 2008a). A sherd of a fourteenth century AD Longquan mallet-shaped (*kinuta*) vase with fish/dragon handles was noted. This ware is considered to be very valuable by modern connoisseurs, and it is similar to specimens from the Sinan ship dated to around AD 1323 (Information Section 1984). Its relation to the actual monument is not clear (Okinawa Kenritsu Maizō 2008a, 24). The rarity of this type in Shuri suggests that it was deposited intentionally. On either side of the Madama Road were other important stelae.

Between the Shurei Mon and the Kankai Mon there was a long, wide paved roadway and a plaza (*hiroba*) that must have functioned as an assembly area (Okinawa Kenritsu Maizō 2007a).

In excavations outside the eastern end of the castle wall, archaeologists undertook exploration of the Kuninakagusuku Utaki, which is said to have had royal patronage (Okinawa Kenritsu Maizō 2005c). This area was damaged not only by the war, but also by postwar construction. An *utaki* exists in this area at present, and it was not possible to dig under it. Trenching uncovered walls and a pavement that may be part of a path leading from the castle. Chinese ceramics from the fourteenth to nineteenth centuries were recovered.

The Tenzan Ryō

Near the castle was the Tenzan Ryō, mausoleum of King Shō Hashi, who died in AD 1439. Thought to have been a completely enclosed cave with a walled front so

Figure 9.4. Carved stone platform for a coffin, Tenzan Ryō, Shuri, fifteenth century AD. Redrawn from a photo by R. Pearson.

that the sarcophagus was hidden from view, it was destroyed in World War II, but drawings remain. At present only the imposing base for a sarcophagus (Figure 9.4) remains in a secluded site in Shuri (Asato Shijun and Morimoto 1984). In an earlier stage of royal burial (thirteenth century AD), in the Yōdore mausoleum at Urasoe described in Chapter 7, the royal burials were displayed in open manmade caves; however, in the renovations of the Urasoe Yōdore Mausoleum in the early fifteenth century AD, the artificial caves were walled up and protected from view by anterior walled courtyards (Asato Susumu 2009). The Tenzan Ryō corresponds to the second stage of protection, thought to reflect the rise of the sun god cult in which the king took on added power, and royal burials were shielded from view. In the early fifteenth century AD both mausolea were furnished with monumental stone sarcophagi imported from Quanzhou, China. The carved base has decorative motifs including turtles and deer, which may be related to Daoist ritual (Tomiyama 1992, 144).

Adjacent Buddhist Temples

Although it seems that Buddhism never became widely accepted by the common people of the Ryukyus, it was important at the official level. China Teikan (2008) has proposed that the Ryukyu Kingdom had a deep relationship with Buddhism; however, since much of the discussion of Okinawan popular religion has been undertaken by students of popular religion and folklore who emphasized local religious practice, the strong Buddhist connection has not been appreciated. The earliest temple, the Gokurakuji at Urasoe, may well have been founded by Chinese priests (China 2008, 33–35). Thereafter strong connections were maintained with Japan. A substantial number of temples were built in the late fourteenth and early fifteenth centuries AD, some seventeen being built by the reign of Shō Shin (AD 1477 to 1526). From tabulations in the *Naha rekishi chizu* (Historical atlas of Naha City) (Naha Shi 1986, 208–212), some forty temples and branch temples are presumed to have been built before AD 1700, mostly in the Shuri and Kume areas. Shuri had at least three Japanese Zen Buddhist temples, all of the Rinzai sect, including the Tenkaiji, the Enkakuji, and the Tennoji, which were family temples for the Shō family (Tōma Shi'ichi 1986, 305). Buddhist sutras were given to the Tenkaiji by the Korean court in the mid-fifteenth century AD (China Teikan 2008, 86).

Partial excavation of the Tenkaiji (Naha Shi 2000; Yamamoto Masa'aki 2003), built by King Shō Taikyu from AD 1450 to 1456, yielded the remains of part of a village found beneath the temple features, confirming that there were settlements in the area at the time of the construction of Shuri Gusuku (Miyagi and Tamashiro 2005, 177). In the mid-fifteenth to early sixteenth centuries AD, there was a main structure with two lateral extending corridors, a separate rear building for the priests quarters (*hōjo*), and a main gate and side buildings. The powerful Ōuchi daimyo family of northern Kyushu maintained close connections with the Tenkaiji, using its power to advance their attempts to establish diplomatic and commercial relations with the Ming court. In AD 1530 the Ōuchi gained the rights to manage Japanese tribute missions to Ming, which gave them an advantageous commercial position in relation to China and other countries in East Asia. However, they later lost their power, and the Shimazu became preeminent (Itō Kōji 2008, 89).

Construction of the Enkakuji was completed in AD 1496, and it was rebuilt in 1588. Excavations from 1997 to 2002 located all of the main buildings. It contained a rectangular pond crossed by a bridge, a main gate at the top of a flight of stone stairs, a main Buddha hall, a side building for the royal memorial tablets, priests' living quarters, a garden, and a Lion Cave area (Okinawa Kenritsu Maizō 2002a).

The establishment of Buddhist temples in Shuri typified the complexity of relationships linking the Ryukyu Kingdom to the Japanese main islands. Who bore the costs of construction of these temples? What was the composition of artisan groups who designed and built these complexes? Sakihara (1987, 170) mentions that the Chinese envoy Chen Kan found in AD 1534 that the Enkakuji was closed to Okinawan local people. Perhaps it was open only on certain days of the year. It seems that the main function of these temples was to legitimize Chūzan sovereignty within East Asia. Although there is less archaeological evidence compared to the remains of Zen institutions, Shingon or Esoteric Buddhism also played an early, important role in the development of Ryukyu cosmology and state ideology, being particularly important in the reign of Shō Shin (AD 1477 to 1526) (Smits 2000).

Shrines to Confucius and to the Heavenly Consort (Tian Hou in Chinese) were constructed in the Chinese port community of Kume but not near Shuri Castle. These were linked to trade but not directly to royal authority.

Naha

The main road leading from the castle to the port of Naha passed by the Sogenji temple, which housed the royal memorial tablets, on its way to the port community of Tomari and to the Chōkotei, a raised causeway about 1 km long that led to the island of Naha (Uezato 2009). The port community of Naha was located on a low island (Ukishima) with brackish estuaries to the north and south. To the north was the port of Tomari, the port for boats traveling to offshore islands such as Kumejima. On the southern side of the island was the main port for foreign shipping. Excavations have located a small triangular island (Watarichi Shima) with a cluster of buildings (Watarichi Mura) immediately inside the port on the north side and separated from Ukishima by a slip that was the berth for ships from China (Okinawa Kenritsu Maizō 2007c; Seto 2010b, 48). This small island was across from Omono Gusuku, a walled warehouse sitting on another small island in the middle of the channel to the inner harbor. On Watarichi Shima there was a warehouse for storing sulfur and separate warehouses for tributary goods from Miyako and Yaeyama. A trench 6 m × 62 m, dug to below sea level, yielded a large deposit of fourteenth to fifteenth century AD Chinese celadon, early remains of iron and copper working, and some 4,970 roof tile fragments, 2 percent of which were of the Koryo or Yamato Types of the Gusuku Period, indicating the presence of some kind of official structure at an early date. The rest of the tiles dated to the Early and Late Ryukyu Kingdom Periods. A total of 464 coins were recovered, including one specimen of the mysterious Ryukyu coin Taisei Tsūhō, said to be minted in AD 1454 (Okinawa Kenritsu Maizō 2007c, 29). The two distinctive characters for Taisei stand out sharply compared to the two characters for Tsūhō. The authors of the report conclude that coinage in general may have circulated in villages near the port (ibid., 188).

In the sixteenth century AD the entrance to the harbor was protected by two long arms, with the fortifications of the Omono Gusuku and Mie Gusuku at their tips. Nearby Watarichi Mura was a stone-faced platform from which officials and others could greet ships entering and leaving the harbor. From that point the north arm included the Oki Gū Rinkaiji temple and two fortifications, Naka Mie Gusuku and Mie Gusuku. Tana (2010) notes that fresh water flowing from three convergent small rivers must have kept the inner harbor free from coral. An interior harbor protected from the open sea would have been easier to defend, resembling ports visited by Ryukyu traders such as Fuzhou, Quanzhou, and Ayuthaya.

At present, tidal flats separating the island of Naha from the mainland have long since been filled in, and there is a continuous urban zone extending from the edge of the East China Sea to Shuri and beyond. Prehistoric sites such as the Sachihijah Shellmound and Nazakibaru Site of the Gusuku Period show that the port area was an important region in prehistory. Along the Ajagawa River on the northern edge of present Naha, many sites yield *kamuiyaki,* whitewares of the Birosuku and Nakijin Types, and incised-flower-type celadon bowls, indicating that the antecedents of Naha port may lie in this inner area. Kin (2008a) notes that investigations around the present Naha port have not yielded materials from the twelfth to fourteenth centuries AD.

The "floating island" of Ukishima contained the Chinese residential area of Kumemura and the Japanese area of Wakasa Machi (Uezato 2008; 2009) (Figure 9.5). Kumemura was a residential walled compound for the Chinese, whereas the Japanese lived among the Okinawans. On the island were various religious and commercial buildings that served the trading community. The Oyamise and the Tenshikan were the center of trading activities with China. There were also religious institutions such as the Daoist Tensonbyo, Shintō shrines, mostly of the Kumano Gongen Sect (Uezato 2009, 74), and Buddhist temples. A number of Buddhist temples were located in the port and waterfront areas (Uezato 2009). A temple to Confucius was built in the seventeenth century (Itō Yoji 2010) near the cliffside temple of Naminoue, and places devoted to Mazu (Tian Hou), the Heavenly Protectress of sea travelers, were built in Naha, Naminoue, and Kumemura (Takahashi Yasuo 2010).

The Wakuta kilns at nearby Izumizaki appear to have operated in the latter half of the sixteenth century AD. They produced roof and paving tiles for Shuri Gusuku. The structure of the kilns is different from the general subterranean kilns of Kyushu and Honshu, being a single horizontal semisubterranean chamber. The ceiling portion has not been preserved, but from what remains it seems to be of a type not seen in south China but only seen in the area around Peking, indicating that Chinese craftsmen migrated directly to Okinawa from the Ming capital (Morimoto 2004). The tiles made there were stamped with the character *dai* sitting in a circle. Roof tiles and paving tiles for Shuri were made there. Ishii (2008, 90) noted that round eaves tiles from Locality R of Wakuta resemble Song dynasty examples found in Ningbo, Zhejiang.

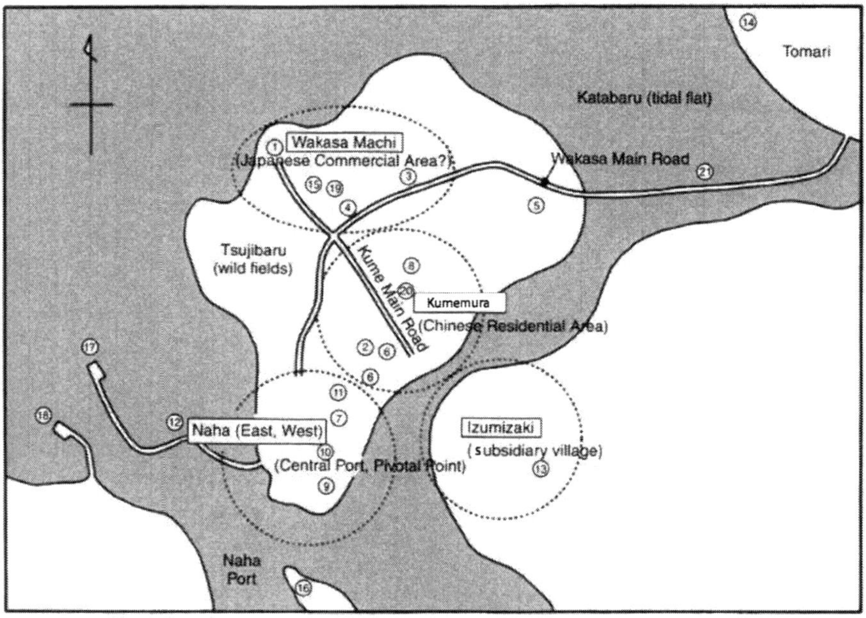

Figure 9.5. Map of Naha in the Early Ryukyu Kingdom Period. From Uezato 2009, 73. Courtesy of Uezato Takashi; reproduced by permission of Okinawa Kenritsu Maizō Bunkazai Sentā.

1. Naminoue Kumano Gongen, Gokokuji
2. Tenmangū, Chōrakuji
3. Wakasa Machi Ebisu Den
4. Wakasa Machi Jizōdō
5. Ukishima Jinja Chōjuji
6. Tenpi Gū
7. Oyamisei
8. Keirinji
9. Naha Jizōdō
10. Ebisu Den
11. Tenshikan
12. Oki Gū, Rinkaiji
13. Wakuta Jizōdō
14. Ameku Gū, Seigenji
15. Tenson Byō
16. Omono (Mimono) Gusuku
17. Mie Gusuku
18. Yarazamori Gusuku
19. Kōganji
20. Tōzenji
21. Chōkōtei

The Expansion of the Ryukyu Kingdom into the Sakishima Islands

Archaeology provides a picture of independent agricultural communities in contact with traders from the north, bringing *kamuiyaki* and soapstone cauldrons, and from Fujian, bringing whitewares and celadons, in the period from the twelfth to fifteenth centuries AD. Elite burials indicate that chiefs were buried in distinctive stone cist chambers. A period of prosperous trade is attested by abundant trade ceramics. Evidence of the historically documented conquest of Chūzan at the beginning of the sixteenth century AD is scarce, consisting of administrative sites and warehouses.

While Chūzan was consolidating its power in the Okinawa Islands in the fourteenth and early fifteenth centuries AD, it was beginning its expansion into Sakishima. The Miyako Islands first came under its control. Relations were first established with Miyako at the end of the fourteenth century AD. In the late fourteenth and early fifteenth centuries AD, Miyako chiefs offered allegiance to Chūzan and started sporadic raids on Yaeyama. They may have been somewhat unified by AD 1390, when the leader Nakasone Toyomioya pledged allegiance to King Satto. They must have relied on the Yaeyama Islands for timber, stone tool material, wild boar, and other products. Different factions within Yaeyama received support from Chūzan and Miyako, finally defeating the local lord Ōyake Akahachi in AD 1500. This brought an end to a period of independence and prosperity for the Yaeyama Islands from AD 1200 to 1500, when islanders were actively engaged in private trade with China (Ōhama 2005), indicated by abundant Chinese trade ceramics, particularly celadon. According to Ōhama, the Ryukyu Kingdom invaded in order to gain control of overseas trade and profit from it, and to control piracy. Local products traded to China include shells, marine products, medicinal plants, and woven hemp (Ōhama 2009). Ōhama proposes that Chinese cargoes were assembled in Fujian and offloaded by small boats in the Sakishima Islands. Profits from the private trade with Fujian may have attracted migrants from the Northern Ryukyus, since the total number of sites increased in the fourteenth and fifteenth centuries AD. The six ancestral shrines of Taketomi Island, thought to date from this period, are devoted to deities from Yakushima, Okinawajima, Kumejima, and Tokunoshima, indicating population movements from the north (Kin 2008b, 49).

For Miyako and Ishigaki, I describe below villages that flourished during the period of independence from the twelfth to fifteenth centuries AD and sites associated with local leaders around AD 1500, when the Ryukyu Kingdom consolidated its power over Sakishima.

In the archaeological sequence of Yaeyama, the period in which these developments occurred is known as the Nakamori Period, fourteenth to seventeenth centuries AD. Ethnohistorical sources describe a network of simple chiefdoms. Various historical sources shed light on Miyako and Yaeyama during this period, the most useful being the account of a group of shipwrecked Koreans who spent twenty-nine months on eight islands. The Koreans were repatriated to Korea via Hakata in AD 1479 (Iha 1974; Pearson 2003).

Archaeologically the most diagnostic artifacts are soft red earthenware wide-mouth jars with external lugs, found along with abundant Yuan, Ming, and rare Southeast Asian trade ceramics. Stone tools were replaced by iron tools, and the presence of slag and tuyeres indicates ironworking. Cultivation of rice, millet, and barley is thought to have begun around AD 1200. Burials and village sites give a picture of life in this period.

Miyako Sites

Village sites dating from the twelfth to sixteenth centuries have ground-level houses (not pit houses) with paved floors as well as elevated storage houses. Many are located inland behind protective coastal vegetation. They yield the usual suite of cereal grains and bones of fish, cow, horse, goat, pig, and chicken.

Imposing stone tombs in both the Miyako and Yaeyama Islands have been linked, by writers such as Inamura Kenpu (1972), Kaneko (1964), and Tōma Shi'ichi and Nakama (1983), to the chiefs of the sixteenth century AD who came under the control of the Ryukyu Kingdom. The most elaborate examples, termed *miyāka,* are found in the Miyako Islands, in Hisamatsu (Matsubara), Irabu, and Hirara. The Hisamatsu examples are large stone cists sitting in or on a terrace enclosed by a large row of upright stone slabs (Kaneko 1964, 122–133). Inamura (1962) provides an account of an excavation in AD 1897 of an unnamed tomb. It was covered with soil and tree roots at the time of its discovery. It yielded a stone adze, hammerstone, stone weight, and other stone artifacts. Reddish brown earthenware vessels, of wide- and narrow-mouthed types, and perforated handles were found on top of the coffin lid. Inamura estimated that it would take six individuals to move the coffin lid into place (1962).

The most imposing of the chiefly tombs on Miyakojima is the tomb of Nakasone Toyomioya, who led the Chūzan forces of the Ryukyu Kingdom against Akahachi of Yaeyama and later became the leader (*kashira*) of Miyakojima (Sunagawa 1983). Built against a steep natural slope, it has two interior chambers, front and back, which are still used by the descendants for burial. The facade consists of seventeen cut limestone steps, and there are seven standing stones on the roof. Nakasone Toyomioya must have lived at the Sumiya Site. His father-in-law, the chief Akagi Tatoya, is said to have been buried at the Hisagai Tomb Site in Hisamatsu. On Taramajima, there is the tomb of Untabaru Toyomioya, a retainer of Nakasone Toyomioya, and his wife, who assisted in the subjugation of Chief Akahachi of Yaeyama. His family genealogy states that he became chief of Taramajima and Yonagunijima (Nakama 1983; Ōyama 1983). Two house- or casket-shaped stone cists with sloping roof are surrounded by a limestone wall 70 cm high with an arched gate. None of the recently investigated large elite burials in the Miyako or Yaeyama Islands dating from the fourteenth to sixteenth centuries AD contain grave goods; later burials often had Japanese, Okinawan, or Fujianese ceramics placed on top or in front of them.

SUMIYA SITE, MIYAKOJIMA

The Sumiya Site has been the administrative center of the Miyako Islands since the fifteenth century AD, first as a chiefly settlement in the fifteenth and sixteenth centuries, when Nakasone Toyomioya lived there. It was the site of the local administrative center of the Ryukyu Kingdom from the early sixteenth to the late nineteenth century AD and became the administrative center for the amalgamated city of Miyakojima, established in 2006. A modern city hall stands to one side of the site, and part of the area that was excavated comprised the Ogden Building for the city Social Welfare Division under the US Civil Administration from AD 1945 to 1972. A large-scale excavation of about 3,300 sq m, consisting of excavation units of 4 m × 4 m, was undertaken for eleven months beginning in April 1990, following an earlier excavation in 1982 (Okinawa Ken Hirara Shi 1983; 1992; Hirara Shi 1999). Analysis of ceramics from the site shows a strong presence of trade ceramics in the fourteenth and fifteenth centuries AD (celadon bowls), fifteenth and sixteenth centuries (blue and white bowls), and seventeenth and eighteenth centuries (Fujian blue and white bowls and Satsuma ceramics) (Pearson 2003).

Judging from numerous finds of *kamuiyaki,* soapstone cauldrons, and Tong'an celadon, occupation of Sumiya and a number of other sites began in the twelfth century AD. Sumiya yielded many features such as building foundations and pavements, postholes, storage and refuse pits, and burials, the interpretation of which has been complicated by extensive disturbance since 1945. Features were divided into the following types: structures, stone arrangements, postholes, pits, hearths, and burials. The relationship of features to the stratigraphy is not clear in the report. Remains of at least twelve structures were recovered, but only two (Nos. 1 and 2) have been dated conclusively by associated artifacts to the fourteenth century AD.

Pit dwellings of an early type (fourteenth to first half of fifteenth century AD) were followed by buildings built on the ground surface (late fifteenth to early seventeenth century AD) and buildings supported by pillars or posts (Takemoto and Asato 1993, 227–229). Structures Nos. 3, 4, and 5 are possibly administrative buildings dating to the seventeenth century AD or later, and No. 9 is also a large building showing successive construction using posts set in holes. No. 4 with its postulated tile roof may be elite or administrative. My interpretation is that the large structures date to the period after AD 1500 when the Ryukyu Kingdom assumed control. Other architectural remains consist of rectilinear areas paved with rough coral chunks. Children's burials, dating to the sixteenth to seventeenth century AD, have been found under these pavements, the remains placed in rough rectangular box-like cists made of chunks of coral limestone. These cist burials are thought to date to the sixteenth and seventeenth centuries AD. Pavement dimensions are roughly 4 m × 4 m. They may be house floors, with child burials beneath the floor. Postholes are scattered through the site, one group in the northwest appearing to be the remains of an elevated granary. A total of 64 pits were dated by associated tradeware sherds; of these, 17 contained sherds dating to the sixteenth century AD or earlier, while 7 contained sherds dating to the sixteenth to nineteenth centuries AD. The others have sherds from both periods, the result of continuous occupation and extensive disturbance.

Analysis of shellfish remains from the site showed that in the lower layers, dating to the fifteenth century AD, shells from the outer ocean and from coral reef areas, such as *Strombus luhuanus* and *Turbo argyrostoma,* were abundant (Hirara Shi 1999, 297–298). Layer 2 and below are the layers of occupation that predate the arrival of officials from Shuri. Shells from this period include *Tridacna,* which could be used for shell weights, or *Turbo* shells, the *operculi* of which were used for tools. Shellfish meat was also eaten. Shells found in the upper layers, very large *Turbo, Trochus niloticus,* and *Tridacna,* were the remains of official feasts for Shuri representatives. The lower-layer shells are similar to those from other fortified sites, coming from inner bays, rocky areas, and tidal river mouths. There are no shells from mangrove areas or terrestrial shells.

Fragments of slag and iron cauldrons were found in the Ogden area, also in Layer 2. Some iron nails were found in the same areas as well as four knife blades, primarily from Layer 2, and two longer blades that could be swords. A few small fragments of iron slat armor were also noted. Metallurgical analysis of iron artifacts indicate that both iron sand and iron ore were used as raw material. Judging from relatively high percentages of manganese oxide, the raw material of some of the artifacts seems to have come from the region of northeast China and Korea. It is likely that the inhabitants used worn out iron cauldrons to make wrought iron and then worked the wrought iron into artifacts (Hirara Shi 1999, 267). There were also four bone spear points from Layers 2 and 3, thought to have been used for hunting or fishing. A review of trade ceramics at the Sumiya Site showed a small but significant number of very large and valuable trade ceramics, suggesting a center of political power (Pearson 2003).

At the beginning of the fifteenth century AD, the Yaeyama chief Ōyake Akahachi, whose residence was the site of Furusutobaru, was subjugated by the Ryukyu Kingdom. In AD 1522 and 1524 respectively, Ryukyu government warehouses for storing tribute were built in the Miyako and Yaeyama Islands. Local textiles were a major tribute item sent from Sakishima to Shuri. It is interesting to note that a relatively high number of spindle whorls, fashioned from earthenware sherds, have been found in Sakishima sites of the fifteenth and sixteenth centuries AD (Uehara 2007, 260).

Sites in Yaeyama

The sequence in Sakishima, with particular reference to Yaeyama, is summarized in Table 4.3. Sites dating to the twelfth to thirteenth centuries in the Shinzato Subperiod of the Suku Period include Birosuku, which yielded early whitewares, *kamuiyaki,* and fragments of steatite cauldrons.

The centrally located, low, well-drained island of Taketomijima was an important center for Yaeyama, from which villagers commuted to agricultural plots on the wet, malarial islands of Iriomotejima and Ishigakijima, which also supplied timber and raw materials for stone tools. A zone of ancient settlement on Taketomijima, Shinzatomura, has east and west components. Shinzatomura East is contemporaneous with Birosuku and has yielded very interesting Chinese white and brown wares (Okinawa Ken 1990b). The fourteenth to fifteenth century AD Shinzatomura West and Hanasuku Sites have both undergone extensive excavation. The Shinzatomura West Site, Taketomijima, shows the distinctive clustered settlement pattern of old villages in the Yaeyama Islands. Such a pattern is not known in the Okinawa Islands. House sites are surrounded by stone walls with only a single narrow entrance to each compound, which was connected to other compounds. There was no central arterial road, although there was a central plazalike space surrounded by compounds. Several house sites contained more than one dwelling. Seventeen house sites were recorded, and four were excavated. The same type of clustered domestic plan of up to nine multiple contemporary dwellings was recorded on Taketomijima in the 1880s AD (Kin 2004). The site of Hanasuku lies on a ridge about 15 m above sea level, with defensive walls as high as 4 m (Nakamori 1999; Okinawa Ken 1994, 29–32; Ono Masatoshi 1997a; Ono 1999, 37–54). Its dimensions are about 500 m east-west, 200 m north-south, containing about forty clustered dwelling sites in bilaterally symmetrical arrangement. In each half, Hanasuku and Kumara, there is a large house in a single enclosure 30 m × 30 m surrounded by seven or eight medium and small dwelling areas comprising a block 50 m × 60 m. Around these are more enclosed dwelling sites, and each of the major blocks has an ancestral shrine (*utaki*) attached to its corner.

There are also a number of beaches in Yaeyama with dense scatters of trade ceramics. George Kerr termed some of these "trading beaches" (Kamei 1982, 117). He proposed that these beaches may have been visited by itinerant trading vessels, that there may have been storehouses nearby, and that the sherds on the beach were from discarded broken wares. The beach at Komi and the offshore island of Pinishijima, Iriomotejima, are good examples. The ceramics found there have been dated by Kamei (1982, 131) to early Ming (fifteenth century AD). The beach at Shitadaru (Kudo), Ishigakijima, may have been the scene of a wreck, since no adjacent storehouse or settlement has been found (Ōhama 1994). Kamei (1982, 135) dated its ceramics to early and middle Ming, and Ōhama (2009) has dated it to AD 1450 to 1500. This is one of the largest beach finds of trade ceramics sherds in Japan, yielding a huge quantity of celadon, brownwares, and whitewares. Stylistic dating of ceramics from these sites indicates that the vigorous trade took place at the time of the heroic leaders, before the consolidation of power by Shuri.

Remains of a large, thriving village dating to the fifteenth and sixteenth centuries AD underlie the shoreline areas of Ishigaki City along the southern coast of Ishigakijima, designated the Ishigaki Shellmound, which was originally a sand dune backed by a low coral limestone terrace and facing a rich reef (Ishigaki Shi 2009). This settlement must have been occupied during the time of subjugation by the Ryukyu Kingdom. Analysis of human burials showed traits of mainland Japanese such as pronounced facial flatness, lending support to the proposal that there was immigration into the Ryukyus as far south as Sakishima at the beginning of the Gusuku Period (Ōhama 2005). In the same general area as the Ishigaki Shellmound, on a sand dune about 3.5 m above sea level, the sixteenth century AD warehouse site of the Chūzan Kingdom has been excavated. Although the site is disturbed, pillar bases for supporting a large building, in association with fifteenth century AD celadon sherds and later Okinawa ceramics, were recovered, along with stone and bone artifacts similar to those from Birosuku and Furusutobaru (Ishigaki Shi 1977). The zone of fifteenth to sixteenth century AD settlement on the old shoreline of Ishigaki City includes the adjacent sites of Hirakawa and Kidamori (Okinawa Kenritsu Maizō 2011). The Ishigaki sites do not show the same walled form as the sites on Taketomi Island. The walls may have been destroyed by the Meiwa Tsunami of AD 1771 or by subsequent construction.

FURUSUTOBARU SITE

As Sumiya was the residence of Chief Nakasone of Miyako, Furusutobaru was the center for Chief Ōyake Akahachi of Ishigakijima (Ishigaki Shi 1977; 1984; 1991; Tōma 1983; Takemoto and Asato 1993, 253–254; Okinawa Ken 1994, 8–13; Shimoji Kazuhiro 1999). The site is situated on a limestone ridge overlooking Miyara Bay (Figure 9.6). Fifteen walled enclosures have been identified. Enclo-

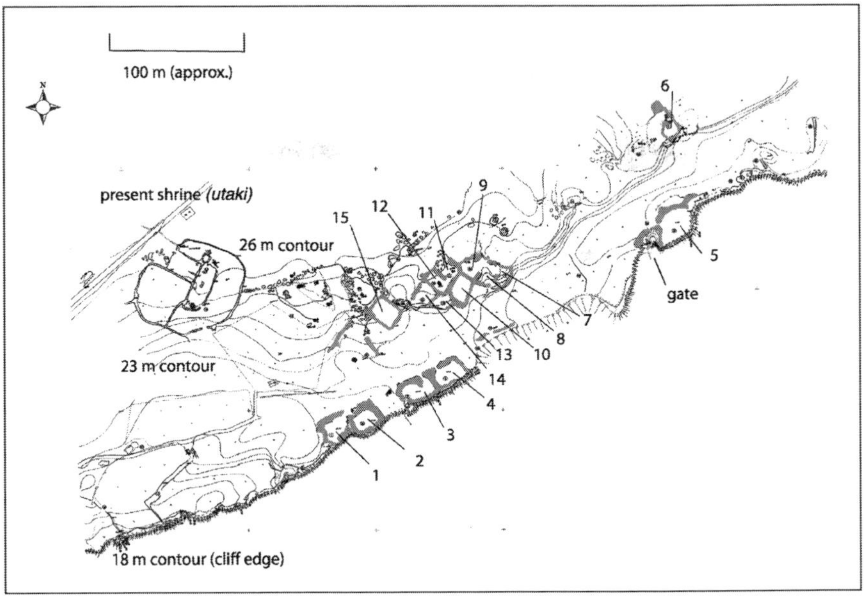

Figure 9.6. Plan of Furusutobaru Site, Ishigakijima, showing fifteen stone-walled enclosures. The contours show a settlement on a gentle slope bounded on the north by a steep cliff. Adapted from Ishigaki Shi 1977 with shading added to show the approximate form of walled enclosures. Courtesy of Ishigaki Shi Kyōiku Iinkai.

sures 1 through 4 are in a line with the seaward edge of the ridge, whereas the others form a row farther inland. Spaces of 190 m between Nos. 4 and 5, 40 m between Nos. 5 and 6, and 40 m between the two rows of enclosures may be the result of damage to the site. Enclosures 1 and 2 have been excavated. No. 2 had walls up to 2 m thick with a single entryway and central hearth. The large hearth was 130 cm × 85 cm and 10 cm deep. In No. 2 there were one hundred post molds, some containing stone wedges. No clear pattern could be interpreted. Enclosure 5 had an interior area of 600 sq m. The walls were 1.8 and 2.5 m thick. Enclosure No. 15 was a rectangle with length and width of 23 m and 20 m respectively. Burials with predominantly eighteenth century AD Tsuboya or Chinese ceramics are later than the main site occupation.

Conclusions

The Ryukyu Kingdom was a maritime entrepôt with economic and diplomatic links throughout East Asia. It arose between territorial powers in China, Korea, and Japan, with minimal defenses and limited agricultural productivity, but flourishing trade. The center of the kingdom was the Shuri capital, where the court formed a distinctive community with its own architecture and ritual program. Through its court and folk culture, language, and religion, it constituted a distinctive cultural community. It contained enclaves of traders and supported foreign and indigenous craftspersons with diverse specialties. Through military expansion to adjacent areas of the Ryukyus, the kingdom gained control over overseas trade and extracted tribute from them. The administrative capital of Shuri reflects the participation of the elite communities in various political and economic networks. The administrative capital and the commercial port were spatially separated and distinctive from the rural population. The kingdom expanded to include the island groups of Amami and Sakishima in addition to the offliers surrounding Okinawajima, and these were linked to Shuri through the extraction of tribute and a network of court officials. The kingdom was also linked to Japanese and Chinese religious and commercial communities.

Chapter 10

Discussion and Conclusions

The main subject of this book has been the archaeological exploration of human communities living on the island arc of the Ryukyus including their migrations, adaptations, interaction, and islandscapes. So far, human fossils are dated to roughly 30,000 to 14,000 BC, although we know virtually nothing about the cultural adaptations, population dynamics, or subsistence practices of the Pleistocene inhabitants of the islands. As island hunter-gatherers, Ryukyuans survived for thousands of years in small communities, dying out on more than one occasion. Repeated migration from surrounding areas was significant for their survival. It is possible that they experimented with growing root crops and pig raising before adopting cereal cultivation. Integration into regional trade networks led to the rise of a substantial trading kingdom with a distinctive civilization within East Asia that took advantage of a special geopolitical location.

Island Communities

More than ten distinctive human population inputs into the Ryukyu Islands from the north, south, and west during the total time period of human habitation can be traced archaeologically. These include Palaeolithic and Jōmon migrants, one or possibly two migrations from the south to the Sakishima Islands, and later groups of traders, officials, religious practitioners and refugees. Different stages of exploration, temporary settlement (sojourning), colonizing, and exchange have been postulated in the chapters above from distinctive configurations of archaeological data.

The earliest inhabitants lived on an archipelago of fewer, larger islands than at present, until the end of the Pleistocene, when rising sea levels created the island chain in its present form. Holocene migrants survived as hunter-gatherers for more than eight thousand years on gathered nuts, seeds and roots, wild boar/pigs, and diverse marine resources. Thus a variety of communities inhabited the Ryukyus from the Late Pleistocene (Table 10.1).

Initial groups formed small, impermanent settlements, which later increased, and engaged in shifting patterns of interaction. Early migration from Kyushu is well documented, but there are still questions about the possibility of continental contacts raised by puzzling information on early suids. Areas with similar pottery styles contracted as population grew, and interaction among various communities was critical to survival and cultural development. Interaction in the Early Shellmound Period or Jōmon Period seems to have focused on the exchange of marriage partners or perhaps raw materials such as lithics; at any rate, it contrasts with exchange in the Late Shellmound Period, which focused on ornaments and bracelets as prestige goods. Final stages of the production of these prestige goods were completed in Kyushu; however, they were at least partially transformed before they left the Ryukyus.

Substantial population inputs, along with the adoption of cultivation, which was brought into the islands by immigrants from the Japanese main islands around AD 800, led to rapid increases in social complexity and the emergence of an island kingdom. Although it might be expected that modern Ryukyuans would show physical resemblances to ancient Japanese populations such as the Ainu and Jōmon remaining in isolated areas such as these remote islands, in fact they resemble modern Japanese, as a result of a major influx in the early mediaeval period (Asato Susumu and Doi 1999).

In the Gusuku and Early Ryukyu Kingdom Period interaction diversified and intensified. As an island state the Ryukyu Kingdom was linked to surrounding areas and depended on its ability to transship goods from external areas to achieve prosperity. This situation contrasts with continental territorial states, in which agrarian production, landownership, and raw materials such as metals were the basis of cultural development and political power. Archaeological research has documented the establishment of a Ryukyuan variant of East Asian high culture.

Distinctive Archaeological Patterns in the Ryukyus

The extremely rich archaeological record of the Ryukyus, built up in the last fifty years, has a number of aspects of interest to archaeologists in other parts of the world.

1. The substantial collection of Pleistocene *Homo sapiens* from Okinawa and the southern Ryukyus is unique in Japan and very unusual in all of East

TABLE 10.1 Communities of the Ryukyus Islands Discovered through Archaeological Research

Community	*Time Period*	*Archaeological Evidence*
Central, Southern Ryukyus: Palaeolithic hunter-gatherers. (Chapter 3)	ca. 32,000 to 18,000 BP	*Homo sapiens* skeletal remains.
Central Ryukyus: Explorers. (Chapter 4)	5000 to 6000 cal BC	Scattered surface finds of artifacts. Kakoinohara-type adzes.
Central Ryukyus: Sojourners. Short-term occupation layers. (Chapter 4)	4000 to 6000 cal BC	Plain Type, Sobata Type, Todoroki Type pottery, Sōgō Guraundo pottery of Kikaigashima. Early suid bones (Noguni Layer IV). Relation to Kikai eruption, 5330 BC?
Central Ryukyus: Colonizers. Longer occupations, conservation of homeland artifacts types, and local adaptation. (Chapter 4)	4000 to 2000 cal BC	Jōkonmon, Omonawa pottery types. Interaction between Amami and Okinawa Islands.
Central Ryukyus: Communities with strong local identity, limited exchange with Kyushu. (Chapter 4)	2000 to 500 BC	Development of Iha, Ogidō, Ōyama pottery types. Exchange of obsidian, Ichiki pottery, bone ornaments.
Southern Ryukyus: Sakishima hunter-gatherers. (Chapter 4)	2500 to1300 BC	Shimotabaru Period, origins unclear. Remains of distinctive pottery, adzes.
Central Ryukyus: Shell traders, island hunter/gatherers, reef fishing communities. (Chapter 6)	500 BC to AD 800	Later Shellmound pottery types, Kaneku pottery. Shell trade systems.
Southern Ryukyus: Sakishima hunter-gatherers, Second group. (Chapter 4)	900 BC to AD 1100	Absence of pottery. Distinctive shell adzes.
Government outpost of Kikaigashima. (Chapter 7)	AD 800 to 1200	Gusuku Site Group, Kikaigashima, administrative and storage buildings, unique early trade ceramics. Distinctive burial practices, substantial ironworking.

TABLE 10.1 *(continued)*

Community	*Time Period*	*Archaeological Evidence*
Kamuiyaki potters, Tokunoshima. (Chapter 7)	AD 1050 to 1350	Kiln sites, no closely related living sites described yet. Extensive distribution of *kamuiyaki* throughout the Ryukyus. Stoneware production techniques show influence from neighboring areas.
Trader communities. (Chapter 7)	AD 1050 to 1600	Hakata traders, Chinese traders, local islanders. Chinese and Japanese communities in Naha.
Agricultural communities. (Chapter 7)	AD 1050 to 1600	Extensive excavation and survey of village and agricultural sites.
Early Gusuku unwalled elite communities. (Chapter 7)	AD 1050 to 1250	Large houses and associated storehouses, some sites with wooden fortifications. Some of these sites lie under later fortified elite sites.
Port communities. (Chapters 8, 9)	AD 1050 to 1600	Beach scatters (place-names).
Late Gusuku Period elite communities. (Chapter 7)	AD 1250 to ca. 1500	Walled *gusuku* structures, separate residential areas for rulers and retainers. Large tradeware vessels. Chiefly administrative centers of Miyakojima, Ishigakijima, Amami Islands.
Royal capitals. (Chapters 7, 9)	AD 1250 to 1600	Urasoe, Shuri. Greater total area, complexity of internal facilities than other *gusuku*. Specialized metal production, complex religious and ritual structures. East Asian luxury trade ceramics.
Religious subcommunities. (Chapter 9)	AD 13th century to 1600	Buddhist sites in Naha, Shuri. Shintō, Daoist, Confucian sites in Naha. Zen memorial temples for Shō royal family.

Note: The 1600 cutoff date is simply the upper limit of the time period covered in this book. Many communities persisted until much later.

Asia. The absence of artifacts and living sites is particularly puzzling. At the same time, the finding of flake tools of similar form to those in the Japanese main islands is tantalizing, but so far the small sites have yielded little information.

2. The proximity of the Northern and Central Ryukyus to a Jōmon "hot spot" (Pearson 2006) is notable. In the Incipient and Earliest Jōmon Period of Southern Kyushu, sites such as Uenohara confirm the existence of sedentary base camps and storage pits, with an adaptation to broadleaf deciduous forests during a cool climatic interval. Finds from Ufuniku Cave indicate that people lived on Okinawa at the time of the Earliest Jōmon, and the implications of this voyaging are still being investigated.

3. An interesting aspect of Ryukyu prehistory is the puzzle regarding origins of pottery left by early voyagers. Usually rapid movements of human groups create broad areas of identical or similar styles ("horizon styles"), such as the Lapita pottery style of Oceania. However, in the Ryukyus, archaeologists have not been able to find acceptable ancestors of the Plain and Nail-Impressed Types of the Northern and Central Ryukyus and the Shimotabaru Type of the Southern Ryukyus, despite intensive investigation. Did the circumstances of voyaging create a lack of continuity? Whereas planned, purposeful voyaging creates artifactual continuity, accidental drift voyaging may lead to disparities among artifact assemblages if the knowledge or appropriate circumstances for the reproduction of the technologies is absent. Historical records of Koreans who were blown off course refer to very small groups who were ill prepared to perpetuate their native ways of living. The absence of dog remains in sites of the Shimotabaru Period may confirm this pattern.

4. A period of island settlement by hunter-gatherers spanning some eight thousand years in the Northern and Central Ryukyus seems to show that, without cultivation, groups can adapt to subtropical island conditions. However, the gap between the Shimotabaru Period and the Non-Ceramic Period in the Southern Ryukyus and the gaps between radiocarbon dates in the Okinawan sequence suggest that, in fact, populations could not survive indefinitely. The survival of hunter-gatherers on small islands has been thought to depend on the exploitation of large marine mammals. However, Ryukyu islanders lived on reef fish and shellfish, edible chestnuts, suids, and seeds, nuts, and roots found in the subtropical forests. Their population does not show the rapid increase displayed by some island agriculturalists. Judging from the presence of what appear to be ranked settlements in the early first millennium AD (Shinzato Takayuki 2003) and the building of multigenera-

tional burial facilities at sites such as Tomachin, Tokunoshima (Shinzato Takayuki 2011), social ranking appeared before the adoption of cultivation. The main cause of the adoption of cultivation is the arrival of agricultural migrants from the Japanese main islands. The actual process of adoption may have involved the preference for cereals as high-status food, to emulate elite food customs of elites in the rice-growing areas of the Japanese main islands. Migration to the Ryukyus was an aspect of a general increase in human movement and interaction that took place in the Mediaeval Period of the Japanese main islands.

5. For some 1,500 years or more, islanders of the Amami and Okinawa Islands exchanged various types of tropical marine shells with the people of the Japanese main islands, Korea, and the coast of China. Social hierarchy emerged in the Ryukyus at the time of this exchange. In Kyushu and Korea, shell ornaments were used as burial offerings and other sumptuary offerings such as saddle decorations. Later they were used for decoration and for trumpets in Buddhist temples. They were essential for the reproduction of elite social relations in a broad area of East Asia. The trade networks extended to several regions of the East China Sea, providing long-range connectivity.

6. The establishment of a government outpost on the island of Kikaigashima from the eighth to twelfth centuries AD makes it clear that Japanese interests were active in the East China Sea at an early period, despite the lack of any substantial written documentation. The Japanese central authorities of the Nara Period (AD 710 to 794) and the Heian (AD 794 to 1185) Period were aware of the East China Sea region from the *kentōshi* tribute voyages to Tang China in the seventh to eighth centuries AD. This outpost must have played a role in the migration of Japanese islanders to the Okinawa Islands and the adoption of cultivation. The presence of Tang dynasty Kaigen Tsūhō coins in the Ryukyus and the growth of trade in *Turbo* shells indicates that Chinese traders were sailing to the Ryukyus. The outpost on Kikaigashima may have served to regulate trade in sulfur, native dye materials (the wood of the *Bischoffia* tree), and other products, and to assert power over the Northern Ryukyus and Amami. The relationship of this community to later polities on Okinawa is not clear but holds considerable anthropological interest in regard to secondary state formation. We need to explore the full range of economic activities that occurred on the sites of the Gusuku Site Group and their political relationship to Yamato and to the Amami and Okinawa Islands.

7. An important contribution of archaeological research to studies of East Asian mediaeval trade is the rich evidence of three centuries of private trade before the establishment of official tributary trade between the Chūzan

kingdom and the Ming dynasty in AD 1372. This evidence consists not only of Chinese ceramics, but also of steatite cauldrons from quarries in southern Kyushu and gray stoneware (*kamuiyaki*) produced on Tokunoshima.

8. Osteological evidence of similarities between Okinawans and mediaeval Japanese suggests that substantial populations moved to the Ryukyus from the north around AD 800 to 1000, creating links between the Ryukyus and the Japanese main islands in the mediaeval period that are not yet fully understood. Further archaeological research is needed to clarify these relations. Can we detect the presence of Japanese main islanders in the Ryukyus from archaeological patterning?
9. The simultaneous establishment of preferential tributary relations with the Ming dynasty and the imposition of the Ming Maritime Trade Ban (AD 1368 to 1567) created particular opportunities grasped by the Ryukyu Kingdom to funnel goods from East and Southeast Asia through Ryukyu to China. While polities in Southeast Asia may have benefited from monopolies created by tributary status, the Ryukyu Kingdom enjoyed the most liberal conditions for transshipping trade. The wide distribution of unusual types of East and Southeast Asian ceramics on Ryukyu sites is an indication of the large volume of trade and the wide social base of consumers.
10. Archaeological investigations of the royal capitals of Urasoe and Shuri reveal the development of a distinctive variant of East Asian culture. In the burials of Urasoe Yōdore, wooden coffins, stone coffins, and tiled structures are configured differently from those in other parts of East Asia. Chinese ceramics of very high quality are mixed with common wares in the Kyōnouchi deposit of Shuri Gusuku, while Yuan blue and white of a type that is rare in China but found in Southwest Asia is found in the Nikaiden deposit of Shuri. Techniques of palace construction in which stone platforms (*kidan*) and tiled roofs are mixed with other styles such as dug post construction and bark-covered roofs show the formation of a distinctive culture that nevertheless resonates with the high cultures of surrounding areas.
11. The unusual archaeological record of Sakishima, in which the source of the initial population is obscure and there is a lapse in the occupation of the islands, is remarkable. Reasons for the disappearance of pottery are not clear.

Conditions Affecting Early Communities

In Chapter 1, I proposed that the relationship between human communities and their physical and cultural environment was one of dynamic interaction. Several aspects of this interaction should be highlighted.

1. The "puzzling pigs" remain a major question, despite a lack of recent publications on this topic. I expect that throughout the Shellmound Period, the suids of the Northern and Central Ryukyus were wild, feral, and domesticated, in varying proportions, and that, from earliest times, suids may have been brought to the islands from outside. Disparate archaeological studies of suids need to be articulated, reevaluated, and rationalized with other kinds of archaeological data.

2. What were the effects of reef development in the Holocene? Tōizumi has indicated that the assemblage of bony reef fish shows little change throughout the Shellmound Period. Studies of shellfish show a high dependency on one or two species of small shellfish in the Early Shellmound Period, with an increase in the diversity of shellfish species in the Late Shellmound Period. However, the most frequently exploited species are all small with limited meat yields, probably being used for soups or condiments. Reef fish, shellfish, and suids, sources of protein, were dispersed but constant and reliable, allowing small populations at a low level of complexity to live in the islands. Current methods of analysis are limited to the study of variability within each group of remains, such as shellfish, suids, or bony fish. They do not illuminate the relative importance of these different kinds of food in the diet.

3. Climatic change has been summarized in Chapter 2. Although climatic change may involve changes in mean temperature, in the subtropical Ryukyus, changes in the intensity of the summer monsoon winds from the south and the strong continental winter winds from the north may be of greater significance. At least four Holocene climatic episodes are of interest to archaeologists. Early occupants of the Northern and Central Ryukyus in the mid-Holocene appear to have enjoyed a moderate climate, but there is clear evidence of a cold climate and strong winter winds around 2000 BC. These winds created extensive dunes in the Ryukyus and were an important factor in the shift of settlement to higher areas in the Middle Shellmound Period. Mild climate and a strong summer monsoon occurred in China at the time of the Song dynasty (AD 960 to 1279). Prosperous agriculture provided optimum conditions for prosperity and commercial development, which in turn led to Song economic expansion to Japan and the Ryukyus. Cultivation began in the Okinawa Islands sometime around AD 800. It is probable that the strong summer monsoon was a factor in the rapid growth of agricultural systems in the Early Gusuku Period, and future research may show cultivation in Okinawa to have some common features with Chinese systems. The Little Ice Age, a period of cold climate, had a profound effect on the economy of the Yuan and Ming dynasties. Increased smuggling along

the China coast at this time may have been stimulated by crop failures and the economic downturn of the fifteenth century AD.

4. Specific aspects of the politics and economy of East Asia allowed the Chūzan and subsequent Ryukyu Kingdom to flourish as an independent state in the fourteenth and fifteenth centuries AD. Chinese trade, both private and tributary, did not involve military or territorial expansion. The Ryukyu Kingdom took steps to fortify itself against the Wakō pirates in the sixteenth century AD (Uezato 2009), but there was no territorial threat. Political instability in the thirteenth to sixteenth centuries AD in Japan made it impossible for the central government to consider expansion into the Ryukyus, allowing the Ryukyus to be independent until the Satsuma Invasion of AD 1609. Japanese interests were managed primarily through Zen Buddhist temples, which were centers for diplomacy and negotiation. These cultural specifics enabled Okinawans to maintain a prosperous and independent polity until the early seventeenth century AD.

Maritime Landscapes and Islandscapes of the Ryukyus

In the prehistory and early history of the Ryukyus, unique cultural landscapes were created. We can place human communities in these landscapes to gain a picture of life in the Ryukyus. In a sense these can be seen as regional "views," like an artist's impression of an area, except that they are based on a temporal as well as a spatial sequence. The following could be termed "eleven views of the Ryukyus."

1. Late Pleistocene islandscape, 20,000 BP (Chapter 3). As mentioned in Chapter 3, the earliest populations of the Ryukyus lived on relatively large islands covered by thick broadleaf evergreen forest and populated by deer, wild boar, and other large ungulates. A retreating shoreline and strong cold continental winter winds must have created an exposed western beach line. Simple boats would have been used to cross from island to island from the south as far as Okinawajima. The Pleistocene remains on Amami Ōshima diverge from those of the Okinawa and Sakishima Islands. Human settlements, for which we have no evidence at present, may have consisted of base camps in rock shelters and seasonal shoreline camps, which have been erased by rising sea levels in the Holocene.
2. Volcanic islandscape of the Northern Ryukyus, 7200 BP (Chapter 4). Following the explosion of the Kikai Caldera, a devastated landscape covered in pyroclastic ash extended from southern Kagoshima to the Tokara Islands, forcing small groups of survivors to move southward. The stark islandscape

would have made a huge impact on the life and psychology of the islanders, affecting their movements and adaptations.

3. Mid-Holocene Warm Period islandscape, 6000 BP (Chapter 4). Small groups living in the Ginowan area of the western coast of Okinawa during a warm episode of the Holocene provide an example of Ryukyu hunter-gatherer communities. In a sheltered shoreline area near a small stream, people processed edible chestnuts and took fish and shellfish from the open sea and small reef. They probably lived in seasonal camps of pit houses, located behind protective strandline vegetation at the foot of marine terraces. Their world included surrounding islands and islands to the north, where they maintained contact with kin groups. Islands on the horizon are definitely part of their islandscape.
4. Holocene Cool Period islandscape, 3500 BP (Chapter 4). A distinctive islandscape was created by very strong winter winds and wave action, sand dune formation, and large settlements on high terraces. People inhabiting large inland base settlements must have moved to coastal fishing camps during the summer. It is not clear whether interaction with Late and Latest Jōmon communities in Kyushu, indicated by exotic pottery, was direct or indirect.
5. Coastal point of exchange in the shell exchange network, AD 100 (Chapter 6). Sites such as Gushibaru Shellmound, Iejima, were fishing villages supplied by smaller communities with shell materials for exchange. They were seasonally visited by trading groups from the north; in the trading season, at the end of the northern monsoon, oceangoing canoes would be beached near the community. Shells were partially processed before transport. Nets with shell weights were used, and lines of stones for weirs and fish traps would be visible in the extensive adjacent lagoon.
6. Yamato outpost, Gusuku Site Group, Kikaigashima, eighth to eleventh centuries AD (Chapter 7). On the limestone terraces of Kikaigashima, looking across 25 km of ocean to the mountains of Amami Ōshima, were a series of settlements with large buildings elevated on posts, some of which were storehouses. They presented a unique landscape in the Ryukyus defined by the Yamato style of buildings, the size of the settlements, and the Japanese main islanders who inhabited them. In adjacent areas agricultural and iron-working sites were scenes of activity. This community must have been in regular contact with centers in Kyushu such as Mottaimatsu and Dazaifu.
7. Urasoe, islandscape of kingship, late thirteenth century AD (Chapter 7). The Urasoe Gusuku Site, described in Chapter 7, commands views of both the Pacific Ocean, including the sacred island of Kudakajima, and the East

China Sea and the port of Machiminato, the source of part of its wealth. The pond, ramparts, palisades, Buddhist temple, and cliffside mausoleum created a landscape of power. Around the site there were numerous dry fields on the ridges and paddies in narrow valleys. Elite residential sites lay outside the ramparts, along with areas for craft production such as metalworking. The structure of Okinawan *gusuku,* with walled sections for the ruler's residence, ritual area, plaza, and storage and activity areas, was achieved in Urasoe. Moreover, the ruler's residence had a tiled roof, which set Urasoe apart from all other *gusuku* except Shuri and Katsuren.

8. Shuri, islandscape of a maritime state, fifteenth and sixteenth centuries AD (Chapter 9). Shuri retained many of the aspects of the Urasoe capital, with additional attributes that confirmed its expanded power, incorporating surrounding islands, and its international role. These included multiple Zen Buddhist temples, a detached mausoleum with distinctive Ryukyu architecture, and substantial neighboring noble residences and production areas. The royal crest of the Shō family, special styles of dress, motifs on monuments, and architectural styles all served to identify the Ryukyu Kingdom as a distinctive islandscape. Groups of inscribed stone monuments at several points listed rulers' achievements and marked the state road to the port of Naha. The island of Kudakajima was visible to the east from the ramparts, and, to the west, the Kerama archipelago and islands beyond showed that the scope of Shuri's power extended to the horizon. The east to west orientation of both palace and plaza followed state ideology of the ruler as the child of the sun.
9. Naha Port islandscape, fifteenth to sixteenth centuries AD (Chapter 9). This landscape combined the port facilities, including storehouses for interisland tribute and official international trade, with a unique array of residences for groups from China and Japan, including Chinese traders' residences, as well as Chinese religious sites and a prominent Shintō shrine. Also included was a dockside promenade for ceremonial greetings for foreign delegations. The high stone walls and distinctive architecture of the royal capital were visible from the port. The combination of Okinawan, Japanese, and Chinese administrative and religious facilities and the variety of cargo, ships, and people are evidence of connectivities to ports and cities throughout East and Southeast Asia.
10. Sakishima prehistoric islandscape, Haterumajima 3500 BP (Chapter 4, 5). Inhabitants of the Shimotabaru Site of Haterumajima, the southernmost island of the Ryukyu Chain, depended heavily on the large, heavily forested island of Iriomotejima, which can be seen on the horizon to the north. They

hunted there and gathered all kinds of raw materials. The site lies on the north shore in front of a small reef, protected by shoreline vegetation.

11. Sakishima fortified house site islandscape, fifteenth century AD (Chapter 9). At the time of vigorous private trade in the fifteenth century and the subjugation by Shuri at the beginning of the sixteenth century, Yaeyama islanders constructed irregular-shaped groups of walled enclosures for protection from outsiders and typhoons. Villagers commuted to field sites on the large islands of Iriomotejima and Ishigakijima, preferring to live on the low surrounding islands where malaria and other diseases were not as common. Chinese and Ryukyu trading ships anchored in nearby bays to exchange iron and ceramics for local products.

Further Questions and Broader Implications

What are the major implications of the findings of countless archaeologists who have worked so hard to understand and protect sites in the Ryukyus? And what are the outstanding questions?

Hunters and gatherers can survive at low population levels for very long periods of time on islands. Preliminary studies of the Andaman islanders show that it is possible to survive on subtropical or tropical islands as hunter-gatherers (Foster and Matsumura 2005). However, it is not possible to achieve large populations or social complexity. Key to their survival in the Ryukyus were reef resources and storable nuts. The conditions under which hunter-gatherers survive and multiply on small islands such as the Ryukyus (rather than high latitude islands where sea mammals are hunted) are still unclear. The reasons for the uncertainty are the unresolved questions about tending of suids and the possibility of early noncereal cultivation. However, both of these subsistence practices would have been supplementary rather than main sources of food. If future research does not support these possibilities, we are left with the unusual case of the survival of hunter-gatherers at low populations levels for as long as eight millennia in the Okinawa and Amami Islands. In Chapter 5, I introduced evidence that the population of Sakishima was discontinuous and the possibility that, in the case of Okinawajima, there may have been periods when the population died out.

After the introduction of cultivation around AD 800, agriculture was hampered by thin soils and destructive typhoons. Overseas trade offset the low yields of cultivation, permitting the development of the distinctive elite culture of the Ryukyu Kingdom. Secondary state formation was dependent on substantial immigration as well as social and economic conditions in China and Japan favoring trade rather than political subjugation.

Although the scope of this book has not included historical linguistics, the arrival of speakers of the Ryukyuan language into the islands appears to be related to the movement of people at the time of the introduction of cultivation, in the latter half of the first millennium AD. Hudson (1999, 91; 2002) has discussed several explanations for the entry of the Japan language into the Japanese islands, favoring a subsistence demography model "where large numbers of people speaking the new language move into the territory." This kind of model is also favored by Takamiya Hiroto (2004, 125) to explain the spread of intensive cereal cultivation to the Ryukyus by speakers of the ancestral Ryukyu dialect. I expect that the actual process of adoption involved emulation of migrants by islanders as well as population replacement. Although the push of people into the Ryukyus explains part of the process of adoption, it does not address the nature of social relations between resident populations and new arrivals. The subsistence demography model is not universally accepted for explaining the spread of other language families, such as Austronesian (Anderson 2005), in which changes in knowledge of navigation and wind patterns are considered to be important. The adaptive advantages that allowed human groups to colonize the islands may have been new knowledge and skills such as mastery of navigation and understanding of wind patterns.

The actual dating of the separation of the Japanese and Ryukyuan languages is difficult to determine. The date of 1,500 to 2000 years ago cited by Hudson based on work by Hokama (1986) fits roughly with the current notions of the dates of adoption of cultivation. A recent analysis of Japonic languages (59 lists of 210 basic items of basic vocabulary) by Lee and Hasegawa (2011) sets the divergence of the Japanese and Ryukyuan languages at sometime between 2182 and 2398 years BP, and the split between the North-Central Ryukyuan and Sakishima dialects at about 1100 years ago. The proposed time of the first split does not correlate with the archaeological evidence of a population input (Chapter 4). At the time of the second split, there was some movement from the North-Central Ryukyus to Sakishima of small groups who may have introduced cultivation to a population of Sakishima islanders thought to have arrived about one thousand years before (Chapter 4). There is a great deal of uncertainty regarding the dates of divergence and the relationship of historical linguistics to archaeological data. The nature of the postulated agricultural migrant groups and historical reasons for their movement is just one of the areas requiring further investigation.

Many unresolved questions are of great relevance to understanding the archaeology of the Ryukyus and island archaeology in general. The process by which an elongated peninsula attached to the East Asian mainland and became a chain of islands needs elucidation. At present we have conflicting theories regarding land bridges. How did the rich population of deer species become extinct? We need clearer geomorphological evidence of the conditions under which the earliest sites in the Ryukyus, both Pleistocene and Holocene, were deposited.

Can we employ palaeoenvironmental analysis to detect human activities in the mid-Holocene, after the arrival of Jōmon populations? How can we formulate and test hypotheses of early noncereal cultivation? How can we learn more about the first populations who colonized the Sakishima Islands? Throughout the Ryukyus, palaeoenvironmental data regarding human impacts on the environment might show whether forest clearance was practiced or whether there is palynological evidence for population changes for the periods during which there are no carbon-dated site remains. New ways of assessing the continuity of human populations and their fluctuations are needed to increase the precision of studies of human adaptation.

From the perspective of historical ecology, human decision making becomes an independent variable in the analysis of human-environmental dynamics. Island hunter-gatherers of the Ryukyus were faced with several choices for subsistence strategies, including hunting of wild boar, raising of domesticated pigs, cultivation of cereal or root crops, harvesting of edible chestnuts, and selective fishing of fish and shellfish living in the evolving coral reefs. These require further investigation.

The "Ryukyu pig puzzle" (Chapter 5) requires systematic investigation using consistent comparison of DNA sampling of archaeological and contemporary specimens with those from surrounding areas, as well as further discussion of the dietary analyses of Minagawa et al. (2005). Samples from Sakishima and Amami need to be included. Optimally, several types of analyses should be attempted and the results cross-checked. Similar studies on DNA patterning in dog remains from the Ryukyus and surrounding areas will no doubt show similar patterns of movements and exchange.

While the Gusuku Site Group of Kikaigashima ranks as a major find in recent Japanese archaeology, many aspects of the social and economic roles of the sites remain unclear from the preliminary reports. Intensive searching for patterning among the artifacts and features in the lists provided in the published reports may help to clarify the context and function of the large buildings and the occupations of the site inhabitants. The Gusuku Site Group is important for understanding the role of Yamato in the emergence of the secondary state of the Chūzan Kingdom. It appears that secondary state development is often stimulated by the presence of outposts of adjacent states. The role of these outposts in stimulating trade and the emergence of elites should be assessed. The extensive use of *Turbo* shell for decoration in some of the most spectacular monuments of

Heian Period art, such as the Konjikidō, Hiraizumi, and the Byōdōin, Uji, needs to be appreciated and investigated, and the significance of the trade of sulfur for medicine and warfare deserves more attention.

Small states such as the Ryukyu Kingdom often make use of religious and trade networks to obtain technical and cultural expertise in the building of their own distinctive culture. The analysis of Japanese and Chinese trading communities in Naha will shed light on their role in the functioning of the Ryukyu Kingdom.

Although the Ryukyus appear to be marginal appendages to the East Asian continent, they have assumed significance that is disproportionate to their geographic size through their strategic location in the East China Sea, equidistant from major centers of East Asia, distant but vulnerable to outside control.

The articulation of local and outside interests in the exchange of tropical shells with Kyushu involved several strategies. Islanders were involved in the collection, processing, and distribution of shells of different types for different markets at different times (Kinoshita 2003d). Although they exchanged shells with agricultural groups along the western coast of Kyushu, they did not adopt cultivation until around AD 800, judging from recent finds. It is difficult to reconcile this late adoption of cultivation with Takamiya's hypothesis that Okinawan populations endured food stress throughout the first millennium. However, many factors hinder the adoption of cultivation (Barker 2011). The dynamics of the shell exchange should be compared with the *Spondylus* trade of the New World and the shell trade of the Mediterranean.

The initiation of the production of gray stoneware (*kamuiyaki*) on the island of Tokunoshima in the tenth century involves a complex set of interactions and decisions among local producers, traders, and groups who bore the cost of establishing the kilns. The scale of production of the kilns and the amount of labor required to establish them make it seem unlikely that they could have been established without outside support, even if they were used only in seasonal production. In the tenth to twelfth centuries islanders grasped opportunities to trade with traders from China and Hakata, and in the late fourteenth century they solicited tributary relations with Ming China. By this time Okinawan communities may have included Chinese traders who had the knowledge and skills to engage in negotiation with state and private trading interests along the China coast. Ryukyu islanders engaged in exchange with both East and Southeast Asian countries, as seen in the *Rekidai hōan* documents (Okinawa Kenritsu Toshokan 1992).

Island archaeology often provides insights into ancient navigation. Evidence from the Ryukyus raises more questions than answers. Recent investigation of underwater sites has supplemented salvage excavations on land, which provide the bulk of our knowledge. Within the Ryuykyus, anchors have been found in several locations, but no actual remains of sunken ships illuminate the technological patterns of navigation.

Travel southward into the Ryukyus from Kyushu must have depended on winter winds from the northwest and summer winds from the southeast. Primitive sails must have been used, although there is no archaeological evidence for them. In order to move southward, the north-flowing Kuroshio must be crossed; negotiating opposing winds and current must have required skill and knowledge. While fluctuations in the monsoon winds are beginning to be assessed as palaeoclimatic research advances, variation in the intensity of the Kuroshio has not been considered. Navigation in the East China Sea seems to have been possible by the seventh to eighth centuries, when the Japanese *kentōshi* tribute ships were able to sail from Kyushu to the mouth of the Yangtze River and return through the Ryukyus; before this, ships followed the mainland coast. Accidental voyages in the East China Sea need to be considered. The drift voyage of the Jeju islanders who drifted to Yonagunijima in the mid-fifteenth century AD is the best known historic example (Iha 1974; Pearson 2003).

Mediterranean and Caribbean Comparative Perspectives

The closest parallels to the Ryukyu Islands are the islands of the Mediterranean, Caribbean, and Andaman Seas; however, lack of available information makes it impossible to discuss the Andaman Islands in detail at this time. In both the Mediterranean and Caribbean cases, colonization began with hunter-gatherers who were probably pushed, rather than lured, into the islands. These archipelagoes are noted for multiple episodes of colonization, limited subsistence opportunities, and the importance of trade. Both cases confirm the importance of cultivation in allowing populations to increase on small islands. Some of these islands are much larger than the Ryukyus and are not visible from the adjacent mainland. For instance, Cyprus, 75 km from Turkey, has an area of 9,251 sq km, and Crete, 160 km south of Greece, has an area of 8,312 sq km. Caribbean islands are variable, Cuba, 145 km from Florida, having an area of 110,860 sq km. In comparison the Ryukyus are minuscule, with Okinawajima covering 1,204 sq km (see Table 1.1). Takamiya Hiroto proposes that islands where hunter-gatherers have colonized "successfully" are nearly all 10,000 sq km or greater in area (2006b, 53).

The general latitude of the Caribbean Islands is 20 degrees north, while that of the Ryukyu Islands is 25 degrees, and that of the Mediterranean, 35 degrees. Cherry concluded that in the Mediterranean, even though it would be difficult to find evidence of Pleistocene colonization since most Pleistocene shoreline sites were destroyed during the last deglaciation, human aquatic dispersal before 10,000 BP was extremely rare in contrast to the high rate of island colonization after that date (1990, 201). Virtually all of the islands of the Mediterranean were colonized in post-Pleistocene times, with a few being colonized at the end of the Pleistocene. Groups remained small through a comparatively short period of hunting and gathering but increased in size with the advent of cultivation. On most islands the Pleistocene fauna became extinct, and mainland fauna were introduced. As in the Ryukyus, rising sea levels may have obliterated Pleistocene sites. Cherry (1990, 202) concluded that the extreme scarcity of Palaeolithic sites in the Mediterranean indicates that the islands were unattractive to potential settlers, not that the people at that time were ignorant of the islands or unable to reach them. It will be important "to learn more about the relative attractiveness of the very different environments of the various islands at successive stages of the post glacial era" (ibid., 202). The "western cereal ovicaprine food production system" (ibid., 202) spread at different rates and degrees from one island to another. It would be instructive to follow the sequences of extinction of endemic fauna and the arrival of introduced fauna.

The first evidence of sea crossing in the Mediterranean, from Italy to Sicily, occurred around 30,000 years ago, when groups were displaced by volcanic activity in the southern Italian peninsula (Broodbank 2006, 206). Broodbank concludes that the true birth of Mediterranean seafaring occurred during the Younger Dryas Period (10,800 to 9,600 BC), when climatic deterioration adversely affected Natufian populations of the Levant and provided a kind of push to explore the eastern Mediterranean. As in the Ryukyu and Caribbean cases, the first stage or colonization was carried out by hunter-gatherers who may have been pushed into the islands or inhabited the islands seasonally.

On Cyprus, the site of Akrotiri Aetokremnos, dated to over 10,000 cal BC, displays some parallels with Noguni B of Okinawajima. Occupied over a span of several hundred years, it contained a huge assemblage of over five hundred individuals of endemic and extinct pygmy hippopotamus as well as numbers of dwarf elephants (Simmons 2009). It is thought that hunting during the relatively brief seasonal occupation of several hundred years pushed the hippopotamus population to extinction, despite the small size of the human population. A shift at the end of the occupation to avian fauna and marine shellfish may represent the demise of the terrestrial fauna. It is not clear if there is a continuity between this early population and later Early Neolithic colonists who introduced domesticated plants and sheep, goats, and pigs, as well as wild deer for hunting. The deer are thought to have been wild because evidence for the domestication of deer on the mainland is rare (ibid., 184–188).

In the Caribbean the first settlement occurred 6,000 to 7,000 years ago.

There were four major and multiple minor migrations. Archaic groups inhabited the islands from about 4000 to 2500 BP, using a stone and shell technology. They transported few if any nonindigenous plants or animals; however, during the Archaic Period sloths, manatees, and some birds became extinct in some areas. Fitzpatrick and Keegan (2007) record heavy exploitation of fish, particularly parrot fish (Scaridae), but also grouper (Serranidae), snapper, and grunts. Horticulturalists of the archaeological Saladoid Culture, who entered the islands around 2500 BP, cultivated introduced root crops including cassava, which was processed into bread. Marine foods were extremely important in the diet, probably more so than cultigens and terrrestrial animals combined. Forest clearance and some overexploitation of both marine and terrestrial resources occurred, judging from the reduced size of individuals in sample populations. Human population grew during this period. The Caribbean Islands had fewer and smaller terrestrial fauna than the Ryukyus, which had deer and wild boar. The period of hunter-gatherers was shorter than in the Ryukyus, with an earlier advent of cultivation. In both areas there was heavy use of reef resources. The Mediterranean and Caribbean cases confirm the importance of cultivation in allowing populations to increase on comparatively small islands. In the Ryukyus agricultural development was compromised by strong typhoons and thin soils.

The Making of the "East Asian Mediterranean"

In this book the processes by which maritime communities of various scales and functions were connected through processes such as migration, colonization, and trade have been outlined, and changes in patterns of livelihood were also described. With improvements in navigation, which allowed the participation of coastal groups, the ability to navigate in all directions was achieved. As Broodbank (2006) observed for the Mediterranean, we can see how seagoing gave way to seafaring and finally voyaging. Similar processes took place in the Ryukyus as islanders learned to sail throughout the islands and far into the South China Sea, creating a broad community by the end of the first millennium AD. Some historians have identified the East China Sea as the "East Asian Mediterranean" (Schottenhammer 2005). Gungwu Wang (2008, 10) has noted important differences between the East China Sea region and the Mediterranean region, which featured "empires characterized by maritime power, and sustained, aggressive tenets of religion." Knapp and Blake perceive a danger of essentializing the nature of the Mediterranean, where integration is the exception rather than the rule (2005, 1, 2). Nevertheless, a "supraregional commercial zone" (Schottenhammer 2007, 58) came into existence in the Ryukyus with the arrival of Chinese traders in the eleventh century AD. The findings of Kaigen

Tsūhō coins of the seventh and eighth centuries in the Ryukyus indicates that Chinese trade actually began several centuries earlier.

Preserving Archaeological Heritage

The cultural heritage of the Ryukyu Islands has been severely damaged by the Pacific War, construction of military bases, and island development of all kinds. The destruction continues as sites are totally excavated and the nonrenewable cultural resource is diminished. The irony is that total excavation and subsequent destruction has brought about knowledge of cultural resources in the process of destroying them. In the creation of enormous level fields for sugarcane, sites are completely demolished to support a heavily subsidized industry that ultimately cannot compete with cane production in the rich tropical regions of the world. Although test pitting and wide area excavation may precede this development, the sites and their environment are lost forever with bulldozing and the introduction of new fill. The Gusuku Site Group of Kikaigashima and the fragile sites of Nagura Bay, Ishigakijima, are examples of this tragic destruction along with countless others. Even agricultural development has become destructive, spreading red clay into reefs and killing them, and affecting the purity of ground water. The problem of balancing conservation with development is complicated in the Ryukyus, with their high population, strategic military importance, and fragile ecosystems. The strategic location of the Ryukyus has brought both profit and destruction throughout history; the islanders should have an active role in this situation. Their active agency can help them to find a new role in East Asia as a center of culture, information, and subtropical research. Although other areas may have superior climatic conditions for tropical agriculture and other industries, the Ryukyu Islands possess a unique and unrivaled central location in East Asia. Can a new order create renewed prosperity through peaceful trade and exchange of ideas?

It is hoped that, in demonstrating the richness of the islands' resources and the success and dedication of Ryukyu archaeologists, this publication will lead to more support for research and preservation as well as new ways to think about the archaeology of the Ryukyu Islands and their future.

Appendix 1

Building a Chronology of Trade Ceramics

In this appendix I introduce the major kinds of Chinese and Southeast Asian trade ceramics found in the Ryukyus up to roughly the beginning of the seventeenth century AD and outline their use in dating sites. One may wonder why archaeologists do not rely primarily on local Ryukyu ceramic seriation, instead of foreign ceramics, to make chronological distinctions in the Gusuku and Early Ryukyu Kingdom Periods. Certainly local ceramics were produced, but their quantity and variability were limited. In the Late Shellmound Period (300 BC to AD 1050) and Early Gusuku Period (AD 1050 to 1250), Ryukyu islanders produced their own earthenware (termed *gusuku doki*); however, by the Late Gusuku Period (AD 1250 to 1429), earthenware production declined because of competition from Chinese hard-fired ceramics. From the late thirteenth century AD roof tiles of Korean style were produced on Okinawa to supply elite sites such as Urasoe, Shuri, and Katsuren. Analysis of the clay material of these roof tiles shows that they were made in Okinawa, although the kiln sites have not been published, if they have recently been found (Yamamoto Masa'aki et al. 2007). In the late sixteenth century AD kilns were established at Wakuta, Naha; at first roof tiles were produced, and in the seventeenth century AD Okinawans began to produce their own stoneware. In the absence of abundant local hard-fired ceramics, archaeologists use the extremely rich corpus of East Asian trade ceramics for chronological studies of trade and consumption.

Trade ceramics can be dated by three different methods, which may be combined.

The first method is through the excavation of kiln sites and the establishment of a relative chronology based on stratigraphy. Pioneering work of Chinese authors has increased our knowledge in this area. Rare historical documents that describe local ceramic production as well as dated coins found in kiln site layers have also been used to provide ranges of dates for certain sites or layers. The investigation of kilns at Dehua, Fujian, demonstrates the use of both stratigraphy and dating by coins (Fujian Sheng Bowuguan 1990, 138). Dated objects such as inscribed celadon plaques and epitaphs have also been used.

The second method is the calendrical dating of "sealed finds" such as burials or shipwrecks. Dated sites of this type in Japan (Ueda 1982; Kamei 1986b, 375) or China (Kamei 1986b, 299) have been described. The dating of objects from such sites may not be absolute, since objects are often retained as heirlooms before burial long after their manufacture and before their burial. This seems to be particularly true in Japan. The Sinan sunken ship, found near Mokpo, Korea, dated to about AD 1323, is very useful for cross-dating finds from Dazaifu, an administrative center near Hakata (Fukuoka), Japan (Yokota, Morimoto, and Yamamoto 1989). In some cases cross-dating between Dazaifu and Okinawan sites has also been attempted (Seto et al. 2007).

The third method is the establishment of a chronology in offshore consumption sites removed from the centers of production by stratigraphy and association of different types of artifacts for which a relative date has been produced. Trade ceramics found in Okinawa can be dated roughly by association with fragments of exotic soapstone bowls from Nagasaki Prefecture that have been dated in Kyushu sites through their association with utilitarian *hajiki* earthenwares, for which there is a very detailed stylistic chronology. In some cases where the archaeological association is particularly precise, archaeologists in Kyushu have been able to date objects within a decade (Kamei 1986a, 49). At present this type of research often provides more precise chronological information than kiln excavation. Ceramics from the same firing may be kept in use for varying lengths of time, depending on many factors, including how precious they are. Variable length of use life can affect the dating of a deposit.

Okinawan field archaeologists have built up a relative sequence of Okinawan trade ceramics based on their context in Okinawan sites (Kin 1990; Seto 2010a). A chronological summary of trade wares and sites is given in Table App 1.1. This has been done independently from the work of Chinese scholars on the kiln sites. When relative dates using this approach are compared with the results from sealed finds and the excavations of production sites, a certain degree of corroboration emerges (Kamei 1992; Kamei 2002b).

TABLE APP 1.1 Chronological Summary of Trade Wares

Period	*Ware*	*Typical Site*
Period I AD 1050 to 1150 In Periods I and II, interaction with Hakata occurred. Soapstone cauldrons were traded. Private trade route existed from Fujian to Hakata through Ryukyus.	whiteware bowls; everted lip whiteware bowls, two types, thickened lip and everted lip; *kamuiyaki* Group A; Gusuku Pottery with square external lugs; soapstone cauldrons	Kominato Fuwaganeku, Amami Ōshima; Kushikanekubaru Layer V, Okinawajima; Ōdomaribama Shellmound, Haterumajima
Period II AD 1150 to 1250 Strong connections with Hakata continued. Fujian celadons from Tong'an and early Longquan celadons are found.	whiteware bowls, comb marked; *kamuiyaki* Group A; square-lug Gusuku Pottery; Longquan celadon with floral pattern or ridged lotus petal	Kurakizaki, Amami Ōshima; Nakanohama, Kumejima
Period III AD 1250 to 1350 Fujian rough whitewares, Nakijin and Birosuku Types, found only in the Ryukyus. Trade ceramics increase. Gusuku Type earthenware disappears in the Okinawa Islands.	Lonquan celadon; floral-shape bowls; bowls with narrow lotus petal exterior incision; plates with grooved rims; *kamuiyaki* B	Nakijin Main Enclosure Levels VII to IX
Period IV AD 1350 to 1400 Tribute missions to Ming begin in the late fourteenth century. Large celadon imperial gifts appear in Shuri, Nakijin. Birosuku whitewares found in Japanese main islands including Hokkaido. Bizen, Japanese soft grayware (*gashitsu doki*) from Nakijin, shows connections with western Japan. Gusuku Pottery and *kamuiyaki* disappear.	celadon large jars and bottles; celadon bowls with everted lip; *tenmoku*; Korean and Vietnamese wares; Yuan, early Ming blue and white	Nakijin Main Enclosure Levels II to VI

TABLE APP I.I *(continued)*

Period	*Ware*	*Typical Site*
Period V AD 1400 to ca. 1450s	celadon bowls with thunder pattern (*raimon*); early Ming blue and white; Bizen stoneware	Shuri SK01 Kyōnouchi; Nikaiden fill deposit; Birosuku, Ishigakijima
Some large "Yuan type" masterpieces may have been produced in first half of fifteenth century AD or imported as antiques.		
Period VI AD 1450 to 1550	Longquan celadon, some with Gu Shi characters; Wakuta soft grayware; Thai, Vietnamese, Bizen, north Kyushu wares; Longquan celadon narrow petal bowls	Shitadaru shipwreck, Ishigaki; Nakijin Main Enclosure Layer I; Shigemajō Enclosure
Naha port facilities were built. Ming-style roof tiles found at Wakuta. Large construction projects carried out, such as Enkakuji and Tenkaiji at Shuri. Village sites expanded. Shitadaru underwater site, Ishigakijima, dates from this period.		
Period VII AD 1550 to 1600	Seto, Mino, Karatsu Japanese wares	Uemura, Iriomotejima; Tenkaiji Okinawajima
Ceramics decrease in quantity throughout the Ryukyus. Blue and white ceramics from Jingdezhen and Zhangzhou, and Hizen (Arita) area of Kyushu are prevalent. Southeast Asian ceramics disappear in the Ryukyus but are abundant in Sakai.		

Source: Based on Seto et al. 2007; Seto 2010a.

Trade Ceramics from the Ryukyus

Although trade ceramics from continental Asia used to be considered a feature of increased contact with China beginning in the Early Gusuku Period, it is now clear that trade ceramics appear much earlier. At least five sites, including the Azamabaru No. 1 site, yielded sherds of Lelang-type earthenware from the Korean Peninsula dating to the first few centuries AD (Shimoji Yasuhiro 1999; Zaidan 2003, 186). As mentioned in Chapter 7, the Gusuku Site Group of Kikaigashima yielded small quantities of unusual trade ceramics of the eighth and ninth centuries AD such as *sueki* ware from Kagoshima Prefecture and Chinese *yue* celadon wares from Zhejiang Province.

Two plates of Changsha Ware, said to be found near an *utaki* shrine in the Sonai area of Iriomotejima (Kin 2008b, 48), are now held by the Tokyo National Museum (Tōkyō Kokuritsu Hakubutsukan 1978, 11) (Figure App 1.1). They are dated to the ninth century AD.

East Asian hard-fired stonewares and porcelains have been recovered from well over two hundred *gusuku* (castle) sites and about four hundred unfortified sites of the same time period in the Ryukyus. Although there are the rare earlier examples noted above, they become increasingly abundant from the beginning of the eleventh century AD. They include Chinese brown, white, celadon, iron-glazed, and blue and white, as well as Korean, Vietnamese, Thai, and Japanese wares. South Chinese Three-Color Wares from Fujian (Kamei 1986b, 339–374) have also been found in a small number of sites. Table App 1.1 and Figure App 1.2 provide a summary of the major types, subperiods, and typical sites.

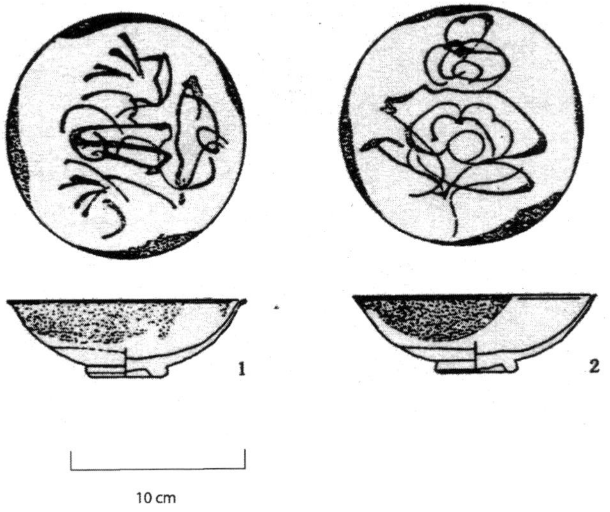

App 1.1. Changsha Ware plates, ninth century AD, from the Sonai area, west coast of Iriomotejima. Redrawn from Kin 1989, 1. Courtesy of Kin Seiki.

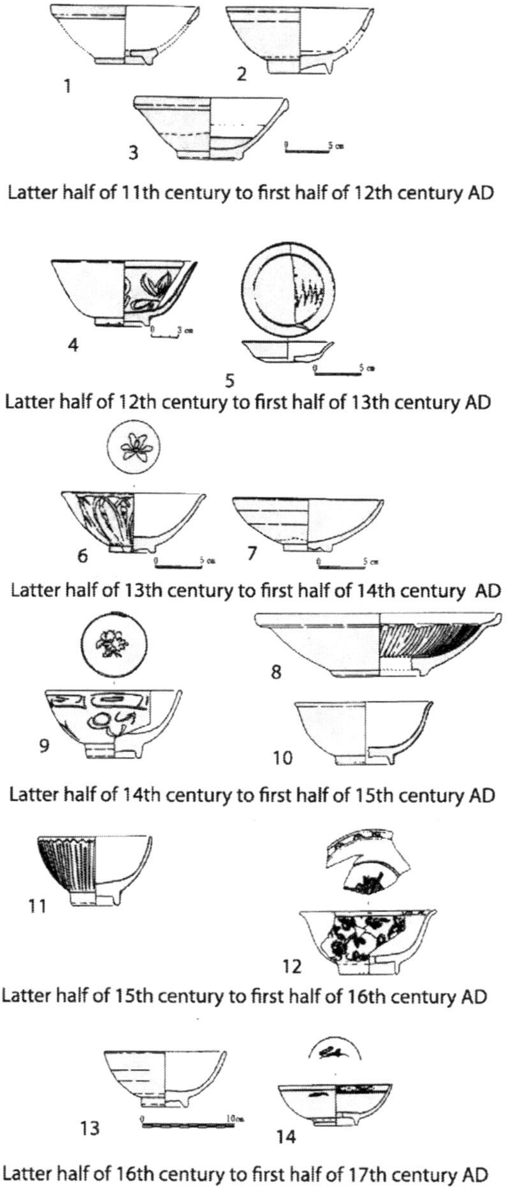

App 1.2. Types of Chinese ceramics found in Okinawa, according to Kin (1993). Courtesy of Kin Seiki.

1, 3. Whiteware bowls with thickened lips
2. Whiteware bowl with everted lip
4. Celadon bowl with incised flower petal decoration
5. Celadon plate with comb decoration
6. Celadon bowl with ridged lotus petal decoration
7. Whiteware bowl, Birosuku Type
8. Celadon plate
9. Celadon bowl with band of thunder pattern decoration
10. Plain celadon bowl
11. Celadon bowl with narrow lotus petal decoration
12. Blue and white bowl
13. Plain celadon bowl
14. Blue and white bowl

The following descriptions and chronology of whitewares and celadons (Figure App 1.3) are taken from Kin 1990, Arakaki and Seto 2005, and Seto et al. 2007 (romanized Japanese terms are Kin's designations).

Whitewares

Bowls

With the exception of the Tang finds mentioned above, the oldest Chinese ceramics are whitewares produced in Fujian Province, dating from the end of the eleventh century AD. Four types of whiteware bowls have been identified by Kin, in addition to plates. Most of the whitewares found in the Ryukyus were produced in Fujian and Guangdong. However, from the latter half of the fourteenth century AD, three types of whiteware bowls from Jingdezhen, Jiangxi Province, can be found (Arakaki and Seto 2005). These are plain bowls with globular shape and high foot ring (mid- to late fourteenth century AD), deep bowls with curving sides and everted rims of the Shufu Type with thick, white glaze and carefully finished body (late fourteenth to early fifteenth centuries AD), and shallow bowls with wide foot ring or no foot ring (sixteenth century AD).

LATE TWELFTH, EARLY THIRTEENTH CENTURIES AD

Kin has identified a white bowl with thickened lip (*tamafuchi wan*) as the earliest whiteware found in the Ryukyus (1988; 1989) (Figure App 1.3: 1–1, 1–2). Thick glaze covers the inner bowl and the outer body, with an unglazed area between the body and the foot. It is dated to the end of the eleventh century and the beginning of the twelfth century AD. Similar bowls with thickened lips have been found in surveys in the Minqing County area (inland from Fuzhou). This area was the largest producer of white and bluish white wares in Fujian (Yeh 1988, 66). These bowls are also similar to certain Type 3 bowls produced at Dehua, Fujian, Lower Layer, , which are thick-walled shallow bowls with thickened rims. The lower layer is dated to the end of the Northern Song (late eleventh and early twelfth centuries AD) (Fujian Sheng Bowuguan 1990, 12).

Other types of whitewares are thought to form a temporal progression. White bowls with an everted rim (*tanhan wan*) and a thick, high, foot ring covered with a thick glaze extending from the interior base of the bowl to an unglazed area near the foot ring have been found in association with Type 1 at the Atta and Ōdomaribama Shellmounds, Okinawajima and Haterumajima respectively, and are dated by Kin to the first half of the twelfth century AD (1990, 2) (Figure App 1.3: 2). Bowls with comb patterns on the outer surface

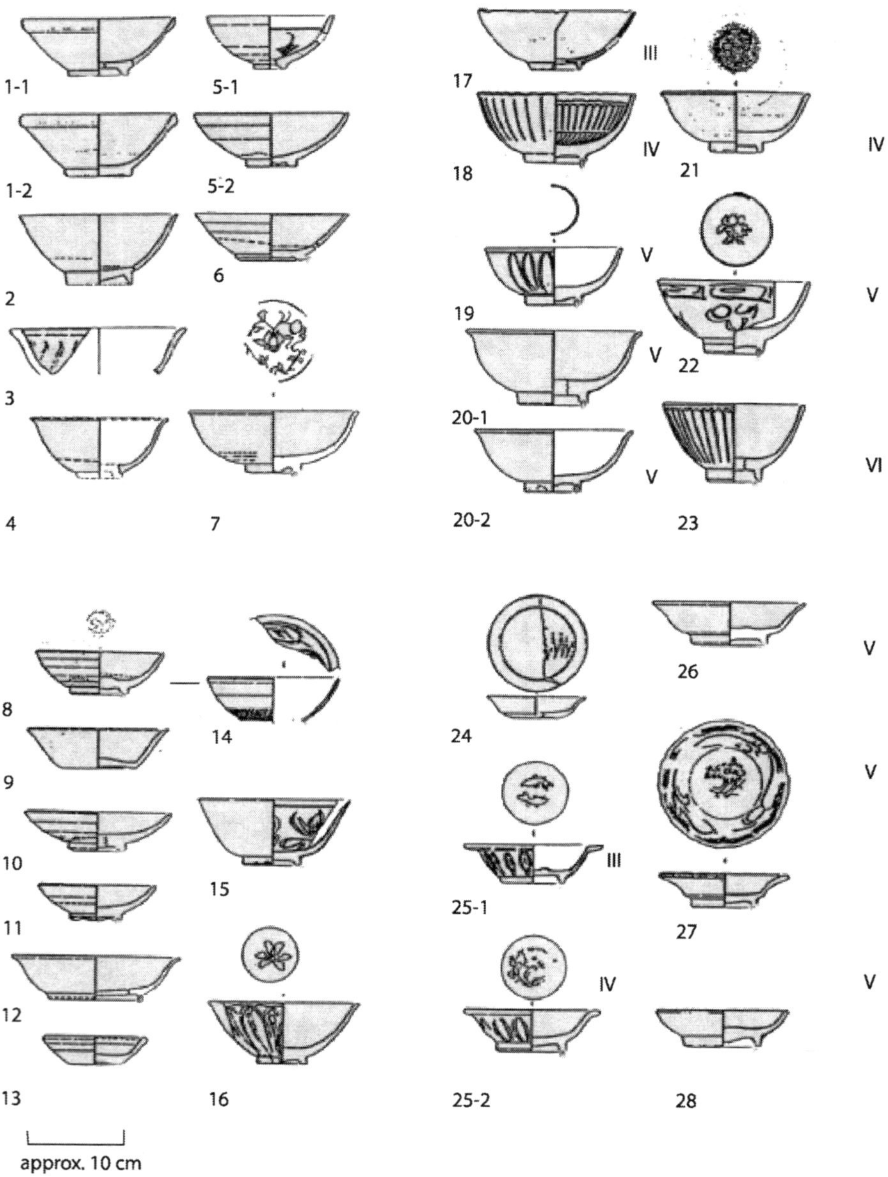

App 1.3. Whitewares and celadons recovered from Okinawan sites (from Kin 1990). Courtesy of Kin Seiki.

App 1.3, *con't.*

Whitewares: 1-1. Bowl with thickened lip (*tamafuchi wan*). Late eleventh to first half of twelfth century AD. Atta Shellmound, Okinawajima. 1-2. Type 2 bowl with thickened lip. Latter half of twelfth century AD. Shinzatomura (west), Taketomijima. 2. Bowl with everted rim (*tanhan wan*). First half of twelfth century AD. Atta Shellmound, Okinawajima. 3. Bowl with exterior comb pattern decoration (*kushigakimon wan*). Latter half of twelfth to first half of thirteenth century. Sashiki, Okinawajima. 4. Bowl with unglazed rim (*kuchihage wan*). Latter half of thirteenth to first half of fourteenth century AD. Nakijin Gusuku, Okinawajima. 5-1 and 5-2. Birosuku Type bowl, with exterior comb decoration. Latter half of thirteenth to beginning of fourteenth century AD. Birosuku Site, Ishigakijima. 6. Birosuku Type thin bowl with straight outward-flaring sides (*usude chokkō wan*). Latter half of thirteenth to middle of fourteenth century AD. Birosuku Site, Ishigakijima. 7. Bowl with everted rim (*gaihan wan*). Latter half of fourteenth century AD. Nakijin, Okinawajima. 8. Thick bowl with outward-flaring straight sides (*atsude chokkō wan*). Fifteenth to sixteenth century AD. Birosuku Site, Ishigakijima; also Main Enclosure, Nakijin, Okinawajima. 9. Plate with unglazed rim (*kuchihage zara*). Latter half of thirteenth to first half of fourteenth century AD. Nakijin, Okinawajima. 10. Concave plate (*naiwan zara*). Latter half of fourteenth century AD. Nakijin, Okinawajima. 11. Small plate with gouged foot ring (*ketsunyū kōdaizara*). Fifteenth to sixteenth century AD. Nakijin, Okinawajima. 12. Thin plate with everted rim (*usude gaihan zara*). Fifteenth to sixteenth century AD. Nakijin, Okinawajima. 13. Small plate with concave bottom, used as lamp (*tōmyōzara*). Fifteenth to sixteenth century AD. Nakijin, Okinawajima.

Celadon wares (roman numerals III to VI indicate type numbers assigned in Dazaifu, Kyushu): 14. Comb pattern decorated bowl (*kushigakimon wan*). Late twelfth to thirteenth century AD. Inafuku, Okinawajima. 15. Bowl with incised floral pattern (*kakkamon wan*). Late twelfth to thirteenth century AD. Birosuku, Ishigakijima. 16. Ridged lotus petal bowl (*shinogi renbenmon wan*). Latter half of thirteenth to first half of fourteenth century AD. Nakijin, Okinawajima. 17. Undecorated flower-shaped bowl (*mumon rinka wan*). Late fourteenth to first half of fifteenth century AD. Nakijin, Okinawajima. 18. Mold-made lotus petal bowl (*katatsukuri renbenmon wan*). First half of fourteenth century AD. Kedasaki, Yonagunijima. 19. Bowl with "ridgeless" lotus petal decoration (*mukō renbenmon wan*). Fourteenth to first half of fifteenth century AD. Nakijin, Okinawajima. 20-1 and 20-2. Plain bowl with everted rim (*mumon gaihan wan*). Fourteenth to fifteenth centuries AD. Nakijin, Okinawajima. 21. Bowl with everted, thickened lip (*tamafuchi gaihan wan*). Latter half of fourteenth to first half of fifteenth century AD. Sashiki, Okinawajima. 22. Bowl with band of thunder pattern decoration (*raimontai wan*). Latter half of fifteenth to first half of sixteenth century AD. Nakijin, Okinawajima. 23. Line-cut narrow lotus petal bowl (*senkokusai renbenmon wan*). Fifteenth century AD. Nakijin, Okinawajima. 24. Comb-decorated plate (*kushigakimon zara*). Late thirteenth to first half of fourteenth century AD. Uganyama, Okinawajima. 25-1 and 25-2. Plates with bent or folded rim. End of thirteenth to first half of fourteenth century AD. Nakijin, Okinawajima. 26. Plate with everted rim (*gaihan zara*). Latter half of fifteenth to first half of sixteenth century AD. Nakijin, Okinawajima. 27. Silhouette flower plate (*ryōka zara*). Latter half of fourteenth to fifteenth century AD. Nakijin. Okinawajima. 28. Straight-rim plate (*chokkō zara*). Latter half of fifteenth to sixteenth century AD. Nakijin, Okinawa.

(*kushigakimon wan*) (Figure App 1.3: 3) are dated by Kin to the latter half of the twelfth century and the first half of the thirteenth century AD.

Late Thirteenth, Early Fourteenth Centuries AD

A whiteware bowl with an unglazed rim (*kuchihage wan*) (Figure App 1.3: 4) was found in the Shinzatomura (East) Site, Taketomijima, and the Shigemajō Enclosure of Nakijin Gusuku, Okinawajima. Kin dates it to the late thirteenth and early fourteenth centuries AD.

Several varieties of concave bowls, with relatively thick walls and fairly wide foot rings that have been cut flat, and with traces of wheel marks on the exterior surfaces, have been identified by Kin as the Birosuku Type. This type is found on many Okinawan sites and has been dated by Kin from the end of the thirteenth century to the beginning of the fourteenth century AD (Kin 1988; 2007a). It is named for the Birosuku Site, Ishigakijima, where it occurred in Layer II. Tanaka (2007) states that the Birosuku Type was made in the Minqing kilns, Fujian, situated in the middle reaches of the Min River. The most typical form is a thick-walled concave bowl with thin white or yellowish white glaze extending from the interior base to the exterior edge of the thick foot ring. In some cases there is comb decoration or a stamped floral pattern in the interior of the bowl. On the exterior body traces of wheel marks are visible (Figure App 1.3: 5, 6). There may be some decoration on the exterior lip, often an encircling line (Figure App 1.3: 6). There may be a Birosuku Type whiteware plate as well, but its range of variation and definition were not clear when Kin published his article on the Birosuku Type in 1988. The Birosuku Type has not been found in Shuri Gusuku, suggesting to Tanaka (2007) that its construction began in the middle of the fourteenth century AD.

A second type of rough whiteware, from about the same time period, was found in Nakijin Gusuku. Thin-walled bowls with straight outward-flaring sides (*usude chokkō wan*), without the interior concavity of the preceding type, have been recovered from the Birosuku Site and Layers V and VII of the Main Enclosure, dated by Kin from the late thirteenth century to the middle of the fourteenth century AD. The bottom of the foot ring is not cut off flat but is beveled so that the bowl rests on the inner edge of the foot ring. The body is grayish white or gray. This type has been identified by Kin (2007a; 2008a) as the Nakijin Type. It is found in Layers IX and VII of Nakijin, in association with dug posthole buildings. Tanaka (2007) states that the Nakijin Type was made in the Pukou kilns, Lianjiang Xian, Fujian Province, some 30 km northeast of Fuzhou, facing Dinghai Bay, the site of famous underwater sites that yield the same wares.

LATE FOURTEENTH TO EARLY FIFTEENTH CENTURIES AD

The bowl with everted rim (*gaihan wan*) (Figure App 3: 7) is the most common white bowl found in castle sites. The methods of finishing the foot and glazing resemble the Birosuku Type. In the excavation of the Shigemajō Enclosure of Nakijin, 55 percent of the whitewares were of this type. Kin expects that it came at the time of the tribute missions of Sanhoku to Ming (AD 1383 to 1415).

LATE FIFTEENTH TO EARLY SIXTEENTH CENTURIES AD

A final type, *atsude chokkō wan* (Figure App 1.3: 8), is a low, shallow bowl with a rounded lip, the foot showing traces of finishing with a bamboo spatula. Glaze extends from the upper portion of the inner bowl to the exterior lip. The inner base of the bowl is unglazed, and examples with a stamped character in this location are abundant. In the Shigemajō Enclosure, Nakijin, this is the next most common bowl type after the bowl with the everted rim. These are dated from the fifteenth to sixteenth centuries AD.

Plates

LATE THIRTEENTH TO EARLY FOURTEENTH CENTURIES AD

Whiteware plates with shape similar to extremely shallow flat bowls have also been recovered. They include plates with unglazed rims (*kuchihage zara*) (Figure App 1.3: 9). These plates have been found together with celadon bowls with the cut petal pattern and comb pattern at the Inafuku, Birosuku, and Nakijin Gusuku Sites, and are dated to the latter half of the thirteenth century and the first half of the fourteenth century AD.

LATE FOURTEENTH TO EARLY FIFTEENTH CENTURIES AD

A concave plate (*naiwan zara*) (Figure App 1.3: 10), glazed from the inner base to the edge of the foot ring, shows use of a bamboo spatula in finishing the foot ring. It has been recovered from the Shinzatomura (East) and Birosuku Sites, and dates to the latter half of the fourteenth century and the early half of the fifteenth century AD.

LATE FIFTEENTH TO EARLY SIXTEENTH CENTURIES AD

A small plate with semicircular gouges removed from the foot ring (*ketsunyū kōdaizara*), which seems to be a smaller version of the previous type with a special foot, is dated to the fifteenth to sixteenth century AD (Figure App 1.3: 11).

These are found in the Shitadaru Shipwreck Site, Ishigakijima, the Sumiya Site, Miyakojima, and Nakijin Gusuku, in contexts dated to the second half of the fifteenth century AD. Sekiguchi (2009) attributes them to the Sidu kilns of Shaowu City, Fujian. A thin, white plate with everted rim (*usude gaihan zara*) (Figure App 1.3: 12) has the same form as blue and white plates and often occurs together with blue and white plates as a set. These are dated to the fifteenth and sixteenth centuries and are the most common whitewares in the Shigemajō Enclosure at Nakijin Gusuku. Small plates with concave bottoms may have functioned as lamps (*tōmyōzara*) (Figure App 1.3: 13). The interior is thinly glazed, while the exterior is unglazed. On the unglazed area near the rim are traces of soot. They have been found in Nakijin Gusuku in contexts dating to the fifteenth to sixteenth centuries AD.

Molded Boxes, Twelfth to Thirteenth Centuries AD

Molded covered boxes, produced in Jingdezhen or related kilns, have been found in a number of sites such as Hanagusuku Furushima, Okinawajima, and Nogusuku, Miyakojima. They are found with sherds of comb-patterned Jukō celadon and are thought to date to the same period (Kin 1989, 13).

Celadon

In the discussion of celadon below, I have followed the analysis of Kin Seiki (1989; 1990), adding information from Seto Tetsuya (2004; 2010a). Seto has used the typology developed at the site of Dazaifu, Fukuoka Prefecture, through decades of research. I have indicated specimens that correspond to Dazaifu types III to VI in Figure App 1.3.

Bowls

TWELFTH AND THIRTEENTH CENTURIES AD

Celadon is the most abundant type of Chinese ceramic found on Ryukyu sites, the earliest types being those produced in Fujian from the end of the twelfth to the first half of the thirteenth century AD. Four bowl types have been recovered. These are comb pattern, floral pattern in silhouette, ridged lotus petal, and undecorated flower shape.

Comb pattern bowls (*kushigakimon wan*) (Figure App 1.3: 14) from the Tong'an kilns in the Ting River area, Fujian, termed Jukō celadon by Japanese scholars, are distinguished by comb patterns as well as floral decoration executed by spatula, and comb patterns and are often dark brownish green in color. The exterior of specimens found in the Ryukyus may be decorated or plain. There are several variations in the shape of the foot ring. Examples from the Inafuku Site, Okinawajima, date from the end of the twelfth to the thirteenth century AD.

Li Xijing (1982) notes that Jukō celadons can have parallel lines on the outer surface. The wares were produced not only at the Tong'an Tingxi kiln, but also in other kilns in the southeast coastal region such as Nan'an, Quanzhou, Xiamen, and Dehua (Kamei 1995). Tong'an celadon bowls have the same general shapes as Southern Song Longquan bowls, with the bulge of the lower body, the foot ring style, and the in-turned rim. They also resemble bowl shapes of Song whitewares. Kin noted that Tong'an celadons have been found in more than ten sites in the Ryukyus, but there are usually only one or two sherds per site (1989, 8). The exceptions are Inafuku and Uganyama, Okinawajima, from which twelve bowls and eight plates were recovered respectively.

Several other types of celadons dated to the twelfth and thirteenth centuries AD appear in Okinawan sites. These are floral pattern bowls, ridged lotus petal bowls, undecorated floral shaped bowls, and cups and plates with everted lips. Incised floral pattern bowls (*kakkamon wan*) (Figure App 3: 15) are of Longquan manufacture. They are abundant on a large number of sites (56 bowls from Birosuku and 15 from Uganyama) (Kin 1989, 8). Incised decoration also occurs on the inner surface. Some of the bowls have plain exteriors, whereas others have some decoration. In distinction to plain incision, the interior floral pattern may be executed with a slanting spatula (*herabori*) or flat lines. A spatula held in a slanting position when the clay is leather hard makes a line with a vertical edge on one side and a sloping line on the other. The sloping line creates a slanting groove from deep to shallow so that the accumulated glaze produces a gradation from dark, where the glaze is thick and the line is deepest, to light, where the glaze is thin and the line is shallowest. The foot ring cavity is shallow, and the foot ring is wide and cut off flat. There is a small unglazed area around the foot ring, and the glaze is relatively thick. Some specimens have four characters stamped in the interior base (Japanese *kin gyoku man dō*: halls full of gold and jade).

There is usually a single circling horizontal line in the interior base of the bowl and around the interior lip. The interior base has a floral pattern produced by the beveled technique or spatula, or no decoration.

THIRTEENTH TO FOURTEENTH CENTURIES AD

Longquan ridged lotus petal bowls (*shinogi renbenmon wan*) (Figure App 1.3: 16) have similar glazing and finishing of the foot to the incised floral pattern bowls. Each lotus petal has a central ridge. The body of the bowl above the foot ring is thick, and there is an unglazed area between the foot ring and the lower body of the bowl. This type has been found in Layer IX, the very bottom of Nakijin Gusuku, and also in Layer VII. Kamei (1986a, 42, 43) states that the ridged lotus petal bowl is the most common type of Chinese celadon found in Japan. He dates this type to the thirteenth to fourteenth century AD, noting that Chinese archaeologists date it to the Southern Song (AD 1127 to 1279).

Undecorated flower-shaped bowls (*mumon rinka wan*) (Figure App 1.3: 17), of Longquan manufacture, have been found in small numbers. The undulating rim is shaped to resemble the tips of flower petals, and the body and base of the bowl are thin. After the bowl was totally glazed, the glaze was wiped from the foot ring, leaving an unglazed portion between the foot ring and the lower body. From the bowl shapes and the style of glazing, this type of bowl seems to belong to the Kinuta type of celadon, which has thick, pale green glaze. The most famous vessel shapes of this ware, seen in art museums, are shaped like a mallet (Japanese *kinuta*). This type of vessel is rare, but from the context of the bowls from Nakijin and Gaja, Okinawajima, the dating is from the latter half of the thirteenth century to the first half of the fourteenth century AD.

FOURTEENTH CENTURY AND THE FIRST HALF OF THE FIFTEENTH CENTURY AD

Mold-made lotus petal bowls (*katatsukuri renbenmon wan*) (Figure App 1.3: 18) have two overlapping rows of lotus petal decoration in the interior, while the outer surface has lotus petals executed with a spatula, their tips being indicated by cuts to the lip of the bowl. From the context of the finds at Kedasaki, Yonagunijima, and Shinzatomura (west), Taketomijima, their date is thought to be the first half of the fourteenth century AD. Five bowl types fall within this span.

Bowls with "ridgeless" lotus petals (*mukō renbenmon wan*) are the second type (Figure App 1.3: 19). The lotus petals have been drawn with a spatula, the mouth of the bowl is flaring, but the upper wall of the bowl is straight rather than curved. The decoration has variable composition, and there are various methods of applying the glaze. These bowls span a considerable time range from the fourteenth century to the early half of the fifteenth century AD.

The third type consists of plain bowls with everted rims (*mumon gaihan wan*). At least two variations occur. Bowl Type 1 (Figure App 1.3: 20-1) has a bulging body and a stamped floral pattern in the inner base. The white body is distinctive. The glaze is thick, and the foot ring has been finished with a bamboo spatula. In Type 2 (Figure App 1.3: 20-2), the wall is a little thinner and the lip everted. The body is grayish. This is the most common type of celadon found in the Shigemajō Enclosure, Nakijin Gusuku.

The fourth type is a bowl with everted, thickened lip (*tamafuchi gaihan wan*) (Figure App 1.3: 21). Both plain and decorated versions are found. It has been found in both the Shigemajō Enclosure, Nakijin, and Sashiki, Okinawajima, and is dated from the latter half of the fourteenth to the first half of the fifteenth century AD.

The fifth type is the thunder pattern band bowl (*raimontai wan*) (Figure App 1.3: 22). The mouth of the bowl is flaring, but the walls of the bowl are straight, and there is a band of thunder pattern (interlocking rectilinear hooks) immediately below the rim. There are several variants of the decoration. This bowl is described by Kamei Meitoku in his discussion of Yamada Gusuku (Kamei 1986b, 301). He noted that the mouth diameter is quite large in comparison to the height, the inner and outer surfaces of the foot ring have been beveled, and the center of the foot ring has a slight protuberance. The glaze is yellowish green, and the foot ring is completely glazed. The thunder pattern near the rim and the lotus petals on the exterior body have been drawn with a bamboo spatula. On the inner base of the bowl there is a stamped floral decoration inside a single ring. In some cases this floral pattern has been incised. This type of bowl was produced in large quantities. The chief motif, the lotus petal pattern, has a scalloped shape, like the lama-shaped lotus petal; inside the petal there is a spiral, springlike motif. Alternately there may be a wide, ridgeless lotus petal made by broad spatula impressions. Kamei dated this type to the middle and late fourteenth to the end of the fifteenth century AD, a span of a hundred years. Ueda groups these into a single type (Type C) and places them at the beginning of the fifteenth century AD (1982, 69). Kamei (1986b, 334) notes that the thunder pattern sometimes occurs on the inner ring of well-made bowls that have human figures, trees, birds, and animals, or Chinese characters, on the interior of the bowl from sites in the Japanese main islands, but this type has not been recovered from Ryukyu sites.

FIFTEENTH TO SIXTEENTH CENTURIES AD

In general, celadon bowls became narrower and higher from the fourteenth to sixteenth century AD (Ueda 1982, 55–70). Kin has identified one type in this time period, the line-cut narrow lotus petal bowl (*senkokusai renbenmon wan*) (Figure App 1.3: 23). This straight-rimmed type has considerable variation in the structure of the decoration. It appears to date to the fifteenth century AD. This type fits within the class designated by Kamei as Celadon Bowl Type B (1986b, 302). The pattern on the exterior of the bowl is composed of narrow single lotus petals, and the edge of the petal is incised with a simple line. Although the petal pattern was derived from Longquan in Southern Song times, by the fifteenth century it became abbreviated and simplified. Type B can be divided into two variants: in most cases, the petal tips are pointed like the end of a spear, and the lines are made with a spatula in the *herabori* technique. In a different version, just below the lip of the bowl a series of curved lines resembling thumbnail impressions constitute the tops of the petals, but they do not clearly demarcate each petal. Both of these variants have the stamped floral pattern inside the bowl, and some have stamped characters. A particular type, with incised Chinese characters Gu Shi, has been identified by Sekiguchi (2009) at the Shitadaru Site, Ishigakijima. This inexpensive ware, made in the Dayao area of Longquan, Zhejiang, was exported to various parts of Japan. Kamei estimates that this type of celadon was produced in the fifteenth and sixteenth centuries AD. Ueda's chronology of celadon bowls indicates that broad lotus petals with ridges change to thin narrow spatula-drawn petals in the late fifteenth century AD.

Plates

TWELFTH TO THIRTEENTH CENTURIES AD

Jukō Type plates of Tong'an, Fujian Province, manufactured with comb pattern decoration (*kushigakimon zara*) (Figure App 1.3: 24), are more common than Jukō bowls. Plates without foot rings occur, but slightly elevated foot rings are more common. Decoration in the interior of the base has been executed by both comb and spatula, but the comb decoration is most useful for dating. Plates of this type have been found in Birosuku, Ishigakijima, and Inafuku and Ugan-yama, Okinawajima, and from their provenience they are dated to the end of the twelfth century and the beginning of the thirteenth century AD, the same time range as Jukō Type bowls.

A second type has a diagnostic bent rim (*kuchi ori zara*) (Figure App 1.3: 25-1). It is of Longquan manufacture. Two forms have been noted. After total glazing, the glaze on the foot ring was wiped away, leaving an unglazed portion on the lower body and foot. Decoration on the outer surface consists of ridged lotus petals, while on the inside there are double fish clay appliqués with glazing over them, lotus petals executed with a spatula, or a plain surface. From Nakijin, dating seems to be from the end of the thirteenth to the beginning of the fourteenth century AD. This dating fits with the Yuan attributions for similar specimens from the Philippines (Tan 1991, fig. 20).

Another type lacks the everted, grooved rim; instead, the rim is rounded (Figure App 1.3: 25-2). There are great differences in the form of the foot and the application of the glaze from the type above. The outer surface may be plain or have ridgeless lotus petals.

FOURTEENTH TO FIFTEENTH CENTURIES AD

Plates with everted rims (*gaihan zara*) (Figure App 1.3: 26) are often plain, but there are also decorated examples.

Silhouette flower plates (*ryōka zara*) (Figure App 1.3: 27), in which the flower is laid out in silhouette around the inner rim of the dish, also have a floral decoration in the center of the plate. They are dated from the latter half of the fourteenth to the fifteenth century AD.

Straight-rim plates (*chokkō zara*) (Figure App 1.3: 28) have thick, straight rims, which are outward flaring. The glaze extends to the outer surface of the foot. Since this type is rare in the Shigemajō Enclosure of Nakijin, it is thought to be later than this deposit and to date to the latter half of the fifteenth to sixteenth centuries.

In addition to bowls and plates, which are relatively abundant, there are rare forms from the important centers of Katsuren and Nakijin. These include large presentation bottles for wine, narrow-necked vases, and very large serving plates from Longquan kilns.

Chinese Blue and White Wares

Mid-Fourteenth Century AD

Yuan blue and white wares (Figure App 1.4) are thought to have appeared in the second quarter of the fourteenth century AD. They are absent from the Sinan ship, dated to AD 1323, but pieces in the David Foundation dated to AD 1351 confirm that the process of manufacture was well understood by that date (Vainker 1991, 82). The Okinawa Islands have yielded an unusually large number of sherds of Yuan blue and white.

With few exceptions, Yuan blue and white in Okinawa is of the type termed "Zhizheng" by ceramic specialists. These are large, fine pieces with meticulous painting in dark blue, rather than small pieces with cursory pale blue decoration, although a jarlet of this latter type was found in Nakijin (see below). The largest number of sherds has been recovered from Shuri Gusuku (as mentioned in Chapter 9). The total amount of Yuan blue and white excavated in the Okinawa Islands is greater than the amount found in China and is roughly 60 percent of the amount found in all of South and Southwest Asia that Kamei could locate (Kamei 2009). This has led Kamei to propose that the Shuri capital played a key role in the distribution of these wares to Southeast Asia. Niijima (2008) reported that 76 percent of all Yuan blue and white found in Japan has been found in Okinawa, and Shuri Gusuku yielded more than 50 percent of all sherds found in Okinawa. The large plate or charger (*ban*) is exceptionally rare

App 1.4. Sherds of a blue and white vessel recovered from Nakijin Gusuku, dating from the latter half of the Yuan period. A blue and white wine jar (*shukai tsubo*), found in the *Shigemajō* Enclosure, Layers I, II, and IV. Reconstruction rendered by Kamei Meitoku and his colleagues. The recovered sherds are shown in darker lines. From Kin 2009, 154. Courtesy of Kin Seiki.

in China but forms 31 percent of the Okinawan assemblage, whereas stemmed cups are common in China but are rare (1 percent) in Okinawa.

Katsuren Gusuku, Okinawajima, has yielded about 250 sherds, a quantity said to be one of the highest from sites outside China. It is possible that within this total an unspecified number of sherds, mostly of jars and bottles, with blurred decoration caused by running of the cobalt are actually early Ming wares (Kamei and Chinen 1983, 41). The nine layers in Enclosure No. 1 of Katsuren Gusuku, the Main Enclosure termed the Honmaru, are 2 m deep. Layers I, III, V, VII, and IX are cultural. Yuan blue and white sherds came from layers III and V, but mostly from Layer III. In Katsuren Gusuku it appears that Yuan blue and white was found only in the Honmaru (Chinen 1980), indicating that it was reserved for persons of the highest rank.

Some twelve jars (*kan*) and five charger plates (*ban*) of Yuan blue and white were recovered from Nakijin, from the Main and Shigemajō Enclosures (see Figure App 1.4.) (Kin et al. 1983). Finds include a cover of a jar, a jar or vase, sherds of a vase of *gyokufu shunbin* (Chinese *yuhucun*) type, sherds of a large jar, and a jarlet with scrolled decoration and chrysanthemum flower. This type of jarlet, very popular in the Philippines, is the earliest example found in Japanese sites. These have been found in association with the following kinds of celadon bowls: Tong'an lotus petal bowls, bowls decorated with simplified lama-style petals and thunder pattern, and dishes with pairs of fishes in relief. The lip of the fish plate is everted and grooved, the exterior surface consists of ridged lotus petals, and the foot ring is unglazed. There are also a bowl with thick brownish green glaze and interior stamped decoration, and a shallow cup with molded petal decoration, both of a type found in the Sinan ship and Izena. Associated whitewares include bowls and plates with unglazed rims and unglazed feet. Some specimens resemble the Birosuku Type. Black-glazed *tenmoku* bowls and tea containers were also recovered.

Some of the Yuan blue and white sherds found at Nakijin Gusuku have three-toed dragon motifs and must have been official presents from China to the Okinawan tribute givers. (The highest imperial wares have dragons with five toes.) These presents are mentioned in the Ming document *Taizu shilu* according to Kin (1993, 351). There is no written record of Ryukyu kings transshipping such objects, which they received as presents from China. Apparently they treated them as special diplomatic gifts.

The style of the depiction of the dragons on one of the jars fron Nakijin Gusuku is similar to Style D identified by Lam (2012, 43), in which the scales are painted in outline with cobalt and are also modeled before firing and left unpainted (Kamei et al. 2007, 240–247). At the time of their production, in the mid- to late fourteenth century AD, blue and white ceramics were given as gifts to foreign dignitaries but were considered vulgar by the Chinese court, which preferred plain ceramics up to the early fifteenth century AD (Lam 2012).

The distribution of Yuan blue and white sherds in Nakijin was restricted almost exclusively to the Main Enclosure (Kin et al. 1983, 38), with a concentration around the main building (Seiden) (Niijima 2008). A few sherds discovered in the Shigemajō Enclosure are thought to have been discarded from the Main Enclosure (Okinawa Ken 1983, 4). The thickness of the sherds varies from 1 to 1.5 cm, indicating that they came from large vessels. Shibata et al. (2009) note that there is a change from the Yuan assemblage of jars and chargers to the early Ming assemblage of bottles, ewers, plates, plum vases (*meipin*), pouring vessels, and stemmed cups.

A large, splendid jar decorated with clouds and dragons and beast head handles was found in a grave in Yomitan, Okinawajima, by collectors (Kamei 1986a, 72, 73). There are four registers of decoration on this vessel. The top register of decoration shows a series of *nyoi* (head of priest's staff) motifs. The second register contains lama-style lotus petals. Two beast heads with open mouths serve as handles. On the top of the beasts' heads, in brownish glaze, is the character for king (Japanese *ō*). Judging from its context and a deliberately fashioned hole in

App 1.5. Ming blue and white bowls found in Nakijin Gusuku. (1) Bowl with everted rim, dating from the first half of the fifteenth to the beginning of the sixteenth century AD. (2, 3) Lotus Seed Type bowls, dating from the latter half of the fifteenth to the mid-sixteenth century AD. (4, 5) Bowls with everted lips, fifteenth to sixteenth centuries AD. (6, 7) Bowls produced in Zhangzhou, sixteenth century AD. The characters below Number 6 are a spurious reign date from the inner foot ring. (8, 9) Plates, late fifteenth to sixteenth century AD. Ceramic images selected from Kin 2009, 129–135. Courtesy of Kin Seiki.

its bottom, it appears to have been used as a burial jar for an elite person. From the reconstructed context of the find (the site has since been destroyed and the jar has disappeared!), the use of the jar as a burial container dates from the seventeenth century AD. From the fourteenth to seventeenth century AD the jar was apparently kept as an heirloom (Kamei and Miyagi 1994). Recently the remains of two imposing jars and three long-neck bottles have been found in Gushikawa Gusuku, Kumejima (Kumejima Chō Kyōiku Iinkai 2005; Niijima 2008).

Ming Blue and White

Seto et al. (2007) based their discussion on older typologies for the Japanese main islands, noting some divergent trends for the Ryukyus. The quantity of blue and white ceramics recovered is small in comparison to celadon and brownwares, with correspondingly fewer complete pieces or diagnostic bases, so that identification and typological grouping are challenging.

Bowls

EARLY HALF OF FIFTEENTH CENTURY TO EARLY HALF OF SIXTEENTH CENTURY AD

The first type of blue and white bowl, termed Group B 1 by Seto et al. (2007), is similar to Ōhashi's Type 1 (Ōhashi 1981). It has a strongly everted lip (*gaihan wan*), resembling the shape of Ming celadon bowls. Underglaze painted decoration consists of lions, intertwining floral patterns (*karakusamon*), and flower petals (Figure App 1.5: 1). The interior bottom of the bowl is decorated with an encircling line, inside which there may be a Chinese character, such as the character for abundance (*fuku*). A few examples have the thunder pattern on the exterior of the rim. Some examples have decoration of alternating lotus and intertwined floral pattern on the bowl exterior as well as a character or floral decoration in the interior bottom of the bowl. This type is dated to early Ming, roughly AD 1420 to 1500. In the Ryukyus it has been found at Zakimi, Okinawajima, thought to have been first built around AD 1420, and Yamabaru, Ishigakijima.

LATTER HALF OF FIFTEENTH CENTURY TO MID-SIXTEENTH CENTURY AD

The major type of the next period, Type II of Ōhashi and Group C of Seto et al. (2007), has the distinctive semiglobular shape of the seed pod of the lotus (Figure App 1.5: 2). Underglaze blue-painted decoration around the rim consists of a wave crest pattern, and on the body there may be arabesques, Sanskrit characters, or so-called leopard skin decoration (Figure App 1.5: 3). Ōhashi's Type IIa (Lotus Seed Pod Type a) is dated to AD 1463 to 1522; IIb, which features repeated geometric patterns on the exterior of the bowl or sometimes plant or floral motifs, dates from AD 1522 to 1566, the Ming Jiajing reign. Ōhashi's Type III also dates to the Jiajing reign. The bowl shape is distinctive, with a comparatively thick, high foot ring and sides that extend upward in a straight line from the base area (Figure App 1.5: 2). A variant, termed C1 by Seto et al. (2007), has an everted lip, a concave inner bottom, and an everted foot rim (Figure App 1.5: 4). It has distinctive decoration that may include human figures on the exterior body (Figure App 1.5: 5). Dating to the mid- to late sixteenth century AD, it has been found in the Main Enclosure of Nakijin Gusuku.

MID- TO LATE SIXTEENTH CENTURY, EARLY SEVENTEENTH CENTURY AD

Several types from Jingdezhen, including the painted landscape pattern, medallions, grouped clouds, and a band of upright banana leaves or the thunder pattern on the exterior, have been recovered at the Tenkaiji and Shuri Gusuku sites. Other types show motifs including phoenix and pine/bamboo/plum; these often have characters resembling reign marks inside the foot ring. There are also rough bowls from kilns in Zhangzhou, Fujian (Figure App 1.5: 6, 7).

Plates

FIFTEENTH TO SIXTEENTH CENTURIES AD

Various plates from local kilns in Jiangxi and Fujian Provinces found in the Ryukyus are difficult to organize into narrow chronological periods because few if any possess reign dates. Motifs include wave crests, upright banana leaves around the exterior base, lions and balls (Figure App 1.5: 8), arabesques, birds and flowers, human figures, and knotted cords. A rare variant is a low dish with a simplified landscape of rocks and plants, sometimes with a human figure in the interior bottom (Seto et al. 2007, 68) (Figure App 1.5: 8, 9).

Thai Ceramics

Kin (1991, 84) reported that sherds of Thai glazed ceramics (Figure App 1.6) have been recovered from eight sites, Nakijin being the richest.

In addition to the glazed ceramics, earthenware lids are particularly distinctive (Figure App 1.6: 4). By 1991, 116 specimens had been recorded from fifteen sites. Two variations in the handles are noted. The lids have been identified as palm sugar pot lids (Harper 1985, 292) or lids for brown-glazed wine jars (see below). The paste contains small distinctive black mineral inclusions.

Brown-glazed narrow-necked jars of small, medium, and large sizes are found as heirlooms and archaeological specimens (Figure App 1.6: 5–7). The paste also contains small black mineral inclusions, similar to the lids described above. On the small jars the ears run vertical to the body of the jar, whereas on the medium and large specimens they sit horizontally. Stoneware jars with four handles are said by Kin to have been containers for "fragrant flower wine" (1991, 99). Kin notes that Chinese Shaoxing wine is shipped in similar containers even today. The jars are

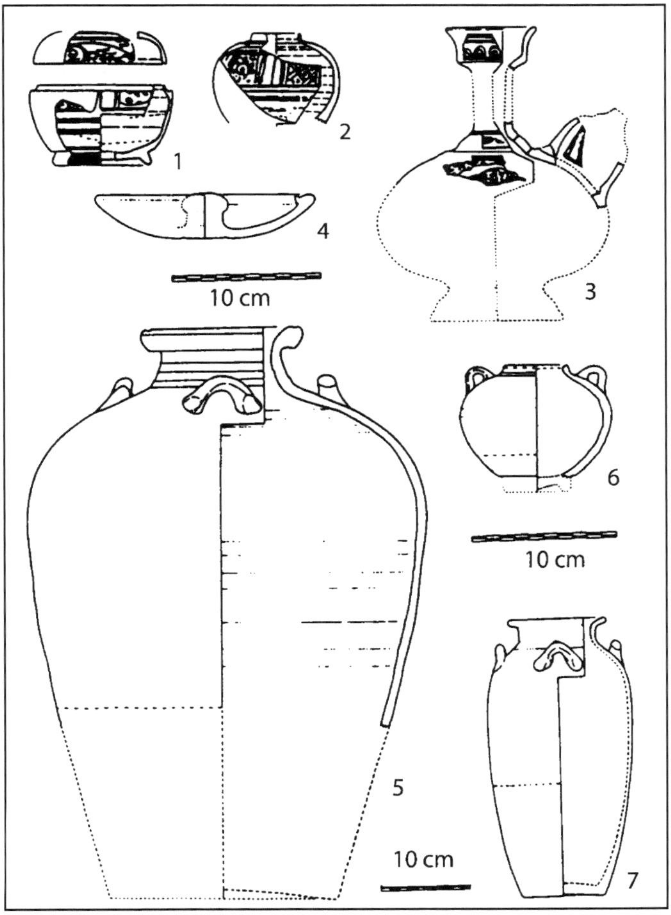

App 1.6. Thai (Siamese) wares found in Nakijin Gusuku. (1–3) Jars and pouring vessel (*kendi*) with iron painted decoration. (4) Earthenware lid. (5–7) Brown-glazed jars. From Kin 1993, 356. Courtesy of Kin Seiki.

rarely found in excavations, but heirloom pieces are well known. The small jars have four small "steps" on the neck, above the ears, a characteristic said to be peculiar to Thai jars. The glaze, which covers the inner upper surface and the exterior, is thick and black. Six large brown-glazed jars with four handles found in the Main Enclosure, Nakijin, had mouth diameters ranging from 11.5 cm to 14.1 cm; the unglazed postulated lids tended to be around 12 cm in diameter.

Wares with decoration painted in iron glaze, consisting of covered boxes, bowls, narrow-necked jars (*tsubo*), and a *kendi* spouted vessel, have been found in Nakijin, Urasoe, Aharen Furushima (Okinawajima), and Uemura (Iriomotejima) (Figure App 1.6: 1–3).

Yellowish glazed bowls and plates covered with a yellowish celadon like glaze, have small black inclusions in the paste, similar to the unglazed lids. A total of 17 rim sherds and 4 base sherds from bowls, and 5 rim sherds and 1 base sherd from plates have been found in Nakijin, along with two forms of bowls, one with everted lip (15 sherds) and one with concave form (2 sherds). The exposed area around the foot ring shows traces of iron oxide.

Thai wares found in the Ryukyus were produced in the kiln centers of Sri Satchanalai and Sukothai in Central Thailand, which are well known for their distinctive celadon, brownwares, iron painted wares, black- and brown-glazed storage jars, and unglazed storage jars. Large unglazed jars from the Maenam Noi River kilns are found on many sites. Earthenware jars from Haripunjaya (Lamphun) have also been found, as well as a few examples of low, wide-mouth earthenware jars from Ayuthaya (Okinawa Kenritsu Maizō 2005e, 84).

Vietnamese Ceramics

Vietnamese trade expanded in the late fourteenth century AD, possibly as a result of the Ming Ban, and reached its height in the fifteenth and sixteenth centuries AD. Brown states that only an estimated 2 to 4 percent of the fifteenth to sixteenth century AD foreign ceramics excavated in the Philippines are Vietnamese, while Thai wares comprise 20 to 40 percent of the total during the same time period (1988, 23). Kin reported that three types of Vietnamese ceramics have been recovered from four Okinawan *gusuku* sites: Nakijin, Goeku, Shuri, and Katsuren (1991, 84).

Sherds from approximately ten celadon bowls thought to be Vietnamese were found at Nakijin Gusuku. These have exterior decorations of lotus petals (Figure App 1.7: 3). The exposed base area is blackish, from the application of an iron slip. Some bowls have marks in the interior from stacking during firing. A thin, clear glaze extends from the inner base to the outer surface of the foot. A bowl with exterior lotus petal decoration and a dark brown "chocolate" exterior foot ring recovered from Goeku Gusuku has been identified by Kin as Vietnamese (1991, 87).

Fragments of a blue and white bottle with four registers of decoration and a wide-mouth jar were recovered from Nakijin Gusuku (Figure App 1.7: 6, 7). The jar is also decorated in four registers; from the top: thunder pattern, panels with alternating wave and plant motifs, dragon motif, and thinly outlined lama-style lotus petals. Bowls, found at Nakijin Gusuku and Katsuren Gusuku, have grayish, fine-textured bodies.

A fragment of an overglaze enamel lid from a covered box, and the lower part

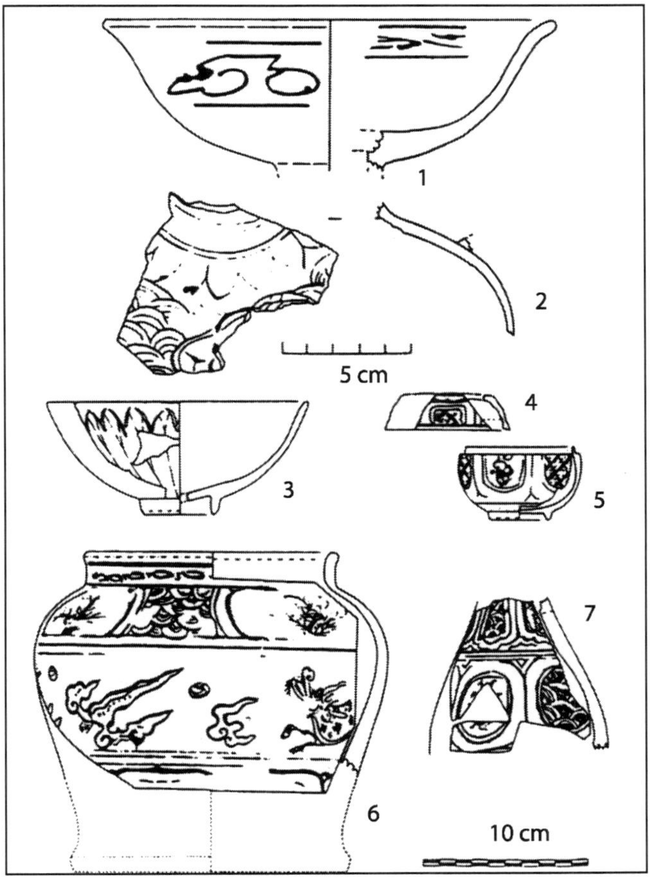

App 1.7. Vietnamese wares found in Okinawan sites. (1, 2) Blue and white vessels from Katsuren Gusuku. (3) Celadon bowl from Nakijin Gusuku. (4, 5) Overglaze red enamel decorated box from Nakijin Gusuku. (6, 7) Blue and white jar from Nakijin Gusuku. From Kin 1993. Courtesy of Kin Seiki.

of a covered box were found in Nakijin (Figure App 1.7: 4–5), as well as fragments of a bowl with overglaze painting of arabesques and intertwining floral patterns.

The Thai and Vietnamese ceramics were found in contexts dating to the fifteenth and sixteenth centuries AD, based on associated Chinese ceramics. At the Main Enclosure, Nakijin Gusuku, two of the unglazed lids were found in the lower part of Layer II, which could be dated as early as the latter half of the fourteenth century AD (Kin 1991, 98). Since Thai and Vietnamese sherds may be mixed with other trade ceramics in Okinawan assemblages, Kin notes that a reexamination of collections may be fruitful. Subsequent to Kin's pioneering work, recent excavations have produced a large variety of Vietnamese ceramics. Excavations of the Nikaiden in Shuri Gusuku produced some 545 sherds, the largest amount found thus far in Okinawa and all of Japan. They were mostly of blue and white ware (Okinawa Kenritsu Maizō 2005e, 74).

Lead-Glazed South Chinese Three-Color Wares

South Chinese Three-Color Wares (Japanese Kanan Sansai, Chinese Huanan Sancai) (Figure App 1.8) are among the most interesting exotic ceramics in Ryukyu and Kyushu because of their pattern of distribution and its implications (Kamei 1986b, 339–354). Distinctive from Fahua three-colored wares made in Shanxi, northern China, they are small objects such as incense containers and water droppers with a soft body and glaze that peels off rather easily. Water droppers come in a large variety of forms such as birds, phoenix, dragon, and lobster, the same types of objects being found in the Philippines and Indonesia. Their dating may be as late as the fifteenth to sixteenth centuries AD; Kamei postulates that they were made around the middle of the fifteenth century and imported into Okinawa at that time but were imported into Japan in the sixteenth century AD. One hundred sherds have been found inside Shuri Gusuku in prewar excavations of an area believed to have been reserved for religious activities (see Chapter 9), and they have been recovered in small quantities from other sites throughout the Ryukyus.

Brownwares

Kin has identified early brownwares (Figure App 1.9) that occur in association with whitewares such as bowls with thickened lips and comb-marked celadon bowls (1989, 13–15). All of these wares are rare. This assemblage has been identified from early sites: Atta Shellmound, Okinawa; Ōdomaribama, Hateruma; Shinzatomura (East), Taketomijima; and Birosuku, Ishigakijima. Interestingly, three of these sites are in Yaeyama.

App 1.8. Lead-glazed South Chinese Three-Color Ware recovered from the Kyōnouchi Area, Shuri Gusuku. From Itō and Kamakura 1937, figures 24 and 25. Intact bird-shape water droppers are about 13 cm in height.

Narrow-necked jars (*tsubo*) (Figure App 1.9: 1–4) may have been made in Guangdong, in kilns such as Taoyuangang, Foshan. The *tsubo* forms have been termed Namban or Luzon jars. The most usual form has four small handles mounted horizontally. The lip is thickened, and the paste has granules of white and black sand. The glaze, which peels from the body, extends from the inside of the neck of the jar to the outer area of the foot. Kamei (1986a, 45) dates these jars to the thirteenth century AD but states that they could be as late as the fourteenth century AD.

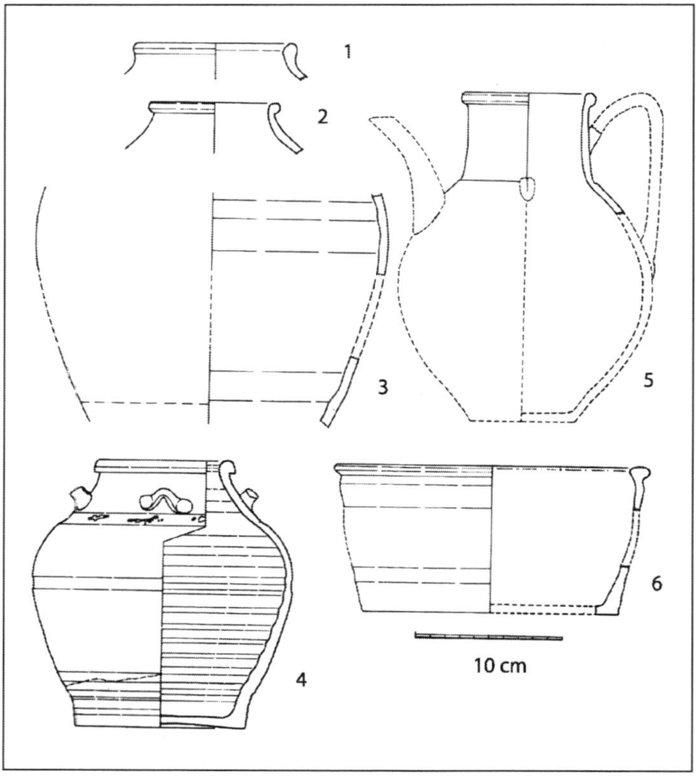

App 1.9. Early brown-glazed ware, twelfth to thirteenth centuries AD. (1) Atta Shellmound, Okinawajima. (2, 5, 6) Shinzatomura East Site, Taketomijima. (3) Ōdomaribama Shellmound, Haterumajima. (4) Shinzatomura West Site, Taketomijima. From Kin 1989, 14. Courtesy of Kin Seiki.

Ewers have been found on a few sites (Figure App 1.9: 5). An example from Shinzatomura East Layer II, has a mouth diameter of 10 cm and a height of 25 cm. The glaze is blackish.

A single example of a wide-mouth jar was found in the Shinzatomura East Site (Figure App 1.9: 6). It has a T-shaped rim profile (thickened on both the inside and the outside). The flat lip extends horizontally to both the inside and the outside of the vessel. This same site yielded a brownware jar sherd stamped with characters in Phags-Pa (Mongol) script, which was used in China from AD 1272 (Ishigaki Shi Sōmubu 2009a, 27).

Later brownwares of the Yuan and Ming dynasties are very common on Ryukyu sites but are in need of typological organization. A precise chronology of types dating to the fifteenth and sixteenth centuries AD is not clear at this time.

By comparing Ryukyu finds with those from Dazaifu, Seto et al. (2007, 68–70) found that brownwares dated before the first half of the fourteenth century AD (using associated celadon sherds) were relatively rare. From the late fourteenth century, storage jars increase suddenly, but shredding bowls and ewers are also found. The jars are often the most common of all ceramic finds since the large vessels break into many small body sherds. Seto et al. (ibid.) classified finds from the late fourteenth to seventeenth centuries into six types, but the relative positions of these types is not precise. Originally containers of shipped goods such as dried food, wine, or sugar, the large jars were recycled for domestic use including water storage.

Conclusions

From the eleventh to fourteenth centuries AD, Chinese ceramics reaching the Ryukyus were plates and bowls for serving food. Storage containers were made of local earthenware or *kamuiyaki* stoneware. In the fifteenth and sixteenth centuries AD, the range of Chinese wares was expanded to include tea, wine, and possibly dried or preserved food containers as well as Thai wine containers. Luxury items included Chinese iron-glazed tea bowls, tea containers, small containers for medicine and possibly cosmetics, as well as food graters, incense burners, and some writing utensils such as water droppers.

Appendix 2

The Successive Rulers of the Chūzan or Ryukyu Kingdom

(from Sakamaki 1963, 288)

The Shunten Dynasty

Shunten 舜天 (AD 1187–1237)
Shunba Junki 舜馬順熙 (AD 1238–1248)
Gihon 義本 (AD 1249–1259)

The Eiso Dynasty

Eiso 英祖 (AD 1260–1299)
Taisei 大成 (AD 1300–1308)
Eiji 英慈 (AD 1309–1313)
Tamagusuku 玉城 (AD 1314–1336)
Sei-I 西威 (AD 1337–1349)

The Satto Dynasty

Satto 察度 (AD 1350–1395)
Bunei 武寧 (AD 1396–1405)

The Shō Shishō Dynasty

Shō Shishō 尚思紹 (AD 1406–1421)
Shō Hashi 尚巴志 (AD 1422–1439)
Shō Chu 尚忠 (AD 1440–1444)
Shō Shitatsu 尚志達 (AD 1445–1449)
Shō Kinpuku 尚金福 (AD 1450–1453)
Shō Taikyū 尚泰久 (AD 1454–1460)
Shō Toku 尚徳 (AD 1461–1469)

The Shō En Dynasty

Shō En 尚圓 (AD 1470–1476)
Shō Sen-I 尚宣威 (AD 1477)
Shō Shin 尚真 (AD 1477–1526)
Shō Sei 尚清 (AD 1527–1555)
Shō Gen 尚元 (AD 1556–1572)
Shō Ei 尚永 (AD 1573–1588)
Shō Nei 尚寧 (AD 1589–1620)
Shō Hō 尚豐 (AD 1621–1640)
Shō Ken 尚賢 (AD 1641–1647)
Shō Shitsu 尚質 (AD 1648–1668)

Shō Tei 尚貞 (AD 1669–1709)
Shō Eki 尚益 (AD 1710–1712)
Shō Kei 尚敬 (AD 1713–1751)
Shō Boku 尚穆 (AD 1752–1794)
Shō On 尚温 (AD 1795–1802)
Shō Sei 尚成 (AD 1803)
Shō Kō 尚 こう (AD 1804–1828)
Shō Iku 尚育 (AD 1829–1847)
Shō Tai 尚泰 (AD 1848–1879)

Glossary

Japanese and Chinese Characters for Okinawan and Coastal Chinese Site Names, Japanese Authors' Names, and Ceramic and Coin Names

Adachi Noboru 安達登
Ahagon 阿波根
Aharen Furushima 阿波連古島
akae 赤絵
Akahoya アカホヤ
Akajangā アカジャンガアー
Akakina Gusuku 赤木名城
Akamine Shinya 赤嶺信哉
Amangusuku 天城
Amitori 網取
Anezaki Tomoko 姉崎智子
Ankei Takako 安渓貴子
Ankei Yūji 安渓遊地
Ankoku 安国
Anzai Eisuke 安斎英介
Ara 阿良
Arafu アラフ
Aragusuku Shichabaru 新城下原
Arakaki Tsutomu 新垣力
Arata Keisuke 荒田敬介
Arita 有田
Asato Kazumi 安里和美
Asato Shijun 安里嗣淳
Asato Susumu 安里進
atsude chokkō wan 厚手直口碗
Atta 熱田
Azama Mitsuru 安座間充
Azamabaru 安座間原
Baba Hisao 馬場悠男
bajōhai 馬上杯
ban 盤
Baxiandong 八仙洞
Beinan 卑南
Benzaitendō 弁財天堂
Betunamu ベトナム
bin 瓶
Birosuku ビロスク
Birosuku Type ビロスク タイプ
Bise 備瀬
Bizen 備前
Bora Motojima 保良元島
Bugeidō 武芸堂
Byōdōin 平等院
chaire 茶入

Chiarabaru 地荒原
Chida Hiroyuki 千田寛之
Chijifuchā チジフチャー
China Teijun 知名定順
China Teikan 知名定寛
Chinen Isamu 知念勇
Chinsenmon 沈線文
chokkō wan 直口碗
chokkō zara 直口皿
Chūzan Tsūhō 中山通寶
Cizao 磁灶
Dabenkeng 大坌坑
dai gōsu 大合子
Danjō Hiroshi 壇上寛
Dazaifu 太宰府
Dehua 德化
Dōgome Hideto 堂込秀人
Doi Naomi 土井直美
Doigahama 土井ガ浜
Ebihara Ippei 蛯原一平
Egami Tomoko 江上朝幸
Eiraku Tsūhō 永楽通寶
Enkakuji 円覚寺
Enkanchi 円鏡 池
Fengtian 丰田
Fensa フエンサ
Fensa Lower Layer フエンサ下層
Fujimoto Hideo 藤本英夫
Fujita Yūki 藤田祐樹
Fukidashibaru 吹出原
fukuromono 袋物
Funaura 船浦
Furusutobaru フルスト原
Furuzamami 古座間味
Fushan 福山
futa 蓋
Fuwaganeku フワガネク
gaihan wan 外反碗
gaihan zara 外反皿
Gaja 我謝
gashitsu doki 瓦質土器
Goeku 越来
Gohezu ゴヘズ
Gokurakuji 極楽寺
gosai 五彩
Goshusen 五銖銭
gōsu 合子
Gotō Masahiko 後藤雅彦
Goya Yoshikatsu 呉屋義勝
Gu Shi 顾氏
Gushibaru 具志原
Gushichan 具志頭
Gushikawa Gusuku 具志川城
Gushikawajima 具志川島
Gushiken 具志堅
Gusukudake 城嶽
Gusuku Site Group 城遺跡群
Gusuku Udun 城御殿
gyokufu shunbin (Chinese *yuhucunping*) 玉壷春瓶
hachi 鉢
hai 杯
Haicheng 海城
hajiki 土師器
Hakata 博多
hakuji 白磁
Hamakita 浜北
Hamayabaru 浜屋原
Hanagusuku Furushima 花城古島
Hanasuku 花城

Handa Motoko 半田素子
Haneji Chōshū 羽地朝秀
hannera ハンネラ
Hanta 半田
Hanta Guchi 半田口
Harunari Hideji 春成秀爾
Hashiguchi Wataru 橋口亘
Hashimoto Hisakazu 橋本久和
Hashimoto Makio 橋本真紀夫
Hashimoto Mika 橋本美佳
Hashimoto Yū 橋本雄
Hateruma Eikichi 波照間永吉
hei 瓶
Heian Kyō 平安京
herabori 箆彫り
Heshikiya Tōbaru 平敷屋トウバル
Higa Naoki 比嘉尚輝
Higa Yoshimori 比嘉賀盛
Higashi 東
Hirata Yukio 平田幸男
Hirota 広田
Hisamatsu 久松
hisuiyū 翡翠釉
Hokama Shuzen 外間守善
Hokuden 北殿
Hōshin Mon 奉神門
Hyakuna 百名
Hyōgo Tsu 兵庫津
Ibaruma 伊原間
Ichijōdani 一条谷
Ichijōin 一条院
Ichiki 市来
Ichimura Takao 市村高男
Iha 伊波
Iha Fuyū 伊波普猷
Ihara Hiroshi 伊原弘
Ijū Tsutomu 伊従勉
Ikeda Yoshifumi 池田榮文
Ikehata Kōichi 池畑耕一
Imamura Mineo 今村峰雄
Imari 伊万里
Inafuku 稲福
Inamura Kenpu 稲村賢敷
Inutabu 犬田部
Iraha Higashi 伊良波東
Ireibaru 伊礼原
Iri no Azana 西のアザナ
iroe 色絵
Isamaebaru 伊佐前原
Ishidō Kazuhiro 石堂和博
Ishigaki 石垣
Ishii Ryūta 石井龍太
Ishimaru Eriko 石丸恵利子
Ishioka Tomotake 石岡智武
Issō 一湊
Itō Chūta 伊藤忠太
Itō Kei 伊藤圭
Itō Shinji 伊藤真二
Itō Yōji 伊藤陽司
Itoigawa 糸魚川
Itokazu 糸数
Izumi 泉
Izumi Sō 泉水奏
Izumizaki 泉崎
Jingdezhen 景德镇
jōkonmon 条痕文
Kadabaru カダ原
Kadena Sōtoku 嘉手納宗徳
Kagomemon 籠目文
Kaifu Yōsuke 海部陽介

Kaigen Tsūhō 開元通寶
Kaijibama カイジ浜
Kajō 嘉門
kakkamon wan 劃花文碗
Kakoinohara 栫ノ原
Kamakura Yoshitarō 鎌倉芳太郎
Kame 甕
Kamei Meitoku 亀井明徳
Kamimura Toshio 上村俊雄
Kamino 上野
Kamiya Kōshō 神谷厚昭
Kamuiyaki カムイヤキ
kan 観
Kan Hironobu 菅浩伸
Kanazawa Yō 金沢陽
Kaneku 兼久
Kanenokuma 金の隈
Kankai Mon 歓会門
Kanna 漢那
Karadake Higashi 嘉良嶽東
karakusamon 唐草文
Karatsu 唐津
Kasari 笠利
Katagiri Chiaki 片桐千亜紀
katatsukuri renbenmon wan 型造り連弁文碗
Katō Shinpei 加藤晋平
Katoku 嘉徳
Katsuren Gusuku 勝連城
katsuyū 褐釉
Kawana Toshio 河名俊男
Kawashima Yūji 川島由次
Kayauchibanta カヤウチバンタ
Kerama 慶良間
ketsunyū kōdai zara 抉入高台皿
Kigahama キガ浜
Kijoka 喜如嘉
Kikai 喜界
Kimura Masa'aki 木村政昭
Kin Seiki 金武正紀
Kinen 喜念
Kinen Tsūhō 金圓通寶
Kinen Uehara 喜念上原
kin gyoku man dō 金玉萬堂
Kinjō Kamenobu 金城亀信
Kinjō Seitoku 金城正篤
Kinoshita Naoko 木下尚子
Kinoshita Shūkai 木下秋海
kinuta 砧
Kishikawa 岸川
Kishimoto Yoshihiko 岸本義彦
Kisshū 吉州
Kitahara 北原
Kiyūna Tōbaru Nubataki 喜友名東原ヌバタキ
Kizaki Kōshirō 木崎甲子郎
Kobashigawa Takeshi 小橋川剛
Kobayashi Ryūta 小林竜太
Kobiki Mon 木曳門
Kōbu Tsūhō 洪武通寶
Kogachibaru 古我地原
Kogusuku 古城
Kohane コハネ
Kokubu Naoichi 国分直一
kokuyū 黒釉
Komi 古見
Kominato Fuwaganeku 古湊フワガネク
Kōmoto Masayuki 甲元真之
kōnan sansai 江南三彩

Konjikidō 金色堂
Kōno Reiko 河野礼子
Kouribaru 古宇利原
kōro 香炉
Koshidake 腰岳
Kozono 小園
Kōzu 神津
Kubirehirasoko くびれ平底
Kubo Tomoyasu 久保智廣
kuchi ori zara 口折皿
kuchihage wan 口禿碗
kuchihage zara 口禿皿
Kudō Yūichirō 工藤雄一郎
Kumemura 久米村
Kuninakagusuku Utaki 国中城御嶽
Kunindō クニンドー
Kuniyoshi Kazuo 国吉和夫
Kurakisaki 倉木崎
Kuroda Tomio 黒田登美雄
Kurokawa 黒川
Kuroshio 黒潮
Kurozumi Taiji 黒住耐二
Kusatobaru 久里原
kushigakimon wan 櫛描文碗
kushigakimon zara 櫛描文皿
Kushikanekubaru 後兼久原
Kuwabara Jitsuzō 桑原隲蔵
Kuwahata Mitsuhiro 桑畑光博
Kuwahata Takeshi 桑波田武志
Kyōnouchi 京の内
Kyūkei Mon 久慶門
Lan Yu 兰屿
Lelang 乐浪
Lianzhang Xian 连江县
Longquan 龙泉
Lü Dao 录岛
Madama 真玉
Maehata 前畑
Maehira Fusa'aki 真栄平房昭
Maezato 真栄里
Makino Kiyoshi 牧野清
Makishi Yōko 真喜志瑤子
Makubaru 真久原
Manabe Aya 眞邉彩
Mashiki Ishikawa 真志喜石川
Matsubara Satoshi 松原哲志
Matsuda Tom'o 松田朝雄
Matsunoto マツノト
Matsushita Takayuki 松下孝幸
Mēbaru 前原
meipin 梅瓶
Meitōsen 明刀銭
Menda 門田
Mie Gusuku 三重城
Migusuku 見城
Mikkabi 三カ日
mimi 耳
Minatogawa 港川
Minō 美濃
Minqing Xian 闽清县
Miyagi Atsumasa 宮城篤正
Miyagi Eishō 宮城栄昌
Miyagi Hiroki 宮城弘樹
MiyashitaTakahiro 宮下孝浩
Miyazato Eiki 宮里栄輝
Miyazato Shinyū 宮里信勇
Miyazato Suehiro 宮里末廣
Mizoguchi Yūji 溝口優司
Momenbaru 木綿原

Momojanabaka 百按司墓
Morikawabaru 森川原
Morimoto Asako 森本朝子
Morimoto Isao 盛本勳
Morimura Ken'ichi 森村健一
Morita Taiju 森田大樹
Moro'oka 諸岡
Mottainimatsu 持躰松
Mukai Wataru 向井亙
mukō renbenmon wan 無鎬連弁文碗
mumon gaihan wan 無文外反碗
mumon rinka wan 無文輪花碗
Murai Shōsuke 村井章介
Muraoka Makoto 村岡誠
Murokawa 室川
Nagabaka 長墓
Nagabaka Fūsōbo 長墓風葬墓
Nagahama Tatsuki 長濱健起
Nagamazuku 長間底
Nagarabaru ナガラ原
Nagarabaru Higashi ナガラ原東
Nagarabaru Nishi ナガラ原西
Nagura 名蔵
naiwan zara 内彎皿
Najima (Midorikawa) Yayoi 名島（緑川）弥生
Naka Shōhachirō 名嘉正八郎
Nakadomari 仲泊
Nakagusuku 中城
Nakagusuku Udun 中城御殿
Nakahara 仲原
Nakama Kushibaru 仲間後原
Nakama Gishō 名嘉真宜勝
Nakamamura 仲間村
Nakamori 中森
Nakamori Ton 仲盛敦
Nakamura Ken 中村健
Nakanohama ナカの浜
Nakasone Motomu 仲宗根求
Nakata Takashi 中田高
Nakaura 中浦
Nakayama Kiyomi 中山清美
Nakaza Hisayoshi 仲座久宜
Nakazato Toshikatsu 中里尋克
Nakijin Gusuku 今帰仁城
Nanden 南殿
Nanzenji 南禅寺
Nazakibaru 那崎原
Nema Nishizato 根間西里
Nihon Kan 日本館
Niijima Natsuko 新島奈津子
Nikaiden 二階殿
Niō Kōji 仁王浩司
Nishi Nagahama 西長浜
Nishime Shō 西銘章
Nishimoto Toyohiro 西本豊弘
Nitta Jūsei 新田重清
Noguni 野国
Nogusuku 野城
Nozaki Takashi 野崎拓司
Obata Hiroki 小畑弘己
Oda Shizuo 小田静夫
Ōdomaribama 大泊浜
Ōgon Odon 黄金御殿
Ōhama Eisen 大濱永亘
Ōhara 大原
Ōhashi Kōji 大橋康二
Okada Teruo 岡田輝雄
Oki Gū Rinkaiji 沖宮臨海寺

Ōkubo Kōji 大久保浩二
Omonawa Zentei 面縄前庭
Omono Gusuku 御物城
Ōnishi Tomokazu 大西智和
Ono Masatoshi 小野正敏
Ono Rintarō 小野林太郎
Onotsu 小野津
Ōnuki Shizuo 大貫静夫
oshigata mon 押し形文
Ōshiro Hideko 大城秀子
Ōshiro Hiroe 大城広江
Ōshiro Kei 大城慧
Ōta Yukio 大田由起夫
Ōtomo 大友
Ouchibaru (Ūchibaru) 御内原
Ouchibaru Shoin 御内原書院
Ōufu オウフ
Ōwada Tomari 大和田泊
Oyadomari 親泊
Ōyama 大山
Ōyama Shunsui 大山春翠
Oyamise 親見世
Ōzato Gusuku 大里城
Ōzawa Masaki 大澤正己
Ozawa Tomo'o 小澤智生
Panari パナリ
Pinishi 平西
Pinza Abu ピンザアブ
Pukou 浦口
Pyutta ピュウッタ
Qilin 麒麟
Quannan 泉南
Quanzhou 泉洲
raimontai wan 雷文帯碗
ruriyū 瑠璃釉
ryōka zara 陵花皿
ryokuyū 緑釉
Ryūfukuji 龍福寺
ryūtaimon 隆帯文
Ryūtan 龍潭
Sachihijah 崎樋川
Saidaiji 西大寺
Saigō Nobutsuna 西郷信綱
Sakai 堺
Sakieda Akasaki 崎枝赤崎
Sakishima 先島
Sakiyama Utaki 崎山嶽
Sanhe 三和
sansai 三彩
sara 皿
Sashiki 佐敷
Sashiki Gusuku 佐敷城
Satō Takao 佐藤孝雄
Satō Yōichirō 佐藤洋一郎
Seiden 正殿
seihakuji 清白磁
seiji 青磁
Sekiguchi Kōji 関口広次
Sekisei 石西
Sekō Tsūhō 世高通寶
senkokusai renbenmon wan 線刻細連弁文碗
Seto 瀬戸
Seto Tetsuya 瀬戸哲也
Shibata Keiko 柴田佳子
Shigemajō 志慶間門
Shimabukuro Yō 島袋洋
Shimabukuro Harumi 島袋春美
Shimabukuro Rieko 島袋利恵子
Shimajiri 島尻

Shimajiri Katsutarō 島尻勝太郎
Shimizu 清水
Shimo Yamada 下山田
Shimoji Kazuhiro 下地和宏
Shimoji Suguru 下地傑
Shimoji Yasuhiro 下地安広
Shimotabaru 下田原
Shīnagusuku シイナグスク
Shinbyōden 寝廟殿
Shinoda Ken'ichi 篠田謙一
shinogi renbenmon wan 鎬連弁文碗
Shinugudō シヌグ堂
Shinzato Akito 新里亮人
Shinzato Takayuki 新里貴之
Shinzatomura 新里村
Shiraho Saonetabaru 白保竿根田原
Shiroma Hajime 城間肇
Shitabaru 下原
Shītachi 岩立
Shitadaru シタダル
Shoin 書院
shukai tsubo 酒会壷
Shurei no Mon 守礼の門
Shuri Gusuku 首里城
Shurimori Utaki 首里森嶽
Sobata 曽畑
Soedō 添道
Sōgō Guraundo 総合グラウンド
sometsuke 染付
Sonai 祖納
Sonohyan Utaki 園比屋武御嶽
sueki 須恵器
suichū 水注
Suigetsu 水月
Sumida Naotoshi 澄田直敏
Sumiya 住屋
Sumiyoshi 住吉
Sunagawa Sachio 砂川幸夫
Sunkuroku スンクロク
suribachi 擂鉢
Sushigā 尻川
Suzuki Kimio 鈴木公雄
Suzuki Yasutami 鈴木靖民
Tai Katsuyū タイ褐釉
Taise Tsūhō 大世通寶
Takahashi Masa'aki 高橋昌明
Takahashi Yasuo 高橋康夫
Takakura Hiroaki 高倉洋彰
Takamine 高峰
Takamiya Hiroe 高宮廣衛
Takamiya Hiroto 高宮広土
Takanashi Osamu 高梨修
Takara Kurayoshi 高良倉吉
Takashima Hiroyuki 高島裕之
Takayama, Jun 高山純
Takayosōridun 高よそうり殿
tamafuchi gaihan wan 玉縁外板碗
tamafuchi wan 玉縁碗
Tamaki Chōken 玉城朝健
Tamaki Nobuhiko 玉城順彦
Tamashiro Yasushi 玉城靖
Tama Udun 玉御殿
Tana Masayuki 田名真之
Tanaka Katsuko 田中克子
Taneishi Yū 種石悠
tanhan wan 端反碗
Taniguchi Sakae 谷口榮
Taoyuangang 逃源崗

Tateiwa 立岩
Tawada Shinjun 多和田真淳
Tenkaiji 天海寺
tenmoku 天目
Tennōji 天王侍
Tenzan Ryō 天山陵
Tezuka Naoki 手塚直樹
Tian Keng, Pinghe Xian 田坑平和县
Tōbaru 塔原
Todoroki 轟
Toguchi Agaribaru 度具知東原
Toguchi Makoto 度久地真
Tōgurubama トウグル浜
Tōizumi Takeji 樋泉岳二
Tokuda Yukino 徳田有希乃
Tōma Kenji 東間研治
Tōma Shi'ichi 当眞嗣一
Tomachin トマチン
Tomari 泊
Tomiyama Kazuyuki 豊見山和行
Tomuru トムル
tōmyōzara 燈明皿
Tonakijima 渡名喜島
Tong'an 同安
Tosaminato 十三港
Tōyama Agaribaru 当山東原
Tōyama Masanao 当山昌直
Toyomioya 豊見親
tsubo 壷
Tsuboya 壷屋
Tsuchihama Yanya 土浜イヤンヤ
Tsumegata 爪形
Tsumesho 詰所
Tsuzuki Shin'ichirō 續伸一郎
Ueda Hideo 上田秀夫
Ueda Kei'ichi 上田圭一
Uegusuku 宇江城
Uehara Nūribaru 上原濡原
Uehara Shizuka 上原静
Uenoyama 上の山
Uezato Takashi 上里隆史
Uezu Yasuyuki 上江洲安亨
Ufudōbaru 大堂原
Ufuniku ウフニク
Ufutōbaru 大当原
Uganhirā Hoppō ウガンヒラア ホッポウ
Uganyama 拝山
Ujiie Hiroshi 氏家宏
Uken 宇堅
Unā 御庭
Urasoebaru 浦添原
Urasoe Gusuku 浦添城
Urasoe Yōdore 浦添ようどれ
Urasoko 浦底
Uruma ウルマ
Ushikawa 牛川
Ushuku 宇宿
usude chokkō wan 薄手直口碗
usude gaihan zara 薄手外反皿
Uzahama 宇座浜
Uzawa Kazuhiro 鵜澤和宏
Wada Hisanori 和田久徳
Wakasa 若狭
Wakuta 湧田
wan 碗
Watarichi Mura 渡地村
Yabuchi 屋部地
Yabumaedabaru 屋部前田原

Yahagi Kenji 矢作健二
Yajiyāgama ヤジヤーガマ
Yamabaru 山原
Yamada Gusuku 山田城
Yamada Hanta 山田ハンタ
Yamaguchi Tōru 山口徹
Yamamoto Masa'aki 山本正昭
Yamamoto Nobuo 山本信夫
Yamanokuchi 山の口
Yamashita Chō 山下町
Yamauchi Shinji 山内晋次
Yamazaki Shinji 山崎真治
Yamazato Jun'ichi 山里純一
Yan 燕
Yanagihara Toshiaki 柳原敏昭
Yarazamori Gusuku 屋良座森城
Yogi Tachinori 与儀達憲
Yokomine 横峯
Yoko'o Masaki 横尾昌樹
Yokota Kenjirō 横田賢二郎
Yokoyama Kōichi 横山浩一
Yōmisaki 用見崎
Yoneda Minoru 米田穣
Yoseman 寄満
Yoshinari Naoki 吉成直樹
Yoshinogari 吉野ガ里
Yotsuyanagi Kashō 四柳嘉彰
yue 越
Yuegang 月港
yuhucun 玉壷春
zōgan seiji 象眼青磁
zōgan tōshitsu 象眼陶質
Zuisen Mon 瑞泉門
Zukeran Chōsei 瑞慶覧朝盛

References Cited

In citations in the text, long names of institutional authors of government documents are abbreviated. The form used in the text is shown in square brackets, whereas the whole name (including the part in brackets) is used in the reference list below.

[Amagi Chō] Kyōiku Iinkai
[Amami Shi] Kyōiku Iinkai
[Chatan Chō] Kyōiku Iinkai
[EAC] Kabushiki Kaisha Ieishi
[Education Commission] of Okinawa Prefecture
[Ginowan Shi] Kyōiku Iinkai
[Hirara Shi] Kyōiku Iinkai
[Hirota Iseki] Gakujutsu Chōsa Kenkyūkai
[Ie Son] Kyōiku Iinkai
[Ishigaki Shi] Kyōiku Iinkai
[Ishigaki Shiritsu] Yaeyama Hakubutsukan
[Ishigaki Shi Sōmubu] Shishi Henshūshitsu
[Kagoshima Ken Amagi Chō] Kyōiku Iinkai
[Kagoshima Ken] Uken Son Kyōiku Iinkai
[Kikai Chō] Kyōiku Iinkai
[Kinpo Chō] Kyōiku Iinkai
[Kinpo Chō Rekishi] Shinpojiumu Jikkōinkai
[Miyakojima Shi] Kyōiku Iinkai
[Naha Shi] Kyōiku Iinkai Bunka Ka
[Nakijin Son] Kyōiku Iinkai
[Okinawa Ken Gushikawa Shi] Kyōiku Iinkai

[Okinawa Ken Hirara Shi] Kyōiku Iinkai
[Okinawa Ken] Kyōiku Iinkai
[Okinawa Ken Nakijin Son] Kyōiku Iinkai
[Okinawa Kenritsu Hakubutsukan] Bijutsukan
[Okinawa Kenritsu Maizō] Bunkazai Sentā
[Okinawa Kenritsu Toshokan] Shiryō Henshūshitsu
[Urasoe Shi] Kyōiku Iinkai
[Yomitan Son] Kyōiku Iinkai
[Yonagusuku Son] Kyōiku Iinkai
[Zaidan] Hōjin Okinawa Ken Bunka Shinkōkai

Abu-Lughod, J. 1989. *Before European Hegemony: The World System A.D. 1250*. New York: Oxford University Press.

Adhikari, P., Fujio Kumon, and Kiyoshi Kawajiri. 2002. Holocene climate variability as deduced from the organic carbon and diatom records in the sediments of Lake Aoki, Central Japan. *Journal of the Geological Society of Japan* 108 (4): 249–265.

Amagi Chō Kyōiku Iinkai. 1988. *Tōbaru* Iseki*: Amagi Chō bunkazai chōsa hōkokusho dai I shu* (The Tōbaru Site: report no. 1 of cultural properties in Amagi Chō). Amagi Chō (Tokunoshima): Amagi Chō Kyōiku Iinkai.

Amami Shi Kyōiku Iinkai. 2008. *Hirujō (Gusuku) hakkutsu hōkokusho* (Report of the excavation of Hiru Castle [Gusuku]). Amami Shi: Amami Shi Kyōiku Iinkai.

———. 2009a. *Akakina Gusuku*. Amami Shi: Amami Shi Kyōiku Iinkai.

———. 2009b. *Amami Shi Kasari Chō Gusuku shōsai bunpu chōsa hōkokusho* (Report of detailed site survey of Gusuku in Kasari Chō, Amami City). Amami Shi: Amami Shi Kyōiku Iinkai.

Anderson, A. 2004. Islands of ambivalence. In *Voyages of Discovery: The Archaeology of Islands*, ed. S. M. Fitzgerald, pp. 252–73. Westport, CT: Praeger.

———. 2005. Crossing the Luzon Strait: archaeological chronology in the Batanes Islands, Philippines and the regional sequence of Neolithic dispersal. *Journal of Austronesian Studies* 1 (2): 25–45.

Ankei Takako. 2011. Sotetsu no kita michi (The routes by which cycad palms arrived). In *Amami Okinawa kenkyūshi shiryō shūsei* (Collection of materials: environmental history of Amami Okinawa), ed. Ankei Yūji and Tōyama Masanao, pp. 363–404. Kagoshima: Nanpō Shinsha.

Ankei Yūji. 2007. *Iriomote no nōkō bunka: kaiyō no michi no hakken* (The cultivation culture of Iriomote Island: discovery of overseas routes). Tokyo: Hōsei Daigaku Shuppan Kyoku.

Aoyagi Yoji. 1991. Trade ceramics found in insular Southeast Asia. *Bōeki tōji kenkyū* 11:35–52.

Arakaki Tsutomu. 2004. Iseki shutsudo no chadōgu kara mita Chadō no tenkai (Development of the tea ceremony seen from excavated tea utensils). In *Gusuku bunka o kangaeru* (Thinking about Gusuku culture), ed. Nakijin Son Kyōiku Iinkai, pp. 437–449. Tokyo: Shin Jinbutsu Ōraisha.

———. 2007. Okinawa ni okeru Chanoyu no fukyū to sono eikyō (The diffusion of the tea ceremony within Okinawa and its influence). *Nantō kōko* 26:209–220.

Arakaki Tsutomu and Seto Tetsuya. 2005. Okinawa ni okeru 14 seiki–16 seiki no chūgokusan hakuji no saiseiri; tsuketari jūyon-jūroku seiki no seiji no yōsō seiri memo (A reexamination of fourteenth- to sixteenth-century whiteware with an appendix, memo concerning the analysis of fourteenth- to sixteenth-century celadon). *Okinawa maibun kenkyū* 3:79–98.

Asato Shijun. 2003. Yonagunijima Tōgurubama Iseki no hen'nenteki ichi no saikentō (Reexamination of the chronological position of the Tōgurubama Site, Yonaguni Island). *Okinawa maibun kenkyū* 1:11–24.

———. 2009. Archaeology of the Ryukyu Islands: major themes. In *Okinawa: The Rise of an Island Kingdom: Archaeological and Cultural Perspectives,* ed. Richard Pearson, pp. 1–4. BAR Series 1898. London: Archaeopress.

———. 2010. Minami Ryūkyū no senshi bunka to Tōnan Ajia (Prehistoric culture of the Southern Ryukyus and Southeast Asia). In *Nankai o meguru kōkogaku* (Archaeology around the Southern Ocean), ed. Imamura Keiji, pp. 159–182. Tokyo: Dōseisha.

Asato Shijun and Morimoto Isao. 1984. Tenzan Ryō no gairyaku (Summary of the investigation of the Tenzan Mausoleum). *Okinawa Ken Kyōiku Iinkai Bunka Ka kiyō* 1:13–34.

Asato Susumu. 1990. *Kōkogaku kara mita Ryūkyū shi, jo* (Ryūkyū history as seen from archaeology, volume 1). Naha: Okinawa Bunko.

———. 1992. Gusuku jidai no kaishiki no saikentō (Reexamination of the beginning of the Gusuku Period). In *Shin Ryūkyū shi—Ko Ryūkyū hen* (New history of Ryukyu—Ko Ryukyu), ed. Ryūkyū Shinpōsha, pp. 63–90. Naha: Ryūkyū Shinpōsha.

———. 1996. Ōgata gusuku shutsugen zenya: ishinabe ryūtsūki no Ryūkyū Rettō (The eve of the appearance of large-scale castles (*gusuku*): the Ryūkyū Archipelago at the time of the exchange of stone cauldrons. In *Atarashii Ryūkyū shizō: Aragusuku Seishō Sensei tsuito ronshu* (A new image of Ryukyu history: essays in honor of Professor Seishō Aragusuku), ed. Takara Kurayoshi, Tomiyama Kazuyuki, and Maehira Fusa'aki, pp. 7–26. Ginowan (Okinawa): Yōjusha.

———. 1997. Shurijō izen no ōgusuku, Urasoe Gusuku no chōsa (Investigation of Urasoe Castle, the royal castle before Shuri). *Nihon rekishi* 585:106–113.

———. 1998. *Gusuku, Kyōdōtai, Mura* (Gusuku, cooperative groups, villages). Ginowan (Okinawa): Yōjusha.

———. 2002. Ryūkyū bunka en to Ryūkyū Ōkoku no keisei (The development of the Ryukyu culture area and the Ryukyu Kingdom). In *Nihon o toinaosu* (Reinvestigating Japan), ed. Nakamura Norio, Akasaka Ikuo, Harada Nobuo, and Miura Sukeyuki, pp. 155–178. Tokyo: Iwanami Shoten.

———. 2003a. Gusuku no naka no gusuku: Okinawa no gusuku to shūraku (Gusuku within *gusuku*: *gusuku* and village in Okinawa). In *Sengoku jidai no kōkogaku* (Archaeology of the Sengoku Period), ed. Ono Masatoshi and Mitsuo Hagihara, pp. 275–286. Tokyo: Kōshi Shoin.

———. 2003b. Ryūkyū Ōkoku no keisei to Higashi Ajia (Formation of the Ryūkyū Kingdom and East Asia). In *Ryūkyū, Okinawa shi no sekai* (Ryukyu, the world of Okinawan history), ed. Tomiyama Kazuyuki, pp. 84–115. Tokyo: Yoshikawa Kōbunkan.

———. 2006. *Ryūkyū ōken to gusuku* (Ryukyu royal power and *gusuku*). Tokyo: Yamakawa Shuppansha.

———. 2009. The emergence of royal authority and Urasoe. In *Okinawa: The Rise of an Island Kingdom: Archaeological and Cultural Perspectives,* ed. Richard Pearson, pp. 57–62. BAR Series 1898. London: Archaeopress.

———. 2010. Yakōgai kōeki futatsu no kuchi to hitotsu no kuchi (One or two entry ways for *Turbo* exchange). In *Kodai makki—Nihon no kyōkai* (The borders of Japan at the end of the Kodai Period), ed. Josef Kreiner, Yoshinari Naoki, and Oguchi Masashi, pp. 131–160. Tokyo: Moriwasha.

Asato Susumu and Doi Naomi. 1999. *Okinawajin wa doko kara kita ka* (Where did the Okinawan people come from?). Naha: Bōdā Inku.

Asato Susumu and Harunari Hideji, eds. 2001. *Okinawa-Ken Ōdomaribama Kaizuka* (The Ōdomaribama Shell Mound, Okinawa Prefecture, Japan). Sakura, Chiba: The National Museum of Japanese History.

Asato Susumu, Miyazato Shinyū, and Kinoshita Shūkai. 2001. Ryūkyū Koku Chūzan Ōryo Urasoe Yōdore shutsudo urushsihin kankei ibutsu karabitsugata urushi shitsugan no fukugen (Reconstruction of a lacquer Chinese-style chest-shaped receptacle and associated artifacts from the Ryukyu Chūzan royal tomb of Urasoe Yōdore. In *Tokubestu ten, Shō kei to Ryūkyū no bi ten* (Special exhibition, the Shō family and Ryukyu art), ed. MOA Bijutsukan, pp. 119–122. Atami: MOA Bijutsukan.

Athens, J. S. 2007. Prehistoric population growth on Kosrae, eastern Caroline Islands. In *The Growth and Collapse of Pacific Island Societies: Archaeological and Demographic Perspectives,* ed. P. V. Kirch and J. L. Rallu, pp. 257–277. Honolulu: University of Hawai'i Press.

Atwell, W. S. 1977. Notes on Silver, Foreign Trade, and the Late Ming Economy. *Ch'ing-Shih Wen-t'i* 3 (8): 1–33.

———. 2002. Time, money, and the weather. *Journal of Asian Sudies* 61 (1): 83–113.

Baba Hisao. 2000. Physical adaptation of the Minatogawa people to island environments. *Nettai* 10 (2000): 231–241.

———. 2003. Minatogawajin wa Ryūkyūjin no sosen ka (Are Minatogawa people the ancestors of Ryukyuans?). In *Okinawa Ken shi kakuronhen daini kan, kōko* (History of Okinawa, separate volume no. 2, archaeology), ed. Zaidan Hōjin Okinawa Ken Bunka Shinkōkai, pp. 525–572. Naha: Okinawa Ken Kyōiku Iinkai.

Baba, Hisao, and Shuichiro Narasaki. 1991. Minatogawa Man, the oldest type of modern *Homo sapiens* in East Asia. *Daiyonki kenkyū* 30 (2): 221–230.

Baba, Hisao, Shuichiro Narasaki, and Seiho Ohyama. 1998. Minatogawa hominid fossils and the evolution of Late Pleistocene humans in East Asia. *Anthropological Science* 106 (Supplement): 27–45.

Balee, W. 1998. Historical ecology: promises and postulates. In *Advances in Historical Ecology,* ed. W. Balee, pp. 13–29. New York: Columbia University Press.

Barker, G. 2005. Agriculture, pastoralism, and Mediterranean landscapes in prehistory. In *The Archaeology of Mediterranean Prehistory,* ed. A. B. Knapp and E. Blake, pp. 46–76. Oxford: Blackwell Publishing.

———. 2011. The cost of cultivation. *Nature* 473:163–164.

Bellwood, P. 2005. *First Farmers: The Origins of Agricultural Societies.* Oxford: Blackwell Publishers.

Bellwood, P., and E. Dizon. 2005. The Batanes Archaeological Project and the "Out of Taiwan" hypothesis for Austronesian dispersal. *Journal of Austronesian Studies* 1 (1): 1–32.

Bocquet-Appel, J. P. 1985. Small populations: demography and paleoanthroplogical differences. *Journal of Human Evolution* 14:683–691.

Bowles, S. 2011. Cultivation of cereals by the first farmers was not more productive than foraging. *Proceedings of the National Academy of Sciences* 108 (12): 4760–4765.

Broodbank, C. 2000. *The Island Archaeology of the Early Cyclades.* Cambridge: Cambridge University Press.

———. 2006. The origins and early development of Mediterranean maritime activity. *Journal of Mediterranean Archaeology* 19 (2): 199–230.

Brook, T. 2010. *The Troubled Empire: China in the Yuan and Ming Dynasties.* Cambridge: Belknap/Harvard University Press.

Brown, R. 1988. *The Ceramics of Southeast Asia: Their Dating and Identification.* Singapore: Oxford University Press.

Brumfiel, E. 1992. Breaking and entering the ecosystem: gender, class and faction steal the show. *American Anthropologist* 94:551–567.

Chadō Shiryōkan. 1998. *Tokubestu ten: Kochin kōro, Fukkenshō shutsudo ibutsu to Nihon no denseihin* (Special exhibition: Cochin incense boxes excavated from Fujian Province and Japanese heirlooms). Kyoto: Chadō Shiryōkan, MOA Bijutsukan.

Chang, Pin-Tsun. 1983. Chinese maritime trade: the case of sixteenth century Fu-Chien (Fukien). Ph.D. dissertation, Princeton University. Ann Arbor, MI: University Microfilms.

Chang, S. T. 1992. Commodities imported to the Chang Chou region of Fukien in the Late Ming Period: a preliminary analysis of the tax lists found in the *Tung-ha-yang-k'ao*. In *Emporia, Commodities, and Entrepreneurs in Asian Maritime Trade c. 1400–1750*, ed. R. Ptak and D. Rothermund, pp. 159–194. *Beiträge zur Südasien Forschung Sudasien-Institut Universität Heidelberg*, vol. 14. Stuttgart: Universität Heidelberg.

Charlton, T., and D. Nichols, eds. 1997. *The Archaeology of City States*. Washington, DC: Smithsonian Institution Press.

Chatan Chō Kyōiku Iinkai. 2004. *Ireibaru C Iseki no katarumono* (Talking about the Ireibaru C Site). Chatan: Chatan Chō Kyōiku Iinkai.

———. 2007. *Ireibaru Iseki* (The Ireibaru Site). Chatan Chō (Okinawa): Chatan Chō Kyōiku Iinkai.

Chen Xiyu. 1991. *Zhongguo fanchuan yu haiwai maoyi* (Chinese junks and foreign trade). Xiamen: Xiamen Daxue Chubanshe.

Chen Yupei. 2009. Taiwan kara mita Taiwan to Ryūkyū no senshi kankei (Prehistoric relations between Taiwan and Ryukyu as seen from Taiwan). In *Yūdoki kara Mudoki e—Sakishima Shotō senshi jidai Mudoki Ki no kurashi* (From the Ceramic Period to the Non-Ceramic Period—life in the Non-Ceramic Period of the prehistory of the Sakishima Islands), ed. Ishigaki Shi Shi Sōmubu Shishi Henshūka, pp. 63–64. Ishigaki: Ishigaki Shi.

Chen, Zhongyuan, Zhanghua Wang, J. Schneiderman, Jin Tao, and Yongli Cai. 2005. Holocene fluctuations in the Yangtze Delta of Eastern China and the Neolithic response. *The Holocene* 15 (6): 915–924.

Cherry, J. 1990. The first colonization of the Mediterranean Islands; a review of recent research. *Journal of Mediterrannean Archaeology* 3/2:145–221.

———. 2004. Mediterranean Island prehistory: what's different and what's new. In *Voyages of Discovery: The Archaeology of Islands*, ed. S. M. Fitzpatrick, pp. 233–248. Westport, CT: Praeger.

Chi, Zhang, and Hsiao-chun Hung. 2010. The emergence of agriculture in South China. *Antiquity* 84:11–25.

———. 2011. Later hunter-gatherers in southern China, 18,000 to 3,000 BC. *Antiquity* 85:1–19.

Chida, Hiroyuki. 2010. Yabumaedabaru Kaizuka Iseki II ku, 3 gō hottate hashira tatemono ato shutsudo no shokubutsu itai hōkoku (Report of plant remains recovered from postholes of No. 3 Structure, Locality II, at the Yabumaedabaru Shellmound). *Nantō kōko* 29:99–112.

China Teijun. 2000. Mēbaru iseki no mizuba ikō to chōzōketsu (The water site and storage pits at the Mēbaru Site). *Kikan kōkogaku* 73:23–26.

China Teikan. 2005. Urasoe Yōdore no ishizushi to butsuzō chōkoku (The stone sarcophagi and Buddhist carvings from Urasoe Yōdore). In *Urasoe Yōdore no Sekizushi to Ikotsu Chōsa no Chūkan Hōkoku* (Preliminary report of the investigation of the stone sarcophagi and human bones from Urasoe Yōdore), ed. Urasoe Shi Kyōiku Iinkai, pp. 28–51. Urasoe Shi (Okinawa): Urasoe Shi Kyōiku Iinkai.

———. 2008. *Ryūkyū Bukkyō shi no kenkyū* (Study of Buddhism in Ryukyu). Ginowan (Okinawa): Gajumaru Shorin.

Chinen Isamu. 1980. Katsuren Jōato no Gen sometsukehen ni tsuite (Concerning the Yuan blue and white sherds found in Katsuren Castle). *Okinawa Kenritsu Hakubutsukan kiyō* 6:15–20.

Clark, H. 1991. *Community, Trade, and Networks: Southern Fujian Province from the Third to Thirteenth Century.* New York: Cambridge University Press.

Collcutt, M. 1981. *Five Mountains: The Rinzai Zen Monastic Institution in Medieval Japan.* Cambridge: Harvard University Press.

Danjō Hiroshi. 2005. Mindai Kaikin no jitsuzō (A true image of the Ming Prohibition). In *Minato machi to kaiiki sekai,* ed. Murai Shōsuke, Rekishigaku Kenkyūkai, pp. 145–177. Tokyo: Aoki Shoten.

Deschamps, P., N. Durand, E. Bard, B. Hamelin, G. Camoin, A. Thomas, G. Henderson, J. Okuno, and Y. Yokoyama. 2012. Ice sheet collapse and sea level rise at the Bolling Warming 14,600 years ago. *Nature* 483:559–564.

Dodo, Yukio, Naomi Doi, and Osamu Kondo. 1998. Ainu and Ryūkyū cranial nonmetric variation: evidence which disputes the Ainu-Ryūkyū common origin theory. *Anthropological Science* 106:99–120.

Doi Naomi. 2003. Jinkotsu kara mita Okinawa no rekishi (The history of Okinawa seen from human bones). In *Okinawa Ken shi kakuronhen daini kan, kōko* (History of Okinawa, separate volume no. 2, archaeology), ed. Zaidan Hōjin Okinawa Ken Bunka Shinkōkai, pp. 573–610. Naha: Okinawa Ken Kyōiku Iinkai.

———. 2005. Urasoe Yōdore no ishizushi to ikotsu chōsa no chūkan hōkoku (Preliminary report of the investigation of the stone sarcophagi and human bones from Urasoe Yōdore). In *Urasoe Yōdore shutsudo jinkotsu no jnruigakuteki chōsa* (A physical anthropological investigation of the human bones from Urasoe Yōdore), ed. Urasoe Shi Kyōiku Iinkai, pp. 18–21. Urasoe Shi (Okinawa): Urasoe Shi Kyōiku Iinkai.

———. 2010. Shutsudo jinkotsu ga kataru Ko Ryūkyūjin no hito to seikatsu (People and living patterns of Ko Ryukyu people as told by excavated bones). In *Okinawa ken shi kakuron hen 3: Ko Ryūkyū* (History of Okinawa separate volume no. 3: Ko Ryukyu), ed. Zaidan Hōjin Okinawa Ken Bunka Shinkōkai Shiryō Henshushitsu, pp. 50–65. Naha: Okinawa Ken Kyōiku Iinkai.

Doi Naomi, Hirata Yukio, Zukeran Chōsei, and Izumi Sō. 1997. Okinawa chiho ni okeru hitokotsu kaku eishitsu no chikiteki, jidaiteki, hen'i ni tsuite (Spatial and temporal morphological variability in human skeletons in the Okinawa region). *Heisei 6–8 nendo Kagakuhi Hojokin Kenkyū Seika hōkokusho* (Research report to the Research Assistance Fund, 1995–1996). Naha: University of the Ryukyus.

Donohue, M., and T. Denham. 2010. Farming and language in island Southeast Asia: reframing Austronesian history. *Current Anthropology* 51 (2): 223–256.

Dupoizat, M. F., and Naniek Harkantiningsih. 2007. *Catalogue of the Chinese Style Ceramics of Majapahit: Tentative Inventory.* Paris: Association Archipel.

Dye, T. S., and E. Komori. 1992. A pre-censal population history of Hawaii. *New Zealand Journal of Archaeology* 14:113–128.

EAC (Kabushiki Kaisha Ieishi), Uruma Shi Kyōiku Iinkai. 2008. *Heshikiya Tōbaru Iseki* (The Heshikya Tōbaru Site). Uruma (Okinawa): Kabushiki Kaisha Ieishi (EAC), Uruma Shi Kyōiku Iinkai.

Ebihara Ippei. 2011. Inoshishi to kyōzon: Amami Okinawa ni okeru shuryō bunka ki (Coexisting with wild boar: accounts of hunting culture in Amami and Okinawa). In *Amami Okinawa kenkyūshi shiryō shūsei* (Collection of materials: environmental history of Amami Okinawa), ed. Ankei Yūji and Tōyama Masanao, pp. 405–438. Kagoshima: Nanpō Shinsha.

Education Commission of Okinawa Prefecture. 1975. *Cultural Assets of Okinawa.* Naha: Education Commission of Okinawa Prefecture.

Egami Tomoko. 2009. Miyakojima Arafu Iseki kara mita kaifū no tsukai hitobito no kurashi (The life of the people who used shell adzes at the Arafu Site, Miyako Island). In *Yūdoki kara Mudoki e—Sakishima Shotō senshi jidai Mudoki Ki no kurashi* (From the Ceramic Period to the Non-Ceramic Period—life in the Non-Ceramic Period of the prehistory of the Sakishima Islands), ed. Ishigaki Shi Sōmubu Shi Shi Henshūka, pp. 70–73. Ishigaki: Ishigaki Shi.

Fitzhugh, B., V. O. Shubin, Kaoru Tezuka, Yoshihiro Ishizuka, and C. A. Mandryk. 2002. Archaeology in the Kurile Islands: advances in the study of human palaeogeography, and Northwest Pacific prehistory. *Arctic Anthropology* 39 (1/2): 69–94.

Fitzpatrick, S., and W. F. Keegan. 2007. Human impacts and adaptations in the Caribbean islands: an historic ecology approach. *Earth and Environmental Science Transactions, Royal Society of Edinburgh* 98 (part 1): 29–46.

Fitzpatrick, S., Hiroto Takamiya, H. Neff, and W. Dickinson. 2006. Compositional analysis of Yayoi-Heian period ceramics from Okinawa: examining the potential for provenience study. *Geoarchaeology* 21 (8): 803–822.

Flannery, K. 1972. The cultural evolution of civilizations. *Annual Review of Ecology and Systematics* 3:399–426.

Foster, Peter, and Shuichi Matsumura. 2005. Did early humans go north or south? *Science* 308:965–966.

Fu Zongwen. 1992. Citonggang dui haishang sichou zhi lu de xuangxiang zhicheng (Two-way support of the the port of Zayton and the maritime silk road). In *Zhongguo yu haishang sichou zhi lu* (China and the maritime silk road), ed. Lianheguo Jiaokewen Zuzhi Weiyuanhui (Unesco Conference on the Maritime Silk Road Committee), pp. 332–343. Fuzhou: Fujian People's Publishing House.

Fujian Sheng Bowuguan. 1990. *Dehua yao* (The kilns of Dehua). Beijing: Wenwu Chubanshe.

Fujimoto Hideo and Naka Shohachirō, eds. 1980. *Hokkaidō to Okinawa* (Hokkaidō and Okinawa), vol. 1: *Nihon jōkaku taikei* (Compendium of Japanese castles). Tokyo: Shin Jinbutsu Ōraisha.

Fujita Yūki and Kaifu Yōsuke. 2010. Minatogawajin no shita gakkotsu o saiken suru (Reexamination of the mandible of the Minatogawa human fossil). In *Nanjō Shi Bugeidō Hakkutsu chōsa gaiyō hōkokusho* (Summary report of excavations at the Cave Site, Nanjō City), ed. Okinawa Kenritsu Hakubutsukan, Bijutsukan, p. 6. Naha: Okinawa Kenritsu Hakubutsukan, Bijutsukan.

Fuqua, D. S. 2004. The Japanese missons to Tang China and maritime exchange in East Asia, seventh to ninth centuries. Ph.D. dissertation, University of Hawai'i.

Furukawa Hiroyasu. 1984. Noguni kaizuka B Chiten oyobi sono shūhen no chishi (Locality B of the Noguni Shellmound and its geological history). In *Noguni Kaizuka B Chiten hakkutsu chōsa hōkoku* (Report of excavations of Locality B of the Noguni Shellmound), ed. Okinawa Ken Kyōiku Iinkai, pp. 3–14. Naha: Okinawa Ken Kyōiku Iinkai.

Furukawa Hiroyasu and Ōshiro Itsurō. 1977. Toguchi Agaribaru shūhen no chikei, chishitsu, toku ni iseki hōgan sō no chishi to hennen ni suite (The geomorphology and geology of the area around the Toguchi Agaribaru Site, particularly geological history of the cultural layer). In Toguchi Agaribaru daiichi, niji chōsa hōkoku (Report of the first and second excavations of the Toguchi Agaribaru Site), ed. Yomitan Son Kyōiku Iinkai, pp. 3–14. Yomitan: Yomitan Son Kyōiku Iinkai.

Gilbert, A., S. Andrefouet, L. Yan, and G. Remoissenet. 2006. The giant clam, *Tridacna maxima* communities of three French Polynesia islands: comparison of their population sizes and structures at early stages of their exploitation. *ICES Journal of Marine Science* 63:1573–1589.

Ginowan Shi Kyōiku Iinkai. 1989. *Tsuchi ni umareta Ginowan* (Ginowan buried in the ground). Ginowan (Okinawa): Ginowan Shi Kyōiku Iinkai.

———. 1993. *Uehara Nūribaru Iseki no kinkyū hakkutsu chōsa no seika gairyaku* (Summary of results of salvage excavations of the Uehara Nūribaru Site). Ginowan: Ginowan Shi Kyōiku Iinkai.

Ginoza Son Kyōiku Iinkai. 1999. *Mēbaru Iseki* (The Mēbaru Site). Ginoza Son (Okinawa): Ginoza Son Kyōiku Iinkai.

Gotō Masahiko. 2008. Ryūkyū to Min Chō, Tōnan Ajia taigai kankei (Ryūkyū and foreign relations with the Ming dynasty and Southeast Asia). *Kōkogaku jānaru* 579:16–19.

Goya Yoshikatsu. 2000. Okinawa Shotō no "hatake" no kentō ni mukete (Toward an examination of "dry fields" in the Okinawa Islands). In *Hatake no kōkogaku* (The archaeology of field agriculture), conference materials, 2000 Convention of the

Japan Archaeological Association, ed. Nihon Kōkogaku Kyōkai, pp. 108–111. Kagoshima: Nihon Kōkogaku Kyōkai.

Griffeth, R., and C. Thomas. 1981. Introduction. In *The City State in Five Cultures,* ed. R. Griffeth and C. Roberts, pp. xiii–xx. Santa Barbara: ABC-Clio.

Groves, C. 2007. Current views on taxonomy and zoogeography of the genus *Sus*. In *Pigs and Humans: 10,000 Years of Interaction,* ed. U. Albarella, K. Dobney, A. Ervynk, and P. Rowly-Conwy, pp. 15–29. Oxford: Oxford University Press.

Guy, John. 1989. *Ceramic Traditions of Southeast Asia.* Singapore: Oxford University Press.

Habu, Junko. 2004. Ancient Jōmon of Japan. Cambridge: Cambridge University Press.

———. 2010. Seafaring and the development of cultural complexity in northeast Asia: evidence from the Japanese Archipelago. In *Global Origins and the Development of Seafaring,* ed. A. Anderson, J. Barrett, and K. Boyle, pp. 159–170. Cambridge, UK: McDonald Institute for Archaeological Research.

Haneji Chōshū. 1983. *Chūzan seikan* (Mirror of the ages of Chūzan). Newly edited version by Okinawa Ken Kyōiku Chō Bunka Ka; original published in 1765. Naha: Okinawa Ken Kyōiku Iinkai.

Hanihara, Kazuro. 1991. Dual structure model for the population history of the Japanese. *Japan Review* 2:1–33.

Hanihara, Tsunehiko, and Hajime Ishida. 2009. Regional differences in craniofacial diversity and the population history of Jōmon Japan. *American Journal of Physical Anthropology* 139:311–322.

Harper, Rosemary. 1985. Summary of ceramic finds from shipwrecks excavated jointly by Thai Australian teams in the Gulf of Thailand. In *Final Report: Technical Workshop on Ceramics (T-W4),* ed. Seameo Project in Archaeology and Fine Arts (SPAFA), pp. 289–310. Bangkok: SPAFA Co-ordinating Unit.

Harunari Hideji and Imamura Mineo. 2004. *Yayoi jidai no jitsu nendai* (The true age of the Yayoi Period). Tokyo: Gakuseisha.

Hasegawa, Yoshikazu. 1980. Notes on the vertebrate fossils from the Late Pleistocene to Holocene of Ryukyu Islands, Japan. *Daiyonki kenkyū* (*Quaternary Research*) 18:263–267.

Hashiguchi Wataru. 2004. Chūsei kōwan Bōnotsu no shokō (Some thoughts on the mediaeval port of Bōnotsu). In *Chūsei Nishi Nihon no ryūtsū to kōtsū* (Circulation and communication in mediaeval Western Japan), ed. Hashimoto Yū and Ichimura Takao, pp. 47–67. Tokyo: Kōshi Shoin.

Hashimoto Mika. 2010. Nankai san kai udewa seisan katsudō no kenkyū (Study of the production activity of shell bracelets produced in the Okinawa archipelago). *Kōkogaku kenkyū* 53 (4): 77–97.

Hashimoto Yū. 2009. Chūsei Nihon no dōsen—Eiraku sen kara Sōsen no sekai o kangaeru (Copper coinage in mediaeval Japan—thinking about the world of Song coins, from Eiraku Coins). In *Sōsen no sekai* (The world of Song coins), ed. Ihara Hiroshi, pp. 129–153. Tokyo: Bensei Shuppan.

Hillson, S. W. 1992. Dental enamel growth, Perikymata and Hypoplasia in ancient tooth crowns. *Journal of the Royal Society of Medicine* 85 (8): 460–466.

Hirara Shi Kyōiku Iinkai. 1999. *Sumiya Iseki (1)* (Sumiya Site [1]). Hirara: Hirara Shi Kyōiku Iinkai.

———. 2003. *Sushigā Iseki* (Sushigā Site). Hirara City: Hirara Shi Kyōiku Iinkai.

Hirota Iseki Gakujutsu Chōsa Kenkyūkai, ed. 2003. *Tanegashima Hirota Iseki* (Tanegashima Hirota Site). Kagoshima: Kagoshima Kenritsu Rekishi Shiryō Sentā-Reimeikan.

Hokama Shuzen. 1986. *Okinawa no rekishi to bunka* (The history and culture of Okinawa). Tokyo: Chūō Kōronsha.

Hokama Shuzen and Hateruma Eikichi, eds. 1997. *Teihon: Ryūkyū koku yuraiki* (Standard edition: Ryukyu country records of origin). Tokyo: Kadokawa Shoten.

Hokama Shuzen and Saigō Nobutsuna. 1972. *Omoro sōshi* (Omoro Sōshi). Tokyo: Iwanami Shoten.

Hong-Schunka, S. M. 2005. An aspect of East Asian maritime trade: the exchange of commodities between Korea and Ryūkyū (1389–1638). In *Trade and Transfer across the East Asian Mediterranean,* ed. Angela Schottenhammer, pp. 125–161. Wiesbaden: Harrassowitz Verlag.

Hongo, Chuki, and Hajime Kayanne. 2009. Holocene coral reef development under windward and leeward locations at Ishigaki Island, Ryukyu Islands, Japan. *Sedimentary Geology* 214:62–73.

———. 2010. Holocene sea level record from corals: reliability of paleodepth indicators at Ishigaki Island, Ryūkyū Islands, Japan. *Palaeogeography, Palaeoclimatology, Palaeoecology* 287:143–151.

Hongo, Hitomi, Tomoko Anezaki, Kiyomi Yamazaki, Osamu Takahashi, and Hiroko Sugawara. 2007. Hunting or management? The status of *Sus* in the Jomon Period of Japan. In *Pigs and Humans: 10,000 Years of Interaction,* ed. U. Albarella, K. Dobney, A. Ervynk, P. Rowly-Conwy, pp. 109–130. Oxford: Oxford University Press.

Hotta, Mitsuru. 1981. The vegetation of Kume. In *Subsistence and Settlement in Okinawan Prehistory—Kume and Iriomote,* ed. Ryūkyū Archaeological Research Team, pp. 154–168. Vancouver: UBC Laboratory of Archaeology.

Hsueh, Y. 2000. The Kuroshio in the East China Sea. *Journal of Marine Systems* 24:131–139.

Hudson, M. 1999. *Ruins of Identity.* Honolulu: University of Hawai'i Press.

———. 2002. Agriculture and language change in the Japanese Islands. In *Examining the Farming/Language Dispersal Hypothesis,* ed. P. Bellwood and C. Renfrew, pp. 311–318. Cambridge, UK: McDonald Institute for Archaeological Research.

Hudson, M., and G. Barnes. 1991. Yoshinogari: a Yayoi settlement in northern Kysuhu. *Monumenta Nipponica* 46 (2): 211–235.

Hudson, M., and H. Takamiya. 2001. Dental pathology and subsistence change in Late Prehistoric Okinawa. *Indo-Pacific Prehistory Association Bulletin* 21:68–76.

Hudson, Mark, and Yū Taneishi. 2007. Miyakojima Shi Shimajiri shozai Nagabaka Iseki no 2006 nendo chōsa gaihō (Report of 2006 investigations of the Nagabaka Site, Shimajiri, Miyakojima City). *Tsukuba Daigaku senshigaku, kōkogaku kenkyū* 18:31–52.

Hung, Hsiao-chun. 2004. A sourcing study of Taiwan stone adzes. *Indo-Pacific Prehistory Association Bulletin* 24 (2): 57–70.

———. 2005. Neolithic interaction between Taiwan and northern Luzon: the pottery and jade evidence from the Cagayan valley *Journal of Austronesian Studies* 1 (1): 109–133.

Hung, Hsiao-chun, and P. Bellwood. 2010. Movement of raw materials and manufactured goods across the South China Sea after 500 BCE: from Taiwan to Thailand, and back. In *50 Years of Archaeology in Southeast Asia: Essays in Honour of Ian Glover,* ed. Berenice Bellina, pp. 215–245. Bangkok: River Books.

Hung, Hsiao-chun, Y. Iizuka, P. Bellwood, K. D. Nguyen, B. Bellina, P. Silapanth, E. Dizon, and R. Santiago. 2007. Ancient jades map 3,000 years of prehistoric exchange in Southeast Asia. *Proceedings, National Academy of Sciences, USA* 104:19745–19750.

Ie Son Kyōiku Iinkai. 1979. *Iejima Nagarabaru Nishi Kaizuka* (The Nagarabaru West Shellmound of Iejima). Ie Son (Okinawa): Ie Son Kyōiku Iinkai.

Iha Fuyū. 1974. Chōsenjin no hyōryūki ni araweta jūgōseiki matsu no Nantō (The southern islands at the end of the fifteenth century as revealed in the account of the drift voyage of the Koreans). In *Iha Fuyū zenshū* (The collected works of Iha Fuyū), ed. Iha Fuyū, pp. 54–99. Tokyo: Heibonsha.

Ijū Tsutomu. 2010. Ikō kara miru Ko Ryūkyū no Shurijō (Shuri Castle of the Ko Ryukyu Period, as seen from excavated features). In *Okinawa Ken shi kakuron hen daisan kan: Ko Ryūkyū* (History of Okinawa, separate volume no. 3: Ko Ryukyu), ed. Zaidan Hōjin Okinawa Ken Bunka Shinkōkai Shiryō Henshūshitsu, pp. 427–450. Naha: Okinawa Ken Kyōiku Iinkai.

Ikeda Yoshifumi. 2004. Okinawa shutsudo bōeki tōji no yōso (Aspects of trade ceramics found in Okinawa). In *Shinpojiumu: Kan Shina Kai sekai to Ko Ryūkyū* (The world around the East China Sea and Ko Ryūkyū), ed. Kyūshū Daigaku 21 Seiki COE Puroguramu (Jinbun Kagaku); Higashi Ajia to Nihon: Kōryū to Henyō), pp. 21–24. Hakata: Kyūshū Daigaku.

———. 2007a. Kodai, chūsei no Nihon to Ryūkyū Rettō (Japan and the Ryukyu Islands in the ancient and mediaeval periods). *Higashi Ajia no kodai bunka* 130:2–19.

———. 2007b. Okinawa shutsudo no Bizen yaki, hoi (Bizen ceramics found in Okinawa—supplement). *Nantō kōko* 26:235–252.

———, ed. 2008. *Kodai chūsei no kyōkai: Kikaigashima no sekai.* (Border area in the ancient and mediaeval periods: the world of Kikaigashima). Tokyo: Kōshi Shuppan.

Ikeda Yoshifumi and Goya Yoshikatsu. 1994. Yayoi-Heian jidai sōtō no Ginowan (Ginowan in the periods corresponding to the Yayoi to Heian). In *Ginowan Shi shi* (The history of Ginowan City), ed. Ginowan Shi Kyōiku Iinkai, pp. 98–114. Ginowan: Ginowan Shi Kyōiku Iinkai.

Ikehata Kōichi. 2008. Kikaigashima no Kodai, Chūsei iseki (Mediaeval and Kodai Period sites of Kikaigashima). In *Kodai chūsei no kyōkai ryōiki: Kikaigashima no sekai* (A border area in the ancient and mediaeval periods: the world of Kikaigashima), ed. Ikeda Yoshifumi, pp. 235–256. Tokyo: Kōshi Shuppan.

Imamura, Keiji. 1996. *Prehistoric Japan: New Perspectives on Insular East Asia:* Honolulu: University of Hawai'i Press.

Inamura Kenpu. 1962. Hisamatsu kyosekibo no hakkutsu hōkoku (Report on the excavation of the megalithic tombs at Hisamatsu). In *Miyakojima kyūki narabi shiba shūkai* (Old records of Miyako Island in light of annotated collections of historical songs), ed. Kenpu Inamura, pp. 496–513. Naha: Ryūkyū Bunka Tosho.

———. 1972. *Miyako shomin shi* (History of the people of Miyako Island). Naha: Kyōdō Insatsusha.

Information Section, Bureau of Cultural Properties (Korea). 1984. *Artifacts from the Sinan Sea Bottom* (in Korean). Seoul: Bureau of Cultural Properties, Republic of Korea.

Ishidō Kazuhiro and Tokuda Yukino. 2007. Kagoshima Minami Tanega Chō Hirota Iseki. *Kōkogaku kenkyū* 54 (3): 111–113.

Ishigaki Shi Kyōiku Iinkai. 1977. *Furusutobaru Iseki* (The Furusutobaru Site). Ishigaki Shi: Ishigaki Shi Kyōiku Iinkai.

———. 1984. *Furusutobaru Iseki hakkutsu chōsa hōkokusho* (Report of excavation of the Furusutobaru Site). Ishigaki: Ishigaki Shi Kyōiku Iinkai.

———. 1987. *Sakieda Akasaki Kaizuka* (The Sakieda Akasaki Shellmound). Ishigaki: Ishigaki Shi Kyōiku Iinkai.

———. 1991. *Shiseki Furusutobaru Iseki hōzon shisetsu keikaku* (Plan for the preservation of the Fusutobaru Historic Site). Ishigaki: Ishigaki Shi Kyōiku Iinkai.

———. 2009. *Ishigaki Kaizuka hakkutsu chōsa hōkokusho* (Report of excavations of the Ishigaki Shellmound). Ishigaki Shi: Ishigaki Shi Kyōiku Iinkai.

Ishigaki Shiritsu Yaeyama Hakubutsukan, ed. 2010. *Idai na tabi* (Great Journey). Ishigaki Shi: Ishigaki Shiritsu Yaeyama Hakubutsukan.

Ishigaki Shi Sōmubu Shishi Henshūshitsu. 1991. *Kerai Kedagusuku yuraiki* (Historical account of Kerai Kedagusuku). *Ishigaki Shi shi sōsho I* (The history of Ishigaki City 1). Ishigaki: Ishigaki Shi Sōmubu Shi Shi Henshūshitsu.

———. 2007. *Kenkyū shi: Yaeyama kōkogaku no ayumi* (History of research: the steps of Yaeyama archaeology). Ishigaki Shi kōkogaku bijuaru han 1 (Archaeology of Ishigaki City visual edition 1). Ishigaki: Ishigaki Shi.

———. 2008a. *Shimotabaru Ki no kurashi* (Livelihood in the Shimotabaru Period). Ishigaki Shi kōkogaku bijuaru han 2 (Archaeology of Ishigaki City visual edition 2). Ishigaki: Ishigaki Shi.

———. 2008b. *Tōjiki kara mita kōryū shi* (The history of trade seen through trade ceramics). Ishigaki Shi kōkogaku bijuaru han 5 (Archaeology of Ishigaki City visual edition 5). Ishigaki: Ishigaki Shi.

———. 2009a. Mudoki kara Yūdoki e (From Non-Ceramic to Ceramic). Ishigaki Shi kōkogaku bijuaru han 4 (Archaeology of Ishigaki City visual edition 4). Ishigaki: Ishigaki Shi.

———. 2009b. *Yūdoki kara Mudoki e—Sakishima senshi jidai Mudoki Ki no kurashi* (From Ceramic to Non-Ceramic: livelihood in the Non-Ceramic Period of Sakishima prehistory). *Ishigaki Shi kōkogaku bijuaru han 3* (Archaeology of Ishigaki City visual edition 3). Ishigaki: Ishigaki Shi.

Ishii Ryūta. 2008. Wakuta koyō no saihyōka: Wakuta koyōseki no nokihiragawara (Reevaluation of the Wakuta old kilns: flat eave tiles from the Wakuta kilns). *Nantō kōko* 27:79–92.

Ishimaru Eriko and Arata Keisuke. 2011. Iseki shutsudo dōbutsu izontai kara mita dōbutsu shizen riyō no rekishi (History of the use of faunal resources from faunal remains in archaeological sites. In *Amami Okinawa kenkyūshi shiryō shūsei* (Collection of materials: environmental history of Amami Okinawa), ed. Ankei Yūji and Tōyama Masanao, pp. 185–300. Kagoshima: Nanpō Shinsha.

Itō Chūta and Kamakura Yoshitarō. 1937. *Nankai kotōji* (Ceramics from the Southern Ocean). Tokyo: Hōunsha.

Itō Kei. 2006. Keishiki hikaku ni yoru Nantō no tsumegatamon doki no chiizuke ni tsuite (Assigning a position for Ryukyu nail-impressed pottery [*tsumegatamon doki*] through typological comparison). *Okinawa maibun kenkyū* 4:41–54.

———. 2007a. Kaizuka jidai ni okeru nōkō mondai kenkyū shi (History of research on the problem of horticulture in the Shellmound Period). *Nantō kōko* 26:97–120.

———. 2007b. Nantō tsumegata doki bunka kenkyūshi—keishiki hikaku ni yoru Nantō tsumegatamon doki to chiizuke ni tsuite (hoi) (History of the study of southern island nail-marked pottery culture [supplement]). *Okinawa maibun kenkyū* 5:25–54.

Itō, Kōji. 2008. Japan and Ryūkyū during the fifteenth and sixteenth centuries. *Acta Asiatica* 95:79–99.

Itō Shinji. 2000. *Ryūkyū Jōmon no kisoteki kenkyū* (Basic study of the Ryukyu Jōmon *Culture*). Tokyo: Myuze Publishers.

———. 2003. The position of the Ryūkyū Jōmon Culture in the Asia-Pacific region. *Indo-Pacific Prehistory Association Bulletin* 23:63–66.

———. 2006. Jōmon bunka no minami no kyōkai (The southern limits of Jōmon Culture). In *Kokugakuin Daigaku 21 COE Puroguramu Kokusai Shinpojiumu, Higashi Ajia sekai ni okeru Nihon kiso bunka no kōkogakuteki kaimei.* (Kokugakuin University 21 COE *Program, International Symposium,* elucidation of the basic culture of Japan in the East Asian world), ed. Itō Shinji and Yamazoe Nanae, pp. 1–14. Tokyo: Kokugakuin Daigaku 21 Seiki COE Puroguramu. http://21coekokugakuin.ac.jp/.

———. 2011a. Ryūkyū Rettō no shinsekka to gendaika o meguru keikan henka (Neolithicization and modernization of the Ryukyu archipelago). In *Senshi, Gusuku Jidai no Ryūkyū Rettō: hito to keikan* (The Ryukyu Islands in the Prehistoric and Primitive Periods: people and landscape), ed. Takamiya Hiroto and Itō Shinji, pp. 293–304. Tokyo: Rokuichi Shobō.

———. 2011b. Senshi Ryūkyū shakai to dantaiteki hatten to sono yōin: Kaizuka Jidai Zen 1 ki setsu (The gradual development of Ryukyu prehistoric society and its factors: the Early Shellmound Period I hypothesis. In *Senshi, Gusuku Jidai no Ryūkyū Rettō: hito to keikan* (The Ryukyu Islands in the Prehistoric and Primitive Periods: people and landscape), ed. Takamiya Hiroto and Itō Shinji, pp. 43–60. Tokyo: Rokuichi Shobō.

Itō Yoji. 2010. Kumemura Kōshi Byō sōken no rekishiteki igi (The historical significance of the foundation of the Confucius Temple in Kumemura). *Nantō bunka kenkyū* 36:101–136.

Jian, Zhimin, Pinxian Wang, Yōshiki Saito, Jilang Wang, Uwe Pflaumann, Tadamichi Oba, and Xinrong Cheng. 2000. Holocene variability of the Kuroshio Current in the Okinawa Trough, Northwestern Pacific Ocean. *Earth and Planetary Science Letters* 184:305–319.

Jin, Guiyin, and Dongsheng Liu. 2002. Mid Holocene climate change in North China, and the effect on cultural development. *Chinese Science Bulletin* 47 (5): 408–413.

Johnson, C. 2004. *The Sorrows of Empire: Militarism, Secrecy, and the End of the Republic.* London: Verso.

———. 2010. Another Battle of Okinawa. *Los Angeles Times,* May 6, 2010.

Jones, R. 2007. *History and Guide to the Cash Copper Coinage of Japan.* Kearney, NE: Morris Publishing.

Kagoshima Ken Amagi Chō Kyōiku Iinkai. 1999. *Tōbaru Iseki (2)* (Tōbaru Site [2]). Amagi Chō: Amagi Chō Kyōiku Iinkai.

———. 2004. *Shitabaru I–IV Iseki* (Shitabaru Sites I–IV). Kagoshima Ken Amagi Chō: Kagoshima Ken Amagi Chō Kyōiku Iinkai.

Kagoshima Ken Uken Son Kyōiku Iinkai. 1998. *Kurakisaki Kaitei Iseki hakkutsu chōsa gaihō* (Summary report of the excavation of the Kurakisaki Underwater Site). Uken Son: Uken Son Kyōiku Iinkai.

Kaifu, Yōsuke. 2007. The cranium and mandible of Minatogawa 1 belong to the same individual: a response to recent claims to the contrary. *Anthropological Science* 11:159–162.

Kamei Meitoku. 1982. Sakishima Shotō saishū no yunyū tōjiki (Trade ceramics collected in the Sakishima Islands). In *Okinawa Shutsudo no Chūgoku tōjiki, jō, George H. Kerr Shi chōsa shūshū shiryō* (Chinese ceramics in Okinawa [I]: collected materials from the investigations of George H. Kerr), ed. Okinawa Kenritsu Hakubutsukan, pp. 127–139. Naha: Okinawa Kenritsu Hakubutsukan.

———. 1984. Katsuren Jōato shutsudo no tōjiki sosei (The composition of ceramics from the Katsuren Castle Site). *Bōeki tōji kenkyū* 4:85–92.

———. 1986a. *Kyūshū no Chūgoku tōji* (Chinese Ceramics from Kyushu). Fukuoka: Nishi Nihon Bunka Kyōkai.

———. 1986b. *Nihon bōeki tōji shi no kenkyū* (Study of the history of trade ceramics in Japan). Kyoto: Dōhōsha.

———. 1992. Chronology of Longquan wares of the Song and Yuan periods. Paper presented at the International Conference on Ceramic Ecology in the Far East—The Manufacture and Export of Zhejiang Green Wares during the Ninth to Fourteenth Centuries, University of Hong Kong.

———. 1993. Nansei Shotō ni okeru bōeki tōjiki no ryūtsū keiro (The changing circumstances of the flow of trade ceramics in the Southwest Islands). *Jōchi Ajiagaku* 11:11–45.

———, ed. 1995. *Fukkenshō yōato shutsudo tōshiki no kenkyū* (Study of ceramics unearthed from kilns in Fujian Province). Kawasaki: Senshū Daigaku.

———. 1997. Ryūkyū bōeki no kōzōteki rikai (Structural understanding of Ryukyu ceramic trade). *Senshū jinbun ronshū:* 60:41–66.

———, ed. 2002a. Mindai zenhanki tōshiki no kenkyū: Shurijō Kyōnouchi SK01 shutsudohin (Study of ceramics of the first half of the Ming dynasty: the objects found in SK01, Kyōnouchi, Shuri Castle). Kawasaki: Senshū University.

———. 2002b. Shuri Jōato Kyōnouchi shutsudo no seika shiki (The blue and white porcelain from the Kyōnouchi, Shuri Castle. *Tōyō Tōji Gakkai kaihō* 46:2–4.

———. 2007. Nantō ni okeru Kikaigashima no rekishiteki ichi (The historical position of Kikaigashima in the Southern Islands). *Higashi Ajia no kodai bunka* 129:85–109.

———. 2008. Changes in the ceramic trade and its modus operandi in Old Ryūkyū. *Acta Asiatica* 9:19–33.

———. 2009. The significance of Chinese trade ceramics from Ryūkyū: focussing on Yuan dynasty blue and white porcelain. In *Okinawa: The Rise of an Island Kingdom: Archaeological and Cultural Perspectives,* ed. Richard Pearson, pp. 63–70. BAR Series 1898. London: Archaeopress.

Kamei Meitoku and Chinen Isamu. 1983. Katsuren Jōato shutsudo no Gen seika (Yuan blue and white ceramics found in the Katsuren Castle Site). *Bōeki tōji kenkyū* 3:41–44.

Kamei Meitoku and Miyagi Atsumasa. 1994. Yomitan kobo shutsudo Gen seika no tsubo o megutte (Concerning the Yuan blue and white jar found in an old tomb in Yomitan). *Urasoe Bijutsukan kiyō* 3:9–14.

Kamei Meitoku, Shibata Keiko, Takashima Hiroyuki, and Niijima Natsuko. 2007. Nakijin Jōato shutsudo Gen seika shi no kenkyū (Study of Yuan blue and white porcelain from the Nakijin Castle Site). In *Nakijin Jōato shūhen iseki III* (Sites in the periphery of Nakijin Castle III), ed. Okinawa Ken Nakijin Son Kyōiku Iinkai, pp. 227–252. Nakijin: Okinawa Ken Nakijin Son Kyōiku Iinkai.

Kamimura Toshio. 1999. Minami no umi no michi to kōryū (Sea routes and exchange in the Southern Ocean). In *Umi o watta Jōmonjin: Jōmon Jidai no kōryū to kōeki* (Jōmon people who crossed the sea: trade and exchange in the Jōmon Period), ed. Hashiguchi Naotake, pp. 303–346. Tokyo: Shogakkan.

———. 2004. Okinawa no senshi, kodai kōryū, kōeki (Trade and exchange in the prehistoric, ancient periods of Okinawa). In *Okinawa taigai bunka kōryū shi: kōkogaku, rekishigaku, minzokugaku, jinruigaku no shiten kara* (History of external cultural relations of Okinawa from the point of view of archaeology, history, folklore, physical anthropology), ed. Kamimura Toshio, pp. 1–72. Tokyo: Nihon Keizai Hyōronsha.

Kamiya Kōshō. 2007. *Ryūkyū Rettō monogatari* (Story of the Ryukyu Archipelago). Naha: Bōdā Inku.

Kan Hironobu. 2010. Ryūkyū Rettō ni okeru sangoshō no keisei (Development of coral reefs in the Ryukyu Islands). *Kōkogaku jānaru* 597:24–26.

Kan, Hironobu, Nobuyuki Hori, Toshio Kawana, and Kiyoshi Ichikawa. 1997. The evolution of a Holocene fringing reef and island: reef environmental sequence and sea level changing in Tonaki Island, the Central Ryukyus. *Atoll Research Bulletin* 443:1–20.

Kan, Hironobu, and Toshio Kawana. 2006. Catch up of a high latitude barrier reef by back growth during Post Glacial sea level rise, southern Ryukyus, Japan. In *Proceedings of the 10th International Coral Reef Symposium (2006)*, 494–503.

Kanazawa Yō. 2004. Nakanohama no saishū ibutsu no igi (The significance of artifacts collected from Nakanohama). *Rekishi dokuhon* 49 (11): 239–240.

Kaneko, Erika. 1964. Ryūkyū report 1962. *Asian Perspectives* 7:113–137.

Kaneko, E., and H. Melichar. 1972. *Pura Mutuzuma: Archaeological Research on Miyako Island, Ryukyus.* Honolulu: Social Science Reseach Institute, University of Hawaii.

Kasari Chō Kyōiku Iinkai. 2006. *Matsunoto Iseki* (Matsunoto Site). Kasari Chō (Kagoshima Ken): Kasari Chō Kyōiku Iinkai.

Katagiri Chiaki, Kobashigawa Takeshi, Shimabukuro Rieko, and Doi Naomi. 2007. Gushikawajima Shiitachi Iseki shutsudo jinkotsu no saiseiri: yaketa hone no sonzai kara mita soho no shoten o atete (Reorganization of skeletal remains from the

Shiitachi Site, Gushikawa Island, fired bones and burial method). *Okinawa maibun kenkyū* 5 (2007): 1–24.

Katō Shinpei. 1979. Okinawa no iwayuru sajō kokki ni tsuite (Concerning the so-called double notched bone tools from Okinawa). *Kōkogaku jānaru* 167:72–75.

———. 2010. Suijigai yurai no kizai to moyō (Artifacts and motifs derived from the spider conch [*Lambis chiragra*]). *Kōkogaku kenkyū* 57 (1): 56–67.

Katsuren Chō Kyōiku Iinkai. 1984. *Katsuren Jōato: Minami Kaizuka Oyobi Ninomaru Chiten no hakkutsu chōsa* (Excavation of the South Midden and No. 2 Enclosure, Katsuren Castle Site). Katsuren Chō: Katsuren Chō Kyōiku Iinkai.

———. 1988. *Kuni Hitei Shiseki Katsuren Jōato: kankyō seibi jigyō hōkokusho* (Report on the consolidation of the environment of the National Historic Site Katsuren Castle). Vols. 1 and 2. Katsuren Chō: Katsuren Chō Kyōiku Iinkai.

Kawahata, Hodaka, and Hideaki Ohshima. 2004. Vegetation and environmental record in the northern East China Sea during the Late Pleistocene. *Global and Planetary Change* 41:251–273.

Kawana Toshio. 2008. Ryūkyū Rettō ni okeru kōko iseki to shizen saigai: toku ni tsunami no shūrai to sono kakawari o kangaeru (Archaeological sites and natural disasters in the Ryukyus with special reference to the invasion of tsunami). *Kōkogaku jānaru* 577:3–8.

———. 2011. Ryūkyū Rettō ni okeru sangoshō keisei to jishin, tsunami (The history of the formation of coral reefs in the Ryukyu Islands and earthquakes and tsunami). In *Senshi, Gusuku Jidai no Ryūkyū Rettō: hito to keikan* (The Ryūkyū Islands in the Prehistoric and Primitive Periods: People and Landscape), ed. Takamiya Hiroto and Itō Shinji, pp. 63–86. Tokyo: Rokuichi Shobō.

Kawana Toshio and Nakata Takashi. 1994. Sangoshitsu taisekibutsu no nendai kara mita Ryūkyū Rettō nanbu shūhen kaiiki ni okeru kōki Kanshinsei no tsunami hassei jiki (Timing of Late Holocene tsunami in the Southern Ryukyu Islands, from coral tsunami deposits). *Chigaku zasshi* 103:4 (1994): 352–376.

Kawashima Yūji and Muraoka Makoto. 1984. Noguni kaizukagun B Chiten shutsudo no jūkotsu ni tsuite (Animal bones from Locality B, Noguni Shellmound Group). In *Noguni: Noguni Kaizukagun B Chiten hakkutsu hōkokusho* (Noguni, report of excavations at Noguni Shellmound Group Locality B), ed. Okinawa Ken Kyōiku Iinkai, pp. 181–188. Naha: Okinawa Ken Kyōiku Iinkai.

Keegan, W. F. 2004. Islands of chaos. In *Late Ceramic Age Societies in the Eastern Caribbean,* ed. Andre and Corinne L. Hofman Delpuech, pp. 33–44. Oxford: Archaeopress.

Keegan, W. F., and M. J. de Niro. 1988. Stable carbon and nitrogen isotope ratios on bone collagen used to study coral-reef and terrestrial components of prehistoric Bahamian diet. *American Antiquity* 53 (2): 320–336.

Keegan, W. F., and J. Diamond. 1987. Colonization of islands by humans. *Advances in Archaeological Method and Theory* 10:49–92.

Keegan, W. F., R. W. Portell, and J. Slapcinsky. 2003. Changes in invertebrate taxa at two Pre-Columbian sites in southwestern Jamaica, AD 800–1500. *Journal of Archaeological Science* 30:1607–1617.

Kerr, G. H. 1958. *Okinawa: History of an Island People.* Rutland, VT: Tuttle Publishers.

Kikai Chō Kyōiku Iinkai. 2006. *Gusuku Iseki Gun, Yamada Nakanishi Iseki I* (The Gusuku Site Group: Yamada Nakanishi Iseki I). Kikai Chō: Kikai Chō Kyōiku Iinkai.

———. 2008. *Gusuku Iseki Gun: Yamada Nakanishi Iseki II* (The Gusuku Site Group: Yamada Nakanishi II). Kagoshima Ken Kikai Chō: Kikai Chō Kyōiku Iinkai.

———. 2009. *Gusuku Iseki Gun: Yamada Hanta Iseki* (The Gusuku Site Group: the Yamada Hanta Site). Kagoshima Ken Kikai Chō: Kikai Chō Kyōiku Iinkai.

Kimura Masa'aki. 1996. Ryūkyū Ko no daiyonki chiri (The quaternary geography of the Ryukyu Arc). *Chigaku zasshi* 105 (3): 259–285.

Kin Seiki. 1986. Jūgata sōshingu (Zoomorphic ornaments). In *Okinawa rekishi chizu* (Historical atlas of Okinawa), ed. Miyagi Eishō and Takamiya Hiroe, p. 92. Tokyo: Kashiwa Shobō.

———. 1988. Birosuku taipu jiki ni tsuite (Concerning Birosuku type white porcelain). *Bōeki tōji kenkyū* 8:148–157.

———. 1989. Okinawa ni okeru jūni, jūsan seiki no Chūgoku tōjiki (Twelfth-, thirteenth-century Chinese ceramics found in Okinawa). *Okinawa kenritsu hakubutsukan kiyō* 15:1–22.

———. 1990. Okinawa no Chūgoku tōjiki (Chinese ceramics from Okinawa). *Kōkogaku jānaru* 320:2–6.

———. 1991. Okinawa shutsudo no Tai, Betunamu tōji (Thai and Vietnamese ceramics from Okinawa). *Bōeki tōji kenkyū* 11:81–100.

———. 1993. Hakusai tōjiki kara mita Ryūkyū no kaigai bōeki: Chūgoku tōjiki ni tsuite (Ryukyu foreign trade as seen from imported ceramics: concerning Chinese ceramics). In *Dai Yonkai Ryūchū Rekishi Kankei ronbunshū,* (Proceedings of the Fourth International Ryūkyū China Historical Relations International Conference), ed. Dai Yonkai Ryūchū Kankei Kokusai Gakujutsu Kaigi Kankōkai, pp. 339–363. Naha: Dai Yonkai Kankei Kokusai Gakujutsu Kaigi Kankōkai.

———. 1994. Doki-Mudoki-Doki: Yaeyama kōkogaku hennen no shi'an (Ceramic–Non- Ceramic–Ceramic: a proposition on the archaeological chronology of the Yaeyama Islands). *Nantō kōko* 14:83–92.

———. 1998. Okinawa ni okeru bōeki tōji (Trade ceramics from Okinawa). In *Nihon Kōkogaku Kyōkai 1998 nendo Okinawa taikai shiryōshū* (Distributed materials from the 1998 Okinawa Meeting of the Japan Archaeological Association), ed. Nihon Kōkogaku Kyōkai, pp. 147–158. Naha: Nihon Kōkogaku Kyōkai.

———. 1999. Okinawa shutsudo Tōnan Ajia tōjiki kara mita nangoku kōryū (Exchange with southern countries seen from Southeast Asian ceramics found in Okinawa). *Kōkogaku jānaru* 448:11–15.

———. 2000. Tōjiki kara kataru Gusuku Jidai no shūki (Discussing Gusuku Period ceramic wine containers). In *Ryūkyū, Higashi Ajia no hito to bunka* (People and culture in Ryukyu and East Asia), ed. Takamiya Hiroe Sensei Koki Kinen Henshū Kankōkai, pp. 285–294. Naha: Takamiya Hiroe Sensei Koki Kinen Henshū Kankōkai.

———. 2004. Kōkogaku kara miru Nakijin Jōato no rekishi (The history of Nakijin Castle as seen from archaeology). In *Gusuku Jidai o kangaeru* (Thinking about the Gusuku Period), ed. Nakijin Son Kyōiku Iinkai, pp. 169–194. Tokyo: Shin Jinbutsu Ōraisha.

———. 2007a. Nakijin Jōato to Nakijin Mura ato no hakkutsu chōsa no igi (The significance of the excavation of Nakijin Castle and Nakijin Village). *In Nakijin Jōato shūhen iseki III* (Sites surrounding Nakijin Castle, III), ed. Okinawa Ken Nakijin Son Kyōiku Iinkai, pp. 181–202. Nakijin: Nakijin Son Kyōiku Iinkai.

———. 2007b. Nakijin taipu hakuji to Birosuku taipu hakuji (The Nakijin type and Birosuku type whitewares). In *Chūgoku Fukken no bōeki tōji to Ryūkyū: Sō, Gen dai o chūshin ni* (Trade ceramics from Fujian and Ryukyu, concentrating on the Song and Yuan periods), ed. Naoko Kinoshita, pp. 25–27. Kumamoto: University of Kumamoto.

———. 2008a. Nakijin Jōato to Shuri Jōato shutsudo no tōjiki ni tsuite (Concerning ceramics found in Nakijin and Shuri Castle Sites) *In Nakijin Jōato hakkutsu chōsa hōkokusho III* (Report of excavations of the Nakijin Castle Site III), ed. Okinawa Ken Nakijin Son Kyōiku Iinkai, pp. 40–56. Nakijin (Okinawa): Nakijin Son Kyōiku Iinkai.

———. 2008b. Yaeyama ni okeru bōeki tōji (Trade ceramics in Yaeyama). In *Tōjiki kara mita kōryū shi* (The history of trade seen from trade ceramics), ed. Ishigaki Shi Sōmubu Shishi Henshūka, pp. 46–49. Ishigaki Shi: Ishigaki Shi Sōmubu Shishi Henshūka.

———. 2009. Nakijin Jōato shutsudo no Gen, Min Seika no bunrui to nendaiteki ichizuke (Analysis and chronological position of Yuan and Ming blue and white from the Nakijin Gusuku Site). In *Nakijin Jōato hakkutsu chōsa hōkokusho IV* (Report of excavations of the Nakijin Gusuku Site, IV), ed. Nakijin Son Kyōiku Iinkai, pp. 121–140. Nakijin (Okinawa): Nakijin Son Kyōiku Iinkai.

Kin Seiki, Matsuda Tomo'o, and Miyazato Suehiro. 1983. Nakijin Jōato shutsudo no Gen seika to kyōhan no tōjiki (Yuan blue and white and associated ceramics found in Nakijin Castle). *Bōeki tōji kenkyū* 3:32–40.

Kin Seiki, Tana Masayuki, Chinen Isamu, and Tōma Shi'ichi. 1988. *Okinawa no gusuku monogatari* (The story of the castles of Okinawa). Naha: Mugisha.

Kinjō Kamenobu. 1990. Gusuku doki no shutsugen (The birth of Gusuku Pottery). *Kōkogaku jānaru* 320: 13–16.

———. 1999. Toshi, jōkan no saishin jōhō: Okinawa (Recent news on studies of cities and castles: Okinawa). *Chūsei toshi kenkyū* 6:258–275.

———. 2001. Shurijō (Kyōnouchi) ato no hakkutsu chōsa gaiyō (Summary of the excavations of the Kyōnouchi Site of Shuri Castle). In *Tokubetsu kikaku ten: Shurijō Kyōnouchi—bōeki tōji kara mita dai kōeki jidai* (Special exhibition: the Kyōnouchi in Shuri Castle—the great period of trade seen from trade ceramics), ed. Okinawa Kenritsu Maizō Bunkazai Sentā, pp. 71–80. Nishihara (Okinawa): Okinawa Kenritsu Maizō Bunkazai Sentā.

Kinjō Seitoku. 1971. Min dai shō, chūki ni okeru kaigai bōeki ni tsuite (Concerning overseas trade of the early and middle Ming period). *Ryūkyū Daigaku Bungakubu Hogakubu kiyō, rekishsi, chirigaku, shakaigaku* 15:111–128.

Kinoshita Naoko. 1996. *Nantō kai bunka no kenkyū: Kai no Michi no kōkogaku* (A study of the shell culture of the Southern Islands: the archaeology of the Shell Road). Tokyo: Hōsei Daigaku Shuppan Kyoku.

———. 2000. Kaigen Tsūhō to Yakōgai (Kaigen Tsūhō coins and *Turbo* shells). In *Ryūkyū, Higashi Ajia no hito to bunka* (People and culture in Ryukyu and East Asia), ed. Takamiya Hiroe Sensei Koki Kinen Henshū Kankōkai, pp. 187–220. Naha: Takamiya Hiroe Sensei Koki Kinen Henshū Kankōkai.

———. 2002. Iseki no gaiyō to roku-nana seiki no Ryūkyū Rettō (Summary of sites and the Ryukyu Archipelago in the sixth to seventh centuries). In *Senshi Ryūkyū no seigyō to kōeki—Amami, Okinawa no hakkutsu chōsa kara* (Subsistence and exchange in the Prehistoric Ryukyus—based on excavations in Amami and Okinawa), ed. Kinoshita Naoko, pp. 3–22. Kumamoto: University of Kumamoto.

———, ed. 2003a. *Chūgoku kodai no takaragai shiyō to ryūtsū, sono imi—Shō Shū dai chūshin ni—shiryōshū* (The use and exchange of cowrie shells in ancient China, their meaning, particularly in the Shang and Zhou dynasties—conference materials). Kumamoto: Kumamoto Daigaku Kōkogaku Kenkyūshitsu.

———. 2003b. Higashi Ajia no kairui bunka III (The shell bead culture in East Asia III) In *Kōryū to kōeki* (Exchange and trade), ed. Gotō Tadashi and Mogi Masahiro, pp. 219–260. Tokyo: Dōseisha.

———. 2003c. Kaisei sōshingu kara mita Hirota Iseki (The Hirota Site seen from shell ornaments). In *Tanegashima Hirota Iseki* (The Tanegashima Hirota Site), ed. Hirota Iseki Gakujutsu Chōsa Kenkyūkai, pp. 329–366. Kagoshima: Kagoshima Rekishi Shiryō Sentā Reimeikan.

———. 2003d. Shell trade and exchange in the prehistory of the Ryūkyū Archipelago. *Bulletin of the Indo-Pacific Prehistory Association* 23:67–72.

———. 2005. Kai kōryū kara mita ibunka sesshoku (Cross-cultural contact seen from shell trade). *Kōkogaku kenkyū* 52:25–41.

———. 2006. Yakōgai kōeki no kanosei: roku-hasseiki no Amami Ōshima mittsu iseki no bunseki (Examination of the possibility of trade of the Great Green Turban: analysis of three sites in Amami Ōshima dating to the sixth to eighth centuries). In *Senshi Ryūkyū no seigyō to kōeki: Amami Ōshima no hakkutsu chōsa kara* (Subsistence and Exchange in the Prehistoric Ryukyus based on excavations in Amami and Okinawa), ed. Kinoshita Naoko, pp. 201–230. Kumamoto: University of Kumamoto.

———. 2009a. Shell exchange in the Ryūkyū Islands and in East Asia. In *Okinawa: The Rise of an Island Kingdom. Archaeological and Cultural Perspectives,* ed. Richard Pearson, pp. 13–40. BAR Series 1898. London: Archaeopress.

———. 2009b. Shōsōin denrai no kaiseihin to kaigara—Yakōgai o chūshin ni (Objects made of shells and shells in the Shōsōin, particularly Green Turban Shell). *Shōsōin kiyō* 31:37–60, 188–189.

———. 2010. Sangoshō to enkyori kōeki (The coral reefs and long-distance exchange). In *Okinawa Ken shi kakuron hen 3: Ko Ryūkyū* (History of Okinawa separate volume no. 3: Ko Ryukyu), ed. Zaidan Hōjin Okinawa Ken Bunka Shinkōkai Shiryō Henshūshitsu, pp. 66–85. Naha: Okinawa Ken Kyōiku Iinkai.

Kinpo Chō Kyōiku Iinkai. 1998. *Mottaimatsu Iseki dai ichiji chōsa* (The first excavation of the Mottaimatsu Site). Kinpo Chō: Kinpo Chō Kyōiku Iinkai.

———. 2000. *Kozono Iseki* (The Kozono Site). Kinpo Chō: Kinpo Chō Kyōiku Iinkai.

Kinpo Chō Rekishi Shinpojiumu Jikkōinkai, Kinpo Chō Kyōiku Iinkai. 1999. *Manosegawa kara mieru Nihon, Higashi Ajia—Ata Tadakage to umi no michi* (Japan and East Asia as seen from the Manose River—Ata Tadakage and the sea routes). Kinpo Chō: Kinpo Chō Kyōiku Iinkai.

Kirch, P. 1980. The archaeological study of adaptation: theoretical and methodological issues. *Advances in Archaeological Method and Theory* 3:101–155.

———. 1984. *The Evolution of the Polynesian Chiefdoms.* Cambridge: Cambridge University Press.

———. 1991. Prehistoric exchange in western Melanesia. *Annual Review of* Anthropology 20:141–165.

———. 2010. *How Chiefs Become Kings: Divine Kingship and the Rise of Archaic States in Ancient Hawaii.* Berkeley: University of California Press.

Kirch, P. V., and D. Yen. 1982. Tikopia: The Prehistory and Ecology of a Polynesian Outlier. *B. P. Bishop Museum Bulletin* 238.

Kishimoto Yoshihiko. 1991. Nantō no doki kigen o megutte (Concerning the origins of pottery in the Southern Islands). *Amami kōko* 2:5–28.

Kishimoto Yoshihiko, Nishime Shō, Miyagi Hiroki, and Azama Mitsuru. 2000. Okinawa hennen kōki no doki yōsō ni tsuite (Concerning aspects of the Late Period in the Okinawa chronology). In *Ryūkyū, Higashi Ajia no hito to bunka* (People and culture in Ryukyu and East Asia), ed. Takamiya Hiroe Sensei Koki Kinen

Henshū Kankōkai, pp. 131–152. Naha: Takamiya Hiroe Sensei Koki Kinen Henshū Kankōkai.

Kizaki Kōshirō, ed. 1985. *Ryūkyū Ko no chishitsu monogatari* (The geological history of the Ryukyu Arc). Naha: Okinawa Taimsu Sha.

Knapp, A., and E. Blake. 2005. Prehistory in the Mediterranean: the connecting and corrupting sea. In *The Archaeology of Mediterranean Prehistory,* ed. A. B. Knapp and E. Blake, pp. 1–24. Oxford: Blackwell Publishing.

Koba, Motoharu, Takashi Nakata, and Tatsuo Takahashi. 1982. Late Holocene eustatic sea level changes deduced from geomorphological features and their 14C dates in the Ryūkyū Islands, Japan. *Palaeogeography, Palaeoclimatology, Palaeoecology* 39:231–260.

Kobata, Atsushi, and Mitsugu Matsuda. 1969. *Ryukyuan Relations with Korea and South Sea Countries: An Annotated Translation of Documents in the Rekidai Hōan.* Kyoto: Kobata Atsushi.

Kobayashi, H., T. Hirose, M. Sugino, and N. Watanabe. 1974. Tk-99. Minatogawa. *Radiocarbon* 16:384.

Kobayashi Ryūta, Satō Takao, Midorikawa (Najima) Yayoi, Irina Zueva-Nosova, and Yamaguchi Tetsu. 2010. Sangoshō o tomonau tōsho ni okeru senshi dōbutsu shigen riyō (Prehistoric use of faunal resources on islands with coral reefs: the example of Ishigaki). Poster presentation at the meetings of the Coral Reef Study Association. Tokyo, December 2, 2010.

Kobayashi, Tatsuo. 2004. *Jōmon Reflections: Forager Life and Culture in the Prehistoric Japanese Archipelago.* Edited by Simon Kaner with Oki Nakamura. Oxford: Oxbow Books.

Kokubu Naoichi. 1972. *Nantō Senshi Jidai no kenkyū* (Study of the Prehistoric Period of the Southern Islands). Tokyo: Keiyūsha.

Kokudo Chōsa Okinawa Ken. 1983. *Tochi bunrui kihon chōsa* (Basic soil classification investigation). Naha: Okinawa Ken Kokudo Chōsa.

Kokuritsu Kagaku Hakubutsukan. 1988. *Nihonjin no kigenten: Nihonjin wa doko kara kita ka?* (Exhibition on the origins of the Japanese: where did the Japanese come from?). Catalogue. Tokyo: Yomiuri Shimbunsha.

Kōmoto Masayuki, ed. 2007. *Sakyū keisei to kanreika genzō* (Sand dune formation and climatic deterioration). Kumamoto: Kumamoto Daigaku Bungakubu.

Kōno Reiko. 2010. Dejitaru kaiseki kara mita Minatogawajin. (Minatogawa human seen from digital imaging). *Kagaku* 80 (4): 378–380.

Kreiner, Josef. 2008. Some thoughts on the idea of kingship and the origins of the Ryūkyū Kingdom. In *The East Asian Mediterranean: Crossroads of Culture, Commerce, and Human Migration,* ed. Angela Schottenhammer, pp. 389–402. Wiesbaden: Harrassowitz Verlag.

Kubo Tomoyasu. 2003. Ryūkyū, Ezo chi no kazari (Ornaments of the Ryukyu and Ezo areas). In *Tokubetsu tenrankai, Konjiki no Kazari: kōgei ni miru Nihon bi* (Special exhibition, Kazari in gold: Japanese aesthetics through metalworks), ed. Kyoto National Museum, pp. 240–263. Kyoto: Kyoto National Museum.

Kudo, Yūichirō. 2007. The temporal correspondences between the archaeological chronology and environmental changes from 11,500 to 2,800 bp on the Kanto Plain, Eastern Japan. *Daiyonki kenkyū* 46 (3): 187–194. In English.

Kumejima Chō Kyōiku Iinkai. 2005. *Gushikawa Jōato hakkutsu chōsa hōkokusho I* (Report of excavations of the Gushikawa Castle Site I). Kumejima: Okinawa Ken Kumejima Chō Kyōiku Iinkai.

———. 2008. *Gushikawa Jōato hakkutsu chōsa hōkokusho II* (Report of excavations at the Gushikawa Castle Site II). Kumejima: Okinawa Ken Kumejima Chō Kyōiku Iinkai.

Kuo Su-chiu. 2010. Kōkogaku kara mita Taiwan to Paiwan bunka no kigen (The origins of the Paiwan Culture of Taiwan as seen from archaeology). In *Nankai o meguru kōkogaku* (Archaeology around the Southern Ocean), ed. Inamura Keiji, pp. 131–158. Tokyo: Dōseisha.

Kuroda Tomio and Ōzawa Tomō. 1996. Kafun bunseki kara mita Ryūkyū Rettō no shokusei hensen to ko kikō (Palaeoclimatic and vegetational changes during the Pleistocene and Holocene in the Ryukyu Islands inferred from pollen assemblages). *Chigaku zasshi* 105:328–342.

Kurozumi Taiji. 2003. Kairuigaku kara mita Chūgoku kodai iseki shutsudo kairui no kyokuchi (The source area of shells found in Chinese ancient archaeological sites as seen from malacology). In *Chūgoku kodai no takaragai shiyō to ryūtsū, sono imi—Shō Shū dai chūshin ni—shiryōshū* (The use and exchange of cowrie shells in ancient China, their meaning, particularly in the Shang and Zhou dynasties—conference materials), ed. Kinoshita Naoko, pp. 12–40. Kumamoto: Kumamoto Daigaku Kōkogaku Kenkyūshitsu.

———. 2006. Kairui itai kara mita iseki no richi, kankyō to seikatsu (Environment and human life in sites seen from shell remains). In *Senshi Ryūkyū no seigyō to kōeki 2—Amami, Okinawa no hakkutsu chōsa kara* (Subsistence and exchange in the Prehistoric Ryukyus—based on excavations in Amami and Okinawa), ed. Kinoshita Naoko, pp. 115–134. Kumamoto: University of Kumamoto.

———. 2008. Ryūkyū Rettō no kankyō henka o kairui kara fukameru (Broadening environmental changes in the Ryukyu Islands based on molluscs). *Kōkogaku jānaru* 577:15–20.

———. 2011. Ryūkyū senshi jidaijin to sangoshō shigen: kairui o chūshin ni (Prehistoric people of the Ryukyu Islands and reef resources: shell species in particular). In *Senshi, Gusuku Jidai no Ryūkyū Rettō: hito to keikan* (The Ryūkyū Islands in the Prehistoric and Primitive Periods: people and landscape), ed. Takamiya Hiroto and Itō Shinji, pp. 87–107. Tokyo: Rokuichi Shobō.

Kuwabara Jitsuzō. 1989. *Hojukō no jiseki* (The accomplishments of Pu Shougeng). Tokyo: Heibonsha.

Kuwahata Mitsuhiro. 2002. Kōko shiryō kara mita Kikai Akahoya funka no jiki to eikyō (Age and cultural influence of the Kikai Akahoya eruption as seen from archaeological material in South Kyushu, Japan). *Daiyonki kenkyū* 41 (4): 331–344.

Kuwahata Takeshi and Ōkubo Kōji. 2000. Tanegashima no saisekki: Nishino Omote Ōnakamine Iseki shiryō no shōkai (Microliths from Tanegshima: an introduction to the materials from the Ōnakamine Site, Tanegashima). *Jinruishi kenkyū* 12:71–80.

Ladefoged, T. N., and R. Pearson. 2000. Fortified castles on Okinawa Island during the Gusuku Period, AD 1200 to 1600. *Antiquity* 74 (284): 404–412.

Lam, P. 2012. The David Vases revisited II: the dragon bands. *Orientations* 43 (1): 40–49.

Larson, G., U. Albarella, K. Dobney, and P. Rowly-Conwy. 2007. Current views on *Sus* phylogeography and pig domestication as seen through modern mtDNA studies. In *Pigs and Humans: 10,000 Years of Interaction,* ed. Umberto Albarella, Keith Dobney, Anton Ervynk, Peter Rowly-Conwy, pp. 30–41. Oxford: Oxford University Press.

Lee, S., and T. Hasegawa. 2011. Bayesian phylogenetic analysis supports an agricultural origin of Japonic languages. *Proceedings of the Royal Society B* 278:3662–3669.

Li, Baohua, Zhimin Jian, and Pingxian Wang. 1997. *Pulleniatina obliquiloculata* as a paleoceanographic indicator in the Southern Okinawa Trough during the last 20,000 Years. *Marine Micropaleontology* 32:59–69.

Li, Kanyang. 2007. A study on the Song, Yuan, and Ming monetary policies within the context of worldwide hard currency flows during the eleventh to sixteenth centuries and their impact on Ming institutions. In *The East Asian Maritime World 1400–1800: Its Fabrics of Power and Dynamics of Exchanges,* ed. Angela Schottenhammer, pp. 99–136. Wiesbaden: Harrassowitz Verlag.

Li Kun-hsiu and Yeh Mei-chen, eds. 2001. *Taidong Xian shi—shiqian pian* (History of Taidong County: prehistory). Taidong Shi: Taidong Shifu.

Li Xijing. 1982. Jukō seiji (kushimekakukamon seiji) ni tsuite no kenkyū sensetsu (A brief explanation of Jukō celadon [celadon with comb marks and floral patterns]). *Bōeki tōji kenkyū* 2:21–27.

Liu, Jian, Rixiang Zhu, Tiegang Li, Anchun Li, and Jun Li. 2007. Sediment-magnetic signature of Mid Holocene paleoenvironmental change in the Central Okinawan Trough. *Marine Geology* 239:19–31.

Loo, J. H., J. Trejaut, J. C. Yen, Z. S. Chen, C. L. Lee, and M. Lin. 2011. Genetic affinities between the Yami tribe people of Orchid Island and the Phlippine Islanders of the Batanes archiplelago. *BMC Genetics* 2011 (12): 21.

Machida, Hiroshi, and Shinji Sugiyama. 2002. The impact of the Kikai Akahoya explosive eruptions on human societies. In *Natural Disasters and Cultural Change,* ed. J. Graham and R. Torrence, pp. 313–325. London: Routledge.

Maehira Fusa'aki. 2004. Ryūkyū ōkoku ni okeru Higashi Ajia no chiiki kan no kōeki (The Ryukyu Kingdom's interregional trade in East Asia). *Chūsei toshi kenkyū* 9:191–203.

Maeno, F., and H. Taniguchi. 2010. Geology and eruptive history of the Kikai Caldera. http://www.eri.u-tokyo.ac.jp/fmaeno/kikai/kikaicaldera.html.

Makino Kiyoshi. 1968. *Yaeyama no Meiwa Tsunami* (The Meiwa Tidal Wave of Yaeyama). Kumamoto: Makino Kiyoshi.

Makishi Yōkō. 2012. Ryukyu ōkoku jūgo seiki chūki irai no kinaiseiteki na tokucho to ōjo girei (Kinai-like special features and palace rituals from the middle of the fifteenth century in the Ryukyu Kingdom). *Okinawa bunka kenkyū* 38:155–245.

Manning, S., and L. Hulin. 2005. Maritime commerce and geographies of mobility in the Late Bronze Age of the Eastern Mediterranean: problematizations. In *The Archaeology of Mediterranean Prehistory,* ed. A. B. Knapp and E. Blake, pp. 270–302. Oxford: Blackwell Publishing.

Matsuda, Masahiko. 2002. Taro in Japan and its dispersal in East and Southeast Asia. In *Vegeculture in Eastern Asia and Oceania,* ed. S. Yoshida and P. Matthews, pp. 117–134. JCAS Symposium Series No. 16. Kyoto: Center for Integrated Area Studies, Kyoto University.

Matsui, Akira, Naotake Ishiguro, Hitomi Hongo, and Masao Minagawa. 2005. Wild pig? or domesticated boar? an archaeological view on the domestication of *Sus scrofa* in Japan. In *The First Steps of Domestication: New Archaeological Approaches,* ed J. Peters, J-D. Vigne, and D. Helmer, pp. 148–159. Oxford: Oxbow Books.

Matsukusa, Hirotaka, Hiroki Oota, Kuniaki Haneji, Takashi Tōma, Shoji Kawamura, and Hajime Ishida. 2010. A genetic analysis of the Sakishima Islanders reveals no relationship with Taiwan aborigines but shared ancestry with Ainu and Main-island Japanese. *American Journal of Physical Anthropology* 142:211–233.

Matsushita Takayuki. 2003. Okinawa Ken Yomitan Son Momenbaru Iseki shutsudo no Yayoi Jidai jinkotsu (The human skeletal bones excavated from the Yayoi Period Momenbaru Site, Yomitan Son, Okinawa). *Nantō kōko* 22:67–108.

Matsu'ura, Shuji. 1982. Relative dating of Minatogawa Man by fluorine dating. In *The Minatogawa Man: The Upper Pleistocene Man from the Island of Okinawa,* ed. Hisashi Suzuki and Kazuro Hanihara, pp. 205–208. Tokyo: University Museum, University of Tokyo.

Minagawa, Masao, Akira Matsui, and Naotaka Ishiguro. 2005. Patterns of prehistoric boar *Sus scrofa* domestication, and inter-island pig trading across the East China Sea, as determined by carbon and nitrogen isotope analysis. *Chemical Geology* 218:91–102.

Mithen, Steven. 2004. *After the Ice: A Global Human History, 20,000–5,000 BC.* Cambridge, MA: Harvard University Press.

Miyagi Eishō and Takamiya Hiroe, eds. 1983. *Okinawa rekishi chizu kōko hen* (A historical atlas of Okinawa, archaeology volume). Tokyo: Kashiwa Shobō.

Miyagi Hiroki. 2006a. Gusuku to shūraku no kankei ni tsuite: oboegaki—Nakijin Jōato o chūshin toshite (Concerning relations between *gusuku* and village, memorandum, with Nakijin Gusuku as main concern). *Nantō kōko* 25:27–40.

———. 2006b. Ryūkyū Rettō ni okeru shutsudo tōjiki no kenkyū (Study of ceramics found in the Ryukyu Archipelago). In *Jūsan-jūyon seiki kaijo bōeki kara mita Ryūkyū Koku seiritsu yōin no jisshoteki kenkyū—Chūgoku Fukkenshō o chūshin ni* (A study to verify the factors in the development of the Ryukyu Kingdom from overseas trade in the thirteenth to fourteenth centuries—with particular reference to Fujian Province, China), ed. Kinoshita Naoko, pp. 89–99. Kumamoto: Kumamoto Daigaku Bungakubu.

———. 2007. Okinawa Shotō ni okeru Gusuku Jidai tatemono ato no hensen (Changes in building remains in the Gusuku Period of the Okinawa Islands). *Nantō kōko* 26:157–168.

———. 2009. Ryūkyū sen no michi (The route of Ryukyu coins). In *Umi ga tsunagaida Satsuma—Ryūkyū* (Satsuma Ryukyu, held together by the sea), ed. Minami Satsuma Shi Bōnotsu Rekishi Shiryō Sentā—Kishinkan, p. 8. Minami Satsuma Shi: Minami Satsuma Shi Bōnotsu Rekishi Shiryō Sentā—Kishinkan.

———. 2010. Chūsei no zeni to Ryūkyū ōkoku (Mediaeval Japanese coinage and the Ryukyu Kingdom). In *Okinawa Ken shi kakuron hen daisan kan: Ko Ryūkyū* (History of Okinawa, separate volume no. 3: Ko Ryukyu), ed. Zaidan Hōjin Okinawa Ken Bunka Shinkōkai Shiryō Henshūshitsu, pp. 527–544. Naha: Okinawa Ken Kyōiku Iinkai.

———. 2011. Gusuku Jidai no otozureta daikibo na shima no keikan henka (Looking at large-scale landscape changes of the island landscapes of the Gusuku Period). In *Senshi, Gusuku Jidai no Ryūkyū Rettō: hito to keikan* (The Ryūkyū Islands in the Prehistoric and Primitive Periods: people and landscape), ed. Takamiya Hiroto and Itō Shinji, pp. 217–241. Tokyo: Rokuichi Shobō.

Miyagi Hiroki, Katagiri Chiaki, Arakaki Tsutomu, and Higa Naoki. 2004. Nansei Shotō ni okeru chinbotsusen hakken no kanosei to sono kisoteki chōsa—kaiyō saishū ibutsu kara mita kaiyō kōryū (Preliminary investigation into discovering sunken ships in the Southwest Islands: underwater artifacts and marine transportation). *Okinawa maibun kenkyū* 2:81–108.

Miyagi Hiroki and Tamashiro Yasushi. 2005. Shūraku iseki ni kansuru kōkogakuteki kenkyū (Archaeological study relating to village sites). In *Nakijin Jōato Shūhen Iseki II, Nakijin Jōato Shūhen seibi jigyo tomonau kenkyū hakkutsu chōsa hōkoku* (Site II, Nakijin Castle Site vicinity: report of salvage excavations associated with renovations of the area near Nakijin Castle), ed. Nakijin Son Kyōiku Iinkai, pp. 173–180. Nakijin Son (Okinawa): Nakijin Son Kyōiku Iinkai.

Miyakojima Shi Kyōiku Iinkai. 2006. *Nema, Nishizato iseki* (Nema, Nishizato sites). Miyakojima: Miyakojima Shi Kyōiku Iinkai.

Miyashita Takahiro. 1998. Kagoshima Ken Mottaimatsu Iseki to shutsudo tōjiki (The Mottaimatsu Site, Kagoshima Prefecture, and its ceramics). *Bōeki tōji kenkyū* 18:70–85.

———. 2003. Sangaku jiin to kōwan toshi no ichi ruikei (One type of mountain temple and port town). *Kodai bunka* 55 (2): 35–45.

Miyazato Eiki and Kadena Sōtoku. 1968. Kyūyō bassui (Kyūyō summary). In *Naha Shishi* (History of Naha City), ed. Naha Shishi Henshū Iinkai Sōmubu Henshūshitsu, pp. 15–86. Naha: Naha Shi Yakusho.

Mizoguchi Yūji. 2010. Nihonjin keiseiron e no sasoi: shinario saikōchiku no tame ni (Rising to the challenge of the theory of the formation of the Japanese people: reconstruction of a scenario). *Kagaku* 80 (4): 396–403.

Mokpo Taehakkyo Panmulgwan. 1990. *Chŏlla Namdo Jindo Gun Yongzaesong* (The Yongzaesong [fortress], Jindo, South Chŏlla). Mokpo: Mokpo University Museum.

Morimoto Isao. 2004. Wakuta Iseki Gun (Wakuta Kiln Group). *Okinawa maibun kenkyū* 2: color frontispiece and text.

———. 2008. Gusuku jidai no makuake (The dawn of the Gusuku Period). In *Nichi Ryū kōeki no reimei—Yamato kara no shōgeki* (The dawn of exchange between Japan and Ryukyu—the impact of Yamato), ed. Tanigawa Ken'ichi, pp. 263–284. Tokyo: Rinwasha.

Morimura Ken'ichi. 1998. Sakai ni okeru bōeki tōji (Trade ceramics from Sakai). In *Nihon Kōkogaku Kyōkai 1998 nendo taikai, kenkyū happyō shiryō* (Research paper materials, Japan Archaeological Association 1998 meetings), ed. Nihon Kōkogaku Kyōkai, pp. 123–135. Tokyo: Nihon Kōkogaku Kyōkai.

———. 1999. Gosude: Gosu Akae no seisan yō (The Gōsu style: the production kiln of Gōsu overglaze enamelware). *Tōyō Tōji Gakkai kaihō* 37:5.

———. 2006. Bizenyaki no susa, genzai, yurai Bizenyaki: Momoyama bunka no katachi ni ikiru (The past, present, and future of Bizenyaki: living in the form of Momoyama Culture). *Bizen shi rekishi shiryōkan kiyō* 8:109–124.

———. 2007a. Fukken, Ryūkyū, Sakai ni okeru Zenrin to kaishō (Fujian, Ryukyu, and Sakai Zen temples and maritime merchants). *Nantō kōko* 26:197–208.

———. 2007b. Sakai, Minnan [Sennan no Bukkoku] kokusai kankei ron (The theory of the [Quannan Buddhist Country] and Sakai and the Minnan region). *Kansai kinsei kōkogaku kenkyū* 15:148–166.

———. 2009. Chusei no Sakai to bōeki tōjiki (Mediaeval Sakai and trade ceramics). In *Umi o Koeta Tōjiki to Cha Bunka Shinpojiumu happyō yōshi* (Lecture notes from the symposium Ceramics and Tea Culture That Crossed the Ocean), ed. Bukkyō Daigaku Shūkyō Bunka Mujiumu, pp. 9–12. Kyoto: Bukkyō Daigaku Shūkyō Bunka Mujiumu.

Morita Taiju. 2009. Kuni hitei iseki Sumiyoshi Kaizuka (Sumiyoshi Shellmound, a national historic site). In *Tokunoshima Kamuiyaki Tōki Yōseki kuni hitei shiseki tōroku kinen shinpojiumu kiroku shū—Kamuiyaki no Sato Tokunoshima—Amami Ōshima no jūyōseki no hōzon katsuyō ni mukete* (Materials from the symposium in commemoration of the registration of the Kamuiyaki Kilns as a national historic site), ed. Isen Chō Kyōiku Iinkai, pp. 5–8. Isen Chō: Isen Chō Kyōiku Iinkai.

Mukai Wataru. 2002. Tai, Betunamu no sanchi to nendai (Production area and date of Thai and Vietnamese ceramics). In *Mindai zenhanki tōshiki no kenkyū: Shurijō Kyōnouchi SK01 shutsudohin* (Study of Ceramics from the first half of the Ming dynasty: the objects uncovered in Shuri Castle SK01), ed. Kamei Meitoku, pp. 70–83. Kawasaki: Senshū Daigaku.

Murai Shōsuke. 1994. Jūgo-jūnana seiki no Nichiryū kankei to Gosansō (Relations between Japan and Ryukyu in the fifteenth to seventeenth centuries and priests from the Five Great Temples of Kyoto). In *Okinawa no rekishi to bunka: kaijō no michi tankyū* (Culture and history of Okinawa: research on the sea routes), ed. Kanaseki Hiroshi and Sahara Makoto, pp. 189–203. Tokyo: Yoshikawa Kōbunkan.

———. 2000. Tōnan Ajia no naka no Ko Ryūkyū (Ko Ryukyu as part of Southeast Asia). *Rekishi* 603 (2000): 16–30.

———. 2008. Introduction. *Acta Asiatica* 95:iii–viii.

Nagahama Tatsuki. 2006. Shuri Jōato shutsudo senka no senshu kōsei ni tsuite (Assemblage of coin types found in the Shuri Castle Site). *Okinawa maibun kenkyū* 4:73–80.

Naha Shi Kyōiku Iinkai Bunka Ka. 1986. *Naha Shi rekishi chizu* (Historical atlas of Naha City). Naha: Naha Shi Kyōiku Iinkai.

———. 2000. *Tenkaiji Iseki* (The Tenkaiji Site). Naha: Naha Shi Kyōiku Iinkai.

Najima Yayoi. 2003. Ryūkyū Rettō ni okeru iseki shutsudo gyoshu sosei no hikaku (Comparison of fish species assemblages from sites in the Ryukyu Islands). *Tōkai shigaku* 38:75–95.

Najima Yayoi, Anzai Eisuke, and Miyagi Hiroki. 2008. Ryūkyū Rettō no tanso 14 nendai shiryō no shūsei (Compilation of radiocarbon dates from the Nansei [Ryukyu] Islands). *Nantō kōko* 27:23–48.

Nakagawa, Ryohei, Naomi Doi, Yuichiro Nishioka, Shin Nunami, Heizaburo Yamauchi, Masaki Fujita, Shinji Yamasaki, Masaaki Yamamoto, Chiaki Katagiri, Hitoshi Mukai, Hiroyuki Matsuzaki, Takashi Gakuhari, Mai Takigami, and Minoru Yoneda. 2010. Pleistocene human remains from Shiraho-Saonetabaru Cave, on Ishigaki Island, Okinawa Japan, and their radiocarbon dating. *Anthropological Science* 118 (2010) 3: 173–183.

Nakama Gishō. 1983. Ntabaru Toyūmiyā Miyāka (The Tomb of Toyomoiya of Untabaru). *Okinawa dai jiten* (Encyclopedia of Okinawa) 3:1008.

Nakamori Ton. 1999. Hanasuku Mura Iseki hakkutsu chōsa no gaiyō (Brief report on the excavation of the Hanasuku Village Site). In *Mura ga kataru Okinawa no rekishi*

(Villages tell the story of Okinawan history), ed. Rekishi Minzoku Hakubutsukan, pp. 77–99. Tokyo: Shin Jinbutsu Ōraisha.

Nakamura, Mari. 2006. Early Upper Palaeolithic sites in the Southwestern Islands of Japan: indirect evidence of plant utilization. *Current Research in the Pleistocene* 23:24–26.

Nakasone Motomu. 2004. Gusuku Jidai kaishiki no hottate bashira tatemono ni tsuite no ichi kōsatsu (An inquiry into buildings with dug posts at the beginning of the Gusuku Period). In *Gusuku Jidai o kangaeru* (Thinking about the Gusuku Period), ed. Nakijin Son Kyōiku Iinkai, pp. 269–288. Tokyo: Shin Jinbutsu Ōraisha.

Nakayama Kiyomi. 1995. Kasari Chō Ushuku Kaizuka hakkutsu chōsa (Excavation of Ushuku Shellmound, Kasari). *Kōkogaku jānaru* 397:17–20.

———. 2008. Tomori Matsunoto Iseki (The Tomori Matsunoto Site). In *Hakkutsu sareta Nihon Rettō 2008,* ed. Bunka Chō, pp. 55–58. Tokyo: Asahi Shimbunsha.

———. 2009. *Horidasareta Amami Shotō* (The Amami Islands excavated). Amami Shi: Amami Bunka Zaidan.

Nakazato Toshikatsu. 1995. Kodai Raden no kenkyū—jō (The study of Ancient Raden [shell inlay], part 1). *Kokka* 1199:3–18.

Nakazawa, Yuichi, Akira Iwase, Fumito Akai, and Masami Izuho. 2011. Human responses to the Younger Dryas in Japan. *Quaternary International* 242 (2): 416–433.

Nakijin Son Kyōiku Iinkai. 2005. *Nakijin Jōato shūhen iseki II: Nakijin Jōato shūhen seibi jigyo ni tomonau kinkyū hakkutsu chōsa hōkoku* (Sites in the vicinity of Nakijin Castle: report of salvage excavations associated with renovation of the area near Nakijin Castle, II). Nakijin: Nakijin Son Kyōiku Iinkai.

———. No date. Sekai Isan Nakijin Jōato (World Heritage Site Nakijin Castle). Nakijin (Okinawa): Nakijin Son Kyōiku Iinkai. (Site explanation pamphlet.)

Nakijin Village, Board of Education. 2008. *World Heritage Nakijin—Jo: Site Guidebook of the Cultural Assets of Nakijin Village.* Nakijin (Okinawa): Nakijin Village Board of Education.

Nelson, Thomas. 2006. Japan in the early life of Ryukyu. *Journal of Japanese Studies* 32 (2): 367–392.

Ng, Chin-keong. 1971. The Fukienese maritime trade in the second half of the Ming Period: government policy and elite groups' attitudes. *Nanyang University Journal,* 5, part 2 (Social Sciences and Humanities)*:* 81–100.

Niijima Natsuko. 2005. Ko Ryūkyū ni okeru Naha kōwan kinō: kuni no minato toshite no Naha Kō (The function of the port of Naha as a national port). *Senshū shigaku* 39:41–68.

———. 2008. Okinawa shutsudo Gen seikashi no shosō—kishū sosei no bunseki o chūshin ni (Aspects of Yuan dynasty blue and white ceramics: an analysis of the assemblage of vessel types). *Nantō kōko* 27:49–56.

Nitta Jūsei, Higa Yoshimori, Shimabukuro Harumi, and Nakaza Hisayoshi. 2005.

Urasoe Kaizuka dai ichi, ni ji hakkutsu chōsa no matome (The Urasoe Shellmound, combined report of the first and second excavations). *Okinawa kenritsu hakubutsukan kiyō* 31:13–54.

Obata, Hiroki, Isao Morimoto, and Susumu Kakubuchi. 2010. Obsidian trade between sources on northwestern Kyushu and the Ryūkyū Archipelago during the Jōmon Period. In *Crossing the Straits: Prehistoric Obsidian Exploitation in the North Pacific Rim,* ed. Y. Kuzmin and M. Glassock, pp. 51–71. BAR Series 2152. Oxford: Archaeopress.

O'Connell, J., J. Allen, and K. Hawkes. 2010. Pleistocene Sahul and the origins of seafaring. In *The Global Origins and Development of Seafaring,* ed. A. Anderson, J. Barrett, and K. Boyle, pp. 57–68. Cambridge, UK. The MacDonald Institute for Archaeological Research, Cambridge University.

Oda Shizuo. 1997. Okinawa Ken Kunigami Son shutsudo no marunomigata seki fu ni rei (Two examples of round gouge-shaped adzes found in Kunigami Village, Okinawa Prefecture). *Nantō kōko* 16:3–26.

———. 1999. Ryūkyū Rettō kyūsekki no wakugumi ni tsuite (A framework for the Paleolithic cultures around the Ryukyu Islands). *Jinruishi kenkyū* 11:29–45.

———. 2007. Ryūkyū Ko no kōkogaku: Nansei Rikuhashi ni okeru hito, mono no kōryū shi (Archaeology of the Ryūkyū Arc: history of exchange of people and things on the Southwest Land Bridge). In *Chiki no tayōsei to kōkogaku: Tōnan Ajia to sono shūhen* (Regional diversity and archaeology—Southeast Asia and vicinity), ed. Marui Masako, Aoyagi Yōji Sensei Taishoku Kinen Ronbunshū Henshū Iinkai, pp. 37–61. Tokyo: Yūzankaku.

———. 2009. Minatogawa fuishā iseki ni tsuite (Concerning the Minatogawa Fissure Site). *Nantō kōko* 28:1–17.

Ōhama Eisen. 1994. Nagura Shitadaru Iseki ni tsuite (Concerning the Shitadaru Site, Nagura). *Nantō kōko* 14:93–102.

———. 1999. *Yaeyama no kōkogaku* (Archaeology of Yaeyama). Ishigaki: Sakishima Bunka Kenkyūsho.

———. 2005. *Ōyake Akahachi Honkawara no Ran to Sanyōsei ichimon no hitobito* (The Ōyake Akahachi Honkawara Disturbance and the people who hold the surname Sanyō). Ishigaki: Nanzan Sha.

———. 2008. Yaeyama Shotō no kōeki: Suku Bunka Ki no chūshin ni (Trade in the Yaeyama Islands, particularly in the Suku Period). In *Nichi Ryū kōeki no reimei—Yamato kara no shōgeki* (The dawn of exchange between Japan and Ryukyu—the impact of Yamato), ed. Tanigawa Ken'ichi, pp. 347–382. Tokyo: Shinwasha.

———, ed. 2009. *Nagura Shitadaru kaisoko iseki kyōdō kenkyū hōkokusho* (Joint report of the study of the underwater site of Shitadaru, Nagura). Ishigaki: Sakishima Bunka Kenkyūsho.

Ōhashi Kōji. 1981. Jūgo, jūroku seiki ni okeru Nihon shutsudo no seika wan ni kansuru hennen shian (A tentative chronology of blue and white bowls from the fifteenth and sixteenth centuries found in Japan). *Hakusui* 8:52–63.

Ohgaki, Shun'ichi, and Taiji Kurozumi. 2000. Historical decline of the mangrove gastropods *Telescopium* and *Terebralia* in the Ryūkyū Islands and Taiwan: evidence from shell middens. *Asian Marine Biology* 17:125–135.

Okada Teruo and Kuniyoshi Kazuo. 2000. *Sekai Isan Gusuku* Kikō (World Heritage Sites: accounts of Gusuku). Naha: Ryūkyū Shinpo.

Okamoto, Hiromichi. 2008. Foreign policy and maritime trade in the early Ming period: focussing on the Ryūkyū Kingdom. *Acta Asiatica* 95: 35–55.

Okinawa Ken Bunka Shinkōkai, ed. 2006. Okinawa Ken shi: zusetsu hen kendo no sugata (History of Okinawa: illustrated volume on land forms of the prefecture). Naha: Okinawa Ken Kyōiku Iinkai.

Okinawa Ken Gushikawa Shi Kyōiku Iinkai. 1980. *Uken Kaizuka Gun, Akajangā Kaizuka hakkutsu chōsa hōkoku* (Report of excavations of the Uken Shellmound Group and Akajangā Shellmound). Okinawa: Okinawa Ken Gushikawa Shi Kyōiku Iinkai.

Okinawa Ken Haebaru Chō Kyōiku Iinkai. 1996. *Kunindo Iseki: dai ichi, ni, sanji han'i kakunin chōsa hōkokusho* (The Kunindo Site: site report of excavations to determine the extent of the site, nos. 1, 2, 3). Haebaru Chō: Okinawa Ken Haebaru Chō Kyōiku Iinkai.

Okinawa Ken Hirara Shi Kyōiku Iinkai. 1977. *Furusutobaru Iseki* (The Furusutobaru Site). Ishigaki Shi: Ishigaki Shi Kyōiku Iinkai.

———. 1983. *Sumiya Iseki (Zokusho Shīma) hakkutsu chōsa hōkoku* (Report of excavations of the Sumiya [Shīma] Site). Hirara: Hirara Shi Kyōiku Iinkai.

———. 1992. *Sumiya Iseki* (The Sumiya Site). Hirara: Hirara Shi Kyōiku Iinkai.

Okinawa Ken Kumejima Chō Kyōiku Iinkai. 2005. *Gushikawa Jōato hakkutsu chōsa hōkokusho I* (Report of excavations at the Gushikawa Castle Site I). Kumejima: Okinawa Ken Kumejima Chō Kyōiku Iinkai.

———. 2008. *Gushikawa Jōato hakkutsu chōsa hōkokusho II* (Report of excavations at the Gushikawa Castle Site II). Kumejima: Okinawa Ken Kumejima Chō Kyōiku Iinkai.

Okinawa Ken Kyōiku Iinkai. 1983. *Inafuku Iseki hakkutsu chōsa hokokusho, Iiutaki Chiku* (Report of the excavation of the Inafuku Site, Iiutaki Area). Naha: Okinawa Ken Kyōiku Iinkai.

———. 1984. *Noguni: Noguni Kaizuka Gun B Chiten hakkutsu chōsa hōkoku* (Noguni: report of excavations of Locality B, Noguni Shellmound Group). Naha: Okinawa Ken Kyōiku Iinkai.

———. 1985a. *Pinza Abu: Pinza Abu dōketsu hakkutsu chōsa hōkoku* (Pinza Abu, report of excavations at Pinza Abu). Naha: Okinawa Ken Kyōiku Iinkai.

———. 1985b. *Shinugudō Iseki, dai 1, 2, 3 ji hakkutsu chōsa hōkokusho* (Report of excavations 1, 2, and 3 of the Shinugudō Site). Naha: Okinawa Ken Kyōiku Iinkai.

———. 1986. *Shimotabaru Kaizuka, Ōdomaribama Kaizuka dai 1, 2, 3 ji hakkutsu chōsa hōkoku* (Report of excavations 1, 2, 3 of the Shimotabaru and Ōdomaribama Shellmounds). Naha: Okinawa Ken Kyōiku Iinkai.

———. 1987. *Kogachibaru Kaizuka* (Kogachibaru Shellmound). Naha: Okinawa Ken Kyōiku Iinkai.

———. 1988. *Shuri Jōato Kankai Mon, Kyūkei Mon Uchigawa chiku no fukugen seibi jigyo no kakaru ikō chōsa* (Investigations of features in the area inside the Kankai and Kyūkei Gates of the Shuri Castle Site related to reconstruction work). Naha: Okinawa Ken Kyōiku Iinkai.

———. 1990a. *Ahagon Furushima Iseki* (The Ahagon Old Village Site). Naha: Okinawa Ken Kyoiku Iinkai.

———. 1990b. *Shinzatomura Iseki: Taketomijima shūhen dōro kensetsu ni tomonau kinkyū hakkutsu chōsa hōkoku* (The Shinzatomura Site: report of excavations in association with the construction of a road on the perimeter of Taketomi Island). Naha: Okinawa Ken Kyōiku Iinkai.

———. 1994. *Gusuku: Gusuku Bunritsu chōsa hōkokusho III Yaeyama Shotō* (Gusuku: report on survey of Gusuku Distribution, III, Yaeyama Archipelago). Naha: Okinawa Ken Kyōiku Iinkai.

———. 1995a. *Kitahara Kaizuka: hakkutsu chōsa hōkokusho* (The Kitahara Site: report of excavations). Naha: Okinawa Ken Kyōiku Iinkai.

———. 1995b. *Nanden, Hokudenseki no ikō chōsa hōkoku* (Shuri Castle Site: report of investigation of archaeological features of the Nanden and Hokuden Sites). Naha: Okinawa Ken Kyōiku Iinkai.

———. 1998. *Shuri Jōato Kyōnouchi hakkutsu chōsa hōkokusho* (Report of excavations of the Kyōnouchi, Shuri Castle Site). Naha: Okinawa Ken Kyōiku Iinkai.

———. 2001. *Kai no Michi: senshi Ryūkyū Rettō no kai kōeki* (The Shell Route: shell trade in the prehistoric Ryukyu Islands). Naha: Okinawa Ken Kyōiku Iinkai.

Okinawa Ken Nakijin Son Kyōiku Iinkai. 1983. *Nakijin Jōato hakkutsu chōsa hōkoku I* (Report of the excavation of the Nakijin Castle Site I). Nakijin Son (Okinawa): Nakijin Son Kyōiku Iinkai.

———. 2005. *Nakjiin Jōato Shūhen Iseki II* (Sites in the vicinity of the Nakijin Castle Site II). Nakijin (Okinawa): Okinawa Ken Nakijin Son Kyōiku Iinkai.

———. 2008. *Nakijin Jōato hakkutsu chōsa hōkoku shō III* (Report of excavations of the Nakijin Castle Site, III). Nakijin Son (Okinawa): Okinawa Ken Nakijin Son Kyōiku Iinkai.

———. 2009. *Nakijin Jōato hakkutsu chōsa hōkoku IV* (Report of excavations of the Nakijin Castle Site IV). Nakijin: Okinawa Ken Nakijin Son Kyōiku Iinkai.

Okinawa Kenritsu Hakubutsukan, Bijutsukan. 2010. *Nanjō Shi Bugeidō hakkutsu chōsa gaiyō hōkokusho* (Summary report of excavations at the Bugeidō Cave Site, Nanjō City). Naha: Okinawa Kenritsu Hakubutsukan, Bijutsukan.

Okinawa Kenritsu Maizō Bunkazai Sentā. 2001a. *Isamēbaru Dai Ichi Iseki. Kitanakagusuku Sen (Isa-Futenma) dōro kaichiku jigyō ni tomonau kinkyū hakkutsu chōsa hōkokusho (3).* (Isamēbaru No. 1 Site: emergency excavations in conjunction with renovation of the road between Kitanakagusuku and Ginowan, between Isa and Futenma). Nishihara (Okinawa): Okinawa Maizō Bunkazai Sentā.

———. 2001b. *Shuri Jōato: kanriyō dōro chiku hakkutsu chōsa hōkokusho* (Shuri Castle Site: report of investigations in the area of the administrative road). Nishihara (Okinawa): Okinawa Kenritsu Maizō Bunkazai Sentā.

———. 2001c. *Tokubetsu kikaku ten: Shurijō Kyōnouchi—bōeki tōji kara mita Dai Kōeki Jidai* (Special exhibition: The Kyōnouchi in Shuri Castle—the Great Period of Trade seen from trade ceramics). Nishihara (Okinawa): Okinawa Kenritsu Maizō Bunkazai Sentā.

———. 2002a. Enkakuji Ato: ikō kakunin chōsa hōkokusho (The Enkakuji Site: report of investigations to confirm archaeological features). Nishihara (Okinawa): Okinawa Kenritsu Maizō Bunkazai Sentā.

———. 2002b. *Shinzato Motojima Johōdaichi Iseki, Shinzato Higashi Motojima Iseki* (The Shinzato Motojima Johōdaichi Site and Shinzato Higashi Motojima Sites). Nishihara (Okinawa): Okinawa Kenritsu Maizō Bunkazai Sentā.

———. 2004. *Shuri Jōato: Jōkaku Minamigawa kudari chiku hakkutsu chōsa hōkokusho* (Shuri Castle Site: Report of Excavations of the area below the Southern Castle Wall). Nishihara (Okinawa): Okinawa Kenritsu Maizō Bunkazai Sentā.

———. 2005a. *Okinawa Kaizuka Jidai Chūki no misuterii* (Mystery of the Middle Period of the Okinawa Shellmound Period). Nishihara (Okinawa): Okinawa Kenritsu Maizō Bunkazai Sentā.

———. 2005b. *Shuri Jōato: Shoin Usasunoma chiku hakkutsu chōsa hōkokusho* (Shuri Castle Site: report of excavations in the area of the Usasunoma and Shoin). Nishihara (Okinawa): Okinawa Kenritsu Maizō Bunkazai Sentā.

———. 2005c. *Shuri Jōato Kami no Ke Oyobi shūhen chiku hakkutsu chōsa hōkokusho* (Report of excavations of the Kami no Ke area, Shuri Castle). Nishihara (Okinawa): Okinawa Kenritsu Maizō Bunkazai Sentā.

———. 2005d. *Shuri Jōato Madama Michiseki: Shuri Jōato Shureimon higashigawa chiku, Madama Michiseki kiten oyobi shūhen chiku hakkutsu chōsa hōkoku* (Shuri Castle, the site of the Madama Road: the area on the east side of the Shurei Gate, beginning from the Madama Road: report of excavations). Nishihara (Okinawa): Okinawa Kenritsu Maizō Bunkazai Sentā.

———. 2005e. *Shuri Jōato Nikaiden chiku hakkutsu chōsa hōkokusho* (Report of excavations in the Nikaiden area of Shuri Castle). Naha: Okinawa Ken Kyōiku Iinkai, 2005.

———. 2006. *Aragusuku Shichabaru Daini Iseki: Kyanpu Zukeran nai setsubi kōba kensetsu ni kakaru kenkyū hakkutsu chōsa hōkoku* (The Aragusuku Shichabaru Site No. 2: report of salvage excavations related to construction of facilities at Camp Zukeran). Nishihara: Okinawa Kenritsu Maizō Bunkazai Sentā.

———. 2007a. *Madama Michiseki: Shuri Jōato Madama Michi chiku hakkutsu chōsa hōkokusho II* (The Madama Road Site: report of excavations in the area of the Madama Road, II) Naha: Okinawa Kenritsu Maizō Bunkazai Sentā.

———. 2007b. *Shuri Jōato, Ouchibaru Nishi chiku hakkutsu chōsa hōkokusho* (Report of excavations in the Ouchibaru West area, Shuri Castle Site). Nishihara (Okinawa): Okinawa Kenritsu Maizō Bunkazai Sentā.

———. 2007c. *Watarichi Mura Ato: rinkō Dōro Naha 1 Gō sen seibi ni tomonau kinkyū hakkutsu chōsa hōkoku* (The Watarichi Mura Site: report of salvage excavations associated with the construction of Naha Highway 1 at the edge of the port). Nishihara (Okinawa): Okinawa Kenritsu Maizō Bunkazai Sentā, 2007.

———. 2008a. *Madama Michiseki: Shuri Jōato Madama Michi chiku hakkutsu chōsa hōkokusho III* (The Madama Road Site: report of excavations in the area of the Madama Road, III). Nishihara (Okinawa): Okinawa Kenritsu Maizō Bunkazai Sentā.

———. 2008b. *Shuri Jōato: Shita no Unā Shurimori Utaki chiku hakkutsu chōsa hōkokusho.* (Report of excavations in the region of the Shurimori Utaki, Lower Plaza area, Shuri Castle Site). Nishihara (Okinawa): Okinawa Kenritsu Maizō Bunkazai Sentā.

———. 2009a. *Karadake Higashi Kaizuka, Karadake Tōhō Kobogun* (The Karadake East Shellmound and Karadake East Tomb Group). Nishihara (Okinawa): Okinawa Kenritsu Maizō Bunkazai Sentā.

———. 2009b. *Shuri Jōato—Kyōnouchi Ato hakkutsu chōsa hōkokusho (2)* (Shuri Castle Site—report of excavations of the Kyōnouchi Site [2]). Nishihara (Okinawa): Okinawa Kenritsu Maizō Bunkazai Sentā.

———. 2010. *Nakagusuku Udun ato* (The site of the Nakagusuku Palace). Nishihara (Okinawa): Okinawa Kenritsu Maizō Bunkazai Sentā.

———. 2011. *Kidamori Iseki* (The Kidamori Site). Nishihara (Okinawa): Okinawa Kenritsu Maizō Bunkazai Sentā.

Okinawa Kenritsu Toshokan Shiryō Henshūshitsu. 1992. *Rekidai hōan* (Valuable records of successive generations). Naha: Okinawa Ken Kyōiku Iinkai.

Okinawa Ken Tamagusuku Son Kyōiku Iinkai. 1991. *Itokazu Jōato, hakkutsu chōsa hōkoku I* (Itokazu Castle Site, excavation no. 1). Okinawa: Okinawa Ken Tamagusuku Son Kyōiku Iinkai.

Okinawa Ken Urasoe Shi Kyōiku Iinkai. 1985. *Urasoe Jōato hakkutsu chōsa hōkokusho* (Report of excavations of the Urasoe Castle Site). Urasoe: Okinawa Ken Urasoe Kyōiku Iinkai.

Okinawa Shi Kyōiku Iinkai. 1988. *Goeku Gusuku* (Goeku Gusuku). Okinawa Shi: Okinawa Shi Kyōiku Iinkai.

Ōnishi Tomokazu. 1998. Kagoshima Ken Ōshima Gun Setouchi Chō Katoku Iseki shutsudo doki no saikentō (A reexamination of pottery from the Katoku Site, Setouchi, Amami Ōshima, Kagoshima). *Minami Nihon bunka* 31:31–41.

Ono Masatoshi. 1997a. Mura ga kataru Yaeyama no chūsei (The mediaeval period of Yaeyama as told from villages). *Ōsenkai* 14:80–86.

———. 1997b. *Sengoku Jōkamachi no kōkogaku: Ichijōdani kara no messeiji* (Archaeology of a castle town: message from Ichijōdani). Tokyo: Kōdansha.

———. 1999. Mitsurin ni kakureta Chūsei Yaeyama no mura (Mediaeval yaeyama villages hidden in the jungle). In *Mura ga kataru Okinawa no rekishi* (Villages tell the story of Okinawan history), ed. Rekishi Minzoku Hakubutsukan, pp. 37–68. Tokyo: Shin Jinbutsu Ōraisha.

Ono Rintarō. 2009. Sangoshō gyoro no minzoku kōkogaku (Ethnoarchaeology of reef fishing). *Kōkogaku kenkyū* 55 (4): 75–94.

Ōnuki Shizuo. 2005. Saikin no Yayoi Jidai no nendai ron ni tsuite (Recent debate about the date of the Yayoi Period). *Anthropological Science* 113:95–107.

Ōshiro Kei. 1997. Okinawa no tetsu to sono tokushitsu (Okinawan iron and its special characteristics). In *Kōkogaku yori mita Okinawa no tekki bunka* (The iron culture of Okinawa as seen from archaeology), ed. Okinawa Kenritsu Hakubutsukan, pp. 12–17. Naha: Okinawa Kenritsu Hakubutsukan.

Ōta Yukio. 2009. Sōsen no ryūnyū (The influx of Song coins). *Kōkogaku jānaru* 591:15–18.

Otsuka, Hiroyuki, and Akio Takahashi. 2000. Pleistocene vertebrate faunas in the Ryūkyū Islands: their migration and extinction. *Tropics* 10:1 (2000): 25–40.

Ōyama Shunsen. 1983. Ntabaru Toyūmiyā (The official with the title of Toyomioya from Untabaru). *Okinawa dai jiten* (Encyclopedia of Okinawa) 3:1008.

Ōzawa Masaki. 2006. Nema Nishizato Iseki shutsudo tetsu kanren ibutsu no kinzokugakuteki chōsa (Metallurgical analysis of iron-related specimens from the Nema Nishizato Site). In *Nema, Nishizato Iseki* (Nema, Nishizato Sites), ed. Miyakojima Shi Kyōiku Iinkai, pp. 17–26. Miyakojima (Okinawa): Miyakojima Shi Kyōiku Iinkai.

Pearson, Richard. 1969. *Archaeology of the Ryūkyū Islands.* Honolulu: University of Hawai'i Press.

———. 1981a. Background and conceptual framework. In *Subsistence and Settlement in Okinawan Prehistory: Kume and Iriomote,* ed. Ryūkyū Archaeological Research Team, pp. 1–7. Vancouver: UBC, Laboratory of Archaeology.

———. 1981b. Environments of Kume and Iriomote with reference to prehistoric settlement. In *Subsistence and Settlement in Okinawan Prehistory—Kume and Iriomote,* ed. Ryūkyū Archaeological Research Team, pp. 8–19. Vancouver: UBC Laboratory of Archaeology.

———. 1990. Chiefly exchange between Kyushu and Okinawa, Japan, in the Yayoi Period. *Antiquity* 64 (245): 912–922.

———. 1994. Kairui ibutsu no bunseki hōhō (Some approaches to the analysis of shellfish remains). *Nantō kōko* 14:45–56.

———. 1997a. Archaeology of the Ryūkyū Islands from the Yayoi to the Kofun Period. *Beitrage zur Allgemeinen und Vergleichenden Archaologie* 17:147–168.

———. 1997b. The Chuzan Kingdom, Okinawa, as a city state. In *The Archaeology of City States: Cross Cultural Approaches,* ed. T. Charlton and D. Nichols, pp. 119–134. Washington, DC: Smithsonian Institution Press.

———. 1999. Regional settlement in Okinawa: the Yokatsu Peninsula and its offliers. *Journal of East Asian Archaeology* 1:277–323.

———. 2001. Archaeological perspectives on the rise of the Okinawan state. *Journal of Archaeological Research* 9 (3): 243–285.

———. 2003. Excavations at Sumiya and other Sakishima sites: variations in Okinawan leadership around AD 1500. *Indo-Pacific Prehistory Association Bulletin* 23:95–111.

———. 2006. Jōmon hot spot: increasing sedentism in Southwestern Japan in the Incipient Jōmon (14,000–9250 Cal BC) and Earliest Jōmon (9250–5300 Cal BC) Periods. *World Archaeology* 38 (2): 239–258.

———. 2007 Early Mediaeval trade on Japan's southern frontier: Grey stoneware of the East China Sea. *International Journal of Historical Archaeology* 11 (2): 122–151.

Pearson, R., Susumu Asato, Gregory Monks, and David Pokotylo. 1980. Excavations on Kume and Iriomote, Ryūkyū Islands. *Asian Perspectives* 21 (1): 7–26.

———. 1990. Kumejima to Iriomotejima ni okeru iseki no hakkutsu (Excavations on Kume and Iriomote, Ryukyu Islands). Translated by Kazue Pearson. *Okinawa Ken Kyōiku Chō Bunka Ka kiyō* 6:79–94.

Pearson, R., Min Li, and Guo Li. 2001. Port, city, and hinterland: archaeological perspectives on Quanzhou and its overseas trade. In *The Emporium of the World: Maritime Quanzhou, 1000–1400,* ed. A. Schottenhammer, pp. 177–236. Leiden: Brill.

———. 2002. Quanzhou archaeology: a brief review. *International Journal of Historical Archaeology* 6 (1): 23–58.

Pietrusewsky, M. 2004. Multivariate comparisons of female cranial series from the Ryūkyū Islands and Japan. *Anthropological Science* 112:199–211.

Qiao, Shuqing, Zuosheng Yang, Jingpu Liu, Xiaoxia Sun, Rong Xiang, Xuefa Shi, Dejiang Fan, and Yōshiki Saito. 2011. Records of Late-Holocene East Asian winter monsoon in the East China Sea: key grain-size component of quartz versus bulk sediments. *Quaternary International* 230:106–114.

Qin, Yunshan, Yiyang Zhao, Lirong Chen, and Songling Zhao, eds. 1996. *Geology of the East China Sea.* Beijing: Science Press.

Rainbird, Paul. 2007. *The Archaeology of Islands.* Cambridge: Cambridge University Press.

Rick, J. W. 1987. Dates as data: an examination of the Peruvian preceramic radiocarbon record. *American Antiquity* 52:55–73.

Robb, J. 2001. Island identities: ritual, travel, and the creation of difference in Neolithic Malta. *European Journal of Archaeology* 4:175–202.

Robb, J., and R. H. Farr. 2005. Substances in motion: Neolithic Mediterranean "trade." In *The Archaeology of Mediterranean Prehistory,* ed. Blake, E. and A. B. Knapp, pp. 24–46. Oxford: Blackwell Publishing Ltd.

Robinson, Kenneth. 2000. Centering the King of Chōson: aspects of Korean maritme diplomacy. *Journal of Asian Studies* 59 (1): 109–125.

Rokkum, A. 1998. *Goddeses, Priestesses, Sisters: Mind, Gender, and Power in the Monarchic Tradition of the Ryukyus.* Oslo: Scandanavian University Press.

Ronquillo, W. 2003. Philippine earthenware pottery from the Early Prehistoric Period. In *Earthenware in Southeast Asia: Proceedings of the Singapore Symposium.* ed. J. Miksic, pp. 32–38. London: Singapore University Press.

Ryūkyū Archaeological Research Team, eds. 1981. *Subsistence and Settlement in Okinawan Prehistory—Kume and Iriomote.* Vancouver: Laboratory of Archaeology, University of British Columbia.

Ryūkyū Shikki Jigyō Kyōdō Kumiai. 1991. *Ryūkyū shikki: rekishi to gijutsu, gihō* (Ryukyu lacquer: history, techniques, methods). Naha: Ryūkyū Shikki Jigyō Kyōdō Kumiai.

Sakai Shi Hakubutsukan. 1993. *Hakata to Sakai* (Hakata and Sakai). Sakai: Sakai Shi Hakubutsukan.

Sakamaki, Shunzo. 1963. *Ryukyu: A Bibliographical Guide to Okinawan Studies.* Honolulu: University of Hawai'i Press.

———. 1964. Ryūkyū and Southeast Asia. *Journal of Asian Studies.* 23 (3): 383–389.

Sakihara, Mitsugu. 1987. *A Brief History of Early Okinawa Based on the Omoro Sōshi.* Tokyo: Honpo Shoseki Press.

Sakura, Hajime. 1981. Pleistocene human bones found at Pinza Abu (Goat Cave), Miyako Island—a short report. *Bulletin of the National Science Museum,* series D, 7:1–6.

Satō Yōichirō. 2010. Ryūkyū Rettō no ine no michi (The route of Ryukyu rice). In *Okinawa Ken shi kakuron hen daisan kan: Ko Ryūkyū* (History of Okinawa separate volume no. 3: Ko Ryukyu), ed. Zaidan Hōjin Okinawa Ken Bunka Shinkōkai Shiryō Henshūshitsu, pp. 48–49. Naha: Okinawa Ken Kyōiku Iinkai.

Schottenhammer, Angela. 2005. The East Asian Mediterranean. In *Trade and Transfer across the East Asian Mediterranean,* ed. Angela Schottenhammer, pp. 1–11. Wiesbaden: Harrassowitz Verlag.

———. 2007. The East Asian maritime world, ca. 1400–1800: its fabrics of power and dynamics of exchanges: China and her neighbours. In *The East Asian Maritime World 1400–1800: Its Fabrics of Power and Dynamics of Exchanges,* ed. Angela Schottenhammer, pp. 1–86. Wiesbaden: Harrassowitz Verlag.

Sekiguchi Kōji. 2009. Nagura Shitadaru kaisoko iseki saishū Mindai tōjiki no kenkyū (Study of Ming period ceramics collected at the underwater site of Shitadaru, Ishigaki). In *Okinawa Ken Ishigaki Shi Nagura Shitadaru Kaisoko Iseki kyōdō kenkyū hōkokusho* (Report of joint studies of the Nagura Shitadaru Underwater Site), ed. Ōhama Eisen, pp. 27–86. Ishigaki: Sakishima Bunka Kenkyūsho.

Seto Tetsuya. 2004. Ryūkyū kara miru chūsei kōki no ryūtsū (Distribution in the Late Mediaeval Period, seen from Ryukyu). In *Chūsei Nihon no ryūtsū to kōtsū* (Distribution and communication in Mediaeval Japan), ed. Hashimoto Hisakazu and Ichimura Takao, pp. 139–160). Tokyo: Kōshi Shoin.

———. 2005. Shurijō Kobiki Mon chiku shutsudo no hajiki to omowareru doki zara (*Hajiki*-ware and possible earthenware plates found in the Kobiki Mon sector of the Shuri Castle Site). *Okinawa maibun kenkyū* 3:71–78.

———. 2007. Tōjiki sosei: Honshū san tōki kara mita jūgo-jūroku seiki no Ryūkyū Koku (The fifteenth- to sixteenth-century Ryukyu Kingdom seen from assemblages of ceramics from the main islands of Japan). *Nantō kōko* 26:221–234.

———. 2009a. Minami no kyōkai: Ryūkyū no gashitsu doki (The southern boundary: Ryukyu tilelike pottery). *Chūkinsei doki no kisoteki kenkyū* 22:157–172.

———. 2009b. Okinawa Gusuku Jidai no sōbosei (The burial system of the Gusuku Period in Okinawa). In *Nihon no Chūsei bo* (Burials of Mediaeval Japan), ed. Shin'ichi Sagawa, pp. 127–138. Tokyo: Kōshi Shoin.

———. 2010a. Okinawa ni okeru jūni-jūroku seiki no bōeki tōji: Chūgokusan tōji o chūshin to shita to shosei (Trade ceramics of the twelfth to sixteenth centuries in Okinawa, particularly phases and assemblages of Chinese ceramics). *Bōeki tōji kenkyū* 30:17–40.

———. 2010b. Ryūkyū ni okeru kōkogakuteki seika (Archaeological results from Ryukyu). In *Chūsei kōki no Higashi Ajia no Hakata hōkoku shiryōshū* (Hakata and East Asia in the Late Mediaeval Period, conference materials), ed. Hakata Kenkyūkai 20 Shunen Shinpojiumu Jikkōinkai, pp. 29–56. Hakata: Hakata Kenkyūkai 20 Shunen Shinpojiumu Jikkōinkai.

Seto Tetsuya, Niō Kōji, Tamashiro Yasushi, Miyagi Hiroki, Azama Mitsuru, and Matsubara Satoshi. 2007. Okinawa ni okeru bōeki tōji kenkyū: jūyon-jūroku seiki o chūshin ni (Trade ceramics study in Okinawa, focusing on the fourteenth to sixteenth centuries). *Okinawa maibun kenkyū* 5:55–76.

Shibata Keiko, Takashima Hiroyuki, Niijima Natsuko, Kamei Meitoku, and Handa Motoko. 2009. Nakijin Jōato shutsudo Mindai zenhanki seikashi no kenkyū (Study of blue and white from the early half of the Ming dynasty at the Nakijin Castle Site). In *Nakijin Jōato hakkutsu chōsa hōkoku IV* (Report of excavations of the Nakijin Castle Site IV), ed. Nakijin Son Kyōiku Iinkai, pp. 141–169. Nakijin (Okinawa): Nakijin Son Kyōiku Iinkai.

Shimabukuro Harumi. 2009. Iwayuru jūgata kaiseihin ni tsuite (Concerning so-called zoomorphic-shaped marine shell pendants). *Nantō kōko* 28:19–32.

Shimajiri Katsutarō. 1983. Ankokuzan jukaboku no kihi (Stele of trees and flowers on Ankoku Hill). *Okinawa dai jiten* (Encyclopedia of Okinawa) 1:132.

Shimoji Kazuhiro. 1999. Miyako no "Gusuku Jidai": doki, tōjiki o chūshin ni (The "Gusuku Period" of Miyako, with particular reference to earthenware and hard-fired ceramics). *Hōsei Daigaku Okinawa Bunka Kenkyūsho shohō* 51:15–20.

———. 2008. Tōki kōeki to Miyako: "Miyako Jin" to Chūzan Ōchō ni tsuite (The ceramics trade and Miyako: "Miyako people" and the Chūzan Kingdom). In *Nichi Ryū kōeki no reimei—Yamato kara no shōgeki* (The Dawn of Exchange between Japan and Ryukyu—the impact of Yamato), ed. Tanigawa Ken'ichi, pp. 327–346. Tokyo: Shinwasha.

———. 2010. Sakishima no senshi bunka (The prehistoric culture of Sakishima). In *Okinawa Ken shi kakuron hen daisan kan: Ko Ryūkyū hen* (History of Okinawa, separate volume no. 3: Ko Ryukyu), ed. Zaidan Hōjin Okinawa Ken Bunka Shinkōkai Shiryō Henshūshitsu, pp. 559–574. Naha: Okinawa Ken Kyōiku Iinkai.

Shimoji Ketsu. 1999. Hakkutsu sareta mura: Ishigakijima Furusutobaru Mura (An excavated village: Furusutobaru, Ishigakijima). In *Mura ga kataru Okinawa no rekishi* (Villages tell the story of Okinawan history), ed. Rekishi Minzoku Hakubutsukan, pp. 10 1–112. Tokyo: Shin Jinbutsu Ōraisha.

Shimoji Yasuhiro. 1999. Okinawa Ken Kajō Kaizuka kara shutsudo no Rakuro doki (Lelang-style pottery unearthed from the Kajō Shellmound, Okinawa Prefecture). *Jinruishi kenkyū* 11:17–24.

———. 2004. Urasoe Gusuku to shūhen iseki (Urasoe Gusuku and surrounding sites). In *Gusuku bunka o kangaeru* (Thinking about Gusuku culture), ed. Nakijin Son Kyōiku Iinkai, pp. 44–49. Tokyo: Shin Jinbutsu Ōraisha.

Shimoyama, Satoru. 2002. Volcanic disasters and archaeological sites in southern Kyushu, Japan. In *Natural Disasters and Cultural Change,* ed. R. Torrance and J. Graham, pp. 326–341. London: Routledge.

Shinoda Ken'ichi. 2005. Urasoe Yōdore shutsudo jinkotsu to DNA bunseki (The human bones from Urasoe Yōdore and analysis of DNA). In *Urasoe Yōdore no ishizushi to ikotsu chōsa no chūkan hōkoku* (Preliminary report of the investigation of the stone sarcophagi and human bones from Urasoe), ed. Urasoe Shi Kyōiku Iinkai, pp. 22–23. Urasoe Shi (Okinawa): Urasoe Shi Kyōiku Iinkai.

Shinoda Ken'ichi and Adachi Noboru. 2010. DNA ga kataru [Nihonjin e no tabi] no fukuganteki shiten (DNA tells the story of the [Journey to the Japanese people] from multiple viewpoints). *Kagaku* 80 (4): 368–377.

Shinzato Akito. 2003. Ryūkyū Rettō ni okeru yōgyō seisan no seiritsu to tenkai (Formation and development of pottery-industry production in the Ryukyu Archipelago). *Kōkogaku kenkyū* 49 (4): 75–95.

———. 2009. Kamuiyaki and early trade in the Ryūkyū Islands. In *Okinawa: The Rise of an Island Kingdom: Archaeological and Cultural Perspectives*, ed. Richard Pearson, pp. 41–56. BAR Series 1898. London: Archaeopress.

———. 2010. Ryūkyū Rettō no nōkō o meguru shomondai (Some problems regarding cultivation in the Ryukyus). *Kōkogaku jānaru* 597:12–14.

Shinzato Takayuki. 1999. Nansei Shotō ni okeru Yayoi heikōki no doki (Pottery in the Nansei Islands that parallels the Yayoi Period). *Jinruishi kenkyū* 11:75–106.

———. 2000. Kyushu, Nansei Shotō ni okeru Yayoi Jidai heikōki no doki idō ni tsuite: kisoteki sagyō (Movement of pottery in the parallel stage of the Yayoi Period in Kyushu and the Southwest Islands: a fundamental study). *Taiga* 7:237–257.

———. 2001. Butsuryū netowaku no ichi sokumen: Okinawa shutsudo no Yayoi kei ibutsu no sozai toshite (One aspect of distribution networks: raw materials of Yayoi-type artifacts found in Okinawa). *Nantō kōko* 20:49–66.

———. 2003. Distribution networks in the Okinawa Islands in the period parallel with the Yayoi (300 BC to AD 300). *Bulletin of the Indo-Pacific Prehistory Association* 23:73–82.

———. 2007. Kinen, Saben Sunahama Iseki Gun Tomachin Iseki hakkutsu chōsa gaiyō hōkoku: Tomachin Iseki dai ichi-sanji chōsa no gaiyō (Preliminary report of the excavation of the Tomachin Site of the Kinen Saben Beach Site Group, excavations 1–3). *Jinruishi kenkyū* 14:13–28.

———. 2008a. Nansei Shotō Tokunoshima Tomachin shutsudo no hisui tama (Jade beads from the Tomachin Site, Tokunoshima, Nansei Islands). *Gyoku bunka* 5:76–86.

———. 2008b. Shimotabaru shiki ki ni heikō suru Amami, Okinawa chūki no senshi jidai (The prehistory of Amami and Okinawa in the parallel time period to the Shimotabaru time period). In *Shimotabaru Ki no kurashi* (Livelihood in the Shimotabaru Period), Ishigaki Shi kōkogaku bijuaru han 2 (Archaeology of Ishigaki City visual edition 2), ed. Ishigaki Shi Sōmubu Shishi Henshu Bu, p. 62. Ishigaki: Ishigaki Shi.

———. 2011. Kagoshima Ken Tokunoshima Tomachin Iseki (The Tomachin Site, Tokunoshima, Kagoshima Prefecture). *Kōkogaku kenkyū* 228:122–124.

———. 2012. Nansei shoto no senshi jidai sōbōsei (Prehistoric burial system of the Nansei Islands). *Hosei Daigaku Okinawa Bunka Kenkyūsho shohō* 69:4–6.

Shiro Kazuto, ed. 2010. *Zusetsu Okinawa no tsuriuo* (Game fish of Okinawa, illustrated). Okinawa Shi: Fuishingu Okinawa Sha.

Shiroma Hajime and Ueda Kei'ichi. 2007. Iwayuru shokusaikon ni tsuite ichi kosai: Okinawa Ken nai ni okeru tahata kanren iseki no shūsei ni mukete (A consideration of traces of cultivation: toward a compilation of cultivated field sites in Okinawa Prefecture). *Nantō kōko* 26:133–156.

Shogakukan, ed. 2004. *Kokogaku shiryō taikan* (Compendium of archaeological materials). Tokyo: Shogakukan.

Shurijō Fukugen Kiseikai. 1987. *Shashinshū Shuri Jō* (Collection of photographs of Shuri Castle). Naha: Naha Shuppansha.

Simmons, A. H. 2009. The earliest residents of Cyprus: ecological pariahs or harmonious settlers? In *The Archaeology of Environmental Change: Socionatural Legacies of Degradation and Resilience,* ed. C. T. Fisher, J. B. Hill, and G. Feinman, pp. 177–191. Tucson: University of Arizona Press.

Smits, Gregory. 2000. Ambiguous boundaries: redefining royal authority in the Kingdom of Ryukyu. *Harvard Journal of Asiatic Studies* 60 (1): 89–123.

———. 2008. Money in the Kingdom of Ryūkyū. *Bunka wenhua* 17:107–117.

———. 2010. Examining the myth of Ryukyuan pacificism. *Asia-Pacific Journal* 37-3-10, http://www.japanfocus.org/-Gregory-Smits/3409.

Spriggs, M. 2008. Are islands islands? Some thoughts on the history of chalk and cheese. *Terra Australis* 29:211–226.

Spriggs, M., and A. Anderson. 1993. Late colonization of East Polynesia. *Antiquity* 67:200–217.

Sumida Naotoshi. 2008. Gusuku Isekigun (The Gusuku Site Group). In *Hakkutsu sareta Nihon Rettō* (The Japanese Islands excavated), ed. Bunka Chō, pp. 59–61. Tokyo: Asahi Shimbun Shuppan.

Sumida Naotoshi, Dōgome Hideto, and Ikehata Kōichi. 2003. Kikai Chō Sōgō Guraundo Iseki Kyudōjō shutsudo no doki (Pottery found in the Community Ground, Archery Field, Kikai Township). *Kagoshima kōko* 37 (7): 25–32.

Sumida Naotoshi and Nozaki Takashi. 2008. Kikaigashima Gusuku Isekigun (The Gusuku Site Group, Kikai Island). In *Kodai Chūsei no kyōkai ryōiki: Kikaigashima no sekai* (A border area in the Ancient and Mediaeval Periods: the world of Kikaigashima), ed. Yoshifumi Ikeda, pp. 153–170. Tokyo: Kōshi Shuppan.

Summerhayes, G., and A. Anderson. 2009. An Austronesian presence in Southern Japan: early occupation in the Yaeyama Islands. *Bulletin of the Indo-Pacific Prehisory Association* 29:76–91.

Sunagawa Sachio. 1983. Nakasone Tuimiyaa Genga (Nakasone Toyomioya Genga). *Okinawa dai jiten* (Encyclopedia of Okinawa) 3:18.

Sutcliffe, A. J. 1973. Similarity of bones and antlers gnawed by deer to human artifacts. *Nature* 246:428–430.

Suzuki, Atsushi, Yusuke Yokoyama, Hironobu Kan, Kayo Minoshima, Hiroyuki Matsuzaki, Nozomu Hamanaka, and Hodaka Kawahata. 2008. Identification of 1771 Meiwa Tsunami deposits using a combination of radiocarbon dating and oxygen isotope microprofiling of emerged massive *Porites* Boulders. *Quaternary Geochronology* 3:226–234.

Suzuki, Hisashi. 1982. Dentition of the Minatogawa Man. In *The Minatogawa Man: The Upper Pleistocene Man from the Island of Okinawa,* ed. Hisashi Suzuki and Kazuro Hanihara, pp. 7–50. Tokyo: University Museum, University of Tokyo.

Suzuki, Hisashi, and Kazuro Hanihara. 1982. *The Minatogawa Man: Upper Pleistocene Man from the Island of Okinawa*. University of Tokyo Museum Bulletin No. 19. Tokyo.

Suzuki Kimio. 1999. *Shutsudo senka no kenkyū* (English title: *The Dynamics of Money Circulation in Fourteenth to Eighteenth Century Japan*). Tokyo: Tokyo Daigaku Shuppan Kai.

———. 2002. *Zeni no kōkogaku* (The archaeology of money). Tokyo: Yoshikawa Kōbunkan.

Suzuki Yasutami. 2008. Kikaigashima Gusuku Isekigun to kodai Nantō shakai (The Gusuku Site Group of Kikaigashima and society of the Southern Islands in the Kodai Period). In *Kodai Chūsei no kyōkai ryōiki: Kikaigashima no sekai* (A border area in the Ancient and Mediaeval Periods: the world of Kikaigashima), ed. Ikeda Yoshifumi, pp. 17–48. Tokyo: Kōshi Shuppan.

Tagaya, Akira, and Jiro Ikeda. 1976. A multivariate analysis of the cranial measurements of the Ryukyu Islanders (males). *Journal of the Anthropological Society of Nippon* 83 (3): 204–220.

Takahashi Masa'aki, ed. 2011. *Taira Kiyomori: ōchō e no chōsen* (Taira Kiyomori: challenge to the monarchy). *Taiyō* special edition. Nihon no kokoro 190. Tokyo: Heibonsha.

Takahashi, Ryohei, Naotaka Ishiguro, Akira Matsui, Tomoko Anezaki, and Hitomi Hongo. 2012. Morphological and molecular phylogenetic characteristics of dwarf *Sus* specimens from the Noguni Shell middens in the Ryukyu Islands. *Anthropological Science* 120 (2012):39–50.

Takahashi Yasuo. 2010. Ko Ryūkyū Ki Naha no mittsu no Tenpi gū (Three shrines to Matsu, Heavenly Princess, in Naha in the Ko Ryukyu Period). *Okinawa bunka kenkyū* 36:49–100.

Takakura Hiroaki. 1981. *Yayoi Jidai shakai no kenkyū* (Study of Yayoi Period society). Tokyo: Azuma Shuppan Neirakusha.

Takamiya Hiroe. 1990. *Senshi jidai no Okinawa* (Okinawa in prehistory). Tokyo: Dai'ichi Shobō.

———. 1993. *Okinawa Jōmon doki josetsu* (Introduction to Okinawa Jōmon pottery). Tokyo: Dai'ichi Shobō, 1993.

———. 1994. The Neolithic Age of the Ryūkyū Islands. In *Okinawa no senshi iseki to bunka* (Prehistoric sites and cultures of Okinawa), ed. Takamiya Hiroe, pp. 23–43. Tokyo: Dai'ichi Shobō.

———. 1995. Kaigen Tsūhō kara mita senshi shumakki no Okinawa (Okinawa at the very end of the prehistoric period as seen from Kaigen Tsūhō coins). In *Ōchō no kōkogaku* (Dynastic archaeology), ed. Ōkawa Kiyoshi Hakase Koki Kinen Ronbunshū Kankōkai, pp. 267–286. Tokyo: Yūzankaku.

———. 1997. Kaigen Tsūhō to aji no shutsugen: yosatsu (Kaigen Tsūhō coins and the emergence of local lords (*aji*): a working hypothesis). *Nantō bunka:* 19:1–27.

Takamiya Hiroe, Kishimoto Yoshihiko, Chinen Isamu, and Nakamura Ken. 1993.

Yomitan Son Ufutōbaru Kaizuka hakkutsu chōsa gaihō (Preliminary report of the excavation of the Ufutōbaru Site, Yomitan Village). *Yomitan Sonritsu rekishi minzoku shiryōkan kiyō* 17:1–47.

Takamiya Hiroe, Shimoji Suguru, Asato Kazumi, and Ōshiro Hiroe. 1985. *Okinoerabujima Kamino Kaizuka hakkutsu chōsa gaihō A1 Torenchi* (Preliminary report of excavation of the Kamino Shellmound, Okinoerabujima, A1 Trench), Okikokudai kōko 7. Okinawa: Okinawa Kokusai Daigaku.

Takamiya, Hiroto. 1996. Initial colonization and subsistence adaptation processes in the late prehistory of the Island of Okinawa. *Indo-Pacific Prehistory Association Bulletin* 15 (1996): 143–150.

———. 1997. Subsistence Adaptation Processes in the Prehistory of Okinawa. Ph.D. dissertation, University of California, Los Angeles.

———. 2004. Okinawa Shotō no Senshi Jidai ni okeru hūdosutoresu ni tsuite (Food stress in the Prehistoric Period of the Okinawa Islands). *Nantō kōko* 23:51–57.

———. 2005. *Shima no senshigaku: paradaisu de wa nakatta: Okinawa Shotō no Senshi Jidai* (Prehistory of the Okinawa Islands: it was not a paradise). Naha: Bōdā Inku.

———. 2006a. Nantō Chūbuen ni okeru shokubutsu riyō fukugen no igi (The significance of reconstruction of plant utilization in the Central Region of the Ryūkyū Archipelago). In *Senshi Ryūkyū no seigyō to kōeki* 2, ed. Kinoshita Naoko, pp. 89–100. Kumamoto: Kumamoto University.

———. 2006b. An unusual case? Hunter gatherer adaptations to an island environment. *Journal of Island and Coastal Archaeology* 1 (1): 49–66.

———. 2007. Nantō Chūbuen ni okeru nōkō no hajimari (The beginning of horticulture in the Central Area of the Southern Islands. *Nihon Kōkogaku Kyōkai 2007 nendo Kumamoto taikai kenkyū happyō shiryōshū* 2:420–431.

———. 2009. Yamada Hanta Iseki yori shutsudo shita shokubutsu itai (Botanical remains from the Yamada Hanta Site). In *Gusuku Iseki Gun: Yamada Hanta Iseki* (The Gusuku Site Group: the Yamada Hanta Site), ed. Kikai Chō Kyōiku Iinkai. 177–182. Kagoshima Ken: Kagoshima Ken Kikai Chō.

———. 2011. Hito wa itsugoro Okinawa Shotō no tekiō shita no ka: Kaizuka Jidai Zen IV Ki setsu. (In which period did humans adapt in the Okinawa Islands? The Early Shellmound Period IV hypothesis). In *Senshi, Gusuku Jidai no Ryūkyū Rettō: hito to keikan* (The Ryukyu Islands in the Prehistoric and Primitive Periods: people and landscape), ed. Takamiya Hiroto and Itō Shinji, pp. 25–42. Tokyo: Rokuichi Shobō.

Takamiya, Hiroto, and Hiroki Obata. 2002. Peopling of Western Japan, focussing on Kyushu, Shikoku, and Ryūkyū. *Radiocarbon* 44:495–502.

Takamiya Hiroto, Obata Hiroki, Manabe Aya, and Akamine Shinya. 2011. Nago Shi Yabumaedabaru Kaizuka shutsudo akkon doki (Pottery with impressions in it from the Yabumaedabaru Site, Nago City). *Nantō kōko* 30:85–88.

Takamiya, Hiroto, L. Pavlish, and R. Hancock. 1991. Instrumental Neutron Activation

Analysis (INAA) of Okinawan pottery: can it be used to identify prehistoric contact? *Bulletin of the Indo-Pacific Prehistory Association* 12:292–306.

Takanashi Osamu. 2005. *Yakōgai no kōkogaku* (The archaeology of Yakōgai [*Turbo marmoratus*]). Tokyo: Dōseisha.

———. 2007. Nantō no rekishiteki dankai: Kaneku Shiki Doki shutsudo no iseki no saikentō (Historical stages of the Southern Islands: reexamination of sites yielding Kaneku Type Pottery). *Higashi Ajia no kodai bunka* 130:53–81.

———. 2008a. Gusuku Iseki Gun to Kikaigashima (The Gusuku Site Group and Kikaigashima). In *Nichi Ryū kōeki no reimei—Yamato kara no shōgeki* (The dawn of exchange between Japan and Ryukyu—the impact of Yamato), ed. Tanigawa Ken'ichi, pp. 121–149. Tokyo: Rinwasha.

———. 2008b. Kodai heikōki ni okeru Amami Shotō no zaichi doki no hennen (Chronology of Amami Islands pottery of the period parallel to the Kodai Period). In *Kodai Chūsei no kyōkai ryōiki: Kikaigashima no sekai* (A border area in the Ancient and Mediaeval Periods: the world of Kikaigashima), ed. Ikeda Yoshifumi, pp. 257–284. Tokyo: Kōshi Shuppan.

———. 2008c. Yakōgai kōeki: Ryūkyū Ko to kodai kokka (Exchange of *Turbo marmoratus:* the Ryūkyū Arc and the ancient state). In *Nichi Ryū kōeki no reimei—Yamato kara no shōgeki* (The dawn of exchange between Japan and Ryūkyū—the impact of Yamato), ed. Tanigawa Ken'ichi, pp. 209–235. Tokyo: Shinwasha.

———. 2010. Rettō nansen ni okeru kyōkai ryōiki no yōsō (Aspects of the border region in the south of the Japanese Archipelago). In *Kodai makki Nihon no Kodai Kyōkai* (The frontiers of Japan at the end of the Ancient [Kodai] Period), ed. Josef Kreiner, Yoshinari Naoki, and Oguchi Masashi, pp. 85–130. Tokyo: Moriwasha.

Takara Kurayoshi. 1987. Ryūkyū Ōkoku no rekishi to Nihon shakai (Ryukyu and the history of Okinawa and Japanese society). In *Rettō naigai no kōtsū to kokka* (Communications inside and outside the Japanese archipelago and the state), ed. Asao Naohiro, vol. 1: *Nihon no shakai shi,* gen. ed. Amino Yoshihiko, pp. 354–384. Tokyo: Iwanami Shoten.

———. 1993. *Ryūkyū Ōkoku* (The Ryukyu Kingdom). Tokyo. Iwanami Shoten.

Takayama Jun. 2001. Sakishima no shakōgai teono wa Fuiripin kigen ka? (Is the origin of the Sakshima *Tridacna* shell adze in the Philippines?). *Nantō kōko* 20:1–27.

Takayasu, Katsumi. 1978. "Ryūkyū Limestone" of Okinawa-Jima, South Japan: A stratigraphical and sedimentological study. *Memoirs of the Faculty of Science, Kyoto University, Series of Geology and Mineralogy* 45 (1): 133–175.

Takemoto Seishun and Asato Shijun. 1993. *Okinawa.* Nihon no kodai iseki (Ancient sites of Japan) 47. Osaka: Hoikusha.

Tamaki Chōken, Shimabukuro Yō, and Kishimoto Yoshihiko. 1981. Doki (Pottery). In *Kusatobaru Kaizuka* (Kusatobaru Shellmound), ed. Okinawa Ken Iheya Son Kyōiku Iinkai. pp. 104–252. Iheya Son: Iheya Son Kyōiku Iinkai.

Tamaki Nobuhiko. 2010. Ko Ryūkyū no sōbosei (Burial system of Ko Ryūkyū). In *Okinawa Ken shi kakuron hen daisan kan: Ko Ryūkyū* (History of Okinawa separate volume no. 3: Ko Ryukyu), ed. Zaidan Hōjin Okinawa Ken Bunka Shinkōkai Shiryō Henshūshitsu, pp. 545–558. Okinawa Ken Kyōiku Inkai, Naha.

Tan, Rita. 1991. Chinese greenware found in the Philippines. *Arts of Asia* 21 (6): 152–161.

Tana Masayuki. 2010. Minato machi Naha no tenkai (The development of Naha port). In *Okinawa Ken shi kakuron hen daisan kan: Ko Ryūkyū* (History of Okinawa separate volume no. 3: Ko Ryukyu), ed. Zaidan Hōjin Okinawa Ken Bunka Shinkōkai Shiryō Henshūshitsu, pp. 387–408. Naha: Okinawa Ken Kyōiku Iinkai.

Tanaka Katsuko. 2007. Okinawa shutsudo no bōeki tōji no mondai; Fukkensan sosei hakuji o megutte (Problems of trade ceramics from Okinawa: concerning whitewares produced in Fujian). In *Chūgoku Fukken no bōeki tōji to Ryūkyū: Sō, Gen dai o chūshin ni, Kōza Shiryō, Okinawa Kenritsu Maizō Bunkazai Sentā kōza 25 gō* (Trade ceramics from Fujian and Ryūkyū, concentrating on the Song and Yuan periods, conference materials, Okinawa Prefecture Archaeological Center lecture no. 25), pp. 21–24.

Taniguchi Sakae. 2009. Nissō bōeki to *Heike Monogatari* (Japan-Song trade and the *Heike monogatari*). *Kōkogaku jānaru* 591:3–6.

Tateiwa Iseki Chōsa Iinkai, ed. 1977. *Tateiwa Iseki* (The Tateiwa Site). Tokyo: Kawade Shobō.

Tawada Shinjun. 1980. *Koki kinen Tawada Shinjun senshu* (Selected essays at the seventieth birthday of Tawada Shinjun). Naha: Koki Kinen Tawada Shinjun Senshu Kankōkai.

Temple, D. H. 2010. Patterns of systemic stress during the agricultural transition in prehistoric Japan. *American Journal of Physical Anthropology* 142:112–124.

Terrell, J. E. 1997. The postponed agenda: archaeology and human biogeography in the twenty-first century. *Human Ecology* 25 (3): 419–435.

Tezuka Naoki. 2000. Jūniseidai no bōeki tōji o shutsudo suru Okinawa Hontō no iseki (Okinawa Main Island sites which have yielded twelfth-century trade ceramics). In *Ryūkyū, Higashi Ajia no hito to bunka* (The peoples and cultures of Ryukyu and East Asia), pp. 295–314. Naha: Takamiya Hiroe Sensei Koki Kinen Ronshu Kankōkai.

———. 2004. Jūni seiki kōhan no bōeki tōji no ikatsu shuryō no kenkyū (The study of a new group of materials concerning trade ceramics of the latter half of the twelfth century). *Rekishi dokuhon* 49:238–239.

Thomas, F. R. 2002. An evaluation of central-place foraging among mollusc gatherers in western Kiribati, Micronesia: linking behavioral ecology with ethnoarchaeology. *World Archaeology* 34 (1): 182–208.

Toguchi Makoto. 2000a. Nakagusuku Jōato (Nakagusuku Castle Site). *Nakagusuku kōhō* 102:16–17.

———. 2000b. Nakagusuku Jōato (Nakagusuku Castle Site). *Nakagusuku kōhō* 103:4–5.

———. 2000c. Nakagusuku Jōato (Nakagusuku Castle Site). *Nakagusuku kōhō* 105:4–5.

Tōizumi Takeji. 2002. Sekitsui dōbutsu itai kara mita Amami, Okinawa no kankyō to seigyō (Environment and subsistence of Amami, Okinawa, seen from vertebrate remains). In *Senshi Ryūkyū no seigyō to kōeki—Amami, Okinawa no hakkutsu chōsa kara* (Subsistence and exchange in the Prehistoric Ryukyus—based on excavations in Amami and Okinawa), ed. Kinoshita Naoko, pp. 47–66. Kumamoto: University of Kumamoto.

———. 2006. Sekitsui dōbutsu itai ni miru Amami to Okinawa (Amami and Okinawa seen from vertebrate remains). In *Senshi Ryūkyū no seigyō to kōeki 2—Amami, Okinawa no hakkutsu chōsa kara* (Subsistence and exchange in the Prehistoric Ryukyus 2—based on excavations in Amami and Okinawa), ed. Kinoshita Naoko, pp. 115–134. Kumamoto: University of Kumamoto.

———. 2007a. Ireibaru iseki kara shutsudo shita sekitsui dōbutsu itai gun (Groups of vertebrate remains from the Ireibaru Site). In *Ireibaru Iseki: Ireibaru B Iseki hoka hakkutsu chōsa* (The Ireibaru Site: excavation of Ireibaru B and others), ed. Chatan Chō Kyōiku Iinkai, pp. 480–534. Chatan Chō: Chatan Chō Kyōiku Iinkai.

———. 2007b. Nakijin Jōato shūhen iseki shutsudo no sekitsui dōbutsu itai gun, IIIb Ku, Higashi Ku, Shinigunni (Groups of vertebrate remains from the sites around Nakijin Castle, Area IIIb, East 7, and Shinigunni). In *Nakijin Jōato shūhen Iseki III* (Sites surrounding Nakijin Castle, III), ed. Nakijin Son Kyōiku Iinkai, pp. 253–282. Nakijin: Nakijin Son Kyōiku Iinkai.

———. 2007c. Senshi Ryūkyū no gyogyō katsudō fukugen ni kansuru gyokotsu bunseki hōhō no sho mondai, toku ni shiryō shūshū ho to dotei bui ga dotei kekka ni yobazu eikyō ni tsuite (Several problems concerning fish bone analysis in relation to reconstruction of fishing practices in the prehistoric Ryukyus, especially methods of gathering data and influence of identification of body parts). In *Chiiki no tayōsei to kōkogaku—Tōnan Ajia to sono shūhen* (Regional diversity and archaeology—Southeast Asia and vicinity), ed. Aoyagi Jōji Sensei Taishoku Kinen Ronbunshū Iinkai, pp. 308–320. Tokyo: Yūzankaku.

———. 2008. Heshikiya Tōbaru Iseki de saishū sareta sekitsui dōbutsu itai gun ni tsuite (Groups of vertebrate remains collected from the Heshikiya Tōbaru Site). In *Heshikiya Tōbaru Iseki* (The Heshikiya Tōbaru Site), ed. Kabushiki Kaisha Iieishi (EAC), Uruma Shi Kyōiku Iinkai, pp. 88–101. Uruma Shi (Okinawa): Kabushiki Kaisha Iieishii (EAC), Uruma Shi Kyōiku Iinkai.

———. 2011. Ryūkyū senshi jidaijin to dōbutsu shigen riyō: honyu dōbutsu itai chūshin ni (Use of faunal resources by prehistoric Ryukyuans: based on mammal remains). In *Senshi, Gusuku Jidai No Ryūkyū Rettō: hito to keikan* (The Ryukyu Islands in the Prehistoric and Primitive Periods: people and landscape), ed. Takamiya Hiroto and Itō Shinji, pp. 109–131. Tokyo: Rokuichi Shobō.

Tōkyō Kokuritsu Hakubutsukan. 1978. *Nihon shutsudo no Chūgoku tōji* (Chinese ceramics found in Japan). Tokyo: Tōkyo Kokuritsu Hakubutsukan.

Tōma Kenji. 2009. Ireibaru Iseki (Ireibaru Site). In *Hakkutsu sareta Nihon Rettō* (The Japanese Archipleago excavated), ed. Bunka Chō, pp. 21–24. Tokyo: Asahi Shinbunsha.

Tōma Shi'ichi. 1983. Furustobaru Iseki (Furusutobaru Site). *Okinawa dai jiten* (Encyclopedia of Okinawa) 3:397–398.

———. 1986. Toshi, jokan no saishin jōhō: Okinawa (Recent news on studies of cities and castles: Okinawa). *Chūsei toshi kenkyū* 3:303–310.

———. 1988. Gusuku no ishi zumi ni tsuite, jo (Regarding castle stone wall building, part 1). *Bunka ka kiyō* 5:18–37.

———. 1997. Gushichan Gusuku hokutō gakeshita dōketsunai de hakken sareta Meitōsen ni tsuite (Concerning Meitosen coins found in a cave in the northeast cliff below Gushichan Gusuku). *Okinawa Kenritsu Hakubutsukan kiyō* 23:97–110.

Tōma Shi'ichi and Nakama Gishō. 1983. Hisamatsu Miyāka Iseki (The Hisamatsu Miyako-style grave site) *Okinawa dai jiten* (Encyclopedia of Okinawa) 3:294.

Tōma, Takashi, Tsunehiko Hanihara, Hajime Sunakawa, Kuniaki Haneji, and Hajime Ishida. 2007. Metric dental diversity of Ryūkyū Islanders: a comparative study among Ryūkyū and other Asian populations. *Anthropological Science* 115:119–131.

Tomiyama Kazuyuki. 1992. Tōitsu kokka keiseiki no taigai kankei (Foreign relations at the time of state unification). In *Shin Ryūkyū shi—Ko Ryūkyū hen* (New history of Ryukyu—Ko Ryukyu), ed. Ryūkyū Shinpōsha, pp. 141–162. Naha: Ryūkyū Shinpōsha.

Torrence, R., and G. Grattan. 2002. The archaeology of natural disasters: past and future trends. In *Natural Disasters and Cultural Change,* ed. J. Torrence and R. Grattan, pp. 1–18. London: Routledge.

Torres, J. M., and R. R. Ramos. 2008. The Caribbean: a continent divided by water. In *Archaeology and Geoinformatics: Case Studies from the Caribbean,* ed. B. Reid, pp. 13–29. Tuscaloosa: University of Alabama Press.

Trinkaus, E. and C. Ruff. 1996. Early modern remains from Eastern Asia: the Yamashita Chō 1 immature post crania. *Journal of Human Evolution* 30:299–314.

Tsang, Chen-hua. 2000. *The Archaeology of Taiwan.* Taipei: Council for Cultural Affairs.

———. 2011. Changbin wenhua yanjiu de jige wenti (Several problems concerning Changbin culture). *2010 nian Taiwan kaogu gongzuo huibao* 13 (1): 1–12.

Tsang, Chen-hua, Wen-shan Chen, Kuang-ti Li, Yu-hsuan Cheng, and Wen-lien Chen. 2011. Baxiandong Yizhi kaogu diaocha qishu xian chaiduan de faxian (Discoveries made in planning for archaeological research on Baxiandong). *2010 nian Taiwan kaogu gongzuo huibao* 7 (1): 1–16.

Tsuzuki Shin'ichirō. 2011a. Sakai Kangō Toshi Iseki kara shutsudo shita Chūgoku sei tōjiki no yōsō ni tsuite (soan) (Aspects of Chinese ceramics excavated from the Sakai Moated City Site [basic introduction]). *Hakata Kenkyūkai ki,* twentieth anniversary special edition, pp. 3–12.

———. 2011b. Sakai kangō toshi iseki ni okeru ryūtsū no yōsō: bōeki tōjiki kara mita Ryūkyū bōeki to shuinsen bōeki) The nature of circulation in relation to the Sakai moated city: the Ryūkyū and Vermilion Tally trade as seen from trade ceramics). In *Kōkogaku to Muromachi, Sengokki no ryūtsū: Setonaikai to Ajia o musubu michi* (Archaeology and circulation in the Muromachi and Sengoku Periods: routes connecting the Inland Sea and Asia), ed. H. Hashimoto, pp. 93–118. Tokyo: Kōshi Shoin.

———. 2012. Sakai Kangō Toshi Iseki ni okeru "Nanban Bōeki Ki" no bōeki tōji (Trade ceramics from the "Period of Nanban Trade" in the Sakai Moated City Site). *Bōeki tōji kenkyu* 32:66–75.

Turner, C. 1990. Main features of Sundadonty and Sinodonty, including suggestions about East Asian microevolution, population history and Late Pleistocene relationships with Australian aboriginals. *American Journal of Physical Anthropology* 82:295–317.

———. 2006. Dental morphology and the population history of the Pacific Rim and Basin: comment on Hirofumi Matsumura and Mark J. Hudson. *American Journal of Physical Anthropology* 130:455–461.

Ueda Hideo. 1982. Jūyon-jūroku seiki no seiji wan no bunrui ni tsuite (Classification of celadon bowls from the fourteenth to sixteenth centuries). *Bōeki tōji kenkyū* 2:55–70.

Ueda Kei'ichi, Yahagi Kenji, and Hashimoto Makio. 2009. Ryūkyū Rettō no taido bunseki kenkyū: Okinawa Ken shita no taido bunseki to sono koka (Analysis of ceramic pastes from the Ryukyu Islands: results of analysis from Okinawa Prefecture). *Nantō kōko* 28:83–94.

Uehara Shizuka. 2004. Ryūkyū Rettō ni okeru yōgyō iseki no chōsa (Investigation of kiln sites in the Ryukyu Islands). *Rekishi dokuhon* 49 (7): 246–249.

———. 2007. Ryūkyū Rettō shutsudo yūkō banjō seihin, kotsusei hera nado ni tsuite (Concerning perforated disks and bone spatulas found in the Ryukyu Islands). *Nantō kōko* 26:253–274.

———. 2009a. Okinawa Shotō ni okeru no izō gijutsu to seisan (Metal casting techniques and production of the mediaeval and early modern periods in the Okinawa Islands) *Nantō kōko* 28:33–60.

———. 2009b. Shuri Jōato Iri no Azana ato no kōji, chūzō kōbō (The forging and casting workshop in the Iri no Azana, Shuri Castle). *Okinawa maibun kenkyū* 6:71–111.

Uezato Takashi. 2002. Ko Ryūkyū no guntai to sono rekishiteki tenkai (The military of Ko Ryukyu and its historical development). *Ryūkyū Ajia Shakai bunka* 5:105–128.

———. 2005. Ko Ryūkyū Naha no (Wajin) kyoryūchi to kan Shina Kai sekai (The Japanese settlement in Naha at the time of Ko Ryukyu and the China Sea maritime world). *Shigaku zasshi* 114 (7): 1–33.

———. 2008. The formation of the port city of Naha in Ryukyu in the world of Maritime Asia: from the perspective of a Japanese network. *Acta Asiatica* 95:57–77.

———. 2009. The architectural landscape of the kingdom of Ko Ryūkyū. In *Okinawa: The Rise of an Island Kingdom: Archaeological and Cultural Perspectives,* ed. Richard Pearson, pp. 71–80. BAR Series 1898. London: Archaeopress, 2009.

———. 2010. Ko Ryūkyū no kinkōhin seisan no ryūtsū (The production and exchange of metalwork of Ko Ryukyu). *Nihon no bijutsu* 533:84–94.

Uezu Yasuyuki. 2004. Ko Ryūkyū no Shurijō (Shurijō in the Ko Ryukyu Period). In *Gusuku bunka o kangaeru* (Thinking about Gusuku culture), ed. Nakijin Son Kyōiku Iinkai, pp. 40–43. Tokyo: Shin Jinbutsu Ōraisha.

Ujiie Hiroshi. 1998. Rikkyō to Kuroshio hendō: Okinawa Turafu kara no hasshin (English title: Late Quaternary changes in the Kuroshio Current due to Ryukyu-Taiwan land bridge formation: evidence from the Okinawa Trough piston cores). *Daiyonki kenkyū* 37 (3): 243–249.

Ujiie, H., Y. Tanaka, and T. Ono. 1991. Late Quaternary paleoceanographic record from the Middle Ryūkyū Trench Slope, Northwest Pacific. *Marine Micropalaeontology* 18:115–128.

Ujiie, Hiroshi, and Yurika Ujiie. 1999. Late Quaternary course changes of the Kuroshio Current in the Ryukyu Arc region, Northwestern Pacific Ocean. *Marine Micropaleontology* 37:23–40.

Urasoe Shi Kyōiku Iinkai. 1996. *Shiseki Urasoe Jōato seibi kihon keikaku shū* (Collection of basic plans for the organization of the historic site of Urasoe Castle). Urasoe: Urasoe Shi Kyoku Iinkai.

———. 2001. *Urasoe Yōdore I: Ishizumi Ikō hen* (Urasoe Yōdore I: stone built features). Urasoe (Okinawa): Urasoe Shi Kyōiku Iinkai.

———. 2005a. *Urasoe Yōdore II: kawara damari ikō* Hen (Urasoe Yōdore II: the accumulation of roof tiles). Urasoe (Okinawa): Urasoe Shi Kyōiku Iinkai.

———. 2005b. *Urasoe Yōdore no ishizushi ikotsu chōsa no chūkan hōkoku* (Preliminary report of the investigation of the stone sarcophagi and human bones from Urasoe Yōdore). Urasoe: Urasoe Shi Kyōiku Iinkai.

———. 2007. *Urasoe Yōdore III: kinzoku kōbōato hen* (Urasoe Yōdore III: the metal workshop). Urasoe: Urasoe Shi Kyōiku Iinkai.

Urasoe Shi Shishi Henshū Iinkai. 1986. Urasoe no kogawara (Ancient roof tiles of Urasoe). In *Urasoe Shi shi, daini hen: Kōko* (History of Urasoe City, part 2: archaeology), ed. Urasoe Shi Kyōiku Iinkai, pp. 173–206. Urasoe: Urasoe Shi Shishi Henshū Iinkai.

Uzawa Kazuhiro, Tōizumi Takeji, Anezaki Tomoko, and Nishimoto Toyohiro. 2001.

Ōdomaribama Kaizuka shutsudo sekitsui dōbutsu itai (The vertebrate faunal remains from the Ōdomaribama Shellmound Site). In *Okinawa Ken Ōdomaribama Kaizuka* (The Odomaribama Shell Mound, Okinawa Prefecture, Japan), ed. Asato Susumu and Hideji Harunari, pp. 41–101. Sakura City, Chiba: National Museum of Japanese History.

Vainker, S. J. 1991. *Chinese Pottery and Porcelain from Prehistory to the Present.* New York: George Braziller.

Wada Hisanori. 1975. Ryūkyū Koku no Sanzan tōitsu ni tsuite shin kōsatsu (A new interpretation of the unification of Sanzan into the Ryukyu Kingdom). *Ochanomizu Jinbun kagaku kiyō* 28 (2): 13–39.

———. 2006. *Ryūkyū Ōkoku no keisei: Sanzan tōitsu no zengo* (The shaping of the Ryukyu Kingdom: before and after the unification of Sanzan). Ginowan: Gajumaru Shorin.

Wang, Gungwu. 1993. Merchants without empire: the Hokkien sojourning community. In *The Rise of Merchant Empires: Long Distance Trade in the Early Modern World 1350–1750,* ed. J. Tracey, pp. 400–421. Cambridge, UK: Cambridge University Press.

———. 2008. The China Seas: becoming an enlarged Mediterranean. In *The East Asian Mediterranean: Maritime Crossroads of Culture, Commerce, and Human Migration,* ed. Angela Schottenhammer, pp. 7–22. Wiesbaden: Harrassowitz Verlag.

Wang Zhongshu. 2001. Lun Liuqiuguo Wangguo Jinliang Zhizhong de zhizhoudi wenti (Discussion of the problem of the place of casting of the Bell That Bridges Myriad Lands). *Kaogu* 6:555–566.

Watanobe, T., N. Ishiguro, M. Nakano, A. Matsui, H. Hongo, K. Yamazaki, and O. Takahashi. 2004. Prehistoric Sado Island populations of *Sus scrofa* distinguished from contemporary Japanese wild boar by ancient mitochondrial DNA. *Zoological Science* 21:219–228.

Watanobe, T., N. Ishiguro, M. Nakano, H. Takamiya, A. Matsui, and H. Hongo. 2002. Prehistoric introduction of domestic pigs into the Okinawa Islands: ancient Mitochrondial DNA evidence. *Journal of Molecular Evolution* 55:222–231.

Watanobe, T., N. Ishiguro, N. Okamura, M. Nakano, A. Matsui, H. Hongo, and H. Ushiro. 2001. Ancient mitochondrial DNA reveals the origin of *Sus scrofa* from Rebun Island, Japan. *Journal of Molecular Evolution* 52:281–289.

Watt, J. C., and B. Ford. 1991. *East Asian Lacquer: The Florence and Herbert Irving Collection.* New York: The Metropolitan Museum of Art.

Whitehead. 1998. Ecological history and historical ecology. 1998. In *Advances in Historical Ecology,* ed. W. Balee, pp. 30–41. New York: Columbia University.

Wolf, E. 1982. *Europe and the People without History.* Berkeley: University of California Press.

Xiang, Rong, Youbin Sun, Tiegang Li, Delia W. Oppo, Muhong Chen, and Fan Zheng.

2007. Palaeonvironmental change in the Middle Okinawa Trough since the last deglaciation: evidence from the sedimentation rate and planktonic foraminiferal record. *Palaeogeography, Palaeoclimatology, Palaeoecology* 243:378–393.

Xiang, Rong, Zuosheng Yang, Yōshiki Saito, Dejiang Fan, Muhong Chen, Zhigang Guo, and Zhong Chen. 2008. Paleoenvironmental changes during the last 8400 years in the southern Yellow Sea: benthic foraminiferal and stable isotopic evidence. *Marine Micropaleontology* 67:104–119.

Yamamoto Masa'aki. 2003. Tenkaiji kō: hakkutsu chōsa kekka o sankō ni shite (Consideration of the Tenkaiji temple based on excavation results). *Okinawa maibun kenkyū* 1:35–46.

———. 2007. Jūyon, jūgo seiki ni okeru shūraku to gusuku no shosō (Several aspects of fourteenth- and fifteenth-century villages and *gusuku*). *Nantō kōko* 16:169–186.

Yamamoto Masa'aki, Ueda Kei'ichi, Yahagi Kenji, and Ishioka Tomotake. 2007. Shuri Jōato Ouchibaru chiku hakkutsu chōsa shutsudo kawara no taido bunseki to sono kenshō (Temper analysis and verification of artifacts excavated in the Ouchibaru Site, West Sector, Shuri Castle Site). *Okinawa maibun kenkyū* 5:77–110.

Yamamoto Masa'aki and Uezato Takashi. 2004. Shuri Gusuku shutsudo no bugu shiryō no ichi kōsai (Arms and armor excavated in Shuri Gusuku). *Okinawa maibun kenkyū* 2:43–64.

Yamamoto Nobuo. 1997. Kyūshū, Nansei Shotō (Kyushu and the Nansei Islands). *Kokuritsu Rekishi Minzoku Hakubutsukan kenkyū hōkoku* 71:237–309.

———. 2003. Jūni seiki zengō no tōjiki kara mita Mottaimatsu no hyōka (An assessment of the Mottaimatsu Site from ceramics dating to around the twelfth century). *Kodai bunka* 55 (2): 5–12.

Yamauchi Shinji. 2009. *Nissō bōeki to Iō no Michi* (Japan-Song trade and the Sulfur Route). Tokyo: Yamakawa Shuppan.

Yamazaki Shinji. 2008. Senshi jidai ni okeru Koshidakekei kokuyōseki no ryūtsū to kakki (Problems concerning distribution routes of obsidian from Mt. Koshidake and their temporal significance in prehistory). *Okinawa Kenritsu Hakubutsukan, Bijutsukan Hakubutsukan kiyō* 1:27–34.

Yamazaki Shinji, Yoko'o Masaki, and Ōshiro Hideko. 2010. Nanjō Shi Oyakebaru Ufuniku Cave saishū no ibutsu ni tsuite (Concerning specimens collected in the Ufuniku Cave, Oyakebaru, Nanjō City). *Nantō kōko* 29:113–128.

Yamazaki Shinji, Katagiri Chiaki, and Yoneda Minoru. 2010. Shiraho Saonetabaru dōketsu iseki no hakkutsu chōsa to Okinawa ni okeru Kōshinsei jinrui kenkyū no gen dankai (Excavations of Shiraho Saonetabaru Cave on Ishigaki Island and current study of Pleistocene human remains in Okinawa). *Kōkogaku kenkyū* 57 (3): 1–5.

Yamazato Jun'ichi. 2010. Nana—jūni seiki no Ryūkyū Rettō (The Ryukyu Retto in the seventh to twelfth centuries). In *Okinawa Ken shi kakuron hen daisan kan: Ko Ryūkyū* (History of Okinawa separate volume no. 3: Ko Ryukyu), ed. Zaidan Hōjin

Okinawa Ken Bunka Shinkōkai Shiryō Henshūshitsu, pp. 90–109. Okinawa Ken Kyōiku Iinkai, Naha.

Yanagihara Toshiaki. 1999. Chūsei zenki Minami Kyushu no minato to Sōjin kyoryūchi ni kansuru ichi shiron (An essay concerning ports and residential areas of Song Chinese in Southern Kyushu in the Early Mediaeval Period). *Nihon shi kenkyū* 448:102–134.

———. 2003. Heian Sue—Kamakura ki no Manosegawa karyū chiiki (The Lower Manose River area in Late Heian and Kamakura Times). *Kodai bunka* 55 (2): 5–12.

Yeh, Wencheng. 1988. Qingbai kilns in Yiyao and Qingyao, Mingxing Xian, Fujian. In *Ancient Ceramic Kiln Technology in Asia,* ed. Chuimei Ho, pp. 60–73. Hong Kong: University of Hong Kong.

Yiengpruksawan, M. H. 1998. *Hiraizumi: Buddhist Art and Regional Politics in Twelfth Century Japan.* Cambridge, MA: Harvard University Press.

Yogi Tatsunori. 1995. Gusuku jidai no buki, bugu ni tsuite (Weapons and armor of the Gusuku Period). *Kōkogaku jānaru* 379:6–9.

Yoko'o Masaki. 2008. Murokawa Kasō Shiki doki no shibungu ni tsuite ichi kōsai—Kauragai o chūshin ni (Tools used for applying decoration on Murokawa Lower Layer–type pottery, particularly *Fragrum unedo* shells. *Nantō kōko* 27:69–87.

Yokota Kenjirō, Morimoto Asako, and Yamamoto Nobuo. 1989. Sinan chinsen to Dazaifu, Hakata no bōeki tōji (Trade ceramics from the Sinan sunken ship and Dazaifu and Hakata). *Bōeki tōji kenkyū* 9:13–45.

Yokoyama Kōichi, ed. 1986. *Kyushu, Okinawa,* vol. 6: *Zusetsu hakkutsu ga kataru Nihon shi Kyūshū, Okinawa* (Illustrated history of Japan told by excavations), ed. Kiyotari Tsuboi. Tokyo: Shin Jinbutsu Ōraisha.

Yomitan Son Kyōiku Iinkai. 1977. *Toguchi Agaribaru dai ichi, niji hakkutsu chōsa hōkoku* (Report of first and second excavations at the Toguchi Agaribaru Site). Naha: Yomitan Son Kyōiku Iinkai.

Yonagusuku Son Kyōiku Iinkai. 1988. *Yonagusuku Son no iseki: shōryaku bunpu chōsa hōkokusho* (Archaeological sites of Yonagusuku Village: report of detailed survey). Okinawa: Yonagusuku Son Kyōiku Iinkai.

Yoneda Minoru. 2010. Shoku seitai ni miru Jōmon bunka no tayōsei (Jōmon cultural diversity seen from food ecology). *Kagaku* 80 (4): 383–388.

Yoshinari Naoki. 2010. Kodai, chūsei no nanpō sekai (The world of the Southern Islands in the ancient and mediaeval periods). In *Kodai Makki—Nihon no kyōkai* (The frontiers of Japan at the end of the Ancient [Kodai] Period), ed. Josef Kreiner, Naoki Yoshinari, and Masashi Oguchi, pp. 15–56. Tokyo: Moriwasha.

Yoshiwara, S. 1901. Geologic structure of the Riukiu Curve, and its relation to the northern part of Formosa. *Journal of the College of Science, Imperial University Tokyo* 16 (part 1): 1–67.

Yotsuyanagi Kashō. 2006. *Urushi* (Lacquer). 1 and 2. Tokyo: Hōsei Daigaku Shuppankai.

Yu, Hua, Yingqian Xiong, Zhenxia Liu, Serge Berne, Chi-yue Huang, and Guodong Hua. 2008. Evidence for an 8,200 BP cooling event in the Middle Okinawa Trough. *Geo-Marine Letters* 28:131–136.

Zaidan Hōjin Okinawa Ken Bunka Shinkōkai. 2003. *Okinawa Ken shi kakuronhen daini kan: kōko* (History of Okinawa separate volume no. 2: archaeology). Naha: Okinawa Ken Kyōiku Iinkai.

Zhang, Feng. 2009. Rethinking the "Tribute System": broadening the conceptual horizon of historical East Asian politics. *Chinese Journal of International Politics* 2:545–574.

Zhang, Pingzhong, Hai Cheng, R. Lawrence Edwards, Fahu Chen, Yongjin Wang, Xunlin Yang, Jian Liu, Ming Tan, Xianfeng Wang, Jinghua Liu, Chunlei An, Zhibo Dai, Jing Zhou, Dezhong Zhang, Jihong Jia, Liya Jin, and Kathleen R. Johnson. 2008. A test of climate, sun, and culture relationships from an 1810-year old Chinese cave record. *Science* 322:940–942.

Index

Page numbers in **boldface** type refer to figures and tables.

About the Author

Richard Pearson has spent a lifetime studying ancient societies and economies in the East China Sea region. He studied anthropology at the University of Toronto and the University of Hawai'i, receiving his Ph.D. from Yale University in 1966. He taught at the University of Hawai'i from 1966 to 1971, and the University of British Columbia from 1971 to 2000. He is currently professor emeritus at UBC.

Pearson's major fieldwork in the 1960s and 1970s was centered in Japan and the Ryukyu Islands. In his books he has attempted to introduce the work of local Asian archaeologists while bringing a Western perspective to the interpretation of new discoveries. Examples of this approach can be seen in his earlier works *Windows on the Japanese Past* (1986) and *Ancient Japan* (1992).